STO

Masterplots

2,010 Plot Stories & Essay Reviews
from the World's Fine Literature

Revised Edition

Including the Four Series
and Further Critical Evaluations

Edited by
FRANK N. MAGILL

Story Editor
DAYTON KOHLER

Volume Nine
POE - REP
4909 - 5524

SALEM PRESS
Englewood Cliffs, New Jersey 07632

LIBRARY OF CONGRESS CATALOG CARD NUMBER 76-5606

REVISED EDITION
First Printing

PRINTED IN THE UNITED STATES OF AMERICA

LIST OF TITLES IN VOLUME NINE

THE POETRY OF DRYDEN

Author: John Dryden (1631-1700)
First published: Astraea Redux, 1660; *Annus Mirabilis,* 1667; *Absalom and Achitophel,* 1681;
The Medall, 1682; *MacFlecknoe,* 1682; *Religio Laici,* 1682; *The Hind and the Panther,*
1687; *Alexander's Feast,* 1697; *Fables Ancient and Modern,* 1700

John Dryden the Restoration poet and critic, has been justly praised as the father of modern English. In spite of the three centuries separating his age from our own, his works in both verse and prose are surprisingly contemporary in his diction and sentence structure. Dryden had an uncanny instinct for avoiding fads and selecting those elements in the language of his day that were to be relatively permanent, and his style exerted a powerful influence on succeeding generations of writers.

Dryden's reputation as a poet rests upon his control of language, his ability to treat widely different subjects with equal skill, and his remarkable gift for expressing complex ideas clearly in verse. His work does not often convey great emotional or imaginative power, and he was generally most successful when he could apply his wit and clarity of expression to someone else's plot. His best known satire, *Absalom and Achitophel,* is based upon Old Testament history and a contemporary political intrigue; his finest play, *All for Love,* owes much to Shakespeare's *Antony and Cleopatra.* His talents were especially well-suited to the journalistic chronicling of events in works like the *Annus Mirabilis,* an account of the war with the Dutch and of the great fire of London that marked the year 1666, and to translations. His versions of the fables of Chaucer and Boccaccio and of Vergil's *Aeneid* have merited special praise for their smoothness and their fidelity to the original texts.

Dryden is best known for his satirical poetry, which depends for its effect chiefly upon devastating, succinct character sketches and pungent witticisms. Writing without the personal bitterness of the great eighteenth century satirists, Swift and Pope, Dryden humorously ridicules the corrupt politicians and bad poets of his day. "The Medall" attacks the Earl of Shaftesbury, the Achitophel of *Absalom and Achitophel,* who was involved in a plot to name the Duke of Monmouth, illegitimate son of Charles II, heir to the throne. Dryden based his satire on a medal struck by Shaftesbury's supporters to celebrate his release from the tower of London, comparing the Earl to this commemorative piece:

> Never did Art so well with Nature strive,
> Nor ever Idol seem'd so much alive:
> So like the Man; so golden to the sight,
> So base within, so counterfeit and light.

"MacFlecknoe," an amusing mock heroic poem, is a witty attack upon several minor poets, notably Richard Flecknoe and Thomas Shadwell. Much of the poem's humor is derived from the contrast between the absurd subject, the coronation of a new king of the realm of Nonsense, and the lofty style in which Dryden couches his account of the ceremony. The poem opens with an elevated moral sentiment, then dignifies the old king, Flecknoe, by comparing him to the Emperor Augustus:

> All human things are subject to decay,
> And, when Fate summons, Monarchs must obey.
> This Flecknoe found, who, like Augustus, young
> Was call'd to Empire, and had govern'd long;
> In Prose and Verse, was own'd, without dispute,
> Thro' all the Realms of *Nonsense,* absolute.

Dryden punctures the epic elevation of his beginning with the word "nonsense" in line six, but he gives no indication of awareness that his subject is less significant than that of the *Iliad*, preserving the essentially serious tone of the mock epic.

In describing his hero, Shadwell, Dryden again makes skillful use of the satirical portrait. Flecknoe says:

> Shadwell alone my perfect image bears,
> Mature in dullness from his tender years:
> Shadwell alone, of all my Sons, is he
> Who stands confirm'd in full stupidity.
> The rest to some faint meaning make pretence,
> But Shadwell never deviates into sense.

Dryden handles the heroic couplet brilliantly for comic effect in the satires, working within the confines of its two lines for pointed criticism and exploiting the humorous potential of rhyme. He achieves a very different result with the same verse form in his two major theological works, the *Religio Laici* (*The Religion of a Layman*), a discussion of his Anglican faith, and *The Hind and the Panther,* an allegorical beast fable written in defense of its doctrines after his conversion to the Roman Catholic Church. He places less emphasis on rhyme in these works and often carries his thoughts through several couplets as he deals with such knotty questions as the doctrine of invincible ignorance, the interpretation of scripture, and the power of reason. These are not poems designed for light entertainment, but the clarity and logic with which Dryden presents his arguments are impressive. Many passages, among them these lines from the *Religio Laici*, are worthy of comparison with the philosophical poems of Lucretius and Vergil:

> Dim, as the borrow'd beams of Moon and Stars
> To lonely, weary, wand'ring Travellers,
> Is Reason to the Soul; and as on high,
> Those rolling Fires discover but the Sky,
> Not light us here; So Reason's glimmering Ray
> Was lent, not to assure our doubtful way,
> But guide us upward to a better Day.
> And as those nightly Tapers disappear,

> When Day's bright Lord ascends our Hemisphere;
> So pale grows Reason at Religion's Sight:
> So dies, and so dissolves in Supernatural Light.

Outstanding, too, is the rare autobiographical statement from *The Hind and the Panther*:

> My thoughtless youth was wing'd with vain desires,
> My manhood, long misled by wand'ring fires,
> Follow'd false lights; and when their glimpse was gone,
> My pride struck out new sparkles of her own.
> Such was I, such by nature still I am,
> Be thine the glory, and be mine the shame.

The Hind and the Panther suffers to a degree from its lack of action; the fable is not developed fully enough to carry the weight of the extended theological disputes between "the milk-white hind, immortal and unchanged," who represents the Church of Rome, and the Anglican panther, "sure the noblest, next the Hind, and fairest creature of the spotted kind." Dryden briefly characterizes the English Protestant sects as the Baptist Boar, the Presbyterian Wolf, the timorous Quaker Hare, and others, but he gives these creatures almost no part in his narrative.

In some respects Dryden was even more gifted as a lyric poet than as a philosophical one; his control of language enabled him to create fine musical effects, and he was a skillful manipulator of tone. Three of his odes have won special praise: "To the Pious Memory of Mistress Anne Killigrew," "A Song for Saint Cecilia's Day, 1687," and "Alexander's Feast." The first of these, written in the irregular stanzas of the Cowleian ode so popular in the mid-seventeenth century, is an elegy for a talented young woman who is described as a goddess-saint, patroness of poetry and painting, who could redeem the arts from their current degradation. There is

little sense of personal grief in the poem;
the dignified classical tribute of these
lines is typical of the prevailing tone.

> Art she had none, yet wanted none;
> For Nature did that Want supply:
> So rich in Treasures of her Own,
> She might our boasted Stores defy:
> Such Noble Vigour did her Verse adorn
> That it seem'd borrow'd, where 'twas
>   only born.
> Her Morals, too, were in her Bosom
>   bred
> By great Examples daily fed,
> What in the best of Books, her Father's
>   Life, she read.

Both "A Song for St. Cecilia's Day"
and "Alexander's Feast" were written to
be sung at the annual celebration honor-
ing the patron saint of music, legendary
inventress of the organ, and both show
Dryden experimenting with language
and rhythm in an attempt to capture the
various shades of emotion conveyed by
different musical instruments and harmonies. The "Song" opens with a majestic
tribute to music, then describes the
effects of several instruments:

> The Trumpet's loud clangor
> Excites us to arms
> With shrill Notes of Anger
> And mortal Alarms.
>
> The double double double beat
> Of the thund'ring Drum
> Cries! "Hark! the foes come;
> Charge, Charge, 'tis too late to retreat."
>
> The soft complaining Flute
> In dying Notes discovers
> The Woes of hopeless Lovers,
> Whose Dirge is whisper'd by the
>   Warbling Lute.

Dryden employs the same technique
for a more complex effect in "Alexander's
Feast," where he shows the court musician, Timotheus, drawing his master,
Alexander the Great, to moods of revelry, love, pride, and revenge through
his music. The rhythms and sounds in
the refrains of each stanza echo the hero's
changing emotions:

> With ravish'd ears
> The Monarch hears,
> Assumes the God,
> Affects to Nod,
> And seems to shake the Spheres.
>
> The Prince, unable to conceal his
>   Pain,
> Gaz'd on the Fair
> Who caus'd his Care,
> And sigh'd and look'd, sigh'd and
>   look'd,
> Sigh'd and look'd, and sigh'd again:
> At length, with Love and Wine at once
>   oppress'd,
> The vanquish'd Victor sunk upon her
>   Breast.

The poem ends with the customary tribute to St. Cecilia, skillfully linked to the
preceding stanzas:

> At last, Divine Cecilia came,
> Inventress of the Vocal Frame;
> The sweet Enthusiast, from her
>   Sacred Store,
> Enlarg'd the former narrow
>   Bounds,
> And added Length to solemn
>   Sounds,
> With Nature's Mother-Wit, and Arts
>   unknown before.
> Let old Timotheus yield the Prize,
>   Or both divide the Crown;
> He rais'd a Mortal to the Skies;
>   She drew an Angel down.

A number of graceful songs, most of
them about love, were written to be sung
in Dryden's plays. The poet used a great
variety of meters and stanza forms, preserving a melodic quality in all of them.
These verses, from *Troilus and Cressida*,
show the flexibility of Dryden's language:

> Can life be a blessing,
> Or worth the possessing,
> Can life be a blessing if love were
>   away?
> Ah, no! tho' our love all night keep us
>   waking,
> And tho' he torment us with cares all
>   the day,
> Yet he sweetens, he sweetens our pains
>   in the taking;

There's an hour at the last, there's an hour to repay.

A famous lyric, from *Tyrannick Love,* is typical of Dryden's songs in its tinge of melancholy, its smoothness, and its simplicity of expression:

Ah how sweet it is to love!
Ah how gay is young desire!
And what pleasing pains we prove
When we first approach Love's fire!
Pains of Love be sweeter far
Than all other pleasures are.

Another important group of poems is Dryden's "occasional verse," written to commemorate public events and milestones in the lives of his friends. While some of these poems are as ephemeral as the activities that inspired them, many others are among Dryden's best work. Two, *Astraea Redux,* which celebrated the return of Charles II to the throne in 1660, and *Annus Mirabilis,* helped to establish the poet's reputation as a man of letters. The heroic couplets of *Astraea Redux* introduce the plight of kingless England in elaborate mythological terms, then shift into a less ornate mode as Dryden addresses the returning monarch:

And welcome now, *great monarch,* to your own;
Behold th'approaching Cliffs of Albion:
It is no longer Motion cheats your view,
As you meet it, the Land approacheth you.
The Land returns, and in the white it wears
The marks of Penitence and Sorrow bears.

Dryden employs a four-line stanza in *Annus Mirabilis* for his description of battle scenes between the English and the Dutch, his analysis of the causes of the war, and his account of the great fire of London. The Duke of York, later James II, is, as the commander of the Navy, the major figure in the first part of the poem; Charles II takes the center of the stage in the second half, comforting sufferers as flames engulf his capital city:

No thought can ease them but their Sovereign's care,
Whose praise th'afflicted as their comfort sing:
Ev'n those whom want might drive to just despair,
Think life a blessing under such a King.

Meantime he sadly suffers in their grief,
Out-weeps an Hermit, and out-prays a Saint:
All the long night he studies their relief,
How they may be suppli'd, and he may want.

While the *Annus Mirabilis* shows Dryden's skill as a journalist in verse, many critics feel that the more than three hundred stanzas of panegyric and patriotism would have benefited from judicious cutting. A number of shorter occasional poems have greater appeal in their clarity and directness. The elegy on the satirist John Oldham is of special interest both for its moving opening lines and for what it reveals of Dryden's sense of his function as a poet:

Farewell, too little, and too lately known,
Whom I began to think and call my own;
For sure our Souls were near allied; and thine
Cast in the same Poetic mold with mine.
One common Note on either Lyre did strike,
And Knaves and Fools we both abhorr'd alike:
To the same Goal did both our Studies drive;
The last set out the soonest did arrive.

Dryden seldom surpassed the dignity, precision, and appropriateness of his fine brief epigram on Milton:

Three poets, in three distant ages born,
Greece, Italy, and England did adorn.
The first in loftiness of thought surpass'd,
The next in majesty, in both the last:
The force of Nature could no farther go;

To make a third, she join'd the former
two.

Dryden was a professional man of letters throughout his maturity, and the
whole body of his poetry shows his
awareness of his public role. Wide as was
the range of his subject matter, it never
encompassed the exposure of his deepest
personal emotions. He wrote with restraint, urbanity, and good humor,
whether he was satirizing political corruption, setting forth the tenets of his
faith, or complimenting a friend on a
new play. He could and did create passages of striking wit and majestic dignity,
but even at his lesser moments he maintained a remarkable level of competence.
His judgment could not always make his
poetry great, but it could prevent serious
lapses in taste.

Dryden well deserved the praise be-
stowed upon him by the eighteenth century critic and poet, Samuel Johnson:
"Perhaps no nation ever produced a
writer that enriched his language with
such variety of models. To him we owe
the improvement, perhaps the completion
of our meter, the refinement of our language, and much of the correctness of
our sentiments. By him we were taught
to think naturally and express forcibly
. . . What was said of Rome, adorned
by Augustus, may be applied by an easy
metaphor to English poetry embellished
by Dryden, 'He found it brick, and he
left it marble.' "

THE POETRY OF DU BELLAY

Author: Joachim du Bellay (1522-1560)
Principal published works: L'Olive, 1549; *Vers Lyriques,* 1549; *Recueil de poésies,* 1549;
La Musagnoeomachie, 1550; *XIII Sonnets de l'honnête amour,* 1552; *Les Antiquités de
Rome,* 1558; *Les Regrets,* 1558; *Poemata,* 1558; *Le Poète courtisan,* 1559

In a short life, marked by illness and disappointment, the Angevin nobleman Joachim du Bellay wrote some of the finest elegiac and satiric poetry in the French language. His earliest verses, written before 1546, were poor imitations of Clément Marot. Jacques Peletier du Mans, whom Du Bellay met in 1546, turned him from these sterile efforts to composing odes and sonnets, still in imitation, but now of Latin and Italian models, with a view to enriching the French language and demonstrating its potential.

Du Bellay, Ronsard, and Baïf, pupils of the Hellenist Jean Dorat, inspired by Peletier, had long thought about a renewal of French poetry Thomas Sebillet, taking Marot and his school as guarantors of a new poetry, published his *Art Poétique* in 1548. Though his definitions were confusing, Sebillet's thesis was essentially the same as that of Du Bellay and Ronsard, who found themselves doubly frustrated by the theory and the choice of model. Du Bellay had a number of sonnets and odes already written. To publish these without commentary would be to range himself under Sebillet's standard. No short preface, what he wrote grew into *La Défense et Illustration de la langue française,* published in 1549. Apparently the manifesto of the young poets known as the Pléiade, the work was in fact a personal text, though Ronsard and the others had their say in outlining the aims of the group: defense of a potentially great language against the Latinizing traditions of Church, University, and Humanism itself; enrichment through the prudent use of neologisms, archaisms, infinitives and adjectives used as nouns, antonomasia, and other devices; illustration (that is, ennoblement) requiring imitation, then emulation of Antique literature (already undertaken, if hesitatingly, by Marot). The poet, a priest, might deliberately obscure truths, divinely inspired (hopefully revealed through love, through a synthesis of Christianity and Platonism) but must combine inspiration with hard work. Mythology would enshrine such truths, the "vestiges de rare et antique érudition" thus being more than ornamental. Poetry, inseparable from music, should be "doux" (sweet) in intention, thrilling the soul and senses—but might also be "utile" (didactic). Although all these ideas were expressed in the *Défense,* they represent the thinking of the young poets at the outset of their careers.

With the *Défense,* Du Bellay published *L'Olive,* a kind of "canzoniere" of fifty sonnets, over half of neo-Petrarchan inspiration. Despite its literary inspiration, its frequent Petrarchan antitheses, the world of *L'Olive* is rich and sensuous in its blending of mythological references, impressions of color and sound, nature images, and intellectual subtlety.

Published with *L'Olive* were the *Vers Lyriques* or *Odes.* Here the poet seems to dominate the Horatian inspiration of his work, resulting in a more sincere expression of his thoughts than in *L'Olive.* Typical themes are the rapid flight of time and the fragility of all worldly goods.

The program stated, Du Bellay's activity was tireless. In 1549 he published a *Recueil de poésies,* containing official, mediocre flattery—yet not forgetting his art (the ode *D'écrire en sa langue*). An augmented edition of *L'Olive,* with sixty-five additional sonnets, appeared in 1550. In the additions there is a change of tone. The poet seeks and achieves solace for the loss of his lady in Christianity. At this moment, Petrarchism becomes diluted with a fervent Platonism, of which one may see, in the famous Sonnet 113, a precise statement. The poet is liberated from the problems of time and earthly beauty by the soul's winged ascent to re-experience (reconnaître) the eternal Idea of Beauty, Goodness, and Truth. A striking example of Du Bellay's syncretism is to be seen in Sonnet 114 of *L'Olive*, where Platonic terms are combined with a text from Saint Paul's Epistle to the Romans. There also appeared in 1550 the *Musagnoeomachie* (*Battle of the Muses against Ignorance*). François I, Henri II, great contemporary statesmen, and poets join in the struggle.

If his poetry had won the poet glory and immortality for his patrons, the latter had not responded well. Du Bellay was by now a sick man, and his poetic vein seemed to be drying up. What value might the esteem of posterity have after all? But poetry seems to have had at least a therapeutic function. Having turned to Christianity for support, Du Bellay found a new purpose: to champion Christian morality. Love poetry in the earlier manner was rejected, Petrarchism being an ethical issue involving deliberate falsehood such as exaggeration of one's feelings or inordinate flattery. But love poetry in Platonic form was acceptable; hence the *XIII Sonnets de l'honnête amour,* a distillation of the researches of Pontus de Tyard, published in 1552, along with a translation of Book Four of the *Aeneid,* and a collection of pieces including the poignant *Complainte du Désespéré.*

In 1553 a new edition of the *Recueil de poésies* appeared containing the humourously satirical ode *A une dame,* in which the postures and clichés of Petrarchan love poetry are rejected in favor of a more human, Gallic, brand of love. Du Bellay mocks too the *topoi* of neo-Platonic love poetry; but he is far from abandoning Platonism and even returns to Petrarchan conceits in the late poems of the *Amours.*

Du Bellay's satiric genius had reached maturity. His voyage to Rome as secretary to his cousin, Cardinal Jean du Bellay provided him with ample material. Spellbound by the pathetic debris of the great city, perhaps inspired by a sonnet of Castiglione, Du Bellay began to write historical, philosophical, and gnomic meditations on time, fatality, decadence, and morality in the sonnets of the *Premier livre des Antiquités de Rome.* Both in form and in subject the *Antiquités* represent a transition from the earlier works of literary inspiration to the personal manner of the *Regrets.* Sonnets in decasyllabic verse alternate with those in Alexandrines, the standard form of the *Regrets.* Often closely imitating Horace, Virgil, and Lucan, Du Bellay creates a poetry of eloquence and of striking images, the first in French literature to celebrate the melancholy beauty of ancient ruins and their significance. One myth in particular translates Du Bellay's vision of Rome. It is the *Gigantomachy,* a myth of origins, violent struggle, burial, immobility.

Fascination for Rome soon turned to bitter disillusionment. In an intimate account of daily impressions, fashioned into the sonnets of the *Regrets,* Du Bellay, suffering nostalgia, pitilessly exposes the state of his heart and denounces the intrigues, vices, nonchalant immorality of Roman society, and the Curia. This collection of 191 sonnets contains du Bellay's greatest elegiac and satirical poetry, mature and original. Its purpose, as the poet explained in the exquisite dedicatory *Ode à Jean d'Avanson,* was to ease the sorrow of his exile and by an act of poetic creation, achieve oblivion to misfortune.

Scorning the learned and ornamental manner of *L'Olive,* Du Bellay begins the *Regrets* with a profession of naturalness and simplicity: "Je ne veux feuilleter les exemplaires grecs" he writes, "Je ne veux point chercher l'esprit de l'univers" ("I don't want to leaf through Greek texts, search out the soul of the universe"); rather "Je me contenterai de simplement écrire" ("I'll satisfy myself with writing simply"). Such simplicity, such facility, is misleading, as the poet well knew when he maliciously discouraged would-be imitators of his vigorous, sinewy alexandrines.

What is striking in the *Regrets* is Du Bellay's gift for noting the gesture, attitude, color, or detail that characterizes a person or a place. Frequent repetition of the verb "voir" (to see) suggests his habit of looking at things, his remarkable faculty for seeing the picturesque detail, often presented by the accumulation of precise technical terms. The theme of a sonnet may be expanded in the last line, often through irony, causing the reader's imagination to yield in silence to the creative impulse it has received. Antithesis, however, is the usual instrument of Du Bellay's wit. It appears as a procedure of composition as well as a device of style. The sonnet itself is an antithetical form, and the subject matter of du Bellay's poetry lends itself to antithetical treatment. Thus in Sonnet 6 he contrasts his past life and poetic manner in the quatrains to his present in the tercets. Du Bellay's refusal to be artificial or erudite functions in fact as an artistic device, as J. C. Lapp has shown in the case of mythological imagery, which, sparingly used, becomes ironic by lending relief to an idea in contrast to the "simple" language of the whole. The great myth that does dominate the poems is, of course, that of the exile: Ulysses or Jason, or both together, as in the famous Sonnet 31.

While confiding personal meditations to his verses ("mes plus sûrs secrétaires"), Du Bellay wrote, as recreation, some forty pieces, highly differing in tone, published as the *Divers Jeux Rustiques*. Among them are the celebrated little ode *D'un vanneur de blé aux vents*; the *Hymne de la surdité* (dedicated to Ronsard, comparing their poetic manner, humourously treating the deafness they shared); a reworking of *A une dame* as *Contre les pétrarchistes*. The *Poemata*, or Latin poems, were published at this time.

In 1557, Du Bellay returned to France to flattering acclaim but also legal difficulties, which, with increasing illness, embittered his last three years. *Le Poète courtisan*, a kind of satirical last will and testament, appeared in 1559. Through his ironic advice to the would-be court poet on how to succeed—where he had failed—Du Bellay antithetically takes up again the arguments of *La Défense* that the true poet is learned, inspired, an indication that he, Ronsard, and their group had not yet achieved an uncontested victory.

One of Du Bellay's early translators was Edmund Spenser:

> It was the time, when rest, soft sliding downe
>   From heavens hight into men's heavy eyes,
> In the forgetfulness of sleepe doth drowne
>   The carefull thoughts of mortall miseries;
> Then did a ghost before mineeyes appeare,
>   On that great rivers banck, that runnes by Rome;
> Which, calling me by name, bad me to reare
>   My lookes to heaven, whence all good gifts do come,
> And crying lowd, "Lo! now beholde," quoth hee,
>   "What under this great temple placed is:
> Lo, all is nought but flying vanitee!"
> So I, that know this world's inconstancies,
>   Sith onely God surmounts all times decay,
>   In God alone my confidence do stay.

>   . . . . . .

> I saw a wolfe under a rockie cave
>   Noursing two whelps; I saw her little ones
> In wanton dalliance the teate to crave,
>   While she her neck wreath'd from them for the nones:
> I saw her raunge abroad to seeke her food,
>   And, roming through the field with greedie rage,
> T' embrew her teeth and clawes with

lukewarm blood
Of the small heards, her thirst for
    to asswage:
I saw a thousand huntsmen, which
    descended
Downe from the mountaines bordring
    Lombardie,
That with an hundred speares her
    flank wide rended:
I saw her on the plaine outstretched
    lie,
Throwing out thousand throbs in her
    owne soyle;
Soone on a tree uphang'd I saw her
    spoyle.

Andrew Lang translated "A Sonnet to
Heaven" as follows:

If this our little life is but a day
In the Eternal,—if the years in vain
Toil after hours that never come
    again,—
If everything that hath been must de-
    cay,
Why dreamest thou of joys that pass
    away,
My soul, that my sad body doth re-
strain?
Why of the moment's pleasure art
    thou fain?
Nay, thou hast wings,—nay, seek an-
    other stay.
There is the joy where to each soul
    aspires,
And there the rest that all the world
    desires,
And there is love, and peace, and
    gracious mirth;
Behold the Very Beauty, whereof now
    Thou worshipest the shadow upon
    earth.

Du Bellay's miserable end in 1560
must have convinced many poets that the
Pléiade's early aim of seeking immortality through one's poetry was somewhat
unpractical. The judgment of posterity,
however, sees Du Bellay as one of
France's greatest satiric and lyric poets,
second only to Ronsard in his own age,
an uncontested master of the sonnet
whose work helped to found modern
French poetry.

THE POETRY OF EBERHART

Author: Richard Eberhart (1904-   )
Principal published works: A Bravery of Earth, 1930; *Reading the Spirit,* 1936; *Song and Idea,* 1940; *Poems, New and Selected,* 1944; *Burr Oaks,* 1947; *Selected Poems,* 1951; *Undercliff: Poems 1946-1953,* 1953; *Great Praises,* 1957; *Collected Poems,* 1960; *Collected Verse Plays,* 1962; *The Quarry,* 1964

Richard Eberhart is one of the least easily classified of modern poets. The directness of his statements and forcefulness of his language prevent his being within the realm of the moderns who remain aloof and intricate. His moralistic tendency to explain his allegories removes him from the sophisticated circles of understatement. As many critics have pointed out, Eberhart is a Romantic in an age of anti-Romanticism. He is also a quasi-mystic. He calls himself a relativist, a modern dualist. As a result of his two-sides-to-every-issue stand, much of his poetry seems contradictory; the "truth" of one he denies in another. His almost militantly individualistic use of language has been compared to D. H. Lawrence's. Finally, his philosophic poetry deals with everyday questions which are dramatized in everyday experiences. Thus his "metaphysical" poetry concerns not the heavenly, but the mundane. Yet it is exactly his romantic impulses, his Whitmanesque egocentricity, his apparent inconsistencies, his idiosyncratic language, and the realm from which he draws his poetry which make it difficult to read him without becoming involved.

Eberhart's major theme is death, which he explores both as an active man and as an intellectual. The irreconcilable duality between action and intellect has long been a concern of poets; Eberhart's concern in, for example, "In a Hard Intellectual Light," is neither revolutionary nor overwhelmingly modern in a scientific age.

One of Eberhart's first answers for the active man who seeks escape from mechanization is in nature. Hence much of his poetry, especially relatively early work, is easily Romantic, as is his deification of the age of innocence recorded in "Recollections of Childhood." Loss of innocence comes, however, with the knowledge of death, and even his most fervently Romantic poems do not escape a persistent questioning about when death will come. Romanticism deserts him completely when he sees man in "Maze." To transcend reality as seen in this poem, Eberhart creates visionary states close to the mystical. The reality which he questions most frequently is death; his visionary poetry, therefore, seeks to transcend death, as in "Imagining How It Would Be To Be Dead." Eberhart is not, however, willing or able to maintain the wholly visionary level; for he feels that it is not human.

Both his romanticism and his mysticism consistently return to a persistent concern with the reality of death and of God. His lyric longing for death is expressed in "Cover Me Over." But in "What If Remembrance?" this mood of longing is deliberately questioned. Again, in "The Groundhog," both lyricism and questioning are rejected when the dead animal reminds the poet of his own mortality and coming decay. Such deliberately polemic statements are not a flaw in Eberhart's philosophy; rather, they illustrate what he means when he says that he tends to philosophize on everything but to arrive at no conclusions. He claims also that he is by nature contemplative, but active.

Perhaps one of his most forceful examinations of the recurrent anguish of a man faced with religious abstractions, is "Reality! Reality! What Is It?" Eberhart comes back again and again to his assertion that there are few things that man can be certain of, but death is always one of them. Although each individual poem presents only one side of the issue, his attitude about death remains nebulous: sometimes Romantic, sometimes mystical, sometimes protesting its interruption of human joys. He allows his poetry to be inconclusive, so seemingly contradictory, because he finds life contradictory. Furthermore, he believes that poetry is a matter of fleeting, perhaps fragmentary flashes of inspiration, and his poem must capture that moment for the part of truth it contains. The next blinding inspiration will contain a new insight, perhaps contradictory, but nonetheless true. He must, therefore, report that moment and let it speak for itself.

As a craftsman, Eberhart seldom revises because the inspiration has passed and the revision would not be faithful to the original truth. For this reason objection has been raised against the fast-moving fury of some of his poems. Critics regretfully point out that sometimes it seems as though Eberhart loses control and the poem directs or misdirects him. Eberhart would not disagree, but neither would he object. The uncontrolled poems, whether we approve of them as true works or not, are written as he wants them, agitated by violent speculation and equally violent contemplation.

Many of his most recent poems deal explicitly with poetry. "Winter Kill," for example, is at first a dramatic regretting of the death of a bear, then becomes an allegory on the nature of poetry, its elusiveness, its hold upon the known, its flashing insights into the unknown.

The most conclusive statement that one can make about Eberhart's poetry is that it is inconclusive. He is a personal poet. Therefore much of his poetry seems almost confessional, or at least self-examining. Just as Whitman used himself as an archetypical democratic man, Eberhart uses himself as a representative of modern man in a confused world. Honest readers at whatever literacy level recognize their own questions in Eberhart's poems. Whether or not we always agree, it is not difficult to identify with the only answer he offers: love.

THE POETRY OF EDITH SITWELL

Author: Edith Sitwell (1887-1964)
First published: Clowns' Houses, 1918; *The Wooden Pegasus* 1920; *Façade*, 1922; *Bucolic Comedies*, 1923; *The Sleeping Beauty*, 1924; *Troy Park*, 1925; *Elegy on Dead Fashion*, 1926; *Rustic Elegies*, 1927; *Poems Old and New*, 1940; *Street Songs*, 1942; *Green Song and Other Poems*, 1944; *The Song of the Cold*, 1945; *The Shadow of Cain*, 1947; *Poor Man's Music*, 1950; *Gardeners and Astronomers: New Poems*, 1953; *The Collected Poems of Edith Sitwell*, 1954

Notoriety was achieved by Edith Sitwell instantly when she and her brothers, Osbert and Sacheverell, burst upon the London literary scene during the period of World War I, each of them striving in flamboyant and self-mocking fashion to live eccentrically against the grain of a dull industrial world. This early pose was maintained by Edith Sitwell all her life.

Extravagant too were the verses of her earliest period, well suited for the brittle musical setting given *Facade* by her composer friend, William Walton. The music was performed with the poet herself chanting her hypnotic and quasi-nonsensical lines about Daisy and Lily. Equally absurd but dazzling to the ear is the poem "Sir Beelzebub."

Only a perceptive few noted, however, that Miss Sitwell's extravagance was serious and that in her own amusing, provocative way she was forging a poetic instrument that would eventually do as much as the poetic practices of the better-known poets Pound and Eliot. When she began to write, she said later, the conventional rhythms, outworn language, and stale imagery made necessary a new direction and more immediate effects of sight and sound in poetry. So when she wrote of the morning light in its "creaking" descent she was endeavoring to make the reader hear the morning as well as see it, and thus feel a new dimension to the dawn. The same deepening of sensuous experience is found in many of her poems during this period. Trees, for example, are compared to hissing green geese; the wind is a blue-maned horse that whinnies and neighs. Some of Miss Sitwell's experiments in synesthesia are strained and excessive, but just as often she does achieve that newness called for by Ezra Pound that is the goal of all good poets. Every reader of Miss Sitwell's criticism of her own work and of that of others, in essays and prefaces, instantly recognizes her keen ear and her constant concern with the relation between sense and sound in poetry, a concern that lay behind all her experimentation and made her deliberately strain or even break old associational patterns in her quest for fresh effects.

Miss Sitwell was obviously a student of the later Yeats and of Gerard Manley Hopkins, but her own work had a different cast and, as the years went by, a meaning all its own. Though the verbal techniques of *Facade* are clearly on display in *Gold Coast Customs*, its structure presented ideas and feelings never imagined by dazzled and largely amused audiences of Miss Sitwell's earlier work. Still chic, on one level her re-creation of savagery and cannibalism is obviously part of the 1920's movement that brought primitive art into modern culture, to be found in sculpture and in the early music of Stravinsky and Prokovieff. But like the novelist Conrad, Miss Sitwell shows, as the poem goes on, that the river of darkness flows through London as well as through The Congo. Cannibal feasts become the equivalents of Lady Bamburgher's stupid but fashionable parties, and Miss Sitwell creates a depiction of a spiritual wasteland that has not achieved the fame of T. S. Eliot's, but is not unworthy of comparison with it. The Negro worships a black stone that stands upright on a bone. But Lady Bamburgher's god never lived at all. Unable to live or die, her god suffers as one in a trance, capable of hearing and bearing everything and yet remaining immobile.

The spirit of Blake, perhaps, tries to sing out here above her images of cannibalism new and old. Through most of the 1940's Miss Sitwell devoted herself to criticism and biography (most notably in her volume on Alexander Pope). But World War II challenged her concern, by now become agony, and found a talent that was worthy of the suffering of the time. Christ's image is now fundamental and right in her "Still Falls the Rain," called by C. M. Bowra, among others, one of the most moving, memorable poems in English about the war. From the magnificent ambiguity of the first word "still" as "always" and also as profound quietness, the comparison between man and god both dying forever is evoked in a contemporary hymn that purges finally profound terror through profound pity. In the poem the still-falling rain eventually becomes the blood from Christ's side, still shed for mankind.

More and more, as war's horror increased, Miss Sitwell found herself capable of turning the traditional images of light, of blood, of the rose of love into poems that somehow made the present meaningful through placing it in perspective with the past. Man's inhuman use of technology creates a new ice age in "The Song of the Cold," in which the poet finds the deadly chill in the heart of man himself. In "The Shadow of Cain" the whimsy of *Facade* has become frozen in a new kind of terror.

Hiroshima provided her with a new vision of the cities of Cain, where the sun descended and the earth ascended in a totemic emblem of destruction and loss. Throughout her famous "Three Poems of the Atomic Age," Miss Sitwell evokes the terrible contrast between the old sun that nourished and gave life, and this new one of man's that kills and destroys. Yet the terrible cloud that brilliantly blossoms also evokes the rose, the traditional image of love both physical and spiritual, and through Miss Sitwell's nightmare vision Christ appears in the terrible rain and walks on seas of blood.

The craft that merely seemed so fashionably clever in the 1920's came a long way before its end, unlike many of the lesser talents of that promising day. Though Miss Sitwell did not write so much as Yeats, or so intensely as Eliot, she nevertheless wrote a body of work that promises to live.

THE POETRY OF EICHENDORFF

Author: Josef von Eichendorff (1788-1857)
Principal published works: Poems, 1837; *Julian,* 1853; *Robert und Guiscard,* 1855; *Lucius,* 1857

Josef von Eichendorff, the most popular poet among the German Romanticists was born March 10, 1788. He spent his childhood at the castle of his parents at Lubowitz in Silesia. These childhood years in the beautifully situated castle became the reservoir for his outpouring of romantic lyricism until the end of his life. It is said that nobody did more to help Germans appreciate the beauty of nature, and German Wanderlust owes much to Eichendorff's glorification of the wanderer. Eichendorff declares in his poem "The Happy Wanderer":

When God, His graciousness bestowing,
Sends man forth in the world so wide,
He unveils Life, His wonders showing
In wood, field, stream, and mountainside.

The slothful, who at home are lying,
Are not refreshed by dawn's clear red;
They only know of children's crying,
Of sorrow, pain, and need of bread.

Many Germans living in a motorized age still agree with him.

Although Eichendorff was a wanderer, he was not trying to wander away from something. All his pilgrimages are inward. He was a member of the old Silesian aristocracy, and one literary critic named him the "last knight of knights." His feelings correspond to the experience of ordinary people, however, and folkloristic elements are always present in his work. The Napoleonic Wars overshadowed his childhood paradise in Silesia, and to shelter young Eichendorff from proximity to war his parents sent him to the universities of Halle and Heidelberg. In Heidelberg he met the two writers credited with starting the German movement of Romanticism: Achim von Arnim and Clemens Brentano, who had published, in 1806, *Des Knaben Wunderhorn,* a major collection of German folksongs.

The romantically inclined Eichendorff became above all a lyricist, probably the most important one of the whole movement with the possible exception of Brentano. Eichendorff also wrote many prose pieces, but few are remembered now. Even his best known humoristic prose work *Aus dem Leben eines Taugenichts* is mainly remembered for its lyrical qualities. His poems are always simple in theme and expression. He used a varied meter, and, refusing to develop a set pattern, adjusted the rhythm of language to the theme of the poem. His recipe for a poet was this: ". . . Rise early in the morning; write under an open sky, in beautiful scenery when the soul is alert and the trees are singing. . . ." All subjects dear to the Romanticist are present in his poems: worship of nature, homesickness, eternal roaming, moonlit nights, old chapels, deserted ruins, and moods of melancholy.

I wander through the quiet night;
There glides the gentle moon so white,
Oft breaking dark cloud-banks away,
And sometimes in the vale
Awakes a nightingale:
Then once more all is still and gray. . . .

In one regard, however, Eichendorff differs from his fellow Romanticists: he had committed himself to Catholicism. He was opposed to the prevailing trend of his time of esthetical Catholicism, but there was never any doubt in his mind about his faith. Romanticism, which has been frequently interpeted as a substitution of adoration of nature for the adoration of God served Eichendorff only to display his belief in God's orderly world:

The small child rests from playing,
Soft Night knocks on the pane,
The angels at God's saying
Are keeping watch again.

In many other poems this theme is repeated:

> I let the dear God guide my going;
>   To brook and lark and wood and
>   field
> And Earth and Heaven favors show-
>   ing,
> My life He will from all harm shield.

His Catholicism was an almost revolutionary approach if one considers the prevailing liberal trends in literature at his time, as well as the fact that the preceding classicism was mainly expressed in Protestant terms. It is true that Eichendorff did not offer any great new ideas and his poems are without a passionate climax. He is not a philosopher, but this fact is probably the key for his enduring popularity. His poems, written with ease and charm, are free from tension and moralizing. When he paints with the dark colors of grief, he never fails to contrast them with the soft colors of consolation. Always present in his work is a sense of the great order of things, in which man becomes a part of the whole when he is only willing to take time to reflect upon himself while observing the wonders of nature.

> There's a sleeping song in all things,
> Which dream on in peace unheard;
> Yet the world awakes and loud sings,
> If you know the magic word.

One of his poems describes how he was saddened by an encounter with evil, and yet while he was composing his poem the angels came and opened a door which radiated so much life that he could no longer see the evil. The melancholy of lost love found its greatest monument in his poem and folksong "The Broken Ring," which can be found in every collection of German folksongs:

> In a spot cool and shady,
> A mill wheel turns in state.
> My loved one has gone from me,
> Who lived there but of late. . . .

> Hear I that mill wheel turning,
> I know not what I will:

> For death I most am yearning,
> That all cares might be still.

The grief described here is not the tragic pain to be found in Goethe's *The Sorrows of Young Werther,* which caused a suicide wave among unfortunate lovers after its publication. This poem shows the faraway wanderer and his remembrance of a loved one. A longing for faraway places (*Fernweh*) is frequently contrasted with homesickness (*Heimweh*), but grief is sublimated to increase sensibility, a participation in universal suffering (*Weltschmerz*) and joy.

In Heidelberg he also met another friend of Arnim and Brentano, Josef Görres, who was a Romanticist and the literary leader of German Catholicism. Görres succeeded in converting Eichendorff, by temperament a dreamer, into a member of a national resistance movement against the conquerer, Napoleon. Thus, in 1813, Eichendorff became a member of the much glorified voluntary Prussian Corps Luetzow. In 1814 he married Luise von Larisch, the daughter of a country squire. After Napoleon returned from Elba he joined the army once more, but before he reached the front the Battle of Waterloo had decided Napoleon's fate. Eichendorff was now twenty-seven years old. He could not return to his childhood paradise in Silesia, for the castle and his father's fortune had been lost as a result of the war. He also was determined not to isolate himself as a poet. Especially he abhorred the scatter-brained scurrility which he described as the usual malady of poets. He took a position as a government official.

Eichendorff remained in government service for religious and educational affairs until 1844. When conflicts arose between his faithful adherence to the Catholic Church and the increasing government policy to reject Church influence in public life, he resigned. In 1837, Eichendorff published his first collection of poems. After his resignation he was able to devote even more time to his writing.

When he visited Vienna, he was well received and declared in surprise, "By all means, they want to make a famous man out of me." In Vienna he also completed the first part of his history of literature under the title *Romantic Poetry*. Here he met the philosopher Friedrich Schlegel, a convert to Roman Catholicism, and a great friendship developed. Eichendorff's marriage was a happy one; he had two sons and two daughters. His most beloved youngest daughter died at an early age and her death was the greatest tragedy he ever experienced. What he said in his poems, he acted out in his life. He was able to find comfort in the belief that even his daughter's early death must be a part of God's plan. In 1855, Eichendorff retired with his family to the country estate of his son-in-law in Neisse. In the same year his wife died. Two years later Eichendorff followed her.

Eichendorff's life, with the exception of his daughter's death, was free from any dramatics. A happy childhood, an education in Germany's best universities, a life among friends with common interests, and a happy marriage gave him the opportunity to lead the life he desired. Even when he joined the army he was spared the sight of battle. And he always found time for reflection:

When man's pleasure cry for rest,

Earth soft whispers as in dreams now,
  Strangely sighing through each green
    bough
What the heart has hardly guessed:
  Of old times, mild sorrow's shimmer,—
And there flashes awe's pale glimmer,
Swift like lightning through the breast.

A justified question is whether a poet of such a period and such experiences can have any meaning for later generations who have problems about which the dreamer Eichendorff never imagined. The continued popularity of the Romanticists answers this question. People compelled to cut their traditional roots as the result of force or voluntary decision as members of a more mobile society are grateful for the rest haven of Romanticism, which permits a pause for re-examination and rejuvenation.

The breeze in the wood stirs the tree-
  tops
From dreams of the cliffs that thrill;
For the Lord moves over the hill-tops
And blesses the land so still.

The consolation of Eichendorff, the belief that everything is right in this world if we can learn to understand that even our grief is part of something greater than we, is the message from the wanderer of the nineteenth century to the wanderer of the twentieth century.

THE POETRY OF ELINOR WYLIE

Author: Elinor Wylie (1885-1928)
First published: Nets to Catch the Wind, 1921; *Black Armour,* 1923; *Trivial Breath,* 1928;
Angels and Earthly Creatures, 1929; *Collected Poems of Elinor Wylie,* 1932; *Last Poems,*
1943

Elinor Wylie lived in those regions of the spirit where only poets and saints are allowed to enter, saw life as a harsh riddle, and withdrew from a material world to concentrate on the intense, personal drama inside herself. Within the diminished mirror of her own mind she viewed men and landscapes, weaving in her small tapestries the record of man's doom. Her exile guarded her from the inhumanity of life. She sketched ardent and somber portraits with firm lines.

Elinor Wylie appeared late upon the literary scene, for she was thirty-five when her first book of poems was published. She had written poetry before, but these were collected in a limited edition which was sent only to her intimates and family friends. Meanwhile she was publishing poems in various magazines and early in 1921, at the request of a publishing company, she assembled her first book of poetry, which was published later that year as *Nets to Catch the Wind.* But publishing poetry is not a lucrative business and she began writing magazine sketches.

Her personality was contradictory, her moods fleeting and intense. One critic compared her to iced chalk, for she could be high-handed and aloof. But she could also be friendly and generous, almost childish in her delight in simple things. Like her writing, her speech revealed the wit and vigor of her mind. She had become a figure of literary legend when in 1923 she married William Rose Benét. That same year she published her second book of poems, *Black Armour,* and her first novel, *Jennifer Lorn.*

Seventeenth century writers were the source of Elinor Wylie's wit. She loved and admired a mind partly critical, partly imaginative, wholly subtle and ironic in its perceptions of life. Her wit is evidenced by her use of subtle thought, aristocratic scorn, the sharpened epithets, and an imagery of symbolic birds and beasts, jeweled metals, rare, exotic things of this world. These are also the lyric gifts which add sharp, dry precision to the poetry of John Donne. Like him and other metaphysical poets, she inhabited countries of the imagination. The grave was her answer to the problem of desire. She received from Donne the pride and courage of a lively mind, an instrument to use against the world's inhumanity and man's desire of the flesh. Thus, even if diaster strikes, the brave spirit may still preserve its own integrity.

Dante was a great metaphysical poet, as were Donne, Webster, Blake, and Emily Dickinson. To analyze or define metaphysical verse is difficult, for its aesthetic principles are based upon a system which exhibits all the precision of logic while being contained in its own imaginative wildness. This type of poetry is a literary culture which has appeared in every age in slightly different form and is based on passion and intelligence. God and the universe and the human soul lie beyond the physical world and it is in this area that metaphysical poetry attempts to express meaning in symbols of the poet's imagination and to relate all human experience to the one great cycle of life, death, and immortality. For that reason life becomes a pattern which the poet uses to create the solid and essential fact. An image which becomes the exact likeness of both thought and feeling is one of the most characteristic devices of metaphysical poetry. By use of this image the poet's experience becomes objective so that thought and emotion assume a new vitality of imaginative concentration. The element of surprise is another device provided by the association of apparently unrelated objects to suggest a wider range of experience than these objects commonly reveal in real life. Thus Elinor Wylie belongs to the tradition of older writers she admired, poets who used abstract ecstasy of thought and emotion as an approach to essential truths of the spirit. Her work, although original, is not free from the succession of literature.

She was extremely sensitive to the powers contained in language. The quality of her prose reflected the quality of her poetry, for actually her prose was poetic in its style and effects. She wrote with amazing precision, but this precision never sacrificed her excellent ability of phrasing, expression, or use of words. She knew exactly what she was going to say and made very few changes in a work once it was on paper.

Shelley had a great influence on Elinor Wylie. Adoring the man, she wrote about him in both poetry and prose. Her "red carpet to Shelley," to use the title of her sonnet sequence, was her novel *The Orphan Angel*. But the past was not her only literary contact, for she could list among her friends such literary figures as Edna St. Vincent Millay, Dorothy Parker, Sinclair Lewis, Aldous Huxley, Rebecca West, Virginia Woolf, Ford Madox Ford, and, of course, her brother-in-law, Stephen Vincent Benét. She was constantly trying to fill social obligations while working on her poetry or novels. She would escape to England whenever she could, but still she was not alone.

It was Elinor Wylie's brilliance of technique which gave her first book, *Nets to Catch the Wind*, its appeal to the readers of the period. Many of the poems in this collection are songs of knowledge, and they contain much bitterness. She scorned her familiar world, preferring instead empty landscapes, leaden skies, silver streams, white, frozen wintry sleep. There are times when her poems echo resoundingly; again her lines are brief, blood-dripping daggers, and at rare intervals, tears. Life was her durable foe, she insisted, and "A Proud Lady," "Sanctu-

ary," and "Valentine" bear evidence of this battle. "The Eagle and the Mole" records with bitter didacticism her wish to live free of the common world, to live alone.

Her desire to be free is a recurring theme in her later poems. *Black Armour,* the title of her second volume of poetry, takes on added significance in the light of her desire to escape. Elinor Wylie used poetry as her defense against the world, but death would be her only true escape from a too-oppressive mortality. Man touches infinity when he is finally in the grave. Beneath her lines she reveals deep personal emotion, and she gained courage from her own feeling of martyrdom.

Trivial Breath, her most uneven collection, is divided between lyrics of her own personal experience and a payment of literary debts. Her dedication to the volume is a graceful acknowledgment of her debt to the English language. Elinor Wylie spent a great deal of time reading, collecting old books until her work area was practically covered with them. Her poetry and her prose show the rich coloring of the writings of the past. She could adapt her reading to her own works without destroying her own style or originality. In *Trivial Breath* we see the true metaphysician trying to show us that mind rather than heart governs the emotions. This philosophy is explicit in such poems as "Desolation Is a Delicate Thing," "False Prophet," and "Last Supper." Death, she said, was not something to fear or hate. She welcomed the transmutation of the body and admonished her soul in bright, brittle images and metaphors.

In such poems as "Confession of Faith" and "Lament for Glasgerion," she wore her heroic mask like a challenge. Criticism cannot discount the greatness of portrait poems such as "Miranda's Supper," "The Puritan's Ballad," and "Peter and John." These poems show the passion and vigor of her earlier poems along with awareness of too scrupulous discrimination in her work.

Angels and Earthly Creatures, published shortly after her death, exhibits the fullest scope of her talent. There is little of the "over-fine" in the elegiac moods which pervade this collection. Without question this volume reveals a lyric power mature in its integrity but simple in freshness of vision. Beneath a severe articulation of phrase her poetry holds beauty and meaning. It has lost the dark didacticism shown in much of her earlier poetry, yet it retains its wisdom and intellectual clarity. It is abstract, but it is alive with passion. These poems are records of moments captured and held within firm imagery; the lyrics soar with ecstasy and bitterness that are the triumph of life over death through art.

The sonnet sequence, "One Person," fits into the great tradition of English poetry. In it the fear of death is overcome by an exultant affirmation of love and faith. It is her most passionate revelation of the woman and poet, just as "This Corruptible" and "Hymn to Earth" are the complete expression of her philosophy.

Collected Poems of Elinor Wylie contains a number of poems not previously published in book form. One of the best is "A Tear for Cressid," which Elinor Wylie had set to a tune of her own composing. Some of the poems were written when Elinor Wylie was working on the collection titled *Black Armour.* "The Heart's Desire" was an experimental work which she liked extremely well. There are several pieces of lighter verse written chiefly for her close friends. In this group of witty and skillful pieces is a short portrait of herself, "Portrait in Black Paint, With a Very Sparing Use of Whitewash." The humorous poem, "Cri du Cœur," is also typical. Although she distorts the image, Elinor Wylie is still evident through the mask lightly worn.

Elinor Wylie has left behind a collection of poetry bearing the stamp of a dedicated artist. She proved through her own work what endeavor and a courageous spirit and a free mind can accomplish in a few years in a confusing world where life is constantly showing a strange, new side, but where she managed to find her purpose in life and be the master of it. Now, only her work is left to speak for her, at times seriously, sometimes half-jokingly, as in such lines as those in which she expresses a keen desire to display a generous mind rather than the polish and precision most frequently associated with her poetic style.

THE POETRY OF EMERSON

Author: Ralph Waldo Emerson (1803-1882)
First published: Poems, 1847; *May-Day and Other Pieces,* 1867; *Selected Poems,* 1876

In his essay "The Poet," Emerson expresses his belief that poetry, like any art, should be organic rather than simply metrically or musically beautiful:

> For it is not metres, but a metre-making argument, that makes a poem, —a thought so passionate and alive, that, like the spirit of a plant or an animal, it has an architecture of its own, and adorns nature with a new thing. . . . The poet has a new thought: he has a whole new experience to unfold; he will tell us how it was with him, and all men will be the richer in his fortune.

It is Emerson's thesis that poetry should not be an embellished art, but a living form which corresponds to higher truth. Like Poe, Emerson believed that true art is the creation of beauty, but he had quite different ideas about what can be considered beautiful. Where Poe believed that the chief merit of poetry is found in its rhythmical beauty and ability to arouse emotion, Emerson held that the worth of a poem lies in its philosophical truth. Emerson likewise believed that the mind of the poet is not "a music-box of delicate tunes and rhythms," but an instrument by which mankind is enlightened. In other words, the verse itself is worthless unless it is an integral part of the truth it conveys:

> For verse is not a vehicle to carry a sentence as a jewel is carried in a case: the verse must be alive, and inseparable from its contents, as the soul of man inspires and directs the body.

Emerson is no less specific in his views concerning the way in which a poet proceeds to create this type of poem. The true poet, to Emerson, is one who is able to intuit impressions from the "Over-Soul" (that universal truth and spirit of mankind which directs all thinking men) and to relate, through verse, instructive truth found within these impressions. This process entails first a testing of the authority of the impressions (whether they be inferior or superior) and then a spontaneous translation of them, without revision, into poetry. Thus the poet is not a carpenter of entertaining sounds, a man of talent, but rather one who instructs, a man of genius.

Finally, Emerson believed that poetry should be of a specific thematic nature: ideally, a poem should show the unity in nature. Beauty, to Emerson, is that quality of likeness in all of nature's objects; consequently, in order for a poem to be truly beautiful it must demonstrate the unity which exists in the diverse objects in nature.

Emerson views the poem, the poet, and the creative process as being integral parts of true poetry. The poet must be of a certain character, in effect a philosophical mystic who intuits truth. He must be able to place this truth on paper with strict economy and without revision, with the resulting poem being an unembellished, organic chronicle of the unity of nature.

Emerson's poetic theory is extremely Platonic and typical of his whole Transcendental doctrine concerning the objectives of the true genius, or "man thinking." Yet Emerson would probably be the first to admit that, while his theory is quite beautiful, its practical application is difficult. Emerson himself applied it completely to only one of his own poems, "Days." The poem, which is concerned with the duality of the ideal and the real, is a sort of poetic parable of man's mortality.

> Daughters of Time, the hyprocritic Days,
> Muffled and dumb like barefoot der-

vishes,
And marching single in an endless file,
Bring diadems and fagots in their hands.
To each they offer gifts after his will,
Bread, kingdoms, stars, and sky that
holds them all.
I, in my pleached garden, watched the
pomp,
Forgot my morning wishes, hastily
Took a few herbs and apples, and the
Day
Turned and departed silent. I, too late,
Under her solemn fillet saw the scorn.

About these lines Emerson said, "I have written within a twelve-month verses which I do not remember the composition or correction of, and could not write the like today, and have only, for proof of their being mine, various external evidences as the manuscript in which I find them. . . ."

On the whole, Emerson's shorter poems are considered superior to his longer ones, and of these "Days," "The Rhodora," "The Snow-Storm," "Concord Hymn," and "Each and All" are the most representative of Emerson's verse. "Days," for example, is one of the best of Emerson's personal poems. "The Rhodora," on the other hand, shows nature generalized. In this poem Emerson presents the organic theme of the unity in nature's plan symbolized by the beauty of a secluded flower.

Rhodora! if the sages ask thee why
This charm is wasted on the earth and
sky,
Tell them, dear, that if eyes were made
for seeing,
Then Beauty is its own excuse for being.

Another approach used by Emerson was to present the beauty of nature in simple, descriptive verse. In "The Snow-Storm" the poet describes the power and beauty which exist simultaneously in this natural force.

Announced by all the trumpets of the
sky,
Arrives the snow, and, driving o'er the
fields,

Seems nowhere to alight: the whited
air
Hides hills and woods, the river, and
the heaven,
And veils the farm-house at the garden's end.

Equally as uncomplicated in theme and presentation are Emerson's occasional poems such as "Concord Hymn," which was composed for the dedication of a monument to those who fought at the Battle of Concord.

By the rude bridge that arched the
flood,
Their flag to April's breeze unfurled,
Here once the embattled farmers stood,
And fired the shot heard round the
world.

The most significant of Emerson's poems, however, are those in which he attempts to present his ideas of the organic unity in nature. One of the best known of these poems is "Each and All," a well-organized work concerning the interdependence of all created objects. Emerson begins with the general statement that

All are needed by each one;
Nothing is fair or good alone.

He then substantiates this belief by listing three representative instances of objects losing their beauty when they are removed from the whole natural context: the sparrow's song without the river and sky, the delicate sea shells without the seashore, and the graceful maid without the "virgin train." Finally, the poet sees the woodland and is able to recall the joy of nature which he experienced as a child, and he concludes:

Again I saw, again I heard,
The rolling river, the morning bird;
Beauty through my senses stole;
I yielded myself to the perfect whole.

"Brahma" is another of Emerson's attempts to explain his philosophy of nature in verse. Here Brahma, the first-person speaker, symbolizes to Emerson the "world soul" or "Over-soul" which gives meaning to all creation:

> If the red slayer think he slays,
> Or if the slain think he is slain,
> They know not well the subtle ways
> I keep, and pass, and turn again.
>
> . . . . . .
>
> They reckon ill who leave me out;
> When me they fly, I am the wings;
> I am the doubter and the doubt,
> And I the hymn the Brahmin sings.

One cannot help noticing the similarity between the theme in these lines and the overall idea of Whitman's poetry: the belief that there is a divine plan and a divine order in which nothing is without significance.

Closely akin to the theme of the organic nature of things is Emerson's description of the problem of artistic creativity which he depicts in his essay "The Poet" and in the poems "The Problem" and "Merlin." In "The Problem" the poet states that, like nature, art must be organic, and he uses the Parthenon and the Pyramids as examples of organic art:

> Earth proudly wears the Parthenon,
> As the best gem upon her zone;
> And Morning opes with haste her lids,
> To gaze upon the Pyramids.

In order to be in tune with nature, the artist must be free from any tradition or routine which could stifle his creativity and prevent him from being artistically organic. Thus the priest in the poem represents one whose creative freedom is suppressed, and he is contrasted with the poet-speaker:

> I like a church; I like a cowl;
> I love a prophet of the soul;
> And on my heart monastic aisles
> Fall like sweet strains, or pensive
> smiles:
> Yet not for all his faith can see
> Would I that cowléd churchman
> be.

Emerson first found this philosophy of organic art in the works of Coleridge, and it was his ambition as a poet to become such an artist. In "Merlin" he expresses

his belief that poetry like that of Poe, which relies on meter and rhyme, is devoid of any real depth:

> No jingling serenader's art,
> Nor tinkle of piano strings,
> Can make the wild blood start
> In its mystic springs.

It was, rather, mystical verse such as Coleridge's own "Kubla Khan" that was Emerson's goal.

Emerson wrote his first poem at the age of ten, was chosen class poet at Harvard, and published only three volumes of poetry during his lifetime. Although he had a wide range of knowledge extending from Oriental mysticism to Plato, and though he knew what he wanted to write and how it should be written, nevertheless he could not become the free-spirited poet he describes, nor could he break with the traditions which he fought.

Many critics believe that Emerson's primary ability was as a poet, not as a prose writer. Certainly his poems are more concise than his prose and lack the slow development of thought, while containing the essence of his ideas. Like his essays, however, his poems are poorly organized and are lacking in the organic quality which he speaks of so frequently. Actually, his descriptions of what poetry should be serve as an excellent preface to a study of Whitman's poetry; for it is the style and theme found in Whitman's works that Emerson probably would have liked to produce. Only in a very few of his own poems did Emerson succeed in becoming an inspired, organic poet.

Whatever else may be said, Emerson showed the desire of American writers to express themselves in a truly creative fashion rather than through the traditional modes. While Emerson may have failed to produce great works of art, one must consider that what he was attempting was extremely new and that the ideas he tried to present are by no means simple. Indeed, many of his poems are excellent, and in a relative sense he was a good poet. Nevertheless, it is for his poetic theory that he should be valued. His theory of organic art was truly modern and heralded the age which was to follow. If one contrasts his poetic theory with that of the eighteenth century tradition which he faced, one can realize that Emerson was not the traditional poet that he is generally said to be.

THE POETRY OF EMILY BRONTË

Author: Emily Brontë (1818-1848)
First published: Poems by Currer, Ellis, and Acton Bell, 1846; *Selections from the Poems of Ellis Bell,* 1850; *The Complete Poems,* edited by C. W. Hatfield, 1941

In criticism today a poem is read first as an entity in itself; difficulties in reading may be clarified by reference to the author's other poems, his life, his other writings, his times, and the like. Exceptions to this rule are the units of a poetic sequence which are lesser entities within a greater whole. But scholarship often imposes two kinds of superior entity on a single work: its place in the author's canon and its significance as an artifact of its time. Emily Brontë's poems may be read simply as single works of art; when understood, however, as a body of work —apart from the reflection of biography or their significance as mid-nineteenth century English verse—they form not one but two larger entities. Her two hundred poems, some still in manuscript, belong to the "Gondal Chronicles" which she and her younger sister Anne composed from the summer of 1832, when Emily was fourteen and Anne twelve, until Emily's death in 1848; thirty-nine of these poems appeared in 1846 and 1850 as the work of "Ellis Bell" without any reference to Gondal. In the case of Emily Brontë, the smaller number of poems—her "selected poems"—have the greater universality of appearing as complete entities and are here treated as to all intents and purposes the collected poems of Emily Brontë as "Ellis Bell."

The moot point in such a course is whether "Ellis Bell's" poems make complete sense without the remaining poems of Emily Brontë, constituting the "Gondal Chronicles" as we have them. The affirmative depends on two grounds: how the "Ellis Bell" poems came to be published in the lifetime of Emily and her older sister Charlotte and the amount of Gondal reference in the original poems necessary to their meaning. If there is little significant reference in a poem, it can be easily released from its original frame and considered separately. *Poems by Currer, Ellis and Acton Bell* is the fourth step in transforming the Gondal poems into those of "Ellis Bell." The first and third steps were taken by Emily Brontë herself. In the winter of 1843-1844 she transcribed some of the Gondal poems from the small printed notebooks of the "Chronicles" into two manuscript books of fair copies. One is dated February, 1844. In October of the following year Charlotte accidently read one of these books and, breaking the family code of the "secret plays," began insisting that the poems be published simply as a book of verse. Emily reluctantly agreed, probably so that the poems of Charlotte ("Currer") and Anne ("Acton") could appear with hers and thus help Charlotte's desperate gamble to capitalize on the writing ability of the three sisters against the looming possibility of their father's death and their own return to teaching simply in order to live. Charlotte, as a mature literary connoisseur of thirty, was right in her belief in the imperishable quality of Emily's best verse, and her decision—the most significant event in the lives of all three sisters —had three important results: it ended the "Angrian Chronicles" on which she had labored for twenty years with Branwell—the dangerously compulsive "web of childhood" that Miss Fannie Ratchford has shown it to be; it opened the way for the novels which did bring Charlotte money (but no privision against death); and, in Emily's double insistence on keeping her identity secret and erasing the Gondalian references in the poems, it provided a body of her poetry which differs textually from the Gondal canon and appears before the world as the work of "Ellis Bell." The transformation was completed when twenty-one of these poems appeared in the 1846 volume and eighteen in the 1850 *Selections from the Poems of Ellis Bell*, edited considerably by Charlotte but along the lines Emily had begun.

A final reason for following Emily's decision to publish her poems as "Ellis Bell" is that the "Gondal Chronicles" are incomplete; thus the full Gondal matrix is irrecoverable. Thanks, however, to Miss Ratchford's *The Brontë's Web of Childhood* and the work of other scholars the story can be outlined.

In this outline the lonely landscapes are sometimes called "moors" in order to stress that the "Gondal Chronicles" are as much sources for *Wuthering Heights* as they are the inspiration of Emily's poems; these occur at static moments in the action and celebrate the emotions of the character concerned (identified by initials used in the headings to the poems, most of them now lost in Emily's editing the poems for publication); the poems may refer to past events in Gondal and to the present situation of the character but the emphasis of the poem is on the emotion, and this is the prime justification for treating the "Ellis Bell" poems as the "selected poems" of Emily Brontë. A comparison of two such poems, both from the 1846 volume, will show the varying amount of Gondalian reference still in the poems and pose the question whether that reference is essential to understanding the works.

The two poems entitled "Remembrance" and "Death" were written to express Queen Augusta's continuing desolation at the loss of Julius; both poems resolve to continue mourning because the first "May" ("Death") or first "morn" ("Remembrance") is the "Sweet Love of youth" ("Remembrance") and is now gone forever. The resolution is achieved only after two different temptations have been resisted. In "Remembrance" the "Sweet Love of youth" is asked to forgive "if I forget thee," not because the speaker wants to forget "memory's rapturous

pain" but because she apparently cannot die until her appointed time, even though it is her "burning wish to hasten Down to that tomb already more than mine." In "Death" the speaker has been tempted by the return of Spring (or the healing passage of time):

> Little mourned I for the parted Gladness,
> For the vacant nest and silent song;
> Hope was there, and laughed me out of sadness,
> Whispering, "Winter will not linger long."

But the speaker rejects the available hope: "Time, for me, must never blossom more!" She asks Death to strike down the budded branch and return it to Eternity, and thus she rejects "Life's restoring tide." There are more overt references to Gondal in "Remembrance" than in "Death," but in each case they simply give the emotion of the poem an objective correlative to sustain turning the emotion into a poem. In "Death" the references to Augusta's love for Julius can be seen in the phrases "when I was most confiding/In my certain Faith of Joy to be" and "the vacant nest." In "Remembrance" they are more concrete ("that northern shore" and "fifteen wild Decembers"), but in sum the references amount to a very small percentage in poems each of more than two hundred words. In effect these references, in the versions published by "Ellis Bell," are no more essential to a satisfactory reading of the poems than is a knowledge of Arthur Henry Hallam necessary in order to understand Tennyson's *In Memoriam*.

The emotion of the speaker in the two poems is conventional in poetry and natural in life; Emily Brontë's claim to being a poet is her personal variation on that theme of loss of the loved one. In some of her other poems there is more reference to Gondalian names and situations—the mother who loses her baby on the moor in "The Outcast Mother" or the references to "Irene" in "Faith and Despondency" and to "Edward" in "A Death-Scene"—but it is still possible to see these as the necessary though extraordinary furniture of the poem.

Emily Brontë's poems depend on the conventional antithesis of inner reality to superficial appearances, a reality discovered or celebrated in the course of the poem. Her unique handling of the convention was to prefer the eccentric or perverse to that normally celebrated in poetry; she seeks the moors, not a pleasant landscape (as Charlotte observed in introducing her *Selections from the Poems of Ellis Bell*); she chooses December before May; she prefers solitude to company and does not make the conventional return to society at the close of the poem; above all she seeks death, and she really means it. She conveys the intensity of her own emotions by dramatizing the situation and focusing on concrete objects, generally aspects of nature, to sing of sorrow; as in "Song":

> The linnet in the rocky dells,
> The moor-lark in the air,
> The bee among the heather-bells
> That hide my lady fair:

Needless to say the "fair" lady is in her grave and "in her tranquil sleep" where Emily rejoiced to go; as Charlotte dryly observed "the colour and perfume of the flowers [i.e. poems] are not such as fit them for festal uses." Charlotte's famous dictum—"Liberty was the breath of Emily's nostrils"—is shown in most of the poems, where the speaker chafes against restrictions and principally that of the body itself, especially in her three most famous: "The Old Stoic" (as it is misnamed), and the stanzas beginning "Often rebuked, yet always back returning" and "No coward soul is mine." The popular choice of these is improved by acquaintance with the other "Ellis Bell" poems; together they sum up her rejection of the unreal world of "riches," "long-past history," and temporal doubts of God's being. The poet affirms her faith only in the moors "where my own nature would be leading" and, given that nature, she achieves a resounding vision of earth which "can centre both the worlds of Heaven and Hell" and of total and real existence only in God.

THE POETRY OF EMILY DICKINSON

Type of work: Poetry
Author: Emily Dickinson (1830-1886)
Principal published works: Poems, 1890; *Poems: Second Series,* 1891; *Poems: Third Series,*
1896; *The Single Hound,* 1914; *Further Poems,* 1929; *Unpublished Poems,* 1936; *Bolts
of Melody: New Poems,* 1945; *The Poems of Emily Dickinson,* 1955

The life and literary career of Emily Dickinson were filled with irony. In deciding that some of the poems she sent him were not strong enough for publication, the essayist and critic Thomas Wentworth Higginson is said to have remarked that they were "too delicate." This judgment is only one of the many strange blunders made in connection with a woman who has finally been accorded the rank of a major poet.

Proper evaluation of a contemporary writer is an uncertain business in any era, but literary criticism in Emily Dickinson's time produced some especially ironic judgments. Of those who saw her poems during her lifetime, only Helen Hunt Jackson seems to have appreciated their real worth; Emily herself (and Emerson, who was astute enough as a critic to recognize the genius of Walt Whitman) thought Mrs. Jackson to be one of the great poets of her time, but she is now remembered almost solely for her championing of Emily. "Creative editing" is another irony that has plagued the work of the inspired recluse of Amherst. Only six of her poems appeared in print before her death; the mutilation of these by zealous editors who wanted to "correct" her vagaries of rhyme, meter, and punctuation was a factor in her decision not to seek publication but to take her chances with fame after death. Well-meaning editing continued to haunt her work long after she died and only recently, in *The Poems of Emily Dickinson,* edited by Thomas H. Johnson and published in three volumes in 1955, has the world been allowed to read her lyrics as she wrote and punctuated them.

The bare facts of the life of Emily Dickinson were so simple that they would seem to permit no garbling, no misinterpretation, but even here what might be called "creative tampering" has also been at work. Legend says she fell madly in love with the Reverend Charles Wadsworth and he with her. Supposedly he was willing to give up family and career for Emily, to renounce everything for love; but true to her Puritan background, she refused him. Now biographers are certain that no such double renunciation ever took place, that while she was greatly influenced by her feelings for Wadsworth and addressed to him many of her finest poems, their acquaintance was largely restricted to letters and he was probably never aware of her deep attachment.

Out of these tangles that have long surrounded her life and career, the reader is now able to judge and enjoy the work of one of America's most original and remarkable poets. Using the Bible as her chief source of inspiration and the rhythms of the hymn books as a metrical starting point, Emily Dickinson developed with care a technique that produced poems breath-taking in construction; they are full of the magic of a child who balances blocks on top of one another, performing feats impossible for a shaky adult hand. Almost as daring as the rhythms are her experiments in all the variations on part rhymes. With the help of Whitman, Emily Dickinson pushed open the door through which the "modern" poets have rushed to find new ways of expressing themselves. Here is an example of her metrics and musical effect:

Success is counted sweetest
By those who ne'er succeed.
To comprehend a nectar
Requires sorest need.

Not one of all the purple Host
Who took the Flag today
Can tell the definition
So clear of Victory

As he defeated—dying—
On whose forbidden ear
The distant strains of triumph
Burst agonized and clear!

Poems in this characteristic style were what brought forth Higginson's pronouncement—"too delicate." The judgment now seems particularly obtuse, for the very delicacy he objected to is one of the poet's chief charms; and sometimes that delicacy conceals the strength of iron:

The Soul selects her own Society—
Then—shuts the Door—
To her divine Majority—
Present no more—

Unmoved—she notes the Chariots—
    pausing—
At her low Gate—
Unmoved—an Emperor be kneeling
Upon her Mat—

I've known her—from an ample nation—
Choose One—
Then—close the Valves of her attention—
Like Stone—

The spirit of Emily Dickinson's poems has been compared with that of the great metaphysicals, John Donne and William Blake; she is indeed like them in her ability to expand the little particularities of her everyday existence into ideas that are timeless and universal. For Emily Dickinson, who as her life slipped by confined herself almost entirely to her home and its grounds, these particularities were birds, flies, frogs, sunrises and sunsets, cups, saucers, doors, even a snake, that "narrow Fellow in the Grass" whom she never met "without a tighter breathing and Zero at the Bone." Broadening these simple subjects, the poet expresses her feelings about God, death, and immortality.

Her relationship with God is an interesting one, for even in her childhood she could not force herself to be orthodox. As a schoolgirl she had great difficulty in professing herself to be a Christian. The harsh God of the Old Testament—the God who created man in His own image, restricted him with all sorts of "thou-shall-nots," and then destroyed the image with death—had little appeal for Emily. In her poems her God is a very personal one, to be treated like a friend, praised for his good deeds and chided for his faults. Pompous piety has no place in any of her religious poems and when her feelings of intimacy lead her to address the Deity as "Papa above!" we are charmed rather than shocked by poetry that lets us become a part of a delightful woman to whom the trivialities of existence and the untouchable verities are of equal importance.

Like most poets, Emily Dickinson was intrigued by death; characteristically, she made it seem just another event in human experience. In one of her best-known poems, death is the driver of a carriage which picks her up, slowly takes her past a school where children are playing during recess, past fields, past the setting sun, until finally

We paused before a House that seemed
A Swelling of the Ground—
The Roof was scarcely visible—
The Cornice—in the Ground—

Since then—'tis Centuries—and yet
Feels shorter than the Day
I first surmised the Horses Heads
Were toward Eternity—

But death is not something the poet takes lightly. The loss of those she loved—particularly her father and Dr. Wadsworth—were blows from which she reeled; to one whose circle of acquaintanceship was so constricted each death assumed such great importance that it inspired a flood of little elegies in which the poet records both her grief and her love.

"Time," "eternity," and "immortality" are words that are insistently repeated in these poems. Always a skeptic, she once asked the question, "Is immortality true?" and like a proper metaphysician she lets her mind play with the two possible answers. In one of her last poems she seems to say that a person's identity can never be blotted out; the poem concludes with this stanza:

> To die is not to go—
> On Doom's consummate Chart
> No Territory new is staked—
> Remain thou as thou art.

Many readers of Emily Dickinson feel that she is a poet whom one may like or not like, that those who judge her a major poet have developed a sort of gourmet's taste in literature, preferring the delicate and dainty to the robust and wholesome. There are indeed times when her poetry is quaint to the point of being cranky, when her eccentricities, compressions, and indirections lead to incomprehensibility; but if the reader will give her a second or third chance he, like others before him, will find that her best poetry provides the essence of great literature—contact with a powerful, original, fascinating mind.

THE POETRY OF ESENIN

Author: Sergei Esenin (1895-1925)
Principal published works: Radunitsa, 1916; "Ionia," 1919; *Moscow of the Taverns,* 1922

After 1910 a general reaction occurred in Russian literature against the vagueness and obscurity of Symbolism. Acmeism, led by Gumilyov, and Futurism, under Mayakovsky, represented two of the directions taken by this reaction. A third direction was that followed by the so-called "peasant poets." These writers, led by Nikolai Klyuyev, expounded a mystical faith in the Russian peasantry and worked folklore and religious liturgy into their poems. The greatest of the peasant poets was Sergei Esenin. Beginning as a student of Klyuyev, he soon surpassed his master in the form and content of his poetry.

The term "peasant poet" is extremely apt in Esenin's case, for he always lamented the passing of traditional Russian life, the village, and the unsophisticated religion of the peasants. In one of his prose works, *Mary's Keys,* published in 1920, Esenin wrote about the origins of Russian art and culture and about the disintegration of Russian religiosity. He felt that without religious traditions the very source of folk art would disappear; whereas the earlier peasant had been able to orient himself in his environment, Esenin now felt that the peasants were uprooted and spiritually lost in an increasingly industrialized world. One critic of Esenin, V. Zavalishin, has said that Esenin knew and understood the meaning of folk art and the peasantry not as a learned scholar but as a man who had lived with them since childhood.

In 1916, Esenin published his first collection of poems, *Radunitsa,* a quasi-pagan spring ritual for the dead. These early poems resemble Klyuyev's work and often glorify the tranquil beauty of nature. In the following year Esenin welcomed the Revolution, but he saw it as a religious and not a political event. He felt that Bolshevism would wear itself out in time and would be superseded by a reli-

gious paradise. He saw only one obstacle to this earthly paradise: peasant fear and servility. The poem "Ionia," written in 1918, urged the peasants toward courage and daring and predicted the advent of a proletarian Eden. Esenin's religion was that of the Old Believers, a group which had split from the Orthodox Church, ostensibly over the question of whether the sign of the cross should be made with two fingers or three. The Old Believers had since dedicated themselves to dogma and fanatical faith, but Esenin reduced this faith to an earthly scale in such poems as "Returning Home" and "The Comrade." Before long, however, Esenin realized the Revolution was not strengthening religion but substituting other ideas for it. In the poem "Mare's Ships," Esenin finally, though impressionistically, condemned the Revolution for the suffering and death it had caused.

Esenin feared the industrialization brought about by the Revolution. As an outward sign of increasing disillusionment, he founded, along with other younger writers, the Imaginism movement which flourished in Moscow from 1918 to 1920. The Imaginists, asserting that the distinctive nature of poetry lay in its imagery, tended to make their poems collections of word pictures, often far-fetched and exotic when they set coarse and crude images next to pathetic and sublime ones in their search for effects. But far more striking than their theory of literature was the kind of life they led. These writers took up a bohemian life of orgies and scandals, and it is said that Esenin outdid them all in license and violence.

Esenin recorded his psychological experiences during these years in "A Hooligan's Confession," published in 1921, and in a collection called *Moscow of the Taverns,* appearing a year later. Soviet critics have condemned these poems as full of filth and vice with nothing to elevate them. But at the same time these verses are something of a personal confession. It is as though Esenin realized that his depression could not be dissolved in vodka, and only too well he also realized he was out of step with the times. In one of his poems, full of despair, he considers himself the last poet of the peasants. And in another poem he feels that his poetry has fallen from grace, and, probably, so has he. In 1921, Esenin wrote a play in verse entitled *Pugachey*. It is a collection of lyrical fragments which, although not historically true, does possess an element of social veracity colored by Esenin's passionate sympathy for the enslaved peasants.

With many poets Imaginism was simply a literary pose, a desire to shock the bourgeoisie as the Futurists had done before them. But for Esenin this life was more tragic. He felt the full force of its pessimism. His disillusionment with the Revolution which had led him into the Imaginist circle continued unabated, forcing him to say in one poem that he has been deceived. By 1920 the anti-peasant aspect of the Revolution had become even more pronounced, and Esenin culminated this period of drunkenness and scandal with his marriage to Isadora Duncan, the American dancer, in 1922. Without a common language between them, they found a bond in high living. A year later, after an unsuccessful and shabby world tour, their marriage ended.

These events seem to have sobered Esenin, and on his return to Russia he tried to adjust to the new order and to regain and reconsider his ideas and feelings about the rural Russia he had given up for Moscow. Although he returned to his native village, he could not recapture his past, and the lyrics he wrote in this period are sad and reflective, foreshadowing his death. In one poem he said that he was destined to die in the back alleys of Moscow, not in the village of thatched houses where he had been born. In another poem Esenin calls himself the last of the village poets. He celebrates the beauty of nature and complains about the coming of machinery to destroy the beautiful fields. The loss of his youth and joy in the village, the changes created by his urbanization, cause him to grieve, and his poem reflects his later death by his own hand. Most of his tavern poems contain a tragic reflection.

Eventually Esenin turned from Imaginism and chose Pushkin for his new model; and in "Persian Themes" Esenin's verse does resemble the lucid, simple verse of his new model. During the last year of his life Esenin wrote the long, autobiographical poem, "Anna Snegina," which portrays a Russian village during the Revolution, and "The Black Man," a narrative poem in which a man confesses his many sins. In several of his shorter lyrics of this period Esenin prophesied his own death, and on December 27, 1925, he hanged himself in a Leningrad hotel room after writing a farewell poem with his own blood. The verses ended with the now famous lines in which he declared that death is not new, but life is no newer.

Esenin's last poems are simple and melodious, sometimes sentimental and sometimes nostalgic. During the 1920's he was extremely popular for these verses. His lyrical, melancholic poems of the rural landscape, village life, and animals appealed both to Communist youth and to older Russians who still remembered pre-revolutionary days. Esenin seemed to have a special feeling for animals, calling them "younger brothers" and dedicating several of his poems to them, as in "The Cow" and "Song About a Dog."

Because Esenin rejected the Revolution and because he led a life of riot, Eseninism was officially condemned by the Communist Party. Officialdom described him as a *kulak* (rich peasant) poet and did not allow his work to be reprinted. Censorship did not dim Esenin's popularity; in fact, one critic has called him the most widely read twentieth century Russian poet, both at home and abroad.

In a sense Esenin's personal fate was symbolic of a Russia in transition. During his lifetime his country changed from an agrarian society to a complex industrial state. The conflict between what had been and what was emerging, and the failure of many of the hopes people had for the Revolution, were expressed personally in the poems of Esenin. Perhaps this is the secret of his great appeal. Esenin, unlike Mayakovsky, refused to compromise himself for the Revolution. He remained openly critical of the government, never diminishing the vigor of his own poems as Mayakovsky had done. And when he could take no more, when both his personal and public life offered him nothing more, he chose death.

THE POETRY OF FLECKER

Author: James Elroy Flecker (1884-1915)
Principal published works: The Bridge of Fire, 1907; *Forty-Two Poems,* 1911; *The Golden Journey to Samarkand,* 1913; *The Old Ships,* 1915; *Collected Poems,* 1916; *Hassan,* 1922

It is possible to risk the generalization that there are two types of the minor poet. To one type belongs the writer who fits neatly into the style prevailing at the moment, echoing all of its mannerisms so faithfully that his poems cannot be distinguished from those of any other equally minor figure of the day. Then there is the opposite type, the minor writer who never seems able to settle on any style and whose poems, in consequence, seem to have been written by half a dozen people. It would not be unfair to place Flecker in this second category.

According to J. C. Squire, who wrote the introduction to the *Collected Poems,* Flecker was much impressed by the poetic theory of the French Parnassians. Squire then quotes a passage from the preface to *The Golden Journey to Samarkand* in which Flecker expressed his admiration for that school of poetry, which had come into being under the leadership of Charles Marie Leconte de Lisle as a protest against the excessive emotionalism and subjectivity of the Romanticists; in addition, the Parnassians wished to return French prosody to something like its former strictness. According to their point of view, a poem should be purely objective and should rigorously exclude the exploitation of the author's private feelings. The doctrine of the school has been described as "Spartan"; its culmination as the hundred and eighteen sonnets of José Maria de Hérédia, a Cuban-born French poet whom Flecker greatly admired. Except for George Moore, who rejected from his *Anthology of Pure Poetry* in 1924 any verse with a taint of subjectivity, on the grounds that the only permanent world is the world of things, Flecker seems to have been the only English writer influenced by the Parnassian doctrine. He described that which was contrary to the Parnassian principles as dull, vulgar, or obscure versifying.

Flecker's theorizing is revealed as basically a part of the revolt against Victorianism that began in the 1880's and continued until World War I. Also, he illustrates another aspect of the *rapprochement* with French literature that marked this same period; instead of turning to the French Symbolists, as the poets of the generation before his had done, he turned to the Parnassians. Yet it is difficult to find in Flecker's work (though he translated one of Leconte de Lisle's poems) any obvious influence of the French school that he so much admired. Indeed, some of his early poems, such as the "First Sonnet of Bathrolaire," sound amazingly like products of the 1890's. And there is the inevitable translation from Baudelaire—this time of the "Litany to Satan," an attempt of which it can be said only that he fared better than did Arthur Symons, a statement that is no great compliment.

But whatever Flecker's poetic theories may have been, a reading of his verse will reveal a poet working in the Romantic tradition. The years just before World War I represented a turning point in English poetry. There were the Georgians who, reacting against the artificialities of the 1890's, let sunlight and fresh air into poetry by rediscovering the beauty of the English countryside and the speech of everyday life. At the same time, the hard, dry, intellectual poetry predicted by T. E. Hulme was coming into being; 1915, the year of Flecker's last volume, saw the publication of T. S. Eliot's "The Love Song of J. Alfred Prufrock," which might be said to have turned modern poetry in its present direction. In only one poem did Flecker attempt the style that we now think of as "modern." That poem is "Oxford Canal." On the other hand, such a poem as "Brumana" is very much in the Georgian style, some of its lines recalling the work of Rupert Brooke, with whom Flecker has often been compared.

In 1910, Flecker, who had entered the consular service, was sent to Constantinople and spent most of the few years of life remaining to him in the Near East. What might be called his "Oriental" poems date from this period. These are the poems by which he is best known, and some of them were incorporated into his posthumously produced play, *Hassan*. These poems are quite beautiful, even thought somewhat artificial in their carefully cultivated Arabian Nights manner: "Gates of Damascus," "Yasmin," "Saadabad."

It is difficult to believe that the lush, romantic lines of Flecker's "Oriental" poems were written by the same man who wrote "Oxford Canal" or the terse "Tenebris Interlucentem."

Although *Hassan* is written in prose, this play should be mentioned here, for its posthumous publication and production in 1922 brought Flecker more attention than he had received during his life; and through it he is known to the generation that can remember the 1920's. Mario Praz, in *The Romantic Agony*, dismisses the play as a "sadistic fantasy," and it is true that the concluding scene, in which the lovers are tortured to death, is sufficiently gruesome. The plot, which has its roots in *Measure for Measure*, has a certain degree of tragic intensity, and the dialogue, written in a deliberately overblown, pseudo-Oriental style, is also effective within the framework of the romantic plot. Into the play were incorporated several of the "Oriental" lyrics written earlier, and as part of this adventure of Haroun Al-Rashid, they appear to better advantage than as individual poems. The epilogue to *The Golden Journey to Samarkand* was used as a grand finale to the play, where it makes a moving and memorable conclusion to the tragedy.

Comparison has often been made between Flecker and Rupert Brooke, undoubtedly because they were contemporaries and died during World War I, in which Flecker could not serve because of his ill health. There are some points of similarity, and Flecker's unfinished "Burial in England" shows that he could have written war poetry of no mean order had he not been a dying man. But Brooke was by all odds the finer poet of the two. In his later poems that emerged from his experiences in the South Seas, he had begun to show what he might have become; he had developed a "style" that was his own. To this point of development Flecker, perhaps because of his physical condition, never attained. He was still groping, still trying to find his own voice, when he died. Hence, he is now remembered for a few individual poems, very different from each other, rather than for a body of work that somehow fitted together. He was a late Romantic, writing at the end of a period.

THE POETRY OF FRENEAU

Type of work: Poetry
Author: Philip Freneau (1752-1832)
Principal published works: A Poem on the Rising Glory of America, 1772 (with H. H. Brackenridge); *The American Village,* 1772; *General Gage's Confession,* 1775; *The British Prison Ship,* 1781; *The Poems of Philip Freneau,* 1786; *Poems Written Between the Years 1786 and 1794,* 1795; *Poems Written and Published during the Revolutionary War,* 1809; *A Collection of Poems . . . Written Between the Year 1797 and the Present Time,* 1815

The fact that Freneau's collected poetic works, at least in a definitive edition, were not published until over a hundred years after he had stirred the American conscience heightens the irony of the title of the best biography of the poet, *That Rascal Freneau: A Study in Literary Failure* (1941). The phrase comes from George Washington, who more than anyone had occasion to be grateful to Freneau, not only for the several laudatory poems addressed to him but also for lifting soldier morale during the nadir of the Revolution. Freneau's political poetry served the same purpose as Paine's incendiary essays, and was perhaps more effective.

These facts alone would make Freneau interesting historically, but his poetry of nature, of American life and culture, add an important dimension to his memory. Most literary historians and critics consider Freneau our first outstanding poet, a liberal in form as well as content. He dared to introduce native themes and idioms into poetry at a time when other writers remained slavishly Anglophile. While a student at Princeton he wrote a poem in collaboration with Hugh Henry Brackenridge, "A Poem on the Rising Glory of America," a cue to later cleverly designed propagandist pieces, written first in praise of British imperialism and then revised to express sharp denunciation of British usurpation. Significantly, the account that the poem was received at commencement, 1771, "with great applause," mentions only Brackenridge's name. In blank verse and dramatic dialogue, the work traces the history of America as the story of freedom-seeking men, establishing on this Eden-like continent, prophetically, a haven for all the oppressed:

And when a train of rolling years are past,
(So sung the exiled seer in Patmos isle)
A new Jerusalem, sent down from heaven,
Shall grace our happy earth,—perhaps this land,

. . . . . .

and such America at last shall have
When ages yet to come, have run their round,
and future years of bliss alone remain.

From this patriotic writing Freneau turned to the often-quoted "The American Village," a poem in praise of this land in contrast to "The Deserted Village" of a decadent England. Though written in heroic couplets, the sentiments expressed, the names, and the idiom are American.

To yonder village then will I descend,
There spend my days, and there my ev'-nings spend;
Sweet haunt of peace whose mud' wall'd sides delight,
The rural mind beyond the city bright.

Perhaps the neglect of his early poems caused him to retreat to a more romantic life in the West Indies. Some memorable verse came out of this period in the 1770's, notably "The House of Night," a poem worthy of Poe with its vivid description of death attended by weird phantasms and graveyard symbols:

Around his bed, by the dull flam-beaux' glare,
I saw pale phantoms—Rage to madness vext,

Wan, wasting grief, and ever musing
care,
Distressful pain, and poverty perplext.

Several times Freneau was captured
by the British while going to and fro
among his island paradises. Finally he
was so incensed over the ruthless war on
the sea and the sad disposition of prisoners that he wrote in 1781 his most
powerful early work of condemnation,
"The British Prison Ship," which contains a notable picture of horror on the
high seas:

The various horrors of these hulks to
tell,
These Prison Ships where pain and
horror dwell,
Where death in tenfold vengeance
holds his reign,
And injur'd ghosts, yet unaveng'd,
complain;
This be my talk—ungenerous Britons,
you
Conspire to murder those you can't
subdue.

Though these were not Freneau's first
satiric thrusts, his earlier diatribes had
not the stuff of conviction. But the war
on the sea he had suffered at first hand
and he wrote about it from personal
knowledge.

From that time on, Freneau followed
closely the progress, or lack of it, of
the Revolution, writing stirring patriotic
pieces to boost morale, scourging lines to
incense the colonials against their op-
pressors, rollicking ballads and celebrations of American victory or British defeat. He edited and editorialized during
the latter days of the war, his poems
being a special feature of various journals with which he was associated. For
this work he was credited by Jefferson
with saving the Constitution from the
Monarchists and the Federalists. Attacked
by critics and forgotten by his countrymen, he abandoned poetry and spent the
years immediately following the war as
a captain of coastal vessels. A collection
of his early poetry and essays was published in 1786. He was aroused to cele-

brate the French Revolution to some
memorable lines written in 1793, on
Bastille Day:

The chiefs that bow to Capet's reign,
In mourning, now, their weeds display;
But we, that scorn a monarch's chain,
Combine to celebrate the DAY
Of Freedom's birth that put the seal,
And laid in dust the proud Bastille.

This partisan feeling eventually gave
rise to the *Probationary Odes by Jonathan
Pindar, Esq.*, some of the most mature
of Freneau's satires against the decay of
liberal, democratic sentiments. At the
same time he wrote masterful, idiomatic
prose under the pseudonym of Robert
Slender. These together brought the
wrath of the pompous against him, a
prelude to the journalistic battle of the
United States Gazette vs. the *National
Gazette*, Hamilton vs. Freneau. From
this affair came the abuse from which
Freneau never recovered during his lifetime.

Freneau was first a poet, then a politician and patriot, as these very late lines
in "The Brook in the Valley" reveal:

The world has wrangled half an age,
And we again in war engage,
While this sweet, sequestr'd rill
Murmurs through the valley still. . . .

But, with all your quiet flow,
Do you not some quarrels know!
Lately, angry, how you ran!
All at war—and much like man.

Of his work, the poems remembered
and anthologized today are his unpre-
tentious, indigenous nature lyrics such
as "The Wild Honey Suckle" ("Fair
flower, that dost so comely grow") or "On
a Honey Bee" ("Thou, born to sip the
lake or spring"). Also, his celebration of
the first Americans deserves mention, especially "The Indian Burying Ground":

In spite of all the learned have said,
I still my old opinion keep;
The posture that we give the dead
Points out the soul's eternal sleep.

Recently, Freneau's verse has been reclaimed from neglect, very much as his reputation has been cleared of calumnious attacks by his contemporaries. Near his former home at Mount Pleasant, New Jersey, stands a monument inscribed:

> Heaven lifts its everlasting portals high
> And bids the pure in heart behold their God.

THE POETRY OF FROST

Type of work: Poetry
Author: Robert Frost (1874-1963)
Principal published works: A Boy's Will, 1913; *North of Boston,* 1914; *Mountain Interval,*
1916; *New Hampshire: A Poem with Notes and Grace Notes,* 1923; *West-Running
Brook,* 1928; *A Further Range,* 1936; *A Witness Tree,* 1942; *A Masque of Reason,*
1945; *Steeple Bush,* 1947; *A Masque of Mercy,* 1947; *How Not to Be King,* 1951

They would not find me changed from
   him they knew—
Only more sure of all I thought was
   true.

Far in the pillared dark
Thrush music went—
Almost like a call to come in
To the dark and lament.

In a sense this early prediction by Robert Frost is an accurate description of the course of his writing career: Frost's poetry has not changed; it has simply grown stronger. The dominant characteristics of his work—his impeccable ear for the rhythms of speech; his realistic handling of nature that transcends the ordinary "love" we ascribe to poets of the outdoors; his revelation of human character by means of dramatic events his warm philosophy that combines a whimsical poet with a dirt farmer whose feet are not only planted on the ground but in it—all these qualities were apparent (at least to some readers) early in his career. And they are still there, handled with greater precision, displaying more depth. As an example of this strengthening process, this growth of sapling into tree, look first at the little poem, "The Pasture," the last stanza of which invites the reader into Frost's *A Boy's Will:*

I'm going out to fetch the little calf
That's standing by the mother. It's so
   young,
It totters when she licks it with her
   tongue.
I sha'n't be gone long.—You come too.

The Frost charm is evident in these lines, but there is also a somewhat juvenile, Rilevesque quality. When one compares "The Pasture" with "Come In," a much later and firmer treatment of the same general theme, the superior diction is immediately apparent in such magnificent lines as these:

But equally apparent is a greater depth of psychological complexity, a stronger suggestion of the "death wish" that John Ciardi discusses in his controversial analysis of "Stopping by Woods on a Snowy Evening," the more famous lyric to which "Come In" is certainly a superb companion piece.

Frost has not changed, only grown surer; but there has been an amazing change, down through the years, in the attitude taken toward his poems. First, his fellow Americans could not see this most American of writers as a poet at all; it was necessary for him to go to England to be hailed for his talent. Secondly, when the English had pointed him out to us, we catalogued him as another cold New England poet who saw everything in black and white. This astonishing judgment becomes superegregious when we consider that *A Boy's Will* contains a poem of such warm understanding as "The Tuft of Flowers" and that *North of Boston,* his second volume, includes "The Death of the Hired Man," "Home Burial," and "The Fear," three dramatic poems that are intensely emotional. After Frost's reputation finally became established, the critics forced him into a third stage of his career: he was recognized as a major poet, but one not very interesting to talk or write about because his poetry was thought too simple and because Frost held aloof from the free-verse poets whose efforts, he felt, lacked discipline. Now, at last, Frost has entered a fourth period in which his great talents are fully recognized, and he is regarded as a poet of far more depth and subsurface complexity than anyone had previously realized. Two of Frost's poems that are provocative enough to satisfy the most eager analyst are "Directive," with its Grail imagery, and "The Subverted Flower," with its tantalizing psychological horror.

But Frost will always be a poet more loved than analyzed. He expresses himself in such an attractive way that his readers identify themselves with the poet; they would like to be Frost. The descriptive lines one finds in "After Apple Picking," for example, have a perfection that seems the only, the inevitable, way of describing the dream that the poet feels coming on. Many other poems by Frost contain this same perfection of word choice. "Two Tramps in Mud Time" is so meticulously written (and yet so effortless, with its touches of the famous Frost wit) that the reader feels surrounded by April weather; and he clearly sees those two hulking tramps who stand around idly, waiting for the poet to hire them to chop his wood.

If Frost had limited his poetry to descriptive and philosophical lyrics, he would still rank as a major poet; fortunately, his poems are also full of people, characters who are understandable and vividly real. In "The Death of the Hired Man" four people come alive: Mary, the sympathetic wife; Warren, the practical, somewhat cynical husband; Harold Wilson, the boy "who studied Latin like the violin because he liked it"; and Silas, the harmlessly wastrel hired man who had come "home" to die. Other people are scattered like old friends throughout the poems: Magoon, the timid professor, and Lafe, the burly bill collector, in "A Hundred Collars"; the casual witch in "The Witch of Coös"; the newlyweds who philosophize so well in "West-Running Brook"; the old farmer in "The Mountain" who lives at the foot of a mountain he refuses to climb simply because he sees no practical reason for doing so; and

that other dour farmer in "Brown's Descent" who takes a hilarious ride down a mountain on a slick crust of snow.

There are others equally memorable, but perhaps the outstanding character in all the poems is Frost himself. Everything he writes is warmed by his own personality, and he emerges from his volumes as a great and charming man who feels deeply but who never breaks the restraining tether of good taste. Emotional but never overly sentimental, he is dramatic but never melodramatic, conservative but not reactionary, sometimes pessimistic but never defeated, humorous without being flippant.

Trying to sum up the beguiling effect of Frost's outlook on life is difficult, for his writing personality is many-sided. Certainly he strikes the reader as a man who looks at life in a way that is both poetic and practical. The concluding lines of "Birches" beautifully illustrate this remarkable blend. In the poem the speaker has expressed a desire "to get away from earth awhile" and then come back for a new start:

I'd like to go by climbing a birch tree,
And climb black branches up a snow-
  white trunk
Toward heaven, till the tree could bear
  no more,
But dipped its top and set me down
  again.
That would be good both going and
  coming back.
One could do worse than be a swinger
  of birches.

Frost's wise outlook is not always concerned with only the broad generalities of life; sometimes he becomes specific about the events of our times, as in "To a Thinker," which gives advice to a President, and in "U. S. 1946 King's X," which is a mordant piece of irony:

Having invented a new Holocaust,
And been the first with it to win a war,
How they make haste to cry with fin-
  gers crossed,
King's X—no fairs to use it any more!

A poet must be more than a dramatist,

an analyst of human emotion, a humorist, and a philosopher: he must above all be a poet. Frost meets this difficult test. He chooses to write in the rhythms of human speech, and by sounding as natural as a man talking to his neighbor in simple language he has produced some of America's greatest poetry. His approach seems casual and disarming, rather like that of a champion athlete who breaks records without straining, who never tries too hard. To claim perfection for anyone—athlete or poet—is absurd. Frost has his defects. At times he is like a kindly teacher whose whimsicality is so sly as to be irritating, whose wisdom sometimes descends to mere crankiness. But Frost has written magnificent poetry—simple, sure, strong. Listen to this beautiful (but not often quoted) lyric called "Moon Compasses":

I stole forth dimly in the dripping pause
Between two downpours to see what
    there was.
And a masked moon had spread down
    compass rays
To a cone mountain in the midnight
    haze,
As if the final estimate were hers,
And as it measured in her calipers,
The mountain stood exalted in its place.
So love will take between the hands a
    face.

THE POETRY OF GABRIELA MISTRAL

Author: Gabriela Mistral (Lucila Godoy Alcayaga, 1889-1957)
Principal published works: Desolación, 1922 (*Desolation*); Ternura, 1925 (*Tenderness*);
Preguntas, 1930 (*Questions*); Nubes Blancas, 1930 (*White Clouds*); Tala, 1938

Gabriela Mistral was born Lucila Godoy Alcayaga, on April 7, 1889, of Spanish and Basque lineage; her father, who deserted the family when Lucila was but a child of three years, was a teacher and a poet. Her early years were spent among the peasants, and the poet, who speaks of herself as one of the *campesinos*, put the peasant's love of the land and the countryside into her poetry.

To understand the poetry of Gabriela Mistral, one must know something of her life. To begin with, she always thought of herself as a teacher first and a poet second, even after she had been awarded the Noble Prize for Literature in 1945. She began her teaching career at the age of fifteen, with unusual success. In 1912 she became a teacher in secondary schools, moving up from primary schools, with the help, it is said, of Pedro Aguirre Cerda, who later became President of Chile, the poet's native land. During the years 1918-1922 the poet served as director of *liceos* at Punta Arenas, Temuco, and Santiago. In 1922 she had become so well known in educational circles that she was sent to Mexico to help in the educational reforms in that country. Her fame spread, and in later life she held a host of educational and official positions. She taught in the United States at Columbia University, Vassar, and Middlebury College. She was Chilean representative on the Committee of Intellectual Co-operation of the League of Nations, in Geneva. She was Chilean consul in Naples, Madrid, Lisbon, Nice, and Santa Barbara, California. She died in New York City in 1957.

Gabriela Mistral's first fame as a poet came when three sonnets on death were read for her (though she was in the audience) at Chile's Juegos Florales, in 1914.

These poems, which brought her national acclaim, were, ironically, the indirect result of a suicide. Gabriela had fallen in love with a young man about five years before. The young man, Romelio Ureta, killed himself with a gunshot when he was unable to repay money he had "borrowed" from the railroad which employed him, to help a friend in need of funds. Also ironically, her first published volume of poems appeared, not in her native Chile, but in the United States, in 1922, after interest in her poetry had been generated by Federico de Onís, in a lecture on her poetry at the Columbia University Instituto de las Españas. This volume was *Desolación*.

Part of the poetry in *Desolación*, in the section entitled "Dolor," was also the direct result of the death of the young man she loved. But there are also poems which show the poet's interest and feeling for religion, her deep maternal feeling for children, and her inspiration in teaching. There are also some poems for children, as well as those written for the adult public. The poems about love show that love for her, at least as a poet, was not a sensual gratification, nor was it joy. The poet tells the reader that it is a bitter experience that ends with death, unless it is the kind of love that becomes almost a religion, so that it can transcend mortality. Her own love, as she writes about it, was an overpowering, jealous love, so strong that it made her, a plain woman, into one of beauty. She describes in "El Ruego" (The Prayer) how she wants her dead lover, a sinner because he took his own life, admitted to the presence and grace of God, despite his sinful end; she pleads humbly, but at times even forcefully, for him. Herself childless, another side of love that Gabriela Mistral celebrated is maternity, the fruits of love. The poet says that sterility which brings forth no child is a source of shame, and the woman who suffers it a tragic figure. Woman, she says, is instinctively maternal.

Maternity and teaching fused together for Gabriela Mistral. In her "Teacher's Prayer" she begs God to make her more maternal than an ordinary mother, so that she may love her young charges as a mother, though they are not of her flesh and blood. In "La Maestra Rural" she compares the rural school-teacher with Christ, saying that the teacher's kingdom, like Christ's, is not of men; she exclaims that the teacher must be pure and glad of heart, that she must be willing to accept misunderstanding and hurt, if necessary, to be a successful teacher of children. This same love of children is also reflected in her poems for children. And along with her love for children she reveals in her poetry, and in her public statements about her career as a teacher and educational administrator, a love for the poor, the unfortunates of the world, which is akin to maternal love.

As a poet Mistral began with the theme of death, following the loss of her beloved, and death recurs in her work throughout her career. Death often appears in the poetry as impurity, or as a process of disintegration. In writing of death, as in writing on other topics, she uses concrete details. Her figures of speech, her descriptions of death, are graphically specific; she seems often to emphasize even a lurid aspect to death.

Life, death, and religion are for the Chilean poet inextricably intertwined, as they are for most poets in the Christian tradition. Religion seems for Gabriela Mistral an emotion, rather than a ritual of faith. She seems to feel that Christianity is the hope of the peoples of the world, not of the individual alone; but it is a Christianity that is neither doctrinal nor conventional. She is reputed to have regarded herself as strongly anticlerical, though very religious. That she evaluated herself correctly as religious, one may

guess from poems that are actually prayers or hymns.

In the early poetry of Mistral one finds little lightness or gaiety; she is sad, at least serious, when her tone is not tragic. Her poetic vocabulary is filled with words of suffering, pain; notably, she uses verbs of violence and pain. Her language is suggestive, too, of underlying violence and turbulence. Even when she writes of nature, it is viewed as the peasant knows it—not a smiling nature, but one from which a living must be wrung.

Mistral's later poetry, as one finds it in *Tala,* published in 1938, is more complex, showing greater maturity of view and craft. Insofar as subject matter is concerned, the reader notes immediately a greater objectivity and a wider scope of subject matter in the later poems. One whole section of *Tala* is called "América" and is devoted to the country that Gabriela Mistral knew and loved. But in the other sections of the volume, too, one finds a wider interest. Her America is a larger land than her native Chile; it is the whole of Latin America, the land of many mountains, a land of varied climates, and a land of many people with long histories. She writes of the Indians of her America, their tragedy, their poverty, and their hopes. In her poems, writing about the Incas, the Mayas, the Quiches, the Quechuans, the Aymará, she displays her love of people, her concern for the poor and the unfortunate. In the later poetry she could write of her own experience as well. The death of her mother, which affected the poet deeply, is the subject of a poem in this volume, as was the death of her beloved a source of earlier poetry.

By 1938 the poet had become conscious of her craft; this fact is borne out by the notes she included with *Tala.* In these she comments on her poetic vocabulary, justifies her use of certain words, and notes her use of specific rhyme schemes. Her choice of words with a distinctly rural flavor is commented upon. She notes that she is influenced by the popular dialect of her own region and country, as distinct from the language from the Spanish classics.

Among historians of Hispanic-American literature, Gabriela Mistral has been regarded as a woman poet who simply ignored the traditional place of women in her culture and, by so doing, became a great writer and public figure. She has been regarded as a romantic (in the literary sense) rebel against the formality of the literary trends of the 1880's and 1890's, one who began as a poet of disillusion but became a voice of love for the suffering mankind of her time—the children, the mothers, the peasants, the Indians, and the Negroes. Critics have seen in her work such varied influences as the Bible, the poetry of Tagore, the poetry of Amado Nervo, of Mexico, and the poetry of Ruben Darío, of Nicaragua. Her best-known poems are reputed to be her *Canciones de Cuña (Lullabies)* and *Rondas de Niños (Songs of Children)*, known and sung throughout South America. Even before she was awarded the Nobel Prize she was heralded and acclaimed as a moral force throughout the South American continent, both as a poet and as a teacher.

THE POETRY OF GARRETT

Author: George Garrett (1929-   )
First published: The Reverend Ghost and Other Poems, 1957; *The Sleeping Gypsy and Other Poems,* 1958; *Abraham's Knife and Other Poems,* 1961; *For a Bitter Season,* 1967

When a poet has made his mark, sharp and distinctive, on the language of poetry (whether that mark is felt immediately as influence upon his contemporaries or not), he can be said to have succeeded in his craft, to have excelled in his art. Of the younger poets in America who have come into their own or begun their progress since World War II, few have made that mark. There are, of course, Richard Wilbur and Robert Lowell, both of whom are of the first order, and there are those shaggy poets, the Beats, who made themselves heard collectively if seldom singly. And there are some younger poets, testing their abilities and finding their strengths, avoiding both the dull drone of the academy or the hysterical howl of the streets of night. Among these young poets is George Garrett, best known perhaps for his novels and short stories, who is a poet of true distinction with a voice clearly and originally his own.

The poems, collected so far in his three books and appearing in journals, were written during and, without being topical and thus temporally restricted, speak for the last twenty years, from 1947 to the present. Garrett is a poet of the cold war years, striving in his verse to understand and accommodate the lost world of heroism and faith, the traditional realm of poetry, to this age of anxiety, shattered hopes, and leering fears. His poetry records a personal journey through the army and a time in Rome, his years in school and after, the growth of his love into a family, and his own growing recognition of his frailty and his mortality in a world in which everything tastes of death and where every skull grins a lewd secret. It is a dark journey, an Augustinian journey through life, fraught with doubts and terrors, lighted by love and a real faith in God and His awesome and awful grandeur, and in the human spirit with its failings and its real achievements.

Garrett's personal odyssey is but a part of his poetry, the mainstream with connecting smaller streams of amazing variety. He has written witty poems of genuine eighteenth century satirical brilliance ("Three from the Academy," "Four Characters in Search of a New Dunciad"); he has evoked the moods and essences of real places ("Fall Landscapes, New England," "In North Carolina," "Crows at Paestum," "Old Slavemarket: St. Augustine, Fla."); he has written poems which approach real people with telling insight ("Congreve," "Matthew Arnold," "Caedmon," "Swift"); and he has re-created larger figures from a real and mythic past ("Tiresias," "Eve," "Abraham's Knife," "Salome"). This variety is evidence of the vitality of the poems, and that vitality, along with Garrett's technical skill, gives the poems, for all their variety, a real unity of vision and manner.

George Garrett's poems, first of all, have a clearly recognizable sound, an uncommon virtue among his contemporaries. They achieve a working fusion between the heightened diction of poetic meditation and the fresh and exciting immediacy of colloquial speech—a living voice, a real meeting of thought and word. His rhythms are subtle and widely varied, at times musically regular and at others wildly free beyond ordinary scansion. His images are vivid and functional, seldom drawn for their own sake, always working in their context. But his metaphors are perhaps the most distinctive quality of the texture of his verse; they arise cleanly and crisply from a context of theme. He does not, as is so often the case since Pound and Eliot, make the familiar landscapes and events of this world seem new and significant by giving them metaphorical overtones of man's archetypal dreams, myths, and faiths; rather, he gives those dreams and fading faiths new life and relevance by clothing them in the things of this real and present world, by incarnating idea in fact.

In "Meditation on Romans," a long and very fine poem which is deeply religious without being pietistic, as are all of his overtly Christian poems, Garrett uses his kind of metaphor to great advantage, as when he cries out his appeal directly to Christ, a carpenter, a physician, and a king.

Here the universal is made real in the specific, and the specific is a very real present of nails and dollar bills stated in a language as ordinary as its objects and as new and clean as its juxtapositions are unexpected and startling. It is a poem of spiritual doubt and desire made real in words and images of this world, just as soul itself lives in the flesh of a dying animal.

The matter of George Garrett's poetry is appropriate to his manner, for in those poems which constitute the mainstream of his work he is a seeker, involved in a long and arduous quest for meaning in the madness of this world, for truth in absurdity, for faith in a time of disbelief and doubt, for that lost age of innocence and heroism and purity. He once defined this quest and his view of that old human dilemma in a preface to Swift's *Gulliver's Travels,* a book which is in many ways parallel to much of his own work, when he said that "we still cling to the hope that with the exercise of reason and with a change of heart we may yet have a new birth of history and recover a lost and shining world that haunts our deepest dreams."

The heroes of the quest are many, for Garrett is no pure romantic who sees only self in everything and describes the world in terms of self. There are true heroes in the ancient sense, the few who have risked everything that they can lose, as he says in "A Bargain"; there are the professionals, those who make their way in the world simply by doing their jobs and who praise God in pragmatic action; and there are the possessed, the saints and sinners alike who are raped by God's love into vision and purity. The practical buzzard, ugly and beautiful at once, comes down to this world's business in "Buzzard"; the itinerant and lusty preacher of "Holy Roller" is a con man and a sinner, but he is of the chosen of God.

The most immediate and real of his heroes is the bearer of saving grace in this life, the lover. In his poem "Eve," Garrett's wounded Adam is healed only by Eve, a part of himself torn apart, whose hand he takes for all time, finite and infinite. Garrett's love poems are rich with idea but richer still with a purity of unabashed feeling which is rare in our self-conscious and cynical time. The last stanza of "Proposition" gives at least a taste of the quality of his love poetry, but even love can fail in the poems as in the world. Garrett's view of things is a dark one, a world of fists and failures, pains of an aging flesh and a corrupted spirit. Lost Eden is long gone, but as long as the vision remains and the artist can give it even ephemeral reality, then that lost purity exists. In his long and surely major poem, "Salome," he brings together the fallen man and the artist in that doomed dancer's flesh. She speaks her dreams and her horrors, of the blank and naked face of truth and that saving vision.

Possessed of a dark vision but not one which has surrendered to despair, often bitter, often sorely wounded, George Garrett's hero strives in this world of transforming figures, sustained by his honest awareness of that world, his artistic vision of a purer world of spirit, and his ability to love and be loved. This is a hero of our time, familiar to us all in life and in art, but seldom figured in poetry with such wisdom and such skill. With a language as lively and as startling as a string of firecrackers, Garrett gives us ourselves and our old dreams made new.

Perhaps the best conclusion to any examination of his poetry is the closing of his poem "For My Sons" in which idea and language are formed, in a way most typical of the best of his work, to shape a litany of the world's ancient wisdom, echoes of Old Testament knowledge and precept. Here we read the words of a wise and humble man, of an honest and skilled artist whose work is still very much in progress.

THE POETRY OF GASCOIGNE

Author: George Gascoigne (1535-1577)
Principal published works: A Hundred Sundrie Flowres Bound Up in One Small Posie,
1573; *Posies of George Gascoigne,* 1575; *The Steele Glas, A Satire,* 1576; *Complaynt of Phylomene,* 1576; "The Grief of Joye," 1577

From the time *A Hundred Sundrie Flowres Bound Up in One Small Posie* was published in 1573, until the twentieth century, most readers have taken the prefatory letters to the volume at face value and believed that George Gascoigne was responsible for only a few of the works included; but now G. T. Prouty has proved beyound doubt that Gascoigne was responsible for all of them. This unquestioning acceptance in Gascoigne's time was fortunate for him: when the volume first came out, he was in Holland fighting for his country, and he was not the only one blamed in the severe attack on the work. Yet, in 1575, when Gascoigne had had time to go over the volume and revise it somewhat, he brought out a new edition in which he acknowledged authorship of the previous volume, openly repented what he had done, and vowed that he would write in the future only works which would have a definite positive influence on the nation. Then he showed how he had revised the volume and how even it could be used for a good purpose. He was equally unsuccessful in this attempt at revision, but he continued to pursue a career in writing. Since the *A Hundred Sundrie Flowres* and *Posies* contain essentially the same material, they may be considered together.

The volumes can be broken down into three main groups: the drama, the fiction, and the poetry. In the drama section are two plays translated into English— the Greek tragedy *Jocasta,* by Euripides, and the Italian comedy, *I suppositi,* by Ariosto. The fictional section contains "The Adventures of Master F. J."; in the later edition this work is considerably revised and is called a translation of a work by an unknown Italian writer, Bartello. In still a later work, Gascoigne reveals that he himself is Bartello.

Gascoigne used another method of division in *Posies.* He divided his material into sections which he called "Flowres, Hearbes, and Weedes." He justifies this classification by saying, "I terme some Floures, bycause being indeed invented upon a verie light occasion, they had yet in them some rare invention and Methode before not commonly used." The herbs are "more profitable than pleasant," and in this section he includes *I suppositi* and *Jocasta.* The value of the "Weedes" may be questionable, but none is "so vile or stinking but that it hath in it some vertue if it be rightly handled." As one might expect, it is in this section that Gascoigne places "The Adventures of Master F. J."

Various poems are scattered throughout Gascoigne's three sections. The first poem is typical of the age in the way it is "The Anatomye of a Lover." This poem is typical of the age in the way in catalogues the physical features of the lover, not the loved one. Starting at the top of the head with "unkempt lockes" and progressing down through the body all the way to the feet, Gascoigne shows what happens to one snared by love. The poem is so typical that a certain humorous tone creeps in and hints that Gascoigne is actually parodying the conceit instead of copying it. This tone of humor continues in the next poem, "The Arraignment of a Lover." Love was a stable topic during this Elizabethan period, and Gascoigne used it over and over in his poems. These titles are typical: "The Passion of a Lover," "The Divorce of a Lover," "The Lamentation of a Lover," and "The Lullabie of a Lover."

A paraphrase of "The Lullabie of a Lover" might go like this: As women sing to quiet the child, so do I sing, for I have many children to quiet. First, silence my youth for I am now an aging man. Next, rest my eyes; I have wandered too much for pleasures of the flesh. Third, let my passion rest and be ruled by reason for a change. Fourth, let my little "Robin" rest and let "lust relent." Thus may my whole body rest. Now that pleasures are past, welcome pain.

"The Lamentation of a Lover" follows the same general theme. Gascoigne is saying that once he enjoyed many pleasures, but since he is no longer able to enjoy them, his sadness is double because he knows what once was and can no longer be.

One of the longer poems in "Flowers" is "Dan Bartholmew of Bathe," a verse narrative. This poem is actually a linking together of verses written at various times by putting them in a narrative framework, rather than a group of verses written in chronological order. The poem did not appear in its completed form in *A Hundred Sundrie Flowres*. Because of its concern with a single love affair, some consider the poem to be a forerunner of the sonnet sequence. The story is of Dan Bartholmew and his love for Ferenda Natura. Not until he is middle-aged does the hero fall in love, but when he does, his passion is so great that even when his love proves faithless he cannot forget her. The only way he can soothe his torment is by telling his sad story. In the end, Ferenda writes a letter in her own blood, begging forgiveness, which Bartholmew quickly grants, even though he suspects his beloved Ferenda will soon be searching for a new lover.

Another long poem appearing in the "Flowers" section of *Posies* is "The Frutes of Warre," which has the subtitle "Dulce Bellum Inexpertis." In it is found in verse form the story of Gascoigne's war experiences in Holland. His discussion of the nature of war can be summed up in his definition of war: "I say that warre is even the scourge of God,/Tormenting such as dwell in princelie plight."

After the "Flowers" comes a section of "Herbs." First in this section are the translated plays, and after these are some eighteen short poems on such various subjects as reconciliation, friendship, virtue, and, of course, love. In "Gascoigne's Woodmanship," the poet is reviewing the various events in his life for his patron, Lord Grey of Wilton. In the form of dialogue, Gascoigne answers the question of why he always misses the mark with his bow, by showing that he has always missed the mark; he has missed as student, lawyer, courtier, and soldier:

> For proofe he beares the note of follie now,
> Who shotte sometimes to hit Philosophie,
> And aske you why?
> . . . . . .
> Next that, he shot to be a man of lawe,
> . . . . . .
> Yet in the end, he proved but a dawe,
> . . . . . .
> From thence he shotte to catch a courtly grace,
> And thought even there to wield the world at will,
> . . . . . .
> But now behold what marke the man doth find,
> He shootes to be a souldier in his age,

Thus he has failed in each attempt, yet he still has hopes of being a successful professional writer.

Still more short poems appear in the section called "Weeds," including "The Frute of Fetters," "The Greene Knights Farewell to Fansie," and "The Praise of Phillip Sparrowe." This last poem shows the Gascoigne must have known John Skelton. One stanza should be sufficient to show the similarities:

> And yet beside all this good sport
> My Phillip can both sing and daunce:
> With new found toyes of sundry sort,
> My Phillip can both pricke and praunce:
> As if you saye but fend cut phippe,
> Lord how the peat will turne and skippe.

After witnessing the acceptance, or rather, the refusal of acceptance of the revised *Posies*, Gascoigne realized that the people could not believe that his repentance was sincere; he resolved "to bestow [his] time and talent in matters both serious and moral" in order to convince them of his sincerity and thus make amends for the lost time of his misspent youth.

With this purpose in mind he published, in Apirl, 1576, *The Steele Glas, A Satire,* and dedicated it to Lord Grey of Wilton. Schelling calls it the "first original composition in blank verse." The design is typical of its age, and it is similar to *A Mirror for Magistrates.* Gascoigne proposes to show the society as a whole what it really is, hoping that when the people see themselves in all their ugliness they will change.

The poem begins with the allegorical story of the birth of Satira and Poesy, as the children of Plain Dealing and Simplicity. This story closely parallels that of Philomene, which Gascoigne was finishing about this time. Nevertheless, Poesy is married to Vain Delight; and later, when Satira goes to visit her wedded sister, she is ravished and consequently has her tongue cut out by Vain Delight with the Razor of Restraint. But, like Philomene, Satira's song is not over for "with the stumps of my reproved tong,/I may sometimes, Reprovers deeds reprove,/And sing a verse, to make them see themselves."

The satire that Gascoigne has to sing is not a personal vendetta; it is of a more general nature and is directed against, the whole social order, not individuals. Typical of the poetry of his day, Gascoigne explains with much detail every aspect of his scheme. He is following the legacy of the Latin satirist Lucylius "who at his death, bequeathed the christal glasses,/To such a love, to seeme but not to be,/And unto those, that love to see themselves,/How foule or fayre, soever that they are,/He gan bequeath, a glass of trustie Steele." Thus it is from the father of Roman satire that Gascoigne gets the name for this satirical poem.

Like a true reformer, Gascoigne first holds up this glass of steel to himself to show the people that he is not now what he once was. He is trying to demonstrate to his countrymen that he has repented for his reckless youth and is now trying to make amends for his earlier days. "I desire to see myself in deed,/Not what I would, but what I am or should."

The next reflection to appear in the steel glass is that of the ideal commonwealth, that type of commonwealth set forth by Solon and Lycurgus. While the crystal glass might reflect rich towns and a rule by just law, the steel glass shows not a commonwealth but a "common woe." This woe can be prevented by the four estates of king, knight, peasant, and priest. Gascoigne then attacks each of these four estates at length, showing what they are doing and should not be. and what they are not doing but should be.

While discussing the second estate, that of the knights, Gascoigne goes into the subdivision of the soldiers and shows that they, the stoic defenders of the kingdom, are but drunken, cruel, and boasting lechers. If the reflection of the soldiers seems to be more vivid than some of the other reflections, the reason is that Gascoigne can recall his own experiences in this profession.

Nor does Gascoigne stop with only the four estates; he expands his reflection mirror to include some of the middle class, the merchants, the lawyers, and others. Yet he continues to use the same method of showing the vices of the present day by comparing them to those of ancient days when the same occasion brought forth virtue.

In his attack on the clergy, Gascoigne follows the tradition by implying their vices, not stating them explicitly. He praises the priests of another day, saying they were not proud, gluttonous, envious, lustful, wrathful, slothful, or avaricious. It is in the lowly plowman that there exists a spirit of truth and there will be a place in heaven for this man, says Gascoigne, for he is truly humble; because he has no interest in seeming, but only in being he will enter heaven "before the shaven crownes" even though "he stink for sweat."

In the *Complaynt of Phylomene*, companion piece published with *The Steele Glas*, Gascoigne turns an exercise of poetic paraphrase into a didactic poem on the evil of lust. He first started working on the piece, as he states in his introductory letter, while in a carriage returning from Chelmsford and on his way to London; but a sudden cloudburst interrupted his work, and he did not return to it until April of 1575, when he was working on *The Steele Glas*. The legend of Philomene was a commonplace to the schoolboys of Elizabethan England. Gascoigne probably used the Latin version of the myth as told by Ovid, and probably in an edition which had some useful notes, such as he may have used as a student.

The Ovidian version tells how Pandion gives his elder daughter, Progne, in marriage to Tereus, King of Thrace. After the wedding rites, Progne returns with Tereus; some time passes and Progne desires to see her sister. Finally she persuades Tereus to go to Athens and ask for permission to take Philomene to Thrace for a visit with Progne. While Tereus is persuading Pandion to allow the visit, he is overcome by the charm and beauty of Philomene, and his lust for her makes his plea so eloquent that Pandion relents and gives his permission.

Returning to Thrace, Tereus takes Philomene to a deserted stable, rapes her, and cuts out her tongue. Tereus then tells Progne that Philomene is dead. Twelve years pass while Philomene remains a prisoner in the sheepcote. Finally she decides how to let her sister know what has happened. She sews a garment, stitching into it the story of her rape, and gives it to a servant to deliver to the queen. When Progne finds out what has

truly happened to her sister, she silently plots revenge. During the rites of Bacchus, she rescues Philomene, disguising her in the dress of the festival. While Progne is trying to decide the best way to revenge the wrong of her husband, her son, Itys, comes in. His close resemblance to his father helps Progne make up her mind. Love and devotion for her sister overcame her love for her own son. She kills him, cuts him into small pieces, cooks him, and serves up the dish to Tereus. After the meal, when Tereus calls for his son, Progne can keep quiet no longer. "The thing thou seekst (ô wretch quoth she)/Within thee doth abide." Tereus does not believe her and in searching for his son, comes upon Philomene who flings the head of Itys at Tereus.

Tereus enraged seeks revenge, but before he can catch the Greek sisters the gods intervene and change all the family into birds. The elder sister

A *Swallowe* was assignde,
And builds in smokey chimney toppes
And flies against the winde.

The king him selfe, condemnde
A *Lapwing* for to be,
Who for his yong ones cries alwais,
Yet never can them see.

Itys is changed into a pheasant. Philomene becomes a nightingale, and as such she can sing her song and please the ears of man, but from fear of force, she sings only at night.

To tell this story, paraphrased from Ovid, Gascoigne uses the framing device of a dream in which the goddess of just revenge, Nemesis, appears to him and tells the tale. Then she interprets the meaning of the nightingale's song: "And for hir foremost note,/*Tereu, Tereu*, doth sing,/Complaining stil upon the name/Of that false *Thracian* king." The second note of the nightingale's song is *"phy."* This is interpreted as disdain for everything. "Phy filthy lecher . . . Phy coward phy . . . Phy monster." The nightingale's third note is "Jug, Jug, Jug." Not even Nemesis is sure of the meaning of this part of the song. She conjectures that it may be the Latin for cutthroat or murderer, or possibly a Latin word for the symbol of humiliation. Eric Partridge, gives another possible interpretation of the word. The fourth and final note of the nightingale's song is "*Némesis*":

> She calles on *Némesis*
> And *Némesis* am I,
> The Goddesse of al just revenge,
> Who lets no blame go by.

With this interpretation of the song, the dream ends and Gascoigne then interprets the meaning of the dream. Through this final interpretation the didactic nature of the whole work is revealed. First, Gascoigne sums up the lesson to be learned in two lines: "I seeme to see [my Lord] that lechers lust,/Procures the plague, and vengaunce of the highest. . . ." He then treats these themes separately and much more extensively. He shows how yielding to an unhealthy desire leads to the suffering of the innocent, sometimes to the third and fourth generations. And he shows that no sin goes unpunished, that God sees all sins, and that all eventually receive their just reward, as did Progne and Tereus.

In closing, Gascoigne reminds his Patron that the poet's days of youthful lust are over; if he is ever tempted again, he needs only to be reminded of the story of Philomene.

Gascoigne's last song was intended to be a gift to the queen, and he thought an imitation of Petrarch would be both pleasing and suitable for the occasion. The poem, "The Grief of Joye," published in January, 1577, deals with the transience of bodily pleasures and the inevitability of death. It is divided into four songs. The first is called "The Greeves or Discomodities of Lustie Youth." The second is a discourse on "The Vanities of Bewtie." The third reveals "the faults of force and strength," and the fourth is concerned with "the vanities of activi-

tyes." All four are written in rhyme royal.

As in most of his work, Gascoigne interjects his own experiences into the poem. While he is pointing out the vanity of delight in material things, he is at the same time mourning the passage of such delights. In the song on youth he says, "Trew joye cannot, in trifleng toyes consist/Nor happiness in joyes which soon decaie/Then looke on yowthe, and marke it he that list/Somtymes both borne and buried in a daye./Yea thoughe it should, contynew [green] alwaie,/I cannot finde, what joy therein doth grow,/Which is not staynd, with undertwiggs of wo."

In the second song, "The Vanities of Bewtie," Gascoigne pays tribute to the queen:

> This is the *Queene* whose onely looke
>   subdewed,
> Her prowdest foes, withowten speare
>   or sheeld
> This is the *Queene*, whome never eye
>   yet viewed,
> But streight the hart, was forst thereby
>   to yeelde
> This *Queene* it is, who (had she sat
>   in feeld,
> When *Paris* judged, that *Venus* bare
>   the bell.)
> The prize were hers, for she deserves
>   it well.

He then catalogues a procession of other ladies of the court he had known; and since the allusions to them are sometimes vague, he is careful to put their initials in the margin. Then he speaks of those who do not have true beauty yet think they do and thus deceive themselves. "They strive to seeme, but never care to be." This line is certainly an echo from *The Steele Glas*.

In his third song of the poem, that on strength, Gascoigne shows that if women are vain because of their beauty, then man is vain because of his strength. In the final song he lists many activities that are considered pleasures and shows the folly of these activities. Among the activities are music, dancing, wrestling, and riding.

The poem gets its name, according to the poet, from the fact that, in essence, all joys are transient. Death is not only always very close; it is always drawing closer. And it was in the year that Gascoigne presented this poem to the queen that he met his death.

THE POETRY OF GAUTIER

Author: Théophile Gautier (1811-1872)
First published: Poésies, 1830 (*Poems*); *Albertus,* 1833; *La Comédie de la mort,* 1838
(*The Comedy of Death*); *España,* 1845; *Émaux et camées,* 1852 (*Enamels and Cameos*)

Théophile Gautier's poetry forms the transition between Romanticism and the Parnassus school in France. As a young man, Gautier was a prominent member of the group surrounding Victor Hugo in the battle of *Hernani.* Later, however, though he did not formally renounce his support of Romanticism, his name was to become associated with the doctrine of Art for Art's sake, and it is especially in connection with his body of ideas that his name is remembered.

Gautier's earliest poetry was collected into a volume entitled, simply, *Poésies,* first published in 1830. A pronounced taste for the Middle Ages, a love of lonely places, an impression of alienation, all traditional sources of inspiration for the Romantic poets, find a place in this collection, which is remarkable mainly for its lack of originality.

"Albertus, or the Soul and Sin," a long narrative poem describing a young painter's fatal infatuation with a witch, appeared in 1833. This work is little read today and indeed has little to recommend it. Worthy of note, however, is Gautier's use of the stock-in-trade of the somewhat unwholesome lesser Romantic writers: slugs and toads, phantoms and vampires all have their place in this work.

"La Comédie de la mort," a long poem, which came out in 1838, is in two parts. In the first, titled "Life in Death" and involving a dialogue in a graveyard between a worm and a corpse, the poet's intention to shock his reader is obvious. In the second part, "Death in Life," Gautier again tends to reveal the grotesque if superficial side of his Romanticism. Yet here the intensity with which the poet insists that death overshadows all of life would seem to suggest in Gautier a deep-seated pessimism with which he has not always been credited. This impression is reinforced by several pieces in his *Poésies diverses.*

Poésies diverses is the title of a collection of poems which appeared in one volume with *La Comédie de la mort.* Especially worthy of mention is a short piece called "La Caravane." Gautier develops beautifully the symbol of a caravan crossing the Sahara as suggestive of mankind in the world. The only oasis, the only resting place, claims the poet, is the graveyard; this idea is evoked in the simplest of terms:

> . . . a wood of cypresses strewn with
> white stones.

However, not all of the poems in this collection are pessimistic. "Chinoiserie" ("Chinese Fantasy") illustrates Gautier's taste for distant lands and things exotic. The poet affirms that his love goes out not to Shakespeare's Juliet, nor to Dante's Beatrice, nor yet to Petrarch's Laura. Rather, he loves a girl in China who lives in a tower of porcelain:

> The one I love, at present, is in China;
> She is living with her old parents,
> In a tower of fine porcelain,
> At the Yellow River, where the cormorants are. . . .

In no way profound, "Chinoiserie" is a delightful piece which has been set to music. It is worth remarking that even at this relatively early stage in his development, Gautier could offer his dream vision in a precise, finely executed form.

In 1840, Gautier went to Spain and stayed there for six months. The first edition of *España* appeared in 1845; in it the reader has the impression that the starkness and acute relief of the Spanish landscape and the paintings in the art galleries of Spain appealed to, and even sharpened, Gautier's eye.

In "Ribeira" and "A Zurburan," two poems in *España* which are written in *terza rima*, Gautier reveals a remarkable talent for giving a life in verse to the paintings of the two Spanish masters. Moreover, in trying to understand Ribeira's love of ugliness, and the cruelty and violence of Zurburan's studies of early Christian martyrs, Gautier makes his art criticism into a powerful art form in its own right. Elsewhere in this edition, Gautier's approach to his art is perhaps more characteristic of the plastic arts than of poetry. In "Le Pin des Landes," for example, it is the scene viewed which calls to mind the symbol, whereas more commonly a poet will seek out a symbol to illustrate or clothe an idea.

Gautier describes how in the Landes, an area of southwest France, the only tree to be seen is the pine, with a gash in its side, to allow its resin to drip into a bowl. He develops the symbolic value of the tree beautifully; the poet, standing upright and alone, is like the tree. For the poet is cut off from others by his superiority and their jealousy. When he is unhurt, he keeps his treasure, Gautier claims; he needs a deep wound in his heart to make him release his works, his golden tears:

> Without regretting its blood that flows drop by drop,
> The pine pours out its balsam and its frothing sap,
> And still it stands upright by the side of the road,
> Like a wounded soldier, who wishes to die on his feet.
>
> The poet is thus in the wastes of the world;
> While he is unwounded, he keeps his treasure.
> He must have a deep gash upon his heart
> To release his verses, these divine, golden tears!

"Dans la Sierra" which is also in *España*, involves a landscape as a symbol, too. Here Gautier, inspired by the arid mountains of Spain, insists that he prefers them to the fertile plains. The cult of beauty for its own sake, suggested in this poem, was to be worked up into a whole new poetic doctrine by Gautier.

Émaux et camées was first published in 1852. This collection, to which additions were made in the five new editions until 1872, marks a major development in his poetry; it is the collection for which Gautier as a poet is best remembered, that which illustrates his doctrine of Art for Art's sake.

In order to understand this doctrine, it is worth recalling that, about 1930, writers were being urged to participate in the general effort toward social progress. As early as 1832, in the preface to his *Poésies*, Gautier declared that the value of art lay in its beauty and not its usefulness: it was not the artist's business to exercise an influence on the crowd. "In general," he wrote, "as soon as a thing becomes useful, it ceases to be beautiful." Art, he claimed, was a luxury, offered to a small, elite public capable of understanding it. In the preface to his novel *Mademoiselle de Maupin,* moreover, Gautier went on to say that only that which serves no purpose is beautiful. In an article in *L'Artiste* he insisted that the artist's sole aim was to capture beauty.

While it is dangerous to seek an explanation of Gautier's poetic doctrine in his life, two possible influences might be considered. In the first place, it should not be forgotten that if the subordination of idea to form brings to mind the plastic arts, Gautier did in fact start his career as a painter. In addition, it is worth mentioning that he earned his living as a journalist, drama critic, and art critic at a time when the writer risked becoming a commodity, the prey of unscrupulous editors and publishers. He was only too aware of the difficulties a writer faced in trying to retain his integrity.

On the other hand, Gautier had lived too close to the Romantic movement and was too much of a critic not to see that in trying to follow all the movements of their soul, the Romantics had frequently sacrificed accuracy for effect; he was aware that his companions had on occasion been guilty of expressing more than they had to say. It is against this background that one must understand the doctrine of Art for Art's sake.

In *Émaux et Camées* one is witness to an attempt to return to precision and clarity, even at the expense of subject matter. The title of the collection is of course significant; the poems grouped under it are highly polished, exquisitely crafted pieces. The tone of the edition is set by the preface. Here Gautier states that just as Goethe at Weimar cut himself off from the world to write, so he, Gautier, has disregarded the storms lashing his windows and has written *Émaux et camées.*

If Gautier's aim in poetry was now beauty, he tells how the poet might achieve this effect in a poem written in 1857 and added as a conclusion to *Émaux et camées.* In "L'Art," Gautier claims that like painting or sculpture, poetry is both an art and a skill to be learned. The poet, a craftsman, must have a firm grip on all the resources of the language. If he succeeds in overcoming all the problems of rhyme and syntax and vocabulary, while creating no artificial obstacles, the work of art will resist the ravages of time as no other human creation can:

> All things pass on.—Robust art
> Alone possesses eternity;
>   The bust
> Survives the city.
> The very gods die,
> But verse, sovereign,
>   Remains
> Stronger than the sword

In this collection Gautier's extreme attachment to form results in carefully executed, sophisticated poetry, which is generally more impersonal than anything he had previously done. On the other hand the subject matter is often very slight:

"Study of Hands," "To a Red Gown," and "The Tea-Rose" are representative titles.

In *España,* especially, Gautier had already attempted artistic transpositions, trying to achieve or reproduce in verse the effect obtained by a work of art in another medium. In *Émaux et camées* such attempts become more ambitious. In "Variations on the Carnival of Venice," for example, the poet offers a series of four pieces in which the point of departure is a musical phrase from a Venetian song. In rhythmic, colorful verse, Gautier creates a picture of Venice as he imagines it once was.

In "Symphony in White Major," Gautier again attempts an artistic transformation, showing all the nuances and associations of white. This is perhaps a fine display of virtuosity, but there is little development within the poem, and the question arises whether poetry is in fact a suitable medium for such an exercise.

The appeal of *Émaux et camées* is by its very nature limited. In trying to banish himself from his work, Gautier is on occasion guilty of creating "cold" poetry. By shutting himself off from the world, he severely restricts his choice of subjects. It might be argued, moreover, that Gautier's choice of art for its own sake is made at the expense of content—that beauty of form is not enough.

It must be recognized that the "impersonal" poetry of the Parnassus owed much to Gautier, while his artistic transpositions were of great consequence for Baudelaire and the Symbolists. Moreover, if Gautier's creative talents were limited, he did, nonetheless, by his respect for his calling and for the word, renew a tradition which began with Malherbe. Baudelaire no doubt lavished excessive praise on Gautier, but in writing that Gautier was a poet for whom the inexpressible did not exist he was probably paying his compatriot a compliment he merited.

THE POETRY OF GOLDSMITH

Author: Oliver Goldsmith (1728-1774)
First published: The Traveller, 1764; *The Deserted Village,* 1770

Oliver Goldsmith, the little Irish writer and sometimes physician who was the friend of Samuel Johnson and Joshua Reynolds and the butt of countless rude jokes from the pen of James Boswell, tried his hand at almost every literary genre popular in his time. His novel, the *Vicar of Wakefield,* his domestic comedy, *She Stoops to Conquer,* and his gently satirical essays, the *Citizen of the World,* have made a lasting niche for him in English literary history. He was also a creditable minor poet, with two long reflective poems, several charming songs, satirical lyrics, a literary ballad, and even the libretto for an oratorio to his credit. He was not an original poet, but he could capture the essence of the techniques of others and make them his own, moralizing like Johnson or satirizing like Swift.

Goldsmith's best poetic works are unquestionably *The Traveller* and *The Deserted Village,* long didactic, reflective poems that show their author's sensitive awareness of the pleasures and pains of the life of the common man. In the first of the two poems Goldsmith speaks as one who wanders over the continent of Europe, rejoicing that the world has been laid open for his pleasures. Yet he feels the pains of this world, too:

> Yet oft a sigh prevails, and sorrows fall,
> To see the hoard of human bliss so small;
> And oft I wish, amidst the scene, to find
> Some spot to real happiness consign'd
> Where my worn soul, each wand'ring hope at rest,
> May gather bliss to see my fellows bless'd.

He surveys the countries he knows, hoping to find this happiness in one of them, but he sees grave faults in each. Italy, bountifully endowed by nature, suffers through the indolence and sensuality of her people:

> As in those domes, where Caesars once bore sway,
> Defac'd by time and tottering in decay,
> There in the ruin, heedless of the dead,
> The shelter-seeking peasant builds his shed.

The sturdy Swiss peasants are happy with their lot, content with the barest necessities; but their pleasures, as well as their desires, are few. In sharp contrast to their stern existence is the gay life of the French, whom Goldsmith finds slaves to their own desires for flattery and frivolity:

> Here vanity assumes her pert grimace,
> And trims her robes of frieze with copper lace;
> Here beggar pride defrauds her daily cheer,
> To boast one splendid banquet once a year.

The industrious Dutch have created a prosperous nation out of the sea, yet brought elements of "craft and fraud," even slavery, into their lives with their undue reliance on commerce:

> At gold's superior charms all freedom flies,
> The needy sell it, and the rich man buys.

The traveler turns his attention finally to England, where he sees the proud desire for independence and the love of liberty sowing the seeds of destruction; this quest for freedom breaks down ties of family and class, and men turn on one another:

> Here, by the bonds of nature feebly held,
> Minds combat minds, repelling and repell'd;
> Ferments arise, imprison'd factions roar,
> Repress'd ambition struggles round her shore,

Till, over-wrought, the general system
    feels
Its motions stop, or frenzy fire the
    wheels.

As this chaos grows, men are enslaved by
avarice, and all learning and the arts decline. Goldsmith protests with special
passion the eviction of villagers by their
landlords, noblemen seeking to enlarge
their estates or their grazing land. This
problem was especially critical in Goldsmith's native Ireland, and he speaks of it
at much greater length in *The Deserted
Village*.

The final passage of *The Traveller*,
which is said to have been written partly
by Samuel Johnson, gives a new turn to
Goldsmith's central idea. Ultimately, the
poem concludes, man's happiness rest
with himself:

How small, of all that human hearts
    endure,
That part which laws or kings can
    cause or cure!
Still to ourselves in every place con-
    sign'd,
Our own felicity we make or find.

The Deserted Village, like *The Traveller* written in the heroic couplet so popular in the eighteenth century, is generally considered Goldsmith's best poem.
His description of the idyllic life in the
village of Auburn before disaster, in the
form of a greedy landlord, struck it, has
great appeal, especially in the brief vignettes of the vicar and the schoolmaster.
Goldsmith's interest in detail of nature
and in the lot of the common man ally
him rather with the poets of the next
generation than with his neoclassical contemporaries.

The Deserted Village is a personal
meditation; its form gives the author
freedom to comment bitterly on the harm
that trade has wrought on the English
people and to lament that he will never
fulfill his lifelong dream of spending his
last years in Auburn, listening to the
night noises of animals, children, and
young lovers. He describes the former

gaiety of the village when children
danced, played games, and whispered
under the hawthorn bushes, then contrasts the present scene:

No more thy glassy brook reflects the
    day,
But, chok'd with sedges, works its
    weedy way;
Along thy glades, a solitary guest,
The hollow-sounding bittern guards its
    nest;
Amidst thy desert walks the lapwing
    flies,
And tires their echoes with unvaried
    cries.

Goldsmith then pictures himself stroll-
ing around the deserted town; the ruins
of the vicarage remind him of the saintly
man who once inhabited it, dispensing
charity to every passing beggar, watching
benevolently over the children in his parish, and dwelling always half in Heaven.
Farther along was the home of the
schoolmaster, a stern yet kind man,
deeply devoted to learning, and a local
celebrity:

While words of learned length and
    thund'ring sound
Amazed the gazing rustics rang'd
    around;
And still they gaz'd, and still the
    wonder grew
That one small head could carry all
    he knew.

The remainder of the poem emphasizes Goldsmith's sense of loss in the destruction of the village with its "simple
blessings" and "spontaneous joys." He is
highly indignant at the wealthy, who let
their horses and hounds inhabit the former homes and lands of the villagers.
The poor find no refuge in the city,
where they see wealth they cannot share,
where the lost village maiden starves in
the streets "near her betrayer's door." The
unhappy alternative is to travel west to
the new world, to face "the various terrors of that horrid shore." The destruction of the villages seems to Goldsmith
the first step in the degeneration of the
whole country. With the villagers depart

the "rural virtues," "contented toil, and hospitable care, and kind connubial tenderness . . . and piety . . . and steady loyalty, and faithful love." Poetry, too, will depart, and Goldsmith implores her to flourish in other lands:

> Still let thy voice, prevailing over time,
> Redress the rigours of th' inclement clime;
> Aid slighted truth; with thy persuasive strain
> Teach erring man to spurn the rage of gain . . .
> That trade's proud empire hastes to swift decay,
> As ocean sweeps the labour'd mole away.

Goldsmith was not always the serious moralist; his clever lyrics are kin to those of the Cavalier poets and the Restoration dramatists, generally hinging on a witty conclusion for their effect. One poem, "The Gift," begins:

> Say, cruel Iris, pretty rake,
> Dear mercenary beauty,
> What annual offering shall I make
> Expressive of my duty?

After considering and rejecting various possibilities, his heart, gems, or gold, he concludes:

> I'll give thee—ah! too charming maid,
> I'll give thee—to the devil.

The poet skillfully and openly imitated the galloping tetrameter couplets, the absurd rhymes, and the sense of man's grotesqueness that characterize much of the poetry of Jonathan Swift. In "The Logicians Refuted," Goldsmith argues that man is basically irrational, in spite of philosophers' statements to the contrary. The instinct of the beasts is better:

> Who ever knew an honest brute
> At law his neighbor prosecute . . .

> No politics disturb their mind;
> They eat their meals, and take their sport
> Nor know who's in or out at court.

"The Double Transformation," the tale of a marriage between a country scholar and a London belle, is reminiscent of both Swift and Pope in its description of the lady, whose beauty was all artifice, "powder, shreds, or lace." Unlike his more cynical predecessors, however, Goldsmith provides a happy ending. The lady is stricken with smallpox, loses her numerous beaux, and contents herself with trying to please her husband:

> Jack soon was dazzl'd to behold
> Her present face surpass the old;
> With modesty her cheeks are dy'd,
> Humility displaces pride . . .

> No more presuming on her sway,
> She learns good-nature every day;
> Serenely gay, and strict in duty,
> Jack finds his wife a perfect beauty,

"Edwin and Angelina" reveals still another side of Goldsmith's interests; it is modeled on the medieval folk ballad and again foreshadows the work of the Romantic period. It is not an exceptionally good ballad; its diction is too artificial to carry the immediate human appeal of the folk lyrics, but it is an interesting foretaste of things to come. The narrative is simple. A youthful traveler, dressed as a boy, takes refuge at a hermit's cell and confesses to him that she is really Lady Angelina, who has left home to search for the worthy lover she scorned and drove away. Now she fears his death. Inevitably, the hermit proves to be the lost Edwin, and the lovers are happily reunited:

> "No, never from this hour to part,
> We'll live and love so true;
> The sigh that rends thy constant heart
> Shall break thy Edwin's too."

Perhaps the most familiar of Goldsmith's poems is the song from the *Vicar of Wakefield*, which begins:

> When lovely woman stoops to folly,
> And finds too late that men betray,
> What charm can soothe her melancholy?
> What art can wash her guilt away?

The simple language of this lyric shows Goldsmith's natural poetic talent to far greater advantage than the lofty rhetoric of "Edwin and Angelina" or of the choral pieces.

The *Threnodia Augustalis,* a memorial poem for the Princess Dowager of Wales, falls into the genre of choral odes, best represented by Dryden's *Alexander's Feast.* Like most of the poems addressed to royal personages, it is full of hyperbole:

Bless'd spirit, thou, whose fame, just born to bloom
Shall spread and flourish from the tomb,
How hast thou left mankind for Heaven!

The poem is divided into solo and choral parts, with sharp changes in mood, ranging from grief and terror to quiet acceptance of death. The second part of the ode pictures pilgrims coming to Augusta's tomb, which is to be a haven for Faith, Religion, and Virtue. Somehow Goldsmith's sense of poetic decorum prevents this effusive tribute from becoming ludicrous.

The Captivity, the libretto for an oratoria, is based on the Biblical account of the Babylonian captivity, with Israelite prophets, Chaldean priests, and women of both nations as the principal speakers.

Goldsmith skillfully varies his verse forms for recitatives and arias, and the work ranks creditably beside others of the same genre, though it is by no means the poet's best effort.

It is, perhaps, remarkable that these choral pieces are even readable. Fortunately, Goldsmith's reputation does not rest on them. Far more natural to his talents were the humorous verses that make up a large part of his collected poetry. Typical is his "Elegy on the Death of a Mad Dog," with its surprise conclusion:

The man recover'd of the bite—
The dog it was that died.

"Retaliation" is a selection of portraits of his circle in London, Johnson, Reynolds, Edmund Burke, David Garrick, and "magnanimous Goldsmith, a gooseberry fool."

No one claims real greatness for Goldsmith's poetry, but his work still gives pleasure to his readers. His interests were as wide as the scope of eighteenth century poetry, and he simultaneously reveals the neoclassicist's interest in satire, urban society, moral generalizations, and polished verse and the Romantic poet's concern for the countryside, the common man, nature, and simplicity of expression.

THE POETRY OF GRAVES

Author: Robert Graves (1895-   )
First published: Over the Brazier, 1916; *Fairies and Fusiliers,* 1917; *Country Sentiment,* 1920; *The Pier Glass,* 1921; *Whipperginny,* 1923; *Mock Beggar Hall,* 1924; *Welchman's Hose,* 1925; *The Marmosite's Miscellany,* 1925; *Poems: 1914-1926,* 1927; *Poems: 1929,* 1929; *Poems: 1926-1930,* 1931; *Collected Poems,* 1938; *No More Ghosts,* 1940; *Poems: 1938-1945,* 1946; *Collected Poems: 1914-1947,* 1948; *Poems and Satires,* 1951; *Collected Poems,* 1955; *Collected Poems,* 1959; *More Poems,* 1961; *The Penny Fiddle,* 1962; *New Poems,* 1963; *Man Does, Woman Is,* 1964

Like the weather, the reputations of even the best poets are subject to change, and the middle years of our century have revealed in a somewhat different light of appraisal and judgment a group of writers whose places, only a short time back as literary generations are measured, seemed fixed and final in the critical canon.

The reason for this change in poetic climate is not hard to determine. Twenty-five years ago the air was expectant with the promise of a bright new day in English poetry. Yeats had achieved the full stature of his later period. Eliot had taken an affirmative stand in *Ash Wednesday* and was at work on his *Four Quartets.* Pound had broken a trail into new terrains of history and art. Auden and others of his generation were stripping drabness and false sentiment from the paraphernalia of ordinary life, bringing witty new insights and values to the contemporary experience. Dylan Thomas had already brought his passionate sensibility to bear on the joined inner and outer worlds and was hymning his findings with full-throated orchestration All this has now changed, however, for the anticipated new day proved only a false dawn. Yeats and Thomas are dead, the latter with the promise of his early work unfulfilled. Eliot turned playwright before his death. Pound has added to the *Cantos* without extending his range or influence. The poets of the 1930's are still honored, but their occasional thin volumes no longer generate excitement in either readers or critics. As for the young apprentice poets on the English scene, their muted voices can scarcely be heard among the strident echoes of our time.

But this situation has produced one good result. Criticism is now willing to take a second look at some poets previously taken for granted or disregarded— the otherworldly lyricism of Walter de la Mare, for example, and the ebullient, idiosyncratic, but always brilliant performance of Robert Graves. Certainly the latest edition of his *Collected Poems* reveals a poet who makes greater demands on our attention than do many contemporary writers of more gilded reputations.

Some poets outlast their periods, others their public. The fact that Robert Graves has done neither is easily explained. During his long career—his first book of verse appeared in 1916—he has never allied himself with any movement or group, never cultivated an eclectic or school style; consequently, he had nothing to lose when critical fashions changed. Also, he has never mistaken current popularity for lasting fame or courted the favor of his readers. A veteran of many hard-fought literary skirmishes, he has battled for only one cause, his own integrity as a poet.

The means by which he has maintained his hard-bitten, roughly achieved literary independence help us in understanding both the tart native flavor of his best verse and the defensive attitude he sometimes assumes toward his poorest.

Graves has often stressed the fact that he is not addicted to any poetic "school." One should not believe, then, that his interest in unusual items of medieval literature makes him automatically a writer of romantic temper. There is in Graves's poetry, and has been since World War I, a strong element of the satirical, evidence of dissatisfaction with many aspects of the world around him—the times, war, England, even himself. Perhaps even the years he resided outside England seem further evidence of such inner dissatisfaction, the kind that is evident in "To Lucia at Birth," a sonnet written relatively late in life.

The earnest thought, the hope that the individual can resist changes which will make him or her conform to the world, instead of resolutely maintaining individuality, recurs in the last stanza of "At the Savoy Chapel," a poem written on the occasion of his daughter's marriage in 1945.

Despite the ever-recurring satire in the poems directed against the world as it is, in poems as diverse as "Vain and Careless," "Angry Samson," "Sergeant-Major Money," "Down, Wanton, Down," and "The Fallen Tower of Siloam," there is also a touch of true sentiment in Graves's poems. It appears sometimes as if the facade of the poet were stripped away temporarily, so that one can see the man and note that the poet and the man, contrary to the traditions of poetry, are not one and the same. In "Coronation Address," for example, Graves writes in the first person, describing the reactions of a family, particularly the husband's, to the death of Queen Victoria, an incident that may well have a historical basis in the poet's own life. A five-year-old boy brings in the edition of the *Times* telling of the monarch's death, news which sends tears rolling down the father's cheeks. In response to his wife's remark that the queen was, after all, only a woman, the husband retorts that to honor the king is honorable, but to have a queen to serve is lovely. He adds that he hopes his son, the five-year-old, may someday serve a queen. The poem closes with an admonition to Elizabeth II to think well of her great-great-grandmother, who so earned the love of her subjects.

Graves is really at his best when least abstruse. The simpler, explicit style, the homely yet well-chosen idiom of a poem like "Recalling War," which looks back to World War I from the distance of a score of years, is poetically indicative of the poet at his best. In this poem Graves captures with extraordinary brilliance the attitudes of young men toward war's activity and their attitudes in later years as they remember what happened.

Graves began as a young poet mingling country sentiment and personal war experiences, but over the years the war poems have almost completely disappeared from his collections and his country themes have been reshaped to show the symbolic particularities of things. Meanwhile he has been formulating his own theories on the origin and nature of poetry, as set forth in *The White Goddess,* a highly controversial examination into the sources of poetic being and truth in the buried anthropological past. At least a third of the poems now collected have their roots in his theory of poetic myth, either directly in the love poems or indirectly in his ballad themes and his adaptations from the ancient Gaelic.

One of his attempts to repossess the past, to substitute the White Goddess for Apollo and Zeus as the source of poetic magic far back in the dim beginning of all things, is "To Juan at the Winter Solstice," surely one of the notable poems of the century. The poem contains an array of images and references which bring into relationship the mythology of the seasons, the ancient, doomed heroes of Aegean and Celtic legends, and the Goddess in her persons as mother, lover, and layer-out of the dead, all a part of old fertility myths of predestined death and miraculous rebirth. The same theme is presented in "The White Goddess."

Graves has had a great deal to say— and most of that destructive—about the work of other poets but surprisingly little about his own, for he believes that the poem should be allowed to speak for itself. Also, he has stated that his writing belongs to the Anglo-Irish tradition into which he was born. This comment explains the mixture of irony and passion that we find in so much of his verse. He stands in the great tradition of Swift and Shaw, but with strange Celtic overtones of his own, and like them he shows the working of a mind that is partly imaginaive, partly critical, and wholly committed to some individual concept of truth.

In "Rocky Acres" the images of some secret country of the heart and mind match perfectly the spirit of Robert Graves's best poems. For the landscape of his imagination is no barren land; it shelters and nourishes the poet who shuns the crowd.

How he has made his solitary position a post of strategy and advantage is reflected in the various editions of his *Collected Poems,* especially in the consciousness of man's burdens that we find in "Children of Darkness" and "Trudge, Body," the acceptance of human mortal-

ity in "Surgical Ward: Men," the reaching back into the dark corners of racial memory in "To Juan of the Winter Solstice," the outrageous ribaldry of "Ogres and Pygmies" and "Down, Wanton, Down," the droll foolery of "Mid-Winter Waking," and "Traveller's Curse After Misdirection," the self-mockery of "A Pinch of Salt," and the emotional depths of love revealed in "The Sharp Ridge" and "The Dangerous Gift."

Poems such as these present Graves as a writer of considerable pith and variety, of occasional excellence so beautifully and precisely centered and controlled that his true quality deserves the recognition which criticism has so often withheld in the past. These poems, like all good poetry, offer first the shock of surprise and then take gradual possession of mind and mood. This is the true magic of poetry as Robert Graves conceives it.

THE POETRY OF GRAY

Type of work: Poetry
Author: Thomas Gray (1716-1771)
Principal published works: Elegy in a Country Churchyard, 1751; *Six Poems by Mr.
T. Gray,* 1753; *Odes by Mr. Gray,* 1757; *Pindaric Odes,* 1758; *Poems by Mr. Gray,* 1768

Although the poem now titled "Elegy Written in a Country Churchyard" is justly the most famous of Thomas Gray's poems, anyone reading through the whole of his work will decide that he is not a poet of only one tone or one mode of sensibility. True, Gray could strike and maintain admirably a specific mood, such as that of gentle melancholy and regret that informs the "Elegy." This, however, was only one of his effects. The poetry of his great contemporary, Samuel Johnson, is sustained in one mode from beginning to end—abstract, moralistic, improving—but not so Gray's.

Although Gray's poetry was expressive of his time and displayed often enough the neo-classic qualities admired by eighteenth-century critics and readers, its small body displays a wide variety of interest that must be recorded in any report of a poet who withdrew as a boy from the playing fields of Eton (he was not one of the "idle progeny" who knew how to "chase the rolling circle's speed,/Or urge the flying ball") and spent a quiet adult life as a fellow-commoner at Cambridge. He did, in his twenties, take an extended Grand Tour with his friend Horace Walpole, and to the end of his life he varied the quietude of his life at Cambridge with frequent journeys. But Gray, in his travels, showed the qualities of the observer, the tourist. Capable of wide ranges of curiosity and considerable imaginative response to what he saw, he was willing to be entertained and diverted by sights and experiences that Samuel Johnson would simply have dismissed as foreign and barbarous. Gray also resembled other men of his time, even his friend Walpole of Strawberry Hill fame; he was willing to be amused, but the one price he would not pay for his amusement was his self-possession.

This reserve is what gives Gray's poetry the kind of unity it has. He attempts many things, and the variety of his poetry gives him minor importance as a forerunner of the Romantic Movement, both in the subjects he sometimes chose and in the simple language he sometimes employed. But those who want to claim Gray for the eighteenth century and neo-classicism have no trouble in doing so. Even Gray's best work, poems like "Ode on a Distant Prospect of Eton College," "Hymn to Adversity," and the "Elegy" abound in the elevated, figurative diction and the excessive personification popular in his time. In some of his verse fish hardly swim, and the poet himself is overshadowed by a thick penumbra of such literary abstractions as Adversity, Melancholy, and others. Often there cluster in the same poem so many of these that the effect becomes clotted and obscure. Consider these lines from "Ode on the Pleasure Arising from Vicissitude":

> Smiles on past Misfortune's brow
>   Soft Reflection's hand can trace;
> And o'er the cheek of Sorrow throw
>   A melancholy grace;
> While Hope prolongs our happier
>   hour. . . .

Succeeding verses present "rosy Pleasure," "a kindred Grief," "Misery," "Bliss," and a line which announces: "Humble Quiet builds her cell."

These tendencies are the marks of some of Gray's greatest poems, lines which have gained the immortality of proverb. The lines of the "Eton" ode ring with many a remembered, self-possessed phrase, such as ". . . where ignorance is bliss,/'Tis folly to be wise." Similarly, a moving and notable sadness, admirably kept within bounds, throws out phrase after phrase in the "Elegy" and enriches our common speech: "The paths of glory lead but to the grave"; "Full many a flower is born to blush un-unseen,/And waste its sweetness on the desert air"; "Some mute inglorious Milton here may rest. . . ." Truly noble is Gray's contemplation of the burial mounds, the rude inscriptions on the stones, the truncated careers, and the unanswerable silence of the modest graveyard at Stoke Poges. For the inglorious Miltons a tear is shed. This shedding of tears may, it is true, anticipate future Romantic glorification of the emotions; but the measured shedding keeps Gray the child of his century. Significantly, most of Gray's poems were written for sympathetic friends and were published only when pirated versions, as with the "Elegy," were about to appear.

The fact of Gray's self-control—the fact that he possessed a considerable range of feeling and powers of taste but was not possessed by them—is testified to by several items. He was a master of the going eighteenth-century style and could, for example, compose restrained and sincere epitaphs ("Epitaph on Mrs. Clerke," "Epitaph on Sir William Williams"). At the same time, with brilliant if trivial results, he could compose his "Ode on the Death of a Favorite Cat." He could be really dull, as in his "Alliance of Education and Government"; yet this sober earnestness did not inhibit his "Satire on the Heads of Houses," in which he ridicules the university masters to whom he was speaking soberly in his "Alliance."

Similarly, Gray had enough taste and curiosity to initiate the use of "Barbarian" materials in "The Fatal Sisters," "The Bard"—called a "Pindaric ode"—and "The Triumphs of Owen." True to the tone of his sources, he speaks in accents quite different from those of neo-classic convention; screams, mantic possession, and direct language sustain many passages in these pastiches from the Norse and other languages. But the Cambridge resident was no more possessed by savagery than he was by the refined sensibility expressed in the "Elegy" or the "Eton" ode. He moved from sincere epitaphs to a lament for a cat; he moved, at least once, from his recreation of bardic song to "A Long Story," in which much of the general machinery of Romantic narrative is burlesqued in advance.

As Gray indicated in "The Progress of Poesy," he believed that he lived in an age of twilight; the great luminaries of Greek, Roman, and English poetry had long since set ("Oh! Lyre divine, what daring Spirit/Wakes thee now?"). He shows us, however, that a conscientious connoisseur can find his way through twilight—perhaps toward a new dawn—and throughout follow a memorable course.

THE POETRY OF HALL

Author: Donald Hall (1928-   )
Principal published works: Exiles and Marriages, 1955; *The Dark Houses,* 1958; *A Roof of Tiger Lilies,* 1964

Donald Hall has edited a number of collections of contemporary poetry, has written a Recitatio on Robert Frost and, in 1961, an autobiographical reminiscence of his childhood in New England, *String Too Short To Be Saved.* It is as a poet, however, that he is best known. His first volume of poems, *Exiles and Marriages,* won the Lamont Poetry Prize for 1955. In 1958, *The Dark Houses* was published; *A Roof of Tiger Lilies* appeared in 1964.

These volumes comprise, generally speaking, a single chronicle of a man's increasing separation from persons and places, and a consequent search for personal identity. Increasingly cut off from the old New England that nurtured him, the poet struggles to live self-reliantly without, at the same time, isolating himself completely. Here the word *poet* means the speaker of most of the poems and not inevitably Mr. Hall personally. The main themes which run through the three volumes are nostalgia for the past, or a region, which the modern world has left in decay; some bitterness and scorn for the kind of life which has displaced rural New England; and, of most importance, the problem of individual freedom.

Technically, the volumes also show a progression. Beginning with a preponderance of closely rhymed, evenly metered stanzas, Hall's later work moves toward greater freedom in style and structure. Less reliance on rhyme, more irregular lines which move less to a meter than to syntactic patterns, and a diction and syntax closer to spoken speech and prose come to characterize the later poems. Such a movement in style is not unusual in contemporary poetry. In "Apology," from *Exiles and Marriages,* for example, he uses rhyme, alliteration, caesurae, and meter to create a formal effect to which the poet himself objects. In contrast, in

some of the poems in *The Dark Houses,* he allows the repetition of the syntactic unit to provide the prosodic form. The effect is at times deceptively prosaic.

In his later verse Hall made, along with a change from metrical to syntactic prosody, a movement toward a more direct utterance, with the poet speaking in a more nearly normal voice to the listener. From a quiet, conversational start in a poem, Hall will often attempt to build gradually toward emotional intensity and even shock. He is likely to move from whimsey or unadorned observation to fantasy or the surrealistic, and sometimes to violence. Perhaps the technique mirrors a theme: beneath the surface of the normal, even the humdrum, lurks the bizarre, the unsettling, even the terrifying. Poem after poem follows such a procedure, and treats such a theme. "A Child's Garden," from *Exiles and Marriages,* is an example. The poet relates the tale of a boy whose revered grandfather has died and who cannot return to the garden where they once were so close. That the grandfather is, in many other poems, characterized as representing the old New England serves to relate the poem to the theme of loss. The effect on the boy is at first whimsical, then frightening. Childish innocence gives way to confusion, violence and fear. Hall is often about the task of resurrecting that lost innocence nostalgically, or exploring the psychological results of having lost it. Coloring everything is a sense of dying. For all its whimsy, its boyish fantasy, and its slightly academic wit, Hall's verse is finally somber, sober, and perhaps a bit over-serious. The note of puritanism is strong: the love of a hard land; respect for those who work long for little; introspection and even moral righteousness. Such qualities are more evident when considering the whole bulk of the poetry than in any one poem, where they are likely to be rather concealed.

Often Hall appears to overwork the theme of a lost past. He is possibly most interesting when he explores the tensions of a man attempting to salvage and maintain a viable identity. The term *perversity* is important in a good many poems by Hall; and it will be examined further. The term leads to an understanding of the psychological conflicts underlying the verse.

Two poems especially in *Exiles and Marriages*, "Lycanthropy Revisited" and "Exile," work out in some detail the theme which is Hall's greatest concern: a love rooted in innocence must, by the nature of things, forsake the "woods" and become part of experience; its innocence is doomed, therefore, by exposure, sex, knowledge, and changing circumstance. "You always hurt the one you love," as the song goes. There is guilt, as well as ego, and in "Lycanthropy Revisited" the poet humorously converts them both into a burlesque parody of Satan and the Wolf-man. Beneath the studied humor, however, there is an irony bitterly directed at the self. Even the guilt seems as silly as the attempt to match Satan in sin. The roles pile up until identity is lost and guilt is submerged in fantasy. In "Exile," Hall begins to pull the strands together and perversity becomes more and more difficult to explain. It leads on to betray the present for a past which it had ruined to begin with. In "A Relic of the Sea," the final poem in *Exiles and Marriages,* a young father climbs to the attic of his childhood home to visit the place where he was master. He climbs back down, vowing to say good-bye to his youth and the lie of being free and only to be concerned with Self. It becomes clear at last that perversity is finally to be equated with the falsehood of isolation—a false sense of the self and of freedom. The past is, really, peopleless; the state of innocence is really only one of self-escape through fantasy and self-gratification through cultivated loneliness. Love, then,

must be murdered or come out of the attic; love must be to know your own self and her's; love, therefore, is painful, the devil in the flesh, the thorn in the rose of the self. To be perverse, then, is to be unable to accept either oneself or another; it is, at last, to deny life by indulging in fantasies of the past, of alter egos, or by entombing oneself in the "jail" of a secure, middle-class, development—the "dark houses."

Toward the end of *Exile and Marriages* comes a short, and well-known, poem titled "Epigenethlion: First Child," which momentarily submerges "perversity" beneath a fatalistic and austere vision of birth, death, and rebirth.

Since the beginning Hall has turned his attention more and more to overcoming perversity by attacking escapism and attempting to define a meaningful kind of relationship with others as in "Marriage: to K." The knowledge he gains is, at least, the human need for a touching of hands, even though all men are separate and free. Yet, the scene and tone of this poem remains a bit furtive and fearful, and the reader senses that the conflicts are not wholly resolved.

The Dark Houses takes up the theme of freedom: isolation is opposed to the possibilities of communion with others, a communion based on self-knowledge free from the curse of egoism. "Christmas Eve in Whitneyville" takes the poet back to his childhood home. But New England has changed completely, and the poet notes almost scornfully how the present inhabitants make prisons of their houses and refuse the risks that freedom entails. This volume shows the poet moving always in opposition to seclusion, isolation, as a protection against suffering and doubt. "The Clock-Keeper," "The Foundations of American Industry," "Residential Streets," "The Adults," "The Umbrella," "Oysters and Hermits," and "The Hut of the Man Alone" are all poems which, in one way or another, speak out against the modern willingness to hide in a crowd, or to be hide-bound, to escape or insulate oneself from the raw edge of experience. Yet, there are notes of uncertainty, as if the poet yet sympathizes with the impulse to hide. The nervous energy displayed is due to the poet's being both objective in his depiction of neurotic escape and subjective in his expression of defiant independence.

Many poems in this volume explore these themes in abstract, intellectualized meditations. Then the abstract is given, suddenly, a palpable body or quality. "Coldness" becomes a key word, both a sensation and an idea. An elemental, detached, very objective viewpoint is taken toward human experience. Past, present, future; love, hate, guilt; the muck and mire of human life is viewed with aesthetic austerity. And the austerity seems to have a quality of cleanliness, a cold, purifying, bedrock reality which in turn suggests an idea or a conception of freedom and renewal. The conclusion to "Cold Water," the final poem in *A Roof of Tiger Lilies,* shows an emphasis on pure sensation, coldness, ritual rebirth, contact with the primitive and elemental, suggesting that it is a beginning, a start to a new view of human relationships and self-awareness.

THE POETRY OF HARDY

Author: Thomas Hardy (1840-1928)
First published: Wessex Poems and Other Verses, 1898; *Poems of the Past and the Present,* 1901; *Time's Laughingstocks and Other Verses,* 1909; *Satires of Circumstance,* 1914; *Moments of Vision,* 1917; *Late Lyrics and Earlier,* 1922; *Human Shows, Far Phantasies: Songs and Trifles,* 1925; *Winter Words,* 1928

It is frequently said of Thomas Hardy that he turned to the writing of poetry as a result of his anger and disappointment at the shortsighted and discouraging critical response to his last novel, *Jude the Obscure,* which appeared in 1895. The truth of the matter appears to be that he had always preferred writing poetry to writing novels, and that he had written poetry before he presented himself to the reading public as a novelist and short story writer. He returned to his first love and decided to publish his poems only after he had established for himself a firm reputation as a novelist. Some of the verses which he included in his first volume of poems, *Wessex Poems,* had been composed more than thirty years before. He was then fifty-eight years old, and for the next thirty years he devoted himself exclusively to writing or rewriting his poems until his death in 1928.

His *Collected Poems,* retains almost a thousand poems which had appeared in eight preceding volumes of verse. This number testifies to his affection for and dedication to poetry, but it is too large an output to allow him to maintain consistent excellence. A few, relative to the large total, must be deemed outright failures, deficient either because of metrical inconsistency or inappropriateness, eccentric, excessive inversion, awkward diction, or an imagery and idea of embarrassing sentimentality. At the other end of the spectrum of his achievement, however, there are a few poems, again relatively speaking, which are extremely successful and claim the right to a permanent place in the ideal anthology of great and memorable poems in the English language. These poems, together with the large number which are at least interesting and competent, constitute a respectable body of work worthy of attention and high regard.

As might be expected, Hardy's poetry complements and intensifies the unhappy vision of life depicted in most of his novels. Hardy protested in an introductory note to his final volume of poems, *Winter Words,* that he had not attempted to present a "harmonious philosophy" in that book or in any of his earlier poetic work. Despite these protestations, however, there can be no question that an easily discernible, special "Hardyesque" vision of life emerges from his poetry as well as from his prose. Cast in the form of imaginative art, it may not have the rigidity or discipline of what we call philosophy, but it offers, nevertheless, a very consistent, even relentless view of life as a series of adventures in frustration and defeat. Man as an individual, man as a creature of society and the cosmos, is simply acting out the whims and dictates of an inexorable life force, a blind, indifferent, neutral Immanent Will. Though the Will (variously called Fate, Chance, Hap, Destiny, and Necessity) is ostensibly neutral about man's fate, the general reality is that man usually becomes "time's laughstock," his efforts to achieve love and dignity and significance simply create "satires of circumstance." These concepts emerge so clearly and triumphantly from his novels and poems because, while they may be few and schematic, they were for him matters of fundamental, abiding concern, and he used them constantly as the basis and the framework of his vision.

The themes and the vision which emerge from the poetry is almost wholly clouded and pessimistic. This was the way Hardy himself summed up the consensus of many reviews of his poetical work ("Apology," *Late Lyrics and Earlier*) a judgment which he deemed "odd." But the real oddity is that he should think this judgment strange because there can be little question that the corpus of his work is in general and quite consistently dark and sad and pessimistic. Hardy contended that the alleged pessimism was in truth a way of questioning and exploring the nature of reality, a first step, as he called it, toward the betterment of man's soul and body. To this end he quoted in his defense a line from an earlier poem, "In Tenebris":

If a way to the Better there be, it exacts
a full look at the Worst:

a perspective which he labeled, perhaps in desperation, "evolutionary meliorism." To point a way to the Better may have been his intention, but the fact is that he succeeded all too well in giving us a full look at the Worst; in his poetry there is very little, indeed only the barest hint scattered here and there, about the way to the Better. What little there is stresses the conjectural "if" in his poetical statements and the many qualifications which abound in his prose clarification. In his poetry there is very little of loving-kindness operating through scientific or any other kind of knowledge, and what free will we can see apparently works to the detriment of all, victor and victim alike.

In form, the poetry is fairly conventional. Hardy frequently exploited the forms of folk tradition: popular ballads, hymns, country songs, but there are many sonnets, couplets, dramatic monologues, narratives, and conversational anecdotes. Most are poems with a plot; that is, Hardy develops his theme through a highly concentrated, epitomized dramatic situation. This method has the value of establishing a distance between Hardy the man and Hardy the poet. The poem may actually be the outpouring of Hardy's secret heart, but the externalized narrative or dramatic situation presents the theme in a way that detaches it from Hardy himself. The poems which are narrative monologues or dialogues, and there are many, are not concerned with the creation of character. They are concerned with presenting a view of the world, Hardy's "dramatic truth" for which the speakers or their situation are more or less the actors. There are a few (relatively speaking again) "philosophical" poems which deal directly and explicitly with Hardy's thesis. They represent only a small proportion of the total poetic production but they have attracted a disproportionate amount of attention precisely because their didactic and abstract quality, stripped of character and situation, reveals Hardy's viewpoint so clearly and starkly. Actually, they are like footnotes that clarify a text; if we want a fair characterization of the bulk of Hardy's poems we must not take the footnotes for the text.

The meters in many of the poems are not skillfully handled, especially in some poems which we know were of early composition. To the modern ear, there is a vaguely anachronistic quality about some of these poems, much of it sounding "poetical" in an old-fashioned way. There is some use of dialect terms, some word-coinages, a few obsolete words. On occasion, Hardy attracted too much attention to these words—most of them making for clumsy, gnarled lines—by inverting normal syntax for the sake of the regularity of his meter or to meet the demands of a rhyme. These inversions contribute to the artificial and contrived quality of his unsuccessful poems.

The basic theme of these varied forms and meters is the cruel irony of a universe which does not, and apparently cannot, answer man's desire, indeed, his hunger, for order, justice, equity, or even a rationale for his suffering. The forces or phenomena which oppose and frustrate man can be identified from the various forms—narratives, situations, characters, settings—through which this basic theme is illustrated and dramatized.

In Hardy's world time erodes and corrodes the promise of youth, talent, hope, beauty, freshness, enthusiasm, and vibrancy. Love, in time, wastes away simply by being. Dreams grow weak and vague in time and soon lose their ability to inspire. If they survive, it is only to stand in mocking contrast to the disappointing reality outside. The body weakens; eyes dim; beauty vanishes in time, and too soon: death.

Death always seems to come too early or too late to provide whatever relief it may have offered; or it takes away the wrong person, meaning the good, and spares the ne'er-do-well.

Sex is a powerful force which victimizes all; which betrays unmarried girls into bearing illegitimate children; which compels them to betray the men they love; which distracts young men from their rightful careers and rightful destinies; which breaks up families, defies the security of traditional mores, and frequently leads to crime.

Love is fleeting, short-lived, and vulnerable; easily swayed, tempted, diverted, betrayed or betraying. Love is best at a distance, whether of time or in space, best when unconsummated and only dreamed of. When realized, it withers. It is a trap for women who must marry the wrong man and yearn for another, and who must therefore live in spiritual infidelity.

Society is viewed either as a system of tradition or security that is rapidly disappearing, or as the embodiment of outmoded ideas which destroy true lovers whose natural passions have betrayed them into defying the code. The rich girl may love the poor boy who loves her, but they are doomed to part because of the class system of society.

War is senseless, vicious, and inhumane. Invariably it is fought bravely but in ignorance by its victims, leaving wives, illegitimate children, and betrayal behind. The settings for these poems are Greek wars, Roman wars, colonial wars, Continental wars, world wars, culminating in the bitter "Christmas: 1924."

Nature is generally seen as a power-ful, blind force, an unknowing, well-intentioned, but blundering Mother, herself helpless in the grip of the heedless, inexorable Immanent Will. In the sense of the physical world about us, it is most often described as barren and bleak, shivering in the cold rain or snow or sleet, an outer weather to reflect the inner weather of the broken, desolate heart. If the scene is the beauty of spring or summer it is only to provide a mocking background to grief or to warn of the winter or death which lurks in or just behind the innocent beauty of the scene.

The setting for these experiences in frustration is frequently a graveyard, a sad, haunted house, an empty, crumbling church, or a desolate moor. Occasionally, we confront the whirling rapids of a river, suitable for a suicide or a killing. Sometimes it is a tavern where riotous drinking and dancing are betraying a young girl into straying, or a young wife into adultery.

Hardy's is a poetry of action and drama, rarely a poetry of mere description. It is not often a poetry of song, but a poetry which moves at the pace of thoughtful speech or spoken thought. If we follow a division of poetry which Hardy himself once made, we may say that his poetry falls roughly into four categories: (1) passionate poems—his ballads and narratives of ballad-like incident; (2) sentimental poems—his poems of recollection and nostalgia, poems about love and lovers. (3) meditative poems—his introspective, first-person monologues. (4) fanciful poems—his poems of philosophical dialogues with Nature and such Powers or his poems of conversations with ghosts. For the most part, in these poems, Nature complains, God argues, and Man questions. But these poems, like most of Hardy's poems, are designed to give dramatic identities and significances to the abstract idea that man, nature, and the universe are in the hands of the Immanent Will which operates powerfully but blindly, quite indifferent to the individual fate or destiny.

THE POETRY OF H. D.

Author: H(ilda) D(oolittle) (1886-1961)
Principal published works: Sea Garden, 1916; *Hymen,* 1921; *Heliodora and Other Poems,*
1924; *Collected Poems of H. D.,* 1925; *The Usual Star,* 1928; *Red Roses for Bronze,*
1931; *Collected Poems of H. D.,* 1940; *By Avon River,* 1942; *The Walls Do Not Fall,*
1944; *Tribute to the Angels,* 1945; *The Flowering of the Rod,* 1946; *Selected Poems,*
1957

The poetry of H.D., as Hilda Doolittle chose to call herself, represents the most Imagistic poems of the school of Imagism. This school of "new" poetry, flourishing during the first two decades of the twentieth century, was finally triumphed over and controlled by Amy Lowell. The proponents had as their credo of poetry (1) the use of common speech; (2) the creation of new rhythms; (3) absolute freedom in subject matter; (4) the use of image; (5) the writing of hard, definite, and clear verse; and (6) the concentration of poetry in its very essence. Although most poets associated with this group later wandered from its narrow statement of beliefs or accomplished little, Hilda Doolittle adhered faithfully to the tenets and produced poetry that is very effective.

The first poem in her first collection called *Sea Garden* reveals her art and accomplishment. In "Sea Rose" with unemotional words, sharp and hard in their clarity, she describes the desiccated sea roe, stunted and blown with the sand in the wind, and yet, despised and abandoned, it has more real fragrance than another flower, the conventional lovely rose, supposedly more fragrant. The poet's room for maneuver and accomplishment is narrow. She uses sixteen lines and only sixty-four words. But the poem is a fine and delicate cameo chiseled in marble.

Another such poem is "Sea Lily." In this work the poet addresses the reed that has been broken and torn by the wind. The myrtle is speckled from this reed, the scales are torn from its stem, and it is cut by sand that is sharp as flint, yet through it all the reed stands lifted up despite all the efforts of enemy elements to cover it. Such poems are triumphant successes.

Many, however, are poignant cries which, because of the author's technique, her assiduous use of the credo of the Imagists, somehow fail to come through to full development. They suggest and hint, but they are underdeveloped and therefore are generally unsuccessful.

A poem of this kind is "Mid-Day." The poet says that the light and heat are beating her down into nothingness. The wind rattles the seed-pods, and her thoughts are scattered like the seeds. But in the midst of this dryness she looks up and sees the deep-rooted poplar spreading among the other trees on the hill, and she addressed the poplar, pointing out how much more vital and alive it is on the hill than the writer is, perishing as she is on the rocks.

Another such work is "Pursuit." In it the speaker is following a man whose footsteps are half hidden, interrupted here and there, but distinct enough to be followed. She follows him past the wild hyacinth stalk that he has snapped in passing, through the grass he has brushed, past the forest ledge slopes and the roots that his hand snapped with its weight, on up the hill, then down where he fell, bruising his thigh and thereafter limping. Then the trail is lost and the writer can no longer find any trace of him in the underbrush and the fallen larch cones.

H.D.'s knowledge of Greek was extensive. More than half her work consists of poems on classical subjects and, to a smaller extent, translations of such writers as Euripides. One poem based on a Greek theme is the poignant "Eurydice," which tells how Orpheus descended to Hades, charmed Pluto with his music, and was allowed to lead Eurydice back to earth on the condition that he would not look back until he reached the upper air. The age-old story is, however, told from a different point of view, by Eurydice after she has been condemned to go back to Hades. She blames her fate on the arrogance and ruthlessness of Orpheus. In Hades she had been forgotten by the world and might have remained in peace but he came and disturbed her. Time and again she pathetically asks Orpheus why he turned and looked at her just when their goal was at hand. Because of his actions she has lost the earth. But she consoles herself with the thought that her hell is no worse than his, though he lives on earth with the sun and flowers. In hell she has more light than he has on earth; she has herself for flowers and her own fervor and her own spirit for a light. She realizes that before she can be lost, hell must allow the passing of the dead.

In other poems she passes from Greek mythology to literature, to Homer. Her poem "Helen" paints a death's-head black-and-white portrait of the wife who by her behavior caused the war between the Greeks and the Trojans. One of the great sufferers of that conflict, Penelope, is the subject of a powerful poem of passion and pride in "At Ithaca." Penelope, Ulysses' wife, is at home hiding behind her ruse for not marrying any of the suitors who are eating her into poverty: weaving the funeral pall for her father-in-law, Laertes, during the day and unraveling it at night. After years of work she thought her duty was done, and she longed passionately that one of the suitors would tear her weaving aside and conquer her with a kiss. But each time she saw her work in its entirety she was reminded of the greatness of her husband, and in contrast with him all the suitors around her faded into nothingness.

Sometimes, in a single simple sentence, H.D. pours feeling that rends the heart, for example, in "Circe." Circe is alone after Ulysses has thwarted her and gone away. She recalls how easily she bent the other men to her will, changing them into beasts as she chose. Man was easy to conquer because he prayed for a sight of her face or a touch of her hand. She could call men from the corners of the world—all except one, Ulysses. And she would give them all up for a glance from him.

The same poignancy enriches the poem "Leda," which concerns itself with the daughter of Thestius and wife of Tyndarus, King of Sparta, seen bathing nude in the river by Zeus, who took the form of a swan in order to love her. This poem is voiced by Leda. She remembers the wonder of love and sighs for the return of the red swan, the soft feathery flutter of his wings, the warmth of his breast.

The poet's same artistic motivations, control, and skill carry over into her translations. There are the same short lines, sometimes only a word, the identical hard, sharp, precise language and images, and the same quite fine artistic triumphs, as in the "Choruses from the *Iphigeneia in Aulis* and *The Hippolytus of Euripides.*" The women in the "Chorus of the Women of Chalkis" cross the hills of sand and the sea to see the battleline. To them, Menelaus is golden and Agamemnon is proud; both command the thousand ships of the Greek forces. They are determined to return Helen to Menelaus. The women see Achilles, with the wind strapped about his feet, flying to battle. The women are awed by the number and beauty of his ships. The number of Greek vessels is uncountable, and life will no longer be the same. The ships etch the mind.

Miss Doolittle published a considerable bulk of poetry after her *Collected Poems* of 1925. *Hippolytus Temporizes*, although probably a failure as true classical tragedy, is successful as a lyrical development of her thesis that beauty lies in the heart and is inviolable. Increasingly her poetry centered on the ancient world, as in *Red Roses for Bronze*. The escape to the Classical world, or perhaps more properly the use of it for present-day problems, is continued in *The Walls Do Not Fall*, which starts in London during the war years but immediately reaches back to an older world, in *Tribute to the Angels*, and in *The Flowering of the Rod*. A departure in subject matter and in style is *By Avon River*, praise in poetry and prose of Shakespeare and his numerous contemporaries. At her death H.D. was still writing and some of her work remained unpublished.

The power and thrust of her work was quickly recognized. She was one of the Imagists whose accomplishment was solid and whose influence was considerable though short-lived, for her later poems did little to broaden her subject matter or to create any momentous changes in style.

THE POETRY OF HENLEY

Author: William Ernest Henley (1849-1903)
Principal published works: A Book of Verses, including "In Hospital," 1888; *The Song of the Sword and Other Verses*, 1892; *London Voluntaries and Other Verses*, 1893; *Poems*, 1898; *For England's Sake*, 1900; *Hawthorn and Lavender*, 1901; *A Song of Speed*, 1903; *Collected Works*, 1908

The poetry of W. E. Henley reveals a man of various postures, of fundamentally slight mental accomplishments, but of great variety in subject matter and verse forms.

His poem sequence "In Hospital" sets the pattern for most of his subsequent work. Presenting a rather new idea for a series of poems, he attempts the unhackneyed in his treatment. The volume chronicles his hospital experience from his moment of entry to his exit, and he gives brief sketches of most of the other people in the hospital at that time. He begins with "Enter Patient," continues with "Waiting" for the operation, then the "Operation" itself, and with his other experiences until he is "Discharged." He also sketches the nurses, the surgeons, and various other people confined as patients. These poems are essentially topical, but in some instances his language is realistic and powerful enough to convey his themes with vividness. The probe used on him while he is waiting for the operation feels like a crowbar, and life he believes is a blunder. The nurses almost come alive, and "Kate the scrubber" is magnificently portrayed in her macabre ballet performance before the patients.

"The Song of the Sword," which was dedicated to and strongly influenced by Rudyard Kipling is a half-successful effort to imitate heroic poetry in having the author speak in the person of the sword. The sword is the long and righteous arm of England. Today this note of imperialism, powered by Kipling's philosophy, has an offensive ring.

"Arabian Nights' Entertainments" is an effort to re-create the wonder of childhood dreams in the make-believe world of Sindbad, Scheherazade, Pan, wizened leprechauns, and dozens of other such characters. Washington Irving's "Rip Van Winkle" held an especial attraction to the author in his memories that were thirty-five years "deep." But the poem is not a success. It gushes and names, trying to recall a lost magic; it does not evoke and re-create in the real sense. The magical words are given but the spirits of the words are not reawakened.

"Bric-A-Brac," written between 1877 and 1888, continues to a certain extent Henley's experimentation in form and subject matter. Most of the works are entitled the "Ballade" of one thing or another, as "Ballade of Youth and Age," and end with an "Envoy," but these efforts at archaism are generally unsuccessful. Far more noteworthy are such efforts at realism as "In Fisherrow." The sentiment in the poem is embarrassing rather than poignant, but the realistic picture of the ugly old woman selling fish is vividly presented. Fifty years old, she has a bronzed and shriveled face and neck; her feet are large, her legs bowed and spare and strong; and as she walks along imploring would-be purchasers to buy her fish she has the "spirit of traffic" ever in her eye.

Another poem in the volume that reveals one unfortunate aspect of Henley is "We shall surely die." Crippled as he was, Henley often postured a bravado that attempted to outstare age and debility but generally failed. Here, recognizing that man must die, he affirms that he and his love will accept their fate and not resent and scold it.

The poems he called "Echoes," (written between 1872 and 1889) contain some of his best and his most widely known works. The smooth and even "O, gather me the rose, the rose" hauntingly affirms the value of love as an antidote to fate. Another of the same kind, "Praise the generous gods for giving," is less successful, too easy an acceptance and affirmation of living. Quite successful is the Byronesque "We'll go no more a-roving by the light of the moon." In it he consciously twits the Byronic pose yet reveals in light parody the fun of the active life, though the poem concludes that the poet will not go roving anymore but will weep at home instead.

Another accomplished poem in "Echoes" is the ballad-like "O, Falmouth is a fine town with ships in the bay." The burthen and third stanza are derived from an old song; the remainder is a lively, muscular rendition of seventeenth and eighteenth century sentiment in sea songs. The most popular of the "Echoes" is "Invictus," with its first line, "Out of the night that covers me," and its concluding declaration that the author is the captain of his own soul.

"Rhymes and Rhythms" reveals little progress in technique, though more in experimentation. In the prologue the author asserts that since something about life is dead it is time to pull back to the fire of meditation and retrospection. These poems are more brooding about matters that can loosely be called philosophical. He experiments with new verse forms, and occasionally he strikes new depths in language.

Hawthorne and Lavender does not differ significantly from the earlier volumes. In the "Envoy" Henley says that his songs which were formerly of the sunrise are now of the sunset; yet they were joyfully written. They are still songs of joy that show little diminution from his earlier works. Occasionally the simple statement of affirmation is marred by the posing that was never far from Henley's nature. For example, in "Will I die of drink?" he feigns a cocksureness that he does not feel. Will he die of drink? Why not? Will he rest and think? Why? Why brood on mortality? Everybody must die, so why not the sooner the better?

For England's Sake: Verses and Songs in Time of War sounds most of Henley's worst faults. The poems are bellicose and chauvinistic. Two, for example, "The Man in the Street" and " 'Our Chief of Men,'" rattle the sword in the manner of Henley's friend Kipling. Another, "Pro Roge Nostro," asks what the author has done for England and asserts that there is nothing he would not do for the race of mighty men raised on that island.

Henley's best poems are those contained in "London Types." In approach they go back to his first poems, "In Hospital." In execution they approach a Dickensian orchestration of the seamy side of London life. Almost exclusively the characters described are lowly and Henley treats them with an unusual honesty, in a language which he had not otherwise indulged in, slangy, earthy, and realistic. "The 'Bus-Driver" is a lively and truly etched portrait. The driver hogs the road, shouts from his vehicle, curses those who cross him, "meets / His losses with both *lip* and £ *s. d.*" and has no gods "but *Fake*."

"'Liza" bristles with slang, and realism. Her *old man's* not always on the up-and-up, her *old woman's* a boozer, but Liza herself is a perfect lady, with feathers and fringes to prove it. She uses her *pearlies*, her *barrer* and *jack* to impress her *bloke*. But other than her "gay and giddy whirl," Liza is only a stupid girl who works hard.

The "Barmaid" reveals a girl named Elizabeth who tries to butter her image by calling herself Elise. She apes the fashion in her cheap clothes and reads penny novels to improve her taste. But she is a mere shadow, not a person at all, and after she has served her time at the bar she simply disappears.

Henley's poetry in total has little weight in the history of literature. A few items are interesting as period pieces, influenced by the spirit of naturalism that influenced English literature at the end of the century; others survive because they reveal the personality of their writer.

THE POETRY OF HEREDIA

Author: José María de Heredia (1803-1839)
Principal published work: Poems, 1825

José María de Heredia y Campuzano, born in Cuba at a time when the island was beginning to resent its position as a territorial possession of Spain, was regarded by Spaniards as "the compendium and epitome of all enmity toward Spain." Yet, at least in his early period, he considered himself a Spaniard and referred in his poetry to "tender Mother Spain." During his youth, his father was chief judge in a court in Caracas that had to try rebels against the tyranny of Monteverde. Because of leniency, the judge was demoted to a position in Mexico where José María lived until his father's death. Then he went to Havana to complete his law studies.

There he became a member of a club of revolutionists called Soles de Bolívar (Suns of Bolívar), who were plotting for Cuban independence. Heredia supported the 1820 revolution in Spain of Rafael del Riego and wrote angry poems against a "stupid Spain" for executing him. It is no wonder that after he had been admitted to the bar in 1823 and had begun to practice law in Matanzas, he was picked up at the outbreak of a revolution that same year and sentenced to perpetual banishment. With all the poetry he had written in Mexico and Cuba, he went to New York. There he spent two years as a journalist, writing literary and theatrical criticism, and in 1825 publishing his first volume of poems, which contains practically all that are best known. A later supposedly "augmented edition" from Toluca in 1832 contained only a few unimportant new original poems, some translations, and a philosophical dissertation in verse on immortality that added little to his reputation. The New York printing contained a preface in English extolling the virtues of the volume as an aid for North Americans wanting to learn Spanish. Heredia added: "May the readers accept this small service from an exiled young man as an expression of gratitude for the asylum he has found in this happy country."

Among the long poems in this volume were "En el teocalli de Cholula" ("On the Temple Pyramid of Cholula"), "En una tempestad" ("In a Hurricane"), "A Niágara" ("Ode to Niagara Falls"), and "Al sol" (To the Sun"). They were well received. Possibly their tinge of melancholy, so like his own poetry, made William Cullen Bryant decide to translate two of them, "In a Hurricane" and "Ode to Niagara Falls," that were published in the *United States Review and Literary Gazette,* in 1827, the first Latin American poetry to appear in English.

In 1830 the youthful Argentine poet Esteban Echeverría returned to his native Buenos Aires after spending five years among the Romantic poets of France; his advice to his fellow writers was to break away from literary dependence on Spain and to hymn the natural beauties of the New World. Heredia was already painting in poetry the American scene and expressing romantic ideas in classic verse forms. In "On the Temple Pyramid of Cholula" he used ten-syllable unrhymed lines resembling English blank verse.

Seated in the ancient Aztec temple, the youthful poet watched the sun setting behind the volcano Iztaccihual, whose snowcap was tinged with gold. The stars came out, and as the moon descended, the shadow of Popocatepec, like a colossal ghost, extended till it covered the earth. This eclipse of nature caused the poet to ponder on the passing of the cruel Aztec rulers and all their glory. In this passing he saw how temporary is human fury and madness.

In the poem, the reader finds such classical touches as a mention in the American landscape of the olive tree "sacred to Minerva," and of Titan and his struggle against the gods of Olympus. With the subjectivity of later romantic poets, Heredia, though describing a scene in Mexico through the eyes of a seventeen-year-old, was actually poetizing his soul and its agony at what it sees.

In his "Ode to Niagara Falls," Nature stirred his emotions to take lyrical form. Confronting this marvel, he thought of the still greater marvels of God and Time. In the awesomeness of the scene, he was filled with nostalgia for his native Cuba. Cynics may remark that the sense of absence is a common theme of literature, and Heredia had scarcely spent enough years of his life in Cuba to become very closely attached to it. He had never been happy or felt at home there, any more than he had in Mexico or in the United States. In reality he had no roots. But melancholy is an emotion common to much poetry, and Heredia was a poet. The sight of the rushing water set his poet's heart pounding. As Bryant translated the opening lines:

My lyre! Give me my lyre! My bosom feels
The glow of inspiration. Oh, how long
Have I been left in darkness, since this light
Last visited my brow! Niagara!
Thou with thy rushing waters doth restore
The heavenly gift that sorrow took away.

Though the poet had never been so moved before, he felt that something was missing from this scene:

The delicious palms that on the plains
Of my own native Cuba spring and spread
Their thickly foliaged summits to the sun.

But a few moments of contemplation changed his mind.

But no, Niagara,—thy forest pines
Are fitter coronal for thee.

A few lines later, bemoaning his hopeless situation and wondering how an unfrozen heart can be happy without love, he expressed a wish that some one worthy of being loved could share his walk. At the end, however, the longing for glory swept over him, and while he knew he would be dead within a few years, he expressed the hope that his verse, like Niagara, might be immortal and that in heaven he could "Listen to the echoes of my fame." At one point in the poem Heredia declared:

From my very boyhood have I loved . . .
To look on Nature in her loftier moods,
At the fierce rushing of the hurricane.

The full intensity of his temperament is revealed in his "Ode to the Hurricane." "Hurricane, hurricane, I feel thee coming," he begins. Then he ascends to poetic heights in a description of the color, the fury, the roar, and the horror of the storm. The poet's personal reaction concludes the poem. The sublimity of the storm makes him forget the vileness of the world. He raises his head in delight. Amid the roar, he rises to the throne of God and with hot tears streaming down his cheeks he adores God's lofty majesty.

Ardor and passion also fill a number of Heredia's political poems that voice love of liberty and hatred of oppression. Cato, Riego, and Napoleon are admired as champions of liberty in excellent sonnets. His "Himno del desterrado" ("Hymn of the Exile"), written in 1825 and prophesying Cuba's freedom from Spain, served as a rallying cry for three quarters of a century until independence was finally won.

THE POETRY OF HODGSON

Author: Ralph Hodgson (1871-1962)
Principal published works: The Last Blackbird and Other Lines, 1907; *The Bull,* 1913;
Eve and Other Poems, 1913; *The Mystery and Other Poems,* 1913; *The Song of Honour,*
1913; *Poems,* 1917; *Hymn to Moloch,* 1921; *The Silver Wedding and Other Poems,*
1941; *The Skylark,* 1958; *Collected Poems,* 1961

Ralph Hodgson wrote very little but remarkably fine poetry through a long life that was mostly removed, though conscious choice, from the bustle of the busy world. A self-educated pressman and draftsman from Yorkshire, he did not publish any collection of verse until he was thirty-six, when *The Last Blackbird* appeared in 1907. The volume included such polished lyrics as "The Linnet" and the title poem, and Hodgson was immediately granted a place of prominence among lyricists of his generation. With his appearance in the second Georgian anthology in 1915, he was indelibly linked, for better or worse, with that group of pre-World War I British poets who have been termed "Georgian" because of King George V and because Edward Marsh, editor of the anthology prophesied another Georgian Age as a result of their talent.

The group with which Hodgson was thus associated consisted of poets as varied as Lascelles Abercrombie, Gordon Bottomley, Rupert Brooke, W. H. Davies, Walter de la Mare, W. W. Gibson, John Drinkwater, John Masefield, James Stephens, Siegfried Sassoon, and the early D. H. Lawrence and Robert Graves. They had no formal aesthetic— few British poetry groups have ever had —but they did have a number of poetic aims and attributes that linked them, although they themselves were not too much aware of this connection at the time. Though not as resolutely formal in technique as Ezra Pound, or as ready to plum the emotional limits of despair as T. S. Eliot, all the Georgians were like that more famous pair in moving away from late Victorian rhetoric and moralizing towards a more realistic depiction in poetry of the world in which they lived.

Reacting against scenes of romantic and patriotic glamor in the poetry of Tennyson and against his obtrusive moralizing, they also avoided the hypnotic rhythms and eccentric themes of Swinburne. They deliberately endeavored to return to the roots of Romanticism associated by them, in scenes of rural simplicity, with the woods, birds, and animals of Blake, Wordsworth, Keats, and Shelley.

This was not merely an attempt to imitate long-dead poets or to retreat from the complex disappointments of the industrial world, but also a genuine effort to re-create the original elements of the Romantic Movement. *Poems,* Hodgson's second book, contains several lyrics which succeed in achieving these effects admirably. His short poem, "Stupidity Street," reprinted countless times since its appearance in this volume, is Hodgson at his quiet but succinct best in his vision of singing birds offered for sale as food in Stupidity Street shops. Following the destruction of the world of nature, he warns, the shops will be empty, with nothing left to sell.

This simple but profound depiction of man's brutalization of the world is constructed with the compactness of William Blake. In this same volume appeared the longer lyric, "The Bull", for which Hodgson was awarded the William Polignac Prize in 1914. The poem is also characteristic of the transitional movement that carried forward the foremost themes of English Romanticism into an age of aircraft and computers. The old bull is not sentimentalized or made to stand for nature outraged by the ravages of man (as is so often the case in minor Romantic verse). The poem, of thirty sextets in length, dramatizes raw life itself, with the deposed pride of the herd now a gaunt shape of skin and bones standing alone by the edges of the lake waiting for death. Dreams of his younger days, his prowess, his potency, his battles and victories are swiftly recorded, finally returning to the moment of decay when he will become food for the vultures.

Toughness and precision were Hodgson's constant hallmark when his lyric gift was at its best. "Eve," his frequently reprinted poem about the fall of man (or woman) in the garden of Eden is also familiar to many who do not know of Hodgson's career or even his name. There is in the poem a sensuality unusual for Hodgson's time, which was often characterized by prudery, and a lyrical tautness equal to that of Thomas Hardy. The actual seduction of Eve by the serpent—here a cobra—is watched from afar by a chattering titmouse and a wren, and Eve's fall is made ominous by this distancing. Even more than the triumph of lewd evil is sensual joy itself—Eve with the berry part way to her mouth—that the reader remembers. A similar effect is created in Hodgson's brief song about a vagrant girl degrading herself to sell ring tosses at a carnival booth, ancient wildness in her dark eyes like beasts in a den. Such springtime paganism is rare in English poetry at any time, but is perfectly depicted by Hodgson in joyous lyricism set to a musical refrain in "Time, You Old Gypsy Man."

Though Hodgson's verse was not escapist, it was not of the 1920's either. All his work was in adaptation of the ballad meter, and his best efforts were in a dozen lines or so; the few long poems tend to dissipate intensity through repetitious meter and failure to sustain drama from inherently static situations. When Hodgson is at his best, we still think of Hardy. Perhaps this unwillingness or inability to develop led Hodgson to abandon poetry with the 1917 volume. He left England in 1924 for Japan, where he taught English literature at Sendai University until 1938, when he moved to the United States with the Ohio missionary and school teacher he married in the Orient. This most authentic of the British Georgians spent the last twenty-four years of his life, until his death at ninety-one in 1962, residing on a small farm in Minerva, Ohio, a figure almost unknown to the outside world. A small volume, *The Skylark*, was published in 1958, but this group of resolutely archaic lyrics merely confirmed the indications that his modest but firm talent had had its real fulfillment in pre-World War I London, forty years before.

THE POETRY OF HOFMANNSTHAL

Author: Hugo von Hofmannsthal (1874-1929)
Principal published works: Ausgewaehlte Gedichte (Selected Poems), 1903; *Die gesammelten Gedichte (Collected Poems),* 1907

All efforts to classify Hugo von Hofmannsthal as a member of a period or a literary school have failed. Terms such as romantic symbolist, neoclassicist, neoromanticist, expressionist, aesthetician, mystic, or naturalist may all be partially true, but they are still insufficient to encompass his work. His success as a librettest for Richard Strauss operas has obscured his even greater contributions as a poet. Followers of literary fashions tended to ignore Hofmannsthal, who refused to be typified. The turn of the century "melting pot" atmosphere of Vienna —German, Italian, Slavic, Jewish—and Hofmannsthal's own Jewish, German, and Italian parentage had considerable influence on his development. He was open to all manifestations of his surroundings, including all new literary trends. Needless to say, the psychological findings by his famous fellow Viennese citizens, most notably Freud, Jung, and Adler, were among those influences.

Hofmannsthal was born in 1874. During his last three years in high school he published his first poems under a pen name. As a student at the University of Vienna he had already gained fame as a poetical "Wunderkind." Under his pen name, Loris, he became a member of the habitués in Vienna's literary coffeehouses.

His early age was also his major period of poetic writings. The poems express some of the anguish of Goethe's well known lament: " . . . If pain forbids a man to talk, God gave me the gift to speak."

Many truly down below must perish
Where the heavy oars of ships are passing;
Others by the helm up there have dwelling,
Know the flight of birds and starry countries.

In the same poem the young Hofmannsthal also indicates his recognition of the interdependence of all things.

I can never cast off from my eyelids
Lassitudes of long-forgotten peoples,
Nor from my astounded soul can banish
Soundless fall of stars through outer distance.

Many destinies with mine are woven;
Living plays them all through one another,
And my part is larger than this slender
Life's ascending flame or narrow lyre.

In a Vienna coffeehouse he met Stefan George; a friendship developed, which led to his contribution in a literary magazine ("Blaetter fuer die Kunst") published by George. George was greatly impressed by Hofmannsthal and wrote him: "You and I could have exercised a most beneficial dictatorship in literature for many years," yet Hofmannsthal refused to become a follower of George's strict concept of art for art's sake, and he did not share the loyalty of George's disciples known as the "George Circle." The second meeting with George ended in an argument and a request for a duel by George. Later he was again invited by George to make contributions to his magazine, but in 1906 the correspondence came to an end. Hofmannsthal was too eager to study new developments to be concerned by only one literary point of view. Like Goethe before him, he tried to interpret his environment in terms of all available knowledge; however, the pace of expanding knowledge in Hofmannsthal's time had accelerated to such a degree that any effort to obtain a true universal knowledge was bound to fail. His intensive readings of contemporary authors were not used to fortify a personal point of view, but rather to absorb more manifestations of the complexity of life.

He did not build an ivory tower, as George did, with a priestly concept of poetry. His poetic effort always centered around the importance of life as a whole, and not as a selective process. Speaking about his poetry he stated: "How from any abyss of the world could it bring back anything more than human feelings, when poetry itself is nothing more than the language of men." He admitted, that he experienced unusual states of exhaltation which he termed the "lyrical state," but even under these conditions he remained on firm ground. His language is musical and graceful in style. Hofmannsthal is more easily accessible than George. Comparisons with Rilke and Verlaine are justified. Water and water-related terms, such as *river, well, fountain,* and *bridge,* are his most favored symbols. His poem "Reiselied" is frequently compared to Goethe's in style:

> To engulf us waters eddy,
> Down the boulders roll, to crush,
> And to bear us off already
> Birds on powerful pinions rush.

Poetry is not an easy task for a man who is subject to many influences. In his epigram, "The Art of Poetry," he states:

> Perilous, terrible art! This thread I
>   spin out of my body
> And at the same time the thread serves
>   as my path through the air.

By describing a landscape he expresses the reward he receives from his perilous and terrible efforts:

> The breath of flowers spoke to him,
>   but only
> Of alien beauty—and in silence he
> Breathed in the pristine air, but without longing:
> Only the need of serving made him glad.

His desire to understand his contemporaries gave many liberal critics an opportunity to attack him as an imitator and to accuse him of trying to maintain the status quo of Austria. Conservatives were equally ready to reject him. Hofmannsthal considered himself as a patriotic Austrian, but he was thinking about Austria as a state with a cultural mission. Although the old Austrian universality was still in existence, it showed signs of disintegration. That Hofmannsthal retained his sanity during his efforts to diagnose all symptoms of the era, without being himself defeated by the virus of disintegration, is attributed mainly to his unwavering Catholic faith. In the field of religion he was inquisitive, and he read with particular interest William James's *The Varieties of Religious Experience* and Kierkegaard's works; but the universality of the Roman Catholic Church and belief in the mystical body of Christ, which encompasses all that was and all that will be, made it possible for him to subordinate all other influences. The major crisis in his life became public knowledge when he permitted publication of the Chandos letter in a Berlin newspaper in 1901. This letter, addressed to Sir Francis Bacon and signed by Lord Chandos, was immediately identified as autobiographical. Hofmannsthal originally intended to address the letter to George, but he mailed him a copy instead. This letter speaks about his increasing skepticism and the fear that his analytical mind might paralyze his creative powers. He claimed, that he was not able anymore to speak coherently and that he had a physical aversion to words like *spirit, soul, body.* Under minute analysis, all assumptions seemed to him to be without foundation and therefore kept him from expressing an opinion on anything. Here he also gives evidence of his empathic power: "A pitcher, a harrow abandoned in a field, a dog in the sun, a neglected cemetery, a cripple, a peasant's hut—all these can become the vessel of my revelation." Word skepticism and work mysticism (his terms) were subjects close to him even before the Chandos letter. In 1895 he wrote that "people are tired of talking, they feel a deep disgust with words. For words have pushed themselves in front of things. This has awakened a deep love for all the arts that are executed in silence."

Fortunately the Chandos crisis did not lessen his creativity. It may have had influence in leading Hofmannsthal from lyric poetry to the dramatic poetry which ultimately led to his work as a librettist. Yet many passages of his dramatic verse plays and playlets could fill volumes of lyrical poetry. The first play, *Little Theater of the World* opens with the lines:

> I bathed, till by the open window's glare
> Glancing between my fingers I could tell
> That slantwise now the low sun's rays were falling
> On golden trees, long shadows gloomed the fields.
> Now up and down I pace the narrow path;
> Bird-catcher you would think me from a distance.

Hofmannsthal's poems have also been compared to those of William Butler Yeats ("Crossway," "The Rose," "The Shadowy Water"). If it is true that lyrical drama survives as poetry but not as drama, the statement applies to Hofmannsthal as well as to Yeats. However, the case of *Everyman* seems to represent an exception to this rule. The poetic and dramatic qualities of this play make it a perennial favorite at the Salzburg Festival and on many other famous stages. His earlier play *Death and the Fool*, first presented in 1893, gives evidence of his ever-present lyricism:

> Now the last mountains lie in gleaming shrouds,
> Clothed in the moistened glow of sun-steeped air.
> There hangs a wreath of alabaster clouds
> Above, here rimmed with gold, grey shadows there:
> So once did Masters of past centuries
> Paint clouds which bear Our Lady through the skies.

Opera lovers will be richly rewarded if they explore the poetic values of the librettos in the Strauss operas. It is not surprising that Strauss, who was describing a transitional period in musical terms, should be attracted by a poet who had inherited Romanticism and was trying to express feelings meaningful to the twentieth century. In 1929, while he was preparing for the funeral of his eldest son, who had committed suicide, a brain hemorrhage ended Holmannsthal's life at the age of fifty-five.

It is too early for a verdict on Hofmannsthal by literary history. At present it seems that the names of his contemporaries, Rilke and George, are more frequently mentioned in German literature. But it is inconceivable that a poet who encompassed the diversities of two centuries should not gain a greater significance when the perspective from another century permits a more objective judgment. Hofmannsthal was always conscious of the transitoriness of all striving and of the indestructible relationship of all things created:

> Then: that in lives a century old I share
> And kinsmen laid in coffins long ago
> Are yet as close to me as my own hair,
> Are no less one with me than my own hair.

THE POETRY OF HÖLDERLIN

Author: Johann Christian Friedrich Hölderlin (1770-1843)
First published: Gedichte (*Poems*), 1826

Hölderlin is classified as a German Romanticist, but in most of his poems he praises the ideals of Greek mythology. Born in 1770, he was educated in a secularized Protestant monastery school. His father died two years after his birth, and his mother, who had a very strict conception of Protestantism, became the major influence in his life. Neither the study of theology nor his mother's efforts to transfer her religious ideas to her son made him a theologian. Hölderlin was not able to find in his mother's strict disciplinarian idea of Christianity the vehicle for his soaring idealism. However, reflections about God are woven into most of his poems ("Man is God when he dreams, a beggar when he reflects"), but for most of his life the personalized gods of Greece were to him a welcome contrast to his imagined remoteness of Christianity. At the age of fifteen he began to write poetry. His only other interest was music, and he displayed great skill with the flute, the violin, and the piano. This musicality, combined with his extreme lyrical sensitivity, gives Hölderlin's poetry an almost musical flow, which in the opinion of some admirers surpasses the poetry of Goethe. His idealistic dreams about Greece separated him from his great contemporaries (Schiller, who tried to help in his early years; Goethe, who rejected most of his efforts; Hegel, who was his schoolfriend). The preoccupation with Greece made him also a strong critic of Germany.

He was always conscious of his eccentricity, and he broke an engagement to his first love, Luise Nast because he considered himself temperamentally too unstable for marriage. At the end his extreme isolation drove him into an imaginary world; he suffered a complete mental breakdown and was insane during the last forty years of his life.

The writing of poetry was a sacred task for him. In one of his youthful poems, which he classified as "eccentric enthusiasm," he stated:

Holy vessels are the poets,
In which the wine of life,
The spirit of heroes is preserved. . . .

His poems are usually constructed on the "thesis, antithesis, synthesis" basis, and never are witty. He objects to novelty: "On no account do I wish that it were original. For originality is novelty to us; and nothing is dearer to me than the things which are as old as the world itself." His strength lies in the power to evoke visions without striving for originality. One of his most widely used symbols is the flower representing birth and death.

In 1795 he found a position as tutor in a banker's house in Frankfort, a post which permitted him to devote most of his time to writing. Here he also had the most important encounter of his life, when he met Susette Gontard, the wife of his employer. She fulfilled his dream of Greek perfection, and he renamed her Diotima. In the same year he wrote his first poem about Diotima. Many more were to follow:

. . . When Time's burden lay upon
    me,
And my life was cold and pale,
And already, bowing downwards,
Yearned   for   the   still   shadows'
    realm . . .
You appeared in all your radiance,
Godly image, in my night . . .

Most romanticists deal with the subject of love in the light of rebellion against the age of reason. Hölderlin uses love as the great unifying factor of material and spiritual forces. In Frankfort he also wrote his only major prose work, *Hyperion*. Subtitled "The Hermit in Greece," the work reflects his love for Diotima and his struggle for a renaissance of the golden age of Greece. In "Hyperion's Song of Fate" his fatalistic attitude finds expression:

> But it is our fate
> To find no resting-place,
> And suffering men
> Dwindle and fall
> Blindly from one
> Hour to the next,
> Hurled like water
> From rock to rock,
> Downwards for years to uncertainty.

Susette Gontard responded to his youthful adoration. It is probable that the love affair was discovered, for two years later Hölderlin left Frankfort and Diotima. It is doubtful that he was ever able to overcome the tremendous grief of separation. The period of eccentric enthusiasm came to an end, but the lyric power of Hölderlin increased. Shortly after his Frankfort experience he finished his major work in dramatic verse, *The Death of Empedocles*. Empedocles sacrifices himself to return to eternity, because a man of purity must disintegrate among men who have lost their connection with nature and the universe.

> O flowers of heaven! beauteous stars,
> Will you now also fade, and will the night
> Descend upon your soul, O Father Aether!
> If your youths, the splendid ones, are grown dim
> Before you? Now I know: what is divine
> Must perish. By his fall I'm made a seer. . . .

Hölderlin had many forebodings of his doomed fate:

> High my spirit aspired, skywards, but down to earth
> Love soon drew it; still more suffering humbled it.
> So I follow the curve of
> Life and return to my journey's start.

Between 1800 and 1803, Hölderlin re-examined his position toward Christianity and Greece. The "Archipelago" gives some indication of his findings:

> . . . And if impetuous Time too forcefully seizes
> My head, and want and wandering among mortals shatter
> My mortal life, on stillness, in your depths, let me ponder. . . .

The transition from Greece to Christianity is also apparent in "Bread and Wine":

> For when some time ago now—to us it seems distant—
> They all ascended by whom life had been favoured with joy,
> When from human kind the Father averted His visage
> And all over the earth sorrowing, rightly, began,
> When at last had appeared a quiet Genius, consoling
> Sacredly—He that proclaimed daytime's conclusion and went—
> Then as a sign that they had once been here and again would
> Come, the heavenly choir left a few presents behind . . .

About 1802 he also departed from the hexameters of his style and began to use rhythms in his poems, which later became influential among many modern German poets. His preoccupation with Christianity had not the characteristics of a conversion, though the domineering influence of his mother, combined with his strong sense of obedience may have been of some importance. However, the conflict between his ideas and his mother's desire to transform him into a God-fearing man was never resolved. In 1802, after many failures to obtain employment, he found a position as a tutor in France. But in the summer of the same year he returned home. Reports of his mental breakdowns became more frequent. He also received the news that Diotima had died. At this period Hölderlin's poetic capabilities were still high, and he wrote some of his most important poems. Among these is his powerful "Patmos":

Near is
The God, and hard to grasp.
But where there is danger,
The Saving powers grow too.

In darkness dwell
The eagles, and fearless across
The abyss go the sons of the Alps
On lightly built bridges. . . .

In "Germania" he entered a new phase
of naturalistic poetry, but without forgetting his spiritual home Greece:

Not them, the blessed, who once ap-
peared,
The images of Gods in the ancient
land,
These, it is true, I may call no more,
but if,
You waters of home, now with you
The love of my heart laments, what
else does it desire,
The sacredly sorrowing? For full of
expectation
Lies the land while, as if lowered
In sultry days, you yearning ones, to-
day a heaven,
Foreboding, casts its shadow about you.

Again his premonitions of years to come
is apparent:

Alas, where shall I find when
Winter, comes, flowers, and where
Sunshine,
And the shadows of earth?
The walls stand speechless and cold, in
the wind
Weathercocks clatter.

In 1805 his illness became serious. A
doctor reported that his speech was no
longer understandable, composed as it
was of German, Greek, and Latin sounds.

Tragically, it was only at this time that
many influential Germans became conscious of Hölderlin's genius. But now he
had to live in obscurity because his behavior did not permit social contacts
except for occasional short visits by understanding friends. He spent the last thirty-
six years of his life in the house of a
friendly carpenter. But in spite of his
frequent attacks he continued to write
poetry. Unfortunately, most of those

writings were destroyed. The poems
which were saved indicate that Hölderlin's art was never completely exhausted,
as these lines found penciled on a
wooden board indicate:

The lines of life are various; they
diverge and cease
Like footpaths and the mountains' utmost ends;
What here we are, elsewhere a god
amends
With harmonies, eternal recompense
and peace.

Many of the letters written to his mother
during this period show that until the
very end she tried to influence her son to
return to her way of Protestantism.
Hölderlin, however, expressed more and
more interest in Roman Catholicism. He
died, apparently without pain and in
prayer, at the age of seventy-three in
1843.

Many early German editions ignored
the poems written during his illness. It
was not until 1923 that the first complete
edition of his works was published. His
illness became the subject of many studies. One of these states that Hölderlin
was not destroyed by weakness or his inability to cope with his environment, but
precisely by his firm purity incapable of
any compromise. Among the twentieth
century German poets Stefan George and
Rainer Maria Rilke, especially, acknowledged their debts to Hölderlin and caused
a revival of appreciation of his work.

The loneliness of his vision in a depersonalized society makes Hölderlin a favorite among many devoted friends of
poetry who give preference to the lone
idealist over his more famous Romantic
contemporaries. The insurmountable difficulty in translating Hölderlin's sensitive
lyricism adequately makes it improbable
that his work will ever be appreciated by
a world-wide audience. But if there is a
borderline between music and poetry,
Hölderlin came closest in crossing from
one to the other.

THE POETRY OF HOPKINS

Type of work: Poetry
Author: Gerard Manley Hopkins (1844-1889)
Principal published works: Poems of Gerard Manley Hopkins, Now First Published, with
Notes by Robert Bridges, 1918; Complete Poems, 1947

Twenty-nine years elapsed from the time the poet Robert Bridges first published his edition of Gerard Manley Hopkins' *Poems* to publication of the definitive collection edited by the great Hopkins scholar, W. H. Gardner. Within that time Hopkins had been firmly established as an important if not a major British poet, not of his age but of the present. Undoubtedly, many of the conflicts over his life and work will have been resolved by the hundredth anniversary of the year Bridges first presented a small number of Hopkins' poems in important anthologies (1893).

Certain it is that the interest when this brilliant genius was in vogue, during the decade after 1918, has changed to something more deeply critical and scholarly. The letters, notebooks, and essays as well as the complete poems—no one now believes the best of the poet's work was destroyed—are now available to all, and hardly a year passes without the appearance of a volume of criticism or biography of the extremely paradoxical G. M. Hopkins.

Of utmost importance in understanding the very powerful poetry of this often misunderstood poet is his eclecticism, his wide knowledge and deep insights. While it is true that the preponderance of criticism has dwelt on Hopkins' innovations in rhythm-rhyme and imagery ("instress" and "inscape" summarize the two main facets), his whole poetic output indicates that he followed in the great European poetic tradition from Homer to Matthew Arnold. Hopkins' greatest poems are unique in powerful rhythmic effect, equal to or surpassing that of any other poet of like output; historically speaking, his poems prove that the genius of our language lies in stress-rhythms (often "sprung") of our oldest traditional poetry, at least as important as syllabic meters in effect. His poetic diction, his use of common idiom as well as ingenious coinages, is without exact parallel. His ear for language was so acute, though highly individual, that he helped restore poetry as an oral-aural art, a fact the late Dylan Thomas so brilliantly demonstrated.

The lack of bulk, the slender volume of three hundred pages encompassing less than two hundred poems or fragments, makes arbitrary the distinction of whether Hopkins was a major poet. Certainly he is a classic in a very special sense. His central vision was deeply Christian, Jesuit, even mystical, often ecstatic though intellectually controlled. One of his greatest poems, "The Wreck of the *Deutschland*," was inspired as much by the "happy memory of five Franciscan Nuns" as their tragic death in 1875 by drowning. By his own account, the thirty-one-year-old theologian, deeply affected by the newspaper account of these nuns, exiled by the Falk Laws, who drowned in the Thames on a ship carrying them from Germany to America, responded to his rector's suggestion that a commemorative poem should be written of this. Hopkins was eager to try a new rhythm which had been haunting his ear, as he puts it. In spite of Robert Bridges' disapproval, he kept the rhythmic "oddnesses" because the technique was irrevocably bound to the sentiment he wanted to express, the sprung rhythm or "expressional rhythm . . . a vital fusion of the internal rhythm of thought-and-emotion and the external rhythm of sounds," as Gardner describes this phenomenon. As a threnody the poem is unique. An invocation to God to master rebellious feelings, a narrative of the tragic event, an elegy of one nun's heroism, a meditation on God's beneficence, a plea for intercession—all these and other arguments within the poem demanded a flexibility and felicity of form. The result is one of the great poems in English or any language. Stanza thirty-two, a poem of praise to a merciful God, will illustrate these subtleties:

> I admire thee, master of the tides,
> Of the Yore-flood, of the year's fall;
> The recurb and the recovery of the gulf's sides,
> The girth of it and the wharf of it and the wall;
> Stanching, quenching ocean of a motionable mind;
> Ground of being, and granite of it: past all
> Grasp God, throned behind
> Death with a sovereignty that heeds but hides, bodes but abides.

While no one definition of "inscape" or "instress" will suffice, this stanza contains both: the former is seeing of the internal and fundamental, significant form or nature of, say, the ocean in motion; and the latter would include the access to God's grace and a celebration of this, though the rhythmic expression is also implied.

Perhaps the searching eye and the recording ear are best illustrated in Hopkins' most famous lyric, "Pied Beauty." Here the poet as painter and musician is displayed, showing his deep concern for bringing to bear in a poem all the senses:

> Glory be to God for dappled things—
> For skies of couple-colour as a brinded cow;
> For rose-moles all in stipple upon trout that swim;
> Fresh-firecoal chestnut-falls; finches' wings;
> Landscape plotted and pieced-fold, fallow, and plough;
> And áll trádes, their gear and tackle and trim.

> All things counter, original, spare, strange;
> Whatever is fickle, freckled (who knows how?)
> With swift, slow; sweet, sour; adazzle, dim;
> He fathers-forth whose beauty is past change:
> Praise him.

Here are rhythmic contrasts, dramatic juxtapositions, unique word manipulations, a compelling meter as dappled and iridescent as the things described.

Another facet of Hopkins' talent, one of his most pronounced achievements, was his variation on the sonnet form, a revolt against the stilted structures and concepts of Victorian poesy. This is not to say he wrote loosely or without thought; quite the contrary is true, for his critical writings reveal the depth of his study and experimentation. Ascetic by habit and temperament, he elevated the form to a new lyricism by breaking with or modifying many old systems and establishing his own.

"The Starlight Night," a well-known sonnet not too revolutionary, illustrates the nervous counterpointed rhythms, the startling pauses, the jarring sound clashes, the harmonic word fusion among many other interesting poetic, semantic, and linguistic devices:

> Look at the stars! look, look up at the skies!
> O look at all the fire-folk sitting in the air!
> The bright boroughs, the circle-citadels there!
> Down in dim woods the diamond delves! the elves'-eyes!
> The grey lawns cold where gold, where quickgold lies!
> Wind-beat whitebeam! airy abeles set on a flare!
> Flake-doves sent floating forth at a farmyard scare!—
> Ah well! it is all a purchase, all is a prize.

> Buy then! bid then!—What?—Prayer, patience, alms, vows.
> Look, look: a May-mess, like on orchard boughs!

Look! March-bloom, like on mealed-
with-yellow sallows!
These are indeed the barn; withindoors
house
The shocks. This piece-bright paling
shuts the spouse
Christ home, Christ and his mother
and all his hallows.

This sonnet also illustrates Hopkins'
childlike joy in fairy lore, his deep love
of nature, and a metaphysical rapture
over God's munificence, a simple joy born
of a deep religion. In the *Deutschland*
poem Hopkins is critical of man's questioning of God's ways, but his later poems
show this questioning in his own lack of
balance—a conflicting of personal desires,
private impulses, and his theology. This
unrest is perhaps best expressed in the
priest-poet's sonnet "Peace" (1879):

When will you ever, Peace, wild wood-
dove, shy wings shut,
Your round me roaming end, and under
be my boughs?
When, when, Peace, will you, Peace?
I'll not play hypocrite
To own my heart: I yield you do come
sometimes; but

That piecemeal peace is poor peace.
What pure peace allows
Alarms of wars, the daunting wars, the
death of it?

O surely, reaving Peace, my Lord should
leave in lieu
Some good! And so he does leave
Patience exquisite,
That plumes to Peace thereafter. And
when Peace here does house
He comes with work to do, he does not
come to coo,
He comes to brood and sit.

Here he seems to have found some measure of this peace through virtuous acts,
selfless serving of an often thankless mankind.

As most critics point out, Hopkins
combined in his interesting person a
depth of humanity with a height of mystical insight, with a whole spectrum of
emotions and attitudes infused. Most of
the contradictions in his nature, the ambiguities within his poetry, can be resolved by a thorough reading not only of
his poems, but of his letters, diaries, and
essays.

THE POETRY OF HORACE

Type of work: Poetry
Author: Horace (Quintus Horatius Flaccus, 65-8 B.C.)
Principal transcribed works: Satires, 35, 30 B.C.; Epodes, 30 B.C.; Odes, 23-13 B.C.; Carmen Seculare, 17 B.C.

Born two years before the Emperor Augustus, Horace, the son of a freed slave, was sent to Rome for the education he could not get in Venusia, Italy. In 44 B.C. he went to Athens for further study. There he met Brutus, after the assassination of Julius Caesar, and was appointed an officer in the republican army routed at Philippi in 42 B.C. Back in Rome, disillusioned, with his possessions confiscated and his father dead, he began verse writing. Vergil, attracted by his poetry, presented the country boy to Augustus' cultured minister, Maecenas.

Horace had the good taste to destroy his early angry poetry. His first published poems were his *Satires* in 35 B.C., followed by his *Epodes*. Then, still more mellow, he published three books of *Odes* in 23 B.C. During the last years of his life, Horace wrote his *Epistles*. In one ode, III, xvii, having heard of Maecenas' illness, he wrote: "If any untimely stroke snatches you away, you the half of my life . . . that day shall bring the end of us both." His wish was granted. He died in 8 B.C., only a few weeks after his protector, and their ashes were buried on the Esquiline hillside.

The early poetry of Horace betrays lack of self-confidence, as in his references to his "pedestrian Muse." But the publication of his *Odes* gave him assurance, and after the death of Vergil, in 19 B.C., he was commissioned by the emperor to compose and read an ode for the imperial secular games. Later Augustus demanded odes to celebrate the military victories of his stepsons, Drusus and Tiberius.

In his poetry, especially in his *Satires*, Horace re-creates his era with tolerance and good humor. He attacks the vanity of human desires, yet stresses the need to enjoy the pleasures of the world. While professing the epicurean philosophy, he generally practiced stoicism. Though praising the pleasures of wine, his health was too delicate to let him drink deeply. And his poems to women were just as conventional. For only one woman, Cinara, did he show real feeling. His affection was reserved for the men he knew; and his sincerity and ability to project himself beyond the lines of his poems have won him innumerable friends through the centuries.

The poetic satire was the invention of the Roman Lucilius, "untouched by the Greeks," as Horace declared, with its name derived from a dish composed of a variety of ingredients. Horace composed eighteen satires, in two volumes, but he made them more a friendly conversation than the bitter lampooning of his predecessor.

Book I, containing ten satires presented in no chronological order, was completed between his introduction to Maecenas in 38 B.C. and their appearance three years later. Number I, appropriately addressed to his patron, deals with Horace's favorite theme, the folly of the discontented man who wants something he does not have: "Oh, happy trader!" cries the soldier, while the trader, in his ship belabored by the south winds, envies the soldier. The poet follows this craving to its most unreasonable form, the hoarding of money, though he does not advocate being a spendthrift. His council is that a man should so live that he can leave his life, as he leaves a banquet table, contented.

In Satire IV, Horace explains why he uses this form: his father trained him for a good life by pointing out as bad examples those who lived it evilly. Besides, the form allows him "smilingly, to tell the truth." Satire V, describing a journey made with his protector, contains the poet's reply to those who charged he was cultivating Maecenas for personal profit, a subject taken up again in Satire IX. His first contacts with the wealthy statesman are described in the following poem, which take a side glance at the vice of aspiring to a higher position than one merits.

The eight satires of Book Two, which appeared five years later, are longer and generally in dialogue form. In one, the Lawyer Trebatius Testa clears the poet of the charge of being too bitter in his first volume. Paradoxes serve as themes for two others: All except the wise are mad, and all but the wise are slaves. Three express Horace's delight in plain living and his disgust at the vapid conversations overheard at formal banquets. He ends with an outburst against a woman he calls Canidia, who also figures in his later writings.

The earliest form of Horace's lyric poetry is his collection of epodes, as the grammarians called them. Horace named them "Iambi," a meter of alternating long and short lines designed by Archilochus for invectives. In these poems he expresses his pet dislikes, sometimes humorously, as in Number III, where he inveighs against the garlic in the food served at Maecenas' table. At other times he really hated the object of his verse, as in Number IV, written about a freedman who proudly strutted along the Via Sacra, or in the poem which expresses his hope that the ship will be wrecked when the poet Maevias goes on a sea voyage. In two epodes, V and XVII, he comes back to Canidia, first accusing her of being a witch who uses her spells on men, and then, when he apologizes, portraying her as threatening to use her vile charms against him.

Several others have the form, but not the substance, of an epode, as in Number I, written when Maecenas was departing for the battle of Actium and begging his patron not to endanger himself. Best known of all is probably the "Beatus ille," classified as an epode because of its surprise satirical ending:

How happy is his low degree,
How rich in humble poverty is he
Who leads a quiet country life
Discharged of busyness and void of strife.

After an enumeration of the joys of life in the country, the poem is revealed as the idle words of the usurer Alphius:

He called his money in,
But the prevailing love of pelf
Soon split him on the former shelf.
He put it out again.

To lovers of poetry, Horace probably makes his greatest appeal through his *Odes,* the artistic work of a mature writer. Composed after Actium, these poems were written between 23 and 13 B.C. The ideas are commonplace—the uncertainties of life, the joys of friendship—but they endure because they express sentiments that appeal to all readers. Number III, for instance, contains the much-quoted line, "Sweet and fitting it is to die for the fatherland." Poets good and bad ever since have enjoyed translating these poems into their own idiom.

In his *Odes,* Horace used a variety of meters to suit his subjects. The earliest are the gayest; the later odes, reflecting his own failing health and the deaths of friends, reveal an artist of subtle elegance and an effective arrangement of words. Even his pensive reflections conceal subtle humor.

The culminating form of Horace's genius was his *Epistles.* "You were the inspiration of my earliest Muse, Maecenas, and must be of my latest," he says, beginning this form. One, Number IX, is a fine example of a letter of introduction, presenting Septimus to the future Emperor Tiberius. The others, however, are letters only in form, being more in the nature of informal moral essays. "Modernism is wisdom" is the theme of the first; but instead of angrily attacking vice, the aging but kindlier poet gently rebukes folly. At the end he sets himself up as critic of the poets and poetic movements of his age. Surprisingly, Horace devotes little time to Lucretius and Catullus, the greatest of his predecessors. Carelessness marred the verses of both; perhaps the fault which he considered the gravest of all blinded him to their many virtues.

Having completed twenty-two epistles, Horace wrote: "You have played and eaten and drunk enough. It is time for you to depart the scene." He died, at the age of fifty-seven, one of the most genial and attractive of poets who have written undying verse.

THE POETRY OF HUGO

Author: Victor Hugo (1802-1885)
First published: Odes et poésies diverses, 1822; *Odes et ballades,* 1826; *Les Orientales,* 1829, (*Poems of the Orient*); *Les Feuilles d'automne,* 1831, (*The Leaves of Autumn*); *Les Chants du crépuscule,* 1835, (*Twilight Songs*); *Les Voix intérieures,* 1837, (*Interior Voices*); *Les Rayons et les ombres,* 1840, (*Rays and Shadows*); *Les Châtiments,* 1853, (*Punishments*); *Les Contemplations,* 1856-1857, (*Contemplations*); *La Légende des siècles,* 1859, 1877, 1883 (*The Legend of the Centuries*); *Les Chansons des rues et des bois,* 1865, (*The Songs of the Streets and the Woods*); *L'Année terrible,* 1872; *L'Art d'être grand-père,* 1877, (*The Art of Being a Grandfather*); *La Pape,* 1878; *La Pitié suprême,* 1879; *L'Ane,* 1880; *Les Quatre Vents de l'esprit,* 1881, (*The Four Winds of the Spirit*); *La Fin de Satan,* 1886; *Toute la lyre,* 1889-1893; *Dieu,* 1891

The name and the work of Victor Hugo fill the whole of the nineteenth century. Hugo the poet has been neglected, although few critics would deny that most modern French poetry has in one way or another been marked by him.

It matters little that one of Hugo's first major collections, *Les Orientales,* seems to have been inspired by his watching the sun set over Paris. Nineteenth century artists were often to turn to the Orient, observed or only imagined, for their inspiration. In France, certainly, where imaginations had been expanded by the Napoleonic adventure, it was hardly surprising that poets and painters should, around 1830, turn their gaze away from the internal political and social scene. Hugo, like others, seems to have sought in the East a sharpness, splendor, and color that he could not find in the French domestic scene. The technical innovations to be found in *Les Orientales* indicate that Hugo was fully conscious of the severe limitations on French as a language of poetry, compared to other European languages.

In the 1829 collection, many poems are fascinating experiments with rhyme and rhythm, in which Hugo's affection for color, contrast, and movement—later to become legendary—is already obvious. The best-known piece in this collection is undoubtedly "The Djinns." It owes its name to spirits of popular Mohammedan belief, said to be associated both with good and evil, though Hugo considers only their malevolent aspect. "The Djinns" is very obviously conceived as a whole from the first to the last line. It is a splendidly successful technical experiment. The opening stanza, of two-syllable lines, describes a scene of perfect calm before the approach of the Djinns. Stanza by stanza, the line expands, the pace becomes more rapid, until, to describe the arrival of the Djinns and their full, terrifying fury, Hugo makes use of a ten-syllable line. With the retreat of the spirits, the movement loses pace and volume; in the final strophe, the poet has returned to the two-syllable line; calm has once again fallen over the scene. The poem is fascinating, for it shows what effects could be obtained when a French poet, without losing precision, was prepared to discard outmoded conventions.

While Claude Roy's remark to the effect that Hugo's poetry was a form that eventually found a content seems a little unjust, there is certainly a progression in his work away from brilliance for brilliance' sake towards a realization and expression of deeper patterns of meaning in life. The signs of an evolution may be observed in *Les Feuilles d'automne.* The title is significant, as in the frontispiece of the original edition, showing two men, wrapped in cloaks, crossing a graveyard at sunset. The fundamental problems of life and death, the frailty of man, the unchanging face of nature, and the basic emotions that center around the family are the recurring themes in this volume. One of the finer poems of *Les Feuilles d'automne,* and there are many that are good, is called "When the Child Appears." Here, as is so often the case in other collections, Hugo selects a simple, almost banal, theme and makes out of it a finely executed, moving poem that is not overdone. Characteristically, the poet makes use of contrast throughout this piece, to enhance the impression he wishes to leave, and it closes with a philosophical meditation.

Some general differences are to be found between the collection titled *Les chants du crepuscule,* which appeared in 1835, and the two others that followed it, *Les Voix intérieures* and *Les Rayons et les ombres.* Yet they have much in common. In all three one notices the more frequent or urgent presence of social or political themes; Hugo's vision of the world now seems wider and deeper than before, and better able to distinguish the general pattern behind the particular example. Everywhere new facets of Hugo's creative genius are to be discovered; his seeking out of new sources for poetry is evident in his lively interest in Napoleon Bonaparte. In "To the Column," Hugo not only traces the history and legend of Napoleon in breath-taking fashion, but reveals a fine talent for taking an inanimate object—in this case the column in the Place Vendôme in Paris—and exploiting all its power as a symbol. His, too, is the gift of bringing to life an extremely precise vision, with great economy, by a judicious choice of a few telling details; and he displays this talent to perfection in "The Cow." He could make himself new in every circumstance, apparently; behind every image he detected an idea, behind every idea an image, and some of his genius may be explained by this ability. Increasingly, Hugo seems to have been attracted by the mysteries of life and death, an attraction especially obvious in *Les Rayons et les ombres.* In "Oceano Nox," which is in this collection, Hugo conveys with great power the idea of nature, in this case the sea, as a force that shows only its surface to man, reveals little while suggesting much:

Where are they, these sailors that foundered in the darkness of night?
O waves, how many dismal stories you surely know!
Deep waves, dreaded by mothers down on their knees!
You tell each other the stories while coming in on the rising tide,
And that is what gives you these desperate voices
That you have in the evening when you come towards us!

The unfortunate or tragic events in Hugo's private and public life in the 1840's divide his life and poetry into two parts. However regrettable these happenings may have been for Hugo the man, they did serve to restore to the public Victor Hugo the poet. After being exiled from Imperial France in 1851, and finally settling in the Channel Islands, Hugo at last seemed to find the time and energy to take up his pen once more.

In *Les Châtiments,* the first fruit of his exile, Hugo too often fails to hold in check his wrath or indignation at the injustice of Napoleon III. Yet elsewhere, recent misfortunes and grievances act as a catalyst to release a brilliant display of swift, even language or vivid imagery. It would be wrong to condemn Hugo outright for being too closely involved in the movements of upheaval of his century; he was involved, and if this is sometimes a reason why his poetry dates so rapidly, it is also, on occasion, one of the greatest strengths of his verse.

Poems in which the mood is essentially serene find a place alongside the other, angrier ones in Les Châtiments. "Stella," for example, recalls similar pieces by Lamartine and Musset. The poet seeks in the sky and sees in Venus, as it stands bright in the midst of darkness, announcing morning, a symbol of light and truth, a promise of a better fate for mankind. The poet of contrasts was to become increasingly, in exile, the visionary, the prophet.

Contemplations is one of the collections for which Victor Hugo's name is best remembered. In it, the poet is truly mature. Not only does he show himself to be in full possession of all the resources of the language, but much suffering seems to have given a new depth and intensity to his thought. The collection is divided into two parts: *Formerly* and *Today*, that is to say poems dating from before and after the death of his daughter Leopoldine. The predominant note that is struck is not one of protest, but rather of resignation. Hugo seems to say, in effect, that without understanding the mysterious workings of God, he accepts them. Nowhere is this more obvious than in "Villequier," an elegy, one of many fine poems dedicated to the memory of Leopoldine:

> I come to Thee, Lord! confessing that
>   Thou art
> Good, clement, indulgent, gentle; O
>   living God!
> I acknowledge that Thou alone under-
>   stand Thy workings,
> And that man is nought but a reed
>   that trembles with the wind. . . .

In an epic series as enormous as *La Legende des siècles*, with its ambitions as great as the title suggests and its intertwining of history, legend, and prophecy, it was perhaps inevitable that Hugo would at times test the patience and credulity of his readers. However, considered individually, the finer poems of this collection bear comparison with the best French poetry can offer. Many critics have admired "As Boaz Lay Sleeping." Every line of this beautiful poem seems to strive toward, and obtain, an effect of fusion and harmony which matches the subject perfectly. Hugo is impressively successful in investing with life a Biblical universe in which past, present, and future are fused, and the thoughts and feelings blend smoothly with the setting:

> Ruth was dreaming as Boaz slept; the
>   grass was black;
> The bells of the flocks stirred faintly;
> The great goodness of God came down
>   from the Heavens;
> It was the peaceful hour when lions
>   go to drink.

Les Chansons des rues et des bois, an uneven collection, seemed to announce an appreciable weakening of Hugo's poetic inspiration. In fact, in *L'Art d'être grand-père,* the poet showed himself capable of writing moving, lyrical verse, while in *Les Quatre Vents de l'esprit* he gave a conclusion to a body of thought that had not been completed in a *Legende des siècles*.

Victor Hugo has not by any means been fully understood. The vastness of the man and of his literary production has intimated too many people for too long. Out of the reappraisals that are now at last being made, two conclusions are likely to arise: on the one hand, the full extent of Victor Hugo's influence on the development of French poetry is probably much greater than has generally been supposed; on the other, it seems certain that one can no longer safely and glibly sum up the poetry of Victor Hugo in a few words. He did more than think he thought, and it seems certain that his thought cannot be reduced to any simple, single formula.

THE POETRY OF JARRELL

Author: Randall Jarrell (1914-1965)
First published: Blood for a Stranger, 1942; *Little Friend, Little Friend,* 1945; *Losses,*
1948; *The Seven-League Crutches,* 1951; *Selected Poems,* 1955; *The Woman at the
Washington Zoo,* 1960; *The Lost World,* 1965

By the time of his death, Randall Jarrell had become one of the recognized leading poets in America. His writing includes a satiric novel, *Pictures from an Institution,* two books of essays, literary and social-critical, two children's books, several translations from German works, and seven books of poetry which collect the work of more than twenty years.

Perhaps his most important book was his second, *Little Friend, Little Friend.* These poems, published in 1945, marked the true beginning of his successful career. The book is largely composed of war poems—the title is the repeated name of an airplane—and the best of Jarrell's work on this theme is here. The most famous, possibly because the shortest, of these is "The Death of the Ball Turret Gunner."

Some critics have viewed this as a poem dealing with the theme of the individual in the modern world. This interpretation seems removed from the content of the poem, but we can see the line of reasoning which may lead to it: the gunner hunched in the belly of the State, which is also associated with the womb of his mother (see Jarrell's note—"he looked like a foetus in the womb"); the transition is from the apparently prenatal life of dream to the waking "nightmare" of the fighters, a waking which is simultaneous with death. Presumably critics have felt that his epiphanic awakening to the fatal horror of the State symbolizes the general power of the mechanized State to crush out the life of an individual, to press him into dormancy. A less sympathetic critic has said of the poem that the last line, with its matter-of-fact expression of the grotesque, leaves much to be desired; that although horror may be unrelieved in poetry, a fuller vision of the implications of

death must be present: the poem stops too soon.

Both of these views hurt the poem. The former finds so much that the poem becomes a sterile, rather trite idea; the latter demands so much that he does not see what is there. For us, the poem is a good capsule summary of three of Jarrell's major themes: death, especially in war; the relationship of mother and child, and childhood in general; and social criticism of the kind that finds prose expression in his essays titled *A Sad Heart at the Supermarket.* Further, one finds in many of Jarrell's poems, as in this one, the exploration and use of dreaming.

"Losses" was published in the 1945 volume, and its title was used for the next book, *Losses,* of 1948. The men killed, as pictured in the poem, were not sufficiently alive, not old enough to have been quite alive; and only at the moment of vision which transcended cities could they die. It is the idea of Keats, that at the most intense moment of life there is death, and at death there is life.

In "The Dead Wingman" death and dream again merge, as a sleeping pilot dreams of searching for his wingman who was shot down. "Fires" is repeated in each of the stanzas, and it is implied that the sleeping pilot's own plane is in trouble; so when we are told only at the end that the pilot is sleeping, we assume his death. In fact, were it not for Jarrell's explanatory note, this would be the inevitable conclusion. This documentation raises a very real question in evaluating Jarrell's work, for although he insisted that his notes are unnecessary, still they are often quite necessary to the understanding of the poems. Often rather than notes the necessary information is given at the head of the poem: often, as in the last two books, there are no notes and the reader finds that the poems require close concentration. The poet must decide what his poems will be, how self-contained they are, but readers will decide the depth to which they are willing to go in apprehending the whole poem.

"Burning the Letters," which appeared in *Losses,* is one of Jarrell's finest. The wife of a pilot delivers a dramatic monologue to herself while burning his letters to her. A metaphorical equation is presented, that by a Man's (Christ's) death man lives, so by her husband's death she lives. She wants now to disentangle her life and the pilot's death, so she burns the letters and beseeches his grave, the "Great grave of all my years," to bury him. Her memory, not herself, will be his resting place. Specifically Christian associations are rare in Jarrell's poetry, possibly accounting for his apologetic headnote that the woman was formerly a Christian, a Protestant. At the opposite extreme from "Burning the Letters" there are poems which are almost entirely description with little "philosophy." "Pilots, Man Your Planes" from *Losses* is a good example, a simple narration of the ironic destruction of a plane by a fire from its own carrier. The lines are chilling and evocative, as those in which the poet describes the pilot entering his plane and taking off the deck of a carrier.

The transition from the world of death and dreams to the world of childhood is an easy one after the Romantic poets. In fact, "The Skaters," from Jarrell's first book, *Blood from a Stranger,* might remind one of Wordsworth's skaters in *The Prelude;* the sudden transformation of landscape at the end of "A Game at Salzburg" is likewise Wordsworthian. We should also look to Rilke for influence on the "childhood" poems—Jarrell translated several of them. The title of one book, *The Seven-League Crutches,* itself juxtaposes childish fancy and morbidity. "Come to the Stone . . ." from *Little Friend,* makes several connections with the poetry we have been discussing. A child sees some bombers, asks why people punish people, and answers easily that everything is childlike except his own death. The death of a child is his arrival into manhood. The theme of the poem is not the brutality of war, but the loss of innocence. This theme becomes increasingly important in Jarrell's poetry until, in his 1965 volume, the title suggests the new theme: *The Lost World.* The world lost is that of childhood.

The title poem is roughly pentametric, seldom decasyllabic, as are many of Jarrell's verses; but here we find a rhyme scheme, *terza rima,* very thoroughly hidden. This is an achievement in itself for nearly 250 verses. The poem is a narrative whose viewpoint shifts from childhood to adulthood with Proustian ease. In the opening of the third part the smell of Vicks Vaporub from a factory reminds the adult of the California eucalyptus tree he used to climb—Proust's *madeleine* —just as in the sequel, "Thinking of the Lost World," at the end of the volume the chain of memory is set off by a spoonful of chocolate tapioca. The lost world is associated with classical and Biblical myths, along with the myths of our age: Tarzan, Peter Pan, and science fiction. In the opening lines toy weapons made by the child and his father's coppersmith work remind us of Hephaestus; a play seen by the child becomes Shakespeare's "Green Wood," Crusoe's island, Eden, and at the end he returns to the world of servants and masters, where no one is generous or noble.

This real world is the subject of a third major theme of Jarrell's poetry, the criticism of a mechanized society which has lost the innocence and mythos of childhood. "The State," from *Little Friend, Little Friend,* portrays a child accepting fascist encroachment until they take his cat; then the child wants to die. "Sears Roebuck," from *Losses,* is a rare humorous poem: unlucky Honest John, who becomes associated with the John of Patmos, author of Revelation, has a vision of the apocalypse as he falls into a wilderness of women's undergarments in the catalogue. In *The Woman at the Washington Zoo*, the title poem whose creation was detailed in an essay Jarrell wrote for *Understanding Poetry*, is a sharp contrast between the bureaucratic world of Washington and the freedom of the ironically caged animals. The form, like that of "Burning the Letters," is a woman's soliloquy—a favorite form of Jarrell's exploited again in this book in "The End of the Rainbow," the confession of a woman who missed her chance in life, who lives in dreams.

Three of the best of the new poems appeared in his children's book *The Bat-Poet*: "The Mockingbird," "Bats," and "The Bird of Night." In these Jarrell avoided two of his major flaws: occasional flatness and a tendency toward philosophizing and intruding ideas prosaically. In this respect *The Lost World* is less frequently faulted than the others, more concerned as a whole with smaller "themes" and tighter form and more careful language, a promise of developing craftsmanship and deeper insights left unfulfilled by the poet's accidental and tragic death.

THE POETRY OF JEFFERS

Author: Robinson Jeffers (1887-1962)
Principal published works: Flagons and Apples (1912); Californians (1916); *Tamar and Other Poems* (1924); *Roan Stallion, Tamar and Other Poems* (1925); *The Woman at Point Sur* (1927); *Cawdor and Other Poems* (1928); *Dear Judas and Other Poems* (1929); *Descent to the Dead* (1931); *Thurso's Landing and Other Poems* (1932); *Give Your Heart to the Hawks* (1933); *Solstice and Other Poems* (1935); *Such Counsels You Gave to Me* (1937); *The Selected Poetry of Robinson Jeffers* (1938); *Be Angry at the Sun* (1941); *Medea* (1946); *The Double Axe and Other Poems* (1948); *Hungerfield and Other Poems* 1954; *The Beginning and the End,* 1963

The history of Robinson Jeffers' reputation might be represented diagrammatically by the figure of a sharp, inverted V, the apex marked, perhaps, by the year 1933. In 1919, when Jeffers had already published two volumes, Louis Untermeyer did not consider him worthy of inclusion in his famous anthology of American poetry that mirrored the taste of the period as definitely as had Palgrave's *Golden Treasury* in 1861. In 1933, William Rose Benét, in his anthology titled *Fifty Poets,* spoke of Jeffers as "the Western Titan of our contemporary poetry" and quoted George Sterling's statement that "Jeffers clasps hands with the Great Greeks across Time." In 1950, a critic considered *The Double Axe* beneath critical notice. Today, Jeffers is neither well remembered nor widely read. Has poetry taken a different direction, or was there some flaw in Jeffers' work, unnoticed thirty years ago, that has slowly caused the disintegration of a reputation once so massive?

Two facts of Jeffers' biography seem important to his poetry: first, his study of medicine and, second, his long residence on the coast of California. The first of these gave him the "scientific" point of view, of which much has been made in discussions of the intellectual content of his poems. The second, his home on Carmel Bay, Tor House, which he built in 1914 and occupied until his death, gave him the geographical, the scenic background of so many of his poems, the rocky coast that "clasped hands," to repeat Sterling's phrase, with the stony landscape of ancient Greece and its citadels built from the primeval stone. It might almost be maintained that for Jeffers there existed only these two worlds, the coasts of Greece and of California.

After two false starts, Jeffers made his reputation with *Tamar and Other Poems,* published in 1924, and then continued until 1954, ending with a total of fifteen volumes that spanned a period of forty-two years, surely an impressive achievement. It was, however, on the long narrative poems—long, that is, by modern standards—contained in these volumes that Jeffers' reputation was based: "Tamar," "Roan Stallion," "The Loving Shepherdess," "Give Your Heart to the Hawks," "Hungerfield," and others, at least one of them running to a hundred pages. These works were written in a period when it was said that a long poem was impossible. There is another group equally long: Jeffers' rehandling of the Greek myths, although these myths also often stand in the background of his narratives with modern settings. In "The Tower Beyond Tragedy" he rewrote the Orestes legend; "At the Fall of an Age" is a short drama, the climax of which is the death of Helen; "The Cretan Woman" is based on the *Hippolytus* of Euripides.

A reading of these long narratives, with their setting on the coast of California, or these reworkings of the Greek legends will reveal easily enough the weakness of Jeffers as a poet. His fault was not his utter pessimism, not his utter contempt for humanity. Rather, it was his extremely narrow range, his constant repetition. In this respect, the only modern poet with whom he can be compared is A. E. Housman, who shared Jeffers' tragic view of life, who repeated his theme of the transience of youth and beauty, the peace that comes with death, throughout his two volumes. But Housman had the great virtue of compression; his poems were pared down to three or four quatrains, whereas Jeffers stretched out the agony for page after page. It can even be said that to read one of his narrative poems is to read them all; they are alike in their preoccupation with drunkenness, lust, incest, and murder. It is not the violence that offends, for violence has become a commonplace in modern literature; it is the sameness, for violence can quite easily become as monotonous as virtuous placidity. We grow weary of drunken, lecherous husbands, of frustrated, rebellious wives, of incestuous relationships. The murders and the incendiarisms pall. The characters do not seem real, so complete is their degradation. We detect in them the same unreality, the same lack of social or moral sense, that T. S. Eliot found in the characters in Lawrence's fiction. It is not that they are immoral, for immoral characters are perfectly recognizable as human beings; it is that they seem to exist in a world completely devoid of all moral values. Each of these doomed families, although it may live in a perfectly real section of the coast of California and may even have contacts with other families, is shut into a kind of private madhouse where horror is the daily fare. Without indulgence in undue sentimentality, we may say that this state of affairs is not recognizably human.

Nor is it quite accurate to assume that because Jeffers depicted such unrelieved tragedy he was clasping hands with the great Greek writers. To be sure, the Greek myths often stand behind his narrative poems: the Pasiphaë story is discernible in "Roan Stallion"; in "Hungerfield," a woman with the implausible name of Alcmena Hungerfield has a son who wrestles—or thinks he does—with Death, just as the classical Alcmena's son, Herakles, contends with Death in the *Al-*

cestis of Euripides. But to use the great myths of classical antiquity does not make one a Greek. The tragic narratives of Jeffers are not such in the Aristotelian sense of a reversal of fortune; they do not depict the fall of a great man from the heights of prosperity and happiness to the depths of misery. The characters in these stories have never known happiness; they are drunken, lecherous, cruel, and degraded. Jeffers' real kinship is not with the Greeks but with the late Elizabethans; he "clasps hands" with such men as Webster and Tourneur and, beyond them in time, with Seneca. As the tragedy of blood developed on the post-Shakespearean stage, the dramatists piled murder upon murder, horror upon horror, until the spectator was driven either to disgust or to a refusal to take the drama seriously. The complicated story of "Tamar" is as unreal in its sensationally gruesome details as those of *The Atheist's Tragedy* or *The Revenger's Tragedy*, and it seems as remote from actuality, yet we are asked to accept this nightmare as a story taking place on the California coast today.

In one of his short poems Jeffers said that the sole purpose of poetry is to feel and completely understand natural beauty; and it is in his ability to put into words the wild, primitive loveliness of the area in which he had made his home that Jeffers was at his best as a poet. Despising humanity, he loved nature—the age-old rocks of the California coast, the gulls, and, above all, the hawks. The rock and the hawk were his main symbols: the rock which will remain long after mankind has vanished and the hawk which represents power and freedom. To Jeffers, nature was not the guide, philosopher, and kindly nurse that it was to Wordsworth; it was indifferent to man, who is, after all, only an incident in the vast history of the planet. In one of Jeffers' most quoted lines he said that mankind was the mold from which the world should break away. Again, in writing of the defacing of Carmel Point by a housing development, he added that given time nature knew that what man had created would dissolve. But the granite of the cliff at Carmel will remain. In "The Tower Beyond Tragedy," he gave voices to the stones of which the citadel is built; they speak to one another of men as loud, boisterous, and mobile, saying that before the world ends man will be gone. Man, as Jeffers saw him, is not merely an animal; he is below the animals, for he is a blight upon the earth. His empires rise and fall; America will fall like the rest, whereas the hawk will still wheel above the cliffs.

Jeffers' medical studies provided him with a certain amount of scientific vocabulary and, perhaps, with his coldly objective view of humanity. One gets the impression of a clinically detached attitude, the attitude of the doctor who has treated so many patients that he can no longer think of them as people. Surely many of the characters in the narrative poems are walking examples from a psychologist's casebook.

In American poetry of this century, Jeffers appears as strictly *sui generis;* he does not fit into any of the recognized schools or influences. Superficially, on the printed page, his long, flowing lines resemble those of Whitman, but the rhythm of his verse is very different from that of the older poet. Except for his general reaction against the conventionalities of the late Victorians, Jeffers was unlike anyone else writing during his period, and he has apparently exerted no influence on the succeeding generation, as have Pound and Eliot.

In *Hungerfield,* Jeffers wrote that poets who forget about the agony of life while singing its praises are fools and liars. The statement is certainly true; yet perhaps Jeffers, in an attempt to avoid all false sentiment, went to the other extreme. He was capable of writing beautiful lines, even beautiful short poems. The weakness was that he never varied, never developed; he merely repeated himself. In "To the Stone-Cutters," the poem which in 1933 he considered his best, he said that eventually man, the earth, and the sun would die, the sun blind of eye, black to the heart. This grim theme of vision and statement rings throughout all of his work.

THE POETRY OF JIMÉNEZ

Author: Juan Ramón Jiménez (1881-1958)
Principal published works: Almas de violeta, 1900 (*Violet Souls*); Rimas, 1902 (*Rhymes*); Arias tristes, 1903 (*Sad Airs*); Diario de un poeta recién casado, 1916 (*Diary of a Recently Married Poet*); Estío, 1917 (*Summer*); Sonetos espirituales, 1917 (*Spiritual Sonnets*); Eternidades, 1916-1917 (*Eternities*); Poesías escogidas, 1899-1917, 1917 (*Selected Poems*); Segunda autología poética 1917-1923, 1922 (*Second Anthology of Poetry*); Poesía en prosa y verso, 1923 (*Poetry in Prose and Verse*); Animal de Fondo, 1949 (*Brute*); Tercera antología poética, 1898-1953, 1957 (*Third Anthology of Poetry*)

One of a group of intellectuals classified as the "Generation of '98" and concerned about Spain's political and literary position following the Spanish-American War, was the Andalusian poet, Juan Ramón Jiménez, born in Moguer, near Cádiz, in 1881.

At his father's urging, he had gone to Seville to study law. While there he became interested in poetry and painting, possible reasons why he failed in his studies and returned to Moguer. There occurred an incident that explains much about his later life. One night his sister awakened him to report his father's death. Despite a long illness, the sudden passing was such an emotional shock that Jiménez was filled with presentiments of his own sudden death and continued to have periods of melancholy that several times sent him to a sanitorium.

He wrote much poetry. Submitted to publications in Seville and Madrid, they attracted such attention that poets in the capital, especially Francisco Villaespesa and Rubén Darío founder of a movement called Modernish, invited him to join them in Madrid.

Because Modernism in poetry meant pretty verses, a cult of form, and refined but artificial emotions, one can imagine the sort of verse Jiménez had been writing. His friends encouraged publication. Darío titled one volume *Almas de violetas* (*Violet Souls*) and Villaespesa suggested *Ninfeas* (*Waterlilies*) for the second. Both volumes appeared in 1900. Like Rubén Darío, however, Jiménez soon turned his back on many of the ideals of Modernism. Many years later when Gerardo Diego questioned Spain's outstanding poets about their inspirations, Jiménez listed as his models Luis de Góngora, Rubén Darío, Gustavo Adolfo Bécquer, and the *Romanceros,* sixteenth century collections of ballads.

Declaring that modern Spanish poetry began with Bécquer, Jiménez now looked for inspiration to the delicately wrought, simply expressed poetry of his acknowledged master. In fact, he called his third volume *Rimas,* the name Bécquer gave to his own poems. His poetic purpose, as Jiménez expressed it, was to give permanence to what he saw and felt was beautiful. To transmit that beauty became a sort of religion. He wrote that what he thought poetic was also deeply religious but not limited by the tenets of any creed.

With his next volume, *Arias tristes* (*Sad Airs*), published in 1903, Jiménez felt he had fully embarked on his career. In fact, later in life he rejected the lyric fire of his early period and directed that nothing published before 1903 be reprinted.

To him, life was a succession of imperishable moments. In 1912 came one of those moments, his meeting with Zenobia Camprubí Aymar, a Vassar graduate, vivacious, intelligent, but not sure that she wanted to marry a poet. When she went to New York to visit her brother, José Camprubí, the founder of *La Prensa,* Jiménez's thoughts followed her and before long he did the same. In *Diario de recien casado* (*Diary of a Recently Married Poet*), published in 1917, he distilled his experience and impressions of his marriage to the woman who was to contribute so much to his career as a poet. Better than most foreigners, he interpreted the United States in impressionistic word pictures of New York, Boston, and other places. Jiménez called it the first in a new period of his art.

It was followed the same year by other volumes, *Estío* (*Summer*) and *Sonetos espirituales*. Although Jiménez had been reading Irish poets and had translated Synge's *Riders to the Sea*, his experiments in free verse in *Summer* cannot be ascribed to them. The simplicity of the sonnets, full of his obsession with death, represented a departure from the sonorous and brilliant exteriorized sonnets loved by baroque and romantic poets. Jiménez had become an original poet, able to assimilate and transmute.

Eternidades, published in 1916-1917, shows what might be called the intellectual side of his poetry. It contained "Poetry," a much quoted poem in unrhymed lines of six, eight, and ten syllables. It says that poetry garbed in pure innocence first appeared to him, but then changed, and when he did not understand the change to richer dress he became angry. But when he saw her once more, disrobed, a vision of naked purity and as innocent as before, he realized that she was basically the same and forever his.

The purification of poetry, simplicity, the abandonment of any ornamental embellishments, and a freer poetic style which he called "naked poetry"—these became the characteristics of Juan Ramón, as his followers called him. He sought the essence, simplicity attained by the fewest separate elements, as achieved by the ballad writers who appeared in the Spanish *Romancero general* of 1600. But Jiménez added another quality, a delicacy not always found in primitive poetry. The poetry also embodied a sad tone, an authentic melancholy, and not the self-pity of the Romanticists.

Since so much of his poetry had appeared in slight volumes and small editions, in 1917 under the sponsorship of the Hispanic Society of America he completed the first of his collections, *Poesías escogidas, 1899-1917* (*Selected Poetry*). In 1922 appeared *Segunda autología poética 1917-1923*, and in 1957 *Tercera antología poética 1898-1953*. For readers wanting to sample all his styles found in thirty-nine separate volumes, this is the book to consult.

Every time Jiménez reprinted a poem, it had to be carefully scrutinized. Though to him poetry was an inspiration, a wellspring rising from deep within the poet, silently, covertly, yet the poem once visible, demanded a second inspection before republication. Sometimes he changed a word, or inverted the sentence order; sometimes he changed a title. "Mañana de la cruz" reappeared as "Mañana de la luz." The British critic J. B. Tread tried to explain Jiménez's penchant for revision by saying that the changes from the original text were not intended for smoothness of line or greater clarity of thought, but to relate them more closely to the vision of nature expressed in the whole unified body of his work.

Jiménez believed that the force of nature resides in everything, a mountain or a person that has the life proper for it. So he felt that a poem would live if it were filled with cosmic force.

In 1956 the Nobel Prize for Literature was awarded to this writer to whom poetry was an end, not a means. He believed in poetic expression for itself and not for its relation to the emotions it tries to express. He could dwell anywhere without having his surroundings interfere with his existence as a poet. Everywhere he could continue his search for absolute Beauty.

THE POETRY OF JOHNSON

Author: Samuel Johnson (1709-1784)
First published: London, 1738; *The Vanity of Human Wishes,* 1749

The poetry of Samuel Johnson is closely related in both content and tone to the rest of his work. His pervasive moral vision of the transitory nature of all human existence and the consequent folly of man's striving for worldly success provides the central themes for his two best known poems, *London* and *The Vanity of Human Wishes,* as well as for his oriental fable, *Rasselas,* his Shakespearian criticism, many of his periodical essays, and several of the *Lives of the Poets.* In his verse, as in his prose works, Johnson moves from the treatment of specific incidents to general application of their meaning. His primary interest was always in presenting universal truths, and he chose detailed episodes that he felt would illustrate them.

Like most of the other writers of his day Johnson received his early training in the composition of poetry in school, making verse translations of Latin works; several of these early efforts survive, either in manuscript or in Boswell's *Life of Samuel Johnson,* and they show young Johnson as a skilled handler of language, capable of creating dignified, striking lines in his adaptations of Vergil and Horace. His mastery of language was no doubt increased by his lifelong practice of writing original Latin poetry and translating English works into Latin, a language that notoriously demands great precision and exactness.

Johnson's English works include a number of occasional pieces, complimentary verses to ladies, prologues and epilogues to theatrical performances, and elegies for friends and acquaintances; but his reputation as a poet rests squarely on *London* and *The Vanity of Human Wishes,* the two long satires modeled on the works of the Roman moralist Juvenal.

The imitation of the classical satire was a popular eighteenth century verse form. The English poet's method was to choose a classical poem whose general premises seemed to him especially applicable to the conditions of his own day, then to replace specific incidents relating to Roman life with those more relevant to his time. The felicity with which an author could apply his source to present-day conditions and his skill in adapting single lines and phrases marked his success with the genre. The most outstanding imitations are generally considered to be Alexander Pope's Horatian epistles, but Johnson's works rank high.

London, published in 1738, the year in which Pope's brilliant *Epilogue to the Satires* also appeared, is based on the third satire of Juvenal, a condemnation of the evils of life in the city of Rome. Johnson uses Juvenal's general plan to point out the perils and corruption of London, attacking in particular the government of Robert Walpole, the general submission of virtue and honor to greed and flattery, and the degrading effects of poverty. The speaker throughout most of the poem is Thales, identified by some scholars as Richard Savage, a minor writer who is remembered chiefly as the subject of Johnson's first biography. Thales, accompanied to Greenwich by his friend, the author of the poem, is embarking for Wales; he can no longer bear to live amidst the corruptions of the city, and he attacks it as he explains his reasons for leaving. Johnson pictures himself as sympathetic with Thales' views: "I praise the hermit, but regret the friend."

Much of the power of the satire in the poem derives from Johnson's use of the heroic couplet for sharp, abrupt, ironic effects in such lines as these:

By numbers here from shame or censure
  free,
All crimes are safe, but hated poverty.
This, only this, the rigid law pursues,

This, only this, provokes the snarling muse.

Sometimes contrast in the relative seriousness of the two lines of the couplet provides the effect:

Their ambush here relentless ruffians lay,
And here the fell attorney prowls for prey;
Here falling houses thunder on your head,
And here a female atheist talks you dead.

While the greater part of the poem consists of direct attacks on contemporary vices, Johnson alludes to chapters in England's past to underline the faults of the present age. There is a brief tribute to Elizabeth I as the poet sets the scene in Greenwich, her birthplace, which calls to mind the "blissful age" when England triumphed over Spain, "Ere masquerades debauch'd, excise oppress'd,/Or English honour grew a standing jest." A reference to the spirit of Edward III, one of England's great military heroes, evokes scorn for "the warrior dwindled to a beau . . . of France the mimic, and of Spain the prey," and the mention of the victories of Henry V underlines the folly of imitating the vices of the French immigrants who have flocked to London.

While Johnson generally confines his attack on specific vices to a couplet or two, there are a few extended satirical portraits that provide an effective change of pace. In the latter part of the poem he describes the fortunes of the pompous and powerful Orgilio, a character taken directly from Juvenal. This unfortunate man's home is destroyed by lightning, but before many days pass flatterers and hangers-on have provided for his new estate treasures far surpassing those he lost. This description is followed immediately by an idyllic account of a country estate, available "for less than rent the dungeons of the Strand," where the landholder may enjoy nature, garden, and dwell in peace and security.

The satirical gifts shown by Johnson in *London* are developed to a far greater extent in *The Vanity of Human Wishes,* published eleven years later. In this work Johnson exercised more freedom in departing from his model, Juvenal's tenth satire, and consequently he created a more coherent work than the earlier poem. *The Vanity of Human Wishes* is not directed so completely at specific abuses as *London* was; the theme, expressed in the title, lent itself to a more general treatment. In the introductory passage Johnson points out the futility of all human undertakings in every corner of the globe, emphasizing his assertion with imagery of mist, clouds, and mazes. After commenting on the universal evils of wealth, "the gen'ral massacre of gold," the uselessness of the quest for military and political power, and the shaky foundations of fame and adulation from the multitude, he relates the histories of several famous men. Cardinal Wolsey's fate is seen as a kind of parable. At the peak of his career this man held "law in his voice, and fortune in his hand," but when the favor of his sovereign changed, "with age, with cares, with maladies oppress'd, he seeks the refuge of monastic rest."

Another specific illustration is the career of the scholar, one which Johnson knew well. If a "young enthusiast" can escape the perils of doubt, praise, difficulty, novelty, sloth, tempting beauty, disease, and melancholy, there await for him "toil, envy, want, the patron, and the jail." Archbishop Laud, executed by Cromwell's forces, reached the pinnacle of scholarly achievement, the archbishopric of Canterbury, then "fatal learning leads him to the block."

The last of Johnson's examples of the fleeting nature of all human achievements is the account of Charles XII of Sweden, who won great military victories until his encounter with a superior Russian army. He died an ignominious death in a later conflict, and Johnson makes this comment on the significance of his life:

He left the name, at which the world

grew pale,
To point a moral, or adorn a tale.

Shunning material advantages, other men desire long life, but there is no happiness in that course, either:

Time hovers o'er, impatient to destroy,
And shuts up all the passages of joy.

Even when a man has been blessed throughout the prime of his life, he must face the end. Again Johnson combines general judgments with specific examples for great effect:

In life's last scene what prodigies surprise,
Fears of the brave, and follies of the wise!
From Marlb'rough's eyes the streams of dotage flow,
And Swift expires a driv'ller and a show.

Even beauty can be a bane rather than a blessing: "Sedley [mistress of James II] curs'd the form that pleas'd a king."

Johnson concludes his poem by asking, then answering the question that inevitably arises from so pessimistic a view as his:

Must helpless man, in ignorance sedate,
Roll darkling down the torrent of his fate?

The only possible solution, in his view, is to trust in God:

Implore his aid, in his decisions rest,
Secure, what'er he gives, he gives the best.

The gifts that make life tolerable, those for which men must pray, are love, patience, and faith.

The variety of both tone and subject matter in Johnson's numerous shorter poems is vast. His "Prologue spoken by David Garrick at the Opening of the Theatre-Royal, Drury Lane" is a judicious, stately survey of the decline of the English stage from the time of "Immortal Shakespeare" to the mid-eighteenth century. A collection of brief verses shows a number of complimentary lyrics addressed, apparently extemporaneously, to various ladies on their playing a spinet, plucking a laurel, or celebrating a birthday. One of the wittiest of these pieces is a clever tribute to the poet's friend, "To Mrs. Thrale on her Completing her Thirty-fifth Year," a *tour de force* of brief lines and amusing rhymes:

Oft in Danger yet alive
We are come to Thirty-five;
Long may better Years arrive,
Better Years than Thirty-five;
Could Philosophers contrive
Life to stop at Thirty-five,
Time his Hours should never drive
O'er the Bounds of Thirty-five.

One of the most moving of Johnson's minor works is the poem "On the Death of Dr. Robert Levet," a mild, kindly, undistinguished man whom the poet had loved and respected. The simplicity of the stanza and the language mirrors the character of the man:

Yet still he fills affection's eye,
Obscurely wise, and coarsely kind;
Nor, letter'd arrogance, deny
Thy praise to merit unrefin'd.

Johnson's poetic gifts are not sparkling, immediately striking ones, but the dignity, the appropriateness, and the wisdom of his works are lastingly satisfying. Johnson had an almost infallible sense of decorum; his lines are not often beautiful or remarkably original, but they are almost never, if ever, unsuitable. He successfully avoids the lapses in taste that plagued many of his contemporaries and conveys those truths he discovered about life in language that rewards continued rereading.

THE POETRY OF JONSON

Author: Ben Jonson (1573?-1637)
First published: The Workes of Benjamin Jonson, 1616 (Containing *Epigrammes* and *The Forrest*); The Workes of Benjamin Jonson. *The Second Volume*, 1640 (Containing *The Under-wood* and *Horace, His Art of Poetrie*); Ben Jonson's *Execration against Vulcan. With divers Epigrams by the same Author to severall Noble Personages in this Kingdome*, 1640; Q. *Horatius Flaccus: His Art of Poetry. Englished by Ben Jonson. With other Workes of the Author never Printed before*, 1640

Ben Jonson was an overpowering individual. People who knew him were rarely neutral: they liked him, some almost to idolatry, or they disliked him with an intensity that vibrates through the centuries. His vigorous personality intrudes and makes dispassionate appraisal of his poetry difficult. A second factor which interferes with cool judgment of his work is the time-hallowed tradition of contrasting portraits of Shakespeare and Jonson. In these conventional portraits, Shakespeare stands for genius, humanity, and native woodnotes; Jonson for labor, bookish pedantry, and classical imitation. It is ironic that one of Jonson's two most popular poems is the noble tribute to his supposed bitter rival.

Unlike Shakespeare—who may or may not have unlocked his heart with his sonnets, but certainly left posterity little personal allusion in his other writings—Jonson wrote to and about many people who had a share in his life. He had been classified as primarily an occasional poet, except in his dramatic works. Perhaps his earliest extant poem is a brief lament on the death of his six-month-old daughter Mary:

Whose soule heavens Queene, (whose
name shee beares)
In comfort of her mothers teares,
Hath plac'd amongst her virgin-
traine. . . .

The distinguished scholar C. H. Herford pointed out the poem's indebtedness to Martial, who wrote an epigram on the death of a small slave girl, Erotion; however, it is more deeply indebted to medieval Christian tradition than to the classics.

Jonson left two other moving poems on the deaths of children: "On my first Sonne," which contains the couplet:

Rest in soft peace, and, ask'd, say here
doth lye
Ben. Jonson his best piece of poetrie . . .

and the "Epitaph on S. P.," which tells of the death of a boy actor who acted old men so well that he deceived the Fates. Though prematurely and mistakenly carried away from earth, Heaven has vowed to keep him. The personal note is also sounded in the epigram "To William Camden," the poet's former schoolmaster:

Camden, most reverend head, to whom
I owe
All that I am in arts, all that I know,
(How nothing's that?) to whom my
countrey owes
The great renowne, and name where-
with shee goes,
Then thee the age sees not that thing
more grave,
More high, more holy, that shee more
would crave. . . .

This high praise is less extravagant than the uninitiated might think, for Camden, formerly a promising fellow student of Sir Philip Sidney, was a poet, an antiquarian praised by Edmund Spenser, and a leading historian and geographer of his country. His works are still mined by scholars. Several of his pupils became important and influential men. He fired Jonson with enthusiasm for scholarship and poetry.

One of Jonson's fairly early poems was an "Ode *Allegorike*" prefixed to Hugh Holland's *Pancharis*. This poem pays a tribute to a former fellow student under

Camden. It portrays Holland as a black swan and foreshadows the more famous poem on the Swan of Avon. It also points the way to passages in Milton's "Lycidas" and John Dryden's odes. Jonson's fondness for the ode as a literary type began early in his career and continued into his old age; one of his most ambitious poetic efforts is a Pindaric ode in memory of Sir Henry Morrison, friend of Lord Falkland, noblest of the Sons of Ben. Sir Henry was killed in 1629, eight years before Jonson's death. This impressive ode is best remembered for a single strophe, often quoted out of context as a separate lyric:

It is not growing like a tree
In bulke, doth make man better bee;
Or standing long an Oake, three hundred yeare,
To fall a logge, at last, dry, bald, and seare:
A Lillie of a Day,
Is fairer farre, in May,
Although it fall, and die that night;
It was the Plant, and flowre of light.
In small proportions, we just beauties see:
And in short measures, life may perfect bee.

The Forrest in the 1616 Folio of Jonson's works contains fifteen poems, three of which are connected with the Sidney family. Like his master Camden, Jonson obviously had great admiration for Sir Philip Sidney as author and man. One of the poems is a somewhat playful birthday ode written to Sir William Sidney, the youthful nephew of Sir Philip and son of Sir Robert, who became Earl of Leicester. Another is an "Epistle to Elizabeth Countesse of Rutland," the daughter of Sir Philip; and the third is "To Penshurst," a favorite of many Jonsonians. This last piece, more than a hundred lines long, begins with praise of the austere architecture of the building to which the poem is addressed, proceeds to admiration of its natural setting and its resources for hunters and fishermen, pays graceful compliments to members of the family who have dwelt therein (including Sir Philip himself), and honors the present family for its hospitality and graciousness and for the deserved love of the neighbors and retainers. Particularly, in the final portion, the satirist shows his face and makes clear that not all the nobility share the qualities of Sir Robert Sidney and his wife. This poem is representative of many tributes to noble and prominent individuals, though the literary device of addressing the building instead of the persons is unusual. Especially notable among the numerous commendatory pieces are those written to noble ladies, since Jonson is often portrayed as a misogynist.

The poet also wrote tributes to many who made their marks in the arts rather than in politics or worldly affairs. The most famous of these poems is the majestic "To the Memory of my Beloved, the Author, Mr. William Shakespeare," included in the Shakespeare First Folio. The late Hazelton Spencer praised this as the finest occasional poem in the English language. Although this praise may be somewhat extravagant, the poem, like "To Penshurst," is a noble composition with several themes harmoniously unified. It contains epithets which have become part of the English inheritance: "Marlowes mighty line . . . Thundering Æschilus . . . the merry Greeke, tart Aristophanes . . . neat Terence, witty Plautus . . . sweet Swan of Avon . . . Soule of the Age"; and it contains prophetic utterances not bettered by the idolaters of Shakespeare:

Thou art a Moniment without a tombe,
And art alive still, while thy Booke doth live,
And we have wits to read, and praise to give . . .
Triumph, my Britaine, thou hast one to showe,
To whom all Scenes of Europe homage owe.
He was not of an age, but for all time!

In spite of Jonson's numerous poems of

praise, many critics think of him primarily as a savage satirist and consider his satires as personal as his other poems. He did indeed have an acid gift of irony or downright invective. It is worth noting, however, that his poems attacking individuals by name are excluded from the collections of verse he himself published. In these, like Swift, he chose to lash the vice but spare the name. Undoubtedly his most masterful handling of satire is in his plays rather than in his poems; but there is strong mutual influence between his "comicall satyre" and his satirical poems. No doubt he heightened his satirical characterizations with traits borrowed from individuals; but the nineteenth century tendency to identify every satirical portrait with a living individual was unsound, and happily seems to have subsided. Sometimes in the poems, though not in the First Folio, the object of the attack is named: Alexander Gill, son of John Milton's schoolmaster, and Inigo Jones, the King's architect and Jonson's collaborator on the masques, are lashed by name. True, in both cases the provocation was great.

In "An Execration upon Vulcan" the poet attacks the fire god with mock fury. He lists works destroyed by a fire (probably in 1623), including some of his own compositions and manuscripts borrowed from antiquarian friends. He takes advantage of the incident to list also works which thoroughly deserved the fire: flamboyant romances, popular journals, alchemic and mystical writings, and extravagantly artificial verses. The poet's good-humored fortitude under adversity serves as a warning to take his strictures with a grain of salt: he probably read with pleasure many of the works he suggested were fit food for Vulcan, including those in "the learned Librarie of Don Quixote."

Jonson wrote a number of translations and adaptations of classical writers; but he had a way of making such works his own. The most famous so-called translation by Jonson is the love lyric "To Celia" ("Drink to me only with thine eyes"). This song, with its combined appeal of music and words (the origin of the music is disputable), has retained its popularity for centuries. It is not really a translation, but a pulling together of scattered prose sentences from the *Epistles* of the Greek rhetorician Philostratus (c. 170-245); these passages are combined and transformed into a unified poem, a new and original piece.

This lyric is but one of many written by Jonson to be sung, not merely read. Music for many of them still survives. The poet's collaboration with musicians of his day and his familiarity with musical techniques shaped many of the lyrics. Eccho's song in *Cynthia's Revels* begins:

> Slow, slow, fresh fount, keepe time
>   with my salt teares;
>   Yet slower, yet, O faintly gentle
>   springs:
> List to the heavy part the musique
> beares. . . .

The same play contains another of Jonson's popular lyrics, "The Hymn to Diana (Cynthia)":

> Queene, and Huntresse, chaste, and
>   faire,
> Now the Sunne is laid to sleepe,
> Seated in thy silver chaire,
> State in wonted manner keepe:
>   Hesperus intreats thy light,
>   Goddesse, excellently bright.
>
> Earth, let not thy envious shade
> Dare it selfe to interpose;
> Cynthias shining orbe was made
> Heaven to cleere, when day did close:
>   Blesse us then with wished sight,
>   Goddesse, excellently bright.
>
> Lay thy bow of pearle apart,
> And thy cristall-shining quiver;
> Give unto the flying hart
> Space to breathe, how short soever:
>   Thou that mak'st a day of night,
>   Goddesse, excellently bright.

Another of the songs which still has life on the concert stage is "Have you seen but a bright lily grow?"

In the masques there are a number of songs with the flavor of nursery rhymes or folk poetry. Three of these are:

CATCH
(from *Oberon*)

Buz, quoth the blue Flie,
Hum, quoth the Bee:
Buz, and hum, they crie,
And so doe wee.

In his eare, in his nose,
Thus, doe you see?
He eat the dormouse,
Else it was hee.

CHARM
(From *The Masque of Queens*)

The owle is abroad, the bat, and the toad,
And so is the cat-a-mountayne,
The ant, and the mole sit both in a hole,
And frog peepes out o' the fountayne;
The dogs, they doe bay, and the timbrels play,
The spindle is now a turning;
The moone it is red, and the starres are fled,
But all the skie is a burning: . . .

SONG
(From *The Gypsies Matamorphosed*)

The faery beame upon you,
The starres to glister on you;
A Moone of light,
In the noone of night,
Till the Fire-drake hath o're gon you.
The wheele of fortune guide you,
The Boy with the bow beside you
Runne aye in the way,
Till the bird of day,
And the luckier lot betide you.

In his lament for his daughter, Jonson demonstrated at an early date his interest in religious themes. This interest lasted throughout his career, for his longest, perhaps his last, original non-dramatic poem, "Elegie on my Muse," (the ninth poem in *Eupheme,* a memorial to Lady Venetia Digby) is steeped in the traditions of medieval Christianity. In "An Execration upon Vulcan" Jonson lists among the works lost in his fire:

. . . twice-twelve-yeares stor'd up humanitie,
With humble Gleanings in Divinitie;
After the Fathers, and those wiser Guides
Whom Faction had not drawne to studie sides.

The fruits of this twenty-four-year period of religious study are scattered through the poet's works. In "The Forrest," published in the 1616 Folio edited by Jonson himself, appears a poem in the penitential tradition with a highly personal tone: "To Heaven." The collection of poems called "The Under-wood" in the 1640 Folio (published three years after Jonson's death) opens with three "Poems of Devotion": "The Sinners Sacrifice," "A Hymne to God the Father," and "A Hymne on the Nativitie of my Saviour." All three of these pieces are in subject matter and form much like the penitential poems of the fourteenth and fifteenth centuries. A brief quotation from each will show its quality:

All-gracious God, the Sinners sacrifice,
A broken heart thou wert not wont despise,
But 'bove the fat of rammes, or bulls, to prize
    An offering meet,
For thy acceptance. O, behold me right,
And take compassion on my grievous plight.
What odour can be, then a heart contrite,
    To thee more sweet?
  . . . . . .
  Heare mee, O God!
  A broken heart
  Is my best part:
  Use still thy rod,
    That I may prove
    Therein, thy Love.
  . . . . . .

I sing the birth, was borne to night,
The Author both of Life, and light;
  The Angels so did sound it,
And like the ravish'd Sheep'erds said,
Who saw the light, and were afraid,
  Yet search'd, and true they found it.

In summary, much of Jonson's non-dramatic poetry is personal; much of it is grounded in his learning, particularly his classical learning; but much of it escapes the limitations laid down by critics of the past. Although it leaves an impression of considerable variety, it is, on the whole, poetry of statement rather than poetry of suggestion. When it is difficult to understand, the difficulty usually lies in linguistic changes wrought by three centuries or in stylistic compression, rather than in far-fetched imagery or vague mysticism. Though it is intellectual poetry, it is far from empty of feeling. Its influence on later poetry, particularly that of the Cavaliers and Dryden and Pope, was potent.

THE POETRY OF KIPLING

Author: Rudyard Kipling (1865-1936)
First published: Departmental Ditties, 1886; *Barrack-Room Ballads and Other Verses,* 1890; *The Seven Seas,* 1896; *Recessional and Other Poems,* 1899; *The Five Nations,* 1913; *Puck of Pook's Hill,* 1906; *Rewards and Fairies,* 1910; *The Years Between,* 1919; *Sixty Poems,* 1939; *Rudyard Kipling's Verse* (definitive edition), 1940

Kipling began writing poetry in 1876 at the age of eleven; sixty years later he was forgotten, mistrusted, or despised for his popularity that had begun with *Departmental Ditties* fifty years earlier. Kipling's early success led to the Nobel Prize and his rejection of the Order of Merit, to be followed by later obloquy; today he is honestly respected for his short stories but still reluctantly for his verse, in spite of the selection of his poetry edited by T. S. Eliot in 1941. Yet Kipling is remembered most for his poems—"Recessional," "Gunga Din," "Mandalay," "The Land," "Danny Deever," "The 'Mary Gloster'"— and for such quotable lines as these from "The Ladies":

> . . . The Colonel's Lady and Judy O'Grady
>   Are sisters under their skins!

The inescapable fact remains that if poetry is memorable speech, Kipling had the gift, used it, and was loved for it. He was the latest and the most prolific of the *popular* poets and perhaps the last in this century. His popularity came from his felicitous handling of the lolloping and hence memorable meters of anapest and dactyl, his wide range of novel, picturesque material, and his clear distinction in each poem between right and wrong. The lack of depth in his perceptions is balanced by the strength of his convictions and emotions. His material gave a voice or at least an echo to the people from whom it was drawn, and his easy superficiality of form and content made those people, generally at an elementary or largely oral level of literacy, read him eagerly and quote him frequently. His well-known "If" is an example of his popular, didactic appeal. This is not the whole of Kipling, but it is essential in the ballad-laureate of Empire.

The sources of Kipling's style are the ballad, the music-hall song, and the Psalms. The last gives him the long, prophetic line in which he sent home the dispatches in verse from the outskirts of the British Empire. Much more of his verse is accompanied by the choruses which perform the same iterative function. The ballads, of which "Sestina of the Tramp-Royal," is typical, are among his simplest and best though not most memorable verse, such as the quietly noble ballad stanzas of "The Veterans," written for "the gathering of survivors of the Indian Mutiny" in 1907, or the gentle raillery of "The Three-Decker." Many poems depend on prologues and epilogues set in italics which bring the poem round to a repetition of the opening lines, again for emphasis. The most characteristic feature of his verse is its introduction not so much of clichés like "the White Man's Burden" in a poem of that title (addressed with considerable foresight to America) but of foreign terms. There are too many of these in the Indian poems, in which the Anglo-Indian is showing off to his British cousins: "all along of abbynay, kul, an' hazar-ho"; but a large number of poems stemming from the South African war and the larger number celebrating British regiments use native and military terms easily, such as *kopje* and *voorlooper* in "Two Kopjes." The worst feature of the verse is the hackneyed Cockney that his private soldiers speak; this dialect sounds better in prose.

A curious feature of Kipling's work is that he published in a unique form, most of his volumes combining stories and poems, sometimes with the same titles, such as "The Benefactors." Both are so related in *Puck of Pook's Hill,* which contains ten stories and sixteen poems that it is a moot point whether his poems can be considered apart from the stories they illustrate (the subtitles often refer to these) or the events they celebrate, as in "The Rowers: 1902: When Germany Proposed that England should help her in a Naval Demonstration to collect debts from Venezuela." At least once his topicality misfired. "The Ballad of the 'Clampherdown' " records the boarding of a cruiser in battle; it was intended to mock the notion of boarding but was taken as Kiplingesque exaltation of the good old days.

Kipling's range of material was in facts, not ideas. The occupations of the folk heroes of his ballads, from the water-carrier in "Gunga Din" to the ship's engineer in "McAndrew's Hymn" to the Viceroy of India in "One Viceroy Resigns: Lord Dufferin to Lord Landsdowne," are exalted as the cogs of Empire, without his realizing, as George Orwell later pointed out, that an empire exists to preserve and extend an imbalance of trade.

Kipling's first success came when he told inside stories about the Indian Civil Service, for which his father worked, and in the next volume about the Indian Army: the materials were new in literature, the attitudes perhaps necessarily romantic as in the similar pioneer work of Bret Harte. Kipling mocks those who get promotion to the top of the ladder in the first volume and exults in the code and lore of subalterns and privates at the bottom of the scale in the second. When he turns later to English affairs, his preference is not for the artisan but for the traditional yeoman, for the Hobdens of "The Land"; he alternately scolds and praises the leaders and people of England as they falter in or carry out their manifest destiny of guiding mankind, his deepest contempt being reserved for the mob and the inept leaders, as in "The Islanders," whom he blamed when the balance of trade evened and began to shift the other way after World War I. Kip-

ling was born and bred on the British frontier where the issues were simplified, and his poems show his continual interest not only in India but also in South Africa, Canada, Australia, and New Zealand, as in "The Parting of the Columns" and "The Song of the Cities," stanzas on sixteen capitals of the Empire in four continents; he responded to the stimulus at the margin of Empire but found the heart of it, London, too sophisticated for his abilities and too preoccupied to heed his strident warnings.

He works mainly in the buffer area between the real center of imperial power and its subjects, often relating Eastern tales but mainly concerned with "the far-flung battle-line" between the civilized and the savage (English and fuzzy-wuzzy) and the "dominion over palm and pine" of "Recessional." But the buffer area is the meeting place of semi-civilized and semi-savage which accounts for the brutality of one and the nobility of the other. Orwell's termed this "colonial literature." His phrase is accurate if one remembers that the Roman "colonus" was a military settler on the Roman imperial frontier. Here the distinctions between right and wrong are expressed in physical, not ethical force, though a simple insular ethic lies behind them.

Kipling was always conscious of the greater mass of Empire behind him whether he was confronting the Indian or the English native, and the greater is always to be imposed on the lesser; he sings the greatness of Empire in many poems. This is frontier-bred psychology always at odds with its environment whether it be the native civilization surrounding the proconsul or the settled life at "Home." Consequently Kipling's most dated poems show not his glorification of Empire but his continual hectoring of those who do not respond to his own vision of the "far-flung, fenceless prairie" as in "The Native-Born," or the "Never-never country . . . behind the ranges," which in "The Explorer" becomes "God's present to our nation." He is at his best when the glorification is not an oratorio on a set occasion but a lyric like "Mandalay," or when he uses the first person plural as in "The Lesson"—"We have had an Imperial lesson. It may make us an Empire yet."—and not the second person pronoun, as in "The Islanders"—"then was your shame revealed, At the hands of a little people, few but apt in the field."

Kipling's metier was light journalistic verse; it became awkwardly and strenuously didactic when he used it as a vehicle for the urgent lessons he was trying to teach the English before it was too late, and his chief enemy was apathy and ignorance about the enormous area and populations under the control of a ruling race on a small and distant island. If the authority of the knowledge he claimed turned to bullying, the sense of inescapable service was often elevated to sacrifice; he rejoices when a British Army Sergeant, "Whatsisname," reforms the Egyptian Army ("Pharoah and the Sergeant"), or when, as in "Two Kopjes," the British Army at last learns how to fight the Boer. Kipling weeps for the young men sent abroad untrained and forgotten, as in his commemoration of the veterans of the charge of the Light Brigade in "The Last of the Light Brigade." His greatest success was "The Absent-Minded Beggar," set to music and making over a quarter million pounds for the relief of the dependents of the British Tommy.

Amid the sprawl of his topics over time and space and the hustle of his many meters in hundreds of poems, it is difficult to find any guiding philosophy except a belief in the job well done. He had the pride of his own craft, and several of his best poems illuminate that craft: "The Story of Ung," the dissatisfied Neolithic cave painter; "The Conundrum of the Workshops," in which the Devil insists, "Is it Art?"; the famous "nine and sixty ways of constructing tribal lays" in "In the Neolithic Age." Apart from an occasional lyrical response to nature, as in "The Way Through the Woods" and a frequent response to English history, his poetry is of the world of military and political affairs and sometimes that of other men who know their job: Noah in "A Truthful Song," the smugglers in "A Smuggler's Song," a colonial farmer in "The Settler," the Boer farmer-fighter in "Piet," the Sudanese in "Fuzzy-Wuzzy," the self-made shipping magnate of his dramatic monologue, "The 'Mary Gloster.'" The smaller the object, the sharper is his observation ("The Sergeant's Wedding"); conversely, as the object of his poetic interest enlarged Kipling hated it, as he hates "The People" in "MacDonough's Song." His complementary belief in the competence of the lesser object against the greater mass is rarely defined, but it lies in the body of his own verse, the "tribal lays" in which, as in life, "The Gods of the Copybook Headings" provide all the answers before a man begins his task. From that given base all Kipling had to do was to attack inefficiency and novelty and to glorify the difficult work of the laboring few, Kipling among them, against the many. For his mass he used the British Empire at its apogee; his individual hero is "Thomas Atkins," the British Regular soldier to whom he formally dedicated *Barrack-Room Ballads* and, in spirit, all his work.

THE POETRY OF LAFORGUE

Author: Jules Laforgue (1860-1887)
Principal published works: Les Complaintes, 1885; *L'Imitation de Notre-Dame la Lune,*
1886; *Derniers Vers,* 1890; *Le Sanglot de la Terre,* 1903

Although Jules Laforgue's span of creative activity was tragically brief (about nine years), his poetry attests a prolific and versatile innovator whose artistic evolution carried him from the traditional Alexandrines and somewhat oratorical poems of the posthumous *Le Sanglot de la Terre,* written between 1878 and 1882, to experimentation with the rhythm and mood of *chansons populaires* in *Les Complaintes,* and culmination in *Derniers Vers* with the frequent use of free verse and with what Laforgue described as psychology in dream form presented in melodic and rhythmic patterns of verse.

"Funeral March for the Death of the Earth," the most celebrated of the poems found in *Le Sanglot de la Terre,* reveals a young poet who is not adverse to indulging in an uninhibited display of his personal views and to capitulating to a rather bleak pessimism concerning the state of the universe; the poet's cries of despair as he depicts bombastically the horrors of civilization and the corpse of the Earth are rarely muted, as they will be in succeeding works. Certain lines ("The nocturnal silence of echoless calm,/Floats, an immense and solitary wreck") are reminiscent of Baudelaire, the precursor of Symbolist poetry whose spell and sphere of influence were ubiquitous in the late nineteenth century.

One of the most distinctive qualities of Laforgue's own personal manner appears with effectiveness in *Les Complaintes:* the poet cultivates a witty and mocking detachment as an antidote to the blunt expression of personal feelings. The theme of death recurs often in Laforgue, but it is not personified as a sinister figure in "Complaint about Forgetting the Dead"; Laforguian irony changes death into the "good gravedigger" who scratches at the door, and if you refuse to welcome him,

If you can't be polite,
He'll come (but not in spite)
And drag you by your feet
Into some moonlit night!

The "complaints," named for a folk-song style which the poet imitates, also reveal a flair for inventing humorous anecdotes and dialogues couched in colloquial language; a case in point is the "Complaint of the Outraged Husband," an amusing conversation in verse form which takes place between an irate husband, who insists he saw his wife flirting with an officer in church, and his wife, who maintains with injured innocence that she was piously conversing with a "life-size Christ."

A predilection for creation of a cast of characters and for dramatization of experience remains a permanent characteristic of Laforgue's style; it reappears most notably in 1886 in the form of a verse drama called *The Faerie Council.* This work, which again demonstrates the poet's preference for depersonalized expression of his sentiments, places on stage the Gentleman, who bemoans the indifference of the cosmos and the tedium of existence, and the Lady, who offers her charms as a cure for his ennui. The subject is typically Laforguian; love is painted as lacking in glamor, as being somewhat sordid, but it is still an acceptable escape from the disenchanting realities of the world. The structure of this verse drama, as in many of Laforgue's poems, presents an ironical commentary on experience, since a certain frame of mind is developed in the course of the drama and then negated at the end; the Earth is round "like a pot of stew" and we are mired in its banalities; but, since this is all men can possess, acceptance of our lot is preferable to some sort of impassioned and futile revolt ("Why don't you see that that is truly our Earth!/And all there is! and the rest is nothing but tax/About which you might just as well relax!") Gaiety and disdain are the prevailing moods of Laforgue in preference to bitterness and melancholy.

Perhaps the most startling and engaging product of Laforgue's imagination is to be found in the collection entitled *L'Imitation de Notre-Dame la Lune.* This work contains a gallery of "choirboys of the Moon," all of whom are named Pierrot. These bizarre individuals prefer lunar landscapes because the moon seems to symbolize aspiration to some obsolute, whether it be savoring the love of an ideal and idealized female, or giving in to the temptation of suicide and blissful nothingness. However, the thirst for self-extinction inevitably ends with an antithetical declaration of a prosaic determination to enjoy the present moment:

—Of course! the Absolute's rights are nil
As long as the Truth consists of living.

Clowns are a favorite source of inspiration for modern painters and poets; few are more individualized and appealing than the Pierrots of Laforgue. They are uniformly white except for a black skullcap and a scarlet mouth:

It's, on a stiff neck emerging thus
From similarly starchèd lace,
A callow under cold-cream face
Like hydrocephalic asparagus.

The eyes are downed in opium
Of universal clemency,
The mouth of a clown bewitches
Like a peculiar geranium.

Parenthetically, it is worth noting that Ezra Pound was struck by the phrase "like hydrocephalic asparagus" and, in general, by Laforgue's frequent reliance upon a scientific lexicon to revivify patterns of poetic expression. In this domain also, the French poet stands out as an important innovator.

The Pierrots, who "feed on the absolute, and sometimes on vegetables, too," are distinguished not only by their acute awareness of death and by their refusal to seek solace and protection from their fate, but also by the inexplicable spell they cast over the opposite sex. They rhapsodize extravagantly when they talk of love, but they speak "with toneless voices." As amusing embodiments of contradictory elements, they offer another example of Laforguian irony. In addition, the portraits of these "dandies of the Moon" permit Laforgue to assume an imaginary identity and expound behind a mask a blasé and mocking view of love, life, and death.

Laforgue was one of the first poets in the nineteenth century to exploit successfully the possibilities of the free verse form. "Solo by Moonlight" in *Derniers Vers* is an excellent illustration of his talent for molding the length of the verse line to conform to the flow of thought and the association of images: stretched out on top of a stagecoach moving rapidly through a moonlit countryside, the poet's composure, as well as his body, is jolted, for he remembers a promising love that ended in misunderstanding; the rhythm and mood are partially created by the lines of radically different length. At the same time, the poem is infused with a dream-like atmosphere; impressions are nebulous and the woman is only briefly glimpsed and partially understood as the poet attempts to recall the past. The theme of frustrated love is left purposely ambiguous and contributes to the evocation of psychology in dream form; a kind of paralysis engendered by boredom and a vague malaise prevented the poet from declaring himself; a simple gesture would have elicited a warm response in the woman but,

Ennui was keeping me exiled,
Ennui which came from everything. So.

Familiar themes recur in *Derniers Vers;* "The Coming Winter" is a poem on autumn which suggests encroaching deterioration and imminent death. However, startling verbal juxtapositions help avert dangers of overstatement and sentimentalism ("Rust gnaws the kilometric spleens/Of telegraph wires on highways no one passes") and Laforgue's sense of humor remains very much in evidence ("Oh! the turns in the highways,/And without the wandering Little Red Riding Hood . . .").

In the foreword to Patricia Terry's translations of a selected number of Laforgue's poems Henri Peyre notes the debt which numerous French writers of imposing stature owe to Laforgue's original handling of irony, of versification, of imagery, and of colloquial language. At the same time, along with Verlaine, his example has inspired composers as different as Schonberg, Milhaud, and Ibert. In addition he influenced with profound effect the poetry of T. S. Eliot, Ezra Pound, and Hart Crane.

THE POETRY OF LAMARTINE

Author: Alphonse de Lamartine (1790-1869)
Principal published works: Poetic Meditations, 1820; *Poetic and Religious Harmonies,*
1830; *Jocelyn,* 1836

As a young man, Lamartine's first literary attempts were in the area of the epic and the drama. In 1848, after the Revolution of that year, Lamartine was made head of the provisional government of France. His liberal sympathies were known throughout the nation, and he was immensely popular. Yet it is neither as an epic poet, nor as a dramatist, nor still less as a politician that Lamartine is best known. His lasting fame has depended principally on his *Poetic Meditations,* lyrical elegies about love and nature, life and God.

The French public had no doubts about the originality of the *Poetic Meditations* when they first appeared in 1820. They had a resounding success; added to by Lamartine, they later ran into many editions. It is worth recalling that at this time, with the extension of public education, first by the men of the Revolution, then by Napoleon, it was possible to reach a much wider public than had ever before been the case. This factor needs to be cited in a consideration of the literature of the period. To a public living with the memory of Napoleonic splendor, yet tired of wars; with a great appetite for literature, while scarcely intellectual, Lamartine's idealistic poetry of spirituality and sensibility appealed greatly.

By his dates, Lamartine may be situated among the French Romantics. In fact, his themes are the eternal themes of poetry, the prerogative of no single school. Moreover, the form of his poetry does not, at first sight, offer any noticeable break with the past. Yet by its lyrical qualities—its musicality and its intimate expression of deep, personal feelings—this verse must situate its creator in the vanguard of the French poets generally held to be Romantic.

The reputation of Lamartine has not remained constant. Toward the end of his life, poor and neglected, he wrote to make money and considered himself a galley slave of writing. One of the reasons for this neglect was the vogue, under Napoleon III, of the Parnassians, to the exclusion of others. In part, the Parnassians may be viewed as reacting against Lamartine, or at least against his example. Poetry, wrote Lamartine, is "the incarnation of that which is most intimate in man's heart, and most divine in his thought." This and many similar pronouncements must be held partly responsible for the chaos that marks the attempts at finding a Romantic doctrine in France. The best of Lamartine has been highly esteemed by many critics, granted grudging praise by others. Even that element often considered the greatest attribute of Lamartine's poetry, its insubstantial, ethereal quality, has been deplored by those who long for high relief, color, precision, solidity.

The most famous of the Meditations is "The Lake." It was originally entitled "Ode to the Bourget Lake." This finest of love elegies seems to owe much, directly and indirectly, to Jean Jacques Rousseau. The theme of a return alone to a place filled with memories of love and happiness recalls *The New Héloïse* by the eighteenth century writer. The direct inspiration for the poem, as for many in the collection, is Mme. Charles, the "Elvire" of the *Poetic Meditations.* Lamartine had met her at Aix-les-Bains and immediately formed a very deep attachment for her. A proposed reunion between them did not take place because of her illness and death. "The Lake" was written before her death in December, 1817, when her illness prevented her from coming to meet the poet.

In this piece the writer has returned

alone to the lake. He feels forlorn at the thought that his happiness, which had been of short duration, is already threatened. He cannot help expressing his anguish at the rapid flight of time:

> Jealous time, can it be that these moments of intoxication
> When love pours happiness for us in long draughts,
> Fly far from us with the same speed
> As days of misfortune?

He wishes his love to be preserved at least as a memory. Aware of the transitory nature of all of man's life, the poet implores the lake and its environs—those reflections of an unchanging, permanent nature—to be a temple to his love, a shrine which will forever contain the memory of it:

> What! Gone for ever? What! Entirely lost?
> This time which gave them, which now wipes them out,
>   Will never give them back?
>
> O lake! Silent rocks! Caverns! Dark forest!
> You whom time spares or whom it can make young again,
> Keep, fair landscape, keep at least
> The memory of that night!

The poem, rather than offering the thoughts and sentiments of one man, seems to express the eternal problems of all men, while appearing to make of them a unique experience. The themes, man's awareness of the fragile and ephemeral character of happiness and his seeking of some consolation in nature, are to be found throughout the collection.

"Alone" is, after "The Lake," one of the best known of the *Poetic Meditations*. It was written shortly after the death of Mme. Charles and bears the direct, profound trace of the poet's grief. His love for Elvire has been refined and purified by her death: it is now an ideal, spiritual love. His longing to be with her is associated with an aspiration to a higher reality, for he feels an exile on earth. Even nature cannot now console him:

> What are they for me, these valleys, these palaces, these cottages,
> Vain objects which have lost the charm they once had?
> Rivers, rocks, forests, once-cherished solitude,
> One person is missing, and the world is deserted!

The emotion expressed here is anything but new to French poetry. By this time the laments and exaltations of sensitive souls in some nature setting were less than unusual. The secret of the beauty of the poem cannot therefore be found in the nature of the emotion expressed. Similarly, it is at first too hard to perceive any originality in the vocabulary or versification. The latter is quite regular; its only remarkable feature seems the frequency of perfect rhyme. The vocabulary involves a fair number of very conventional, classical periphrases and standard "poetic" words checked out from the classical armory. If one seeks an explanation in the person of the narrator or his mistress, it cannot be found; no telling detail reveals their appearance or character. Even the setting is so vaguely described as to be any one of countless sites having a lake, a river, mountains, and forests. If no color, sound, or person limits the poem to any one place, it is also impossible to say what time is being described, beyond an awareness that it is evening. In thus leaving his horizons wide open, Lamartine was running a considerable risk; by being so vague, he might very well have fallen into the danger of making his poem so imprecise as to be meaningless or unrecognizable. Instead, he has succeeded in revealing his setting as a state of mind of the person contemplating it. The reader fills in the scene for himself. By leaving it open, the poet is able to present memories of the past alongside a scene in the present, with a suggestion of a future life beyond this world. He is able to intermingle sadness with beauty and an aspiration to happiness. He suggests much more than he states or shows, and an impression of tenderness and sincerity arises from the work. The standard, regular form seems to underline this sincerity. Finally, by a remarkable deployment of alliterations and emotive words and phrases, Lamartine bestows upon this poem a free-flowing sound and movement strongly suggestive of the qualities of music. The techniques used in "Alone" are no different from those to be found throughout the *Poetic Meditations*.

In other fine pieces from the *Poetic Meditations*, Lamartine builds up an ambience rather than a view; "Immortality," "The Valley," and "Autumn" are only a few examples. In each, Lamartine proceeds by deft touches until the atmosphere has been diffused. The reader is then able to add to the scene by drawing upon his own background.

Like du Bellay, a spiritual if not a real predecessor of Lamartine, the author of the *Poetic Meditations* lived for a time in Italy, as a representative of his country. It was in Florence, from 1826 to 1828, that he worked on the *Poetic and Religious Harmonies*, which were published in 1830. Composed of forty-eight pieces, this collection contains some of the best of Lamartine, but is not perhaps so uniformly successful as the *Poetic Meditations* of 1820. Running through the *Poetic and Religious Harmonies* is a definite, spontaneous, religious ardor. Most of the poems are hymns of praise to God. In some there can be no doubt about the Christian inspiration. One of the finest examples is "Hymn to Christ." Yet the reader comes away with the impression that Lamartine's inspiration is perhaps less Christian than deistic or even Platonic. Although, unlike du Bellay, Lamartine seems to have enjoyed to the full his stay in Italy, one of the finest pieces in the collection, "Milly or the Native Land," contains the poet's affirmation of his preference for his humble village in France over the splendors of Italy.

Jocelyn is a long epic poem recounting the sacrifices and tribulations of a priest. The latter is scarcely orthodox. He is a practitioner of social Christianity, preaching by example, with sympathy for the spirit of the gospel, but little for Church pomp or literal dogma. Though there are magnificent descriptions of nature and rural life, the poem has many weaknesses.

It seems a pity that many imitations of Lamartine's work by lesser poets have tended to detract from the original. Also, it is unfortunate that in defining poetry in a passive way, as something received, Lamartine seems to have helped the movement toward imprecision and verbiage that one finds in many writers of the first half of the nineteenth century. It is regrettable that in a large part of Lamartine's work, looseness and inaccuracy are common. However, if this poet is granted the right extended to most, that only his finest works be considered in an evaluation of lasting value, his place among the most outstanding poets of the nineteenth century is by no means that of a usurper.

Lamartine's poetry is both conventional and original. On the one hand a just comparison may be made with writers of a previous age. On the other hand, similarities between his poetry and that of Paul Verlaine are striking.

THE POETRY OF LANDOR

Author: Walter Savage Landor (1775-1864)
First published: Poems, 1795; *Gebir,* 1798; *The Hellenics,* 1847; *Poemata et Inscriptiones,*
1847; *Italics,* 1848; *Last Fruit off an Old Tree,* 1853; *Antony and Octavius,* 1856; *Dry
Sticks Fagoted by W. S. Landor,* 1858; *Heroic Idylls,* 1863

Walter Savage Landor, who has been described as a classic writer in a romantic age, was an isolated figure who outlived by many years the period of the Romantic triumph in England. Possessing from his earliest youth a strong attachment to both the ideals and the styles of Greek and Latin literature, he nevertheless admired and sympathized with the artistry of Byron, Shelley, and Keats. On the whole, however, the more restrained manner of his own poetry tended toward the temper best exemplified by Browning and Tennyson. Often he composed first in Latin and then translated his work into English, consciously preserving the classical qualities of the original.

Having studied at Rugby, Landor matriculated at Oxford in 1795, when the tide of republicanism and revolutionism was running high. His active sympathy with the ascendant ideals of liberty brought him into difficulties with the university officials and eventually led to his withdrawing from Oxford without a degree. But the excellent training in Latin which he received there was to leave a distinctive mark on all his writings. Unmistakably and pervasively it is evident in the noble restraint and chastened expression which give Landor's poems a typically classical touch.

At the same time, with the Romantics, he was a worshiper of nature and an unflinching defender of the downtrodden and helpless. In actuality, there is in the man, as in his poetry and prose, not a diametric clash of classical and Romantic contraries but, rather, a mingling of these opposing tendencies. Landor declared sincerely that he was not seeking wide popularity as a poet. To explain this attitude he used the effective metaphor, "I shall dine late, but the dining room will be well-lighted, the guests few and select." Although their mutual influence seems not to have been great, he appreciated, and was appreciated by, such notable contemporaries as Carlyle, Dickens, Browning, and Wordsworth.

In his first volume of poetry, *Poems,* which appeared in 1795, Landor displayed considerable dignity of phrase and artistry of style. Yet this volume appears inconsequential when compared to *Gebir,* an Oriental tale in blank verse written during two solitary years in Wales and published in 1798. In its seven books this epic recounts the adventures of the mythic founder of Gibraltar. The elevated style and cadence of the poem suggest that Landor's models were Milton and classical authors such as Pindar. *Gebir* drew attention and admiration from a number of Landor's discriminating contemporaries, but was too weak in characterization and narrative content to appeal to the general reader. The one passage of the poem which has achieved lasting recognition is the episode of "Tamar's Wrestling," in which the outclassed shepherd loses to the "nymph divine" both the wrestling match and the sheep he has wagered.

"Shepherd," said she, "and will you
  wrestle now.
And with the sailor's hardier race engage?"
        . . . .
"Whether a shepherd, as indeed you
  seem,
Or whether of the hardier race you
  boast,
I am not daunted, no: I will engage."
        . . . .
Now she came forward, eager to engage;
But, first her dress, her bosom then,
  survey'd,

And heav'd it, doubting if she could
deceive.
Her bosom seem'd, inclos'd in haze like
heav'n,
To baffle touch; and rose forth undefined.
Above her knees she drew the robe succinct,
Above her breast, and just below her
arms:
"This will preserve my breath, when
tightly bound,
If struggle and equal strength should
so constrain."
Thus, pulling hard to fasten it, she
spoke,
And rushing at me, closed. I thrill'd
throughout
And seem'd to lessen and shrink up
with cold.
Again, with violent impulse gushed my
blood;
And hearing nought external, thus absorb'd,
I heard it rushing through each turbid
vein,
Shake my unsteady swimming sight in
air.
Yet with unyielding though uncertain
arms,
I clung around her neck; the vest be-
neath
Rustled against our slippery limbs en-
twined:
Often mine, springing with eluded
force,
Started aside, and trembled, till re-
placed.
And when I most succeeded, as I
thought,
My bosom and my throat felt so com-
prest
That life was almost quivering on my
lips,
Yet nothing was there painful! these
are signs
Of secret arts, and not human might,
What arts I cannot tell: I only know
My eyes grew dizzy, and my strength
decay'd,
I was indeed o'ercome!—with what re-
gret,
And more, with what confusion, when
I reached
The fold, and yielding up the sheep,
she cried,
"This pays a shepherd to a conquering

maid."
She smil'd, and more of pleasure than
disdain
Was in her dimpled chin, and liberal
lip,
And eyes that languished, lengthening,
—just like love.
She went away. . . .

The uneven quality of *Gebir* has been
best described by Coleridge, who referred
to its beautiful passages as "eminences
excessively bright and all the ground
around and between them in darkness."
Indeed, Landor's longer poems, generally, are best remembered in extract. "I
must read again Landor's *Julian*," Charles
Lamb wrote in 1815, "I have not read it
for some time. I think he must have
failed in Roderick, for I remember nothing of him, nor of any distinct character
as a character—only fine-sounding passages."

Landor devoted the first twenty-six
years of his literary career almost wholly
to verse. He then turned for a time primarily to the writing of prose, of which
his *Imaginary Conversations* and the creative romance *Pericles and Aspasia* are
the most noteworthy. Then followed the
period of Landor's Latin poetry, during
which he produced Latin verse of all
kinds—elegiac, idyllic, lyric, and satiric
—directly as well as indirectly imitating
various Roman writers, among them
Catullus, Horace, Juvenal, and Vergil. In
1847 he published these poems under the
title of *Poemata et Inscriptiones;* and that
year he also published in English *The
Hellenics,* a series of poems on Greek
topics, many of which had been written
long before. A second version appeared
twelve years later.

The Hellenics contains imaginary dialogues of moderate length in poetic form.
A number of them having been written,
like parts of *Gebir,* first in Latin, these
poems are very much like their classical
models. The settings and situations generally are dramatic; the characters are
harmoniously arranged to set off their distinctive qualities, and the entire design is

carefully proportioned. Although the products of this craftsmanship frequently resemble sedate, cool sculpture rather than intense drama, they are not devoid of an inner life of human emotion. Two poems in the collection which especially demonstrate the latter quality are the tragic "Iphigeneia" and the idyllic "Hamadryad."

In the former poem, Iphigeneia, daughter of Agamemnon, is to be sacrificed to the gods so that her father's ships will have a safe and prosperous journey.

Iphigeneia, when she heard her doom
At Aulis, and when all beside the king
Had gone away, took his right-hand,
    and said,
"O father! I am young and very happy.
I do not think the pious Calchas heard
Distinctly what the Goddess spake. Old
    age
Obscures the senses. . . ."
The father placed his cheek upon her
    head,
And tears dropt down it, but the king
    of men
Replied not. . . .
"But father! to see you no more, and
    see
Your love, O father! go ere I am gone!"
Gently he moved her off, and drew her
    back,
Bending his loftly head far over her's,
And the dark depths of nature heaved
    and burst.
He turn'd away; not far, but silent
    still. . . .

An aged man now enter'd, and without
One word, stept slowly on, and took
    the wrist
Of the pale maiden. She lookt up, and
    saw
The fillet of the priest and calm cold
    eyes.
Then turn'd she where her parent
    stood, and cried
"O father! grieve no more: the ships
    can sail."

Aside from *Gebir, The Hellenics,* and several "closet" dramas, the most nearly successful of which is *Count Julian,* almost all of Landor's poetry was in the form of occasional lyrics. Easily and regularly over a period of more than fifty years, he produced short poems, among which are his best poetic creations. There are several hundred of these occasional verses, forming a record of cheerfulness, gallantry, and affection, as well as of sad retrospect. Some of them, notably "Rose Aylmer," have achieved lasting success. Perhaps the best and most genuinely felt words in all of Landor's poetry are these eight lines of *Rose Aylmer:*

Ah what avails the sceptred race,
    Ah what the form divine!
What every virtue, every grace!
    Rose Aylmer, all were thine.
Rose Aylmer, whom these wakeful eyes
    May weep, but never see,
A night of memories and of sighs
    I consecrate to thee.

Other lyrics possess qualities which range from engaging charm to playful triviality and roguish trifling. The verses Landor wrote in old age are majestic in their own way. Of these, "I Strove with None" is the most famous, and it is typical in the author's proclaiming his apartness of temper. His announcement, "I hate the crowd," is like Ben Jonson's pose which could not entirely hide the genuine feeling underneath. Seldom successful in spontaneous poetry, and sometimes far wide of the mark, Landor yet displays sensitiveness, mastery of the exquisitely beautiful phrase, exceptional proliferation of imagery, and graceful, though fastidious, dignity.

Landor declared: "Poetry was always my amusement, prose my study and business." Although his literary reputation is based mostly on his prose, it is in poetry that he has achieved his few works of genuine greatness. During the last decades of his life, although his disposition grew increasingly aloof, he continued to produce poetry of high quality. The volume titled *Last Fruit off an Old Tree* is notable mainly for a group of five dramatic scenes on the trial and death of Beatrice Cenci, the heroine of Shelley's poetic drama *The Cenci. Antony and Octavius,* a group of twelve dramatic dialogues, appeared in 1856. In 1858 he published a miscellany of poetry entitled *Dry Sticks Fagoted by W. S. Landor*. His final volume was the *Heroic Idylls*.

Landor's own proud, resonant voice was heard over an amazing span of years; and although we readily acknowledge the truth of Swinburne's epitaph,

And through the trumpet of a child of Rome
Rang the pure music of the flutes of Greece,

we must immediately qualify it by the recollection that throughout Landor's creative life, his classically based verse idylls such as the beautiful "Hamadryad" and its sequel "Acon and Rhodope" are in essence not only Landorian but also "Romantic" and modern. Landor's works are products of the age of Keats and the age of Tennyson.

THE POETRY OF LANIER

Type of work: Poetry
Author: Sidney Lanier (1842-1881)
Principal published works: Poems, 1877; Poems of Sidney Lanier, 1884

The poetic fame of Sidney Lanier, after Poe the most important nineteenth-century poet of the Southern United States, rests upon a small body of poetry found in the posthumous volume, *Poems of Sidney Lanier,* which contains the verse Lanier included in his *Poems,* along with a number of pieces which had received only magazine publication before the poet's death in 1881, plus a group of unrevised early poems that his wife felt were worthy of publication. Of approximately one hundred titles in the posthumous volume, only fifteen or twenty are known today except to students especially interested in Lanier. Most of the critical discussions of Lanier's poetic significance cite primarily these some fifteen or twenty poems in illustrating both his merits and his defects.

Lanier was a poet of both theory and practice. His theory of technique was influenced by his great love for music. Precociously musical, he was in manhood a brilliant flutist who played with symphony orchestras in Dallas and Baltimore. His moralistic theory of poetic content was possibly influenced by his early training in a devoutly Christian family as well as by his own fundamentally religious nature, which shows itself, in some of his nature poems, as a passionate love for God's plants and creatures approaching that of St. Francis of Assisi.

Lanier's theory of prosody is expounded principally in *The Science of English Verse* (1880), which develops in extensive detail and with copious illustration the thesis that the same laws govern both versification and music. Three brief quotations will illustrate this thesis:

> . . . when we hear verse, we *hear* a set of relations between sounds; when we silently read verse, we *see* that which brings to us a set of relations between sounds; when we imagine verse, we *imagine* a set of relations between sounds.

> When those exact co-ordinations which the ear perceives as rhythm, tune, and tone-color are suggested to the ear by a series of *musical sounds,* the result is . . . MUSIC.
> When those exact co-ordinations which the ear perceives as rhythm, tune, and tone-color, are suggested to the ear by a series of *spoken words,* the result is . . . VERSE.

> . . . there is absolutely no difference between the sound-relations used in music and those used in verse.

Lanier's application of his prosodic theory may be studied in many of his poems, but it may be easily seen in such poems as "The Symphony," "The Marshes of Glynn," and "Song of the Chattahoochee."

In "The Symphony," Lanier attempted the difficult task of composing a poem somewhat as a musician would. Such instruments as violins, flute, clarinet, horn, and hautboy (oboe) are personified and used to develop the theme of Love, the enemy of Trade (materialism), which pervades the poem. Nowhere is Lanier's belief in the essential identity of sound-relations in music and in verse better illustrated than in the four lines which introduce the horn passage in the poem:

> There thrust the bold straightforward horn
> To battle for that lady lorn.
> With hearthsome voice of mellow scorn,
> Like any knight in knighthood's morn.

It has been objected that Lanier tried the impossible in "The Symphony" and that his achievement, though notable, is successful only in part. Perhaps his theory is better illustrated in "Sunrise" and "The Marshes of Glynn." In "Sunrise," one easily catches the sibilance of the forest:

Ye lispers, whisperers, singers in storms,
Ye consciences murmuring faiths under
forms,
Ye ministers meet for each passion that
grieves,
Friendly, sisterly, sweetheart leaves.

In "The Marshes of Glynn" the sounds and even the silence of the great marshes near Brunswick, Georgia, may be heard and felt by the reader. A passage near the close of the poem describes in this fashion the coming of the high tide of evening:

The creeks overflow: a thousand rivu-
lets run
'Twixt the roots of the sod; the blades
of the marsh-grass stir;
Passeth a hurrying sound of wings that
westward whirr;
Passeth, and all is still; and the currents
cease to run;
And the sea and the marsh are one.

In these lines the sounds of the moving waters and grasses and of the whirring wings are followed by a silence that is palpable.

Because of Lanier's repeated use of onomatopoeia in his verse he has often been compared with Poe; but Lanier's theory of poetic content is quite different. Poe, in "The Philosophy of Composition," concedes that "passion, or even truth, may . . . be introduced, and even profitably introduced, into a poem"; but, he asserts, "Beauty is the sole legitimate province of the poem." In another essay, "The Poetic Principle," Poe attacks what he calls "the heresy of *The Didactic*." "Every poem, it is said, should inculcate a moral," he reminds us; "and by this moral is the poetical merit of the work to be adjudged." But, he continues,

would we but permit ourselves to look into our own souls, we should imme-diately there discover that under the sun there neither exists nor *can* exist any work more thoroughly dignified—

more supremely noble than this very poem—this poem *per se*—this poem which is a poem and nothing more—this poem written solely for the poem's sake.

Lanier loved art as much as Poe did, but Lanier was on the side of the moral-ists. In the series of lectures posthumously published as *The English Novel and the Principle of Its Development* (1883), he leaves no doubt as to his position when he states that

We may say that he who has not yet perceived how artistic beauty and moral beauty are convergent lines which run back into a common ideal origin, and who therefore is not afire with moral beauty just as with artistic beauty—that he, in short, who has not come to that stage of quiet and eternal frenzy in which the beauty of holiness and the holiness of beauty mean one thing, burn as one fire, shine as one light within him; he is not yet the great artist.

Although Lanier wrote occasional poems such as his verse narrative "The Revenge of Hamish," in which the moral element is not a major one, most of his poetry is charged with moral purpose or shines with "the beauty of holiness." "The Symphony" bitterly indicts the cruel, greedy practices of Trade and sings the gospel of brotherly love. In "The Marshes of Glynn," he writes:

As the marsh-hen secretly builds on the
watery sod,
Behold I will build me a nest on the
greatness of God.

Even a dialect poem like "Thar's More in the Man than Thar Is in the Land" contains a moral lesson, as the title itself suggests. Occasionally his moral earnest-ness dims Lanier's artistic sight, however, as in "Song of the Chattahoochee," in which the river is made to say:

. . . I am fain for to water the plain.
Downward the voices of Duty call—.

This is a flagrant example of what John Ruskin called the "pathetic fallacy." Peo-ple may act with moral purpose; when the Chattahoochee River flows downward, however, it is not because it knows that

> The dry fields burn, and the mills are to turn,
> And a myriad flowers mortally yearn,

but because, as Lanier himself very well knew, the law of gravity is a part of the earthly scheme of things.

Though Lanier is not primarily a regional poet, many of his lines sing eloquently of his Southern origin. He is in love with the beautiful Marshes of Glynn, with their "moss-bearded live-oaks." He mourns that "Bright drops of tune, from oceans infinite/Of Melody" were ended when a pet mockingbird "died of a cat, May, 1878." He grieves in "Corn" that the rich soil of his native state is being washed away because of the greed of cotton farmers who lay the surface bare and then leave their erosion-ruined areas and head for Texas to repeat their folly. In "A Florida Sunday," he holds "in my being" rich-scented orange trees, pea green parrakeets, 'pranked woodpeckers that ne'er gossip out," palmettos, pines, and mangroves. In such poems Lanier is as clearly a Southern poet as Robert Frost is a New England one when he describes his New Hampshire countryside.

A fault that many readers have found with Lanier is that, as a poet, he too often lets his heart overflow and his whole being "quiver with the passionate thrill"; at times a noble emotion may descend into sentimentality and at others the poet's feeling may blur the expression of "the great thought." The lush music of Lanier's lines may also create the lulling mental effect that one finds in Swinburne. Part of Lanier's trouble seems to be that he is striving too hard to attain the right combination of "rhythm, tune, and tone-color." He sometimes forces his comparisons so that they become too-obvious poetic conceits, as in "Marsh Song—at Sunset," with its metaphors drawn from Shakespeare's *Tempest*. Some of his sentences, such as the thirty-six-line one which opens "The Marshes of Glynn," lack clarity because of their great length and intricate structure.

In spite of the undisciplined emotionalism, hazy thought, and strained effects of his lesser poems, Lanier seems well assured of a permanent place in American literature. The melody of his best lines; the love of God, man, and nature found in poems like "The Marshes of Glynn" and "The Symphony"; the simple beauty of "A Ballad of Trees and the Master"; and the stoic acceptance of "The Stirrup-Cup," in which the consumptive poet says uncomplainingly to Death, "Hand me the cup whene'er thou wilt" —for these Lanier will continue to be loved.

THE POETRY OF LARKIN

Author: Philip Larkin (1922-   )
First published: The North Ship, 1945; *Poems,* 1954; *The Less Deceived,* 1955; *The Whitsun Weddings,* 1964

Where does the mainstream of English poetry lie? Admirers of the contemporary British poet, Philip Larkin, see its source to be Wordsworth, its exponents Thomas Hardy and Edward Thomas, those quiet introverted men who refused to follow any but their own individual bent. It is a stream that moves underground when intensely classical or romantic spirits are abroad—an Eliot or a Dylan Thomas—but which is encouraged into the light by the ironic, contemplative aura of the later Auden. It was in the early 1950's that "The Movement" declared itself again, in Robert Conquest's anthology, *New Lines;* and the British public revealed itself as ready for Wordsworth's "real language of men." Novelists and poets began to take a hard look at changing social patterns: at middle class mentality, suburban mediocrity, the uncaring anonymity of "I'm all right, Jack." It was a world shorn of metaphor and myth whose poets almost desperately declared themselves as humanists, dedicated to the revelation of "the real person or event." Honesty or the awareness of honesty was their religion.

Philip Larkin was one of the first, along with Kingsley Amis and John Wain, to reflect the new attitudes. He had started off at the beginning of the war as a promising young novelist. His first novel, *Jill,* was published in 1940, when he was twenty-one. It depicts the struggles of a scholarship boy thrust into the upper class world of Oxford and resolving his problems through fantasy. However, Larkin's 1955 book of poems, *The Less Deceived,* indicated that he had stripped himself of the dream and was forcing himself to become at home in a world essentially alien to the dreamer. He was seeking a way to deal with things as they are, not as they seem; without distortion. Possibly for this reason the first poem in the book, and one that has been much anthologized, is most revealing of his approach and method. It is titled "Lines on a Young Lady's Photograph Album."

With its evocation of a real girl in a real place this poem sets the colloquial, self-mocking tone reminiscent of Hardy's ballads or of Meredith's lyrics. The structure, too, of this poem is as complicated and controlled as Hardy's: a loose iambic stanza of five lines with a consistent rhyme scheme, yet contemporary in its use of half-rhymes and assonances.

In his poem, Larkin is not satisfied merely to record, to photograph, even though he can flick out the exact word to create a picture. He can do more by commenting on the scene and involving the listener in his commentary. A purely "imagist" poet would be content to leave the picture objectively before us, implying only its emotional direction. But Larkin plunges right into exposition, and he goes over the scene again, peeling away leaf after leaf to reveal the frustration.

"Lines on a Young Lady's Photograph Album" reveals his control over his vehicle which is a characteristic of all of Larkin's work. He is an intent craftsman, creating within a set form an amazing variety of rhythmic variations. And he is steadily concerned with the evocative power of assonance and alliteration. This poem is aptly illustrative of Larkin's nostalgic, ironic mood; of his reasonable acceptance of an unsatisfactory world; and of his *angst* which never becomes self-pity. There is, in his best work, a stoicism which keeps the artist apart from the crowd yet not superior to it, as in "Reasons for Attendance" when he looks through a ballroom window at the jiving dancers.

Integrity and honesty are the keynotes

in Philip Larkin's volume of poems titled *The Whitsun Weddings.* Here he is willing himself to identify more closely with other men, other houses, other streets and communities. Many of the poems are less introverted, consisting of more objective recording and less private comment. The result is lively, as a newspaper is lively; but one wonders whether the poems in this volume may not be more ephemeral, concrete though they appear. The colloquial tone makes them highly topical, but the sense of timelessness so strong in *The Less Deceived* is somehow missing. Throughout all these later poems it is remarkable to note how often the last line, which in *The Less Deceived* was often a *tour de force* of strength and confidence, has become wearily negative.

The title poem, "The Whitsun Weddings," is the longest and most ambitious. In all eight stanzas the iambic pentameter is skillfully handled; the structure, even the rhymes, seem as natural as everyday speech. Inevitably the tone brings to mind a trenchant, detached observer of the noisy wedding parties: the loud-voiced mothers, an uncle mouthing smut, genteel dress, cheap jewelry. The poem expresses a desperate sense of time spent uselessly. At the end it is no longer merely ironic; it has become a bitter commentary on the meaningless in life. "No exit" faces the poet. Is it that Philip Larkin, who began by assuming a steady unflinching view of the human condition, is now disturbed or terrified by the spectacle of humanity's nakedness? The world that had seemed so interestingly photogenic now forces him to examine its flesh and blood.

THE POETRY OF LAWRENCE

Author: D. H. Lawrence (1885-1930)
First published: Love Poems and Others, 1913; *Amores,* 1916; *Look! We Have Come Through,* 1917; *New Poems,* 1918; *Bay* 1919; *Tortoises,* 1921; *Birds, Beasts, and Flowers,* 1923; *Pansies,* 1929; *Nettles,* 1930; *Last Poems,* 1932; *Fire and Other Poems,* 1940; *The Complete Poems of D. H. Lawrence,* 1964

In a note to his *Collected Poems* of 1928, D. H. Lawrence explains that he tried to arrange the poems in chronological order "because their personal nature made them, in effect, a biography of inner life and experience. Lawrence's poetry, which is not widely read, succeeds for just this reason; reading through the volumes, one must agree with the poet, for the poems, rough as they often seem, sometimes even crude and apparently rapidly composed, are everywhere alive; they pulse with the currents and cross currents of their author's tempestuous life and affairs. This effect is remarkable in any body of poems, and Lawrence's are also remarkable for their haunting, incantatory cadences. In other words, the poems are seldom witty or intellectually complex; they do not sustain, nor often require, a great deal of explication or analysis. Perhaps better, they require, even demand, that the reader open himself to them, to the gusts of emotions—anger, bitterness, tenderness, outrage, nostalgia, regret, love—which make up their form and content, and which are artistically controlled and expressed chiefly in haunting though generally a-metrical rhythms.

The poems, up to 1923, revolve around Lawrence's early loves, and his mother, especially. The background of these poems, which are all rhymed, may be supplied easily by anyone familiar with his autobiographical novel, *Sons and Lovers.* Then there is the death of his mother, which completes the volume of rhymed poems and forms, as Lawrence says, the "climax" of the first volume of the collected poems. Chronologically overlapping these poems, which run through the war into 1918, are the unrhymed poems of *Look! We Have Come*

Through, the poems which deal mainly with the love and torments of his marriage to Frieda, who left a husband and two children to marry Lawrence, and their life in Austria and in England during the war. The poems in "Birds, Beasts and Flowers" are mainly of the Mexican and New Mexico sojourn of 1920-1923, and conclude the first volume. Beyond these, Lawrence's poems, most notably in *Pansies* and *Nettles,* become stridently political and anti-social. Roughhewn and full of disdain, anger, and even hate, often near hysteria, full of preachings and pronouncements, these poems are mostly ephemera. Then, with last poems like "The Ship of Death," he reaches the apex of his poetic career. Haunting, mysterious, religious, the poem is a unique contribution to modern verse.

It is nearly impossible to illustrate the nature of Lawrence's poetry with short quotations, for the poems build slowly from a perception, an image, to a flash of realized emotion. They are deceptively simple, for the curve of feeling is often very complex. They are organic growths, and the art with which Lawrence can build a poem to a climax is disarming. Details are introduced; they slowly become focused and symbolic as a *persona,* a viewpoint, is established, a conflict—emotional, sexual—is gradually engaged and developed through incremental repetition. Then the full experience blossoms forth, usually directly stated, and the poem, a little drama built out of the countercurrents of image and response, is completed. To quote a line or stanza hardly reveals the process, for it is a process, a chaffing, rhythmic movement building a tension and bringing a release, that is Lawrence's method. There is, therefore, more intensity and significance in the cadences and reiterations of detail than in single images or memorable lines. The poems grow, develop; they are not set pieces at all. Of course, all poems work in some such way, but Lawrence's more purely so, and with the attendant risk of flatness, prosaic-ness, and loss of form.

At his best, however, the accumulating reiteration of line, image, and thought has the effect of a chant or incantation. The poem becomes, as in "The Ship of Death" or in "Bavarian Gentians," a kind of ritual; or, in a poem like "Snake," it is as if the poet's nerves were laid bare, quivering. In one of his early poems, "The Scent of Irises," Lawrence displays the facility with which he can develop a response, in this case to a jar of iris in the classroom where he was teaching. The iris and his lonely slavery as a school-teacher take him back to an earlier time, in the country, with a girl. The internal rhyme and alliteration, the way the lines are "rove-over," the strongly cadenced anapestic-like rhythm with the beautifully manipulated double stresses, the repetition of syntactic phrases and clauses, may, in their chanting effect and syncopation, remind one of Hopkins or Whitman or Dylan Thomas, and rightfully so. The developing tensions between the girl and the flowers, between sexual blossoming and the reminder, in the last line, of death, illustrates, in part, the manner in which Lawrence characteristically works. There is strife here, between the "you" of the girl and the "me" of the poet; the tone is half-nostalgic, half-bitter. The love and the simultaneous hate vie for precedence with desire and scorn: cross currents of emotion. The "Scent of Irises" is a very typical and compelling poem, as are the better-known "Love on the Farm," "Lightening," and "Monologue of a Mother," all from the early poems.

"Piano," from the last volume of the rhymed poems, *Bay*, is one of Lawrence's best-known poems but is often dismissed with the charge of sentimentality. The poem relates how the poet, listening to a woman sing, is reminded of his mother singing to him as a child, and how that remembrance sweeps his manhood away. The poem is *about* the dominion of mother over even the adult man, and one may say that the poem is *about* a particularly pernicious sentimentality, but the *poem* is not sentimental, for Lawrence has objectified and dramatized the experience. His tormenting love for Frieda is well expressed in "A Young Wife," from *Look! We Have Come Through.* The experiences reflected in this volume begin in 1912 and extend to the winter of 1916. In the poem the ambivalent feelings, the tension between love and fear, are expressed in images of darkness and night. The darkness becomes a favorite image for Lawrence, as it appears to symbolize or suggest both death and the profound, mysterious, and instinctual inner life. Lawrence, who grew up in the raped countryside of the Midlands, whose father was a victim of the mines, became in "philosophy" a primitivist who felt that modern society had buried man's instinctual, most human self. He advocated a retreat from rationality and a rediscovering of the primitive "blood-consciousness" of emotional and instinctive being. His novel *The Plumed Serpent* depicts a revolution in Mexico, behind which lies the revival of the ancient Indian god Quetzalcoatl, whose "return" is accompanied by rituals which include the shedding of blood. The forms of modern culture were to be swept away; and the original man, including his cruelty, was to be resurrected. In another poem, "Snake," Lawrence vividly describes his horror at seeing a snake emerge from a hole in the ground and drink at the water fountain. He throws a stick at it, signifying modern man's fear of the primitive, the secret, and, by extension, the sexual. Then the poet is disgusted with himself for such a reaction of fear and cowardliness. The snake is described in terms which relate him to the ancient, primitive past, to the mythic.

In Lawrence's view it is that modern "voice" of education which must be overcome, so that men can live as men again, and not as machines or as slaves to machines and the bloodless, passionless machine-owners, such as Lady Chatterley's symbolically crippled husband.

Lawrence's movement, in his verse, toward themes dealing with ancient myth and ritual is evidenced by this first stanza from "Middle of the World," one of his last poems, in which he asserts that the sea will never grow old, lose its blueness, or fail to raise its watery hills in the dawn-light as the ship of Dionysos, grape vines decorating its masts and attended by leaping dolphins, sails the waves.

Here is cadenced verse, working very close to prose, but highly poetic in its control, in its patterning of syntax, and the movement of symbolic images. Dionysos is, of course, a symbol and the repository of the life of passion, of instinct, and of freedom from the bindings of rationality. The sea is a symbol of fruition and life.

Lawrence searched the globe for a place where he could feel the ancient pulse of life still beating, but perhaps nowhere did he feel it more than in the burial caves of the ancient Etruscans; the vaults are vividly decorated with images of hunting and of other activities. From the Etruscan caves Lawrence drew the main images and primitive conception of death which informs "The Ship of Death." Perhaps his greatest poem, it was rewritten many times, but the reader will find it fully rewarding simply to read as one poem the many versions. It is a ritual chant in praise of death and man's journey toward obliviousness. In this poem Lawrence refers to the Etruscan belief in a kind of rebirth, when souls will need their tools and crockery, and the ship, which sails to oblivion, sails on through to a new life, where peace is renewed within the heart.

No quotation can communicate the poem. Alternately elegiac and joyful, the cadences subtly modulated to fit the moods, Lawrence here plumbs, as it were, his vision of death and touches on the rock of belief he found in ancient ritual and culture.

"Bavarian Genetians" also depicts an imaginative journey to the underworld, where in the mysterious life in darkness Lawrence chants, in images of Pluto's hell and of Persephone, his mythic sense of death and rebirth in the darkness of lost and legendary time.

THE POETRY OF LEOPARDI

Author: Giacomo Leopardi (1798-1837)
Principal published works: Versi, 1826; *Operetti morali,* 1827; *Canzi,* 1831

Giacomo Leopardi, Italy's most distinguished contribution to European Romanticism, was one of the great lyricists of the nineteenth century. Virtually a contemporary of Keats, he demonstrates many similarities to that brilliant, short-lived Englishman. More useful, however, is the comparison with Wordsworth. Like him, Leopardi uses rural scenes and idioms and writes much verse superficially in the same mode. A typical poem of both will begin with a scene rich in natural, simple details, from which the poet weaves both message and mood out of his impression of nature. Nothing could be farther from the divine power in nature that Wordsworth depicts, however, than the bleakly pessimistic mood which is the characteristic impression of a Leopardi lyric. Undoubtedly as a result of his tortured and pathetic childhood, joined to his darker cast of mind, Leopardi's work is almost anti-Wordsworthian in tone and depicts a welcome although a morbid contrast to other nineteenth century Romanticists who conventionally, almost mechanically, found in birds and flowers solace from social disappointments. The season of rebirth in Leopardi's "To Spring" is a thing of irony more than of joy, for the seasons to him merely remind one of the irrevocable coming of eternal winter. Though "fragrant spring breathes upon the frozen heart" now, soon the ice of death and disintegration will descend upon man, creating a stillness that no spring will ever touch. This same lyric contrasts the lost world of classical Greece, in which the world seemed to live in dynamic rapport with the divine in myth and legend, with the world of today, where "blind thunder" wanders over the valley and the rain falls on good and evil alike. The poet concludes by asking the spirit of nature to affirm that there is a divinity even though the deity

be but a "pitiless" spectator of meaningless comings and goings.

Undoubtedly Leopardi's remarkable but pathetic upbringing had much to do with the bitterness and sadness of his verse. The lonely, brilliant child of ambitious but stodgy parents, his intellect was recognized at an early age, but was then pressured by his family at a terrible rate. At fifteen he could both read and write Greek, but at eighteen he was broken in body and spirit, with eyes permanently damaged, spine prematurely crooked by extraordinary intellectual endeavor, and mind keenly suffering as well. Renouncing classical scholarship through necessity as well as conviction, Leopardi turned to creative literature almost as therapy. As D. H. Lawrence would affirm later about himself, he seemed to shed his illnesses of body and spirit in books.

Too much Leopardi at one sitting is as overwhelming to the reader as Leopardi's life must have been to the poet, but taken in selections his creations have a spirit that helps fill out the literature of European Romanticism with a sad beauty too rarely found in others of the period. In "Memories" the poet sits before the open window and looks at the stars, but such an experience intensifies bitterness more than it dissipates it. Memories flood of his lost boyhood when he had his health and hope, when the stars beckoned instead of glittering coldly and mindlessly. "My heart never told me," he thinks, how "my green age" would be wasted here in "the barbarous town, with a cheap boorish people." The bell that once gave meaning to the day now mocks it; now only death awaits to alleviate the barren dullness of days without hope or love. Then the poet speaks of the loss in death of Nerina, who is another image of the bright past now gone. Here, and again in "To Sylvia," Leopardi creates something akin to Wordsworth's "Lucy" poems, but with the ubiquitous Leopardi difference. For Wordsworth, the death of Lucy is somehow made acceptable through the natural world that took her back but is given life through her death. No such reconciliation is possible for Leopardi, who finds nothing beyond the bare bones of death. The death of Sylvia, like the passage of spring and youth, is another reminder of the deception nature practices on men:

Sylvia, do you still recall
  That time of your life here
  When beauty shone within
  Your laughing, glancing eyes,
  And you, thoughtful and merry, passed across
  The threshhold of your youth?

Love is another unfulfilled promise, a dream to die, and Sylvia's hand bares the only truth, "a bare sepulchre." These poems represent the Romantic lyric tradition in their use of sexual motifs, but they also undoubtedly reflect the frustration of Leopardi's few but intense and all unrequited love affairs, about which his close friend and biographer, Antonio Ranieri, tells. Physically blighted, keenly sensitive and shy, Leopardi found sexuality only another realm in which man could suffer the cruelties of indifferent fate and ineluctable mortality.

But from the bitter fruit came a wine of lyricism that has its own truth as well as its own beauty. In a prose dialogue between Tasso and his familiar spirit, Leopardi's version of Tasso says that man generally oscillates in a tedium between pleasure and pain, but pleasure is wholly a delusion about which he dreams but never achieves. So he lives largely in tedium, which is the true passion that fills his existence. Later this quality will be Baudelaire's *ennui* and to the modern, spiritual alienation, in which intelligent man suffers from the knowledge of that unbridgeable gap between hope and reality, and from the inevitable *angst* that such knowledge brings. What remedy can there be for tedium? So Tasso asks

his dream visitor. "Sleep, opium and pain," the spirit replies. And pain is the only relief, for through suffering man fully knows perhaps all the truth of life he is capable of possessing. This insight is a key to Leopardi's aesthetic, as well as being a virtual axiom for the existentialist writers of today, with whom Leopardi has strong though archaic affinity.

The famous lyric "The Broom, or the Flower of the Desert," written in Ranieri's house on the slope of Vesuvius a few months before Leopardi's death at thirty-nine, is one of his finest achievements in his paradoxical poetry of bitter lyricism. In this flower, which blooms brilliantly but briefly on the side of the volcano that destroyed it before and will destroy it again, Leopardi found the perfect image for men's brief but brilliant hopes that are closed at either end by darkness. In nineteenth century fashion, Leopardi uses this image to begin and end a long poem that comments upon both nature and society.

Here on the naked back
  Of the dread mountain,
  Vesuvius the destroyer,
  Which no other tree nor flower cheer,
  You scatter round your solitary clumps,
  O scented broom,
  Contented with a desert. I saw you too
  Add beauty with your stems to those lone tracts
  Encompassing that city
  Which was mistress once of all mankind,
  And with their grave and silent air they seem
  To act as witness and reminder of
  The empire that is gone.

The flower is expanded into a symbol of Pompeii. Then Leopardi, as bleak in vision as Hardy, notes how "loving Nature" cares here for her own and calls us to witness here "the magnificent progressive destiny of Humankind" as well. (Such sentiments as these account for Leopardi's appeal to James Thomson, who translated Leopardi into English and echoed him in the bitter philosophy contained in his "city of Dreadful Night," that overlong and turgid but occasionally powerful poem of the modern city of unalive men, surrounded by the wasteland that is our spiritual landscape.) Nature has no more care for man than for the ants, and she pours her lava, her dissolution, upon man and all his projects. In a similar mood Leopardi then discourses upon nineteenth century liberalism, prophesying, as Joseph Conrad did later, that the very men crying now for liberty will enslave others who oppose their version of it. Yet the pathetic but perennial broom blooms anyway, like man who, born to perish and reared in pain, ludicrously persists in saying, "I was born for joy."

Leopardi's most characteristic verse form is the *canzone libera,* a stanza largely of blank verse, but punctuated at select moments of intensity with short, rhymed intervals. Though he has a mastery of traditional imagery and diction, he strives for idiomatic simplicity. (His knowledge of classical literature gave him a command of ancient culture more profound than that of almost any other nineteenth century poet. At eighteen he wrote an imitation Greek ode to Neptune that was accepted as genuine by many scholars of his day.) His use of villagers, peasant settings, and rural scenes fulfill the aim he set forth in his famed essay on Mme. de Stael's Germanic Romanticism, when he called upon Italy's young poets to cultivate their own customs, their own scenes, their own folklore and leave those of the Germans to the North. This essay became a manifesto of nationalistic Italian literature, thus giving him a revered place in his country's nineteenth century radical spirit, like Byron's in England and Hugo's in France, despite the quite bleak character of Leopardi's beautiful but dark lyrics.

THE POETRY OF LEWIS

Type of work: Poetry
Author: Cecil Day Lewis (1904-1972)
Principal published works: Beechen Vigil and Other Poems, 1925; *Country Comet,* 1928;
   Transitional Poem, 1929; *From Feathers to Iron,* 1931; *The Magnetic Mountain,* 1933;
   A Time to Dance and Other Poems, 1935; *Overtures to Death,* 1938; *Poems in Wartime,*
   1940; *Word Over All,* 1943; *Short is the Time: Poems, 1936-1943,* 1943; *Poems, 1943-*
   1947, 1948; *An Italian Visit,* 1953; *Pegasus and Other Poems,* 1957

Cecil Day Lewis began writing poetry at Oxford along with his literary friends, W. H. Auden, Stephen Spender, and Louis MacNeice, but his early work shows little resemblance to that of his contemporaries. His first well-known work, *Transitional Poem,* was a long, Whitmanesque, searching work containing different styles and verse forms and filled with classical allusions. Although a few of its sections satirized contemporary life, it was generally diffuse and had little in common with the early sharp, ironic Auden or the early lyric MacNeice. It was followed by another long poem, *From Feathers to Iron.* More carefully controlled and more somber in tone, this work displayed a shrewd observation of contemporary English life. In it, Day Lewis criticized the flat, industrial suburb and contrasted the hardness of the iron life of most men in modern society. The poet also praised the natural process of birth, pitting the idea of creation and the child against the overwhelming industrialism of the age. He felt that there was, however, some limited amount of space left for the natural and spiritual. In this early poem several characteristics of Day Lewis' work are evident: his contemporary references and language and the loose, conversational quality of his style.

Day Lewis' poetry became more like that of his contemporaries, at least in theme, with his next long poem, *The Magnetic Mountain.* Here he attacks the complacent person who ignores social issues, the fool who does not see them, and the escapist who purposely avoids them.

The poem satirizes the old English, public-school tradition, the tradition which assumes that invariable guides for conduct exist, formulas for meeting every problem of society. Day Lewis pleads for all who would reform society, who would fashion a world based on the heart of man, to join him in his journey to the "Magnetic Mountain." The mountain symbolizes both the heart or faith of man and the enduring power or iron in his character, for iron is a magnetic and compelling substance. In his attack on the English colonizing and commercial past, Day Lewis calls for social action, for a "communal sense" in order that man may realize his full potentiality. His stinging reproach to the gray, gritty present and his great faith in the possibility of a new social order, as well as the qualities revealed in his earlier writing, are in evidence throughout this work. In this rhetorical declaration of faith, Day Lewis' writing is loose and allusive, with none of the hard, cryptic quality of Auden's work. Yet the looseness of Day Lewis' structure is frequently, as in the above passage, balanced by unexpected, musical alliteration.

Day Lewis' faith in the new social order began to wane in his next volume, *A Time to Dance and Other Poems,* a volume including a number of shorter lyrics. Although his allegiances were still just as strong to the new social order, he began to demonstrate an awareness of some of the difficulties of bringing about a reformation. He claimed, however, that he still wrote his poems in order to keep his faith and courage. The following volume, *Overtures to Death,* demonstrates an even keener realization that man was not likely to become perfect within a generation or so by joining in a communal assault on the "Magnetic Mountain." The verse in this book is crisper, less shrill, and less rhetorical, conveying a deeper insight into man and the issues that face him. Although Day Lewis still attacks the complacent and those who love tradition for the simple reason that it is tradition, he realizes that he, too, may be bound to some sterile tradition, some impossible notion of human conduct. He develops this theme in one of his best short poems, "Regency Houses." The vague influence of Yeats in this poem has given it a terseness and power not always present in Day Lewis' work. At the same time the introspective quality, the realization of his own limitations, has given the poem a depth not apparent in his earlier calls to social action.

Day Lewis, alert to the dangers of Nazism, had attacked the complacent people who refused to acknowledge that war was imminent. During the war, however, his poetry became less social, less political, more personal. He began to write autobiographical poems dealing with childhood memories and concerns. He also wrote a number of poems on the theme of love, presenting both its pleasures and its difficulties. The range of the subjects he treated widened greatly: the life of the simple countryman, the impact of the war, places, poems in praise of literary figures such as Thomas Hardy and Walter de la Mare, the pleasures of Christmas. His thoughtful and introspective side continued, but his subjects grew more personal, more concerned with direct experience, and less dominated by the intensity of a single vision for mankind's salvation. In this shift of interest to more personal and direct concerns, Day Lewis mirrored the changing trend of a whole generation of English writers and intellectuals. Day Lewis still used satire, as he does in his most recent volume, *Pegasus and Other Poems,* but it was, and

has continued to be, a far more gentle and understanding kind of satire.

In 1953, Day Lewis published *An Italian Visit,* a long versified account of a journey to Italy. This is a thoughtful, descriptive work, full of powerful and often startling images. The style is conversational, like the easy flow of imaginative language and rich contemplation from an urbane and cultured gentleman. It is perhaps this kind of loose, ruminative writing that best suits Day Lewis' talent, for he has never been, save in rare moments, a poet of great intensity or linguistic magic. The poem, in its descriptions of Rome, Florence, and numerous smaller towns, also displays a deep appreciation of both art and tradition. Day Lewis is, for the contemporary reader, far more convincing as the guardian of tradition and culture than he was as the voice crying out for a new order. His conversational ease, along with his skill in fashioning images, is evident in the following passage which can also serve as his final comment on his pseudoprophetic role in the 1930's:

We who 'flowered' in the Thirties
Were an odd lot; sceptical yet suscep-
tible,
Dour though enthusiastic, horizon-
addicts
And future-fans, terribly apt to ask
what
Our all-very-fine sensations were in aid
of.
We did not, you will remember, come
to coo.
Still, there is hope for us. Rome has
absorbed
Other barbarians: yes, and there's no-
body quite so
Sensuously rich and reckless as the re-
formed
Puritan . . .

Day Lewis has become the intelligent gentleman of letters, able, with both richness and humor, to see his past convictions in perspective. Never a poetic innovator, he has been overshadowed, in critical accounts of his generation, by his more brilliant contemporaries. But he has produced a great variety of thoughtful and introspective verse, and he has written with honesty and intelligence on a wide range of subjects. In his maturity he has found the kind of verse and the kind of subject, as well as the gentle and ruminative tone, that he is making definitely his. Poems like the *An Italian Visit* and "Moods of Love" in his most recent volume are admirably readable and demonstrate the poetic attractions of a witty, cultured gentleman reporting on his travels, his observations of people, his feelings about himself. Cecil Day Lewis, though not a great poet, is an honest and attractive one.

THE POETRY OF LINDSAY

Type of work: Poetry
Author: Vachel Lindsay (1879-1931)
Principal published works: General William Booth Enters into Heaven, 1913; *The Congo and Other Poems,* 1914; *The Chinese Nightingale and Other Poems,* 1917; *The Golden Whales of California and Other Rhymes in the American Language,* 1920; *Going-to-the-Sun,* 1923; *Going-to-the-Stars,* 1926; *The Candle in the Cabin,* 1926; *Johnny Appleseed and Other Poems,* 1928; *Every Soul Is a Circus,* 1929

No complete collection of Vachel Lindsay's poetry has ever been published, nor does it seem likely that this would be a profitable venture for publisher, reader, or scholar. The vogue for this poet died out even before his death; the excellent collections of selected poetry and anthologies contain all that is likely to survive; and a consensus among scholars has already been established—Lindsay was a vital minor poet whose interesting experiments and some fifty poems will be remembered.

Setting aside his earliest poems, including the famous "Rhymes to be Traded for Bread," and his late ones, excluding "Johnny Appleseed," the critical reader will find a corpus of poetry which, if no longer startling, is at least substantial. These first collections sometimes include sketches which do not illuminate and poems without substance; they were a part of the poet's years when he considered himself a traveling mystic, an artist-writer with a rather vague creed based loosely on Swedenborgian philosophy. His later years before his suicide were clouded over by a despondency which the poems reflect.

In January, 1913, *Poetry: A Magazine of Verse* published "General William Booth Enters into Heaven," published in book form later that year along with other poems by the same author. The immediate—and lasting—popularity of this poem is justified, perhaps more so than that of the familiarly anthologized "The Congo." With cues for instruments and singing, the writer's very real tribute to the religious leader is a studied cacophony which ends in deep reverence:

And when Booth halted by the curb for
    prayer
He saw his Master thro' the flag-filled
    air.
Christ came gently with a robe and
    crown
For Booth the soldier, while the throng
    knelt down.
He saw King Jesus. They were face to
    face,
And he knelt a-weeping in that holy
    place.
Are you washed in the blood of the
    Lamb?

Here is Lindsay's métier, the rhythmic portrayal of almost legendary persons: Lincoln, Bryan, Chapman, Altgeld, Sullivan, Jackson, and Alexander Campbell, the founder of his religious sect, among others. In these poems he created a new kind of poetic tribute, as unlike the usual versifying obituary as his own life was from those he celebrated.

Less successful, though even more popular on chautauqua and college platforms where he appeared for so many years in so many cities, are the "travel" poems, the sweeping Whitmanesque vistas of the Santa Fé Trail, the Congo, the Great Plains. Here, too, his poetry has its strongly personal and syncopated quality, a stress here and a manipulation there, which stamps it with a form no longer usable because, perhaps, he himself overused it. "The Congo" begins:

Fat black bucks in a wine-barrel room,
Barrel-house kings, with feet unstable,
Sagged and reeled and pounded on the
    table,
Pounded on the table,
Beat an empty barrel with the handle of
    a broom,

Hard as they were able,
Boom, boom, BOOM,
With a silk umbrella and the handle of
a broom,
Boomlay, boomlay, boomlay, BOOM.

This is the four-stress line, with a kind of added syncopation which one critic has called "star-spangled jazz." Poems of this type are most effective when read aloud in keeping with the instructions Lindsay supplied in a marginal gloss.

A third category, and in some ways the most successful because the poems seem so artless, is that of "children's" poetry—the kind which is enchanting to all, the large child reading and the small one listening. "The Chinese Nightingale," although sullied by adult overtones, is the best known of this group with its chiming, clanging pigeon-Chinese symbols:

He lit a joss stick long and black.
Then the proud gray joss in the corner
stirred;
On his wrist appeared a gray small bird,
And this was the song of the gray small
bird:
"Where is the princess, loved forever,
Who made Chang first of the kings of
men?"

A group of poems on all kinds of mice still delights youngsters when they are reprinted in children's anthologies. These little poems are more of a delight than those which Lindsay thought would charm children.

On the other hand, his exploitation of sounds always pleases, as in "The Kallyope Yell":

Music of the mob am I,
Circus day's tremendous cry:—
I am the Kallyope, Kallyope, Kallyope!
Hoot toot, hoot toot, hoot toot, hoot toot,
Willy willy willy wah HOO!
Sizz, fizz . . .

or the second part of "The Santa Fé Trail":

Listen to the iron-horns, ripping, rack-
ing.
Listen to the quack-horns, slack and
clacking.
Way down the road, trilling like a toad,
Here comes the *dice*-horn, here comes
the *vice*-horn,
Here comes the *snarl*-horn, *brawl*-horn,
lewd-horn,
Followed by the *prude*-horn, bleak and
squeaking:—
(Some of them from Kansas, some of
them from Kansas.)

The first echoes calliope dissonances, the latter, the klaxon racket.

From his last volume, *Every Soul Is a Circus*, comes what Lindsay thought was a tribute to P. T. Barnum, but which was really, as the opening lines reveal, an apology for his own works:

My brothers of the poet-trade,
Leave your ivory towers, and stand
On the porch, and watch this ardent
band
And praise, with me,
This Masquerade.
From a cloud by the dark Art Institute
That old Barnum comes,
Followed by serene Greek Gods,
And the lake-breeze hums.

The Art Institute is the place where Lindsay started his career; like Barnum, he ended in the tent. Both brought thrilling moments, Barnum his Lind, Lindsay his Salvation Army hero-leader. A note from the poet suggests this poem is to read "with bardic and troubadour chanting," and Lindsay's postlude might well grace his epitaph:

So, come, let us be bold with our songs,
brothers,
Come, let us be bold with our songs.

THE POETRY OF LOVELACE

Type of work: Poetry
Author: Richard Lovelace (1618-1658)
Principal published works: Lucasta, 1649; *Posthume Poems,* 1659

To most readers, Richard Lovelace is remembered for two lines each of two songs. He caught for all those spirits who have suffered in prison, who have thought or composed thoughts in gaols, the perfect expression of the free will in

Stone Walls doe not a Prison make,
    Nor I'ron bars a Cage;

and he expressed his own high standards as a gentleman, soldier, scholar, and poet in lines which he wrote when going off to war:

I could not love thee (Deare) so much,
Lov'd I not Honour more.

A Royalist by birth and politics, the poet lost a modest fortune upholding his own high standards: he suffered imprisonment twice, ironically, and his entire life he spent surrounded by war's tragedies. He lost his father and a brother in battle, and he and his remaining brothers fought valorously for England (he attained the rank of colonel). His poetry, of limited popularity, was virtuous and modest in extreme and, as critics hasten to point out, the most moral written by the Cavalier poets. His most famous series, *Lucasta* (from *lux casta,* light of virtue), is his testimonial.

No conclusive evidence has yet come to light concerning the Lucasta of Lovelace's first volume, though it is now certain that this idealized figure was not Lucy Sacheverell. The woman to whom he addressed most of his early poems may have been a Lucas, however; hence the play on words.

Lovelace wrote in the age of the "conceit," that witty and often barbed line popularized by John Donne, but he must always rank in second place in its use. His two famous songs, written also in an age of words set to music, surpass those of his betters, but on moral grounds: "To Althea, from Prison," demonstrates Lovelace's indomitable spirit and "To Lucasta, Going to the Warres," his incorruptible soul. Lovelace was an amateur poet, a man of action whose education made of him a man of parts; and he is often compared to Sir Philip Sidney, "A Scholar, Souldier, Lover, and a Saint," as one epitaph verse reads.

The diversified poetry within *Lucasta* indicates that Lovelace followed in that great tradition of the Renaissance gentleman. His varied activities and tastes led sometimes to the exercise of a talent thinly spread, to poor taste, but especially to haste—Lovelace's besetting sin. His first volume lacked care, proofreading (even at a time of variable spellings, indifferent typography, and fanciful punctuation), not to mention chronological arranging, collating of stanzas, and other matters so necessary to a really professional work. One wonders, then, why Lovelace was a favorite poet of an age when better poets went begging for readers. As a contemporary and professional said of him, "He writes very well for a gentleman."

Only twenty-seven copies of the 1649 *Lucasta,* available in the seventeenth century for a few pence, are now known to be extant. The portrait included makes one wonder at the extravagant praise of Lovelace's looks, but not of his poetry, which is courtly, exuberant, at times pleasingly fanciful, though often amateurish in tone and style. This slender book of some sixty poems is dedicated to Lady Anne Lovelace, wife of his cousin John, though not to be thought of as Lucasta. A group of commendatory poems follows the dedication, by his brothers Francis and Dudley, the latter, ten years later, the compiler of Lovelace's posthumous poems. The most interesting poem in this commendatory group is by the author's friend and fellow poet, Andrew Marvell, who suggests the verses will please the ladies more than the critics, those "Word-peckers, Paper-rats, Book-scorpions."

The poems proper begin with two songs, both dedicated to ideal or Platonic love and both related to going overseas and fighting. Of the sixty, about a third were set to music and may still be found in books of "Ayres." Most of the poems conform to the seventeenth-century pattern of odes written on memorable days or for sad occasions, pastorals, sonnets, satires, and elegies. An interesting example of the latter is one of the poet's earliest poems, written when he was twenty and addressed to Princess Katherine "borne, christened, buried in one day." The interesting contrasts of birth and death, swaddling and winding clothes, joy and sorrow, with the overtones of pomp and circumstance befitting her royal-innocent lineage make of this poem a study in contrasts.

In addition to these varied types of poems, Lovelace wrote at least one acted play, a comedy called "The Scholars," the prologue and epilogue appearing in his first collection. Another play, "The Soldier," was a tragedy never acted because of the closing of the theaters in 1642. During the period of the Protectorate songs by Lovelace were probably sung in the so-called masques, thinly disguised plays produced privately for an aristocratic audience.

Lovelace prepared his second book, *Posthume Poems,* before his death, though it remained for his brother to bring out the volume. It is dedicated to Sir John Lovelace, an indication this time of his patronage. The first poem, "To Lucasta: Her Reserved Looks," epitomizes the gay-sad theme so prevalent among the Cavaliers, even at death:

Lucasta, frown and let me die,
  But smile and see I live;
The sad indifference of your Eye
  Both kills, and doth reprieve.
You hide our fate within its screen,
  We feel our judgment ere we hear:
So in one Picture I have seen
  An Angel here, the Divel there.

The poems in this volume show a mature writer, even a practiced one, and the salutary effect of careful editing by Dudley Lovelace assisted by Eldred Revett, makes this edition a more appealing one for the modern reader. Although the volume does not contain as many songs, the same types of poems appear, forty-four in all, with a series of translations from Latin and French appended. There is also a group of nature verses on "The Ant," "The Grasshopper," "The Falcon," "The Spider," "The Snail," and others.

Thought by the critics to be devoid of playful talent, Lovelace disputes the charge effectively in the poem "A Black patch on Lucasta's Face," a sonnet in which a bee "Mistook her glorious Face for Paradise," and the plaster placed on the sting serves as "the sweet little Bees large Monument."

It may be significant that Lovelace's longest poems, in the first volume a pastoral titled "Amarantha" and in the second a satire, "On Sanazar's Being Honoured with Six Hundred Duckets by the Clarissimi of Venice," display the courtier as a gallant and then as a cynic. In the later poem Lovelace sees woman as something less than perfect, but so much gentler is this knight than the other Cavalier poets that he would almost fit Chaucer's famous description of knightly grace.

From the sentiments expressed in a group of elegies in which the poet's friends lament his death, the character of Lovelace was exemplary. Such expressions were a literary convention, of course, but so much of what is said rings true of his life that a backward glance reveals in epitome a man of his age. His brother, revealing something of a family talent, wrote the concluding lines to Richard Lovelace's literary epitaph, lines in which the tragedy of premature death—"Snatcht the bright Jewell from the Case"—is softened by bright memory:

And now, transform'd, he doth arise
A Constellation in the Skies,
Teaching the blinded World the way,

Through Night, to startle into Day:
And shipwrackt shades, with steady

hand
He steers unto th' Elizian Land.

THE POETRY OF MACHADO

Author: Antonio Machado (1875-1939)
Principal published works: Soledades, Galerías y otros poemas, 1907; *Campos de Castilla,* 1912; *Nuevas Canciones,* 1920; *Cancionero Apócrifo,* 1926

The spiritual crisis brought about in Spain by the loss of its last overseas possessions in Spanish America in 1898 found expression through the works of the Spanish writers of the *Generación del 98* (Generation of '98). The resulting attitude of pessimism, analysis of the past, desire for change, and consciousness of history is reflected in productions of Spanish men of letters of that time.

Spain had actually been suffering a prolonged frustration in its national goals. Most of the Spanish-American colonies, discovered, explored, conquered, acculturated, and exploited by the mother country, had obtained their independence during the first quarter of the nineeenth century. A relatively small portion of the old Hispanic empire remained. But when Cuba and Puerto Rico gained their freedom, Spain lost all its political links with the American continent. Four centuries of Spanish rule and influence in the Americas had ended.

A strong reaction appeared among the Spanish intelligentsia. Spain was forced to set new goals, close its eyes to tradition, and re-examine its political life. Philosophers, fiction writers, and essayists put together their efforts to arouse the soul of their country and make it open its eyes to reality and the future.

It could be thought that this generation had no place for poets, men of abstractions and often unconcerned with national affairs. However, writers not only of commitment but also of contemplation appeared. Antonio Machado, the best poet of the *Generación,* fully shared the intellectual and emotional attitude of his age. The development of his themes and his poetic perspective began in those critical years.

From his first poems Machado demonstrated the coordinates of his poetry. He will be in all his books the poet of time, of melancholy memories, of death, of concern for his country, a writer in vain pursuit of the divinity, singer of love in terms of metaphysical speculation.

Perhaps no other Spanish-speaking poet has written so much about the phenomenon of time. For him, poetry is the essential method by which man may communicate with his time. Poetry is a way of bridging time and obtaining permanent, intemporal results. In other words, poetry for him is the result of inner, personal experience, in contact with his world, expressed not only by way of ideas, but mainly by way of intuition, with the intention of giving to such experiences a universal value.

Few writers have felt the burden of time as Machado did. A philosopher and poet, he went deep into the analysis of its essence both as a metaphysical entity and as a reality affecting human life. He did not theorize about it; through poetry he tried to grasp its meaning and to present its pathetic impact upon man.

Among his preferred ways of meeting time and interpreting his own life, Machado finds in daydreams a fit instrument. In this respect he falls in line with Calderón de la Barca, poet and playwright of the Golden Age of Spain, who proclaimed in one of his dramas that "life is a dream." For Machado, poetry is also a daydream; life is a permanent attitude of watchful vision with open eyes. We can frequently discover in his poetry an ecstatic mood. Rather than recalling his memories, he used to dream of them. For him the true interior life was that of dreams and, conversely, these are the best way of knowing his inward being.

These dreams are not the substance of the subconsciousness nor are they expressed in a super-realistic manner. They are simply the manifestation of yesterday that presses upon the poet, causing him to live his life again in recollection. In this way they are made present and converted into poetic forms.

Time is the span between birth and death in man. For Machado, who was reared in an educational environment devoid of religious training, death is only a limit, a state of absolute finiteness, rather than the last act of human life or the beginning of a different one. Since nobody can boast of having experienced death, its apprehension is only an aprioristic idea, the object of belief, not of knowledge. At the same time, death is always possible. Because of this continuous imminence, Machado experiences the anguish of death but meets it with a stoic resignation. In his poetry there is neither the cry of rebelliousness nor belief in the immortality of the soul. Sometimes death appears as something connatural with the poet—a companion.

The presence of death is sometimes so sharp that Machado suddenly thinks that his end is imminent, but he is appeased by the hope of living more days until he may see the bright morning of death.

"Spain aches me," was the poignant cry of Miguel de Unamuno, one of the writers of the *Generation del 98*. It was an attitude shared by all his contemporaries. That generation of Spaniards, receptive and national-minded, took as their own the collective problems of their country. These problems were the consequence of many years without collective values and endeavors. Machado devoted his pen to a poetic dissection of his country. *Campos de Castilla (Lands of Castile)*, published in 1912, is his contribution to the most pungent question of his generation: the past and future of Spain.

A two-fold Spain appears in this book: the "official" and the "authentic" Spain. For Machado, they have been living divorced for many years. The "official" has created a Spain of tradition, laziness, individualism, and presumptions. The "authentic" is the Spain of the people, who dream and fight and think and live after their own ideals of honesty, hard work, and patriotism.

Castile is, for the writers of the *Generación*, the heart and symbol of Spain, because it has played a special role in Spanish life for many years. Machado chooses this region and tries to find in it both the constructive and destructive forces that have molded the Spanish soul. The landscape of his vision is chiefly in Soria, where he spent some decisive years of his life and where he met his wife, dead a few years later. He remembers his childhood in Seville, merry and colorful, in contrast to a less happy youth in the Castilian plateau.

Campos de Castilla abounds in strong, pessimistic poems, written mainly in the most traditional meters of Spanish poetry: the Alexandrinian and the octosyllabic. Machado speaks of poor people, ancient warriors, barren fields, familiar tragedies, and the painful remembrance of his dead wife.

In "The Land of Alvargonzález," the longest poem in the book, Machado depicts the tragedy of a rural family. The poet, in bitter, popular, and lyric *romanzas*, tells a story of envy and murder. The father is killed by his older sons; his farm, which they inherit, becomes arid; and when Miguel, the last born of the brothers, returns rich from the New World, he buys the land from his brothers. The land now flourishes, and his brothers, repentant of their sin, plunge into the Black Lagoon.

The Castilian landscape is frequently associated with his wife, Leonor, dead at the age of seventeen in Soria. This only true love was born, met the poet, married him, and died in the Castilian land. Machado imagines going with her, enjoying the scenery, though the consciousness of her death makes him melancholy.

Machado never gave profound expression of religious origin. His education, based on the principles of secularization of thought and the philosophy of positivism, was not concerned with the relationship between divinity and man. There is an agnostic attitude in most of his books. His interpellations to God are vague and made among dreams.

We find in Machado's poetry some preference toward the metaphysical treatment of love. For him, love begins as an abrupt increment of the vital energy, yet with nothing tangible that needs attention. It is like the explosion of spring, an attitude of being escorted by an impersonal and merely suggested feminine companion. A second step in love comes later when man encounters a real woman, but then, paradoxically, anguish and waste of life plague the lover because in spite of his efforts he cannot yield himself totally to the loved one. When she disappears from the immediate circle of the lover, oblivion comes. Finally, she becomes only a subject of reminiscence and poetry.

Time, the past, dreams, death, God, and love are the eternal questions of man. Poets and philosophers have tried to find some answer to them. Antonio Machado, poet and philosopher, made an attempt to find an explanation of himself and his world in a given time and space. He did not succeed, and he did not expect to, but he left the deep, beautiful, tentative testimony of a man who thinks that he is only a traveler in this world, condemned to the yoke of time and to the sole glimpse of life's mysteries.

THE POETRY OF MacLEISH

Author: Archibald MacLeish (1892-   )
Principal published works: Tower of Ivory, 1917; *The Happy Marriage,* 1924; *The Pot of Earth,* 1925; *Streets in the Moon,* 1926; *The Hamlet of A. MacLeish,* 1928; *New Found Land,* 1930; *Conquistador,* 1932; *Frescoes for Mr. Rockefeller's City,* 1933; *Public Speech,* 1936; *Land of the Free,* 1938; *America Was Promises,* 1939; *Actfive and Other Poems,* 1948; *Collected Poems, 1917-1952,* 1952; *Songs for Eve,* 1954

There is a wide range of achievement in the poetry of Archibald MacLeish, but there is nearly always high technical excellence and the student of technique will be greatly rewarded by discovering in MacLeish's work the subtlety of the rhyme and assonance, the complexity of the metrics, and the variety of his forms. Although many of MacLeish's shorter poems make pleasant reading, the longer poems are perhaps more interesting in that they reveal more fully the fabric of his thought. Among the shorter poems, one might consider "The Happy Marriage," "The Silent Slain," "The End of the World," "Selene Afterwards," "No Lamp Has Ever Shown Us Where To Look," "Hearts' and Flowers'," "Ars Poetica," "You, Andrew Marvell," "Land's End," "American Letter," "Empire Builders," "Invocation to the Social Muse," "Words in Time," "Thunderhead," "The Snowflake Which Is Now and Hence Forever," "Ship of Fools," and "Reasons for Music." One would do well to consider among the longer poems: "The Pot of Earth," "The Hamlet of A. MacLeish," "Einstein," "Conquistador," and "America Was Promises."

It is appropriate to consider MacLeish's poetry in relation to his successful public life, for he holds as one of his ideals that the world of thought should be related to the world of action. His theory is that the public world of our time needs the kinds of meanings that poetry alone can discover. MacLeish feels, moreover, that the thinking man should be actively involved in the political and social movements of his time. In the offices MacLeish has held, as well as in his speeches, one may see to what extent he was himself committed.

MacLeish does not exploit in his poetry, as might be expected, what must have been so close at hand for him, the language of social discourse. In fact, he never makes use of such language in the witty and ironic manner of T. S. Eliot, but speaks nearly always in a tone that might be described as "personal" or "characteristic," sinking at its worst to an undistinguished and lethargic solemnity, but attaining at its best a bardic, although individual, authority. He has sought rather to relate the "public world" to the "private world" in a more direct way. In *Conquistador* he has successfully produced an epic of the Americas and has tried the relations of private sensibility and history. In other instances, MacLeish seems to feel that the role of the thinker in history is to engage in summing up and pronouncement, as in "America Was Promises," in which sociology is grafted upon poetry in such a manner that neither survives.

MacLeish says in his *Poetry and Experience* that the deepest human need is to make life coherent and meaningful, and that poetry is one of the valid means—perhaps the most important—by which such sense and order may be achieved. The poet, he says, quoting the Chinese poet Lu Chi, is one who "traps Heaven and Earth in the cage of form." Poetry is a means of achieving meaning. He says in "Reasons for Music" (written for Wallace Stevens) that in this world there is no rest from the effort to impose order on confusion—order achieved in the still, adamant form of art. One may say of MacLeish in this respect that what should properly have been a hope, and possessed of an appropriate reticence, became a somewhat strident conviction. In his better poetry, in *The Pot of Earth* and *Conquistador,* for example, this predilection for form results in the achievement of an elevated and gracious order, but in his bad poetry the impulse degenerates into banality and truism. Often MacLeish's poetry does not assume, much less suggest, the variety of experience, and often he is even bold enough to violate, with his rigid schemata, the rightful multiplicity of the world.

On occasion MacLeish cannot resist the temptation to make a felicitous phrase, but on most occasions one senses in MacLeish a sincere love of felicity inasmuch as it is an expression of a certain way of achieving order and harmony in the world. But MacLeish does not seem to have examined this tendency of his mind—to alight upon felicity—critically and thoroughly, as have many of the other modern poets. One thinks certainly of T. S. Eliot, when he uses, so cleverly, so tragically, rhyme, rhythm, and high sentiment. To some modern critical minds MacLeish's felicity can only seem facile, for he lacks the modern tough-mindedness. He does not seem to have considered with adequate clairvoyance his altogether human, altogether admirable impulse toward what Wallace Stevens calls integrations of instinct. But it is probably more fitting to say that MacLeish attempts a felicity he does not always achieve rather than to say he voices a sublimity he does not really feel.

A cursory glance at MacLeish's poetry may lead the reader to accuse him of vague thinking. It is not that MacLeish is unaware of the important ideas of his time, but that perhaps he has not examined some of them critically, or has at least not considered with sufficient perspicacity the relationship of these ideas to his own mind.

At times MacLeish seems unaware of the tendency of his mind to reduce experience to formula. He praises in *Poetry and Experience* Keats's negative capability, the ability to live without certainty, in mystery and in doubt, and it is indeed unfortunate that MacLeish himself in his poetry was not always able to maintain this precarious and sacred balance.

In some of his long poems, as in "Einstein," *The Pot of Earth,* and *The Hamlet of A. MacLeish,* he does examine the relationship of the mind to the world, or more specifically to "nature," and one senses here that he is no longer the fabricator of the shorter poems where, with an aestheticism that yields only sterility, he plucks an image from the natural world, pastes it upon his thought, and finds that in the process the image has deprived the thought of its complexity, and the thought has deprived the image of its rich substantiality. He uses as the epigraph to *The Pot of Earth* a description, from Sir James G. Frazer's *The Golden Bough,* of the ancient ceremonies of Adonis, a god of vegetation, and he attempts in the poem to come to terms with nature in the fruitful and mysterious way of the ancients; yet he knows that this is not quite possible. He quotes, after the passage from Frazer, the lines from *Hamlet*: "For if the sun breed maggots in a dead dog, being a god-kissing carrion,—Have you a daughter? . . . Let her not walk i' the sun—" and one feels that MacLeish is suggesting here what might be called the modern "civilized" horror of nature's fecundity, promiscuity, ruthlessness, and even perhaps of her energy. Like Hamlet, MacLeish, in *The Hamlet of A. MacLeish* is bookish and introspective, skeptical that one may not find in nature, as one finds in words, a principle of malleable equivalence.

In "Einstein," MacLeish portrays a mind which can undo the manifestations of nature. Yet even so, nature still resists his attempts at penetration and turns him back to find answers within his own nature. Even though MacLeish in "Einstein" sets himself the difficult task of portraying the relationship of a mind of genius to the world, he does not succeed in doing more than expressing the obvious graciously, although he does create in "Einstein," as he does not in most of his other poems, an illusion of what might be called the living relationship of consciousness to the world.

One may look in vain in MacLeish's poetry for a tough and thought-provoking fabric of meanings, but find in its place the elegant compositions of a mind dominated by sensibility. MacLeish's best achievement is in the genre of lyrical poetry skillfully shaped as an expression of sensibility. It may be said that in some respects he stands to the Modernist movement in poetry as Verlaine stood to the Symbolists. At his best, MacLeish achieves an elegance which is vital and unschematic. There are long descriptive passages in many of his poems, in *Conquistador* and *The Pot of Earth,* for example, which seem intent upon proving nothing except that, as Ezra Pound said of the Imagists, "a hawk is a hawk." These are passages of refined and vigorous sensibility in which the infinite richness of experience is suggested rather than cast into the confinement of form. In like manner, MacLeish sometimes offers brief perceptions of a perfect gratuitousness, sometimes irrelevant to the meaning of the poem, but delightful and veracious in their own right. At his best the poet exhibits the expectation of an aristocratic sensibility: that experience will indeed yield up from its abundance certain felicities.

THE POETRY OF MacNEICE

Author: Louis MacNeice (1907-1963)
Principal published works: Blind Fireworks, 1929; *Poems,* 1935; *The Earth Compels,* 1938; *Autumn Journal,* 1939; *The Last Ditch,* 1940; *Plant and Phantom,* 1941; *Springboard: Poems 1940-1944,* 1944; *Holes in the Sky: Poems 1944-1947,* 1948; *Ten Burnt Offerings,* 1952; *Autumn Sequel: A Rhetorical Poem in XXVI Cantos,* 1954; *Visitations,* 1957; *Eighty-five Poems,* 1959; *Solstices,* 1961; *The Collected Poems of Louis MacNeice,* 1967

Louis MacNeice was associated in the 1930's with Stephen Spender and W. H. Auden and, like them, directed his poetry to recording, and lamenting, the contemporary, metropolitan scene and the breakdown of older values. MacNeice's poems, published steadily since 1929, in recent years become more and more preoccupied with the past, the poet's lost youth and, at times, his sense of having lost his freshness as a poet.

At his best, he succeeded in mingling the commonplace and even trivial with an ironically acute insight to produce a memorable portrait of the modern industrial society. The rather forlorn and wistful attempts of metropolitan man to achieve some satisfaction in a generally treadmill life were chronicled by MacNeice in tones of mild sympathy, more detachment and, sometimes, of condescension. The rhythms are very close to prose or speech, the rhyming is often deliberately banal in order to achieve a caustically comic effect, and, occasionally, doggerel is used to express something of the tired, cheapened quality of a wasteland society. One of his best poems is "Sunday Morning," in which his coupling of the once-valued expanding heart of man and the newly banal, vulgar substitution of working with his car on a Sunday morning illustrates a typical kind of rhetoric as well as MacNeice's sense of how the romantic ambitions of the previous, prewar generations have become cheapened and empty of anything but momentary and shallow diversion. Disillusionment is everywhere, but the poet maintains a detached, resigned pose most of the time. In the poem, the car is readied, and the weekenders speed to Hindhead, trying to recapture something

of the past and hold firmly to it in the flow of time measured by dull days and dragging weeks. Life thus becomes escape from boredom, meaninglessness, and a march of time which only destroys old dreams. There is no escape.

While, especially in his poems of the 1930's, MacNeice is often highly successful in expressing the sadness and wistful regret of modern men caught between two wars, his verse becomes increasingly tired itself, even boring, as the rhythms grow stale and prosaic or "talky"; the constant use of comic or merely doggerel rhyme and the undifferentiated tone of slightly supercilious disillusionment, constantly verging on the merely nostalgic, wear thin. The symbols of planned obsolescence and overproduction which in turn signify the hopeless and helpless vulgarity and sterility of "modern life" cease either to surprise or to shock when constantly juxtaposed with older and "higher" thoughts. The studied use of the banal ends in sinking the poetry beneath its own dead weight. In *Autumn Journal,* which is MacNeice's long counterpart of Auden's "September 1, 1939," the poet is not at his worst, but one can see the direction of his thought in his ironic criticism of the modern world.

MacNeice's ability to use dance-hall rhythms and clichés to good satiric purpose is prominent in his poem "Bagpipe Music." The cleverness of parody and the cliché, like the colloquial idiom, belong strictly to a time and place, and though MacNeice has recorded that time, often tellingly, he has lacked the larger gifts of either Spender or, especially of the protean, effervescent Auden which are necessary for a lasting poetry.

MacNeice constantly counterpoises the

older traditions and values with the present state of society. Playing off the old pastoral illusions, in "Nuts in May" he describes the breakdown of the traditional values.

MacNeice's early influence was Edith Sitwell, and then, like Auden, C. D Lewis and Spender, the war poetry of Sassoon and Owen. The political and moral chaos of the war and the decades following it, the manifestoes of Hulme, Pound, and Eliot for a "harder" and more "classical" poetry, the teeming and dingy metropolis, all lay behind the sort of poetry MacNeice and his friends wrote. It seemed as if all the world had turned a final corner away from the past, and the aestheticism of the 1890's the pastoral poetry of the Georgians, in fact, the whole Keatsian and Tennysonian tradition seemed no longer a possible idiom in which to express the "new world" of quiet terror, cataclysm, and tenements. Instead, the "new" verse, close to colloquial speech, used the clichés of the shopgirl, the banalities of the popular song, the cadences of jazz, and the dance hall. In such a world, the British Museum seemed an anomaly, where one discovered poor scholars, cranks, and hacks.

Another poem, similar to "The British Museum Reading Room," is entitled, simply, "Museums," and jokingly expresses MacNeice's conviction that the Past is now only the past, and the museum is where we go to find a tenuous kind of escape or refuge. MacNeice seldom "reaches" for a metaphor or a poetic effect. He uses materials ready at hand, even clichés, and often produces an adroit and truly poignant image of modern life. His tone, at best, is controlled, detached, yet sad and intelligent. He represented an awareness of self and of reality which is so scrupulous as almost to preclude poetry. He had little or none of Spender's romanticism. His materials sometimes failed him, and do so increasingly with the passage of time away from that period when both the poetry and the disillusionment at least had the grace of novelty.

THE POETRY OF MALLARMÉ

Type of work: Poetry
Author: Stéphane Mallarmé (1842-1898)
Principal published works: L'Après-midi d'un Faune, 1876 (*The Afternoon of a Faun*);
Poésies, 1887; *Vers et Prose,* 1893; *Poésies complètes,* 1899

Because of the highly individual qualities of his writing and in spite of his tremendous impact on modern poetry, Stéphane Mallarmé has never been a popular figure known to the general reader. It is difficult, however, to overestimate his importance as an innovator and as an influence on other poets.

Certainly the most striking characteristic of Mallarmé's poems is their obscurity. The reader meets in them a subjective formation of imagery and a warping of the normal patterns of syntax and grammar that has puzzled, at times even infuriated, students of French poetry for more than a century. This obscurity is no accident, and it plays an important part in the history of poetry. At the end of the Romantic period of French poetry (which paralleled that of English poetry), the figure of Charles Baudelaire loomed large, with his theory and practice of *correspondances* between things concrete and things human and emotional.

Of the followers of Baudelaire, Mallarmé assuredly holds first place as the leading exponent of the Symbolist school. It might be said that to understand Mallarmé, in itself a difficult task, is to understand Symbolism. Rimbaud and Verlaine are not so profound, although their personal lives reflected the rebellion that is often thought an important part of the movement. Mallarmé was a rebel only in his verse; outwardly he led a quiet, decorous life at home and in the classroom.

In a sense, Symbolism is to the regular run of poetry what Surrealism is to representational painting; and there seems little doubt that the early Impressionists in painting may well have had some of Mallarmé's theories in mind, even if only subconsciously. To Mallarmé, a symbol represented a feeling or sensation that cannot be logically explained or clearly expressed. Often, for him, the symbol was a very personal abstraction that remained unexplained even in the poem which it inspired.

This concept of the use of symbols was defended persistently by Mallarmé, who, like Baudelaire, was a *poète-critique.* Unfortunately, many of Mallarmé's critical dicta are as abstruse as his verse. Difficult as the reading of this verse is, however, the concept and the examples of it in the work are intriguing; and those who have been willing to put forth the great amount of effort needed usually declare themselves highly rewarded by their grasp of these poems. For the person who reads only English, or to whom French is a less familiar second language, the difficulty is compounded. Perhaps more so than for any other poet, the English-speaking reader is dependent upon the translator for his interpretation of one of Mallarmé's poems; such a reader will surely be perplexed to observe the important differences in translations of the same poem by different scholars.

In spite of these difficulties there is about Mallarmé's verses a strange, haunting beauty that has captured the fancy of many great minds, from Gide's to Joyce's and T. S. Eliot's. Eliot suggests an important fact that must be known in order to understand Mallarmé's poetry. The poems of Eliot are also difficult for the general reader to understand, but usually for a different reason from Mallarmé's obscurity. Whereas Eliot relies frequently on little-known allusions to convey his poetic meaning, Mallarmé used a very personal poetic diction and a chain of thought that puzzles the reader.

Like Browning, Mallarmé thought that poetry need not be simple and direct and that the reader should be willing to exert himself to discover the poet's meaning. For Mallarmé, however, the word "meaning" must be thought of in a very broad sense, for to say that his poems have "a meaning" may not be quite accurate. Often, all that Mallarmé wished to convey was a state of mind or an emotional mood, and certainly no poet ever worked harder at perfecting a poetic style designed for this purpose.

The basis of Mallarmé's poetic credo is fundamental, coming close to the essential nature of reality itself. To him the reality of an object was not in the object, or even in the poet's mind as he observes the object. True reality, he believed, lies in the poet's observation, his perception of the object; thus the poet must express the impression that he finds in a sort of reverie inspired by contemplation of the object within a twilight zone of awareness. Simply to describe the object is far from the poet's intention. Often the object will be transformed during a poem into one of its qualities, that one which strikes the poet as the true reality. In a well-known short poem, "Brise Marine" ("Sea Breeze"), the sheet of blank paper under the lamp has whiteness as its salient quality, a whiteness that protects the paper and which symbolizes the poetic sterility of the poet.

This obsession with sterility—and Mallarmé's poetic thinking was virtually a series of obsessions—which possessed the poet for a long time in his youth, represents another part of his basic outlook. The poet must find first of all the spirit of nothingness ("le Néant") that pervades and underlies the visible universe. Then the poet must re-create the universe from his own mind. In this framework of thought, Mallarmé concentrated on the movement of his mind, not on the data it possessed.

With such a theory of poetry in his mind, it was easy for the poet to use the "black rock" in the opening line of "Tombeau" ("Tomb"), a very difficult poem written at the grave of Verlaine, to symbolize a black cloud, and the cloud to represent the cloud of somber religious ideas and the notions of sin which shade the earth. This symbolism appears to the penetrating reader, however, only after long consideration of the opening stanza of the poem.

As Mallarmé lost his fear of poetic sterility and began to achieve in his mind the grasp of the spiritual nothingness that was to him a prerequisite to worthy creativity, his verse became more and more obscure, so that his later work remains a mystery to almost all readers, even to some of the most diligent poets and scholars. Throughout his work, however, run more or less regular currents of thought, or obsessions. His preoccupation with absence, silence, and death is part of his central poetic philosophy, as his interest in music reflects his conviction that music and poetry are much akin in their expression of truth. *L'Après-midi d'un Faune* demonstrates and expresses this conviction; the poem, appropriately, was the inspiration for Debussy's famous tone poem.

Side by side in Mallarmé's work the reader finds two other, very dissimilar "obsessions": religious belief—essentially a tragic subject for Mallarmé, as in "Toast Funèbre" ("A Funeral Toast")—and an erotic preoccupation with nudity which is found in *L'Après-midi d'un Faune* and in many other poems.

Mallarmé's later poems evidence not only the profound convolutions of his very personal poetic thinking but also some experimentation with the form of the poem on the printed page. One of his last works, "Un Coup de Dés Jamais N'Abolira Le Hasard" ("A Throw of the Dice Will Never Abolish Chance"), will remind an American reader of the interesting arrangements of the poems of E. E. Cummings. In this poem as in his other work, Mallarmé had the same overall purpose: to express, not clearly but none the less accurately, an impression of reality.

It may be said in Mallarmé's favor that he was, in his way, one of the most sincere of all poets. He was, in fact, so critical of his work and so demanding in his standards that his total poetic output can be contained in one regular-sized volume. Further, Mallarmé's verses have a fluidity about them that the reader at first senses only vaguely. As the poet was preoccupied with the movement of his mind, so the lines of his poems achieve a kind of movement: words flow into words; meanings blend and change; images fade and reappear with new evocations of significance.

Although the Symbolist movement as such can be said to have died with an immediate follower of Mallarmé, Paul Valéry, its influence, particularly in the English-speaking world, is still strong today. The modern poet, trying to impose the discipline of order on his fragmented world, works partly in the shadow of this French writer wholeheartedly devoted to a poetic ideal.

THE POETRY OF MARIANNE MOORE

Author: Marianne Moore (1887- 1972)
Principal published works: Poems, 1921; *Observations,* 1924; *Selected Poems,* 1935; *The Pangolin and Other Verse,* 1936; *What Are Years,* 1941; *Nevertheless,* 1944; *Collected Poems,* 1951; *The Fables of La Fontaine,* 1954; *Predilections,* 1955; *Like a Bulwark,* 1956; *O to Be a Dragon,* 1959; *The Complete Poems of Marianne Moore,* 1967

Marianne Moore, probably the most individualistic American poet writing today, has been "modern" ever since she was first published in 1921. Although she has influenced scores of writers, her poetry is inimitable and unparaphrasable, with an excellence still distinctly her own. She is a rare combination of "poet's poet" and advice-giving moralist. As a "modern" poet in New York in the 1920's, many readers found her poetry "esoteric": it was much admired by the select group of modern poets headquartering there, but almost unintelligible to most readers, and certainly did not seem great because most of her topics appeared inconsequential. Her modernism, contrary to writers influenced by T. S. Eliot during the same period, led her away from philosophy; she was never disenchanted by the world around her.

On the contrary, the enchantment she finds is everywhere, even in "business documents and school books." Her fantastic footnotes are from encyclopedias, newspapers, *National Geographic,* documentary films, Tolstoy's diary—everywhere. She seeks to show reality, the genuine.

Miss Moore's favorite "inconsequential topic" is animals. The descriptions of her often exotic menagerie—"The Pangolin," "The Jerboa," "The Plumet Basilisk," "The Frigate Pelican," and monkeys, snakes, mongooses, a buffalo, fish, elephants, a snail—illustrate above all her uncanny accuracy as an observer. The smallest details are included to characterize her animals. In "The Pangolin" her description could be a stage director's explanation of reasons behind actions so that his cast will make their stage movements believable. One could walk like a Pangolin after hearing Miss Moore's instructions.

There are as many examples of minute observation in her poems as there are lines. Perhaps Miss Moore's observations are somewhat difficult to follow; after all, most readers' minds are not as enchanted as hers. The difficulty results, not from inaccuracy, but from her ability to compress so much description into so few unemphasized words. She is, in a way, trying to train her readers to be observers too.

As it often does, the title "The Fish" serves also as the first line. The size of the sea life diminishes as the poem progresses; both order and structure are carefully planned. Like a scientist, Miss Moore works from specifics to generalizations in all of her poems ("The illustration/is nothing to you without the application"). Her animal poems, more specifically, are like the works of a naturalist interested in animals as animals, not as symbols of people. Nevertheless, Miss Moore is a moralist. Her animal poems, which show what she admires in animals, illustrate what she wants to admire in humans. In fact, most of her animal poems fit into a broader category often termed "essays in verse." She defends the cat, "Peter," for example, by reminding us to be true to our own natures.

As animals are imperfect, so are people. Miss Moore admires honestly imperfect efforts because they demand fortitude; "Nevertheless" points out that the most beautiful design comes from "a struggle" in the strawberry plant, and that even the strongest plants must endure hardships. In fact, that is why they are the strongest.

She sees beauty and bravery in the simplest things, and in "The Face" she identifies the things that help define her aims as a poet: order, ardor, simplicity, inquiry.

Many of Miss Moore's essays in verse are about the poet and the art of poetry. Her most famous, and her most overt statement about content, is found in the earlier, fuller version "Poetry." Miss Moore's poems also discuss style. Her own emphasis on compactness is explained in "To a Snail." In "The Labors of Hercules" she speaks to critics of content and style. It is her straightforwardness "like electricity" which controls her metrical individuality.

The strikingly individualistic form of Miss Moore's verse is neither free verse nor accented rhythms. Her model is French: words are neither accented nor emphasized; neither do they metrically rhyme. Instead, the pattern of syllables per line in each stanza is repeated in the next stanza. This unusual quality and brilliance contribute to the total effect of the previously cited poems.

The conversational effect of unaccented syllabication is consistent with Miss Moore's advice in "Silence," in which she declares that the deepest emotions are always revealed in silence and restraint. The reason for the restraint is given in "The Student," who sometimes appears untouched, not because he is lacking in feeling but because he feels too intensely. The formality of Miss Moore's rigid, yet perfectly controlled, mechanics is indeed formidable until the magic of her tone, some implication of the heart, rescues us. Miss Moore never separates intelligence from emotion and sensitivity.

It is her love in her observations that makes her poems which are so carefully constructed and controlled, so modern and experimental, also so individualistic. While critics and poets are won by her mechanical perfections, by her perceptive wit and intelligence, the public appreciates poetry which dismisses the trivial and talks about important things like real animals, birds, snakes, and toads. Her ability to delight, to record with sensitive perception and appreciation the things of this world, and to convince us of its reality provide the reasons for Miss Moore's popularity and literary reputation among both scholars and general readers. It is just these qualities which make her an individualistic and enchanting part of the American literary tradition.

THE POETRY OF MAROT

Author: Clément Marot (1496-1544)
Principal published works: L'Adolescence clémentine, 1532; *La Suite de l'Adolescence clémentine*, 1533-1534; *Le Premier livre de la Métamorphose d'Ovide*, 1534; *Oeuvres*, 1538 (one edition printed by Dolet, one by Gryphius)

Superficially, unjustly criticized by Du Bellay as being nothing but rhymed prose, the poetry of Clément Marot, by its conscious innovations clearly anticipated and facilitated the work of the *Pléiade* poets in the renewal of French poetry. By reason of its naturalness and freedom, the best part of Marot's work has indeed aged less than the poetry of his illustrious successor, Pierre de Ronsard. Marot's witty, elliptical manner, imitated in epigrams and narrative poetry, appears in the work of no less figures than La Fontaine in the seventeenth century, Voltaire in the eighteenth, while through his sense of fantasy, Marot has been linked with the modern French "chansonniers."

A page to François I's secretary of finance in 1515, Marot, under the tutelage of his poet father, daily practiced the techniques of the largely formalistic Rhétoriqueur poetry. His verses between 1515 and 1526 show the influence of this school of the expiring Middle Ages. Yet there are exceptions.

The "Temple de Cupido" by its subject and by its allegorical form is related to the part-lyrical, part-didactic poetry of the Middle Ages. Marot follows the Rhétoriqueurs here, yet he manages to avoid their excesses, as had Jean Lemaire de Belges, whom he sought to emulate. At the other end of this period is the satirical poem "L'Enfer." Having been imprisoned on the heretical charge of eating "lard en carême" (meat during Lent), Marot here attacks the magistrates and their "justice." In this, his first major poem, Marot begins to free himself from Rhétoriqueur traditions. Allegory is presented through the simple procedure of comparing the Châtelet prison to Hades, its officials to a Rhadamanthus, a Cerberus and so on; introducing his victims

and satirizing them without benefit of the familiar medieval dream sequence, Marot makes a weapon of allegory in which fantasy and reality mixed produce comic and satiric effects.

Youthful works composed mainly between these two longer poems include the Rondeaux, Ballades, Chants royaux, Chansons (a variety of genres set to music). Marot succeeded in giving literary respectability to these latter poems without losing their simple, popular character. The Ballades, personal, political, satirical, show characteristics of Marot's mature manner: the expressive refrain, delicate development of an emotion; wit, caustic gibes, as in the "Chant de Mai," "Ballade à la Duchesse d'Alençon," and "De Frère Lubin." Longfellow translated the last as "Friar Lubin":

> To gallop off to town post-haste,
> So oft, the times I cannot tell;
> To do vile deed, nor feel disgraced,—
> Friar Lubin will do it well.
> But a sober life to lead,
> To honor virtue, and pursue it,
> That's a pious, Christian deed,—
> Friar Lubin cannot do it.
>
> To mingle, with a knowing smile,
> The goods of others with his own,
> And leave you without cross or pile,
> Friar Lubin stands alone.
> To say 'tis yours is all in vain,
> If once he lays his finger to it;
> For as to giving back again,
> Friar Lubin cannot do it.
>
> With flattering words and gentle tone,
> To woo and win some guileless maid,
> Cunning pander need you none,—
> Friar Lubin knows the trade.
> Loud preacheth he sobriety,
> But as for water, doth eschew it;
> Your dog may drink it,—but not he;
> Friar Lubin cannot do it.

Leigh Hunt was another of Marot's

translators. "Madame D'Albert's Laugh" is as follows:

Yes! that fair neck, too beautiful by half,
Those eyes, that voice, that bloom, all do her honor;
Yet, after all, that little giddy laugh
Is what, in my mind, sits the best upon her.

Good God! 'twould make the very streets and ways,
Through which she passes, burst into a pleasure!
Did melancholy come to mar my days
And kill me in the lap of too much leisure,
No spell were wanting, from the dead to raise me,
But only that sweet laugh wherewith she slays me.

The Rondeaux, more personal, express fleeting moments of love, joy, anger, irony ("De sa grande amie," "De l'amour du siècle antique"). The Chants royaux, a kind of double ballade, deal with *topoi* such as the Virginity of Mary, the pleasures and miseries of love.

It was through satire that Marot most quickly and clearly discarded Rhétoriqueur techniques and found his personal manner after 1527, though he continued to compose some official poetry in the old manner. The Coqs-à-l'âne, a genre created by Marot in or about 1531, contain his most personal thoughts, are his preferred satirical medium in attacks against the Church, priests, and his personal enemies. Exuberant fantasy beneath a consciously obscure, incoherent form characterize the coq-à-l'âne, the genre being related, Professor C. A. Mayer believes, to the medieval, didactic "sottie." The old expression "sauter du coq à l'âne" (literally to "jump from Rooster to Ass"), meaning to talk incoherently, suggests the title of this genre. Despite his light "poésie de circonstance," official, command performances (instant poetry?), Marot's work is fundamentally satiric; in contemporary eyes he was a bold fighter attacking the abuses of

his time, sharing that revolutionary Renaissance spirit which found expression in Erasmus or Rabelais. Marot has been linked with medieval tradition through his irreverent "esprit gaulois," yet this connection is somewhat tenuous, to be seen in pieces of lesser importance, the fixed-form ballades and rondeaux.

In large measure, to Marot belongs the honor of breaking with the Rhétoriqueur tradition, of beginning a renewal of French poetry. If one thinks of the *Pléiade*'s work in terms of translation, imitation, emulation of the Greek and Latin poets, Marot has his place here too, before them. In his formally serious lyric poetry he best practices the imitation and contamination of classical models recommended by Du Bellay. This would include the *Epithalames*, the *Eglogues*, the *Elégies* (the least successful), and the *Cantiques*. Professor C. A. Mayer has pointed out how Marot's hesitation in classifying and defining such forms as these show his preoccupation with finding, not always successfully, a vehicle for grave and official lyricism, with reorienting French poetry by re-creating classical forms ten years before Ronsard's *Odes*. (See the *Cantique* "Le Dieu Gard de Marot à la Cour de France"; the *Eglogue* "L'Avant-Naissance du troisième enfant de Madame la Duchesse de Ferrare," with its praise of Renaissance values and confidence in Man; the *Eglogue* "De Marot au Rou, sous les noms de Pan et Robin.")

During the middle and late 1530's the *topoi* of predecessors are thus replaced by intelligent imitation and emulation: the Horatian metaphor of the boatman describing Marot's flight into exile (*Epître* "Au Rou du temps de son exile à Ferrare"); the theme of Ulysses (borrowed from Ovid) anticipating the poetry of nostalgia of Du Bellay (*Epître* "Au tresvertueux prince, François, Dauphin de France"). There is the comment on the poet's function (*Epître* "Au Dauphin") where, anticipating the doctrine of the *Pléiade*, Marot promises the King and the Dauphin immortality through his verses. His concern with the judgment of posterity appears in lines like: "Maint vivront peu, moi éternellement." He is read universally; people say "C'est Clément." This pride of being what he is is surely no less than that of Ronsard himself.

Marot owes his transformation to the Courts of François I and Marguerite d'Angoulême, Italianate and humanizing. In exile at Ferrare, he was influenced by neo-Petrarchan poetry and sentiments, wrote the first sonnet in French, launched the fashion of the *Blasons du corps féminin,* and began putting the Psalms into verse. Here he wrote some of his best *Epîtres,* unexcelled vehicle of his genius. Difficult to define by reason of their variety of tone and subject, the *Epîtres,* letters in verse, free in form, personal, contain Marot's sharpest wit and satire, his bitterest reflections, highest lyricism. (See *Epîtres* mentioned above, also "Au Roi pour avoir été dérobé.")

One aspect of Marot's art, defined by Boileau as "élégant badinage," consists of self-mockery, obvious affirmation, specious denial, jesting (sometimes tense with emotion) through feigned naïveté and reticence. The other principal aspect, Marot's narrative style, is characterized by vividness and picturesqueness deriving from concrete imagery, an elliptical turn of phrase. Fantasy, mixed with reality, results in a satiric weapon of considerable force (light-hearted, sly in "Au Roi pour avoir été dérobé"; direct, indignant in the "Epître de Frippelippes"). As with fantasy, the incoherence of the coqs-à-l'âne is not gratuitous, but directed by satiric intent, which gives a unity to apparently unconnected allusions, rapidly passed in review, as in the second *Coq-à-l'âne.*

Reflected in important parts of his work, Marot's religious faith requires some comment. Introduced to the ideas of the early Reformation at Marguerite's court, he would seem to have adopted the lessons of Evangelism in spirit if not in precept. He went into exile twice, in 1534 and again in 1542, because of his reputed Lutheranism. In 1534 he had written: ". . . Point ne suis Lutériste/ Ne zwinglien, encore moins Papiste." This was before the *Affaire des Placards.* In 1538 (a less relaxed moment) when putting together his edition of the *Oeuvres,* Marot had emended the line: "Ne Zwinglien, et moins Anabaptiste." His protestations to the king, while in exile in 1535 were moving oratory, but ambiguous. Was Marot fickle? Or a coward? It seems likely that his position was in fact dictated more by an independent spirit, rebelling against the stupidity of the Sorbonne, the persecutions of the Papacy, than by any deep religious conviction. He did not remain long with Calvin either, though perhaps he ran out of money and work.

The traditional portrait of Marot as light-hearted, unstable, cowardly seems false. He was impulsive, compromising himself on occasion; independent in spirit, unable to keep his sharp tongue in cheek; obliged by circumstance to flatter; no martyr, but no coward either. In his own age, with Montaigne, he protested against torture in "L'Enfer," read the poem to François himself. Above all, he should be remembered as one of the most gifted and delightful poets of the sixteenth century.

THE POETRY OF MARVELL

Type of work: Poetry
Author: Andrew Marvell (1621-1678)
Principal published works: Miscellaneous Poems, 1681; *Poems on Affairs of State,* 1689;
An Horatian Ode upon Cromwell's Return from Ireland, 1776

Andrew Marvell, influenced by the work of Ben Jonson and John Donne, was the last major poet with their qualities and habits of mind. All his great poems are metaphysical; that is, they present feeling intellectually and synthesize thought and passion. Marvell is always aware of the multiplicity and the unity of the universe and the tension he maintains between them constitutes the peculiar poise and balance of his verse. This metaphysical reconciliation of seeming opposites appears in the imagery of the poems, which with characteristic hyberbole combine many areas of ideas and experience.

"An Horatian Ode upon Cromwell's Return from Ireland," generally acknowledged to be the finest poem of its kind in the language, exemplifies both his political feeling and the balance of thought in his verse. It is probably the last English poem in which the divine right of kings and a totally different type of rule could be presented simultaneously. Marvell celebrates Cromwell's phenomenal rise to power "from his private gardens" to

> . . . cast the Kingdoms old
> Into another mould.

The king's weakness rendered him helpless against the strength of Cromwell, and Marvell records the nobility of Charles I, who "adorned" the "tragic Scaffold." The transition from the account of the king's death to the time of Cromwell's rule are terse and effective:

> This was that memorable hour,
> Which first assured the forc'd Power.

Although he praises the efficiency and energy of Cromwell and acknowledges that he gave the government of the country to Parliament, Marvell sees also the necessity to continue fighting (after Ireland, Scotland remains to be subdued), and he concludes with a muted warning:

> The same Arts that did gain
> A Pow'r, must it maintain.

The equipoise of the "Ode" is maintained through its combination of praise, reticence, and admonition: the recognition of the justice of Cromwell and of the tradition of kingship. Desire for the good of his country outweighs the poet's feelings about specific acts. He both disliked the execution of the king and declared that Cromwell's ability would be beneficial to England. This sustained tension between forces gives the "Ode" its power.

Marvell's reputation rests on a very few poems. Some of the loveliest of these are the poems in which he employs nature images. One of his outstanding characteristics is his use of a simple theme to develop a deeply serious idea. Wit and brilliant imagery enhance the seriousness of his thought, so that an apparently slight subject will thus carry religious and philosophic implications and express the complex sensibility which is so much a part of the metaphysical poetic tradition. In "The Bermudas," Marvell celebrates the joyous exile of a group of nonconformists who left England in the days of Anglican Bishop Laud. Those islands, "far kinder than our own," sheltered and welcomed them and they were able freely to practice their religion. The poem glows with joy and pleasure at God's grace manifested in the tropical luxuriance of the exiles' environment:

> He hangs in shades the Orange bright,
> Like golden Lamps in a green Night.

These images parallel their spiritual freedom.

Religious significance is implicit in "The Nymph Complaining for the Death of her Faun." The huntsmen cannot cleanse themselves of guilt, even though the nymph forgives them; the faun's whiteness and purity are matchless. The tone of gentle grief is perfectly maintained, however, and the precision of the images exactly conveys heartfelt emotion:

So weeps the wounded Balsome: so
The holy Frankincense doth flow.
The brotherless Heliades
Melt in such Amber Tears as these.

The most complex of the poems that draw their imagery from nature is "The Garden." Here Marvell's wit and resilience of mind are almost dazzlingly apparent. Coleridge has described the poetic imagination as a "more than usual state of emotion with a more than usual order." This statement could well describe the impact of "The Garden." The pleasure of recognition symbolized by "the palm, the oak bays," with reference to the slight shade these individual leaves cast, is contrasted with the shade given by flowers and trees. Quiet and innocence are not to be found among men:

Society is all but rude
To this delicious solitude.

No lovely woman is "As am'rous as this lovely green." The tree on which a mistress' name is carved is far more beautiful than she. The hyperbole of these assertions contains its own irony; the passionate insistence with which they are made obliquely denies some of their validity. The fourth stanza describes classical lovers who confirm the thesis that the garden contains all delights:

Apollo hunted Daphne so
Only that she might Laurel grow.

In the sensual delights of the garden, sexual pleasure is no longer sublimated but is provided by the fruit itself:

The nectarine, and curious Peach,
Into my hands themselves do reach.

Along with this sexual identification, the image of Eden and the fall of man is present in the image of "ripe *apples*" and the line, "*Insnar'd* with flowers, I fall on grass."

The sixth verse contains the climax of the poem. Here the tension and poise are most marked. The sensual pleasure has led to intellectual joy, and "the Mind, from pleasure less./Withdraws into its happiness." In the mind are images of all material things and from these it creates transcendent worlds of its own until the quintessence of nature is perceived:

Annihilating all that's made
To a green Thought in a green Shade.

The remaining three stanzas are more relaxed, yet they carry the weight of, and are reinforced by, the previous argument. The poet's soul glides into the trees where "like a Bird, it sits and sings." It will stay there until it is ready to ascend. Meanwhile, it "Waves in its Plumes the various Light." Eden, the poet says, was like this, but the joy of solitude was "beyond a Mortal's share."

Two paradises t'were in one
To dwell in Paradise alone.

The last stanza returns to a man-made garden, where a sundial of herbs and flowers measures the "sweet and wholesome houres." The "skilled Gard'ner" is, of course, God as well as a human craftsman.

The levels of thought and feeling in this complex poem are so carefully wrought together that they could not exist alone. The ideas complement, balance, and reveal one another. The withdrawal of the mind to contemplation of paradise and its wry conclusion that such solitude is impossible are inextricable if their full force is to be appreciated. From the original conceit that all ambition can be satisfied by the delights of a garden, the themes are, through the allusive imagery, totally interdependent.

Marvell's two great love poems, "The Definition of Love" and "To his Coy Mistress," are passionate and urbane, intense and witty, violent and civilized. The reconciliation of opposites is the theme of the definition: it is the metaphysical proposition that in perfect love separation is essential. The validity of this proposition relies on the jealousy of fate. The poet's love was "begotten by despair/Upon impossibility." The decrees of Fate

Us as the distant Poles have plac'd,
(Though love's whole world on us doth wheel)
Not by themselves to be embraced.

The conceit, that heaven would have to fall

And, us to join, the world should all
Be cramped into a Planisphere

before the lovers could be together, emphasizes the inevitability of separation:

Therefore the love which doth us bind,
But fate so enviously debars,
Is the conjunction of the mind,
And opposition of the stars.

The punning conceit in these lines exemplifies the wit and logic of Marvell's verse.

The crowd of images, change of mood, and development of emotional tension combined with a subtle variation of rhythm and pace render "To His Coy Mistress" Marvell's greatest poetical achievement. His theme is the traditional one of "Gather Ye Rosebuds." The opening theme is that if there were time enough the lover would woo endlessly:

My vegetable love should grow
Vaster than Empires and more slow.

An urbane note is sounded in the lines:

For, lady, you deserve this state,
Nor would I love at lower rate.

Then comes the surprising reversal:

But at my back I always hear
Times wingéd chariot hurrying near,
And yonder all before us lye,
Deserts of vast eternity.

The lines ring with passionate desperation and the awful vision of the unknown. The next image is one of destruction in the grave, where the lady's beauty shall no longer exist and honor and lust alike will turn to dust and ashes. From this vision of death the poet turns to an evocation of the lady's present beauty. He adapts the theory that souls shine through the flesh of people of exceptional purity to a reason for consummating their love:

And while thy willing Soul transpires
At every pore with instant fires,
Now let us sport us while we may.

The ardor of the saint has become the heat of physical passion. The conceit of conquering time is developed in images of strength—they will "devour"—time, and will combine their powers "into one Ball" to force their pleasures "Through the iron gates of life":

Thus, though we cannot make our sun
Stand still, yet we will make him run.

The power of this love is conveyed in the witty and determined assault on unconquerable time.

These poems, with the addition of the "Dialogue between The Resolved Soul and Created Pleasure" and "Clorinda and Damon," are those on which Marvell's reputation depends. His poetic ability was seemingly lost after the Restoration, and he wrote, in verse, only political satires. The flowering of his sensibility prior to this period is an outstanding example of that fusion of wit, passion, and intellect which had its roots in Latin culture and its last complete expression in the poetry of Andrew Marvell.

THE POETRY OF MAYAKOVSKY

Author: Vladimir Mayakovsky (1893-1930)
First published: Vladimir Mayakovsky: A Tragedy, 1913; *The Cloud in Trousers,* 1915;
The Backbone Flute, 1915; *War and Peace,* 1916; *Man,* 1917; *Mystery Bouffe,* 1918;
150,000,000, 1920; *Vladimir Ilyich Lenin,* 1924; *My Discovery of America,* 1925-1926;
At The Top of My Voice, 1930

Futurism was founded in 1910 by Viktor (Velemir) Khlebnikov, who was primarily interested in etymology. Under Khlebnikov's leadership, the Futurists created a "trans-verse" language, one which separated words from their meanings and made their sound value all-important. The only kind of meaning a trans-verse poem might have would be a certain suggestive and admittedly very elusive quality. But perhaps more than an experiment with language, Futurism was the natural revolt from Symbolism.

The Symbolist movement had been strong from 1894 to 1910, during which time such poets as Bely and Blok had expounded a personal retreat from reality. They spoke of a rather closed mysticism and its aestheticist cult of pure beauty which had to be preceded by separation from, and unconcern for, all the events of daily life. The Futurists scorned the Symbolist ideals and followed the realities of modern life. But they went much further than simply presenting a new alternative to the Symbolist interpretation of life. Their aim was to shock the bourgeois at any cost. The Futurist Manifesto of 1912, signed by Khlebnikov, Kruchonykh, Mayakovsky, and Burlyuk, was entitled "A Slap in the Face of Public Taste." It called the entire cultural tradition of the past stifling and insufferable. Pushkin, Dostoevski, and Tolstoy were to be thrown aside by the modern trends. The manifesto also called for hatred of the previously used language of literature and for an enrichment of the vocabulary by words arbitrarily chosen.

Although Russian Futurism was an offshoot of Italian Futurism founded by Marinelli, it had little in common with the Italian movement. Russian Futurists wanted to depict twentieth century life,

but they deplored war and laid emphasis on technology. After the 1917 Revolution the Futurists, of all the writers and poets, gained the foremost position in Russian literary society, and their most outstanding representative was Vladimir Mayakovsky.

Although Mayakovsky had signed the 1912 Futurist Manifesto, he did not personally advocate Khlebnikov's "trans-sense" language. The words Mayakovsky invented were not based purely on sound effect; they consisted, rather, of a free and imaginative use of prefixes and suffixes producing blends that were both new and readily comprehensible. In all his poems Mayakovsky used rhyme freely and deliberately created distorted echoes, often extending a single rhyme to four or more syllables involving several words. His poetry tends to have a constant number of stresses to the line but an irregular number of unstressed syllables. Above all, Mayakovsky's poetry was meant to be read aloud, and in his own public readings he gave these meters the rhythm of a drum beat or a march cadence.

Mayakovsky wrote primarily in two genres: that of political patriotic poems and that of love lyrics. He had accepted the October Revolution wholeheartedly, and between 1918 and 1920 he wrote thousands of jingles for propaganda posters. In his more formal political poems he satirized the enemies of the Revolution. In "Our March" he passionately denounced the bureaucrats and philistines of the new order. In *150,000,000,* Ivan, the essence of the Russian people, crosses the Atlantic to fight a hand-to-hand battle with Woodrow Wilson. Written during the American intervention in the Russian Civil War, the poem used Wilson as a symbol of the capitalist West. In

"Paris" the poet tells the Eiffel Tower to instigate a revolution and then journey to Moscow where she will be given better care than in the West.

During the early 1920's Mayakovsky continued to write short propaganda verses in support of socialist reform and government control. Although this was his main preoccupation, he did manage to produce some lyrical poems. One of Mayakovsky's earliest love poems was "The Cloud in Trousers" in which the poet calls a fire brigade to extinguish his burning heart. "I Love" is a poem to Lily Brik, wife of Osip Brik, a critic and editor. In it Mayakovsky states that hearts are found in a person's chest, but that anatomy made a mistake and he is a tingling heart from head to toe. In 1923, Lily left Mayakovsky for another man. "About That" is a desperate lament over her infidelity.

Mayakovsky was well aware of the poet's conflict between devotion to personal themes and to Communism. In the poem "Letter from Paris to Comrade Kostrov on the Nature of Love," the poet claims that such a man as Kostrov cannot understand or prevent a poet's passion. He declares that to the last beat of his heart he will sing simple and human love. In 1925, Mayakovsky undertook a long trip to western Europe and America which resulted in a critical account of his life under capitalism, *My Discovery of America*. Although he admired American technology, he felt it was not exclusively beneficial, and he criticized capitalism as breeding inequality and injustice. On returning to the Soviet Union, Mayakovsky wrote the long poem "All Right" which, without reservation, praised Soviet progress. "Black and White," written during the same period, is a rather biting poem inspired during his Mexican tour. In it he asserts that the white man eats the ripe, juicy pineapples, the black man the weather-rotted fruit; that the white man gets the best jobs, the black man only back-breaking labor.

With his two satirical plays, *The Bed-bug* and *The Bathhouse*, written in the late 1920's, Mayakovsky again directed his attention to political and social themes. But the picture of Soviet society that emerges in them is far from positive. In the first part of *The Bedbug* the main character, a vulgar and repulsive official, has power and a standard of living beyond his deserts simply because he owns a Party card. In the second part, set in 1978, sex, romance, vodka, and tobacco no longer exist, and the protagonist has become a zoölogical curiosity. In this dehumanized world of the future, this repulsive figure becomes a tragic hero searching for love in a loveless state. *The Bathhouse* is a grotesque satire against bureaucracy in the Soviet state.

During the last years of his life Mayakovsky abandoned Bolshevism. He began to feel increasingly that in the new era love was a discarded fiction and his own efforts, a rejected martyrdom. In his last important poem, the unfinished "At the Top of My Voice," Mayakovsky pointed up what he saw as his intentional self-sacrifice to the aspirations of the Revolution, saying that he had subdued himself, trampling on the throat of his song. What had been a craving for melodrama and anarchy turned to tragedy when, on April 14, 1930, Mayakovsky killed himself.

Four years earlier, in the poem "To Sergei Esenin," on the occasion of that poet's suicide, Mayakovsky had written that it is not hard to die; to shape life is more difficult. In 1927, Mayakovsky said he had written this poem not to glorify the beauty of death but to celebrate life and the joy to be found along the most difficult of all roads, the road leading toward Communism.

It has been said that Mayakovsky's tragedy lay in his writing lyric poems in an unlyrical era. Whether this is true or not, Mayakovsky was, finally, overcome by depression and gloom. In his own suicide note he enjoined his comrades not to think him weak-spirited. There was nothing else he could do. Soviet critics denounced his suicide as a bourgeois act, but they have since changed their minds. Today Mayakovsky is considered the greatest poet of the Soviet Revolution, remembered not so much for his ideas as for the spirit of his verse. His ideas are often superficial or naïve, and his propaganda poems after the Revolution are inferior to his other work. But in the intensity and spirit of his lyrical poems he does justify his occupation of the place history has accorded him. Of the utter loneliness of unrequited love he speaks with a moving blend of self-pity and tenderness. But he is at his best in those verses that are at once coarse, lyrical, and passionate.

THE POETRY OF MELVILLE

Author: Herman Melville (1819-1891)
First published: Battle-Pieces and Aspects of the War, 1866; *Clarel: A Poem and Pilgrimage in the Holy Land,* 1876; *John Marr and Other Sailors,* 1888; *Timoleon,* 1891

Though a few of Herman Melville's short poems have been reprinted in anthologies of American literature, he is known almost exclusively for his prose fiction. The Melville biographers and critics who mention the poetry usually pass quickly over it, often giving the impression that it may interest some curious readers but that it has no great importance as compared with his novels and stories. In recent years, however, considerable interest has been shown in Melville as a poet.

Most of Melville's poetry was published during his lifetime, but it drew little attention, partly because the last two volumes were published in editions of only twenty-five copies each. A number of previously unpublished poems did not appear until 1924 in the final volume of the Standard Edition of Melville's works. A critical edition of the poems (not including the lengthy *Clarel,* which occupies two volumes in the Standard Edition) was published in 1947 with explanatory notes and textual notes by Howard P. Vincent. A similar edition of *Clarel,* with a critical analytical introduction by Walter E. Bezanson, came out in 1961. Nearly a century after its original publication, Melville's *Battle-Pieces and Aspects of the War* was re-issued in 1963 as *The Battle-Pieces of Herman Melville* in a handsomely printed and profusely illustrated edition with an introduction and extensive notes by Hennig Cohen. The following year Mr. Cohen brought out a volume of *Selected Poems of Herman Melville,* which contains, in addition to many of the poems in Vincent's edition, several passages from *Clarel* and over eighty pages of comment by the editor on individual poems. Cohen quotes many of Melville's notes to the poems and frequently draws attention to the relationship between certain poems and Melville's various works of fiction.

Melville's first published volume of verse did not appear until 1866, and most of his extant verse was written in the last thirty-five years of his life. But his symbolic novel *Mardi,* published in 1849, contains some romantic effusions by the poet Yoomy and several other brief poems. In 1860, when Melville sailed for San Francisco on his brother's ship, he left with his wife a manuscript volume of poems for which she was to find a publisher if possible. No publisher was found, but many of the poems in *Timoleon,* which came out in the year of Melville's death, may be among those in the earlier unpublished book.

A number of critics and biographers have called attention to the difficulties which face the beginning reader of Melville's verse. Newton Arvin has observed that Melville the poet seems to be a prose writer working with verse. Robert Penn Warren has found the seemingly inept distortions and wrenchings in many lines to represent a possible attempt to develop a style fitted to a man of Melville's masculine temperament. Laurence Barrett sees the violences and wrenchings as often effective, especially upon rereading, and as conscious technical devices being used sometimes awkwardly but occasionally with marked success.

Melville explains in a prefatory note to *Battle-Pieces and Aspects of the War* that most of the poems in the volume were the result of an impulse imparted by the fall of Richmond in 1865. The arrangement is generally chronological but not strictly so. The first poem, "The Portent," concerns the hanging of John Brown on December 2, 1859, and most of the poems at the end of the volume relate to events of 1864 and 1865, though several return to earlier years of the war. Among the best poems are "The Portent," "The Conflict of Convictions," "The March into Virginia," "The Temeraire," "Malvern Hill," and "The Martyr."

In "The Portent" the body of John Brown hangs swaying from the scaffold beam, throwing a symbolic shadow on the green of the Shenandoah Valley which will be stained later with so much red. As the hangman's cap covers Brown's face, so the future is veiled, but the streaming beard of "Weird John Brown" ominously forecasts the "meteor of the war."

"The Conflict of Convictions," with its obvious allusions to the war in Heaven in *Paradise Lost,* shows an indifferent God who will not stop men when they make their choices: "The People spread like a weedy grass, / The thing they will they bring to pass." The boyish soldiers in "The March into Virginia" proceed into the "leafy neighborhood" near Manassas with the lightsome joyousness of picnickers. But, says Melville, some in the next three days will "Perish, enlightened by the volied glare," and others will survive to endure the shame of a second defeat in the same area a few weeks later. In "The Temeraire" an old Englishman fondly and sadly recalls the passing away forever of the glorious oldtime sea battles of the great wooden sailing ships, while he muses on the fight between the small and unromantic ironclads *Monitor* and *Merrimac.*

"Shiloh" is a brief and beautiful requiem for the soldiers who fell there and who lie now "While over them the swallows skim, / And all is hushed at Shiloh." As the swallows in this poem symbolize the indifference of nature to man's bloody conflicts, so do the elms in "Malvern Hill":

> We elms of Malvern Hill
>> Remember every thing;
> But sap the twig will fill:
> Wag the world how it will,
>> Leaves must be green in spring.

"The Martyr" portrays poetically the grief over the land on the day of Lincoln's death, but in its refrain it anticipates the spirit of vengefulness which the murder incited: "Beware the People weeping/ When they bare the iron hand."

Clarel: A Poem and Pilgrimage in the Holy Land, Melville's second book of poetry, is a single poem of twenty thousand lines inspired by a journey to Palestine in 1857 and by Melville's speculations on theology, philosophy, science, belief, doubt, and the nature of the human soul. Newton Arvin has called it a novel of ideas in verse, which suggests the slight significance of its story line as compared with the space devoted to the opposed views of the numerous pilgrims who appear, disappear, and reappear in the 150 cantos. The basic story concerns young Clarel, a spiritually troubled American divinity student who seeks a resolution of his inner conflict between faith and doubt through a journey to the Holy Land. He falls in love with Ruth, whose American-Jewish father is murdered. While she is in mourning for her father, Clarel joins a group of pilgrims on a journey to various parts of Palestine. On his return he learns that Ruth has died of grief, and after he had watched the burial of Ruth and her mother he is left at the end of the poem still pondering the ways of God and the fate of man.

Among the pilgrims with whom Clarel is briefly associated are Celio, a handsome but hunchbacked Catholic, embittered and doubting; Rolfe, a former sailor who somewhat resembles Melville himself in his experiences and his appearance; Vine, an American whose creative ability and moral and aesthetic views suggest that Melville modeled him after his one-time friend Hawthorne; Derwent, an Anglican clergyman with pleasing manners but a superficial mind; Mortmain, a disillusioned idealist; and Ungar, an ex-Confederate officer who, while critical of man and his society and institutions, believes in man's need of a religious faith to sustain him in a confused and confusing world.

Clarel is difficult to read not merely

because of its great length but because, as Willard Thorp has said, it has all the faults of a "private" poem and thus one should come to it only after having learned much about Melville's moods and speculative questings. Though the poem itself leaves Clarel still searching for the sustaining faith he has not found, Melville, in the brief "Epilogue," directly addresses Clarel (and any doubting reader as well, one may assume), urging him to keep his heart to the end when "Emerge thou mayst from the last whelming sea, / And prove that death but routs life into victory."

In *John Marr and Other Sailors,* Melville, now nearing seventy, turned back nostalgically to his years as a sailor. The title poem may perhaps reflect a feeling the poet himself had often had, of being separated forever, through time and distance, from the companions of his youth. John Marr, living on a Middle-western prairie after having lost his wife and child, longs to hear from those he once knew, and he asks wistfully, "Why, lads, so silent here to me, / Your watchmate of times long ago?" Other poems with this mood of reminiscence are "Tom Deadlight," spoken by an old and dying petty officer, and "Jack Roy," which celebrates again the manly, ebullient character of Jack Chase, who was a character in *White-Jacket* and the sailor to whom Melville dedicated *Billy Budd.* Though "Billy in the Darbies" did not appear in the *John Marr* volume but was appended at the end of *Billy Budd,* it may be grouped with the sailor poems and it is one of the best of them. In form it is a ballad represented as having been composed by one of Billy's shipmates in memory of the beloved sailor after his hanging for the accidental killing of a ship's officer.

Two very different poems from the *John Marr* volume are "The Maldive Shark" and "The Enviable Isles." The first conveys poetically the theme that Melville had treated so often in his fiction: the mystery of evil in the world. The

shark is pictured as too stupid to find its own food unless guided by the "sleek little pilot-fish, azure and slim," who are the "Eyes and brains to the dotard lethargic and dull, / Pale revener of horrible meat." The reader is left to wonder, as did Melville, where lies evil? With the shark? with the pilot-fish? Or with the Creator who made them both and all else in creation? Or is the shark's voraciousness simply man's interpretation of evil, but really no evil at all, only a survival of the fittest, the dull-witted shark and his helpful little pilot-fish?

"The Enviable Isles" pictures a green, sleepy land of swaying palms in the uplands and sweet fern and moss in the glades where "myriads lie   Dimpling in dream—unconscious mere,   While billows endless round the beaches die." As Cohen notes, the final word of the poem suggests, as do several other words, that these are the Isles of the Dead whose sleep is endless after the storms of life.

Of the poems in *Timoleon,* Melville's last published volume, many are travel poems related to the poet's trip to Europe and the Middle East in 1856-1857. In the title poem, based on the life of a Corinthian statesman and general, Cohen sees hidden autobiographical relationships. The second poem in the volume, "After the Pleasure Party," has attracted considerable comment and disagreement as to its meaning and even its form. Vincent calls it a dramatic monologue and takes issue with Lewis Mumford for having assigned the monologue to a man, Melville himself. Cohen resolves some of the ambiguity of the complex poem by assigning different parts to two speakers: a woman who is troubled over the discovery of her own strong sexuality; and the poet himself, who warns her of the power of Amor, god of love, and in the closing lines warns also "virgins everywhere, / O pray! Example take too, and have care."

The short poem "Monody" has a special appeal because of its commemoration of the brief friendship of Melville and Hawthorne, the lengthy later separation calling forth after Hawthorne's death the anguished cry in the poem, "Ease me, a little ease, my song," The closing lines, "Glazed now with ice the cloistral vine / That hid the shyest grape," are a reminder also of the Hawthorne-like character Vine in *Clarel*.

Among the poems of Melville not printed until 1924 in the Standard Edition are a group collectively entitled *Weeds and Wildings, with A Rose or Two* which, according to Vincent, were obviously intended for private publication. Though for the most part unremarkable as poetry, they are of interest as reflecting Melville's happy life at Arrowhead, near Pittsfield, Massachusetts, where he had lived with his family from 1850 to 1863. A long prefatory introduction also shows his love for his wife Lizzie, who was in temperament quite different from him. One of the most unusual aspects of these poems written late in Melville's life is that they show a love of rural life and the quiet beauty of a nature very different from the terrifying, destructive natural world of his sea fiction and his sea poetry. Though one poem, "The American Aloe on Exhibition," appears to refer symbolically to Melville's disappointment in having lost his audience of earlier years, many of the other poems seem to suggest that in his closing years Melville was not the embittered man he is supposed by some commentators to have been, but rather a husband living a happy old age with his wife of many years.

THE POETRY OF MEREDITH

Author: George Meredith (1828-1909)
First published: Poems, 1851; *Modern Love,* 1862; *Poems and Lyrics of the Joy of Earth,* 1883; *Ballads and Poems of Tragic Life,* 1887; *A Reading of Earth,* 1888; *A Reading of Life,* 1901; *Last Poems,* 1910

Best known as the author of fourteen novels, most notably *The Ordeal of Richard Feverel* and *The Egoist,* George Meredith may eventually find a securer place in literary history as a poet. *Modern Love,* a sequence of poems depicting the breakdown of a marriage, is already acknowledged as a masterwork of late Victorian verse, but in addition Meredith's mythological poems in praise of Earth are entirely worthy of more acclaim than they have received. A few critics, among them Douglas Bush and Siegfried Sassoon, have praised these poems, but in general, Meredith's verse has been almost entirely overlooked. In six principal volumes published from 1862 to 1901, Meredith wrote about 130 poems which make up his main collection, exclusive of the very early poems, some translations, and numerous epitaphs and occasional poems. His best work was published in 1883 as *Poems and Lyrics of the Joy of Earth,* and in 1888, *A Reading of Earth.* The poems of both volumes chiefly explain Meredith's nearly pagan faith in man as a part of natural process, and celebrate, often in terms of regeneration myths, the natural vitality and renewal which comes to men when they forego selfishness and live at one with nature.

> Enter these enchanted woods,
>   You who dare.
> Nothing harms beneath the leaves
> More than waves a swimmer cleaves.
> Toss your heart up with the lark,
> Foot at peace with mouse and worm,
>   Fair you fare.
> Only at a dread of dark
> Quaver, and they quit their form:
> Thousand eyeballs under hoods
>   Have you by the hair.
> Enter these enchanted woods,
>   You who dare.

This, the first stanza of "The Woods of Westermain," expresses Meredith's belief that nature is essentially mysterious "enchanted," and beneficent. Nature becomes a source of terror only to the man who has lost a sense of his dependence on nature. The man who is guilty of over-weening pride in intellect, who feels superior to nature, is cut off from Mother Earth and so conceives her to be brutish and even fearful. Meredith's attitude toward nature is remarkably advanced for his time. He accepts natural process—both in the way it limits men and also as a creative, evolutionary force—not in the Darwinian sense, nor in the way Tennyson sometimes conceived of science as a possible saving force, but rather in a "mythological" or even "pagan" sense. Man's scientific dominion over nature counts less for Meredith than man as being a part of nature. A man lives a single span of life, and nature provides him with that life. And though the individual dies, as each Spring "dies" in winter, man and nature are continually reborn and renewed within the great cycle of being. Because of this root belief, and because it provides a viewpoint which is essentially one of joy, and because according to it a man's false pride and sense of superiority can be ridiculed, Meredith's "philosophy" is profoundly comic. Indeed, he is one of the few truly comic writers in modern literature.

Influenced in his early poetry by the Keatsian tradition of Tennyson and even by the "Spasmodic School" of, notably, Richard H. Horne's "Orion," Meredith came under the influence of Swinburne, whose friend he was, and then, breaking away from aestheticism, developed his own, highly characteristic and often unique style which Douglas Bush has called "a bright, muscular idiom." His style is very compressed, his thought often overly convoluted, even tangled.

His metaphors, rich in visual observation and sly analogies, come thick and fast and do not normally form a single developing "conceit" or extended metaphor. For these reasons—complexity of thought, ambiguity of expression—Meredith's poetry was greeted by the reading public with some acclaim but more bewilderment. In his verbal tricks, his syncopated rhythms, his compression of language and often confusing use of metaphor, Meredith's poetry bears comparison to that of another contemporary who has been acclaimed as a great innovator, Gerard Manley Hopkins.

> Carols nature, counsel men.
> Different notes as rook from wren
> Hear we when our steps begin,
> And the choice is cast within,
> Where a robber raven's tale
> Urges passion's nightingale.

Such a passage invites a certain amount of study and puzzling out; it will not become clear until the whole poem is studied, but the real point is to assess the immediate effect of the lines. The changing rhythms, the double alliteration, the close rhyming, are intended to produce a mysterious and somehow incantatory effect, as Meredith celebrates, and often preaches, the mysterious influence of nature on the inner man. Unlike Wordsworth, however, Meredith never really abstracts nature, does not perceive behind the concrete forms a quasi-platonic "idea" or ideal. Rather, he finds the deeper meaning within the forms of nature itself. It is in this sense that he has been called "pagan."

The same strong cadence marks "Hard Weather," in which Meredith sings of how storms serve to brace men, to force on them an awareness of nature's vitality. "Contention is the vital force," he chants, and he indicates how such a notion as "the survival of the fittest" can be viewed not with alarm but accepted as a principle of growth:

> Earth yields the milk, but all her mind
> Is vowed to thresh for stouter stock.

> Her passion for old giantkind,
> That scaled the mount, uphurled the rock,
> Devolves on them who read aright
> Her meaning and devoutly serve.

To "read aright" requires the use of brains, believes Meredith. He decries sentimentality as well as crass naturalistic groveling in the gutter. "More brains, more brains," he once cried, testifying to his faith in man's ability to perceive rationally his destiny and being in nature, and so to bring himself into accord with nature, unified then in "blood, brain and spirit."

Meredith finds in Greek legend a character who symbolizes man's communion with nature. Melampus, the physician, preserved some snakes from death, and so was granted the power to understand the language of birds. The theme is not unrelated to that of spiritual renewal in Coleridge's *The Rime of the Ancient Mariner*:

> Of earth and sun they are wise, they nourish their broods,
> Weave, build, hive, burrow and battle, take joy and pain
> Like swimmers varying billows: never in woods
> Runs white insanity fleeing itself: all sane
> The woods revolve: as the tree its shadowing limns
> To some resemblance in motion, the rooted life
> Restrains disorder: you hear the primitive hymns
> Of earth in woods issue wild of the web of strife.

"The Day of the Daughter of Hades," a remarkable poem which celebrates the renewal of spring, is based on the myth of Persephone's return from Hades. Persephone's daughter, Skiagenia, accompanies her mother, spends a day with an earthling, and chants of the joy of earth's fecundity. She understands earth better than earthlings do because she is a daughter of Hades, of darkness. This mysterious linking of life and death, the earth and underground, is the poem's deepest meaning, and again Meredith's vision here is not unrelated to D. H. Lawrence's belief in the deeply-rooted instinctual life.

To accept the good of nature, pain and death must also be accepted, and Meredith had to struggle to keep his faith in earth despite personal loss, ill health, and discouragement. "A Faith on Trial" records this struggle, but *Modern Love,* published in 1862, is the key poem to an understanding of the tragic side of Meredith's vision of life. This sequence is closer in kind to the other dramatic monologues which Meredith wrote, such as "Juggling Jerry" and "The Old Chartist." His first wive, the daughter of Thomas Love Peacock, had deserted him in 1858 and died in 1861. *Modern Love* dramatizes the bitter psychological warfare of a couple who lose their early romantic and somewhat illusory love and proceed to subtly cut up each other and themselves. The wife finally commits suicide. Meredith's conclusion is typically philosophical and humane:

> Then each applied to each that fatal knife,

Deep questioning, which probes to endless dole.
Ah, what a dusty answer gets the soul
When hot for certainties in this our life!—
In tragic hints here see what evermore
Moves dark as yonder midnight ocean's force,
Thundering like ramping hosts of warrior horse,
To throw that faint thin line upon the shore!

And, again:

> I see no sin:
> The wrong is mixed. In tragic life, God wot,
> No villain need be! Passions spin the plot:
> We are betrayed by what is false within.

Nature can be harsh, but never wantonly cruel. Only men, in their illusions and pride, can be cruel. Nature, "read aright" disciplines the unruly passions, brings solace, gives strength. Meredith's renewed faith in Earth is intensely felt and is conveyed not infrequently with great eloquence and energy in poems remarkable both for vigor of thought and compressed, rhythmically exciting verse.

THE POETRY OF MICHELANGELO

Author: Michelangelo Buonarroti (1475-1564)
First published: Collected Poetry, 1623

The fame of Michelangelo Buonarroti as a painter and a sculptor has far outdistanced his reputation as a poet. This is unfortunate, for while it is open to question whether Michelangelo could have ever developed into a world poet of a stature equivalent to his stature in the plastic arts, his reputation as a poet is now established. Modern critics admit that he is an important Renaissance Italian poet, and by many he is considered the best Italian lyric poet of the sixteenth century.

The reasons for the slow growth of Michelangelo's poetic reputation are easy to identify. First, even in his own day, while his poetry was extravagantly praised by a circle of friends, it was Michelangelo's painting and sculpture that drew the eyes of the world at large. Moreover, his poetry was not published until 1623, eighty-nine years after his death, and then only in an incomplete, much edited, and censored edition. By that time the Renaissance style of writing was being rapidly replaced by the neoclassical style throughout Europe, and the poems did not attract major attention. It was not until the early nineteenth century, when the Romantics were rediscovering the Middle Ages and the Renaissance, that complete and well edited editions of the poetry began to appear; and only in our century have completely authoritative editions been published.

Michelangelo never took his poetry seriously enough to collect, revise, or preserve the whole of it. While he considered himself a professional painter and sculptor, he, like almost every poet of the Renaissance, thought of himself as an amateur. For poetry was in that age valued as a social pastime and a gentleman's skill; and even if a man did think of himself as a professional poet, it was bad form to act as if he did. This Renaissance attitude has given scholars much trouble, and only after much searching have they managed to locate in various places 343 separate poems and poetic fragments (and many variants) by Michelangelo. Most of these were composed after 1530.

Though the poetry is sometimes written in the traditional Petrarchan manner, and though the conventions of neo-Platonism are also important in the work, the best poems are characterized by Michelangelo's unique style. The structure and syntax, and even the grammar, are twisted and full of tension; the poems are often obscure, and the poet sometimes seems to pay scant attention to such relatively simple things as rhyme and metrical regularity. The overall impression of the verse, as critics like to point out, is as if Michelanglo in writing was struggling to shape his complex thoughts into hard, unmalleable language the way a sculptor struggles with marble or granite.

The poems fall into several categories. First in importance are the pieces written to Vittoria Colonna, either proclaiming Michelangelo's Platonic love for her (he met her when he was sixty-three), or lamenting her death, as in this sonnet:

So that I might at least be less unworthy,
Lady, of your huge high beneficence,
To balance it, my poor wits at first
Took to plying my own wholeheartedly.

But then, seeing in me no potency
To clear the way to grasp that goal exists,
My evil fault for its forgiveness asks,
And the sin makes me wiser constantly.

And well I see how anyone would stray
Who thought my flimsy, transient work could equal
The grace pouring from you, which is divine.

For wit and art and memory give way;
In a thousand attempts none who is
 mortal
Can pay for Heaven's gift out of his
 own.

Vittoria was herself a poet of some
note and a patroness of the arts, and she
inspired several notable men of her day to
the composition of verse. Generally speaking, there are three levels of love spoken
of in Michelangelo's poetry: human,
fleshly love, which takes the Petrarchan
convention; honest love, a transcendental emotion that takes the neo-Platonic convention; and good love, the spiritual love of God. Good love is the
subject of the greater number of Michelangelo's poems, but honest love is the
dominant theme in the best of his love
poems, most of which are written to Vittoria. Human love is a theme in these
poems too, but as an antagonist to honest
love. In a typical poem to Vittoria, for
example, the poet describes how honest
love has come to him forbidding corrupt
desire (human love) and raising him to
the level of the spirit. This is a conventional, neo-Platonic theme, yet Michelangelo's energetic expression of it reani-
mates the convention and produces a
remarkable unconventional poetry:

I want to want, Lord, what I do not
 want,
An icy veil hides between heart and fire
And damps the fire, making my page
 a liar,
Since my pen and my conduct do not
 fit.

I love you with my tongue, then I
 lament
Love does not reach the heart, and
 can't tell where
To open the door to grace so it can
 enter
And thrust all ruthless pride out of my
 heart.

Tear the veil thou, O break that wall,
 my Lord,
Which with its hardness keeps in check
 the sun
Of your own light; on earth it is put
out.

Send that same ray of light to your fair
 bride
Which we are then to have, so I may
 burn,
And my heart feel you only with no
 doubt.

The poems concerning the good love
of God are next in importance after the
poems to Vittoria. Michelangelo was seriously dedicated to the Christian ideal,
and the religious poems are full of his
deep, though often agonized love for
Christ. Many of them are tortured, self-
debasing confessions. Among the most
frequent themes in these poems are fear
of the judgment day, fear for salvation,
the feeling of moral inadequacy, and
prayer and supplication.

I live on my own death; if I see right,
My life with an unhappy lot is happy;
If ignorant how to live on death and
 worry,
Enter this fire, where I'm destroyed
 and burnt.

Tommaso Cavaliere was a young Roman aristocrat to whom Michelangelo was
strongly attracted; a significant group of
the poems are dedicated to the poet's admiration and love of that youth. He saw
in Tommaso a model of elegance and
grace, a man with manners and a social
style the opposite of that of Michelangelo
himself. The main burden of this group
is Michelangelo's statement of admiration
of the young man, and the poet's offer of
friendship.

I feel how a cold face that fire has lit
Burns me from far, and turns itself to
 ice;
Two lovely arms submit me to a force
That does not move, but moves all other
 weight;

Unique, and grasped by me alone, a
 spirit
That has no death, but others' death
 can compass,
I see and meet, that binds my heart,
 being loose;
From one who helps I feel the only

spite.

Lord, from a beautiful face how can it
be
Effects so far opposed are borne on
mine?
It's hard to give to men what you have
not.

As for the happy life he's snatched
from me,
He may, if you're not kind, act as the
sun,
Which heats the world although it is
not hot.

Michelangelo's overtures were, apparently, coolly received. All in all, these poems speak of a Platonic kind of love very similar to the kind of affection for a young man we are familiar with in Shakespeare's sonnets. Much different are the forty-eight quatrains to Cecchino Bracci, who died at the age of fifteen in 1544. His uncle, Luigi del Riccio, requested of Michelangelo a tomb design and an epitaph for his nephew. Michelangelo had seen very little of Cecchino, and the moods of the poems represent those of the uncle, not of Michelangelo.

Naturally enough, a group of Michelangelo's poems are concerned with art in general and some of his own works in particular. One interesting piece describes the physical difficulties he endured painting the Sistine Chapel ceiling. Two poems are written as speeches for two of the statues (Night and Day) that Michelangelo made for the tomb in Florence of the young Duke Guiliano de Medici. A number of the poems use metaphoric structures drawn from aspects of the practice of various arts, painting and sculpture in particular. Among these is Michelangelo's perhaps best-known poem, the sonnet "Non ha l'ottimo artista alcun concetto" ("No conception the greatest artist can have"). Written between 1538 and 1544, the first four lines of this Platonic love poem became famous immediately. Within a few years they were known in Spain and elsewhere, and they were translated into French by Phillipe Desportes, the only verses of Michelangelo translated into French before the nineteenth century. In these four lines is condensed Michelangelo's idea of art. They can be roughly paraphrased as follows: "No conception the greatest artist can have is not imprisoned in the rough marble block; to break away the excess stone to reveal it is all the mind-guided hand can do." This idea of sculpture (and by extension the other arts as well) as the achievement by skill of the artist's intellectual conception was not entirely new, but Michelangelo's unique and authorative expression of it became, and still is, a touchstone for critics of his art.

Another group of poems is concerned with messages to acquaintances, patrons, and friends, and with the pronouncement of opinion, praise, and condemnations. A friend is lectured on ingratitude; Vasari, the great biographer of artists, is praised for his perservation of the reputations of painters; Pope Julius II is angrily denounced; and the deaths of friends and relatives are eloquently regretted. Some of these poems are cautiously political and complain or condemn the actions of powerful contemporaries of the poet. The best-known of this class of poems is Michelangelo's piece put in the mouth of his statue of Night on the Florentine tomb of Duke Guiliano de Medici. Another poet, Giovanni Strozzi, had praised the statue, carved in the shape of a sleeping girl; Strozzi suggests that since she is so much alive in art she be awakened. In reply, Michelangelo condemns the excesses of contemporary Medici politics in his native Florence. (Michelangelo, who to some extent identified himself with Dante in exile, lived in Rome in self-imposed exile.) He has his statue answer that she would rather sleep than endure the vile corruption which she would witness around her if she were awakened.

The poems that do not fall into any one or more of these major groups cannot be easily classified. Michelangelo wrote in an unsystematic way and, apparently, as the spirit moved him. Many of his poems, for example, have been found jotted down on the back of prints or in the margins of letters or notebooks. It was only in his later years that he wrote consistent groups of poems. Among the unclassified poems are pieces on such various subjects as fire, night, the rustic life, death (he was already writing of his "approaching death" fifty years before he died), cities he had visited, and the manners and morals of his times. Not a few of this last type of poem are satirical burlesques, some full of the earthy language that has always upset censors and self-appointed guardians of public morality.

THE POETRY OF MÖRIKE

Author: Eduard Mörike (1804-1875)
First published: Poems, 1838; *Idylle vom Bodensee, oder Fischer Martin und die Glockendiebe,* 1846

Since the Romantic period was, among other things, a revolt against the Age of Reason, it is frequently asserted that the Romantics were sentimental eccentrics. However, Eduard Mörike cannot be classified as such. He was a sensitive dreamer, a skillful poet, but above all a poet of simplicity. A contemporary critic called him "a human being in nightgown and soft slippers." While purists of the Romantic Period will refer to Hölderlin, Mörike was able to appeal to a larger public. Many of his poems became folklore and folksongs during his lifetime. Brahms, Schumann, and Hugo Wolf set some of his poems to music, and most of them are still to be heard in concert halls all over the world. He was a master of classical meters, but he abhorred strict theoretical principles in his work. D. F. Strauss, his famous theologian contemporary, said: "Thanks to his work, nobody can sell us rhetoric for poetry." Describing the poet's intuitive creativity, he stated that "Mörike takes a handful of earth, squeezes it ever so little, and a little bird flies out."

Mörike made full use of the wealth of inflections which the German language offers. Some critics, however, object to a lack of composition in his poems. Frequently past, present, and future are interwoven without proper sequence. Mörike himself was suspicious of a purely academic approach. In an epigram he replied to his German critics: "You can see in his poems that he can express himself in Latin." He was a representative of the "Schwaebische Dichterschule" (Swabian School) which had formed around the poet Ludwig Uhland. Heinrich Heine, who detested this lack of cosmopolitan ambitions, attacked the school with satirical comments. Mörike always remained a native son, and some of his poems are written in Swabian dialect. He did not leave Swabia except for a few excursions into Bavaria, Tyrol, and Switzerland, and he disregarded the problematic speculations of his time which caused Goethe to examine all aspects of nineteenth century knowledge, and which made Hölderlin seek refuge in the idealistic world of Greece. Goethe tried to explore the unexplorable, while Mörike maintained a childlike vision and radiated in his poems an adoration of life without torturing his mind with a multitude of question marks. This attitude is demonstrated in his most frequently quoted poem "Prayer":

> Lord, send what pleaseth Thee!
> Let it be weal or woe;
> Thy hands give both, and so
> Either contenteth me.
>
> But, Lord, whichever
> Thou giv'st, pain or pleasure,
> O do not drench me!
> In sweet mid-measure
> Lieth true plenty.

A prose translation of the same poem may serve to illustrate the simple choice of words which could not be employed in a poetical translation:

> Lord, send what you will
> Love or sorrow
> I am happy
> That both flows from your hand.
>
> Do not overload me
> With joy
> Or with sorrow
> In the middle lies
> Sweet contentment.

Mörike, the seventh child in a family of thirteen, was born in 1804, the son of a medical doctor. A student of theology, he entered the Lower Seminary at Urach and continued his studies at the Higher Seminary. Although he came to dislike theological study, he nevertheless became a pastor in the small Swabian village of Kleversulzbach, chiefly because his mother felt that the ministry was the proper profession for any educated man. His father had died early, and his mother came from a vicar's family. An attempt in 1828 to establish himself as writer and editor had failed. He admitted feeling "like a tethered goat" when he started his pastoral duties, and he preferred to write poetry instead of sermons. Frequently he had to borrow his Sunday sermons from a colleague. In 1838 he published his first volume under the title *Poems*. His attitude towards his parishioners is described in his poem "A Parson's Experience": "Fortunately my peasants like a 'sharp sermon.' What happens is that on Saturday evening after eleven o'clock they creep into my garden and steal my lettuce and on Sunday in the morning service they expect the vinegar for it. But I make the ending gentle: they get the oil."

After nine years, in 1843, he resigned from his position as pastor for reasons of ill health. But the major reason was his desire to be free from his pastoral duties. His happiest time arrived, when he obtained a position as a professor of literature in a girls' high school. A one-hour teaching assignment each week left sufficient time for writing poetry, and the girls enjoyed being lectured on poetry by a real poet. He even earned an honorary doctor's degree, and the queen attended one of his lectures. His major diversion from his literary work were his delightful drawings, which showed again his ability to create something without strenuous efforts. His drawings, issued as a separate volume, have only recently found a larger audience.

Mörike married in 1851, but his marriage resulted in separation. His close relationship with his sister Klärchen, who lived in the Mörike house, caused many conflicts. Also, in his student days he had had an unpleasant experience with the opposite sex when he fell in love with a beautiful girl who had a doubtful

reputation and who failed to remain faithful to him. Five poems with the title "Peregrina" describe his joy and sorrow. The cycle ends:

Could I forsake such beauty? The old bliss
Returns, and seems yet sweeter than before.
O come! My arms have waited long for this.

But at the look she gives my heart grows sore.
Hatred and love are mingled in her kiss.
She turns away, and will return no more.

Another love affair, which resulted in an engagement, was called off three years later. Retelling his experience, he again demonstrated his ability to evoke deep feelings with simple words:

Fare you well—you could not guess
What a pang the words imparted,
For you spoke with cheerful face,
Going on your way light-hearted.

Fare you well—time and again
Since that day these words I've spoken,
Never weary of the pain,
Though my heart as oft was broken.

In spite of unfortunate love affairs and an unhappy marriage, he never lost his serenity, which was based on a sincere belief in the goodness of his creator and his place in God's creation. In his most famous prose piece, "Mozart auf der Reise nach Prag" ("Mozart on a Voyage to Prague"), he inserted a poem, usually titled "O Soul, Remember," which indicates his sense of tranquillity while speaking about the ever present reality of death:

A sapling springs, who knows
Where, in the forest;
A rosebush, who can say
Within what garden?
Chosen already both—
O soul, remember—
To root upon your grave
And to grow there.

Like most Romantics Mörike used nature as his major source of inspiration. When he was a curate, he was found resting in the grass of the churchyard while the honor of the Sunday sermon was given to young assistants. Restful poems like "Withdrawal" were the result of such leisure:

Let me go, world, let me go!
Come no more with gifts to woo me!
Leave this heart of mine, now, to me,
With its joy and with its woe!

In his adoration of nature he also refrained from the emotional eccentricities which can be noted in the work of his contemporaries. He described his impressions in simple rhymes, which found their way into numerous poetry collections, children's books, and school books, "September Morning" falls in this category:

The world's at rest still, sun not
    through,
Forest and field lie dreaming:
But soon now, when the veil drops, you
Will see the sky's unmisted blue;
Lusty with autumn and subdued,
The world in warm gold swimming.

Many love poems, free from affectations, also flowed easily from his pen. "Question and Answer" is typical:

Whence, you ask me, did the demon
Love gain entrance to my heart?
Why was not long since his venom
Wrenched out boldly with the dart?

Mörike's poems are not a product of tense creative efforts by candlelight in a poet's attic (a setting used by most romantic painters of the era to depict poets). In all of his poems the element of spontaneity is apparent. Nothing sounds labored or contrived. One of his poems, written in bed on a morning, is "The Sisters," now a well-known Brahms duet. A popular love poem "Fair Rohtraut" was started when he saw the name in a dictionary:

Then they rode home without a word,

Rohtraut, Fair Rohtraut;
The lad's heart sang though he made
    no sound:
If you were queen and today were
    crowned,
    It would not grieve me!
You thousand leaves of the forest wist
That I Fair Rohtraut's mouth have
    kissed!
—Quiet, quiet, my heart!

It is not surprising that his deep love of nature and his childlike purity of imagination made him also an outstanding teller of fairy tales and a writer of ballads. The mythical world of ghosts and elves comes alive in the "Song of the Elves" and "The Ghosts at Mummeisee."

In spite of his marriage to a Roman Catholic, he never showed an inclination to become a member of any church after he left his pastoral assignment. He was under the influence of his friend D. F. Strauss, who wrote the most unorthodox biography of Jesus of this time. That Mörike admired the ritual of the Catholic Church is evident, however, in his poem "Holy Week."

Following his separation from his wife in 1873, he lived in several places and at spas, residence made possible by financial help from his friends. He died in 1875, and on his deathbed he was reconciled with his wife.

The simplicity of Mörike's poems made many of them popular during his lifetime, yet at the same time this quality prevented proper recognition of his art by many of his fellow Romantics. But in spite of his unsophisticated writings no critic ever accused him of being trivial. If the test of time is considered the most valid criteria for a poet's work, Mörike easily has passed the test, and he will most probably remain a popular poet for generations to come. Gottfried Keller, a contemporary Swiss poet and novelist, said after his death: "He died like the departure of a quiet mountain spirit . . . like a beautiful day in June. If his death does not bring him closer to the people—it is only the people's fault."

THE POETRY OF MOSCHUS

Author: Moschus (fl. c.150 B.C.)
First transcribed: c.150 B.C.

There is virtually no real biographical evidence about the lyric poet Moschus. Suidas, the lexicographer who lived in the tenth century, and a note appended to the poem of Moschus called "Love in Flight" provide the only sources of information available. For what they are worth, these sources assert that Moschus was born at Syracuse and was a student of the grammarian Aristarchus, who taught at Alexandria from about 180 to about 144 B.C. The year 150 would possibly be about the middle of the life of Moschus.

Moschus is considered the chronological, if not the stylistic, successor to the Greek bucolic poet, Theocritus, and it is a commonplace to say that he is a pastoral poet like Theocritus. The texts of the poems of Moschus, however, do not actually support such an assertion. The pastoral poets assumed the mask of shepherds, or in Greek *pastors,* and in the guise of simple country folk they sang of love and death in a highly stylized and conventional manner. The reputation of Moschus as a Greek poet rests on three poems, "Love in Flight," "Europa," and "Lament for Bion." The other poems attributed to him are fragments surviving as quotations in other works and are of little consequence. These poems, in general, follow the pastoral conventions much less than most critics assume.

The "Lament for Bion" is the closest to Theocritus in manner of all the works by Moschus, but it is agreed by the best authorities that it is not really by Moschus, although traditionally attributed to him. The work was probably written by a student of Bion in imitation of his master's "Lament for Adonis." "Lament for Bion" is an elegy, a song of mourning, for the poet Bion who, as the poem asserts, had drunk poison. The poem has a refrain, "Keen, Sicilian women, keen the cry of grief for him, mourn melodic maidens." This recurring line sets off sections of the poem. The subjects treated in each section are as follows: 1. The poet announces the death of the beautiful musician and calls on the woods, rivers, orchards, and flowers to weep for him. 2. The nightingales are told to tell the Muses that Bion is dead and with him dies all music. 3. Wild swans are called to sing the swan song for Bion. 4. The flocks and herds lack the comforting presence of their shepherd Bion. 5. The gods weep for Bion and all nature droops. The flowers wilt; the flocks give no more milk; bees gather no more honey. 6. Never has such a grief found so vocal expression not even in the old stories and ancient myths. 7. Nightingales and swallows sing in sad choirs the requiem. 8. Who will be able to make music now that Bion is dead? 9. Galatea weeps for her dead lover Bion. 10. Bion compared to Homer is the second greatest loss to the joy of the earth. 11. All cities weep for Bion. 12. As the greenery of the earth is renewed in springtime, so death is part of the natural cycle of nature. 13. Yet, Bion drank poison and died unnaturally. 14. Justice will be done. Moschus would descend to Hell to retrieve the soul of Bion if he could do so. There Bion will sing a Sicilian song to Persephone, the sad Queen of Hell who was carried from her flowering fields in Sicily by the God of the underworld.

"Europa" deals with the story of the Phoenician princess in Greek mythology who was carried off to Crete by Zeus in the form of a bull and who bore Minos, Rhadamanthus, and Sarpedon there. This story, however, is only the vehicle for two extended digressions. First, Europa dreams at some length of the contest of Asia and Europe to possess her. The struggle described is a contest between two women. Second, when Europa awakens, she goes out to gather flowers and her flower basket with cleverly contrived pictures is described in great detail. These pictures, like the struggle between the two women, have an allegorical significance. Zeus looking down at the girl gathering flowers becomes enamoured and changes his shape to that of a bull. He induces her to climb on his back and swims across the sea to Crete with her.

"Love in Flight" is a charming erotic poem in which Cypris, the goddess of love, has lost her mischievous little boy Love, or Cupid. She offers a kiss to anyone who can tell her news of her boy and offers much more to anyone who can catch him and return him to her. Her description of Cupid is of great interest as a reflection of the poet's attitude toward erotic love. Cupid is physically beautiful and talks well, but he tells lies and is cruel and wily. His kiss is a sick kiss and his lips are poison. His arrows are tipped with fire. In short, although intensely desirable, love is represented as dangeous and hectic.

THE POETRY OF MUSSET

Author: Alfred de Musset (1810-1857)
First published: Contes d'Espagne et d'Italie, 1829 (*Romances of Spain and Italy*); *Poésies diverses,* 1831; *Le Spectacle dans un fauteuil,* 1833 (*A Show from an Easy Chair*); *Poésies nouvelles,* 1840 (*New Poems*)

In 1852, the whole body of Alfred de Musset's poetry was gathered into two volumes and published as the *First Poems* and *New Poems*. The first volume is made up of *Romances of Spain and Italy* and *A Show from an Easy Chair*. The second collection contains pieces written after 1833. It is worth recalling that by 1840, when the poet was thirty years old, Musset's creative talents were virtually exhausted. A complete explanation of this premature exhaustion should not be sought in the character of Musset's poetic doctrine. However, in the light of Musset's stated belief that the greatness of verse was commensurate with the magnitude of the poet's suffering, the intensity of his emotion, it will be readily understood that his creative talent was likely to fade relatively early.

Only a handful of people turned up for Musset's funeral in 1857. This seems remarkable now, in the light of Musset's continuing popular appeal both as poet and dramatist. It is all the more remarkable in view of the enthusiastic welcome given him by the members of the Romantic *Cénacle* when he first joined the group in 1828. His precocious poetic talent and dazzling wit could not, and did not, fail to impress its members.

Romances of Spain and Italy was written after the first collected works of Victor Hugo had become available. Just as it is of little moment that Victor Hugo's *Poems of the Orient* was inspired by his watching the sun set over Paris, so it matters little that when Musset's collection first appeared, he was not familiar with either Spain or Italy. The brightness and color of these countries, remembered or imagined, appealed to the young Romantics seeking a vivid contrast with the drabness of France in their day; a rich backcloth in front of which intense pas-

sion could be appropriately represented.

The poems for which Musset is best known are the series of four "Nights": "The Night of May," "The Night of December," "The Night of August," and "The Night of October." All four relate directly to his turbulent, unhappy love affair with the novelist George Sand. Although it is easy to exaggerate the effect of this liaison on Musset, it does seem certain that he was deeply marked by it and that subsequent affairs even served to remind him of it.

The four "Nights" contain some of the finest lyrical passages that may be found in French verse. They take the dramatic form of dialogues between the poet and his Muse, with the latter acting as a confidante who listens, advises, and consoles. In "The Night of May," the Spring Muse vainly begs the poet to give form to his suffering in a work of art; by so doing, he will be participating in the rites of creation and eternal renewal taking place around him. At first, the poet thinks he is only imagining the voice of the Muse, but little by little it grows louder and more urgent, and he clearly makes out her words:

> Poet, take thy lute. . . .

The Muse despairs of banishing the poet's indolence, after insisting however that his very unhappiness would have been a guarantee of the beauty of his verse:

> The most desperate songs are the most
>   beautiful;
> I know some immortal ones that are
>   pure sobs.

The poet breaks his silence to claim that the weight of his grief is such that no form of expression could bear it:

But I have suffered a hard martyrdom
And the least I might say about it,
Were I to try it on my lute,
Would break it like a reed . . .

"The Night of December" presents, beside the poet, a mysterious companion who follows him through all the stages of his life. This brother reveals himself to be the image of loneliness. In "The Night of August" a happier note is struck, the work involves a hymn of praise to the forces of life that allow man to recover from the setbacks in life. However, "The Night of October" contains a return to anguish for the poet. He knows once more wrath and despair; he realizes that he has not in fact recovered from his unhappy love affair.

In his series of "Nights," Musset seems to have moved away from the mainstream of the nineteenth century Romantic movement. Yet in doing so, he renews contact with some of the resources of Romanticism in its ageless aspects. For here the poet places himself at the center of his poetic meditation and, in representing himself sincerely, as directly as possible, admits the reader to a position of privileged intimacy. The reader feels in sympathy with the poet. Musset's sincere, lyrical laying bare of the emotions in the form of confidential poetry was to be imitated frequently in the course of the nineteenth century.

The emotion which recurs with most frequency in Musset's verse is love. His love is in turn generally associated with suffering and a form of regret. A partial explanation of Musset's considerable popularity may doubtless be sought in the lucidity with which he was able to analyze his sufferings and their causes. It is this lucidity and the regret which it provokes that make Musset's unhappiness especially poignant. One of the most moving illustrations of this sincere self-analysis, from which all trace of oratory or rhetoric is excluded, may be found in the short piece entitled "Sadness." This sonnet, collected in the *New Poems* of 1852, was written in June, 1840. It is a confession of failure in life: a loss of pride, a wasting of energy and a sense of shame about the whole situation:

I have wasted my strength and my life,
I have lost my friends, my gaiety;
I have even lost my pride
Which gave confidence in my genius.

The simplicity of the language, its power to suggest the repentance of the sinner, remind the reader of similar confessions by François Villon four hundred years earlier.

In Musset, the dramatist often coexists with the poet, and it is difficult to separate the two. This is readily evident in the dramatic dialogue employed in the "Nights." Regrettably, it also shows up in oratorical aspects of parts of these poems. The double role of poet and dramatist seems part of a greater dualism and even dichotomy in Musset. On the one hand he was truly a child of his century, containing within himself many of its contradictions, much of its anguish. On the other, he was an admirer of the great French classics, too aware of the tradition of French letters ever to subscribe completely to the doctrines of the Romantic *Cénacle.* Some of the distrust with which he came to be viewed by members of the group may be explained by his mischievously parodying some of their excesses. If it is valid to talk of Musset as a poet aiming at a free transfer of emotion from himself to his reader, it is also necessary to remark that irony and whimsical, critical detachment are also components of Musset's poetic repertory.

"A Wasted Evening"—a poem about an evening at the theater—is one of Musset's finest poems. It has the tone of a conversation. Whereas in other pieces by Musset one might regret the absence of those elements of density and surprise which are often held to be essential to a poem, here they are much in evidence. The poem is related to a precise circumstance in his life: a performance of Molière's *The Misanthropist* in Paris in 1840. Musset proceeds from an ironic, effective treatment of current tastes in the theater:

> I was alone, the other evening, at the
> Théâtre-Français,
> Or almost alone; the author had but lit-
> tle success.
> Of course, it was just Molière. . . .

Then, in masterly fashion, he weaves in a new theme: the glimpse of a girl in the theater brings to mind a phrase from the poet André Chénier. This is enough to distract the poet from the task he had set himself: to rehabilitate, and imitate the talent of the seventeenth century drama- tist. Musset succeeds admirably here in calling to life an atmosphere, and in mak- ing a concise, critical commentary on the tastes of men of his day. Moreover, he shows up strikingly the problem of his personal, artistic indolence.

That flippancy and irony were a stud- ied technique becomes obvious in a piece such as "Upon Three Steps of Marble," a poem composed in 1849. The title refers to the stairs of the terrace of the *Orange- rie* at Versailles. The beginning of the poem is a disrespectful description of the palace and park of Versailles:

> I do not believe that there is on earth a
> place
> . . . . . .
> More described, more lauded, more

> sung
> Than the boring park of Versailles.

The flippant beginning, with its implicit criticism of descriptive poetry, gives way however to a magnificent evocation of the century of Louis XIV, with which Mus- set patently feels considerable spiritual affinity.

When Musset's name is mentioned, regret is often expressed. It is felt by many readers that with a more sustained effort, he could have accomplished far more than he did, that his life of dissipa- tion must be deplored. Some have the impression that in his emotional develop- ment Musset never did seem to move far beyond adolescence. The poet himself hints at this possibility in an address to the reader in the *First Poems*:

> My first poems are those of a child
> The second of an adolescent
> The last scarcely of a man.

Even if this is true, and it seems possible, it is to be remembered that Musset is in good company. It could perhaps be shown that many great poets, although they did not write during their actual ad- olescence, frequently referred back to it, consciously or unconsciously, as their pri- mary source of inspiration.

THE POETRY OF NEKRASOV

Author: Nikolai Nekrasov (1821-1878)
Principal published works: Dreams and Sounds, 1840; "Vlas," 1856; *The Pedlar,* 1861; *The Red-Nosed Frost,* 1863; "Russian Women," 1871-1872; *Who Can be Happy and Free in Russia?* 1873-1876; *Last Songs,* 1877

The second half of the nineteenth century produced two outstanding Russian poets who were, however, almost direct opposites. Afanasi Shenshin, better known as Fet, represented the art for art's sake school in his lucid, subjective lyrics. His antagonist was Nikolai Nekrasov, a remarkable, enterprising, and often contradictory man who wrote realistic "civic" poems.

At seventeen Nekrasov was disowned by his wealthy father. Alone in St. Petersburg, the youth was forced to take up hack-writing in order to sustain himself. During this time he wrote a great many rhymed *feuilletons* and acquired a facility for turning out mediocre verse which, unfortunately, he never lost, even in his later serious work. His first collection of poems, *Dreams and Sounds,* appeared in 1840. It was a complete failure and was ruthlessly criticized by Vissarion Belinsky, the foremost literary critic of nineteenth century Russia. Determined to be a success, Nekrasov entered the publishing field and in 1846 bought *The Contemporary,* which, under his editorship, became the outstanding literary journal in Russia.

Nekrasov has rightfully been called a genius as an editor and publisher. He had the ability to get the best writers as contributors and had himself a keen eye for good verse. *The Contemporary* published works by Dostoevski, Turgenev, and Tolstoy. Encouraged by his financial success, Nekrasov again began to write poetry. After many sentimental and prosaic excesses, he succeeded in creating original standards for his work. He deliberately aimed at realistic, rhetorical verse that did not follow traditional aesthetic paths or the Pushkin tradition of which Fet was an heir. Unfortunately, Nekrasov did not have the same skill in judging his own work as he had in judging that of others, and it is only when he abandoned traditional meters altogether and wrote in a folk-song style that his poems achieved a successful, vigorous, and highly original character.

In content, too, Nekrasov broke with the traditionalists. While Fet followed the Romantic school, Nekrasov strongly adhered to Naturalism as Belinsky had formulated it. Belinsky advocated a fidelity to life in literature, a representation of the "inner and outer truth" of Russian life as well as a devotion to positive social tendencies. In other words, literature should be both a protest against social injustices and a compassionate portrayal of the Russian masses. Nekrasov's poems fitted this formula well. His favorite subject was the suffering and misery of the Russian peasantry. In 1856, Nekrasov published a long narrative poem, "Vlas," which tells how a rich peasant suffered a vision of hell, repented his former sins, greed, and miserliness, and became an ascetic. This poem, obvious moral and all, closely resembles a sermon. Later, Nekrasov turned from this kind of moralizing to a more arresting description of the peasantry and at the same time gave his verses a tone of irony that saved them from sentimentality.

In 1866 publication of *The Contemporary* had been suspended. With the aid of Saltykov-Shchedrin and Mikhailovsky, Nekrasov then began to edit *The Fatherland's Annals,* which he had acquired. Under these three the periodical becamed the leading instrument of the "populist" trend of thought.

Nekrasov's 1863 narrative poem, *The Red-Nosed Frost,* describes, almost as in a fairy tale, the beauties of the Russian winter and presented an idealized picture of the peasant woman. Darya, a young widow who has just returned from her husband's burial. The cottage is cold and so she goes out to gather wood to build a fire that will keep her children warm. While she collects logs for the fire King Frost sees her and causes her to fall asleep. As she freezes to death she remembers her happy marriage and her two children, working together with her family in the fields. The poem is beautiful and passionate, deep in feeling and pathos. In another poem, "Russian Women," the sufferings of women are again depicted as two wives follow their husbands into exile in Siberia. *The Pedlar*, written in 1861, is a series of poems about two traveling peasants who sell cloth in the countryside. Their initial adventures, jokes, and tales are followed by "Song of a Poor Pilgrim," which begins "I pass through the meadows, the wind in the meadows is moaning; I am cold, pilgrim, I am cold. I am cold, dear one, I am cold. I pass through the forest, the beasts in the forest are howling: We are hungry, pilgrim, we are hungry! Hungry, dear one, hungry." The tone of foreboding and hopelessness in this lamenting repetition prepares the reader for the tragic end of the poem when the peasants are robbed and murdered in the forest. In this poem Nekrasov approximated the spirit of Russian folk song so closely that the opening lines were later included in an actual song of the people.

In many of his poems Nekrasov used dactylic endings, which were typical of the *byliny*, the oral heroic poems of medieval Russia. He introduced unpoetic peasant words and at times used an almost journalistic style. Nekrasov's most famous short lyric is "Whether I am driving down a dark street at night." The story of a starving couple unable to buy a coffin for their dead child, it is told in intense, direct style. The mother has no alternative but to go out into the streets to earn money for the coffin. The poem ends with the thought: "All without exception will call you by a terrible name. Only within me will curses stir and die away to no purpose."

The extremes of poverty and misery especially attracted Nekrasov. In his epic work *Who Can be Happy and Free in Russia?* the theme is also that of peasant suffering. The poem attempts to give a picture of all Russia after the abolition of serfdom in 1861. The theme is presented as a folk tale. Seven peasants meet and argue over who they think is happy and free in Russia. Eventually they come to blows. They capture a small bird. Seeking freedom, the bird offers them a magic napkin. Agreeing to take the ransom gift, the peasants are delighted with it and proceed to put it to use. When they see the wonders it offers, they decide to follow the commandments of God and to settle their arguments with reason and honor. They then decide that they will not return home until they have discovered who is happy and free in Russia. They meet all types of people during their search. One of the common people, Grisha, dreams that the future holds freedom and happiness for all the people of Russia. This poem has none of the subjective lamentations of *The Pedlar*. The style is vigorous and expressive, the tone good-humored and sometimes satirical. The work shows Nekrasov at his best, and the critic D. S. Mirsky has called it one of the most original works in Russian poetry of the nineteenth century.

Nekrasov's place in Russian literature has been repeatedly reassessed. During his lifetime he was often criticized for his private conduct, and it is true that his personal life was strangely in contrast to the ideas he expressed in his poems. He spent his large income on lavish dinners, mistresses, and entertainment. His name was linked with many scandals, and he was known as an unscrupulous businessman. Nevertheless the radicals of the day praised him for the compassion for the peasantry he displayed in his poems.

In 1878, at Nekrasov's funeral, Dostoevski said that Nekrasov deserved the third place in Russian literature, close to Pushkin and Lermontov. The crowd responded with the cry, "Higher, higher." In contrast, critics of the aesthetic school scorned Nekrasov's poetry. Today a middle ground has been reached, and he is recognized as a highly original and expressive poet. By creating his own standards Nekrasov opened new possibilities for poetry. At the same time, using folk-song techniques, he brought his verse closer to the people, so that his readers were not limited to the intelligentsia. The Symbolists of the early twentieth century, especially Blok and Bely, paid Nekrasov a lasting tribute when they openly imitated his attempts to make poetry out of the prose of life.

THE POETRY OF NERUDA

Author: Pablo Neruda (1904-1973)
Principal published works: Veinte poemas de amor y una canción desesperada, 1924;
Tentativa del hombre infinito, 1926; *Residencia en la Tierra, I,* 1933; *Residencia en la Tierra, II,* 1935; *Un Canto para Bolivar,* 1941; *Tercera Residencia, 1935-1945,* 1947;
Canto General, 1950; *Odas Elementales,* 1954; *Nuevas Odas Elementales,* 1955; *Obras Completas,* 1957

Reading Pablo Neruda's poetry requires patience, tolerance, and high spirit. Very few of the contemporary Spanish-speaking writers have created so much, so incoherently and so poetically, as this Chilean poet. Before his achievement an attitude of indifference or complete adherence becomes almost impossible. Criticism must also take into account the radicalism of his Communist ideology and the resulting controversial opinions of his readers. A literary analysis of his poetry must put aside these perspectives in order to obtain a serene and objective appreciation of his work.

Neruda's poetry is characterized by language and attitudes as visceral as those of D. H. Lawrence. Most of the time his poetry springs tumultuously in a feverish mood, expressing his eroticism, melancholy, anxiety, and protest.

From the very beginning, in his youthful work, he expresses his romantic vein in the limpid, sad lines of *Crepusculario* (*Poems of the Twilight*).

At the same time, while love and beauty are sharpened by erotic desire, the poet tries to avoid them.

Veinte poemas de amor y una canción desesperada (*Twenty Poems of Love and a Desperate Song*) inaugurates, as the title itself implies, the torture of love. Between the poet and the loved woman there is only distance and bitterness. It does not matter whether love has joy in itself; sooner or later anguish crosses the heart as a tempest and whirlwind. To heal his wounds the poet would prefer to escape from everything that would tend to hold him where he is. Since he has found only disaster in woman, it is time to fly away. In "A Desperate Song" he feels his heart broken, rotten, converted into a pit that is bitter and open to the trash of the world.

A milestone in Neruda's poetry is his *Residencias,* three books published successively in 1933, 1935, and 1947. The first two books have as title *Residencia en la Tierra, I* and *II* (*Residence on Earth*); the last of the series is *Tercera Residencia* (*Third Residence*). In these he adheres to surrealism and a philosophical attitude pervades the poems. Subjected to vital experiences, in a world of constant changes, he views everything in a state of disintegration: men, love, stars, waves, life. Everything belongs to the drama of the river that is constant and yet ever changing. The poet's sense of disintegration appears everywhere in these books, in which he abandons logic and syntax as a formal consequence of his inner attitude. The result is a message of disintegration through disintegrated ideas, sentences, and words. It is hard to find a single line in these books in which there is no violence.

In the first book, *Residencias,* this process of disintegration is the scenery in which the poet contemplates perpetual decadence. The only possible ways of escaping from this cosmic cataclysm are love and poetry, though time is always and stubbornly corroding all around it. His lack of faith in something, his feelings of guilt with no possible redemption, emphasizes his anxiety.

"Arte Poética" ("Poetic Art"), one of the most hermetic and at the same time most revealing poems of this book, exemplifies those ideas. The corporal senses establish a relationship with everything that surrounds him as he locates himself among shadows and space. But suddenly there appears, as a true escape, his desire of poetizing and loving, of expressing his prophetic voice and his melancholy, and of answering to a universal call from things that question in a confused and constant manner.

The joy of love and poetry, however, is melted by time and matter. The poet is surrounded by one single thing and one single movement.

As this title suggests, Neruda shares in a semi-pantheistic conception, but with no religious implication, the same destiny of the cosmos. He is not a thing, but the universe is limiting him, restraining his ideals, paralyzing his restlessness. Paradoxically he feels both the companionship and enmity of the universe.

His symbols, with no coherent meaning but expressing his personal vision are rich: *bee, sword, fire, grape, ant, butterfly, dove, fish, salt,* and *rose* are common and meaningful words in Neruda's poetry. Under these symbols hide love, vitality, joy, hostility, negation, dream, fugacity, erotism, plurality—words that include a very personal perspective.

His second *Residencias* possesses a more mature expression within the stream of super-realism. His contact with the Spanish poets who had adopted a visionary attitude orients his production. In these poems he achieves evasion from reality through dreams, subconsciousness, and illogical reasoning. Disintegration and its consequent anguish keep pervading his poems, but he is no more a mere spectator of decadence; he is a human, anguished, and abhors his human quality.

The worship of "ugliness," a trait of super-realism, imposes upon Neruda the use of words, sentences, and stanzas of incoherent and strange effects. But his apparent absurdities in his poetry have an intention. Since the world is for the poet a planet filled with useless, worn things, he chooses some of them to express his nausea, his feeling of futility toward all types of being.

The third *Residencia* begins with a series of poems of the same trend as those included in the second volume. But

from the seventh, "The furies and sorrows," written in 1934, Neruda declares that the world and his poetry have changed, as he indicates in the lines preceding the poem.

With these poems his work takes a radical turn. Until now Neruda had been the poet of egotism, solitude, disintegration, and anguish. The Communist ideology now appears in his verse and he writes political poems, full of vigor and fury.

The Spanish Civil War and World War II influenced this transformation. Neruda even ridicules his concern with his earlier themes. "Spain in my heart," one of the poems of this book, presents his new attitude: he curses wealthy Spanish people because they are responsible for the poverty of the country, blasphemes against God, attacks tradition because of its sterility, condoles with Madrid stormed by Franco's soldiers, and justifies his hatred of tyrannic suppression. He praises the Republican soldiers' mothers, remembers with affection many small Spanish towns, evokes the arrival of the International Brigade, condemns Franco and his generals, wails over the destruction of Madrid, and finishes his tempestuous lines with an ode to the People's Army, hope of salvation for the country.

His poems about Stalingrad, in the period of World War II, also have political and social themes; the tone of indignation is now directed against German soldiers, and praise is given to the Russians. His lines become less hermetic; they are more open and direct. More concerned with ideas and feelings, Neruda puts aside his old poetic techniques and stylistic resources. "New Song of Love to Stalingrad" is explanatory of his "public" poetry of the period.

Canto General (General Song) is one of the most ambitious book of poems ever written in Spanish. It is a work inspired by Neruda's political ideas and his personal interpretation of Spanish-American history. A nationalist attitude echoes through many of the poems, for Chile is very often at the center of Neruda's emotion and thought. We can find some antecedents of these poems on the attitude and production of Andrés Bello, Rubén Darío, and Leopoldo Lugones, who strove through different poetic works to exalt and praise the Spanish-American continent. But no one of them reached the span and influence of Neruda's *Canto General*.

The book is divided into fifteen cantos of unequal length and value. Among lines of great lyric beauty appear also some filled with prosaic expression. Some of the positive features of the book are its almost constant strength, its vast knowledge of Spanish-American history, geography, and flora, and its wide variety of meters, forms and measures of the poems. In the last of the cantos, the poet states the sources and intention of his book.

"Amor América (America, My Love")" stands first in the book. It is a beautiful poem of praise to the continent before the arrival of the Spaniards: the Indians were tender and bloody, owners of the land until blood was spilled and a lamp was extinguished. This initial lyric introduces a series of poems presenting an ecumenical parade of themes and tones. "Alturas de Macchu Picchu" ("Heights of Macchu Picchu"), the fortress city of the Incas, perched high between two mountain peaks, gives Neruda an opportunity for a poem of great chromatic effect.

"Canto General de Chile" ("General Song to Chile") is another poem of imaginative and descriptive strength. Geography, geological disasters, towns, people, and plants are shown amidst a stream of powerful metaphors. Neruda's absence from his country, exile imposed because of his ideology, exacerbates his patriotic feelings, and upon his return he made this feeling clear in "Hymn and Return."

The last series of the poems, *Yo soy* (*I Am*), is a poetic autobiography. Neruda sings to his native place and early childhood, tells his stay in Santiago, his overseas adventures, his dramatic stay in Spain, his pleasant sojourn in Mexico, a country he prefers. He closes this book with his last will, proclaiming his faith in Communism and asserting his freedom.

Neruda's last works, *Odas Elementales* (*Elementary Odes*), *Nuevas Odas Elementales* (*New Elementary Odes*), and *Tercer Libro de las Odas* (*Third Book of the Odes*), are composed of poems written in hendecasyllable and heptasyllable lines; in them a new poetic turn appears. Now simple themes and common things are present, often with the result that the poetry becomes platitudinous and poor. "Oda a la alcachofa" ("Ode to the Artichoke"), "Oda al caldillo de congrio" ("Ode to the Conger Eel Broth") are some titles that speak for themselves. At the same time, however, the poet displays a greater love for nature. In "Ode to the Rose" a tone of tranquillity sharply contrasts with his former protest and violence.

Neruda's poetry, despite its hermetism and obliquity of ideology, is valid testimony of a rebel, an anguished, impotent man of our times. His poetry is hard to understand, too long to be pleasantly read, too slanted to be ideologically shared. But its darkness and rage correspond to the expression of the oniric realm, to the telluric forces of nature, to the instincts, frustrations, and pessimism that corrodes the modern world. He projects into our time that poetic stream, vital and furious, of the *poets maudits* of last century, who revolted against everything and everybody, including themselves, and created a pre-existentialist current of desperation, the mood of many writers in this century.

THE POETRY OF NERVAL

Author: Gérard de Nerval (Gérard Labrunie, 1808-1855)
Principal published works: Odelettes, 1852; *Les chimères,* 1854; *Poésies,* 1924

No poet of the French Romantic group has a more ardent public today than Gérard de Nerval, whose haunting poetic visions have influenced poets from Baudelaire to the Surrealists. Yet his visionary powers also brought him poverty, madness and repeated failure in love, and finally led him to take his own life. Numbering scarcely more than fifty, his poems remain more strangely suggestive than any other writing of the period and reveal a true poet's sense of the secret sources of lyricism. The finest of them carry this lyricism into a world of illusions and shifting forms, where "dream overflows into real life."

Setting aside his earliest poems, Nerval grouped the others under three different headings: the *Odelettes,* short lyric pieces; the poems composed specifically to be set to music, *Lyricism and Operatic Lyrics (Lyrisme et vers d'opéra)*; and finally, separate from the others, the twelve sonnets (plus nine published long after his death) of *Les chimères (Chimerae,* or *Visions).* He also made collections of the folk songs, poems, and legends of his native Valois and some remarkable translations of the German mystical and Romantic poets, including Heine and Richter. His rendering of *Faust* (Parts I and II), a scrupulously careful, yet eminently poetic text which remains the standard French version of Goethe's great poem, earned high praise from the author. Alone among the French poets of his generation, Nerval felt a spiritual kinship with the metaphysical orientation of the German poetic tradition. From the fantastic, hallucinatory tales of E. T. A. Hoffmann he learned what fragile boundaries separate the realms of poetry, dream, and external reality—the central discovery of his life.

Characteristic of all his work is a perfect technical control. The directness of German and folk poetry taught him to avoid the pretentiousness and bombast which mar the work of so many of his more famous contemporaries. From the lightest song to the densest sonnet, meter and rhyme sustain the poetic movement, seconding and enhancing its suggestions. The lyrics achieve that rare feat of retaining their charm in the absence of the musical setting for which they were created. Even his prose expresses delicate nuances of perception with a musicality in which not a word is wasted.

The *Odelettes* are vibrant with the same sort of limpid enchantment. Avoiding the pompous rhetoric, didactic tendencies, and factitious allegory inherited by his contemporaries from the eighteenth century, Nerval looked back for his models to the greatest period of pure lyrical expression in French literature, the Renaissance of Ronsard. In this collection the exuberant rhymes of a bacchic song such as "Gaieté" stand beside shimmering, whispered evocations of the natural world "In the Woods" ("Dans les bois") or in early springtime ("Avril"):

Déjà les beaux jours, la poussière,
Un ciel d'azur et de lumière,
Les murs enflammés, les longs soirs;
Et rien de vert: à peine encore
Un reflet rougeâtre décore
Les grands arbres aux rameaux noirs!

Ce beau temps me pèse et m'ennuie.
Ce n'est qu'après des jours de pluie
Que doit surgir, en un tableau,
Le printemps verdissant et rose,
Comme une nymphe fraîche éclose,
Qui, souriante, sort de l'eau.

(Already there are fine days and dust,
Already a blazing, azure sky,
The walls are on fire, the evenings
     lengthening,
And nothing green; barely visible yet,
A reddish reflection decorates

The towering trees with their black
branches!

This fine weather weighs me down and
wearies me.
It is only after rainy days
That spring should surge up,
A picture going green and rose-colored,
Brought out like a new nymph
Who steps from the water, smiling.)

A lament for lost loves—"Les Cyda-
lises"—follows a sensitive, half-mocking
rumination on "Butterflies," hovering
flowers which "pass like a thought/of poetry or of love." Whatever the subject of
the approach, the result is a gem of pure
lyrical expression. Where his contemporaries posture and declame, Nerval simply sings.

Some of his fundamental preoccupa-
tions appear in the *Odelettes* free from
the obscurity and cypher-like transmuta-
tions of *Les chimères*. Long before Marcel Proust, he asserted the superiority of
affective memory over immediate experience. "It is now three years since my
grandmother died," he says in "La
grand'mère":

Depuis trois ans, part le temps prenant
force,
Ainsi qu'un nom gravé dans une écorce,
Son souvenir se creuse plus avant!

(For three years now, taking strength
from time,
Like a name engraved in the bark of a
tree,
Her memory sinks more deeply into
me.)

The poet had a sense of very real participation in the past, not only his own, but
that of his race, and even the occult,
mythical past of the ancient Eastern-
Mediterranean peoples. In "Fantasy" he
is transported to the early seventeenth
century:

Il est un air pour qui je donnerais
Tout Rossini, tout Mozart et tout
Weber
Un air très-vieux, languissant et fu-
nèbre,

Qui pour moi seul a des charmes secrets.

Or, chaque fois que je viens à l'en-
tendre,
De deux cents ans mon âme rajeunit:
C'est sous Louis treize . . . Et je crois
voir s'étendre
Un coteau vert que le couchant jaunit,
Puis un château de brique à coins de
pierre,
Aux vitraux teints de rougeâtres cou-
leurs,
Ceint de grands parcs, avec une rivière
Baignant ses pieds, qui coule entre des
fleurs.

Puis une dame, à sa haute fenêtre,
Blonde aux yeux noirs, en ses habits
anciens . . .
Que, dans une autre existence peut-
être,
J'ai déjà vue!—et dont je me souviens!

(There is a melody for which I would
surrender
All Rossini, all Mozart, all Weber,
An ancient, langorous, funereal tune,
With hidden charms for me alone.

And every time I hear that air,
Suddenly I grow two centuries younger.
I live in the reign of Louis the Thir-
teenth . . . and see stretched out
A green slope yellowed by the sunset,

Then a brick castle with stone corners,
Its panes of glass stained by ruddy
colors,
Encircled with great parks, and a river
Bathing its feet, flowing between flowers.

Then I see a fair-haired, dark-eyed lady
In old-fashioned costume, at a tall window,
Whom perhaps I have already seen
somewhere
In another life . . . and whom I remember!)

Many of these poems were written before
Nerval's encounter with the actress Jenny
Colon, who, after her death at twenty-
five, came to incarnate in his imagination
the feminine ideal. Only one, the often
anthologized "Une allée du Luxem-

bourg" ("A Lane in the Luxembourg Gardens"), suggests his constant search for the Beloved Woman "who, coming into [his] profound night/would light it with a single glance,"

> Qui venant dans ma nuit profonde
> D'un seul regard l'éclaircirait!

Here the unknown girl is as yet only a passing ray of light ("doux rayon qui m'as lui").

In spite of the variety of forms taken by the *Odelettes,* there is not a sonnet among them. Nerval reserved this lyric form for his most intense, anguished and difficult works, *Les chimères,* composed in a state of "supernaturalistic revery." In such a state, said his friend Theophile Gautier, "the soul becomes aware of invisible relationships, of previously unnoticed coincidences." To express his discoveries, Nerval invented a cypher-like poetic language. So unlike anything being written at the time were the *Chimerae* that recognition of their mysterious beauty has come only recently, the result in part of the Surrealists' explorations of the subconscious. If Nerval's more lyrical poems sing to an Orphic lyre, these sonnets chant in the haunting semi-tones of Eastern mysticism. Insisting on their basically incantatory nature, he remarked that they "would gain nothing by being explained—if the thing were possible." Despite the poet's comment, they have given rise to numerous studies and exegeses and their meaning, if not entirely agreed upon, is at least much clearer today than it was to his contemporaries.

Basic to the whole set is the anguish stated in the "Christ on the Mount of Olives" group of five poems. There, imitating the German mystical poet Jean-Paul Richter, he depicts Christ as the eternal embodiment of man's despair in a silent, godless universe. "Brothers," he cries to his disciples, "I deceived you: All is emptiness! Abyss!/The god is missing at the altar where I am the victim. . . . /There is no God! God is no longer!"

> "Frères, je vous trompais: Abîme!

> abîme! abîme!
> Le dieu manque à l'autel où je suis la victime . . .
> Dieu n'est past! Dieu n'est plus!" . . .

Faced with the inevitability of physical death, and the less of his belief in the Christian salvation, the poet was to find a new hope of immortality in the animism of the pagan past. His Pythagorean conception of a sentient universe is formulated in the final poem of the *Chimerae,* "Vers dorés" ("Golden Verses"). This personal kind of religious eclecticism, which he called "syncreticism," allowed him to see Christ as but one more archetypal incarnation of the "sublime fool"—the visionary, the poet, the discoverer—destroyed by his own aspirations, "this forgotten Icarus who ascended the heavens."

> Cet Icare oublié qui remontait les cieux.

In his desire to force the "gates of ivory" which conceal that ineffable reality of whose existence his mystical beliefs—and his dreams—assured him, he threw himself into the study of the occult like another Faust, no longer aspiring to anything but "knowledge of things supernatural, no longer capable of living within the limited circle of human desires." Events from his life, processed by memory, came to exist on the same plane as myth, illusion, dream, and those historical events which he adopted as part of his personal past. Through these revelations he was assured not only of personally overcoming death, but of recovering his beloved in another world. "It would be consoling," he muses, "to believe that eternity conserves in its bosom a sort of universal history, visible only through the eyes of the soul." If the past continues to exist in the present, then time and death are no longer to be feared. "Artémis," one of Nerval's most beautiful poems, postulates the fusion of past and present, expressed in the opening lines in terms of the indefinable period between the last (twelfth) hour and the first, which is at the same time the thirteenth, continuation and renewal:

La Treizième revient . . . C'est encor
  la première;
Et c'est toujours la seule,—ou c'est le
  seul moment. . . .

(The Thirteenth returns . . . once
  more she is the first;
And she is still the only one, or this is
  the only moment. . . .)

Just as dreams "flowed into real life," revealing the "super-reality" he sought, myth became for Nerval the key to the cycle of universal history, the retainer of archetypes. "Artémis" continues, applying to the lover and his beloved this same principle of eternal rebirth:

Car es-tu reine, ô toi! la première ou
  dernière?
Es-tu roi, toi le seul ou le dernier
  amant? . . .

(For you are surely queen, first and
  last?
For you are surely king, O first and last
  lover? . . .)

In the quest for his personal reality, Gerard Labrunie reveled in pseudonyms—his noble pen name is an example—and identified himself with many a figure of history or myth. The effectiveness of "El desdichado" ("The Outcast"), his most famous poem, is largely due to the interplay of these shifting identifications.

Je suis le ténébreux,—le veuf,—l'inconsolé,
Le prince d'Aquitaine à la tour abolie:
Ma seule *étoile* est morte,—et mon luth constellé
Porte le *soleil* noir de la *Mélancolie*.
Dans la nuit du tombeau, toi qui m'as consolé,
Rends-moi le Pausilippe et la mer d'Italie,
La *fleur* qui plaisait tant à mon coeur désolé,
Et la treille où le pampre à la rose s'allie.

Suis-je Amour ou Phébus? . . . Lusignan ou Biron?

Mon front est rouge encor du baiser de
  la reine;
J'ai rêvé dans la grotte où nage la
  sirène . . .

Et j'ai deux fois vainqueur traversé
  l'Achéron:
Modulant tour à tour sur la lyre
  d'Orphée
Les soupirs de la sainte et les cris de
  la fée.

(I am the dark man, the disconsolate
  widower,
The prince of Aquitania whose tower
  has been torn down:
My sole *star* is dead,—and my constellated lute
Bears the black *sun* of *Melancolia*.

In the darkness of my grave, you who
  have consoled me,
Give me back Posilipo and the Italian
  sea,
The *flower* so dear to my tormented
  heart,
And the arbor of vines where the rose
  twines the branch.

Am I Amor or Phoebus? . . . Lusignan or Biron?
My forehead is still red with the kiss
  of the queen;
In the grotto where the siren swims I
  have had a dream . . .

And twice I have crossed and conquered
  the Acheron:
On Orpheus' lyre in turn I have sent
The cries of faery and the sighs of a
  saint.)

Through the loss of his beloved (his "sole *star*") he has become several almost allegorical types and a figure from medieval legend. Again, when he asks if he is Amor or Phoebus, Lusignan or Biron, he is seeking his true role—lover or poet?—and wondering whether his love has been a real woman or a creature of fantasy. These names, however, are not simply literary symbols. The poem is a distillation of Nerval's mystical experience.

Like so many aspects of his life, his search for the Eternal Feminine developed within the context of a play of opposites. Woman is "saint" or "fée," source of life and light or mysterious apparition from the world of darkness. Although she took on many contradictory forms during his lifetime, there was only one object of Nerval's love. Having twice crossed the frontiers of madness (the Acheron) and returned successfully, he knew that only in death could he find his Beloved. On the night of January 28, 1855, he stepped into that other existence, fulfilling the prophecy in "Artémis":

Aimez qui vous aima du berceau dans
   la bière;
Celle que j'aimai seul m'aime encor
   tendrement:
C'est la mort—ou la morte . . . O
   délice! ô tourment!
(Love the one who loved you from
   the cradle to the grave;/
The one alone I love loves me dearly
   still:
She is death—or the dead one. . . .
   Delight or torment!)

THE POETRY OF NICHOLAS BRETON

Author: Nicholas Breton (1545?-1626?)
Principal published works: Bower of Delights, c. 1591; *Pilgrimage to Paradise,* 1592; *Arbor of Amorous Devices,* 1597; *Melancholic Humours,* 1600; *Poems in England's Helicon,* 1600; *The Passionate Shepherd,* 1604

> Who can live in heart so glad
> As the merry country lad?
> Who upon a fair green balk
> May at pleasure sit and walk?

Thus Breton asks and gives the answer in *The Passionate Shepherd,* just as Marlowe and Raleigh and other Elizabethans, from Sidney and Spenser to Shakespeare and Jonson, lyrically spoke. The pastoral, the idyll, the lyric, and the satire reached classic heights during the period, with Nicholas Breton one of its most artistic voices.

His voice was varied; his background was obscure; he was praised and ridiculed by his eminent peers. He possessed both versatility and refinement as a writer of satire, romance, pastorals in prose and verse, but he excelled in lyric verse. His devotion to letters is unquestioned and attested to by one after another of the Elizabethan giants. As a friend of Sidney, a protégé of Spenser, he was the devoted servant to a great patroness of poets, Sidney's sister, the Countess of Pembroke. Most critics agree that this patronage, especially in Breton's allegorical *Pilgrimage to Paradise,* brought to the highest his considerable talent. Also, in the lines "Nor was the labor little for to climb/The fiery ashes of a phoenix nest" he speaks not only with religious fervor of the risen Christ but of Sidney's memory.

Apparently Breton was one of the first careful anthologizers, including leading artists in his *Bower of Delights* and *Arbor of Amorous Devices* contributing himself to another collection sometimes ascribed to him, *England's Helicon.* His scholarly nature suggests an Oxford background, accented by dedications to "schollars and students of Oxford." His satire, expressed through the pseudonym of Pasquil, is not up to the wittier works of Nashe and Green, though he obviously moved among the university wits, "the tribe of Ben."

The dispute of his religious sympathies does not seem important today. His epitaph to Spenser, his invocation of the memory of Sidney, his devotional fervors, are all full of passionate yearning and rich imagery. His true religion, however, was chivalric and pastoral love, and his most memorable poems serve this cult:

> Good Muse, rock me asleep
> With some sweet harmony;
> This weary eye is not to keep
> Thy wary company.
>
> Sweet Love, be gone awhile
> Thou knowest my heaviness;
> Beauty is born but to beguile
> My heart of happiness.
> . . . . .
> And, therefore, my sweet Muse,
> Thou knowest what help is best;
> Do now thy heavenly cunning use
> To set my heart at rest.
>
> And in a dream bewray,
> What Fate shall be my friend;
> Whether my life shall still decay,
> Or when my sorrow end.

Contrapuntal to such effusions is another vein, richer in both poetry and prose, of country life and rural scenery and customs: "Shall we go dance the hay, the hay?" expresses this theme, and "Sylvan Muses, can ye sing/ Of the beauty of the spring?" celebrates all things of nature, birds, trees, and flowers, with mythological overtones. However, one of his most celebrated poems, "A Sweet Lullaby," has a darker theme:

> Come, little babe, come, silly soul,
> Thy father's shame, thy mother's grief,
> Born as I doubt to all our dole,

And to thyself unhappy chief:
  Sing lullaby and lap it warm,
  Poor soul that thinks no creature
  harm.

The poet asks the "little wretch" born out of wedlock to think kindly of his misguided father and miserable mother and then surprisingly acknowledges the child's paternity:

Come, little boy, and rock asleep!
Sing lullaby, and be thou still!
I, that can do nought else but weep,
Will sit by thee and wail my fill:
  Good bless my babe, and lullaby,
  From this thy father's quality.

Again, the poet anticipates the later metaphysical writers in his use of conceit, elaborate metaphors turned on key phrases: "Lovely kind, and kindly loving,/Such a mind were worth the moving;/Truly fair, and fairly true,/Where are all these but in you?" He elaborates the "Sweet, fair, wise, kind, blessed true,/Blessed be all these in you," in his *Melancholic Humours.* In "An Assurance" he asks, "Say that I should say I love ye,/Would you say 'tis but a saying?" and "Think I think that love should know ye,/Will you think 'tis but a thinking?" and then goes on to vow his love in the high hope that she will love in return. These witty and pretty conceits are of a high order and Breton deserves their fame.

In his prose Nicholas Breton wrote "essaies, Morall and Divine," a "conference between scholler and angler," and *Fantastickes,* prose pictures of months, hours, and festivals. But he also wrote *A Poem to Our Saviour's Passion* and *Toyes of an Idle Head,* a "Floorish upon Fancie." In short, he was a Renaissance Man and exhibited *virtu,* the vigor and the erudition and restless activity of his day, not inferior at times to those better remembered in the history of English literature.

THE POETRY OF OWEN

Author: Wilfred Owen (1893-1918)
Principal published works: Poems, 1920; *The Poems of Wilfred Owen,* edited by Edmund Blunden, 1931

For Wilfred Owen, born and brought up in the Housman country of Shropshire and Shrewsbury, reader of Keats, Tennyson, and Swinburne, a young poet devoted to boyish "loneliness" and the aesthetic cult of Beauty, wounded March 19, 1917, again on May 1, and killed in action November 4, 1918, Beauty was no escape. The horrors of war, in Owen's hands, were transfigured in poems into a terrible beauty.

The war itself did not make Owen a poet, but it did mature his poems, as if overnight; too, the war never completely dissolved his early yearning for a misty, aesthetic Beauty. But the war transformed that Beauty from a literary dream to a stark necessity, held to in the face of the horrors recorded so bluntly, spat out, the devastating "Dulce et Decorum Est."

Owen, who published only three poems during his short lifetime, could find cause for elation, within two months of his death, at being accepted "as a peer" by the generally innocuous Georgian poets, those purveyors of sentiment and pictures of the English countryside. But his poetry had before them moved sharply away from both the literary aestheticism of his youth and the either jingoistic or merely homesick poesy which had been the first two reactions to the war which, begun in August, 1914, was to be "over by Christmas."

Just before the outbreak of war, Owen could write in his diary poems about wind murmuring in the leaves and birds singing. Such evidence of a boy's experiments with sound and celebration of youth and a pastoral setting is obviously a young man's conception of poetry, based not on any real experience but probably on an immature reading of Keats, Tennyson, and Swinburne. His last known poem, "Smile, Smile, Smile," starkly illustrates how daydreams have turned into nightmares, the disingenuous into the ironic, aestheticism into social protest, beauty and truth into a deeply-felt pity which, while expressed with mature artistic detachment, is nonetheless a product of personal pain, fear, and moral outrage. The soldiers read the home-town paper and think of buying homes after the war. The poem also describes the stupid, callous, mawkish sentiment and blindness of the Home Front.

Siegfried Sassoon, Robert Graves, Edmund Blunden, Isaac Rosenburg, and Owen were the first poets to take another look at the war which had at first been regarded as a kind of sacred crusade. In his study of Owen, D. S. R. Welland writes of how, by about 1915, the emphasis in the anthologies of "war poetry" had shifted righteous nature of the crusade to the knightly crusader. The latter response merely replaced national glorification with self-pity, or, at best, evocations of better times in England. Obviously, neither reaction produced much in the way of an honest, fully human poetry. The old ways died hard.

The third reaction was one of protest, and Sassoon, perhaps, or Rosenburg, was most biting in satirical attack. Sassoon met Owen in a hospital in England, and Owen's mature war poetry dates, roughly, from their long discussions (though to say that Sassoon "made" Owen a poet is a vast distortion). Owen, however, expressed his protest not so much satirically as through a mixture of sarcasm, ironic detachment, and, most importantly, of pity. His verse loses the old melodiousness of the "Celtic twilight," and becomes hard, direct, colloquial, strongly cadenced. In this respect he was not different than the other poets of the war. In Owen, however, pity for the "poor wretches" is dominant both over pity for himself (of which there is absolutely none) and satiric protest at the perpetrated outrage of war, or the naïve, even criminal stupidities mouthed at home. And the pity is rooted not in condescension or gratuitous superiority, but in a profound awareness of human fellowship and fellow-suffering.

In "Strange Meeting" the poet meets an enemy he had killed. They meet in Hell, where he had fled to escape the terror of battle in a dream-vision. They must find fellowship in Hell itself, for Earth has become worse. The German is not a fiend, a killer who delights in atrocities and is devoted to crushing freedom and the British Empire, but a man who, like the poet, dreamed and hoped. Neither the dead nor the living indulges in self-pity. The "enemy" refers to the pity the war has distilled, but by "pity" the poet means not for self, but for his fellows, for humanity itself. Indeed, Owen develops finally a viewpoint which is largely characteristic of the poetry of World War II: a poetry not so much of protest but of a recognition of how, in the horror of battle, human fellowship is starkly, and of necessity, thrown into sharp relief. Enforced murder breeds, at last, a kind of gentleness.

Poems like "Apologia pro Poemate Mea" must be understood in this context. Death becomes a joke, and the men laugh in its face, not out of false bravado, but out of a sense of a new awareness of life, death, and fellowship. What seems bravado is, instead, an honest account of actual human response to a living, absurd hell. The death-bound comradeship, both pitiable and defiant of battle comrades, is a theme on which Owen probes the paroxysm of war more deeply and poignantly than any protest alone could. It is the core of his achievement, and his frequently quoted statement that he was not concerned with "Poetry" must be understood in terms of this attitude. Poetry, here, suggests the old illusions, the old "literary" aestheticism, poesy of birds and Greek goddesses and pastoral landscapes. To a large extent it refers to Owen's own youthful effusions and illusions. Now the poetry is in such matters as pity and protest.

In the matter of style, it should be noted that Owen's development away from the vague, vaporous, and pseudo-Keatsian effusions of his youth, his development of a style which is abrupt, chiseled, and colloquially dramatic, corresponds to a general drift in the poetry of the late nineteenth and early twentieth centuries. Parallel developments occur in the poetry of Yeats, and T. E. Hulme (who also was killed in the war). Pater and Pound had called for a more objective, "harder" or "classical" poetry, and this development may be traced in Imagism or, better, in Yeats and Eliot. In Yeats, the line of development is clear from the softly sensuous and evocative "symbolism" of his early poem to the harder and more genuinely symbolic and dramatic specimens of *The Green Helmet and Other Poems,* published in 1910.

But Wilfred Owen, until he met Sassoon in 1917, had had no important contact with the literary world, and his development of terse, "hard" idiom must have been only a natural and necessary way of expressing, without illusions, lies, evasion, and the stark and monumentally un-"Poetic" reality of war.

Owen's experiments with slant and internal rhyme, with nonmetrical cadences and compressions like that of "bloodshed," are significant steps toward a poetry which moves away from the more regular and traditionally "poetic" work of the previous two centuries. Owen influenced, in this respect, later poets like Auden, C. Day Lewis, Stephen Spender, and Louis MacNeice. But it is his individual and searing exposure of both the horror and the pity of war that provides Owen a lasting niche in the history of English poetry. A world changed during his short lifetime. His ability to change with it, and to record the old world's dying anguish, is his unique and memorable achievement.

THE POETRY OF PASTERNAK

Author: Boris Pasternak (1890-1960)
Principal published works: Bliznets v oblake, 1914 (*Twin in the Clouds*); Poerklo baryerov, 1917 (*Over the Barriers*); Sestra moya zihizn', 1922 (*Life, My Sister*); Temyi variotsii, 1923 (*Themes and Variations*); 1905 God, 1926; Lieutenant Schmidt, 1927; Spectorsky, 1932; Vtoroye rozdenie, 1932 (*Second Birth*); Na rannikh poyez dakh, 1941 (*On Early Trains*); Zemnoy Prostor, 1945 (*The Terrestrial Expanse*)

Translation is the sea change for poetry, often giving it a different coloring and new or odd dimensions during its passage from one language to another. For the linguistic artifact which is the poem, by reason of its structure achieved in and its meaning expressed through language, cannot speak in another tongue with the same sonance, precision, or authority that it possesses in the original. The best that the translator can hope to accomplish is to keep as intact as possible those elements of the poem which resist the violence of change: the larger meaning, the revealing image or metaphor, and sometimes, with luck, an echo of cadence. Without these effects the translation falls into toneless literal statement at one extreme or paraphrase, too frequently distorted and irresponsible, at the other.

In the case of Boris Pasternak, a poet of intensely personal vision and idiosyncratic style, the task of translation must appear insurmountable at times. The problem of adequate rendition involves more than the barrier of language and the difficulties arising from the writer's passionate fusion of image and meaning. It is also one of distance, the gap between two parts of a world divided by temperament, culture, and ideology in this century. Pasternak is a Russian as well as a contemporary, and reading him with understanding requires adjustment to a different picture of the world and a different evaluation of the human condition.

In his poems Pasternak's figurative tendency found expression in a joining of symbolist techniques and pantheistic feeling. Historically, he was the heir of Russian symbolism, a tradition he shared with Mayakovsky and Esenin in the post-revolutionary period. Symbolism in Russian literature is not to be confused, however, with the similar movement in France, where it was directed chiefly toward experiment with new modes of poetic expression. The Russian symbolists, although concerned with the re-creation of language, were also interested in a new consciousness of the universe and a new concept of man. Thus Mayakovsky was able to find his themes in the mythology of the revolution; Esenin voiced a lament for archaic peasant Russia, and Pasternak tried to make his poetry an expression and configuration of the essence and uniqueness of being.

In the beginning his images were abrupt, often disparate and startling, always vigorous and imaginative. His images function on both a literal and a symbolic level. A good example showing the poet's vivid imagery is present in his poem entitled "The Racing Stars."

The lines provide an illustration of T. S. Eliot's theory that a poem may be appreciated, its meaning sensed, before it is really understood. In "The Racing Stars" the appeal is almost wholly to the imagination and the senses. The subject proper is Pushkin's composition of a poem, *The Prophet*, worked at with creative energy during a night when the world—humanity—sleeps through the cold darkness. By illustration the poet is trying to express the miracle of artistic creation. A similar idea is expressed in "Definition of Poetry."

Pasternak's images are guideposts pointing to the true subject of his verse. It is the Russian land—not Holy Russia, nor revolutionary Russia, but vast, bleak, irrational, beautiful Russia—that he celebrated in his poems. His pictures are of the land itself: the rain falling in village streets, the dusty roads in summer, the steppes swept by blizzards, silent snows, thunderstorms, railway stations, dandelions, lilacs, birch trees, mushrooms, the smell of plowed earth. He found these things the true feelings guarded in man's heart. He did mention the Sahara, the Ganges, and European cities in his poems, but the place names about which associations cluster are the Moscow suburbs, the Caucasus, the Urals, Kiev, the Gulf of Finland, and the Siberian wastes. The same is true of the people in his poems. He invoked the names of Shakespeare and Beethoven, but his special reverence was for Pushkin, Lermontov, Tolstoy, and Chekhov. Apparently Pasternak thought of these four as the Russians of Russians, writers in whose works the land and its people found expression.

To Western readers, Pasternak's intense Russian feeling makes all the more incomprehensible his isolation and the name-calling to which he was subjected. One answer is that he held aloof from the stratagems of totalitarian dictatorship. Never an opportunist, in literature or in politics, he wrote no poems in celebration of collective farms, factory production, or the dictates of the Party line. Instead, he insisted upon the artist's right to privacy, freedom, and process of thought described as song. The closing lines of "Thrushes" may be interpreted as a statement of his position.

But it should not be supposed, as many readers of *Doctor Zhivago* mistakenly assumed, that Pasternak was the enemy of the revolution. He had accepted it, just as he accepted the feelings of happiness and sturdiness, as a part of the oneness and wholeness of living reality. Many of his images of turbulence relate to the great storm of the revolution in which he had been a spectator, if not a participant, of its violence. In *Lieutenant Schmidt,* the story of a mutinous officer executed for his part in the sailors' uprising at Sebastopol in 1905, he wrote that he stood between the past and the present in conflict, a position he himself had chosen. Here, perhaps, is the clue to his refusal of commitment. He looked from past to present and into the future.

His larger vision of man *sub specie aeternitatis* is the sustaining force of Pasternak's poetry, a vision directed toward the unknown and unexplored future of mankind.

THE POETRY OF PAZ

Author: Octavio Paz (1914-   )
Principal published works: Raíz del Hombre, 1937; *Bajo tu Clara Sombra,* 1937; *Entre la Piedra y la Flor,* 1941; *A la Orilla del Mundo,* 1942; *Libertad bajo Palabra,* 1949; *¿Aguila o Sol? Poemas en Prosa,* 1951; *Semillas para un Himno,* 1954; *Piedra del Sol (Sun Stone),* 1957; *La Estación Violenta,* 1958; *Libertad bajo Palabra: obra poetica 1935-1958,* 1960; *Salamandra,* 1962; *Selected Poems of Octavio Paz,* translated by Muriel Rukeyser, 1963

In Mexico the tradition of poetry extends back into ancient times. Even in pre-Columbian days the country could boast of poets among some of the Indian rulers and an oral poetic tradition of great aesthetic value mingled with rites and mythologies. The Indian poet performed an official function and was the speaker of the community. When the Spaniards arrived, they found, mainly among Aztecs, a rich body of poems, both lyric and epic, chanting the eternal themes of mankind: divinity, death, time, beauty, and the heroic deeds of warriors and gods. During the so-called colonial period, under Spanish rule, Mexico continued to speak with poetic voice. The European literary movements of Baroquism and Neoclassicism found a well-prepared soil in which poetic expression could flourish. Sor Juana Inés de la Cruz, a nun considered perhaps the best feminine poet in Spanish-speaking countries, left a copious testimony of poems of standing value. Later, at the turn of the nineteenth century, Modernism was represented in Mexico by poets of great renown, such as Gutiérrez Nájera, Díaz Mirón, Othón, González Martínez, Nervo, and Urbina, who together with other Spanish-American poets, especially the leader of the movement, Rubén Darío, gave to the Western world the first uncontaminated and original literary expression of Latin America.

In this century, though poetry has been somewhat disregarded, Mexican writers have not completely neglected the poetic attitude. López Velarde, Torres Bodet, Pellicer, José Gorostiza, Novo, and Villaurrutia represent, among others, some of the leading figures of modern poetry in Spanish. As the most recent and famous voice, Octavio Paz has been acclaimed Mexico's greatest living poet.

He began his poetic career under the auspices of the group called *Taller* (Workshop). Some of the traits of this group were opposition to the merely literary expression and the search for the original word, the *mot juste.* A poem is not to be regarded as an excercise of expression but an act of vital affirmation. Man must use poetry as a way of stating not only his inner thoughts and feelings, but his condition of social being. Under these premises we deal with Paz's work. His poetry is not an easy one. Nourished in wide reading, always alert to the deep and wide in every cultural direction, at the same time Mexican and universal, traditional and modern, Paz in his poetry embraces many ideas, attitudes, problems, and forms of expression. He has delved into the study of many philosophic, religious, and aesthetic movements. Proof of this statement is found in his inquisitive books in prose in which he has analyzed the soul of his country, the creative process of poetry, and the problems of artistic expression in different cultures. Having lived as a diplomat in many countries, both in the Western and the Eastern world, in contact with different and sometimes opposite ways of life, he can say, like Terentius, that because he is a man nothing is alien to him.

El Laberinto de la Soledad (The Labyrinth of Solitude) is the title of one of Paz's books in prose. It could be applied to the perspective of his poetry which in some ways resembles a labyrinth, not exactly because it is confusing, but because of its hermetism and intricacies. It is a poetry of solitude because the writer's basic attitude is that of a man who feels alone in the world, always in need of the "other" to attain his own self-realization. As an inference of this attitude, man can be said to be a half-being who strives after his integration and completion. He intends to reach this state of fulfillment by three elements: the poetry, which reveals the unity of mankind; love, which makes the ego realize himself in the "you"; and the sacred, which shows the "other shore" of life. This itinerary begins in solitude, is continuously stimulated by desire, and tends to arrive at the communication.

Paz's literary technique of expression is that of surrealism, so that he may appear incongruous and unnatural on the surface. Though this is true on some occasions, Paz is not, however, a poet of mere free associations and emptiness of message. His poetry has both width and depth. He embraces all the basic problems of man and deals with them in a tragic and sympathetic way. He hates the easy expression because he thinks that poetry is a very serious, complex, almost magic task, not reserved to the multitude but to a very few people capable of delving into the analysis of the most intimate problems surrounding human life.

Libertad bajo Palabra (Freedom and the Word), in its second published edition in 1960, is a collection of the best poems written by Paz between 1937 and 1960. In the prologue to this book he said that he wrote the word freedom, a word that created itself and him. These words mean that the poet creates his poetic universe in spite of himself and others, and that the poetry is a way of liberation, a need and the outmost revelation of the poet.

Poetry becomes a consubstantiation with the poet and makes him feel his true origins.

Images of opposition and conflict cloud the eyes of the poet. He does not find his place in this world, nor does he believe in earth or heaven; he is anchored in a sea of skepticism and desperation, and cries in solitude, as in "Nor Heaven nor Earth."

Prisoner in a contradictory world, man has the obligation of being audacious, though he knows at the same time that he is slave of necessity and is the alpha and the omega of himself in a cyclical process of creation and destruction.

Paz intends also through his poetry to touch the limits of the absolute, mainly through love, which is a hunger of life.

In "The Broken Jar" and "Sun Stone," his best and longest poems, Paz takes ancient Mexican mythologies and symbols to eddy into the most universal and intimate themes of mankind. In the first of these poems, Paz begins by presenting the jewelry of the Mexican sky in a rich enumeration of metaphors. In contrast with such wealth, he looks at the vast wasteland surrounding him, flooded with blood, dust, and misery. He recalls the Aztec gods of abundance and rain, and sees that the only prevailing divinity in this land is the toad, symbol of drought and scarcity.

The poet then makes transference and its mythologies to the spiritual world from the reference to the Mexican land of man. This is also a barren land, a broken jar, in thirsty quest of water, namely, in anxious quest of others. Words and love are the best vehicle for this communication. They give the human being the deep, true, original significance of his existence.

Piedra de Sol (Sun Stone) is Paz's most ambitious poem. There is in it an obvious reference to the Sun Stone of the Aztecs, better known as the Calendar Stone, a huge block representing the history of the world and embodying the statement of the infinity of the Aztec universe. In the center of this stone is the sun set within the sign Four Motions representing according to Aztec mythology, the dates of the four previous ages of the world. Among many other symbols there are two immense fire serpents, symbolic of the year and time, circling the exterior to meet each other at the base.

In this poem, Paz wants to call up the sense of repetition of human life within eternity and the sense of ambiguity and duality of the universe. Written in 584 lines, the same number of days that it takes the planet Venus to complete its synodic period, the poem strives to be cyclical also. The first six lines of the poem are the last ones, signifying the re-entry into a new and identical cycle. After this beginning the poet deals with himself, placed in the world, among past and future, spending an ephemeral life made only of instants. Love is, among all human experiences, the deepest and most rewarding.

However, consubstantial to love is death; therefore, all human experiences, including love, are nothing in contrast with eternity. Under this dimension, life is an instant, a symbol, nothing. The only true way of reaching completeness of oneself is by existing for others.

Finally the poet longs for birth and light amidst death and shadow.

Poet of metaphysical uneasiness, tortured by the most radical human problems, with his sensitivity always prone to perceive and analyze every new mainstream of thought, Paz has reached a prominent position among the poets of his generation. It would not be an exaggeration to say that in him Mexico has her best and deepest-insighted living poet.

THE POETRY OF PÉGUY

Author: Charles Péguy (1873-1914)
Principal published works: Joan of Arc, 1897; *Mystery of the Charity of Joan of Arc,*
1910; *The Portal of the Mystery of the Second Virtue,* 1911; *The Mystery of the Holy
Innocents,* 1912; *The Tapestry of Saint Genevieve and Joan of Arc,* 1912; *The Tapestry
of Notre Dame,* 1913; *Eve,* 1913

Charles Péguy's life, thought, and poetry are inextricably mixed. He was born in total poverty. His intelligence and energy, with the help of scholarships, got him through excellent schools, but he always remained a man of the people both in his life, religion, and poetry. In school he was deeply influenced by the thought of Henri Bergson, and he adopted a philosophy of motion and change rather than the traditional philosophies of static values.

In his youth Péguy became deeply involved in the Dreyfus affair, but when the cause was exploited by selfish politicians, he became a Marxist. Yet he remained an almost mystically patriotic Frenchman, so that, when his socialist colleagues turned to pacifism and internationalism, Péguy (while maintaining his socialist ethic) turned away. He was convinced that war between Germany and France was inevitable, and he wanted to defend France. Also, in 1908, just before he began writing the largest body of his poetry, he returned to the Catholic faith, a strange and, as always with Péguy, very personal brand of Catholicism. He rejected the dogma of damnation, but in the most literal way he accepted the doctrine of salvation and the cult of the saints, especially the Virgin and Joan of Arc. In Joan, who was an important subject of his poetry, Péguy could simultaneously adore God and France. In one way or another these two things were always the poet's themes.

Péguy, who is almost the object of worship by a large cult of admirers in France, has never been well received in the United States. His style is simple, incantory, and free. His most obvious characteristic is quantity; some of his poems are hundreds of pages long. He achieves his effects mostly through repetition and expansion of themes, sometimes to the point of diffuseness. His diction is invariably colloquial and purposely naïve. Yet he is undeniably a powerful, major poet. Except in his last poems, his verse is entirely free and unlike anything else in French. With one exception, all of the poet's major work was written in an incredible four-year burst of energy that ended only with his death in battle, leading an attack, in 1914.

Joan of Arc, an immense three-hundred-page drama, was Péguy's first real attempt at poetry, or, rather, lyricism: the texture of the piece is an intermixture of freely rhymed verse, rhythmical and normal prose, and versets inspired by the rhetoric of the Bible, or, perhaps, the choral movement of ancient tragedy. The text, moreover, is given poetic unity by a structure of symbolism that tends to heighten Péguy's poetic prose still more. The drama, almost impossible to stage, if only because of its great length, is based on the familiar story of Joan of Arc and is divided into three sections: "At the Village of Domremy," "The Battles," and "Orleans." The first section is divided into three parts and ten acts; the second part is divided into three parts and eight acts; and the last section falls into two parts and six acts. The tone is, as was to become usual in Péguy's poetry, one of solemn simplicity. The play, written before the author's return to Catholicism, is revealingly dedicated to "all men and women who will have lived, to all men and women who will have died attempting to cure the universal sickness," and it is further dedicated to "the establishment of the universal Socialist republic." In the play the mysticism of Joan and the humanitarianism of Péguy are interpenetrating.

After his return to belief in 1908, Péguy once more set himself to writing poetry. In 1910 he published his *Mystery of the Charity of Joan of Arc*. This was followed in 1911 by *The Portal of the Mystery of the Second Virtue*, and in 1912 by *The Mystery of the Holy Innocents*. Once more he used the verset and lyrical prose as his medium. These vast plays are an innovation in form. By "Mystery" Péguy meant two things: he was writing dramas which are meditations on the Holy Mysteries of the Incarnation, the Redemption, and the theological virtues (faith, hope, and charity); and he was reviving in modern terms the mystery play genre of the Middle Ages.

The Charity of Joan of Arc is essentially a dialogue between Joan and Madame Gervaise, a fervent, contemplative, simple-hearted young nun who had figured in Péguy's earlier Joan of Arc trilogy. The central theme of the piece is the love, the "Charity" of Joan. In *The Portal of the Mystery of the Second Virtue* and in *The Mystery of the Holy Innocents* it is, for the most part, God who speaks through the mouth of Madame Gervaise. Both of these Mysteries celebrate "Hope," which is the universal animating force. Without hope the world would wither to nothingness; it is everything. God himself is amazed at it. "Faith doesn't surprise me, love doesn't surprise me," says God, "what does astonish me is hope." God's tone and voice in Péguy's poetry are not at all what we hear in Job: mighty, distant, imperious. Rather, Péguy's God, speaking through the mouth of a very simple woman, is familiar, human, and just a little innocent. And he is very French: "Our Frenchmen are favored above all. They are my witnesses. Preferred. They don't need me to tell them the same thing twenty times. Before I've finished talking, they've left. Intelligent people."

After writing *The Mystery of the Holy Innocents*, Péguy in 1912 began writing regular and formal verse. He published a number of shorter lyric poems in regular stanzas in 1912 and 1913. Among the better known of these is "Seven Against Thebes" ("Les Sept contre Thèbes") a remarkable new version of the classical Theban story; "The Loire Chateaus" ("Chateaux de Loire"); and "Seven Against Paris ("Les Sept contre Paris"), a strange paean in praise of the expansion, growth, history, and cultural development of Paris. The major part of this poem is one long sentence, constituted of thirty quatrains, which does not conclude or make sense until the last line. Péguy also wrote during this period of his career a long series of quatrains which he felt were too private to publish; they did not appear until 1941. In the quatrains he dramatized a private struggle between desire and his duty. These poems are apropos of a personal involvement Péguy, for the sake of his family and faith, resisted successfully.

Most important in this change to formal verse, however, are Péguy's *Tapestries* (*Tapisseries*). Once again looking for a new poetic form to carry his artistic and spiritual vision, the poet looked to the Middle Ages. Modeling his poetry, metaphorically, on the carefully worked, slowly woven wall coverings made during the high Middle Ages by master craftsmen of great patience, Péguy sought to weave poems by interlacing threads of theme, symbol, and idea to form an orderly, repeated, but varying design. The poems are written in the way tapestries were woven: the design is slowly worked in until at the end, and only the end, the whole picture becomes visible. These poems, like medieval tapestries that took religious themes for their designs, are meant to grace a holy sanctuary. Like most of Péguy's work, they are of great size and length.

Altogether Péguy published three *Tapestries* before his death: *The Tapestry of Saint Genevieve and Joan of Arc* (1912); *The Tapestry of Notre Dame* (1913); and *Eve* (1913). *The Tapestry of Saint Genevieve* takes the form of a novena in which the patron saint of Paris and Joan, the French national heroine, are paid homage. The piece is made up of nine separate poems, one for each day of the novena—the movement is toward a crescendo in the eighth poem, then to a decrescendo in the ninth. *The Tapestry of Notre Dame* is divided into two large sections, each made up of several smaller poems. The first part is the presentation of Paris to Notre Dame in which Péguy places the city in the care of the Virgin. The second part is the presentation of the countryside of Beauce to the Virgin at Chartres. The presentation takes the form of a pilgrimage to Chartres; it reflects a pilgrimage the poet actually made in fulfilment of a vow he had made when his son was ill with typhoid.

The last of the Tapestries, *Eve*, is thought by many to be Péguy's finest work. It is a single poem made up of about three thousand quatrains, over twelve thousand lines, and it has been called the most impressive piece of Catholic literature produced in France, with the exception of Corneille's *Polyeucte*, since the fourteenth century. Also, in its sweep and size and power it has frequently been compared to Victor Hugo's epic of the world, the *Legend of the Centuries*. The poem is impossible to describe; it is too all-inclusive. It progresses in a series of gradations of "climates," the climate of the earthly paradise, the climates of the Incarnation, the Fall, the Judgment, and so on. If the poem has a single theme, it is the double and interpenetrating spiritual and carnal creation, of which Eve is the archetypal symbol. It is from *Eve* that the most often quoted and best known lines of Péguy come: "Happy are they who die for the carnal land" ("Heureux ceux qui sont morts pour la terre charnelle").

THE POETRY OF PRIOR

Author: Matthew Prior (1664-1721)
Principal published work: Poems, 1709

Many of the poems of Matthew Prior are in the pastoral mode: the poet adopts the age-old pretense of being a shepherd who sings, with rustic honesty, of the fortunes and misfortunes of his love. The woman appears as reluctant shepherdess in the pastoral convention, and the poet as a lovesick swain. Such poems as "Love and Friendship: A Pastoral" invoke a vocabulary familiar to early eighteenth century poetry of this kind. The poem, like others by Prior and his contemporaries, begins with a description of the natural setting, the fields and skies of the rural landscape. A mood is the object of the description, and night is chosen as the fit time to discourse on love and hope. A great part of the poem is devoted to the "charms" of the lady—the rest to their effect on the imagination of the swain. Other minor poems, like "To a Lady," attempt to reinvigorate the ancient poetic metaphor of love as war. The woman is the "victor" and the lover is the "slave." The poem is, of course, an invitation to love; it finds its central expression when it describes the woman who "triumphs, when She seems to yield."

The early poems of Prior have a large concentration of this courtly and pastoral type of art. "Celia to Damon" brings out once more the theme of love as a hopeless war, in which the lover is perpetually doomed to servitude and defeat. He describes the "Excess and Fury" of his love, and the beauty that confounds it. The tone of the poem, faithful to its models of hopeless and adoring passion, is intentionally pathetic. The great contrast the poem strives for is that between the humility of the lover and the "raging Love" and "swelling Seas of Rapture" in his soul. The lover assumes the familiar stance of the half-exalted and half-mad figure of romance. In response to worldly wisdom Prior's "Imitation of Anacreon" states "Love shall be my endless Theme"

—and he invites the critics and all other in the community of the sane and responsible to mind their own business while he goes happily to his fate.

Prior did not confine himself to such poetry, which is often imitative. His "An English Ballad" is both heroic and satirical; perhaps its most obvious theme is that of witty skepticism:

> If *Namur* be compar'd to *Troy;*
> Then Britain's Boys excell'd the Greeks:
> Their Siege did ten long Years employ:
> We've done our Bus'ness in ten Weeks.

The great political and military struggles between England and France, Greece and Troy, are set in the context of parody, a mode which expresses the feeling of the poet that these events are not altogether praiseworthy or even meaningful. The poem is in praise, ostensibly, of William of Orange, but the poem balances "Death, Pikes, Rocks, Arms, Bricks, and Fire" against the Lilliputian moral stature of the combatants. William, of course, comes off much better than his great rival, Louis XIV, but neither comes off very well in terms of the great idea of civilization which the poem raises. If Prior was a parodist of things political, he also was a parodist of matters amatory. Some of his better-known poems satirize the whole institution of love poetry and the courtly conventions to which it subscribed. "An English Padlock" and "Hans Carvel" are both intentionally indecent in that they express a thoroughly Augustan attitude toward romantic love. The first of these is not about pastoral lovers but about a jealous husband. The best way to handle a woman, Prior suggests in this poem, is not to write sonnets, nor is it to declare in limitless hyperbole the nature of one's passion. It is rather to allow her to see the world in all its false beauty, and to sicken of the truth.

"Paulo Purganti" is another of the poems which attacks romance and puts disillusioned objectivity in its place. The importance of the piece is its explicit relationship to the hard insights of Wycherly and Congreve. Prior begins by noting that things true may not be things beautiful, or even things moral. This is a worldly poem defending things "Beyond the fix'd and settl'd Rules." Pride is seen in its conflict with sex, and it is the latter that wins out. The woman is proud, the man is logical, but both pride and logic yield to the imperious instinct that denies all pretensions. The myth of human perfection dies hard. Prior returned to his deflating attack time after time. When he writes about the old story of the Greek gods visiting earth, it is not to expatiate on the piety of the old man and woman who are their hosts, but to reveal the cupidity and weakness of all men at all times. When he writes about learning, as in "Merry Andrew," it is to point out that folly sometimes is better than wit. In short, Prior shares the insights of Pope and Swift into what has been called the human condition. He refuses to be deluded by conceptions of the ideal; he insists that reality is often disappointing.

Prior's lengthy "Alma," written while he was in prison after the fall of the Tory party in 1714, is a sardonic and skeptical review of human history. It begins by stating that the soul has been located by various philosophers in different places, but that it may best be known by the actions it motivates. The animating spirit of man, Prior suggests, enters the body "at the Toes" and then "mounts by just Degrees." The "system" thus described is a parody of philosophy, but it is a useful device to explain Prior's principal point: man begins in mere motion, then feels the effects of emotion as he grows older, and finally, when Alma nears the brain, he learns intelligence. Most men, Prior suggests, never attain the final stage, for Alma never visits their minds. His historical examples are many and comical. One

is the hero of the Trojan War:

> In scornful Sloth Achilles slept;
> And for his Wench, like Tall-Boy, wept:
> Nor would return to War and Slaughter;
> 'Till They brought back the Parson's Daughter.

He then ranges from ancient to modern history, explaining with mock-seriousness how men as different as Mark Antony, Edward IV, and Henry IV were all united by their failure to allow Alma to get past their hearts.

Successive cantos of the poem describe all human folly as the consequence of the natural journey of Alma being interrupted and her powers diverted to serve a single function. The glutton confines the human spirit to his gullet; the lover confines his soul and mind to the senses; even the artist imprisons Alma to serve his "Fancy or Desire." All these corruptions, Prior sums up, "Have got the better of his Mind." The confirmed huntsman will be blind to all things else in life; the girl who thinks of nothing but dancing will become an old woman ridiculous in the same affectation; the man whose Alma "Slip'd up too soon into his Tongue" will never let that weapon lie still. The poem concludes with a moral familiar to the reader of Alexander Pope: the man of full mental and moral development must allow mind and body, emotion and intelligence, their limited domination.

Prior's longest consideration of the state of man is his poem "Solomon on the Vanity of the World." The poem is divided into three parts: knowledge, pleasure, and power. In the first part Solomon convenes the wise men of his kingdom in order to find out the nature of happiness. A dialogue ensues in which he and the wise men discuss all of nature, from vegetative to human life. This discussion leads only to bewildering dilemmas and not to any solutions. No man at the court can satisfactorily explain the physical laws of nature; on the contrary, they reveal only their own ignorance and pride. Solomon concludes this first part by scornfully dismissing them and remarking on "How narrow Limits were to Wisdom giv'n." In the next part of the poem the king asks whether wealth can in fact give happiness, and he considers the principal means whereby men hope to capture happiness in physical objects. He states that he too has tried to make happiness the consequence of material joys, but that he has failed. He has tried luxurious palaces, gardens, feasts, and even works of art, yet none of these was able to give him a pleasure greater than the passing moment. Neither in music nor in dance could he discern any power of lasting pleasure. Disappointed in all these, and especially in love, the king concludes that he must explore not the exterior of all things but the interior of his own mind. The second book ends with a farewell to useless wealth and to both "Lust and Love." The third begins by admitting that, because of the nature of the flesh

itself, there is no real prospect of lasting happiness. The end of all things, Prior says, may be more desirable than the continual and futile search for joy. In short, his central character says, "Who breathes, must suffer; and who thinks, must mourn."

Prior began in pastoral poetry and very quickly wrote the kind of satirical and moralistic verse made popular by Alexander Pope. He became essentially a parodist, interested in the great disparities between the ideal and the actual. As his long poems "Alma" and "Solomon" indicate, he had his share of the satirist's pessimism. Yet he was not a negative thinker; the ending of "Solomon" is especially interesting for the manner in which the "various doubts" of its protagonist are dispelled. In the moral and religious life, and particularly in the enactment of biblical wisdom, Prior suggests that there is a possibility of human fulfillment. Like Pope and Swift, he furnishes a moral standard by which his satire must be measured.

THE POETRY OF RALEIGH

Author: Sir Walter Raleigh (c. 1552-1618)
First published: Selections published in various anthologies during lifetime; *Poems, with Biography and Critical Introduction,* 1813

Sir Walter Raleigh, like so many other Renaissance courtiers, considered the writing of poetry one of the polite arts, to be practiced in one's leisure moments for the pleasure of friends. In his busy political, military, and adventuring career, his poetic efforts apparently carried little weight, and he never seems to have encouraged their publication, though he was much interested in presenting to the public his history and his treatises on his expeditions to the new world. Consequently, over the years countless verses have been attributed to him, and no one can be sure how many of them he actually wrote. The small body of work that is unquestionably his, however, shows him to be a poet of high ability.

Though Raleigh was perhaps second only to Spenser and Sidney as poets in the court of Elizabeth I, he shunned the opulence of the typical poetry of his time for a sparse, dignified, manly style that has many echoes of his predecessors, Wyatt and Surrey. The melancholy quality that pervades much of Raleigh's work is close to that of almost all of Wyatt's poems and to the last lyrics of Surrey, written while he was in the Tower awaiting trial and execution. Raleigh himself spent over ten years in the Tower, hoping against hope for release, and a sense of the constant closeness of death runs through his later work. Yet almost all of his poems, even the early ones, reveal a strong awareness of what Shakespeare in *Love's Labour's Lost* calls "cormorant devouring Time." Life is precarious "beauty, fleeting," and death near at hand for all men. Raleigh's answer to Christopher Marlowe's famous pastoral lyric, "Come Live with Me and Be My Love," is filled with this sense of the transience of all things:

Time drives the flocks from field to fold,

When rivers rage and rocks grow cold,
And Philomel becometh dumb;
The rest complains of cares to come.

The flowers do fade, and wanton fields
To wayward winter reckoning yields;
A honey tongue, a heart of gall,
Is fancy's spring, but sorrow's fall.

Raleigh protests against the actions of time in another lyric, "Nature that washt her hands in milke," where he describes the creation of the perfect woman by Nature, at the request of Love. This paragon no sooner exists than Time, "being made of steel and rust, Turns snow, and silk and milk to dust." The final stanza is the eternal human lament:

Oh, cruel time! Which takes in trust
Our youth, our joys and all we have,
And pays us but with age and dust,
Who in the dark and silent grave
When we have wandered all our ways
Shuts up the story of our days.

While Wyatt's laments are most often those of the Petrarchan lover, scorned by the lady to whom he offers devotion, Raleigh's melancholy seems to derive from a more general vision of the human condition. Even in those sonnets where he takes the conventional stance of the rejected lover, he seems conscious of a larger world. One of these concludes:

And at my gate despair shall linger still,
To let in death when love and fortune will.

Raleigh's sense of the destructive powers of time has particular force in his elegy on Sir Philip Sidney, an excellent poem in which the writer pays tribute to a fellow courtier-soldier-poet. There is in the "Epitaph" a touch of envy of Sidney, who died with an unblemished reputation and was freed from the threats of time and evil men:

What hath he lost, that such great
  grace hath won?
Young years for endless years, and hope
  unsure,
Of fortune's gifts, for wealth that still
  shall dure,
Oh, happy race, with so great praises
  run!

Like many other writers of his century, Raleigh uses his poetry to chastise the court for its hypocrisy, its vice, and its folly. Few men, indeed, suffered more from the false appearances of monarchs and their ministers. The brief stanzas of "The Lie" move over the whole spectrum of society:

Say to the court it glows,
And shines like rotten wood;
Say to the church, it shows
What's good, and doth no good:
  If church and court reply,
  Then give them both the lie.

The tone of Raleigh's poetry is not unmitigated gloom; few men were more vibrantly alive than this courtier-adventurer, and he could compose gay, witty lyrics with the best of his contemporaries, following out a pseudo-logical argument in the manner of Donne, singing lyrically about the beauty of the moon, or defining love in the vocabulary of the common man:

Yet what is love? I pray thee sain.
It is a sunshine mixed with rain;
It is a tooth-ache, or like pain;
It is a game where none doth gain;
The lass saith no, and would full fain:
And this is Love, as I hear sain.

There is much of the medieval heritage in Raleigh's work. Folk wisdom, proverbs, and the haunting quality of many of the early ballads lurk under the surface of several of his poems, notably one addressed to his son. The poem begins quietly and continues in a matter of fact way that reinforces its horror. Three things, "the wood, the weed, and the wag," prosper separately, but, together they bring destruction:

The wood is that, that makes the gallows tree,
The weed is that, that strings the hangman's bag;
The wag, my pretty knave betokens
  thee.
Now mark, dear boy: while these assemble not,
Green springs the tree, hemp grows, the
  wag is wild;
But when they meet, it makes the tim-
  ber rot,
It frets the halter, and it chokes the
  child.
  God bless the child!

Medieval in a different sense is one of Raleigh's last and best poems, "The Passionate Man's Pilgrimage." Its Christian allegory is like that of parts of Book I of *The Faerie Queene* and of Bunyan's *The Pilgrim's Progress,* with all of life described in the imagery of a traveler's journey to salvation:

Give me my scallop-shell of quiet,
My staff of faith to walk upon,
My scrip of joy, immortal diet,
My bottle of salvation,
My gown of glory, hope's true gage,
And thus I'll take my pilgrimage.

Raleigh's irregular metrical pattern is admirably suited to his subject; the simplicity of his acceptance of redemption in the second section is mirrored in the short rhymed lines, the clarity of the language, and the images of silver, nectar, milk, and crystal. The fourth section, with its theme of judgment, is harsher in both rhythm and vocabulary, as Raleigh speaks of Christ as the advocate, pleading the cause of sinful man in a court where bribery and forgery have no place, a compelling allusion to the trial in which Sir Edward Coke, not Christ, was the King's Attorney, and the verdict was, in the minds of most men, a travesty of justice. The concluding stanza has something of the macabre quality of a few of Donne's poems: Raleigh is said to have written these last lines on the night before his execution:

Just at the stroke when my veins start
  and spread

Set on my soul an everlasting head.
Then am I ready like a palmer fit,
To tread those blest paths which before
    I writ.

Raleigh's longest extant poem is a fragment of a still more extensive work called "Ocean's Love to Cynthia." The original version, so far as scholars have been able to deduce, was addressed to Queen Elizabeth about 1587, when Robert Devereux, Earl of Essex, seemed to be replacing Raleigh in her esteem. In its first form the poem evidently served its purpose, for Raleigh was reinstated in Her Majesty's favor until his indiscreet affair and hasty marriage with one of her maids of honor in 1592. It has been suggested that the surviving fragment of the poem was written from the Tower, where Raleigh had been imprisoned with his bride, in an attempt to mollify Elizabeth's resentment.

The quatrains of the extant text are presented as the outpourings of a disillusioned lover of the queen. There is no real narrative link; the whole poem is essentially the exposition of a state of mind. It is written in four-line stanzas with alternate rhymes, a compact form that lends itself to the development of a slightly different point in each quatrain. The extant manuscript is evidently an unfinished version of the poem, for occasionally Raleigh left two, three, or five lines as a separate unit to be revised later. However, even if the poem as it exists is unfinished, it demonstrates forcefully Raleigh's power to convey his deep and intense disillusionment. Toward the end of the fragment the poet, speaking as a ·

shepherd, like Spenser in his "Colin Clout's Come Home Again," another record of a writer's unhappy experiences at court, ponders the paradox of his state of mind. However, his mistress treats him, she is with him forever: *She is gone, she is lost, she is found, she is ever fair.*" He can only take life as it comes, let his flocks wander at will, and live with his despair:

> Thus home I draw, as death's long
>   night draws on;
>   Yet every foot, old thoughts turn back
>   mine eyes;
> Constraint me guides as old age draws
>   a stone
>   Against the hill, which over-weighty
>   lies

He must, in the last analysis, trust in the mercies of God.

Raleigh never entirely fulfilled his promise as a poet. His intense interest in colonizing projects, his career at court during his early maturity, and his later political misfortunes probably combined to prevent his devoting his energies to poetry; and his gigantic project, the *History of the World,* left far from complete at his death, occupied his last years in the Tower. Yet the works he did leave are among the best of what C. S. Lewis called "Drab" poetry in the Elizabethan age. The virtues of his poems are their quiet strength and the melancholy tone which was the almost inevitable result of his skeptical, inquiring mind; and they are almost always clear and satisfying in their own low-keyed way.

THE POETRY OF ROBERT LOWELL

Author: Robert Lowell, Jr. (1917-)
Principal published works: Land of Unlikeness, 1944; *Lord Weary's Castle,* 1946; *The Mills of the Kavanaughs,* 1951; *Life Studies,* 1959; *Imitations,* 1961; *For the Union Dead,* 1964; *Near the Ocean,* 1967

Of the generation of American poets who came to prominence in the years following World War II, Robert Lowell has emerged as the acknowledged master and, evidently, the most likely candidate for greatness, the odds-on favorite to fill the shoes of our century's first generation of poets, the generation which included Pound, Eliot, Williams, Stevens, and Frost. In the 1960's he has managed to win acceptance and unquestioned recognition by all cliques and schools of contemporary poetry and by a dazzling array of critics at home and abroad. While it must be admitted that some of his reputation is the result of pervasive American insistence upon celebrity in all aspects of our culture, still it represents no slight achievement for Lowell and, equally important, seems to indicate an end to the long, tedious, and largely phony cold war between "the academics" and "the Beats." In point of fact, Robert Lowell has been recognized as a poet of repute since his *Lord Weary's Castle* was published and won for him the coveted Pulitzer Prize, but for a poet to fulfill his early promise and to gain steadily in stature and popularity is rare, especially during a period of literary conflict, questioning, and change.

Lord Weary's Castle was a powerful and, within the extremely limited precincts of the world of modern poetry, popular introduction to the new formalism which dominated American poetry for a decade following. World War II interrupted the continuity of American poetry. It is hard, except by going through the books and anthologies of the 1930's, to remember or recapture the pre-war literary milieu, but in general the establishment was characterized by a deep concern for the social problems of the Depression, an attempt to employ the vernacular American idiom in poetry, not only for more freedom and richness and variety in language, but also in the hope of reaching out to a larger audience. The underground movement of that period was composed of the Fugitives, who cultivated journalism in verse, together with ambiguity, intellectual and personal complexity, traditionalism, and an apparently aristocratic view of the poet's function. Politically and socially they called themselves Agrarians, being so at least in their distaste for the excesses wrought by the Industrial Revolution. Regionally they were Middle Southern, and theologically they tended to be high church Episcopalians with definite affinities toward Roman Catholicism. They were academics at a time when the relationship between writers and the academics were not so cozy as they are today. Their leader was John Crowe Ransom and their special hero was T. S. Eliot in England. It is hard to realize the influence these men and women have had on American poetry and fiction. The exemplary amount of either produced by the group has been relatively small. But they wrote a great many reviews and a great deal of criticism, taking over and breathing life into quiet quarterlies, and they taught, directly and in a formal context, many of the young men who would in the years following World War II move to prominence on the literary scene. One of these was Robert Lowell.

It is possible that Lowell, at least in his early books, is the best pupil the Fugitives ever had; and they rallied around him and his work with alacrity and enthusiasm. Yet he seems an unlikely representative of the movement. Coming from a long and distinguished New England tradition, he has shown little sympathy for the South or things Southern or, indeed, interest in these things. His heritage was Puritan, yet he rebelled against it and became a convert to Catholicism, with the additional complexity that he was a conscientious objector during World War II, at a time when his new-found Church did not recognize that position as legitimate. Nor did the courts, and he was punished by imprisonment for his beliefs. This personal courage and commitment became meaningful to the poets, those who survived to write poems, who came back; and Karl Shapiro spoke for many of them when he referred to Lowell as the conscience to which other young poets returned.

There are many conflicts obvious in even this impersonal and casual view of Lowell as poet, and conflict is the essence of *Lord Weary's Castle*. His personal struggles with his heritage and the present and future of the society are reined in tightly in strict forms, strict rhythms, and solid rhymes. The effect is often the moment before an explosion, a highly dramatic moment. The verse is demanding, requiring as was the custom at the time, some notes, ambiguous, allusive, knotty, and what was then called "tough-minded." The transitions were swift and almost cinematic in abruptness. But the essence of any poetry is voice, the language and especially the verbal texture, which distinguishes the work of one poet from another. Lowell showed from the first a good ear for a wide range of language, from the straightforward cadences of the spoken idiom to the high resonance of classical and Biblical rhetoric. The texture was as rough and rocky as the New England earth, almost anti-poetic in its hardness. There was a "tension"—a word very popular with the Fugitives who by this time were called the New Critics—between the rugged texture and the smoothness of felicitous metrics and exact rhymes.

The complexity of Lowell's imagery is vaguely reminiscent of Hart Crane, and it may be relevant that Allen Tate, who was Lowell's teacher and friend as well as a friend of Hart Crane, has written that what prevented Crane from greatness was the lack of an ordered and controlling philosophy or a belief like Roman Catholicism. Finally, it should be noted that Lowell displayed a real affinity toward the Fugitives in his strong dislike for the things of modern civilization.

With *Lord Weary's Castle*, Lowell had arrived. Four years later came *The Mills of the Kavanaughs*, described as "a collection of seven dreams, fantasies, and monologues." These were long poems, basically narrative in form, yet combining the strict formality of his earlier work in the longer forms, and sustaining and expanding the areas of interest demonstrated in the earlier book: history, his heritage, Catholicism, the classics, and the Bible. There was no diminishment of power, and the poems represent a remarkable achievement of sustained power and energy. They carried certain aspects of Lowell's technique to its limits, almost to the breaking point. This book served to consolidate his reputation, yet at the same time it raised a question: where would he go from there? Eight years later *Life Studies* appeared, surprising many with its apparent difference and new directions. During those years the American literary scene had changed somewhat. Men of Lowell's generation, most of them formalists, were now respectable in the academies. Most of them were teaching and already gifted pupils were turning out good and passable imitations of their work. Meanwhile another group, equally academic in education and background, was rebelling. These were the so-called Beats. In one sense they represented a nostalgic return to the prewar poetry. They rejected the rules and idiom of the New Critics. They made an effort to be popular poets, to speak in the vernacular idiom, including obscenity and profanity, to and for a larger audience. They rejected Eliot and set up William Carlos Williams and Ezra Pound as literary heroes. They received a great deal of publicity and they devoted a large amount of their time, effort, and their verse to attacking the "Academics." *Life Studies* came as a great relief to many poets and critics on both sides, for they all knew one another and many had been schoolmates. They wanted some form of negotiated peace, and Lowell seemed to supply the answer. The Academics were willing to listen to reason, willing to relax to keep up with the times, and the Beats were realizing that publicity and popular interest did not increase the reading audience of poetry. There remained a limited audience which would have to be shared by both. The conditions were ripe for settlement. Robert Lowell was acceptable to both sides. He had proved himself to the formalists. His passion, indignation, suffering, and the now widely-known vicissitudes of his personal life qualified him, by definition, as at least an honorary Beat.

Life Studies is a mixture of things. Part One contains a few exciting poems in his earlier manner. Part Two, entitled "91 Revere Street" is a long, personal reminiscence in prose, a kind of short novel. Part Three is a short collection of literary sketches or snapshots, sometimes using rhyme, but more free and colloquial than anything he had done so far. The final section returns to his personal concerns, his family background and present troubles, but with a significant difference. It is now much more explicitly personal, sometimes openly confessional. The verse is often free in form. The old tough texture and the voice is there, but the form and method seem new. Moreover, this quality of the explicit manifests itself in a direct dealing with social concerns. Lowell speaks out against racial prejudice, injustice, urban blight, and President Eisenhower. In short, *Life Studies*, while compromising none of his skill and power, manages to make a wedding of the two dominant and established modes of the period.

In the years following *Life Studies*, Lowell seems to have devoted himself to translation, to assimilation of those voices in the European tradition which interest him. His free adaptation of *Phaedra* was performed and highly praised, and in 1961 *Imitations*, a collection of his translations appeared, together with an introduction which explained his method of translation and, by implication, a part of his developed poetics. The book was intended as a special kind of European poetry anthology, exploring the dark, working against the grain, and in historical time ranging from Homer and Sappho through Boris Pasternak. It was to be called *Imitations* because, in fact, these were original poems, based on the tone and mood of the model in another language and filtered through the consciousness and sensibility of Lowell himself. It is possible that Lowell exaggerated the novelty of his method; for this kind of translation by adaptation and imitation has a long history in our language, and Lowell had already done some similar versions—"War/(After Rimbaud),""Charles the Fifth and the Peasant/(After Valery),""The Shako/(After Rilke),"the "Ghost/(After Sextus Propertius),"and others—in *Lord Weary's Castle*. But the significance of an entire book of these imitations, coupled with an assertive and explicit introduction, was twofold. In a personal sense it was a kind of advertisement for himself, or, perhaps better, an honest recognition that he had now achieved recognition and stature, a boldly open declaration that he was now fully a major poet. Secondly, though not unrelated to the first effect, it was a further declaration of independence from the so-called Academic school. Some of his peers and colleagues had been translating, a bit more strictly, for some time. Among the very finest of these was Richard Wilbur whose two very accurate translations of Molière, *Le Misanthrope* and *Tartuffe*, elegantly rendered line by line and rhyme by rhyme, but always with amazing flexibility, had preceded *Phaedra* in performance. But in any case Lowell's method serves to illustrate his deliberate attempt to dissociate himself from what he believed to be a more academic approach to translation. *Imitations,* accepted on its own terms, was seen clearly as a book bound together by what was Lowell's and thus a major contribution to the canon of a major poet. The book not only was a critical success, but it also sold well, and this fact is quite unusual for a contemporary poet's work. Moreover, the earlier books were brought out again in paperback and sold widely and well. For the first time in many years a serious poet at the peak of his creative powers had managed to achieve the highest critical praise and at the same time reach a wider audience than either he or his contemporaries had ever reached before. Special as it is, *Imitations* was at once a breakthrough and a bulwark to Lowell's already secure position.

By 1965, Lowell had a double bill of plays, *The Old Glory,* successfully produced in New York and had seen published his most important collection of poems to date, *For the Union Dead.* This book, containing poems written between 1956 and 1964, is varied and dazzling in its variety. It can also be seen as exemplary of internal peacemaking, for he includes poems in the earlier, taut manner as well as poems as free in form and more so than those in *Life Studies.* In addition, he acknowledges in a "Note" at the beginning that he has gone back to recast or rewrite some of the earlier poems. There is in *For the Union Dead* not only a greater sense and appreciation of the audience, but also a firm commitment to poetry as a responsible rhetorical dialogue with that audience. Though the same basic subjects and concerns are there, there is at the same time a greater ease, frankness, and open quality than ever before, a confidence in his place and power. The title poem, a set piece of reminiscence and association based on the St. Gaudens bronze relief of Colonel Shaw and the bell-cheeked Negro infantry he led, which had appeared as the final poem in *For the Union Dead,* becomes the key to the "new" Lowell. In the ever-present, very present conflict of racial integration and assimilation, he sides proudly, in fact vehemently for a conscientious objector, with the old New England abolitionist tradition, fire-breathing in his condemnation not only of injustice elsewhere but also in his rage and contempt for the indifference of his own townsmen.

At an age when poets of the recent past, men of great stature like Robert Frost and Wallace Stevens, were just beginning to receive the first preliminary signs of recognition, Robert Lowell has already earned as a matter of course the appellation "leader of mid-century poetry." As his audience has grown and together with it the audience for modern poetry, and as he himself has continued to grow and develop, it would seem that Robert Lowell may stand the best chance of any poet of his generation to earn and receive the laurels reserved for the truly great poets. But there are obstacles ahead. For one thing, it is possible to argue that his poems have changed very little except superficially, not half so much as his critics and he seem to believe, from the earliest poems. There are slight differences in form, but the concerns and attitudes may or may not have deepened and matured. The matter is ambiguous and debatable. Success has not always been kind to American writers. Early and sustained success tends, if history is a guide, to be unkind. The child of Fortune often ends as the slave of Fortune. In recent interviews as well as in the introductory notes to his last two published volumes Lowell has shown a disconcerting and dangerously self-conscious concern for ratings on what Robert Frost called "the literary stockmarket" and his place in it. It has sometimes proved a fatal mistake to try to write history in advance. Finally, now that Lowell's deep personal problems are public property, in the sense that he has made frank and explicit use of them in his poems, there is, inevitably, a genuine question in the mind of his reader as to

The Poetry of Robert Lowell / LOWELL

whether or not he has or ever will overcome some of these problems. So long as they are manageable they are subjects for poetry, but the question remains as to whether these confessional poems are therapeutic and liberating, as Lowell would seem to think, or perhaps symptomatic and ultimately inhibiting. Neither concern and hopeful wishes nor Lowell's firm belief will answer these questions. History will write its own answers in due time. Meanwhile America has a first-rate poet whose art has earned for him a place of honor and distinction.

5125

THE POETRY OF ROETHKE

Author: Theodore Roethke (1908-1963)
Principal published works: Open House, 1941; *The Lost Son and Other Poems,* 1948; *Praise to the End!,* 1951; *The Waking: Poems 1933-1953,* 1953; *Words for the Wind,* 1958; *I Am Says the Lamb,* 1961; *The Far Field,* 1964; *The Collected Poems of Theodore Roethke,* 1966

It used to be a commonplace in discussion of the poetry of Theodore Roethke to emphasize the variety, the differences between his work as he passed through various "phases." It is true that there is variety and there are differences at every stage of his work as he matured as a poet. Now that he is gone, however, and now that it is possible to look at his work as a whole, it is surprising how much of his future work, his interests and the directions he would later explore, veins that he would later mine, is indicated in *Open House,* mostly written during the decade preceding World War II. (It is to be remembered that though Roethke was often grouped with Richard Wilbur and Robert Lowell as one of the three leading poets of his generation, he was, in fact, ten years older than both of these poets and a good deal behind them in receiving an equivalent critical recognition). It was and is easy to be deceived by the poems of *Open House.* They are short, quiet, rather plainly and strictly formal, evidently subdued and modest. Their artistry is understated, and they blithely ignore some of the critical fiats prevalent at the time. They have a kind of hewn and carved simplicity, with minimal attention paid to the intellectual ambiguity, the forms of irony and wit, which were becoming fashionable. They make frequent and familiar use of abstractions, which had become the equivalent of dirty words to poets and critics who took their standards of judgment at second hand from Eliot and Pound. One has to imagine the effect of, for example, the second stanza of the title poem upon the conditioned reader of that period. Except for the poet's obvious use of rhetorical paradox, which was very acceptable at that time, his lines break all the rules. Few, if any

critics caught in the web of time have ever been able to exercise the necessary self-transcendence to acknowledge the validity of another and different approach. It is not surprising that *Open House,* which turns out to have been the first public statement of a poet of acknowledged greatness, was largely ignored. Contemporary literary history would seem to indicate that this is the fate of all the truly important writers of the modern period. It was hard then to see the virtues of this work and altogether too easy to label it as the quiet and unassuming verse of an English teacher who was obviously a little too removed from the action, a little out of touch with the exciting center of the literary scene. Then, also, there was World War II whose gory clamor drowned all but the loudest voices.

The Lost Son came after the war and after the successes achieved by Robert Lowell in *Lord Weary's Castle* and Richard Wilbur in *The Beautiful Changes.* Some changes in method were immediately evident. The shorter lyric poems shied away from abstraction, coming close at times to the purity of imagism in the exact rendering of the concrete image without regard to generalized comment by the poet and, inevitably the texture seemed tougher and more conventionally antipoetic. The final stanza of "Cuttings I" is illustrative and shows as well what the poet can do by intense and precise concentration on a single, small action.

A substantial number of the shorter poems in *The Lost Son* are more explicitly personal than before, deriving directly from his experience of growing up around a greenhouse. Some of the titles tell the story: "Root Cellar," "Forcing House," "Weed Puller," Orchids," "Moss-

Gathering," "Old Florist," "Transplanting," "Child on Top of a Greenhouse," "Flower Dump," "Carnations." For the most part these poems are freer in form than the earlier poems, and when the poet does return to the strictness he had observed, as, for example, in the now widely anthologized "My Papa's Waltz," strict form is used more for humor and irony, which was, at that time, a more acceptable strategy.

With so many poets now engaged in the academic life, either patronized by or servants to the colleges, depending on one's point of view, it was almost inevitable that a genre of the academic poem would develop. As the genre has developed, it is much like the familiar Middle English poem in which the monk or scholar announces the coming of spring and bewails his fate and vocation which requires him to sit at a desk inside with a chained manuscript while outside the world is exploding with new life. Most of our poets have tried a version of this "updated" genre, bemoaning the university's apparent isolation from "real life," and adding the modern element of criticism against a large and impersonal institution. Roethke's "Dolor" is one of the most successful and memorable of this kind, precisely because of its richness and multiplicity of things, its condensation of these things into a single evocative impression. Saul Bellow has said in talks to students that his novel *The Victim*, told exactly in the "correct" method of narration, can be considered his "Ph.D. thesis," a kind of payment to Caesar to be allowed the privilege of rendering his art as he chooses. Yet *The Victim* is a fine and in many ways original novel. Similarly it is possible to view the fine shorter poems of *The Lost Son* as demonstrable proof that Theodore Roethke could do what was expected and demanded and yet in a highly original manner.

But if Roethke paid the piper and handsomely with the shorter poems, it was the long title poem which made people sit up and take notice. "The Lost Son" was something quite new in our poetry. A long poem, in an original and independent form, it was a kind of dramatic monologue, but an interior monologue, an objectification of the nearly ineffable drama and history of the psyche and in this case of a deeply tormented and troubled psyche. Its method can best be illustrated by analogy. To an extent Roethke availed himself of the techniques of surrealism, and to an extent, like other modern painters, he used the resources of primitive arts and forms of expression to create an effect reminiscent of totem objects and cave paintings, on the work of children. But, more important, he found a logic of images, often fleeting and ghostly images to be sure but always palpable and concrete, to represent the shades and states of being far more complex than other poets had been able to suggest when they started from the outside and evoked the inner drama by hints and clues and shards. The given setting was the mysterious landscape of consciousness with the unconscious just at the edge of the horizon, and all this spelled out in words and images. The effect was ragged, nervous, raw, a grotesque vision. The poet dared all and risked everything, moving in unknown territory, a realm with more questions than answers. Out of context, he risked the danger that in his search for meaning and articulation he would come up only with sheer gibberish. This new method showed difficulty and knotty complexity in a new form and with a new intent, by the articulation of these obscurities to bring light; a poetry which by definition trembled on the verge of madness or mysticism.

This new direction caused a considerable stir in the critical world. Roethke could no longer be labeled. If he could not be identified as a member of a "school" and if, at the same time, he was not setting a new direction for some future "school" to follow, he was undeniably an original and attention would have to be paid. "The Lost Son" was, for the poet, the beginning of one of those remarkable bursts of creative energy and inspiration which from time to time seem to come with dazzling largesse into the lives of great writers. In 1951 he published *Praise to the End!* with further and deeper explorations of this new mode, including the much praised "The Shape of the Fire," with its opening lines which shocked those as yet unfamiliar with his method.

With *Praise to the End!* and *The Waking* Roethke established for himself a place. *The Waking* earned him the Pulitzer Prize for 1953, and his literary fortunes had turned for the better. During the 1950's he became one of the most prolific and widely published of our poets, going his own way and marvelously aloof from the sweaty pseudo-struggle between the "Beats" and the "Academics" which riddled and cluttered the literary journals and little magazines.

We have a tendency to rejoice in any success story, but at the same time the American public, including its poets, has an intense desire to classify work, to give the works of an artist a kind of brand name, as if to name a thing were to comprehend it and eventually to own it. Roethke was always much too independent of spirit to be bought and owned by prizes, recognition, or even the knowledge of personal achievement. He pushed himself restlessly to try new and different variations. At the same time that he was writing these profound and knotty psychic monologues he was writing shorter pieces in a variety of modes, delightful and meaningful children's verse and some of the finest love lyrics of our century. His talent was wide and encompassing. He could write, for children of all ages, such delightful poems as "The Cow"; he could write, with high heterosexual gusto, the now celebrated "I Knew a Woman"; and he could take a shopworn, weary form like the villanelle and make it sing as if he had made it for the first time, as in "The Waking."

No wonder that by the middle of the 1950's Theodore Roethke seemed to many of our most responsible critics and the elderly guardians of art to be the most important poet writing in English.

Words for the Wind: Collected Verse of Theodore Roethke, appearing in 1958, won the National Book Award and gave his readers a chance to view Roethke's work as a whole for the first time. It was in fact, more a selected volume than a true collected book, for he dropped and eliminated some poems, revised and rearranged others, but even so it was a volume of impressive length which few if any of his contemporaries could have equaled, running more than two hundred close-packed pages and illustrating all the variety of his past work and indicating in its concluding section of previously uncollected poems, some of the directions he was following at the time. The book opens with the title poem from *Open House* and now only the insentient could fail to recognize how true and how prophetic, how completely stated were the quiet and rigorous lines of the first stanza of that poem. He had said what he was doing and was going to do. He had introduced himself and his subject. But no one had listened then. *Words for the Wind* gave them, to begin, a second chance.

The book brought Roethke immediate recognition. He was now fifty years old and it had taken almost twenty years for this recognition, but it had happened. Of special interest to his readers were the two long poems, "The Dying Man: In Memoriam: W. B. Yeats" and "Meditations of an Old Woman." "The Dying Man" caught the rhythms and cadences of Yeats, yet assimilated them into the manner and vocabulary of Roethke. It was more than a salute and memorial to a great poet. It demonstrated dramatically the influence of the earlier master on the younger poet and helped the reader to see a certain analogy or affinity between the two poets. Yeats, too, by his Irishness and special interests and concerns was just outside the literary scene of his own day. It was possible as well to see that Roethke, like Yeats, was more traditional, part of the grand tradition which ignores or transcends fashions if it can, than anyone had previously realized. Finally, there was a wish, a hope to be derived from this deliberate analogy. Yeats alone of the century's early masters had a career that paralleled his long life. While the others wrote less and less, if at all, standing pat on their finished work, Yeats had written some of his finest poetry as an old man, proving once and for all that maturity need not necessarily stifle lyric impulse. Roethke, after an amazing burst of creativity, had collected his poetry, but, since his powers seemed never stronger, it could be hoped that he might go on to even greater things. "Meditations of an Old Woman," a long and beautifully realized poem in five parts, offered a clue. Here images and pieces from all the early poems, familiar motifs reappeared, but in a new guise. All the intensity of the psychic poems and much of the complexity were present, except that now, through the voice of someone else, a fully realized character, there was a difference. There was a difference, too, in the seeming clarity and logic of the poem; scales of difficulty had fallen away, perhaps partly because the reader was now familiar with the personal conventions, the signs and symbols of the poet, but even more so because the poet seemed more secure in his knowledge of their wider meanings and, thus, more able to use and to apply rhetorically what had once seemed almost incantatory. Some of his personal ease and security shows itself in his ability to focus the kind of concentrated attention upon details which would not have interested him earlier.

The final section "What Can I Tell My Bones?" takes as its theme the terror and release of dying, the fear of death and the aspiration of the caged spirit to be free. On the one hand there is the inexorable logic of the mind and on the other is the eternal cry of the spirit for deliverance. The poem ends with acceptance and affirmation, the mystical wedding of body (including the mind) and soul, a sense of the peace which passes understanding, utterly credible and, at the last, confirmed with a quiet summation which might apply as much to the poet as to his dramatic *persona*.

Ironically, the closing line of this poem, with its emphasis on finality, was to be the last statement in book form that Roethke made in his lifetime. He continued to publish poems in the magazines, but died suddenly in late summer of 1963, leaving his latest poems uncollected. His widow put together these last poems for publication, and *The Far Field*, appearing posthumously, was awarded the National Book Award. It is sad and perhaps pointless to speculate where Roethke might have gone had he lived. We have the book and can celebrate what he had already done. *The Far Field* is his finest work, built on the solid foundation of all his earlier efforts. It is divided into four parts: "North American Sequence," "Love Poems," "Mixed Sequence," and "Sequence, Sometimes Metaphysical." The most impressive single piece is the long "North American Sequence," his longest poem and most ambitious. Here, in a poem as grandly designed in its own way as Hart Crane's *The Bridge*, he goes a giant step beyond the liberty of "Meditations of an Old Woman" by meditating, as poet, upon the history and meaning of his country. To this meditation he brings Roethke the poet we know with all of himself and all the baggage and burden of himself in his encounter with the staggering fact, half-dreamed and half-realized, of America. Time and study will tell to what extent the poet succeeded, but meanwhile there are obvious glories to rejoice in, such as the variation on the epic catalogue which opens Part III of the section called "The Rose."

The poems in the other sections are variations on all the forms and subjects he had worked with, never more eloquently realized. Everything is recapitulated. "The Abyss" is a variation on the earlier psychic mode; the love poems sing and shine as always; a poem like "Song" is suddenly and effectively in the manner of *Open House*. With *The Far Field* we see, with an inner wince of pathos, another element of Roethke's greatness: that nothing was ever lost. Perhaps he did go through stages, for all men do as they grow and learn and become; but few men manage to do so without rejecting what they were and have been. Part of our culture, the literary world places a premium on novelty. Roethke was able to come up with something new which neither offended nor isolated the old. His achievement was in part the result of the knowledge, intuitive and marvelous, which he had spent his life trying to communicate in our language and within the structure of poetry. This knowledge is at once nakedly simple and as indescribable as a veiled mystery (except in his poems), but he stated it all outright in the concluding lines of "Once More, The Round," saying that everything merges into the final unity, the "One," as we dance on and on and on.

THE POETRY OF RONSARD

Type of work: Poetry
Author: Pierre de Ronsard (1524-1585)
Principal published works: Odes, Books I-IV, 1550; Book V, 1552; *Amours de Cassandre,*
1552; *Hymns,* 1555; *Elégies, mascarades et bergeries,* 1565; *La Françiade,* 1572

Pierre de Ronsard was in his own time, and to a less degree in later times as well, the "prince of poets." This was not merely an impression generally held. It was Ronsard's own conviction, and he did not hesitate to admonish a coy mistress by reminding her that her kindness to him was as nothing to his generosity in fixing her name in the midst of immortal lines. But the arrogance can, though infrequently, coincide with just estimate; Ronsard, the kings of France whom he served, and those enemies, Mary Stuart and Elizabeth of England, were at one in their estimate of his verses.

Some poets speak at variance with the conditions of their lives and their own time. Ronsard, however final and universal his accent, always speaks to us of his own era and the circumstances of his life. Great and moving as his poems are, they speak of Renaissance spirit as well as of humanity pure and simple.

The Renaissance, in France as elsewhere, was a time when several tendencies, not necessarily compatible, merged with each other. It was a time when nationalism was taking the place of the feudal loyalties that had once held society loosely together. At the center of Ronsard's political consciousness are the king and his court: from the king flow the favors, including ecclesiastical benefices, which allow a poet to live, and the king's court, the nobility that dine, talk, and dance there day after day, constitutes the audience for whom the poet writes. Ronsard addressed not a general public but a particular one in that it was small and self-conscious in its tastes. It expected a poet to be learned as well as moving, and it accepted and understood references to events known only to the privileged.

Related to this rarefied centrality is the growing patriotism that led Ronsard's friend Du Bellay, also a member of the literary group called the Pléiade to which Ronsard belonged, to write *La défense et illustration de la langue Française* (1549), in which the tendency of the learned to write Latin verse is censured and, perhaps inconsistently, the importance of classical studies to any French-writing poet is underlined. The result was that Ronsard's use of his mother tongue reflected literary conventions as old as Homer, Sappho, Theocritus, and Horace. Nymphs haunt Ronsard's home forest of Gastine; local fountains, like that of Ballerie, have all the grace and romantic significance of the ancient Arethusa; and the real charms of Ronsard's various mistresses—Cassandre, Marie, Astrée, Hélène —receive additions from what Catullus, many centuries before, wrote about his Lesbia.

Like numerous other Renaissance persons, Ronsard was a full-blooded man as well as a literary person. He did not, for example, escape the serious political turmoil of the century which divided Catholic France against Protestant France and, of course, one part of the court against another. Though he could mingle Christian and Greek views of deity in the same poem, Ronsard died enjoying the full rites of the Church, and he earlier lived perceptive of the superior advantages, to a cultured man, of the rich traditions of the Catholic Church as opposed to the stern moralism, the "Hebraism" of many of the "sectaries." Because of his adherence to the Catholic faith, Protestant writers attacked the poet, not for his advocacy of pleasant and amorous pursuit alone, but for darker sins which had once been a part of the pagan world.

The pattern of Ronsard's personal career but intensifies the lines drawn in his world. He was wellborn and demandingly educated; he served at court; he went twice to Scotland and once to England and Germany. Suffering from early deafness, he subsided into the role of court poet; he received the tonsure in order to enjoy ecclesiastical benefices; and the rest of his long life was an alternation between the court and his three country estates. His background provided Ronsard with two of his main themes: the peril and hypocrisy of courts and the charm and natural beauty of a life that is rural and retired. (This contention between city and country finds reflection in the essays of Ronsard's great contemporary, Montaigne.) A poem like "Institution pour l'Adolescence du Roy très-crestien Charles IXe de ce Nom" is a stern, moving record of Ronsard's estimates of the moral perils that threaten a king, and "A la Forest de Gastine" is an account of Ronsard's country pleasures which mingles classical memories with vivid recollections of the real forest, greensward, and flowers.

Testimony to a rich, energetic life that was both patriotic and passionate echoes through Ronsard's poetry; friendship and piety, playful wit and sober reflection mingle in such collections as *Odes, Hymns, Bocage Royale,* and *Elégies.* His one real poetic disaster is the *Françiade,* an epic written at royal command, beginning with the tale of Troy and ending with the history of the Merovingian kings of early France.

No summary of Ronsard's poetic creation can omit the many sonnets which he wrote to his mistresses—some kind, some cruel. Here, too, recollections of Petrarch's Laura shape the diction of many a passionate declaration. But Ronsard, unlike many Elizabethan sonneteers in the last decades of the century, was always in pursuit of a flesh and blood woman rather than the "Idea" of Drayton. Passion was the occasion for extended poetic exercises, but the exercises were never, with Ronsard, an adequate substitute for passion gratified. Two of his mistresses, one early, one late, were cruel—Cassandre Salviati, who disappointed the young Ronsard by marrying; and Hélène de Surgères, who during several years never submitted to Ronsard's passion, dressed in black, and was painfully faithful to the shade of a dead sweetheart and the rites of amorous Platonism. It is to these two women rather than to more indulgent mistresses that his greatest sonnets are addressed. In one Ronsard declares to his servant that he wishes to shut himself up and read the *Iliad* of Homer in three days, unless a message comes from Cassandre. In another the name Hélène suggests to aging Ronsard some moving parallels with Homer's heroine; he adds, hopefully, that he believes *his* Hélène may also turn out to be a Penelope, a comfort as well as a torment. Or, anticipating Shakespearian accents ("Shall I compare thee to a summer's day . . .") Ronsard writes of Hélène's chill perfection: "Shall I compare your beauties to the moon. . . ."

Ronsard's abundance, his revival of certain parts of the medieval French vocabulary, his personal note—all these were censured by Malherbe, the tastemaker of the next century. Ronsard was also too direct for the oversubtle *précieuses,* the finicking, "learned" women of the Hôtel de Rambouillet. These seventeenth-century women, ironically, had a good deal in common with Ronsard's Hélène. But an eclipse of several centuries is now over, and Ronsard's poetic fame has now revived.

THE POETRY OF SHAPIRO

Author: Karl Shapiro (1913-   )
Principal published works: Person, Place and Thing, 1942; *V-Letter and Other Poems,* 1944; *Essay on Rime,* 1945; *Trial of a Poet and Other Poems,* 1947; *Poems, 1940-1953,* 1953: *Poems of a Jew,* 1958; *The Bourgeois Poet,* 1964

When Karl Shapiro published his first two volumes of poetry, *Person, Place and Thing* and *V-Letter,* he joined the generation of poets whose verse shared at least one characteristic: an overriding concern with the texture, the actual feel, of contemporary urban life. Their poetry is, finally, social rather than lyric, if such a distinction can be made. They do not so much sing of the self as speak bluntly about the society which surrounds them. They view with relatively clear and disenchanted eyes a society built upon ideals of individualism, free enterprise, and progress in all its mechanical and political power, personal anonymity, and public conformity. The feelings and thoughts of ordinary people lie buried somewhere beneath the slogans, advertisements, and downright lies of a mass culture dominated by a faceless state. For example, the poignancy of the sound of a human voice beneath all the whirring of machinery may be discovered in Shapiro's poem "V-Letter."

Responding to the same social and political developments as the slightly older British group including Auden, Spender, Day Lewis and MacNeice, the American poets also create no mythologies, celebrate neither a Georgian landscape nor a Golden Age of the past. These poets have given lyricism a tone of irony.

Like the others, Shapiro draws on the materials at hand for the matter of his poems: images of city and suburbia, home, crowds, drugstores, machines, human types drawn from the rigid hierarchies of a democratic society. Also, these poets are somewhat doubtful as to the sense of writing poetry at all. Poetry seems a bit like an effeminate whimper in the face of realities it can never quite express. Shapiro feels this quite strongly.

Power, raw power, is sometimes celebrated in near-lyric fashion, as in Spend-er's poem "The Express"; something of the same is seen in Shapiro's "Buick" and "The Gun." In all cases it is not the machine that is to blame, or frightening, but the men who made it and use it. If only men had the cold authority of steel they could survive, but the flesh is weak. For all his hard-headedness and irony, Shapiro and others of his kind have, not quite a faith or, finally, pity, but a defiant love for the weak human flesh, for the ordinary man. Ultimately that love for the downright human, the essential, brings Shapiro under the influence of a writer whose apparent callousness he once despised—D. H. Lawrence. It is Shapiro's doubt and finally his impatience with poetry as such that led him to abandon the ironic formalism of his original style and write the admixture of prose polemic and Whitmanesque verse titled *The Bourgeois Poet.* But this is to anticipate. Consider the poet's skepticism concerning poetry itself, as expressed in "Poet"; one notes that the tone is fairly bitter and scornful. Shapiro especially, who returned from the Pacific to be lionized by the literary elite, is aware of how the poet can become a cheapened type, sought not for his poetry or for himself, but because he embodies a sentiment.

It is basically Shapiro's sense of himself as a poet in the modern world which led him first to use rhyme and meter as a technique for irony, and later to abandon that technique because it was, finally, contrived, negative, evasive, the neatness of the rhyme scheme providing a shape, a completeness, which the experience recorded does not have.

The anonymity and even gruesomeness of modern life makes it difficult for a poet to be openly lyrical. Of what shall he sing, what celebrate? Instead, he draws back even from himself, and employs the old trappings of lyric verse for ironic purposes. In "The Gun," a thing is given more sensibility than the man. In the poem, Shapiro can move toward a swinging, lyric cadence, a heightened phrasing and diction, because his subject is a gun and not himself. There is rhyme in this poem, but the long lines, among other things, prevent the rhyme from having any ironic or sarcastic effect. "The Gun" is illustrative of the plight of modern men, as Shapiro sees it. There is much guilt, but no blame; the anonymity is worse than the bloodshed. The gun, not the man, protests, cries out, is "manly." Men are seen as dehumanized integers in a cold calculus of abstractions and things. Guns, Buicks, beds, flies—all subjects of poems by Shapiro—take on an ironic human identity. Humans, in contrast, are expendable, weak, pitiable at best. In "Epitaph for John and Richard," both the pity and the ironic disenchantment are expressed. The natural order is reduced to clockwork, a mechanical process. The close rhymes, the near-doggerel cadence, assert both a sense of the maudlin and a pity which cannot be overtly stated. The events of an ordinary man's life are matter only for a bureaucratic file, anonymous statistics. Everyone takes his appointed place in a neat order. Only in *The Bourgeois Poet* does Shapiro at last speak on the side of the ordinary mortal and against the orderliness of a society he feels is superficial and life-denying.

Shapiro was born in Baltimore and educated at the University of Virginia and Johns Hopkins. He is also Jewish. The hypocrisy and cruelty of the South is a pervasive subject for him. The South is also a subject of honest pity in much of his poetry. Shapiro's scorn for the South is matched by his pity for its being an outmoded anomaly. Beyond that, he discovers in both the figure of his father, and in the underlings, the outcasts of an aristocratic order, what he comes to value most, his faith.

The Jew, the outcast, becomes allied with men who are outcasts from society. The common man is exiled from his land, as the Jew was. Having been foresaken, the common man becomes in that very commonness, that alienation, the last bulwark against a sterile, dehumanized social order. In this light, Shapiro can even feel kinship with the Southerner.

Thus the common, substandard man becomes Shapiro's alternative to mechanization, slogan, literary pandering, privilege, and politics. In order to assert this alternative, irony and detachment give way to direct statement, outright expression. The result is, in form and content, *The Bourgeois Poet*. One can go on being ironic only so long. The old feeling that verse is effeminate posturing also remains in his poetry. In his *Essay on Rime* Shapiro had spoken of discovering a new form for poetry, a richly cadenced and suggestive prose, something like Joyce's in *Ulysses*. Whitman, too, is a forerunner.

With Joyce in mind, but even more noticeably Whitman and Lawrence, Shapiro fashioned the ninety-six sections which make up *The Bourgeois Poet*. The style of this work is, largely, a prose which is more closely patterned after spoken speech than the more formalized patterns of syntax and grammar. Images come in rich sequences; mind and imagination dart and leap, as in very excellent conversation; the utterances are given shape through the repetition of phrases and clauses. These elements of style are also characteristic of modern verse; consequently *The Bourgeois Poet* is often called a prose-poem. Actually, it is a special kind of prose-speech. At times, as at the end of the first section, Shapiro is writing verse and using what is called syntactic prosody. The irony here is not so much one of disenchantment, distance, or self-apology, but is, rather, openly satiric and comic. The whole book is notable for its gusto, its humor, its forthright anger, and its honesty. It is also, too often, stale and derivative.

Shapiro intends to embrace experience, and to do so on the real and humdrum level of bourgeois life. He accepts its formlessness, its contradictions, its relativity of values. Echoing Lawrence, Shapiro calls for a revolt by the natural man who is instinctual, honest, many-sided.

Though Shapiro will not dabble in mythology, his primitivism is an analogous attempt to discover and revivify the essential roots of life, the dried radicals buried beneath the modern society in its conformity and superficiality. He and T. S. Eliot share an aversion to that society, to the misleading Liberal-Rationalistic dogmas of Progress, Individualism, and Perfectability. But whereas Eliot counters with an austere and traditional conception of culture based on the authority of the Church and a conviction of Original Sin, Shapiro is directly opposed in urging the natural, the common, even the unregenerate: Humor vs. intellectual austerity; Apeneck Sweeney vs. The Fisher King. Shapiro's very human (as

opposed to theological) views on Original Sin are expressed in a series of poems entitled "Adam and Eve." Their sin produces our world, which is preferred over a mythical paradise.

Shapiro's poet has a comic sense of his own weaknesses, and the ability to reveal them as well as lash out with comic invective at whatever he finds dishonest, posturing, or antihuman. He sometimes resembles Saul Bellow in upholding the unreclaimed, damned, and abidingly human man, the animal with a bothersome but ever-functioning conscience. Shapiro's love for the ordinary man is such that the sophistication of art becomes perverse and debilitating. Irreverent, bawdy, funny, serious, Shapiro identifies accepted poetry with what has happened to too many people. In rebellion, he makes of himself a sort of latter-day Whitman.

THE POETRY OF SIDNEY

Author: Sir Philip Sidney (1554-1586)
Principal published works: Arcadia, 1590; *Astrophel and Stella,* 1591; *Certain Sonnets,* 1598

During the middle of the sixteenth century English poetry was, almost without exception, mediocre. Thomas Wyatt and Henry Howard, Earl of Surrey, had succeeded in bringing some continental polish and new Renaissance ideas into their works, composed during the last years of Henry VIII, but their efforts did not really bear fruit until Edmund Spenser published *The Shepheardes Calendar* in 1579 and Sir Philip Sidney began to circulate his pastorals, sonnets, and songs at about the same time. The metrical variety and the rich Renaissance imagery in the works of these two poets opened new doors for aspiring English writers.

Spenser's contributions to English literature have been widely recognized, but Sidney's influence has been less accurately assessed, in spite of his tremendous popularity in his own time. In a sense the reputation of Sidney the ideal courtier has tended to overshadow that of Sidney the poet, who is remembered chiefly for selected sonnets from *Astrophel and Stella* and for a handful of lyrics. The fine Oxford edition of his poetry, edited by W. A. Ringler and published in 1962, sheds new light on the genius of the young courtier, who died of a battle wound at the age of thirty-one. In moments of leisure in his active career as diplomat and soldier Sidney composed a substantial volume of poetry. Only a few lyrics were published before his death in 1586, but his work was widely circulated in manuscript and his reputation as a poet was high.

Sidney received a standard classical education at the Shrewsbury School and at Oxford, but his years of study and travel on the Continent probably had an even greater effect on his work. The experiments in rhyme and meter of sixteenth century French poets, who were especially interested in recapturing the techniques of the Greek and Roman writers, the beauty of cadence and imagery in the sonnets of the great fourteenth century Florentine, Petrarch, and his disciples, and the courtly tone of French and Italian Renaissance poetry almost certainly inspired Sidney to strive for similar elegance in his own language. Sidney, even more than Spenser, was a European poet; the native medieval tradition of Chaucer and his contemporaries that played a considerable part in the development of Spenser's genius seems to have had much less effect on Sidney.

Among the earliest of Sidney's poems to be widely circulated were lyrics from his charming pastoral entertainment, the *Lady of May,* presented for Queen Elizabeth at Wanstead, home of the poet's uncle, the Earl of Leicester, in 1578. The verse portions of the masque included compliments to the queen and a song contest, in the best tradition of Virgilian pastoral, between a forester and a shepherd:

> Come *Espilus,* come now declare thy skill,
> Shew how thou canst deserve so brave desire,
> Warme well thy wits, if thou wilt win her will,
> For water cold did never promise fire:
> > Great sure is she, on whom our hopes do live,
> > Greater is she who must the judgement give.

Many of Sidney's poems were composed as part of his pastoral romance, the *Arcadia.* A number of lyrics appeared in the body of the narrative, and the five books of the original version of the work were separated by groups of eclogues related to the general themes of the story: unrequited love, the conflict between reason and passion, marriage, and the sorrows of age and death. The poems were

spoken or sung by both the noble characters and the rustics; the shepherds' songs
include amusing parodies of courtly
verses. Alethes' song of Mopsa in the first
book satirizes the conventional catalogue
of the beauties of an adored lady:

Her forhead jacinth like, her cheekies
    of opall hue,
Her twinkling eies bedeckt with pearl,
    her lips of saphir blew.

Sidney had a fine dramatic sense that
enabled him to capture the intense inner
conflicts of his characters in many of his
lyrics. The tormented queen, Gynecia,
laments:

Like those sicke folkes, in whome
    strange humors flowe,
Can taste no sweetes, the sour only
    please:
So to my minde, while passions daylie
    growe,
Whose fyrie chaines, upon his free-
    dome seaze,
Joie's strangers seeme, I cannot bide
    their showe,
    Nor brooke outghte els but well ac-
        quainted woe.
Bitter griefe tastes me best, paine is
    my ease,
Sicke to the death, still loving my
    disease.

The heroes of the *Arcadia,* Pyrocles
and Musidorus, traditional Renaissance
courtier-poets, express their feelings in
highly complicated sonnets, in which
Sidney explores the possibilities of different and demanding rhyme schemes, intricately balanced lines, and ingenious
paradoxes. Musidorus pays tribute to his
beloved Pamela in a sonnet that employs
only two rhymes throughout, a technical
tour de force:

Locke up, faire lids, the treasures of my
    harte:
Preserve those beames, this age's onely
    lighte:
To her sweete sense, sweete sleepe,
    some ease imparte,
Her sence too weake to beare her
    spirit's mighte.
And while O sleepe thou closest up her
sight,
(Her sight where love did forge his
    fayrest darte)
O harbour all her partes in easeful
    plighte:
Let no strange dreme make her fayre
    body starte.
But yet O dream, if thou wilt not de-
    parte
In this rare subject from my common
    right:
But wilt thy self in such a seate de-
    lighte,
Then take my shape, and play a lover's
    parte:
Kisse her from me, and say unto her
    spirite,
Till her eyes shine, I live in darkest
    night.

The four groups of eclogues dividing
the books of the *Arcadia* are a remarkable
demonstration of the breadth of Sidney's
imagination and the range of his technical skill. He employs a number of different verse forms, even within a single
poem, and experiments with various line
lengths and stanza forms, borrowing
complicated meters from the French and
the Italians; he evidently enjoyed setting
difficult technical problems for himself.

While most of the pastoral poems were
written in conventional accentual verse,
Sidney tried in several to reproduce the
quantitative meters of classical poetry,
in which the length of syllables, rather
than accent, was the basis of the poetic
line. On occasion Sidney's adherence to
classical rules produced lines that were
nearer bad prose than good poetry, but he
was in general more successful than
might be expected. Dorus' song in the
second group of eclogues, written in Horatian Asclepiads, a complicated pattern
of short and long sounds in a twelve-
syllable line, has a pleasant, stately
rhythm:

O sweet woods the delight of solitarines!
O how much I do like your solitarines!
Where man's mind hath a freed consid-
    eration
Of goodness to receive lovely direction.
Where senses do behold th'order of

5137

heav'nly hoste,
And wise thoughts do behold what the creator is:
Contemplation here holdeth his only seate:
Bownded with no limits, borne with a wing of hope
Clymes even unto the starres, Nature is under it.

The subjects and tone of the eclogues are as varied as their verse forms. There are love laments, philosophical musings, elegies, an epithalamion, and several comic pieces. The songs of the shepherds, who speak a simple, commonplace language without the archaic diction of Spenser's rustics, are often entertaining. One of the best is a comic imitation of Virgil's third eclogue, a song contest between two impudent young shepherds. Sidney, like Virgil, begins with an amusing interchange of insults, then descends to broad humor as the youths set prizes for their contest and Nico speaks:

Content: but I will lay a wager hereunto,
That profit may ensue to him that best can do.
I have (and long shall have) a white great nimble cat,
A king upon a mouse, a strong foe to a rat,
Fine eares, long taile he hath, with Lion's curbed clawe,
Which oft he lifteth up, and stayes his lifted pawe.

In a more serious vein are the songs of Philisides, who represents Sidney himself. He appears in each of the groups of eclogues, meditating upon his unrequited love for Mira and lamenting the human condition in general in a song taught him, he says, by old Languet, the French Protestant who accompanied Sidney on his European trip in 1573 and 1574.

While the poems in the *Arcadia* show the greatest range of Sidney's poetic gifts, his best works are in his *Astrophel and Stella*, the first of many English sonnet sequences. Sidney used the Italian sonnet form throughout, but he borrowed the English practice, initiated by Wyatt and Surrey, of ending with a rhymed couplet. His use of classical imagery reveals further his indebtedness to French and Italian poets of his day, but his clear, straightforward language gives his poems a distinctly personal quality that lifts them far above the conventional Renaissance sonnets.

Astrophel and Stella tells the story of the poet's romance, real or imaginary, with Penelope Devereux, Lady Rich; her husband's name occasioned several punning sonnets that reveal the identity of "Stella." Sidney describes the development of his love for Stella and his worship of her from a distance, then rejoices at signs that she returns his affection. His passion urges her to yield to him; his reason respects the virtue that makes her refuse and finally brings about their separation.

The sonnets do not form a continuous narrative but are rather reflections of the poet's state of mind, which is occasionally related to particular events: a tournament at court, a stolen kiss, or Stella's illness. Most often Sidney is either praising Stella's beauty and virtue with copious references to Venus and Cupid, or mourning the unhappiness of the scorned lover, Astrophel; there are also a number of sonnets about the writing of love poetry. Astrophel recommends spontaneity in writing to convince the lady of the genuineness of the poet's passion. The famous first sonnet, unusual in that it is written in hexameter, rather than pentameter, lines, states this theme:

But words came halting forth, wanting Invention's stay,
Invention, Nature's child, fled stepdame Studie's blowes,
And others' feete still seem'd but strangers in my way.
Thus great with child to speake, and helplesse in my throwes,
Biting my trewand pen, beating my selfe for spite,
'Foole,' said my Muse to me, 'looke in thy heart and write.'

Even this sonnet owes something to Petrarch; naturalness and originality were conventions, too.

Sidney's simple diction contributes much to the appeal of many of his sonnets. He can capture a state of mind beautifully in poems like this often anthologized one:

> With how sad steps, O Moone, thou climb'st the skies,
> How silently, and with how wanne a face,
> What, may it be that even in heav'nly place
> That busie archer his sharp arrowes tries?
> Sure, if that long with *Love* acquainted eyes
> Can judge of *Love,* thou feel'st a Lover's case;
> I reade it in thy looks, thy languisht grace,
> To me that feele the like, thy state descries.
> Then ev'n of fellowship, O Moone, tell me
> Is constant *Love* deem'd there but want of wit?
> Are Beauties there as proud as here they be?
> Do they above love to be lov'd, and yet
> Those Lovers scorn whom that *Love* doth possesse?
> Do they call *Vertue* there ungratefulnesse?

Sidney frequently inserts bits of dialogue or rhetorical questions for dramatic effect; he complains that court ladies do not take his love seriously because he does not flaunt it:

> The courtly Nymphs, acquainted with the mone
> Of them, who in their lips *Love's* standerd beare;
> 'What he?' say they of me, 'now I dare sweare,
> He cannot love: no, no, let him alone.'

Although sonnets make up the major part of *Astrophel and Stella,* Sidney inserted several songs that carry forward his action. These lyrics were written in various meters and among them are what seem to be the first trochaic stanzas in English. One of the finest poems in this new form is the fourth song, beginning:

> Onely joy, now here you are,
> Fit to heare and ease my care:
> Let my whispering voyce obtaine,
> Sweete reward for sharpest paine:
> Take me to thee, and thee to me.
> 'No, no, no, no, my Deare, let be.'

Another opens with that fresh appreciation of nature that is so characteristic of the best Elizabethan poetry:

> In a grove most rich of shade,
> Where birds wanton musicke made,
> May then yong his pide weedes showing,
> New perfumed with flowers fresh growing,
>
> *Astrophil* with *Stella* sweete,
> Did for mutual comfort meete,
> Both within themselves oppressed,
> But each in the other blessed.

Sidney left a number of works not included in the *Arcadia* or in *Astrophel and Stella.* One of his finest sonnets, often mistakenly associated with the sonnet sequence, is the familiar rejection of love, which opens with the famous lines:

> Leave me O Love, which reachest but to dust,
> And thou my mind aspire to higher things:
> Grow rich in that which never taketh rust:
> Whatever fades, but fading pleasure brings.

Another remarkable demonstration of Sidney's technical skill is his collection of metrical versions of the first forty-three psalms, each in a different stanza form. He modeled his translations upon the French Protestant psalter of Clément Marot and Theodore Beza, attempting to improve on the popular, but unpoetic, English translations of Sternhold and Hopkins. The quality of Sidney's versions is uneven, but he often succeeded in bringing out the majesty of the Biblical passages:

All, all my trust, Lord, I have put in
   Thee,
Never therefore let me confounded be,
   But save me, save me in Thy right-
     eousness,
Bow down thine ear to heare how much
   I need,
Deliver me, deliver me in speed,
   Be my strong rock, be Thou my
     forteress.

It is difficult to estimate the significance of Sidney's contribution to the development of English poetry. He demonstrated the flexibility, beauty, and elegance of the English language without distorting it with obscure or archaic diction, and he conveyed in his poetry the idealism and the sense of beauty that filled contemporary French and Italian literature. He wrote in his *Defence of Poesie*: "Nature never set forth the earth in so rich tapestry as divers poets have done; neither with pleasant rivers, fruitful trees, sweet-smelling flowers, nor whatsoever else may make the too-much-loved earth more lovely; her world is brazen, the poets only deliver a golden." This, perhaps, was Sidney's own gift to his nation's literature—the creation of a new and beautiful world of poetry that inspired other writers to enter it.

THE POETRY OF SKELTON

Author: John Skelton (c. 1460-1529)
Principal published work: The Pithy, Pleasant and Profitable Works of Master Skelton, Poet Laureate, 1568

To place John Skelton in some convenient niche of literary history is difficult, but it is even more difficult to find an appropriate artistic designation for this early Tudor poet. Nearer in time to the writing of Wyatt or Surrey, he is much closer in style to the writing of the Medieval Latinists. Though the first mention of Skelton comes in Caxton's preface to Eneydos, calling him a "humanist scholar," Skelton and the humanists did not have much in common and even indulged in some feuding. While the humanists were reviving an interest in the classical Greek and Latin writers and using them for examples, Skelton continued to copy the style of fourteenth and fifteenth century writers.

The most obvious example of the copying is "The Bouge of Court," which is typical of the medieval tradition in several ways. It uses rhyme royal to tell a dream allegory; it relies heavily on personification and the use of court terms; and it has the usual astronomical opening and closing apology.

The prologue begins with allusions to the sun, the moon, and to Mars. The narrator wishes he could write, but being warned by Ignorance not to try, he lies down and dreams of going aboard a ship, "The Bouge of Court," which is owned by Sans Peer and captained by Fortune. The narrator, who reveals that he is called Drede, is first accosted and frightened by Danger, the chief gentlewoman of Sans Peer. Before Drede can flee, he is soothed by Desire, who persuades him to stay aboard.

After this introduction comes the main body of the poem, which consists of conversation between Drede and seven of the passengers, Skelton's representations of the seven deadly sins. Drede first describes the approaching figure in unforgettable detail; then, as the figure speaks, an even sharper focus of his personality is achieved. The seven passengers are named "Favel" or Flattery, Suspect, Harvy Hafter, Disdain, Riot, Dissimulation, and Deceit.

Harvy Hafter is Skelton's most colorful creation in the poem, and he is still around:

> But as I stood musing in my mind,
> Harvy Hafter came leaping, light as lynde.
>
> Upon his breast he bare a versing-box,
> His throat was clear, and lustily could fayne.
> Methought his gown was all furréd with fox,
> And ever he sang, '*Sith I am nothing plain . . .*'
> To keep him from picking it was a great pain:
> He gazed on me with goatish beard;
> Whan I looked on him, my purse was half afeard.

Thus Harvy Hafter is the typical confidence man, always gay and optimistic, always ready to dispel all doubts and fears with pat answers and stale jokes.

After talking with these seven characters, Drede fears for his life and jumps overboard. The leap and landing awaken him, and he seizes his pen and records his dream. In the final stanza, his apology, he states that what he has recorded is only a dream, but sometimes even dreams contain truth.

> I would therewith no man were miscontent,
> Beseeching you that shall it see or read
> In every point to be indifferent,
> Sith all in substance of slumbring cloth proceed.
> I will not say it is matter indeed,
> But yet oft-time such dreams be found true.
> Now construe ye what is the residue!

Though this poem is typical of the medieval tradition, its importance lies in how it deviates from the tradition: this is Skelton's contribution. His characters are certainly types, as in a dream allegory they must be; but they are more than the mere pictured figures of medieval writing. They are highly individualized characters, as shown by Harvy Hafter's description, and they are characterized not only by description but also by their own speech. Furthermore, Skelton's setting is more concrete than is usual in the medieval tradition.

The allegory depicts the life at court as Skelton saw it. The highest achievement of the courtier was to be recognized by the king and to maintain his favor, no matter what the means. Those who attained his favor were openly praised but privately scorned and envied by the others. Thus, if one succeeded, he failed to maintain the true friendship of his fellow courtiers, for flattery, jealousy, disdain, suspicion and other feelings all joined forces to destroy such friendship. To Skelton, the irony of such a life was that gaining the attention of the king was accomplished purely by chance. Since this kind of court life was demeaning to the dignity of man as Skelton saw it, he attacked it.

Another of Skelton's early poems which shows the poet still working in the medieval tradition is "Philip Sparrow." Following a medieval point of view, Skelton wrote this poem in the short-lined couplets, tercets, and quatrains now known as Skeltonic verse. This poem is Skelton's most playful and most popular work; in it we see the poet in a mood in which he has cast dignity and restraint aside and has indulged himself in a bit of fantasy. He evokes both tears and laughter from the reader as he describes the activities of the bird, its death, its funeral, and as he describes the owner or mistress, Jane Scroop. It is a long and rather loose poem which can be broken into three distinct parts.

The first part, which takes over half of the 1,382 lines in the poem, is a dramatic monologue with Jane Scroop as narrator telling of her Philip. Through her Skelton gives the reader his appraisal of Chaucer, Gower, and Lydgate, and also uses the opportunity to display his wide reading in Greek and Latin. He parodies the funeral mass by having the whole host of birds chant over the dead body of Philip Sparrow. But the most delightful lines are those in which Jane talks of her pet:

> It had a velvet cap,
> And would sit upon my lap,
> And seek after small wormes,
> And sometimes white bread-crumbes;
> And many times and oft
> Between my breastes soft
> It woulde lie and rest;
> It was proper and prest.
>
> Sometime he would gasp
> When he saw a wasp;
> A fly or a gnat,
> He would fly at that;
> And prettily would he pant
> When he saw an ant.
> Lord, how he would pry
> After the butterfly!

In the second part of the poem, "The Commendacione," Skelton commends and defends Jane Scroop as the composer of the first section. He also spends much time reporting "the goodly sort/Of her features clear," and ends each section of the "Commendacione" with a refrain:

> For this most goodly floure,
> This blossom of fresh colóur,
> So Jupiter me succóur,
> She flourisheth new and new
> In beauty and virtúe:

The third part, the "Addition," was obviously added after the other two had been written and was an answer to the critics of the poem and a protest against their criticism.

"The Tunning of Elinour Rumming," more than all the other poems together, has earned for Skelton the title of "scurrilous" or, as from Alexander Pope, "beastly." It is Skelton's most notorious work. The first part of the poem introduces the hostess, Elinour. Then follow seven sections of various scenes in the tavern. This study of Tudor low-life is extremely realistic. To show the stench and squalor of the bar, Skelton eliminates no details, no matter how crude or coarse. Yet, there is a vitality in the realism of the scene, and the impression—no matter how unpleasant it may be to some, though to others it may be only humorous—is an unforgettable one. For example:

Maud Ruggy thither skippéd:
She was ugly hippéd,
And ugly thick lippéd,
Like an onion sided,
Like tan leather hided.
She had her so guided
Between the cup and the wall
That she was there withal
Into a palsy fall;
With that her head shakéd,
And her handés quakéd,
One's head would have achéd
To see her nakéd.

But even Skelton feels he has gone too far in his description of the tawdry existence:

I have written too much
Of this mad mumming
Of Elinour Rumming.

Like many others after him, Skelton excuses himself for his descent by saying that he has written the poem to show others how to escape from such a fall. Yet the gusto of the representation shows a familiarity with the subject that is unexpected in such a scholar and churchman.

Perhaps Skelton's most puzzling work is "Speak, Parrot." There are several reasons for the vagueness of the poem which has led to an appellation "unintelligible." In the first place, there is strong evidence to suggest that the work is a collection of many poems written at various times. Although some of the poems are even dated, the method Skelton used to date them is not conventional, so that any attempt to decipher these dates is mostly guesswork. Another reason for the vagueness is that Skelton feels that to protect himself from charges of treason he must veil his allusions to topical incidents in allegorical language, and he uses the Book of Judges for many terms of this language. Present knowledge of particular events of the day also cloud an intelligible interpretation. Finally, the device Skelton uses as framework for "Speak, Parrot" compounds the vagueness. He puts the whole narration into the mouth of a parrot that relates the poem in no particular chronological sequence, and at times the parrot speaks only gibberish.

In this poem Skelton still relies on the medieval use of allegory and the verse form is basically rhyme royal. But he is much farther from the medieval tradition here than he was in "The Bouge of Court." Since Skelton went to such pains to conceal his message, his targets must have been powerful and the events well known; and the members of the court probably had little trouble understanding just what Skelton was about. Still, by having the parrot speak, he was able to deny any treasonous charges.

With the writing of "Colin Clout" comes Skelton's complete severance from the medieval tradition. He has abandoned the dream structures for one narrator, personification and allegory for direct statement, and rhyme royal for Skeltonic verse. His use of Colin Clout as narrator is fortunate, for Colin simply repeats what he hears during his travels:

Thus I, Colin Clout,
As I go about,
And wandering as I walk
I hear the people talk.

Thus he cannot vouch for the truthfulness of what he hears, nor can he be blamed for his crudeness. This flexible framework also allows him to repeat in any order what he has heard, and this order, or lack of it, is sometimes frustrating.

One of Skelton's attacks in the poem is against the conflict between church and state. He is fighting for the church but, like Erasmus, from a humanistic viewpoint. He argues that the church should be independent, not parasitic on the state; that the selling of salvation leads to total disorganization of the church; and that the clergy are ignorant, mainly because of the careless selection of priests. All of this leads the laity to distrust the clergy. Again, like Erasmus, he is calling upon the church to cleanse itself, to carry out reform from within. He is not calling for a change in doctrine, but rather asks that the old doctrines be more closely followed. His bitterness is directed against those who are defiling the sacraments of the church. and those who allow this defiling. Thus the focus of the attack is Cardinal Wolsey, who, in Skelton's opinion, is the epitome of sacrificing the interests of the church to those of the state. The power of the poem lies not in the bitterness of the invective, but in the appeals for reform which, coming from England's most prominent writer of the time, also a powerful churchman, do carry some weight.

"Why Come Ye Not to Court?" is Skelton's third and most direct indictment against Wolsey. Like "Speak, Parrot" and "Colin Clout," this poem lacks any basic organization, and the lines tumble one upon another with a seeming lack of order. Also, there is no chronological order to the events referred to. This loose structure might lead one to assume that the poem was composed at various times.

In this poem Skelton does not use allegorical language or Biblical terms to describe Wolsey but speaks of him plainly as the Cardinal or "red hat." Because the Cardinal is in complete control of the kingdom, the situation is bad because Wolsey is concerned only with money and lavish living:

> We have cast up our war,
> And made a worthy truce
> With, 'Cup, level suse!'
> Our money madly lent,
> and more madly spent:
> . . . . . .

> With crowns of gold emblazéd
> They make him so amazéd
> And his eyen so dazéd
> That he ne see can
> To know God nor man!
> . . . . . .

> *Why come ye not to court?*
> To which court?
> To the kingés court,
> Or to Hampton Court?
> *Nay, to the kingés court.*
> The kingés court
> Should have the excellence,
> But Hampton Court
> Hath the preéminence. . . .

One of Skelton's last poems, and one of his longest, is "The Garland of Laurel." Strangely enough, it is dedicated to Wolsey; therefore, some degree of reconciliation must have taken place, for Skelton died while living in the protection of the church. Once more the poet reverts to his medieval tradition of the dream allegory, using mostly rhyme royal to tell how the garland of laurel has come to be placed on his head. A long procession of poets, headed by Gower, Lydgate, and Chaucer come to Skelton. He agrees to carry on in the tradition and places the garland on his own head. As Alexander Dyce said, "The Garland of Laurel" is in one respect the most remarkable poem in all literature, for no other poet has ever written sixteen hundred lines to honor himself.

Had Skelton given more time and energy to developing his lyrical poetry, he might be better known today, for he did have a definite gift for shaping verse. However, we have only a few poems as evidence; unfortunately, Skelton did not spend much time or effort on lyrics. Some of his better ones are "Woefully arrayed," "The Manner of the World Nowadays," "Womanhood, Wanton, ye want" and "My Darling Dear, my Daisy Flower."

Skelton is not an imitator of those who went before him, nor is he a founder of any style or school to be copied by those who came after him. True, he did write in the medieval tradition, but not entirely, and he is better in those poems where he does not follow the tradition; also, he did have imitators of his style in his day, but they have made no significant contribution to literature. Thus we have the enigma of Skelton: a poet following the medieval tradition while the other scholars are heralding England's Renaissance, yet a poet creating his own particular style; a tender poet capable of the warm humor of "Philip Sparrow"; a realistic poet capable of the crude grossness of "The Tunning of Elinour Rumming"; a religious poet, loving his church yet calling for its inner reformation; a secular poet knowledgeable in the ways of the world; and most of all, a courageous poet fearless in speaking his mind and in attacking one unequaled in power.

THE POETRY OF SMART

Author: Christopher Smart (1722-1771)
Principal published works: The Seatonian Poems, 1750-1756; *A Song to David,* 1763; *Poems by Mr. Smart,* 1763; *Poems on Several Occasions,* 1763; *The Collected Poems of C. S.,* 1949

Christopher Smart's Seatonian poems won prizes at Cambridge University from 1750 to 1756. These poems cover the attributes of the "Supreme Being" to whom they are addressed: his Eternity, Immensity, Omniscience, Power, and Goodness. The poems are Miltonic not only in the structure of the verse but in the largeness of vision they conjure up. The second of these in particular, "On the Immensity of the Supreme Being," is a landmark of Miltonic adaptation. It begins with an avowal that God is best praised by that poetry which, like nature itself, acknowledges "the grand thanksgiving" of creation. Its prevailing tone is humility; the center of the poem is God and not man. It is, in fact, a poem about human imperfection opposed to the plenitude of the created universe, and in this respect it is quite unlike the mainstream of eighteenth century poetry.

The beauty of the earth is praised for the evidence it gives of the nature of the deity. "Astonish'd into silence" the poet reflects on the variety, beauty, and multiplicity of creation, finding even in the bottom of the sea the evidence of a divine intention in

> th' unplanted garden round
> Of vegetable coral, sea-flow'rs ga.
> And shrubs of amber from the pearl-
> pav'd bottom.

Like the other Seatonian poems, this suggests that the works of civilization are far inferior to those of nature.

Smart's "Hymn to the Supreme Being" was written, as he said, to express his thanks for recovering from a dangerous illness. He begins by relating the sickness of David, a figure ever present in his mind. For Smart, David stands not only for the figure of the psalmist, but for the man who is both "the sovereign of myself and servant of the Lord." When he compares the sickness of David and his own illness, he sees that he has very little to recommend him to the special care of heaven. In going over his life he addresses himself constantly to the great themes of waste and sorrow. He finds that he has no special title to mercy, much less to divine notice, but it is his discovery of this fact which both casts him down and lifts him up. His penitence and his union with a world of sinners, which he sums up as the "contrite heart," are the whole of the defense he offers of his past life. The poem is both a thanksgiving for and praise of charity; it makes clear that the beneficiary is such only by the grace of heaven.

The figure of David is pre-eminent in Smart's "A Song to David," a poem which is both a biography and a spiritual celebration of its subject. Smart begins by pointing out the excellences of David's character which won for him material rewards. He outlines the courage and intelligence of his hero "arm'd in gallant faith." Yet, above all other issues, and infinitely more meaningful than David's success as a warrior and a politician, is the piety of David. It is his consecration to his religion that Smart particularly admires, and the poem is in substance in praise of this. The goodness of David he explains by reference to those occasions when the king showed mercy to his enemies: "To pity, to forgive, to save." Beyond this, according to the poet, is the perpetual prayer of David, the purity of his devotion, his fasting and fear of the Lord. Whether in warfare or in the employments of peace he is the paradigm of the virtuous man and the consecrated leader.

Like Milton, Smart appreciates in David another quality, that of poetic creativity. David as king elicits the praises of Smart. David as the man of "perpetual prayer" draws his admiration, but David as the figure of the artist is perhaps even more central to the poet's vision. Smart writes of the "invention" of David, his capacity to make the form and the language of the Psalms convey the richness of his responses. He praises too the "conception" of the poet-king, or his powers of imagination. His emotional quality is last but not least, the "exaltations" that the poet, above all other men, manages to achieve and to express. David is in fact the model of the poet; he begins in contemplation and ends in creation. In this he repeats, indeed acts out, the first process of all, the creation of the world itself.

Thereafter Smart returns to the character of David, which he compiles from the stories of his reign as well as from the Psalms themselves. It is both the character of a man that is described and that of a symbol. The first of the allegorical qualities of soul that Smart attributes to David is serenity; it intimates the wish of the king for peace in his kingdom and on earth. The next of these is strength, to persist against the great odds of a divided people and hostile external forces. Smart then writes about the constancy, joy, and wisdom of his hero, in terms which may be taken to reveal Smart's consciousness of his own tragic lack of these qualities. Writing shortly after a prolonged attack of insanity, in despair over his private and artistic life, Smart put into this poem a deep sense of the need for these qualities in life as in art.

One of the great themes of Smart's work as a whole is the appreciation of created things. This theme is explicitly connected to the idea of God as He is revealed by the things He has made. "A Song to David" leaves his first subject, the king himself, and turns to a lengthy consideration of this favorite and recurring theme. Smart himself can best convey the depth of his feelings for the plenitude of the created world:

Trees, plants, and flow'rs—of virtuous
    root;
Gem yielding blossom, yielding fruit,

Choice gums and precious balm;
Bless ye the nosegay in the vale,
And with the sweetness of the gale
    Enrich the thankful psalm.

The "thankful psalm" is a good description of the essential character of Smart's work as a whole. He continually seizes upon the variety, beauty and intelligibility of creation and as critics have pointed out, he does not spend as much poetic energy in contemplating his own condition as he does praising what he perceives by his senses. From this point in the poem Smart praises the world of water and that of land, that of sky and that of earth. He uses the ancient conception of the chain of being to give form to the feelings which he tries to convey: from the world of shells and fishes to that of higher life he gives an outline of the harmonic order of the universe. Very little escapes this great catalogue, not even those inanimate things at the base of the pyramid of Being. After this interlude of praise, Smart returns to his ostensible subject, the Hebrew poet and king.

The height of the achievement of David is summarized in Smart's concept of Adoration, the act of submitting the mortal to the immortal. This concluding section of the poem is a vital link in connecting two subjects: the Hebraic tradition and the Christian. In a long and orchestral ending Smart relates the qualities of David to those of Christ, and we see the figure of the warrior and poet emerge as the forerunner of an even greater figure.

This outline would seem to indicate that Smart was almost totally involved in matters of religion; that his own religious mania succeeded, in spite of himself, in coloring all of his writing. The fact is that Smart found time to translate Horace and to provide a translation of the Roman poet of such high quality as to ensure its use even today. Translation was a very great eighteen century craft, if not indeed an art, and Christopher Smart shows the same familiarity with the classical spirit as that shown by Alexander

Pope and other masters of paraphrase. The Odes of Horace are simply and cleanly done. Perhaps their most significant contribution is the expression of classical thought in enlightenment language.

Besides his religious poetry and his translation Smart was able to work in minor veins of poetry. His poem "Of Jeoffrey, His Cat" is certainly slight, but it is strong evidence of Smart's ability to observe and to deduce: we see the cat no longer with the automatic stare of everyday but as Smart does, "wreathing his body seven times round with elegant quickness." In many other minor poems Smart concentrates on his appreciation of the qualities of the senses: he writes about music in "On Gratitude" and celebrates the "Voice & Lyre" just as, in the religious poems, he celebrates all those things which bring beauty to life. In "An Epistle to John Sherratt, Esq." Smart writes that of all the offerings he can conceive of, none so delights the mind as "gratitude expres'd in song." This thankfulness for the rewards of the senses is a constant theme in his work, and he relates it with equal constancy to the intention on God in creating a world full of aesthetic and moral delight. In another poem he writes that "the sweets of Evening charm the mind"—it is an expression quite un-Miltonic in language and tone, but very much related to Milton's consciousness of the nature and meaning of all things experienced by the mind. "Every thing that grows," Smart writes in this poem, is a reminder of "superior natures" and the highest sphere of imagination. In short, his work reiterates, whether it is about figures from history or the experiences of everyday life, the constant theme of thankfulness for the variety and beauty of life. It reiterates, too, something substantially Miltonic: the conviction that all this beauty means something, that it is a key to an understanding of the nature of life itself.

THE POETRY OF SOR JUANA INÉS DE LA CRUZ

Author: Sor Juana Inés de la Cruz (1651-1695)
Principal published works: Inundación Castálida de la única poetisa, musa décima, sor Juana Inés de la Cruz, 1689; Fama y obras póstumas del Fénix de México y Dézima Musa, 1700

Sister Juana Inés de la Cruz, a celebrated Mexican nun, was the greatest literary figure in the colonial New World, not only because of her lyrical ability but also because of her delightful personality. In the early seventeenth century there were few women in Hispanic America who could even sign their names, but with the developing culture, more and more girls received a sort of education in schools called "Amigas." However, it was only a primary education. The University of Mexico, founded in 1551, was only for boys. Girls were not believed to have any need or desire for extensive learning.

This was not true, however, of Juana Inés de Ashbaje y Ramírez de Santillana, born in San Miguel de Nepantla, Mexico, in 1651. To keep her out of mischief, her mother sent her with an older sister to one of the Amigas. There the three-year-old unblushingly told the teacher that her mother wanted her taught how to read. The teacher, at first as a joke, then amazed at Juana's quickness, taught her to read before her mother learned of the deception.

A craving for knowledge followed Juana throughout life. A few years later, having heard that cheese, of which she was very fond, stupefied the brain, the girl stopped eating it. When she thought she was not learning grammar as rapidly as she should, she cut back her hair, vowing not to let it grow long till she conquered the subject, "since a head so naked of knowledge ought not to be adorned with pretty hair." Hearing about the university for men at the capital, she importuned her mother to let her disguise herself in men's clothes and attend classes. At the age of eight, when she finally went to Mexico City to live with her grandparents, she learned Latin in order to read all the books in their library.

Turning suddenly to the religious life, she entered the convent of Santa Teresa la Antigua at the age of sixteen, but the rigorous discipline of the order proved too strict for her frail health and she was released. In 1669 she entered the convent of San Jerónimo. She remained a member till her death.

She early discovered her versifying ability and practiced it for formal and informal occasions. The latter part of the seventeenth century in America was the Baroque Period, with poetry and even prose full of distorted syntax, Latinisms, mythological and classical allusions, and an abundance of metaphors and ridiculous conceits. This Gongorism was the result of imitation of the Spanish poet Luis de Góngora y Argote.

Because of her wide reading, Sor Juana was bound to imitate the prevailing literary fashion when she began to write. Before long, however, she found other models. Critics find the influence of the great lyric poet Garcilaso de la Vega, who wrote in the Italian style with love as his chief theme. Though limited in number, his verses achieved perfection. His thirty-eight harmonious sonnets, in which emotion mingles with beauty, established that form in Spanish verse. At times Sor Juana also followed Lupercio and Bartolomé Argensola, brothers who were among the most classic of poets.

Sor Juana experimented with every type of verse: sonnets, lyrics, ballads, *redondillas* of four line stanzas and a specific rhyme scheme, *villancicos* or rustic Christmas carols, and drama, both short *autos sacramentales* and full-length plays. She synthesized many of the poetic currents, learned and popular, Renaissance and Baroque, with even traces of mysticism. Her subject matter ran from the deeply spiritual to such humor as the *ovillejo* concerning the beauty of Lisarda.

Especially, she wrote love poems. Love versus Reason was a favorite theme. Of her sixty-five sonnets, twenty-two deal with love. Critics argue how much of her work is autobiographical and how much either the result of her observation or conformity to literary trends. There is a tradition that she had an unfortunate early love affair with the Count of Mancera. Several Mexican playwrights, José Rosas Moreno and Octavio Meza, have dramatized the story for the stage.

But was her well-known example of *Redondillas* founded on fact? It begins:

> Stupid men, quick to condemn
> Women wrongly for their flaws,
> Never seeing you're the cause
> Of all that you blame on them!

Was she talking of her own experiences when she went on?

> She who's modest cannot hold
> Man's esteem. We're all thought
> naughty.
> If we don't accept, we're haughty;
> If we welcome you, we're bold.

Is that her personal pronoun in the final stanza?

> Women need be strong, I find
> To stay safe and keep unharmed
> Since the arrogant male comes armed
> With Devil, flesh, and world combined.

Her fellow countryman, Ermilo Abreu Gómez, editor of a volume of her poetry, declared that her poetic reputation rests essentially on her lyric verse, which is for the most part amorous. During her lifetime her personality so charmed everyone that she was called Mexico's Tenth Muse and everything she wrote was accepted uncritically. Before she became a nun, she was lady in waiting to the Marquesa de Mancera, wife of the Viceroy. Later after she had taken her vows, her cell in the convent became a meeting place of the leaders of Mexico's intellectual life.

Two books of her poems were published during her lifetime. The first appeared in Spain in 1689 under the title *Inundación Castálida de la única poetisa, musa décima, sor Juana Inés de la Cruz* (*The Castalian Flood of the Unique Poetess, the Tenth Muse, Sister Juana Inés de la Cruz*). Three years later a second volume was published in Seville. In 1700, five years after her death, a Madrid publisher printed *Fama y obras Poetess, the Tenth Muse, Sister Juana Musa* (*Posthumous Fame and Works of the Phoenix of Mexico and the Tenth Muse.*)

What is known of her early life can be read in one of the greatest autobiographical letters in Spanish literature, *A Reply to Sor Philotea de la Cruz*, written in 1691. An acquaintance, Bishop Manuel Fernández de Santa Cruz, of Puebla, wrote her some admonitions under the signature of Sor Philotea, suggesting that to be holy she spend less time on worldly things and more on religious matters. The letter brought a reply from her telling of lifelong craving for knowledge, of childhood episodes, and stating that she had never written anything of her own volition, but always from outside urging, except "Primero Sueño" ("First Dream") whose subtitle declares it an imitation of the *Soledades* or *Visions* of Góngora. While much of the poem is an arabesque of interwoven images and sentences made difficult by artificial grammar, many of the thousand lines are pure poetry and show her intellectual knowledge of her art. In the silva meter of irregular lines, Sister Juana tells how in a dream her soul caught a glimpse of the whole of creation and in dismay returned in humility to undertake a further search for knowledge, simple and complicated, with attendant doubts and uncertainties. Apparently no one has ever put its baroque verses into an English translation.

However, a number of her sonnets appear in English form. From one of them a reader can get an idea of her style with its Gongoristic ornaments:

> This trickery of paint which you perceive
> With all the finest hues of art en-

wrought,
Which is false argument of colors
  taught
By subtle means the senses to de-
  ceive—
This by which foolish woman would
  believe
She could undo the evils years have
  brought
And conquering in the war against
  time fought
Could triumph over age, and youth
  retrieve—
Is all a futile ruse that she has tried,
A fragile flower tossed against the wind,
A useless bribe the power of fate to
appease,
A silly effort of mistaken pride,
A base desire, and viewed in rightful
  mind,
Is dust, a corpse, a shade,—is less than
  these.

The admonitions of the bishop brought results. Sor Juana sold her private library of four thousand books, surely the largest collection in the New World, concentrated on religious work, and died four years later nursing sisters in the convent during a plague.

THE POETRY OF SPENDER

Type of work: Poetry
Author: Stephen Spender (1909-   )
Principal published works: Nine Entertainments, 1928; *Twenty Poems,* 1930; *Poems,* 1933;
Poems, 1934; *Vienna,* 1935; *The Still Centre,* 1939; *Ruins and Visions,* 1942; *Poems
of Dedication,* 1947; *Returning to Vienna,* 1947; *The Edge of Being,* 1949; *Collected
Poems, 1928-1953,* 1955

Stephen Spender explains in a brief introduction to his *Collected Poems* that the volume does not contain his entire poetic output over a period of twenty-five years, but rather a selection of those poems which he wished to gather together from earlier volumes with an aim "to retrieve as many past mistakes, and to make as many improvements, as possible, without 'cheating.' " He admits that he has altered a few readings here and there in the interest of clarity or aesthetics, but adds that he has retained, in the interest of honesty and truth, certain passages in which he now recognizes youthful imperfections and a few poems which reflect views he no longer holds. As printed, the poems have been grouped to represent roughly his development as a poet, as well as his interest in contemporary history—chiefly the Spanish Civil War and World War II—and in such eternal themes as love and separation. He views his book as "a weeded, though not a tidied up or altered garden."

The volume gives an opportunity for a studied reappraisal of one of a group of English poets who first achieved fame between the two world wars. The members of the Oxford Group, as they have sometimes been called, included W. H. Auden, Christopher Isherwood, Cecil Day Lewis, and Louis MacNeice. Spender dedicates three of his groups of poems to the first three of these poets. Though Spender has written elsewhere of the "teacher-to-pupil" relationship between Auden and himself at Oxford, his later development as a poet has been largely an independent one.

This is not to say, however, that he has followed poetic paths never traveled before. Some of his critics have compared him to Shelley, for the young Spender was also a rebel against the society of his time; and in both poets criticism of their own eras is combined with a vision of a future, better time. Both saw themselves somewhat as prophets of their respective ages. Shelley addressed the West Wind:

> Be through my lips to unawakened earth

> The trumpet of a prophecy! O, Wind,
> If Winter comes, can Spring be far behind?

More than a century later Spender exhorted, in "Exiles from Their Land, History Their Domicile":

> Speak with your tongues,
> O angels, fire your guns

> . . . .

> And let my words appear
> A heaven-printed world!

Though some similarities of attitude and theme are to be found in poems of Shelley and Spender, their poetic techniques are as different as the times in which they lived. Spender is as romantically emotional as Shelley: he believes in the unmistakable love of man for his fellow man; he often opposes the darkness of man's life with the bright sun which brings light and warmth into it. But Spender's poems echo twentieth-century phrasing, though some lines might be described as Shelleyan, as in the beautiful lyric which begins, "I think continually of those who were truly great."

At times Spender reminds one of T. S. Eliot (and Auden too), as in

"The Uncreating Chaos":

> Shall I never reach
> The fields guarded by stones
> Rare in the stone mountains
> Where the scytheless wind
> Flushes the swayed grasses. . . .

Spender himself has said, however, that he was more influenced by Wilfred Owen than by Eliot. Like Owen, Spender often employs subtle combinations of sound effects, as in the lines quoted above: "Where the scytheless wind/Flushes the swayed grasses." Owen's poetry was principally inspired by World War I, which brought early death to the poet whose pity had been stirred by the suffering and dying which he had witnessed. Spender seems to have been influenced not only by Owen's bitterness against the bloody injustices of the world, but also by what he himself had learned of war during his months in Spain and later in the Battle of Britain and even more directly, perhaps, by the content of certain of Owen's war poems. Compare, for example, Spender's "Two Armies," which describes enemy forces resting at night only a few yards apart,

> When the machines are stilled, a common suffering
> Whitens the air with breath and makes both one
> As though these enemies slept in each other's arms,

with Owen's "Strange Meeting," an unfinished poem in which a soldier dreams he meets in Hell the enemy whom he killed and discovers in that "strange friend" the same hope and pity and compassion that was in his own heart.

In a critical essay on Auden which Spender published several years ago in the *Atlantic Monthly* (July, 1953), he pointed out that the essential direction of Auden's poetry has been toward a definition of Love. The reader of the *Collected Poems* discovers that, like his slightly older friend and mentor, Spender has written a series of variations on the same theme. In the early poems the love seems

often like Whitman's "manly love of comrades," even to the point of suggesting Whitmanesque ambiguities, as in the poem which begins "How strangely this sun reminds me of my love" or another which addresses directly an unnamed "Abrupt and charming mover." One is reminded of Whitman again in the hortatory "Oh young men, oh young comrades," in which the theme of loving comradeship is combined with the call to desert the dusty past, to leave the "great houses where the ghosts are prisoned," and to make a new and better world:

> Oh comrades, step beautifully from the solid wall
> advance to rebuild and sleep with friend on hill
> advance to rebel and remember what you have
> no ghost ever had, immured in his hall.

In other lyrics, as in the lovely sonnet "Daybreak," which describes a couple waking at dawn, first the man, then the woman, one finds both tenderness and the passionate intensity that suffuses so much of the poetry of D. H. Lawrence. But the mixture of desire and revulsion which unpleasantly mars so many of Lawrence's love poems is not in Spender. In Lawrence's "Lightning," for example, a lightning flash reveals to a lover the fear in the face of the woman he is preparing to kiss, and his passion is followed by hatred of both the woman and himself. Contrast with this Spender's "Ice," in which a woman comes "in from the snowing air" and is greeted by a kiss:

> Then my lips ran to her with fire
> From the chimney corner of the room,
> Where I had waited in my chair.
> I kissed their heat against her skin
> And watched the red make the white bloom. . . .

The love of man and woman shows no hectic flush in Spender; the colors are those of radiant health.

Another aspect of love is revealed in

Spender's numerous poems about children. Several are about his daughter, but the group titled "Elegy for Margaret" are to or about the niece who died after a long, wasting illness on Christmas Day, 1945. Here, though there are morbid lines which describe the progress of the disease, the whole elegy is filled with pity and sorrow for both the child and her parents; and the final poem, in which he attempts to console his "Dearest and nearest brother," is as moving as anything that Spender has written.

Many of the poems for which Spender is best known were published in his widely reviewed *Poems* (1933). In the *Collected Poems* these are reprinted in a group under the title "Preludes." Here one finds such familiar poems as "The Express" and "The Landscape near an Aerodrome," both of which illustrate Spender's early interest in enlarging the language of modern poetry through the use of terms drawn from science, machinery, and industry. The first opens:

> After the first powerful, plain manifesto
> The black statement of pistons, without more fuss
> But gliding like a queen, she leaves the station.

The blending of the names of mechanical objects with language more usual in poetry is so skillfully achieved that the train becomes a mighty poem in motion. "The Express" is perhaps the finest train poem since Walt Whitman's portrait of a very different train in "To a Locomotive in Winter."

"The Landscape near an Aerodrome" contains poetic beauty like that in "The Express," but it is weakened by the attempt to combine arresting description with social commentary. The poem begins with the picture of a gliding air liner and then contrasts the quiet descent of the great machine with the scenes of squalor and misery which become clearer to the passengers as they approach the aerodrome. It ends with a sudden, trenchant last line that not only surprises the reader but seems totally uncalled-for by the preceding descriptive lines:

> Then, as they land, they hear the tolling bell
> Reaching across the landscape of hysteria,
> To where, louder than all those batteries
> And charcoaled towers against the dying sky,
> Religion stands, the Church blocking the sun.

Several of the "Preludes" and two or three poems in the next group, "A Heaven-Printed World," belong to the literature of protest of the 1930's and reflect Spender's leftwing politics which he later forswore. These poems, as Spender has said, "did not please the politicians." Notable are "The Funeral," "The Pylons," and "An Elementary School Classroom in a Slum." The last is full of the pity which is deep in Spender's poems, political or otherwise.

The introspective poems in the group called "Explorations" are as a whole less impressive than those in the other groups. Rather hazy and inchoate, these "explorations," when compared with Spender's other poems, lead one to conclude that he is a sensitive but not a cerebral poet.

It has been said that Spender is a humorless poet. He does usually take himself seriously, often too much so; but the gracefully witty conceit in one of his later poems called "Word" refutes the charge against him:

> The word bites like a fish.
> Shall I throw it back free
> Arrowing to that sea
> Where thoughts lash tail and fin?
> Or shall I pull it in
> To rhyme upon a dish?

THE POETRY OF STEFAN GEORGE

Type of work: Poetry
Author: Stefan George (1868-1933)
Principal published works: Hymnen, 1890 (*Hymns*); Pilgerfahrten, 1891 (*Pilgrimages*);
   Algabal, 1892 (*Heliogabalus*); Die Bücher der Hirten und Preisgedichte; der Sagen und
   Sänge; und der hängenden Garten, 1895 (*The Book of Eclogues and Eulogies; Legends
   and Lays; and The Hanging Gardens*); Das Jahr der Seele, 1897 (*The Year of the Soul*);
   Der Teppich des Lebens und die Lieder von Traum und Tod, 1899 (*The Tapestry of
   Life and Songs of Dream and of Death*); Maximin, 1906; Der siebente Ring, 1907 (*The
   Seventh Ring*); Der Stern des Bundes, 1914 (*Star of the Covenant*); Das Neue Reich,
   1928 (*Kingdom Come*)

Stefan George was probably the strongest defender of the "art for art's sake" thesis ever to appear in Germany, and his exclusiveness led him to write his first poems in an invented language, a "lingua romana" similar to Spanish. For many years he printed his books privately and not before 1899 were they offered to the public. He disregarded the German rule of grammar which calls for capitalization of all nouns; the resulting loss in reading speed was a most desired effect for the author because he wanted his readers to note that words in themselves were artistic instruments which would evoke as many—or more—emotions as the colors of a painter's palette.

In 1890 George published his first series of poems, *Hymns*. The title of the first poem, "Initiation," indicates how conscious he was of his radical literary departure and of its limited appeal to an audience used to continuous outpour of modern naturalism. Nevertheless the signal was given:

The river calls! Defiant reeds unfurl
Their slender banners to the languid
   breeze
And check the coaxing ripples as they
   swirl
To mossy shores in tender galaxies.

The theme is repeated in "Invitation":

"Let us leave pavements and grime!"
How dear your offer sounded!
"Far, where more light and elate
Thought and breath seem to chime,
We shall enjoy the flower
And resurrection fete."

Not expecting the applause of many— the poems were still published privately —the author treasured his small circle of friends. Most of his works carry dedications; that of his next work, *Pilgrimages*, was written for the Austrian poet, Hugo von Hofmannsthal (the friendship never matured):

Then I journeyed forth
And became a stranger,
And I sought for some one
To share my mournfulness,
And there was no one.

Hymns and *Pilgrimages* reveal the conflict between the author's poetic ideals and the baseness of everyday life. He used for his next work earlier historical periods and the Orient as times and places for escape from the unpleasant realities of the present. Thus *Algabal*, written in Paris in 1892, is his own interpretation of a Roman emperor who moves in a world of time-removed serenity and passionate feelings:

The hall of yellow glitter and of sun!
On level dome among the stairs it
   reigns,
And from the fiery crater flashes run:
Topazes interfused with amber grains.

His sense of remoteness, however, never excluded his knowledge of the "mystical body of Christ" inherited from his Catholic childhood in a small town in the German Rhineland:

. . . For I, the one, comprise the multitude . . .

THE POETRY OF STEFAN GEORGE. Excerpts reprinted from THE WORKS OF STEFAN GEORGE by permission of the publishers, The University of North Carolina Press. Translated by Olga Marx and Ernst Morwitz. Copyright, 1949, by The University of North Carolina Press.

The Book of Eclogues and Eulogies; Legends and Lays; and The Hanging Gardens indicates a turn toward tranquility; the wanderer once in desperate search for beauty finds it in his own back yard:

> Struck with amazement, as though we
> were entering a region
> Frost-bound when last we had seen it,
> yet now full of flowers,
> We, who felt old and sorrowful, gazed
> at each other,
> And our reflections were fused in the
> river below us.

Thus the world of knighthood described in *The Book of Legends and Lays* contains much of this recognition of beauty around him:

> What a morning, what a day!
> Breath of sun on brook and tree
> Tunes your ear more swiftly to
> Melting promise, melting plea
> Which I shyly hid away.

The Year of the Soul, probably George's best-known book, indicates that the author no longer needed to search for remote backgrounds; an old park is sufficient for the description of images symbolizing the principles of nature and love. Beginning with autumn, the seasons of the year are portrayed, with the exception of the much used and abused season of spring. The poet invites an unseen friend:

> Come to the park they say is dead, and
> you
> Will see the glint of smiling shores be-
> yond,
> Pure clouds with rifts of unexpected
> blue
> Diffuse a light on patterned path and
> pond.

In *The Year of the Soul* the lonely prophet speaks again:

> . . . The word of seers is not for com-
> mon sharing. . . .

In 1900 George published *The Tapestry of Life and Songs of Dream and of Death.* Each part contains twenty-four poems. In the prelude he recollects his struggles up to the present:

> When pale with zeal, I searched for
> hidden store . . .

and almost regrets that his stormy period has ended:

> Give me the solemn breath that never
> failed,
> Give me the fire again that makes us
> young,
> On which the wings of childhood rose
> among
> The fumes our earliest offerings ex-
> haled.

The Tapestry of Life, a poet's picture book, gave the author ample opportunity to employ his impressionistic power of words:

> When days are done with memory-laden
> shadows
> In half-forgotten beauty's faded frame,
> Waves of white lambs draw slowly
> through the meadows
> From the broad clearing to the darkened
> stream.

It is not surprising that the author became also well-known for his translations of Mallarmé, Baudelaire, and Rimbaud. *Songs of Dream and of Death* is dedicated to persons or occasions in the poet's life; the sequence ends with a forceful description of everlasting conflict:

> All this whirls, tears and pounds, flames
> and flies,
> Until late in the night-vaulted skies
> They are joined to a bright jewelled
> beam:
> Fame and glow, pain and bliss, death
> and dream.

When George published *The Seventh Ring* in 1907, a decisive factor had entered his life. The partial fulfillment of his poetic vision was his encounter with a young man whom he called Maximin. To George, this youth was the embodiment of a dream and temporarily—Maximin died very young—an end to loneliness. The poet described the appearance of Maximin: ". . . softened by the mobility and vague sadness that centuries of Christian civilization have wrought in the faces of the people . . . youth in that unbroken fulness and purity that can still move mountains. . . ." When Maximin died George considered his death in the light of his mystical evaluation of the youth. He regrets his loss:

The forest shivers.
In vain it clothed itself in leaves of
spring,
The field your foot made consecrate is
numb
And cold without the sun you bring.
The fragile blades on hilly pastures
quiver,
For now you never come.

His death was almost a religious event:

You also were elect, so do not mourn
For all the days which unfulfilment
sheathed.
Praise to your city where a god was
born,
Praise to your time in which a god has
breathed!

George's next work, *Star of the Covenant*, a book of a thousand verses, again deals in its "Introit" with the significance of Maximin. Some of the poems are not rhymed, but a strong rhythmic flow is present at all times:

You took away the pain of inner
schism,
You, who were fusion made incarnate,
bringing
The two extremes together: light and
frenzy!

The poet pleads again for a spiritual life and complains that Germans do not listen to their prophets, as in the case of Nietzsche, who, according to George, delivered his message

. . . With such insistence that his
throat was cracked.
And you? The shrewd or dull, the false
or true,
You acted as if nothing had occurred.

The book ends with a chorus expressing a firm reminder that the power to lead a spiritual life is available to man:

God has locked us in filiation,
God has swept us with his blaze,
God has lit us with elation,
God has steeped us in his grace.

In 1928 George published his last volume, *Kingdom Come*. In this collection he remembered once again the rich literary inheritance of Goethe and Hölderlin. The book also contains a poetic prophecy about war, written during World War I, which seems to anticipate the horrors of future world wars:

You shall not cheer. No rise will mark
the end,
But only downfalls, many and inglorious.
Monsters of lead and iron, tubes and
rods
Escape their maker's hand and rage unruly.

In "Secret Germany," George abhors again the present regime and asks for sincere understanding of the values which will remain part of the true German tradition:

Only what consecrate earth
Cradles in sheltering sleep
Long in the innermost grooves,
Far from acquisitive hands,
Marvels this day cannot grasp
Are rife with the fate of tomorrow.

Until his death in 1933 George abstained for unknown reasons from writing any more poetry.

George appealed to few, but his admirers recognized in him the high priest of German literature, a writer who appeared at a time when the ideals of Goethe were still venerated, but when poetic expression was already in danger of being suffocated by excessive romanticism and sentimentality. Under the leadership of the author a "George Circle" was founded and the idea of transforming life to mystical heights by way of art and not by scientific positivism was promoted by its members, who adhered to strict moral principles. George made the German language an instrument of art and as a poet he was best qualified to carry Germany's classical tradition into the twentieth century. After refusing to become identified with Hitlerian Germany's literary trends, George died in self-imposed exile in Switzerland in 1933. His inventiveness with the German language makes all translation efforts a most difficult undertaking, but *The Works of Stefan George* (1949), translated by Olga Marx and Ernst Morwitz, succeeds in conveying much of George's intensity of feeling into English.

THE POETRY OF STEPHEN VINCENT BENÉT

Author: Stephen Vincent Benét (1898-1943)
First published: Five Men and Pompey, 1915; *Young Adventure,* 1918; *Heavens and Earth,* 1920; *The Ballad of William Sycamore,* 1923; *Tiger Joy,* 1925; *John Brown's Body,* 1928; *Ballads and Poems, 1915-1930,* 1931; *A Book of Americans* (with Rosemary Carr Benét), 1933; *Burning City,* 1936; *Western Star,* 1943

Often mentioned, along with Sandburg, Hart Crane, and Whitman, as a national bard, Stephen Vincent Benét was first and foremost a poet, his stories, novels, and propaganda pieces taking second seat. His topical patriotic pieces, his lyric poems, and some of his children's poetry have scarcely survived him, but his two narrative poems, *John Brown's Body* and *Western Star,* won for him both Pulitzer prizes and an active posterity.

His interest in history manifested itself early. At the age of seventeen he published *Five Men and Pompey,* Browningesque monologues in a form that he often used in his later works. The ballads which followed, while winning a poetry prize at Yale, showed less promise, though one, "The Hemp" fancifully retells an incident from colonial history. The conclusion dramatized the title, indicating the rhythmic effects which became Benét's hallmark.

In his first collected edition Benét rearranged some of his early poems under the division American Names, the title poem being one of his best and a preview of his expert use of place names in *John Brown's Body.* "The Ballad of William Sycamore" is a sustained attempt to present through one character a view of the American way, here the frontier life so important to national development. William Sycamore speaks of a growing nation, a growth which took from him his way of life. His father was a mountaineer and his mother was happy and brave. She bore him, as did so many other mountain women in childbirth, with only nature to comfort her in her labor. He remembers his youth, the tall, thin, brown visitors, and the barn dances. When he grew up, his father could give him only a knowledge of the land. After he married,

he and his wife settled uncleared land and raised their children. His sons all died, the oldest at the Alamo, the youngest with Custer. When he died William Sycamore again felt the freedom he had known in his youth; he now slept like an old fox gone to earth, and he was again with the buffalo.

The ballad evokes our sympathy and strong feelings for the hard, wild, free growth of our nation. In "The Mountain Whippoorwill," Benét used folklore to great advantage and described an old fiddlers' contest, a practice which survives, but in this case won by young Hill-Billy Jim in what the poet subtitled "A Georgia Romance." By taking lines from singing calls and combining them with fanciful ancestry he re-creates a period and achieves effects much as Sandburg does with proverbs in *The People, Yes.*

In a very different vein, but with as great an assurance as in "The Mountain Whippoorwill," the young poet startled readers of *The Nation* with an irreverent "King David," a sophisticated ballad expressing playful disbelief. His college poems of these first collections display a normal sophomoric attitude, though the lyrics are sometimes bright and original, "Memory" in particular. His Gothic themes and fantastic works were better managed in short stories than in sonnets.

To this early period belong poems later collected, love poems to Rosemary Carr, and after their marriage collaboration on *A Book of Americans,* now a standard work in children's literature. These poems celebrate not only famous but infamous figures in American history, both men and women. Much of the pleasure in these lyrics comes from the deft handling and gay daring, the unconventional though carefully patriotic praise and blame, qualities also to be found in his most famous story, "The Devil and Daniel Webster."

Burning City, prophetic poems of doom fortunately not fulfilled for New York City as Benét envisioned, vividly suggests that through war, natural causes, universal sterility, and collective madness we will fall. A modern Everyman is the narrator and the time follows World War III, though the tense is present. The most vivid poem concerns the eating away of skyscrapers by giant steel-hungry termites, while the best artistically is a monologue of the revolting machines that have taken over from nonthinking people. "Notes to Be Left in a Cornerstone" is a somewhat metaphysical poem describing the contradictory nature of New York as we know it, just before the fall that Benét brilliantly envisions. While the entire sequence is noteworthy, coming as it does after the great success of *John Brown's Body* and seven years before the publication of his posthumous *Western Star,* Benét's reputation chiefly rests on his Civil War saga.

Ironically, Stephen Vincent Benét's deep patriotism prevented his completing what might have been his greatest work, comparable even as a fragment to parts of *Leaves of Grass* and *The Bridge.* As Parry Stroud suggests in his critical biography of Benét, *Western Star* was planned to complement *John Brown's Body,* the *Odyssey* of America's westward movement as his Civil War poem had been his country's *Iliad.* He had begun the work in 1928, collected materials constantly though always postponing the final work in order to engage in governmental and other activities. He invoked not the muses but the spirit of the pioneer as his guide.

Around representative individuals, he planned to write a poetic history in ten books for the safeguarding of national unity expressed in the continuous mobility of the people. The fragment of the poem actually written ends with his pioneers looking toward the West, ahead of them the endless wilderness and a guiding star.

Though criticism of Benét in his lifetime and immediately thereafter is divided, and recent evaluations often derogatory, the pendulum seems now to be swinging in his favor. His voice was clear; his meanings were immediate.

THE POETRY OF STEVENS

Author: Wallace Stevens (1879-1955)
Principal published works: Harmonium, 1932; *Ideas of Order,* 1935; *Owl's Clover,* 1936;
The Man with the Blue Guitar, 1937; *Parts of a World,* 1942; *Notes Toward a Supreme
Fiction,* 1942; *Esthétique du Mal,* 1945; *Transport to Summer,* 1947; *Three Academic
Pieces,* 1947; *A Primitive Like an Orb,* 1948; *The Auroras of Autumn,* 1952; *The
Collected Poems of Wallace Stevens,* 1954

Wallace Stevens' poetry has been called both "elegant" and "austere." It has been criticized for "an air of sumptuousness, *chic,* expensiveness, 'conspicuous consumption,' " as well as for bleakness, abstractness, a lack of personal warmth. Neither of these criticisms, however, says much about Stevens, who, according to Northrop Frye, was a rhetorician and therefore expendable, but an essential poet.

Stevens' first and perhaps most "elegant," least "austere," volume of poems, *Harmonium,* was unlike many first volumes in that it contained statements of all the major themes to appear in his later books. *Harmonium,* in other words, was a mature work, differing from the later volumes largely in manner rather than meaning. Thus, throughout Stevens' poetry, whether early or late, one observes recurrent elements: a love for precise language resulting in a selection of words at once elegant and austere; a celebration of the imagination and the power of human creativity; a highly abstract, careful examination of different theories of perception and knowledge couched in highly concrete, colorful, often playful language; and a continuing concern for the myth-making capabilities of poetry in a world of defunct myths.

In *Ideas of Order* and *The Man with the Blue Guitar,* Stevens made a perceptible step toward austerity in statement of theme and in technique, although the themes were the same as those in *Harmonium.* Thus, the title poem of the second volume (containing also "Owl's Clover," "A Thought Revolved," and "The Men That Are Falling") consists of a series of thirty-three re-evaluations of the position of the artist and the meaning of art in a world of "things as they are," a phrase

equivalent to the *"ding an sich"* of the earlier "The Comedian as the Letter C." However, instead of Crispin the Comedian's symbolic journey representing the various philosophical metamorphoses of an artist in a world of *"ding an sich,"* the guitar player in the later poem plucks out various types of "fictive music" corresponding to varying definitions of poetry. Crispin moves from definition to definition in the course of his journey; the guitar player appears to pose all thirty-three variations of "things as they are" without an exact progression. As in "The Comedian as the Letter C," the guitar player is confronted by a world of fact and matter which he transmutes—or tries to transmute—even though they are greatly changed by the player—the artist, the disciplined imagination, the passion for order—on the blue guitar. That they are changed is known; just how they are changed, and to what degree, becomes the central puzzle in a poem dealing at once with aesthetics, epistemology, and something similar to Coleridge's "poetic faith." The general conclusion is the recognition of the importance of poetry as source for "order" and meaning in a world of dazzling, jumbled, apparently purposeless objects—a world without clear meaning. Although it may be that, given the myth-making importance of poetry in a mythless world, the poet cannot entirely succeed in making fact and matter meaningful.

This is Stevens' central quandary: How can the imagination (another word for poetry) fulfill man's craving for beauty, order, and meaning in a world—depending on the point of view—antipathetic to imagination? And Stevens' answers—depending on the poem—are plural, operating as logical alternatives. Thus, at times, no problem seems to arise at all, for "the imagination" may be the only thing which is real in an imagined world. This is the possibility or alternative which gives rise to section XXV of "Blue Guitar," wherein the hero flings and twirls the world. It is, however, only one possibility, the most playful and optimistic, among thirty-three. Perhaps the simplest statement that can be made about "Blue Guitar," then, is that the basis of the poem is poetry — as it is of all of Stevens' work —"poetry" meaning human perception and creativity (one and the same) rather than words on a page.

Stevens' 1935 volume, *Ideas of Order,* contains no poems of the length of "Blue Guitar," but a number of excellent short meditative lyrics such as "Academic Discourse at Havana," "Evening Without Angels," and "The Idea of Order at Key West." Here, Stevens also asks questions leading to an investigation of poetry. Often the form of Stevens' poems becomes a question about the nature of imagination or reality followed by an answer (always tentative or conditional) or series of answers.

Stevens' following volume, *Parts of a World,* continues his examination of poetry, as the titles of some of the poems therein indicate: "Poetry Is a Destructive Force," or, "The Poems of Our Climate." The admired, much-cited "Connoisseur of Chaos" is contained in this volume. The "connoisseur," the poet, Stevens and reader, live, perhaps, mostly in a world of disorder, rather than in the largely historical, now hard-to-come-by world which, having the advantages of "order," has also the disadvantage of dogma.

In the same year as *Parts of a World* appeared a long, difficult poem, "Notes Toward a Supreme Fiction." Therein Stevens, in three sections, defines the qualities such a "fiction" must have: "It Must Be Abstract," "It Must Change," and "It Must Give Pleasure." These statements would be simple enough if Stevens were talking about poetry on a page. He is, however, talking about poetry and "fic-tion" as reality, or poetry as the perception of reality, and consequently "supreme fiction" comes to mean several analogous products of imagination: "the first idea" or "Logos," the created world, the first man, "the idea of man," and, by extension, the imaginative creation which takes place in a human mind. Hence, the qualities which Stevens defines in his three sections are not so much qualities which a poem on a page must have as they are qualities which existence must, and does, have. In "Notes," too, appears the conflict which exists between fact and matter. This conflict explains why Stevens, praising poetry, appears to say that poetry gets in our way.

Transport to Summer includes "Notes" and also "Esthétique du Mal," a poem similar to "The Comedian as the Letter C," in which a poet tries to reconcile a comfortable philosophy or "esthetic" with "pain" and the destructiveness symbolized by Mt. Vesuvius. This comfortable philosophy, "his book," is akin to the romantic theory of the sublime and to the "esthétique du mal" nineteenth century style. We shrink from real pain, the real volcano, and the fact of death. The poet and the poem seek out an "esthétique du mal" which will not shrink or falter, but arrive face to face with *"ding an sich"* and fact and matter as they are, finding a genuine aesthetic merely in living life as it is. All comfortable philosophies and panaceas Stevens counters with *"ding an sich."*

Three Academic Pieces, containing "The Realm of Resemblance," "Someone Puts a Pineapple Together," and "Of Ideal Time and Choice," deals, as the title indicates, almost didactically, but always playfully and elegantly, with the nature of poetry. These pieces were included in the later collection of prose and verse lecture-essays, *The Necessary Angel,* wherein, with a prose style very much like his poetry, Stevens continues to examine art, the subtitle reading, "Essays on Reality and the Imagination."

The Auroras of Autumn, which won

for Stevens his first National Book Award, includes, besides the title poem, "A Primitive Like an Orb" (published separately in 1948), "An Ordinary Evening in New Haven," and "Things of August." If there is drama in "Ordinary Evening," or in most of Stevens's poetry, it is the drama of thought, of re-evaluation and redefinition as in "Blue Guitar." The problem, if imagination is the only reality, is solipsism.

The solution, as elsewhere, tentative, conditional, ironic, is poetry. That is, ironically, in an imagined world poetry offers reality, offers the antidote to imagination, to "romance" and "illusion" and "esthétiques du mal" which do not include all parts of the "sublime." But is poetry able to dispense with tropisms and offer only a "pure reality"? Is it not, finally, the "supreme fiction," merely the illusion of disillusion, the ultimate and hence least real product of the imagination? If so, then reality is also the ultimate product of the imagination, and therefore poetry and reality are one—the same dream or the same fact, whatever one may wish to call it. In any case, what one imagines, what one perceives, what one is, do not depend on the implication that reality is an actuality, or on the implication that imagination produces unreality, but only on changing ideas and on facing them directly or indirectly.

The Collected Poems of Wallace Stevens contains most of the poetry which appeared in his previous volumes, with the exception of "Owl's Clover," which Stevens thought unsuccessful, and two poems from *Parts of a World,* "The Woman That Had More Babies than That" and "Life on a Battleship." It also contained a long section, written when he was about seventy, called "The Rock." There, in poems such as "Not Ideas About the Thing but the Thing Itself" and "Reality Is an Activity of the Most August Imagination," Stevens continued his examinations of poetry. There are overtones of the problems of age and death, but such overtones appeared even in *Harmonium,* and a reading of Stevens from early to late reveals little change in outlook, though increasing perfection of style and language, and perhaps an increasing preference for meditative lyrics, of which "Sunday Morning" is the greatest early example. There followed *Opus Posthumous,* edited by S. F. Morse, drawing together unpublished pieces, Stevens' notebook adages, occasional lectures, and Stevens' early verse plays, "Carlos Among the Candles" and "Three Travellers Watch the Sunrise."

Stevens could write that life is composed of theories about life, and he might also have added that poetry consists of propositions about poetry. Thus Stevens no doubt sounds like the first section of "Notes": "It Must Be Abstract." But while Stevens is "abstract" and does build poetry out of "propositions," that poetry rarely if ever has the dryness of prose philosophy, and is among the most exciting, original, and, as Northrop Frye might say, "essential" verse of modern times.

THE POETRY OF SUCKLING

Author: Sir John Suckling (1609-1642)
Principal published works: Fragmenta Aurea, 1646; Last Remains, 1657

Sir John Suckling, like many of the other writers at the court of Charles I, was an inheritor of the poetic traditions of both John Donne and Ben Jonson, literary masters of the preceding generation. From Donne came the tone of gay cynicism that pervades Suckling's love lyrics, while the classical smoothness of Jonson's verse is reflected in the clarity, precision and easy flow of the brief stanzas of his successor. There is, however, very little of Donne's tough intellectualism in Suckling's poetry; though he occasionally develops a poem as an extended rational argument, his aim seems to have been to produce amusing, polished verses for the entertainment of Charles' court, and the revelation of his own emotions has no place in his lyrics.

Critics have pointed out Suckling's relationship to the *precieux* and the *libertins*, the court and "society" poets of Louis XIII, writers who valued spontaneity, fluency, and witty conceits in the verses they composed for the ladies who headed the popular literary salons. Their concern was, in general, with the manner, not the matter, of poetry; it would have been inconceivable for one of them to write, as Donne did, of the paradoxes of the Incarnation or of his quest for faith. Suckling's appreciation for their kind of spontaneity can be seen in his comments on both Jonson and his friend Thomas Carew in his witty survey of the literary figures of his time, "A Session of the Poets":

> Tom Carew was next, but he had a fault
> That would not well stand with a laureate;
> His muse was hide-bound, and th' issue of 's brain
> Was seldom brought forth but with trouble and pain.

The best known of Suckling's poems are his songs and his "sonnets," which are not sonnets in the technical sense but love lyrics in stanzaic form. Almost any one of these poems would illustrate Suckling's skill with the genre. One of the most familiar is this lyric from his *Last Remains*:

> Out upon it! I have lov'd
> Three whole days together;
> And am like to love three more,
> If it prove fair weather.
>
> Time shall moult away his wings,
> Ere he shall discover
> In the whole wide world again
> Such a constant lover.
>
> But the spite on 't is, no praise
> Is due at all to me:
> Love with me had made no stays,
> Had it any been but she.
>
> Had it any been but she,
> And that very face,
> There had been at least ere this
> A dozen dozen in her place.

The abrupt colloquial opening lines are reminiscent of a number of Donne's early poems, where a similar dramatic effect captures the immediate attention and interest of the reader. Suckling's own particular talent is especially evident in the musical flow of the whole, the carefully worked out assonance and rhyme. The repetition of sound in *love, prove, discover, lover*, in the first two stanzas is reinforced by the smooth, slow movement of *whole, more, moult, world* especially in the second, where the stately meter emphasizes Suckling's mock constancy. The rhythm picks up in the last two stanzas, where the poet uses shorter sounds.

The kind of wit that pervades even the sound patterns of his lyric is characteristic of Suckling's work. The reader cannot take seriously the stately stanza, whose dignified movement implies eternal fidelity, when he knows that this much-vaunted constancy is of three days' duration. Suckling has cleverly contrived in the last two stanzas to turn this demonstration of his own fickleness into a compliment to the lady who alone has beauty sufficient to hold his attention for even so short a time.

Others of Suckling's best-known poems reveal the same cynical attitude toward love and the same mastery of rhythm and sound. This familiar song from *Aglaura*, illustrates again the poet's skillful use of alliteration and assonance, as well as the effective change of tone and rhythm he can achieve in his conclusions:

> Why so pale and wan, fond lover?
>   Prithee, why so pale?
> Will, when looking well can't move her,
>   Looking ill prevail?
>   Prithee, why so pale?
> . . . . . .
> Quit, quit, for shame, this will not move,
>   This cannot take her.
> If of herself she will not love,
>   Nothing can make her.
>   The devil take her!

Although Suckling does not make use of Donne's very involved, intricate conceits in his lyrics, he does occasionally imitate the older poet in developing a poem as an extended argument. In the five stanzas that begin "O! for some honest lover's ghost," a line that echoes Donne's "Love's Deity," Suckling moves wittily over the question of whether greater eternal felicity comes to the scorned lover or to him who was favored by his mistress. Concluding that there would be no paradise in watching his beloved forever embraced by the man she loved, the poet ends his poem with a typically unexpected shift in tone. Since the most the unrequited lover can hope for is that "Some bays, perchance, or myrtle bough,/For difference crowns the brow /Of those kind soulds that were/The noble martyrs here," he will not look to the future:

> And if that be the only odds,
>   (As who can tell?) ye kinder gods,
>   Give me the woman here.

Another group of poems reflect the popularity of the allegorical tradition, especially among the followers of Edmund Spenser. In these verses Suckling takes a single conceit, that courtship is like a battle, or love, a clock, and develops it at length, referring to the ineffectuality of his "cannon oaths," his "engineer" tongue that attacked by whispering sweet nothings, his strategic attempt to starve out the fortress of the heart by removing kisses and amorous looks, and, finally, his hope of deceiving his enemy by removing himself altogether. The mock battle concludes with the revelation, by some spy, that Honor is the commander of the fortress, a formidable foe with whom the lover will not contend.

Another poem in the same manner, more ambitious but less successful, partly because of its greater length, is "Love's World." Here Suckling states his subject in the first stanza:

> In each man's heart that doth begin
> To love, there's ever fram'd within
> A little world, for so I found
> When first my passion reason drown'd.

He then equates the components of the universe with aspects of his own situation. His faith is the earth, quaking sometimes from jealousy; his lady, the sun; his flickering hopes, the ever-changing moon. The remainder of the poem is worked out similarly and cleverly, but this process of equations almost inevitably becomes tedious. Suckling apparently felt this, for after comparing his lady's moods to the weather, he comes to a rather abrupt conclusion:

> But soft, my Muse! the world is wide,
> And all at once was not describe:
> It may fall out some honest Lover
> The rest hereafter will discover.

Suckling's wit is far better displayed in the rollicking iambs and anapests of "A Session of the Poets." Apollo has called all the wits of the kingdom together to bestow the laureateship on him who most deserves it, and the poets gather to plead their causes. Suckling is especially hard on Ben Jonson, to whom he devotes the most space; he satirizes the older poet's confidence in his own gifts and in what was for that time an absurd assumption, that dramatic works were true literature, worthy of preservation:

> And he told them plainly he deserv'd
> the Bays,
> For his were called Works, where
> others were but Plays.

Suckling is no kinder to his contemporaries. His criticism of the effort with which Carew composed has already been quoted. William Davenant is the butt of an old joke about his nose, deformed by his bout with the "malady of France." Suckling does not exempt even himself; he alone was not present, for he did not seek the laurel:

> . . . of all men living he cared not
> for't,
> He loved not the Muses so well as his
> sport;
>
> And prized black eyes, or a lucky hit
> At bowls, above all the Trophies of wit.

Having surveyed the whole rank of English talent, Apollo bestows his honor upon an alderman who happens to wander into the assembly, on the grounds that "it was the best sign/Of good store of wit, to have good store of coin." Suckling concludes with a final satirical touch, hitting at the lack of aid for aspiring writers:

> Only the small Poets clear'd up again,
> Out of hope as 't was thought of bor-
> rowing,

> But sure they were out, for he forfeits
> his Crown
> When he lends any Poets about the
> Town.

"A Ballad upon a Wedding" presents a surprising contrast to Suckling's other works and reveals an added dimension of his talents. This poem is a rustic wedding song, a kind of parody of the classical epithalamion. It has the characteristic elements of this traditional form, a complete description of the wedding procession, the feast, the revelry, and the ceremonies attending the bedtime ritual of the couple, as well as a full account of the beauty and virtue of both the bride and the bridegroom. However, the resemblance of this poem to the epithalamia of Spenser and Donne ends with this rough outline, for Suckling wrote in a country dialect, using a colloquial rhythm and images drawn from rustic life. The bride is not described in terms of the sun, stars, or jewels:

> No Grape that's kindly ripe, could be
> So round, so plump, so soft as she,
> Nor half so full of Juyce.

As she danced:

> Her feet beneath her Petticoat,
> Like little mice stole in and out,
> As if they fear'd the light.

Suckling had many poetic gifts, and had he not, by his own confession, owed greater allegiance to pleasure than to his muse, he might have accomplished far more than he did. As it is, he has left a body of verse which is delightful to read, a reflection of the gay, sophisticated spirit of the Caroline court at its peak, and an indication of the poet's mastery of his art.

THE POETRY OF SWIFT

Author: Jonathan Swift (1667-1745)

First published: Miscellanies, 1708-1711; *Cadenus and Vanessa,* 1713; *On Poetry:* A Rhapsody, 1733; *Verses on the Death of Dr. Swift, Written by Himself,* 1739

Poetry was never the form in which Jonathan Swift's talents were exhibited at their greatest, but his incisive satirical wit made his verses a powerful political weapon and a strong defense of common sense and morality. His poetic works, as well as his prose, stand high in the ranks of Augustan writing.

Swift's first poems were floundering attempts to master the rather formless Pindaric ode popularized by Abraham Cowley, but he soon discovered that the heroic couplet gave him the control and discipline he needed to compress his ideas for the greatest satiric effect. Even the early odes, however, products of the years when Swift lived at Moor, Park as secretary to Sir William Temple, show brief flashes of the poet's characteristic, terrifyingly clear awareness of mankind's hypocrisy, folly, and vice: Describing Philosophy in the "Ode to the Athenian Society," he wrote:

> More oft in Fools and Mad-mens hands than Sages
> She seems a Medley of all Ages,
> With a huge Farthingale to swell her Fustian Stuff,
> A new Commode, a Top-knot, and a Ruff,
> Her Face patch't o'er with Modern Pedantry.

By 1693, when he wrote his ode to the playwright Congreve, Swift had a clear idea of his mission as a poet:

> 'Twas in an evil hour to urge my hate,
> My hate, whose lash just heaven has long decreed
> Shall on a day make sin and folly bleed.

The view of vice and folly as physically disgusting, as well as morally repellent, that was responsible for the creation of the Yahoos in *Gulliver's Travels* is also evident in the Congreve poem. The muse

> Sham'd and amaz'd beholds the chat-t'ring throng,
> To think what cattle she has got among;
> But with the odious smell and sight annoy'd,
> In haste she does th' offensive herd avoid.

Swift had found his true poetic voice in the couplets of the ode to Congreve, and he forced himself to even greater brevity and conciseness in many of his later poems by using a tetrameter rather than a pentameter line and speeding up his rhythm with the occasional use of trochaic feet. Both the brevity and the rhyme of his favorite verse forms lent themselves to the effective juxtaposition of the sacred and the profane, the serious and the trivial, the moral and the immoral in his satires. Typical of his experimentation with this juxtaposition is "Verses Wrote in a Lady's Ivory Table Book," where he notes:

> Here you may read (Dear Charming Saint)
> Beneath (A new Receit for Paint)

> Here (lovely Nymph pronounce my doom)
> There (A safe way to use Perfume).

Much of Swift's poetry was occasioned by particular events, especially those on the political scene. He often attacked, sometimes bitterly, sometimes humorously, public figures who had aroused his enmity, his contempt, or his amusement. Lord Berkeley, Lord Justice of Swift's native Ireland from 1699 to 1707, was an early target; the poet ridiculed his stupidity and his dependence upon his secretary. The poet-architect John Vanbrugh fared worse than Berkeley as Swift attacked his grandiose building plans and his aspirations to be a dramatist in "Vanbrugh's House":

> The Building, as the Poet Writ,
> Rose in proportion to his Wit:
> And first the Prologue built a Wall
> So wide as to encompass all.
> The Scene, a Wood, produc'd no more
> Than a few Scrubby Trees before.
> The Plot as yet lay deep, and so
> A cellar next was dug below:
> But this a Work so hard was found,
> Two Acts it cost him under Ground.

The bursting of the "South Sea Bubble," the economic crisis which followed wild speculative investing in a proposed trading venture, called forth more ridicule from the prophet of common sense. Here, as in his prose, Swift points out the essential absurdity of the scheme by giving physical form to an abstract concept, that of multiplying one's investment ten times:

> Ye wise Philosophers explain
> What Magic makes our Money rise
> When dropped into the Southern main,
> Or do these Juglers cheat our Eyes?
>
> Put in Your Money fairly told;
> Presto be gone—Tis here again,
> Ladies and Gentlemen, behold
> Here's ev'ry Piece as big as ten.

The poet's concern for Ireland and his fury at the exploitation of her people and her lands by the English inspired many of his most powerful poems. In an epilogue to a benefit production of *Hamlet* he pleaded with the English audience to use Irish wool to help alleviate the dire poverty of the Irish weavers. During the 1720's Swift used his verse, as well as the impassioned prose of *The Drapier Letters*, to defend his country's economy from "Wood's halfpence," English-made copper coins which the government of Robert Walpole planned to circulate in Ireland. Swift and other patriots feared the debasing of their currency, and the poet directed a number of attacks at William Wood, the man who was said to be preparing to make his fortune by manufacturing the coins. Typical of his vilification of Wood are these lines from

"Wood, an Insect":

> By long Observation I have understood,
> That three little Vermin are kin to Will. Wood:
> The first is an Insect they call a Wood-Louse,
> That folds up itself in itself for a House:
> As round as a Ball without Head without Tail,
> Inclos'd *Cap-a-pee* in a strong Coat of Mail.
> And thus William Wood to my Fancy appears
> In Fillets of Brass roll'd up to his Ears:
> And, over these Fillets he wisely has thrown,
> To keep out of Danger, a Doublet of Stone.

The last line of this passage refers to the fact that Wood was in debtors' prison.

Perhaps the harshest of the Irish poems is one of Swift's last works, the "Legion Club," a bitter attack on the Irish Parliament, which is described as a madhouse. The poem is filled with the ugly scatological imagery that characterizes the poet's darkest moods:

> Let a royal grant be pass'd,
> That the Club have Right to dwell,
> Each within his proper Cell;
> With a Passage left to creep in,
> And a Hole above for peeping.
>
> Let them, when they once get in
> Sell the Nation for a Pin;
> While they sit a picking Straws
> Let them rave of making Laws;
> While they never hold their Tongue,
> Let them dabble in their Dung;
> Let them form a grand Committee,
> How to plague and starve the City.

General condemnation of the whole legislative body is combined with attacks on specific members for their incompetence and immorality.

Swift, like his friend and fellow poet, Alexander Pope, felt that his function as a satirist extended beyond the correction of particular evils on the political scene, and much of his poetry deals with the evils of social customs and of human nature in general. Inevitably, this part of his work has a wider appeal than that which is closely tied to a particular contemporary situation.

A number of poems satirize, sometimes mildly, sometimes harshly, the foibles of women. "The Furniture of a Woman's Mind" ridicules feminine practices of scandal-mongering, carrying on illogical arguments, and exercising wily deceptions, usually on their husbands. There is an underlying sense of disgust in "The Progress of Beauty," in which Swift describes the hideous appearance of popular belles as they arise in the morning, without the hairpieces and other artificial aids that contribute to their charms, still wearing the remnants of yesterday's makeup. One of the qualities Swift criticizes throughout his work is artificiality, a discrepancy between appearance and reality, and he finds that beauty which rests entirely upon paint to be in some sense morally evil, as well as distasteful or ridiculous.

A lighter, more amusing piece is "The Journal of a Modern Lady," the description of the activities of a woman of fashion from the moment she awakes, aching and bleary-eyed, at noon, lamenting her losses at the card table the night before. At dinner she torments her husband's guests with her sharp tongue, while he wonders at her wit; then she joins her gossipy friends for tea:

> Now Voices over Voices rise;
> While each to be the loudest vies,
> They contradict, affirm, dispute,
> No single Tongue one Moment mute;
> All mad to speak and none to hearken.

Swift skillfully reproduces the acid conversation over the evening's games of cards, when the lady again loses heavily:

> "This morning when the Parson came,
> "I said I should not win a Game.
> "This odious Chair how came I stuck
> in 't,
> "I think I never had good Luck
> in 't...
>
> "Nay, Madam, give me leave to say

> "'Twas you that threw the Game away;
> "When Lady Tricksy play'd a four,
> "You took it with a Matador."

The game ends in the early hours of the morning and Swift's heroine retires again "with empty purse and aching head."

In "Helter Skelter," a poem that rollicks along in trochaic tetrameter, Swift attacks the young Irish attorneys, whom he accuses of attending to their own pleasures at the expense of their clients' needs. The contrast between the gayety of the rhythm and rhyme and the harshness of the content is particularly effective:

> Now the active young Attorneys
> Briskly travel on their Journies,
> Looking big as any Giants.
> On the Horses of their Clients . . .
>
> With some Law but little Justice,
> Having stolen from mine Hostess,
> From the Barber and the Cutler,
> Like the Soldier from the Sutler . . .
> Into this and t'other County,
> Living on the public Bounty.

One of the finest of Swift's satirical works directed at mankind as a whole is "The Day of Judgment," written in an iambic pentameter couplet which gives it unusual elevation and dignity. Swift's vision of the end of the world is a particularly devastating one; the pale sinners who make up the human race gather before the throne of an utterly contemptuous Jove, who finds their activities, even their sins, so meaningless and petty that he cannot be bothered to damn them:

> "Offending Race of Human Kind,
> By Nature, Reason, Learning, blind;
> You who thro' Frailty step'd aside,
> And you who never fell—thro' Pride;
> You who in different Sects have
> shamm'd,
> And come to see each other damn'd;
> (So some Folks told you, but they knew
> No more of Jove's Designs than you)
> The World's mad Business now is o'er,
> And I resent these Pranks no more.
> I to such Blockheads set my Wit!
> I damn such Fools!—Go, go, you're bit."

A similar scorn for men's self-deception underlies "The Beast's Confession," in which animals are shown ignoring their vices and praising themselves for their faults; the ass confesses that he may be overfond of jesting, but praises his beautiful voice, while the swine prides himself on his shape and beauty and his hatred of sloth. Similarly, men deceive themselves as they evaluate their actions. The lawyer gives free advice to the poor and surpasses all his fellows in the speed and efficiency of his work:

> The Statesman tells you with a Sneer,
> His fault is to be too Sincere;
> And, having no sinister Ends,
> Is apt to disoblige his Friends.
> The Nation's Good, his Master's Glory
> Without Regard to Whig or Tory,
> Were all the Schemes he had in View.

Swift concludes by commenting that his tale is false; he has libeled the animals, who never betray their natures. It is only man who deceives himself.

By no means is all of Swift's poetry so bitter and critical as the works discussed here. He and his friends frequently exchanged witty, jocular messages in verse, and he wrote a number of moving poems to his friend "Stella," Esther Johnson. One of the best of these is the lyric addressed to her on her last birthday. Swift realized that they were both growing old, and he sensed the nearness of the end of her life. His poem is an affirmation of the values of the virtuous, unselfish life:

> Say, Stella, feel you no Content,
> Reflecting on a Life well spent?
> Your skillful Hand employ'd to save
> Despairing Wretches from the Grave;
> And then supporting with your Store,
> Those whom you dragg'd from Death
> before:
> (So Providence on Mortals waits,
> Preserving what it first creates).

Another revealing poem is "Cadenus and Vanessa," a thinly disguised description of Swift's relationship with Esther Vanhomrigh in the form of a classical myth. Vanessa was many years younger than the poet, but her love for him was apparently deep, and this poem is an attempt on his part to express the nature of his feeling for her. He pictures himself as the crusty tutor to a beautiful girl who has been raised by Venus and Minerva to restore prestige to romantic love, which had fallen into disrepute. However, Venus' scheme was unsuccessful. Vanessa's natural beauty was scorned by the elegant ladies of fashion whose color came from artifice, and her wisdom made the foolish, ignorant beaux of the day shun her as a bore. Only Cadenus appreciated the virtues of her mind, but much as he was flattered by her affection, he tried to keep his own feelings platonic. The outcome of the relationship is left in doubt; Vanessa was a persuasive debater on the side of romantic love, and the poet refuses to say "whether he at last descends to like with less Seraphic ends."

One of the most popular and appealing of all Swift's poems is the "Verses on the Death of Dr. Swift," in which he comments with wry humor upon the natural human tendency to find something pleasing in any misfortune befalling others. Even his friends will find consolation at his death:

> Poor Pope will grieve a Month; and
> Gay
> A week; and Arbuthnot a Day.

He imagines men discussing him at their club, recalling his defense of the Irish and his independence of the patronage of the wealthy, aspects of his life of which he was justly proud, and he concludes with this brief epitaph:

> He gave the little Wealth he had,
> To build a House for Fools and Mad:
> And show'd by one satiric Touch,
> No Nation wanted it so much:
> That Kingdom he hath left his Debtor,
> I wish it soon may have a Better.

Many more of Swift's poems could be cited to show those aspects of life that particularly disturbed him and to enlarge the reader's affection for the poet, who shows himself in his more personal poems to be a warm, sympathetic man. His hatred for man's faults was prompted by his deep and passionate concern for the human race, and the permanent value of his works lies not simply in their wit and technical brilliance, but in their power to move the reader, a power that undoubtedly derives from the poet's love for mankind and his disgust with human failings.

THE POETRY OF TATE

Author: Allen Tate (1899-   )
First published: Mr. Pope and Other Poems, 1928; *Three Poems,* 1930; *Poems: 1928-1931,*
1932; *The Mediterannean and Other Poems,* 1936; *Selected Poems,* 1937; *The Vigil of
Venus,* 1943; *Poems: 1922-1947,* 1948; *Poems,* 1960

A reader who comes across a volume of poetry by Allen Tate will probably read only a few pages before words such as "obscure" and "rigid structure" from literature survey courses make him put it back on the shelf. Tate is not, in fact, an easy poet to understand. There are four principle reasons why his poetry is not at first as engaging as that of several of his contemporaries; the heirs of our literary tradition will perhaps give these same reasons to explain why his works have survived. Certainly Tate will survive in the myth he has created; four interrelated, yet distinct, aspects of his poetry are component parts of that myth.

Tate himself has commented on the common charge that modern poetry is obscure: in his famous essay, "Tension in Poetry," he says that poetry is bound to be impenetrable and obscure if the reader does not share the poet's feeling. Tate does not, for example, share the feeling of "sentimental" poets, and therefore calls their work "obscure," even though the poems are technically very simple. One of Tate's feelings is evident in his concern with history, man's closest link with the past. He believes that history should be a matter of myth rather than patterns and systems. "The Swimmers" recalls a young boy's feelings as he saw a Negro hanged by a posse. He could not run, but watched what he felt was a matter which concerned the whole town, even though no one would acknowledge the fact. But history is more personal than statistical, as Tate makes it in "Ode to Our Young Pro-Consuls of the Air" with its images taken from the Revolution and the Civil War. History is not as big a thing as war; it is, rather, as small as one man in a war. Or it is a man, like Tate, observing the results of war.

John Orley Allen Tate, who was born in 1899 in Kentucky, began his career through association with the Fugitives, a group of Southern writers including John Crowe Ransom and Robert Penn Warren (his professor and roommate at Vanderbilt), Andrew Lytle, and Donald Davidson. In a literary journal, *The Fugitive,* and a book, *I'll Take My Stand,* this group sought, or at least advocated, the reestablishment of the Old South in opposition to the New. Although this theme of disenchantment with the new was not unusual for the times, Tate's concern was not only for the waste and despair of one world war; his despair went back to and sought relief in the days of the Old South, which became his symbol of the lost tradition of America. Perhaps not many can share his feeling for the Old South, but an understanding of the symbols Tate has structured from his past certainly will help release him from the charge of obscurity.

Some critics feel Tate's poetry indicates that he would have been happier had he been born early enough to be a Confederate soldier in order to fight for his Old South rather than being forced to brood inactively over its death. That view is a literal interpretation of his symbols: the Old South is merely a representative for him of the better tradition which has been replaced by the less noble, less alive, less "human" condition he sees today. "Ode to the Confederate Dead," as Donald Davidson has said, does not eulogize dead soldiers as much as Tate's dead emotion. The "modern" world of science has a nightmarish wasteland quality to men of sensitivity, as implied in "Sonnets at Christmas." In fact, when "Euthenasia" was published in 1922, Harte Crane wrote to Tate saying that he recognized an Eliot influence. Tate, however, had not yet read Eliot. The similarity in theme has been attributed to a similarity in reaction to the times. Both poets were concerned with man's inactivity, the "dry bones," the "wasteland." Both men also believed that civilization must return to religion in order to escape the death-in-life that Tate symbolized as twilight. "The Last Days of Alice" bitterly asserts that it is better to be sinners than twilight dwellers; the premise sounds very like Eliot's "The Hollow Men."

Tate's despair has also been compared with that of Edgar Allan Poe, who predicted that man was becoming dehumanized. Despite the similarity, Tate is not as bleak as Poe because he seeks to reconcile man; the major vehicle he offers us for escape from the twilight is an increased awareness of the double level of language. There is a difference, he insists in "The Man of Letters in the Modern World," between what he calls political communication used for the control of others, and the communion of language used for self-knowledge in literature. Mere communication is a symptom of mechanized society: communion includes love, and to be complete communication must also include communion. Tate's concern for poetry as a symbolic language, a possible safeguard of continuing humanity, can be seen in his translation of the "Pervilgilium Veneris" ("The Vigil of Venus"). The silence of twilight, the lack of communion, lamented by the Latin poets, is also equated with sleep in Tate's "Retroduction to American History."

Because Tate is so concerned with symbolic language as the only escape from non-existence, it is not unusual that his own poetic language is highly symbolic. To obfuscate further his early readers, his symbolic language is based on a polar ambiguity; two levels are juxtaposed with the assumption that neither can be totally correct. In an article on Tate titled "The Current of the Frozen Stream," Howard Nemerov conjectures that Tate's duality is the generating principle of his poetry. He cites a passage from "The Meaning of Life" as the key to Tate's ambiguity indicated in the polar categories of commentary and essence. Tate's poems of commentary have a theme with which they deal explicitly; they are characterized by meditation and reflection; they offer no conclusion; they are usually in blank verse. "Fragment of a Meditation" is an example. The poems which aim at "essence in itself" are organized around subtle thoughts making implicit connections; they are typically brief and concise in formal metrical schemes. "Ode to Fear" is cited as an example. His most frequent symbol for "essence" is blood, as is shown in "The Mediterranean."

Blood is liquid, hot and fluid, and is contrasted with the solid, cold, rigid symbolism of "commentary" that *cracks* the hemispheres. Blood and a cold frieze are set in opposition in "To the Romantic Traditionists."

Extending his symbols still farther, in "To the Lacedemonians," blood represents youth and life, as opposed to the rigidity of age and death.

One could surmise from Tate's preoccupation with the Old South that it represents his world of "essence"; the North represents "commentary." The continuous ambiguity in Tate is the fact that the symbols of both life and death are needed in the paradoxical polarity of his world.

Like many poets, Tate believes that the Man of Letters has a role to play in modern civilization: poets must show the way to interpret society and how to live in it. Typical of the intricately symbolic myth he has created, Tate is a withdrawn scholar. He feels poets should not be actively engaged in politics. It is, Tate says in "To the Lacedemonians," up to poets to see that the polarity remains, that "communication" does not mechanize "communion" as well.

These major themes—history, language and religion—all combine as a major statement on the necessity of a duality in modern life which will prevent our being swallowed in mechanization. It is, therefore, perhaps ironic that Tate once described a good poem as primarily a work of craftsmanship. That Tate is a careful craftsman is obvious in his tightly structured poems with strict metrics and rhyme. But it is equally obvious that the carefully controlled format of his poetry does not entirely control the very personal rage that slashes convention.

Tate insists on honesty; he refuses to produce a forced lyricism which pretends to be relaxed. In most of his poems he does not "strain"; he balances tight structure and an almost casual irony to voice his rage. The myth Allen Tate has created is not an easy one to crack, and it is difficult, as Marianne Moore pointed out, to admire what we do not understand. But once understood, the poetry of Tate's myth is smashing, slashing, consistently paradoxical, and consistently individual.

THE POETRY OF THEOCRITUS

Type of work: Poetry
Author: Theocritus (305?-c. 250 B.C.)
Principal published works: The *Bucolics;* the *Epics*

Theocritus is the originator of pastoral poetry, that form which displays to us the labors, the songs and loves, and the sufferings of more or less simple shepherds. In Western literature it is a poetic tradition that is as deathless as it is—or has become—conventional. When Marie Antoinette and her court played at the simple life in the village near Le Petit Trianon, they were reviving modes of sensibility to which the Hellenistic poet first gave expression. Indeed, it would be possible to say that no society can produce pastoral poetry until it has become keenly aware that it is non-pastoral in actuality, old and sophisticated and worldly.

Although Theocritus composed forms of poetry that fit other classifications, he is best remembered for his idealization in verse of the simple, rustic life of the Sicilian shepherds. In his idyls he tells us of herdsmen and their loves; he writes of country singing contests on a mountain hillside, for which the prize is a new set of pipes; he surrounds the occasions his poems celebrate with pastoral grace and occasional rural crudity. Among the best of his pastoral poems is the elegy *Thyrsis,* a lament for Daphnis, traditional hero of shepherds.

It is highly likely that Theocritus' audiences included very few real country people. The bare facts of his life suggest that his ambition led him to courts and not to the country hillsides or gatherings of his verse. He was probably born in Syracuse in Sicily, and some of his poems were written in Alexandria, at the Egyptian court of Ptolemy Philadelphus: fulsome poems of praise to this ruler as well as to Hiero II of Syracuse suggest that Theocritus knew how to finger courtly instruments as well as oaten pipes. His tales of shepherds—their bucolic existence, simple fare, unsophisticated hopes in love, and rude sports and games—were never destined for country ears at all. Rather might a ruler like Ptolemy Philadelphus, after he had had his considerable fill of praise from the poet, command a song about Daphnis or Theugenus, drawn from Theocritus' recollections of his native Sicilian countryside.

Theocritus' poetry, in short, is one of the chief representatives of the Alexandrian period of Greek poetry. This was a time generally regarded as an era when the direct, authentic utterances of poets like Homer, Hesiod, and Sappho had given away to more self-conscious garlands of verses woven self-consciously and with as much variety as possible, a time when the idyl, the epigram, and the mime were the style. It was a time, too, when verses were first written and then polished and a poet like Theocritus was as aware of the art of poetry as he was of what themes he was expressing.

It is significant that Theocritus often falls back on the traditional stories of the Greek-speaking peoples. He tells us of Cyclops in love with the sea-nymph Galatea—but Cyclops is no longer Homer's monster but a not entirely unattractive swain "sighing like a furnace" for a cold maiden. Or Theocritus takes incidents in the life of Hercules and uses the ancient web of the heroic tale as an occasion for elegant embroidery. We are less struck by the tale of Hercules strangling serpents that attack him in his cradle than we are by the deftness with which the poet elaborates the old brief tale; the gradual approach of the serpents is very gradual indeed, the confusion of the parents is very pretty, and the final triumph of the muscular infant is a foregone conclusion.

Theocritus is perhaps most brilliant and most himself in two fairly long poems that are far from the sloping fields of

Sicily and which reflect the rather fetid, cynical, and jaded life of a city like Alexandria. "Love Magic," or the "Spell," tells of a young woman, Simaetha, and her servant working an incantation to bring back a vigorous young lover who has only recently gone elsewhere. The mixture of sick desire and sicker hatred in the girl's song is remote from the simple lays of shepherds and herdsmen.

Less morbid and certainly wonderfully charming and revealing of busy street life of a Hellenistic city, is "The Women at the Festival of Adonis." In this mime, a brief dramatic sketch not unlike some of the more extended efforts of Menander, two women, Gorgon and Praxinoa, chatter with each other and re-create a world for us. They meet, they plan an outing, comment on each other's costumes, and arrange for their households to be cared for in their absence. Then they go out and walk through the hot, jostling streets; out of their mouths tumble phrases that allow us to see the city streets and their abundant distractions as clearly as if we were there. Then the women, never losing breath or dropping a syllable, come to the palace of Ptolemy, where a famous young woman will sing the lament for Adonis, the slain god. The two women attend the religious rites.

All this should indicate that Theocritus had a considerable range. But his country poems, now elegant, now crude in their language, but always fresh and vigorous, have left a greater mark on the literature of the Western world. Vergil's celebration of the simple life (so far from luxury and the cynicism of Augustan Rome) have for twenty centuries implored readers to go back to a Sabine farm; and Vergil took his cue from Theocritus. From Vergil, if not from Theocritus, many poets have learned to hope for escape from courts and cities. Spenser, Milton, Keats, Tennyson, Arnold are on the long list of English poets who have used the pastoral convention of Theocritus for their special purposes, often weaving into the plaintive rural song of pipe and voice political and religious themes that no shepherd—or even Theocritus for that matter—ever dreamed of.

THE POETRY OF THOMPSON

Author: Francis Thompson (1859-1907)
Principal published works: Poems, 1893; *Sister Poems,* 1895; *New Poems,* 1897

Francis Thompson's poetry resulted from the tortured and tormented mind of a man maladjusted to the world. The son of a successful father with whom he could have little in common, he was a failure in his studies to become a Catholic priest and later a physician. Self-exiled from home, he wandered to London, where, ground down into the direst degradation and poverty and forced to subsist on the inadequate fare he could earn by selling matches on the street, he nevertheless grew in spiritual fervor and integrity.

His first poems, growing out of a promising youth of effort, were published in April, 1888, in *Merry England,* a magazine edited by Wilfrid Meynell, who with his beautiful and talented wife Alice was to have great influence on the personal and poetical life of the poet. These early works include numerous poems about children. One of these, Thompson's first on the subject, is named "Daisy." The poem flirts with the obviously sentimental but rises above it. The poet meets the little girl, in a Wordsworthian fashion, walks with her, like two children walking side by side. When she leaves her walking partner after a short time, he remembers the joy of their companionship and the poignancy of parting, but he reconciles himself with the thought that sadness is the price of all happiness.

Thompson's first volume of poetry, *Poems,* was well received. Spurred on by enthusiastic reviews in numerous magazines, the volume startled the Victorian audience who reacted with approval or shock. It was immediately evident that a poet of considerable power was writing. His verse form was unconventional, running from clipped lines of one word to unusually long ones. The vocabulary was exotic, even bizarre, including old forms of usual words and outlandish coined terms. Latinisms abounded. Most important of all, however, was the powerful mysticism that had energized the great works of the earlier Metaphysical poets, John Donne and Richard Crashaw. William Blake's influence is also immediately evident in several of the poems, as in "Little Jesus," which parallels in subject matter, treatment and rhythms the earlier poet's "The Lamb."

Thompson's second volume, *Sister Songs,* did not meet with the success of the earlier volume. Even the author held reservations about its publication. In approach and language that marks no advance over the previous volume, it catalogues Thompson's love affair—which seems to have been genuine—with the daughter of his landlord.

Another of Thompson's love affairs, entirely chaste and worshipful, is chronicled in "Love in Dian's Lap," begun the year of publication of "The Hound of Heaven." The sequence is made up of poems written about Alice Meynell, the wife of his first publisher, who was herself a poet and a beautiful and charming woman. In Thompson's mystic, powerful style she becomes far more than an earthly woman. She is his spirit, soul, his Heaven. In "A Carrier Song," the poet says that she has "waned" from him and left him in a "darkened cage." Another, "Her Portrait" reveals his approach, his power, and his reaching back to the technique of the Metaphysical poets. The poet wishes that he had the "heavenly grammar" which "angels' tongues" turn to gold. To praise her soul "All must be mystery and hieroglyph." He catalogues her beauties, ending with the statement that in the contemplation of her eyes there is "Passionless passion, wild tranquillities." In another sensuous-mystical statement, "Domus Tua," Thompson states that the perfect woman should be praised because her body is God's Tem-

ple, and he will be glad to say at Dooms-
day that he loved the beauty of that
House.

Evidence of the fact that Thompson
could never write very far from his own
experience—limited as that was—nor on
any subject but himself is seen in the
elegy, written at the request of Wilfrid
Meynell, on the death of the Cardinal of
Westminister, with whom Thompson
had been loosely associated. The poem
begins on the theme of the dead clergyman but almost immediately turns to the
poet himself, who is contrasted in his
failure with the Cardinal in his success.
Thompson was "ex-Paradised" and not
tall enough to lean against the Cardinal's
Christ. Death, which was ever close to
Thompson with his tuberculosis and in-
termittent addiction to opium, moves
nearer here than usual, as he says in one
of his simple and powerful lines that the
grave is in his blood.

The wide range of Thompson's poetry
is further revealed in two works quite
different in subject matter and in treatment. "The Fair Inconstant" is a love
poem in the same mode and treatment as
Shakespeare's Sonnet 18, "Shall I compare thee to a summer's day?" which ends
with Shakespeare's statement that it is his
poem that will eternally give life to the
subject of his song. Thompson's begins
with the same kind of statement, asking
his love if she thinks her beauty will live
after it has ceased being beautiful to him.
He feels that he made her fair, his heart
did tint her cheek with beauty, and she
will eventually discover that he looked
her "into loveliness."

Such a delicate poem is successful.
"Cecil Rhodes" is in every way a failure.
The poem catalogues the glories of this
great man, his saving Africa for England,
and finally devolves into chauvinism in
its appeal for "Colonies on Colonies" to
cling to the skirt of Mother England and
thus be wise.

Among the various influences on
Thompson, both immediate and remote,
one of the most powerful was Coventry
Patmore. Thompson indicates this influence in the dedication to his last volume,
New Poems. The book will attempt to
outface Time under the banner of Patmore's renown, and if it fails, then one
page at least, the dedication, will survive,
"armed" with his great name.

Of all Thompson's poems, none has
the appeal and power of his most widely
known work, "The Hound of Heaven,"
completed during the poet's residence in
London from 1890 to 1892, and translated into most languages of the world
and generally admired. Written by a man
who wanted to become a priest but was
denied this way to serve God, the poem
chronicles the rejected man's pell-mell
flight to other consolations. He fled God
"down the nights and down the days"
and through the "labyrinthine ways" of
his own mind. Even when assured of
"His love Who followed," he continued
to run for fear that God's love would exclude all other things from life. God's
voice behind insisted that nowhere could
the pursued find shelter except in Him.
Excluded from men and women, he
turned to children, but they were
snatched from him. He turned to nature
but his heart was not eased. And the insistent voice asserts that nothing can content the poet that does not content God.
At the end of the long flight, the "long
pursuit," the poet discovers that he is so
"ignoble," so worthless, that only God will
love him. All the certainties of life, the
rest and peace, were taken from man so
that he would "seek" it in God's "arms."
All rest and certainty is "stored" for man
"at home." The poem ends in a glorious
affirmation of faith and certitude.

Thompson's later work, after *New Poems,* consisted mostly of reviewing and
criticism, which was weak and inferior.
Generally, the verse he wrote was also a
failure, vitiated by his weakening powers,
his advanced tuberculosis, and his reliance on opium.

THE POETRY OF THOREAU

Author: Henry David Thoreau (1817-1862)
First published: Poems of Nature, 1895; Collected Poems, 1943; Collected Poems of Henry
  Thoreau, enlarged edition, 1964

Most of Thoreau's best poetry was written between 1839-1842, though he had experimented with verse composition for several years before those years. The poems best known to the public are those which appear in *A Week on the Concord and Merrimack Rivers*—several had already been published in the magazine *The Dial*—and in *Walden,* his only books published before his death. Most of the remaining poems in the collected editions appear in Thoreau's voluminous *Journal,* published after his death.

Carl Bode points out in his introduction to the *Collected Poems* that Thoreau was talked about and judged as a young poet by his contemporaries; a decade before his death, however, he was forgotten as a poet, though celebrated for his remarkable prose. Bode assigns three reasons for the continued neglect of Thoreau's poems: the unevenness of his verse, Thoreau's loss of enthusiasm for poetry, and the mistaken belief of F. D. Sanborn and others that his verses are fragments inseparable from the prose into which they were originally woven. Even such a recent biographer as Walter Harding, in *The Days of Henry Thoreau,* says that most of Thoreau's poems are third-rate. Because so many of the poems in Bode's *Collected Poems* are actual fragments or are marked by aesthetic faults, incomplete revision, or even technical errors of composition, the average reader is likely to agree with Harding. Yet in a few of Thoreau's best poems he achieves a blend of poetic beauty and skill that make these poems at least worthy of serious consideration.

Emerson said Thoreau's biography is to be found in his poems. The hyperbole is typical, but important parts of the biography are to be found there: his personal philosophy of life and his closeness to nature, his love for his brother John, his love for Ellen Sewall and her young brother Edmund, and his concept of love itself.

The paucity of Thoreau's poetic output is explained in part in his couplet "My life has been the poem I would have writ, / But I could not both live and utter it." Like Emerson, his older friend and early inspirer, Thoreau believed in living each day to its utmost and living it in or near Concord, though he did leave several times on what he called "excursions" of varying lengths. This belief is found in the poem which begins "I seek the Present Time, / No other clime, / Life in today, / Not to sail another way. . . ." Poor in worldly goods but rich in his life of the spirit, Thoreau's pride in this life is seen in "Poverty." Like Wordsworth, one of his favorite poets, he stored in memory the beauty of the natural world for the pleasure and the spiritual gain of recollection at other times, as he suggests in the opening lines of "The Inward Morning": "Packed in my mind lie all the clothes / Which outward nature wears. . . ." But unlike the Wordsworth of "Ode: Intimations of Immortality from Recollections of Early Childhood," who mourned the loss of life's freshness and glory by the growing youth, Thoreau was stirred to admiration and love of the mature man who, having passed through the storms of life, faces the world proudly and bravely.

Thoreau's deep love for his older brother John, who died of lockjaw at twenty-seven, is seen in the quatrain "Where'er Thou Sail'st Who Sailed with Me" and in the grief-filled lines of "Brother Where Dost Thou Dwell." Henry's brief but passionate attraction to Ellen Sewall's young brother Edmund appears in "Lately, Alas, I Knew a Gentle Boy" (titled "Sympathy" in the *Dial*). His love for Ellen is expressed in "Love" (reminiscent of John Donne) and in the gay lines of "The Breeze's Invitation." Apparently Thoreau conceived of love as necessarily coexisting with hate though rising above it, and the love-hate motif is found in such poems as "Indeed, Indeed, I Cannot Tell" and "I Will Obey the Strictest Law of Love."

From a man who lived as close to nature as Thoreau did, one would expect to find poetic evidence of his response to the world about him. In "Within the Circuit of This Plodding Life" the poet remembers how in winter he has recalled the beauty of the world in spring or summer and he has been enriched to continue his winter's tasks. "Smoke in Winter," beginning "The sluggish smoke curls up from some deep dell," describes how the just-risen woodsman sends the smoke, his "early scout, his emissary," from his home "To feel the frosty air, inform the day. . . ." In the rhythmic "When Winter Fringes Every Bough" the ice and snow in their beauty remind the poet of summer as if it hid beneath, and the cracking of the ice on the pond hurries him to the scene to join nature in her festival mood. "Rumors from an Aeolian Harp" pictures an imagined vale of beauty, love, youth, and virtue which is contrasted with the real world of toil, strife, and sin. "Low-Anchored Cloud" employs a series of metaphors to paint a poetic canvas: "Fountain-head and source of rivers, / Dew-cloth, dream drapery, / And napkin spread by fays; / Drifting meadow of the air. . . ." "My Books I'd Fain Cast Off, I Cannot Read" follows the advice of Wordsworth in "The Tables Turned," and the poet lies watching a battle of red and black ants on a hummock and even enjoys the sudden rain which drenches him. In "Nature" he desires no high fame or place in the world, only to be a child and pupil of nature living and working in it. "A Winter and Spring Scene" is an interesting experiment in four-syllable lines with multiple rhymes to achieve an effect of lighthearted celebration of early spring in New England.

One chapter of *Walden* is entitled "Sounds"; in it Thoreau tells of those he hears from his cabin, some from nature and some from the world of men. His responsiveness to sounds is found also in his poems. There are the songs of the chickadee, the vireo, and other birds. In "The Cliffs and Springs" the poet, alone, hears at noon the trill of the veery or thrush and feels that the melody is addressed to him from "out the depths of universal being." The bird song ends, there comes the low of distant cattle, and then the cries of farm boys in a neighboring vale remind him that he is a mere denizen of earth. "Upon the Bank at Early Dawn" celebrates the cock that wakes the world and in the "rare bragging of thy throat" makes even God himself appear more young. "The Funeral Bell" contrasts the sad tones of the tolling bell with the silence of lovely flower bells. "Music" reveals the renovating power of musical notes upon the dull, despondent spirit. "I've Heard My Neighbor's Pump at Night," with its comparison of the sound to a bittern's call or the squeak of a meadow hen, anticipates the New England poems of Robert Frost.

No case can be made for Thoreau as more than a minor poet, but his best lines have a memorable quality in them. Nowhere is this better seen than in his "Smoke," first published in the *Dial* in 1843 and republished in *Walden* more than a decade later.

Light-winged Smoke, Icarian bird,
Melting thy pinions in thy upward
    flight;
Lark without song, and messenger of
    dawn,
Circling above the hamlets as thy nest;
Or else, departing dream, and shadowy
    form
Of midnight vision, gathering up thy
    skirts;
By night star-veiling, and by day
Darkening the light and blotting out the
    sun;
Go thou, my incense, upward from this
    hearth,
And ask the gods to pardon this clear
    flame.

THE POETRY OF TRAHERNE

Author: Thomas Traherne (c. 1637-1674)
First published: Poems, c. 1655-1674, first published 1903; *Poems of Felicity,* c. 1655-1674, first published 1910

Thomas Traherne was one of the last seventeenth century inheritors of the Metaphysical tradition of religious poetry, developed to its height by John Donne and George Herbert, who drew on every aspect of the world around them to express their faith and their longing for closer communion with God. Much of their complexity of thought and their awareness of the essentially paradoxical nature of the Christian religion was lost on Traherne, whose concepts and style were much simpler and less compact than theirs. The greatest differences between Traherne and his predecessors undoubtedly resulted from his radically different theology. Both Donne and Herbert struggled with a strong sense of sin, a feeling of man's unworthiness, and as a consequence of this realization they had an equally overwhelming perception of the miraculous, outreaching mercy of God.

Traherne, who was closer in spirit to the great Romantic poets, Blake and Wordsworth, than to his own contemporaries, wrote out of a deep conviction of man's innate innocence. Original sin forms no part of his faith, though he was conscious, intellectually if not emotionally, of man's corruption, which he felt was derived from the world's emphasis on materialism. Evil comes from human greed; gold, silver, and jewels are symbols not of beauty, but of temptation and of that avarice that perverts man's youthful joy in the creation. Nature, not wealth, is for Traherne the greatest of human possessions. He who is an inheritor of the light of the stars and the fruitful soil can desire no more.

Just as Donne's complex metaphorical language reflects his equally involved theology, so Traherne's brief stanzas echo the essential simplicity of his vision. His lyrics have been compared to William Blake's *Songs of Innocence,* though he never achieved the sustained control of the later poet. Both his form and his devotional tone are perhaps closest to the less impassioned poems of Herbert, who may have inspired him to experiment with a wide variety of verse forms, not always successfully. Traherne's work is characterized by lines of striking loveliness in the midst of uninspired, wordy mediocrity. His limitations in his religious thought are partly responsible for those of his poetry: a narrowness of vision, a lack of awareness of many significant sides of life, and a tendency to repetitiveness. He never really mastered the poetic control of Donne, Herbert, or even of Vaughan, another late Metaphysical poet with mystical tendencies, who shared Traherne's propensity for unevenness in his writing. This problem can be clearly seen in a lyric which begins with an unusual and striking vision of "new worlds beneath the water." The intensity of the opening is dissipated by the weakness of the end of the stanza:

> I saw new worlds beneath the water lie,
> New people; yea, another sky
> And sun, which seen by day
> Might things more clear display.
> Just such another
> Of late my brother
> Did in his travel see, and saw by night
> A much more strange and wondrous sight;
> Nor could the world exhibit such another
> So great a sight, but in a brother.

Dominant themes in Traherne's poetry include the innocence of childhood, when human eyes look upon everything with delight and wonder, the glories of the natural world, and the corruptions of the commerce-directed society of the time. Perhaps the best-known and most skillful treatment of these characteristic themes comes in "Wonder," a rather ecstatic statement of the poet's childhood reaction to the world around him:

How like an Angel came I down!
How Bright are all Things here!
When first among his Works I did
appear
O how their GLORY me did Crown?
The World resembled his Eternitie,
In which my Soul did Walk;
And every Thing that I did see,
Did with me talk.

Like Wordsworth, Traherne suggests a kind of platonic pre-existence, when men's souls were united with God. Children retain some of this divine luster until greed gradually wears it away. Though Wordsworth could not have known Traherne's poems, since they were lost until late in the nineteenth century, his "Ode on Intimations of Immortality" has surprising echoes of a poem called "News," in which Traherne ponders his early sense that there was a world of bliss beyond the one he saw. Unlike Wordsworth, however, Traherne finds the creation not a consolation for the loss of heavenly bliss, but this bliss itself:

But little did the infant dream
That all the treasures of the world
were by,
And that himself was so the cream
And crown of all which round about
did lie.
Yet thus it was! The gem,
The diadem,
The ring enclosing all
That stood upon this earthen ball,
The heav'nly eye,
Much wider than the sky,
Wherein they all included were,
The love, the soul, that was the king
Made to possess them, did appear
A very little thing.

In another poem, "The Apostasy," distinguished by a complex, well-handled stanza form, Traherne comments at greater length on his childish appreciation of the natural world, when he seemed to dwell in Eden before the fall:

As Eve
I did believe
Myself in Eden set,
Affecting neither gold nor ermined
crowns,
Nor aught else that I need forget;
No mud did foul my limpid streams,
No mist eclipsed my sun with frowns;
Set off with heav'nly beams,
My joys were meadows, fields, and
towns.

Temptation entered his paradise with "those little, new-invented things, fine lace and silks . . . or wordly pelf that us destroys." His own fall was gradual, but he, like all other men, was corrupted, separated, finally made "a stranger to the shining skies."

Traherne's poetry has a pervasive quality of innocence and purity; even when he speaks of corruption, he seems to be living in an incorruptible world himself, and he preserved a child's uncomplex awareness of existence. Both his language and his images reflect these characteristics. They are expanded, not compressed; a poet of mood, rather than of ideas, Traherne built much of his effect through repetition and restatement, deriving images from the preceding ones, finding new examples to express the same idea, as he does in the following stanza:

A globe of earth is better far
Than if it were a globe of gold; a star
Much brighter than a precious stone;
The sun more glorious than a costly
throne—
His warming beam,
A living stream
Of liquid pearl, that from a spring
Waters the earth, is a most precious
thing.

Traherne's fondness for the exclamatory tone is especially evident in a little verse appropriately entitled "The Rapture," which conveys that joy in existence that is part of so much of his poetry, especially that about childhood:

Sweet infancy!
O heavenly fire! O sacred light!
How fair and bright!

How great am I,
Whom the whole world doth magnify!

The poet does have other voices. In "Insatiableness," a poem faintly reminiscent of Herbert's "The Pulley," in which God is seen withholding the gift of rest from man that "weariness" may turn him back toward the Deity, Traherne restates in three successive stanzas the impossibility of satisfying the "busy, vast, inquiring soul" of man. His conclusion differs from Herbert's; this restless spirit is, finally, proof of the existence of God: "Sure there's a God, (for else there's no delight,) One infinite."

One of the most unusual of Traherne's poems is "A Serious and Curious Night Meditation," where he deals with a theme he rarely touches on—death as a physical process, rather than as a spiritual reunion with God. Some of the images have the harsh, almost macabre realism of the true Metaphysical poets like Donne and Marvell:

What is my Fathers House! and what
    am I!
My fathers House is Earth; where I
    must lie:
And I a worm, no man; that fits no
    room,
Till like a worm, I crawl into my
    Tomb.

Even here there is a suggestion of the awareness of beauty that is characteristic of Traherne, in the lines "Whilst, at my window, pretty Birds do Ring my Knell, and with their Notes my Obit sing." The conclusion is a weaker version of Donne's triumphant affirmation in his sonnet, "Death Be Not Proud":

Sleep is Cousin-german unto Death:
Sleep and Death differ, no more, than
    a Carcass
And a skeleton.

Therefore, since he sleeps peacefully in his bed, he has no reason to fear death.

Traherne's formula for "felicity," a term that recurs frequently in both his poetry and in his fine prose work, the *Centuries of Meditations*, is effectively summarized in "The Recovery." Here he presents his conviction that man's pleasure is God's reward: "Our blessedness to see/Is even to the Deity/A beatific vision." Men see God's glory in his works and worship him through their joy:

All gold and silver is but empty dross.
    Rubies and sapphires are but loss,
    The very sun and stars and seas
    Far less His spirit please:
One voluntary act of love
Far more delightful to His soul doth
    prove
And is above all these as far as love.

Traherne's own joy in the works of God is perhaps the most memorable quality of his poetry; his exuberant praise of nature and the innocence of childhood is for the reader at least temporarily infectious. There is, however, a sameness about his work, a lack of variety in his ideas and in his vocabulary, which makes it difficult to read many of his poems at a sitting without feeling the sweetness and the smoothness rather oppressive. When even evil is described in terms of gold and silver, rubies and sapphires, words which have inevitably been associated with beauty rather than with corruption, one eventually begins to long for a single harsh phrase or metaphor of real ugliness. However, notwithstanding all his limitations. Traherne deserves a place of respect among the poets of his century for expressing, often very beautifully and appropriately, his own unique view of life and the way to human happiness.

THE POETRY OF VALÉRY

Author: Paul Valéry (1871-1945)
First published: La Jeune Parque, 1917; *Album de vers anciens, Poèmes 1890-1893,* 1920; *Charmes,* 1922

Paul Valéry said that while making poems he always watched himself at work on them. This statement is a good place to begin a consideration of Valéry's poetry, for it reveals the super-consciousness of a writer whose major theme and inspiration are super-consciousness. Thought and the process of thought interested Valéry above all other things; and in an effort to make poetry of these concerns he followed the lead of the French Symbolist movement in attempting to write a "pure" poetry in which thought itself would be purely felt without the impurities and lack of clarity that the use of language usually involves.

Valéry's idea of pure poetry was much influenced by the thought of Mallarmé, whom the young Valéry knew and admired. Poetry is not, Valéry insisted, prose dressed up with pretty and poetical devices; a poem cannot be reduced to the expression of a mere idea. The thing we experience when we truly feel a poem is revelation and communication of a poetic state which involves the thinking, feeling being. The experience of a poetic state, which is the whole reason for the poem's existence, cannot be translated into any other form of expression than the poem itself without destroying the unique poetic state. Each poem is a construct that lives only for and by itself. Poetry uses language to make in each individual poem a "language within language" that can only be understood within the world of the particular poem; a language that can be understood only after reading and rereading have brought a full experiencing of the individual poem. When the reader understands this "language within language," he is immersed in the poetic world the poet has created. It is a world of poetic music, harmony, and resonance arising from the interplay of the sound and connotations as well as from the de-notations of the words in the poem. When the reader is thus immersed in the poetic world, the true pure text of the poem is "created" in the sensibility, the structure of aesthetic response.

The union of the reader's mind and the poem is impossible in prose, or in "impure" poetry which is based on the statement of ideas rather than on the exploitation of the meanings within words that the true poet releases by his harmonic and musical arrangement and juxtaposition of words in pure poetry. Pure poetry is poetry that finds its world within the relationship of words, not in the relationship of words and the things they refer to.

Since pure poetry can only be known as it is actually being felt by a reader, pure poetry exists only as it is actually being said aloud, and heard, and experienced: only when we are being made the sensitive instrument upon which the poem plays. As we read the poem our voice, our intelligence, our sensibility are shaped into a single experience by the art of the poet: the letters printed on the page are not the poem; the experience of the poem *is* the poem. Valéry has made his best statement on pure poetry in his *Little Notebook of a Poet (Calepin d'un poète).*

Committed as he was to a poetry of pure intellect, Valéry played down the idea of poetic inspiration in favour of an emphasis on the poet's conscious labor and construction. He did not deny that the poet feels a kind of creative energy as he contemplates and writes. But the task of the poet is to make his readers feel inspired, not himself. To accomplish this task the poet must always be aware of what he is doing, of how he is doing it; he must be in total control. The poet must go beyond mere inspiration. Pure poetry is the product not of enthusiasm and accident, but choice and conscious work by the poet who has the idea of pure poetry constantly in mind.

The poet, for Valéry, is a professional. The characteristics of the poetic profession are patience, conscious effort, and knowing how to discern and use what is poetic in chance ideas and observations. The poet must wait for the germ of a poem to appear. When the germ does present itself, the poet must know how to exploit it and how to resist the impulse to stop work, to "finish" the poem. The poet is an "architect of poems" who is concerned with the problems of expression: it is not with ideas that poems are made, but with words. Feeling this way, it is no surprise that Valéry valued the controlled art of classicism more than the effusions of the Romantics. He did not protest against rigid rules, forms, and restrictions of vocabulary; on the contrary, he saw in such restrictions the very source of poetic greatness. They are devices by which the poet may more fully control his language.

Valéry is often accused of being an obscure poet. His obscurity, however, is not a systematic effect sought after, as it is in the poetry of Mallarmé. It is the result of the genesis of Valéry's poetry and its subject matter. The poems arose from years of examination of his own thought, the processes of thought, and the idea of pure intellect that occupied him for over twenty years. Further, the subtle ideas that obsessed the poet are virtually impossible to catch in language. Valéry claimed that language was not constructed to express precisely the complex states of mind and soul of a complex man: and these things are exactly what he wanted to express in his poetry. Further, obscurity in poetry is a problem both of the complexity of the poem and the complexity of the person who reads the poem. Valéry unhesitatingly affirmed that his poetry was for the happy few. Only a complex man can understand a complex poem, and such understanding will never be easy, for complexity is the opposite of ease.

The poetic production of Valéry is very slim. He published only two small volumes of verse: *Album de vers anciens* and *Charmes*. The first of these, published in 1920, is made up of poems Valéry wrote in his youth in the early 1890's before he had renounced poetry as the result of a personal crisis in 1892. The poems are interesting in that they reflect the formative Symbolist influences on young Valéry and because they foreshadow to some extent the later poetry, and in many ways "Narcissus Speaks," one of these early poems, is a promise of what was to come. In this poem the mythological Narcissus (an appropriate symbol in the poetry of a man almost completely concerned with the nature of his own being) languishes in his pure love for his own chaste beauty. He becomes identified with his image as he kisses the still water of a reflecting pool and vanishes in the resulting crystalline ripple.

When he was asked in 1912 by André Gide to put his old verse together in the volume that became the 1920 edition of *Album*, Valéry still did not intend to write any new poetry. But as he was working over one of the pieces that was to be included in the book, he became engrossed in the problems of writing and began to work on what was to be his first mature poem. After four years of work, and the expansion of a few old lines into a new 512-line poem, Valéry published "The youngest of the Fates" ("La Jeune Parque"), in 1917. At one stroke his new style was achieved. The main theme of the poem is the motion of a consciousness during a sleepless night. The three Fates symbolized to the ancients the various stages of a man's life. Valéry's choice of the youngest Fate as his symbol is proper to this poem in which a consciousness first begins to be aware of itself and to gain self-knowledge. The consciousness in the poem experiences her past and considers the problems of the conscious being conscious of itself: a young girl in the adolescent crises.

All the rest of Valéry's poetry appeared in his *Charmes*. This volume contains only twenty-one poems—Valéry's entire *oeuvre* totals a mere forty-three. The poems in *Charmes* had first appeared in literary magazines after the publication of "The Youngest of the Fates" and they, like the "The Youngest," had attracted a great deal of attention. Valéry was elected to the French Academy in 1925 on the strength of *Charmes*.

The première piece in *Charmes*, Valéry's greatest and best-known poem, is "The Cemetery Beside the Sea" ("Le Cemetière Marin"). This poem, like all of Valéry's work, is untranslatable, if only because of its dependence for effect on the music of the French language. Every language has its own musical possibilities which are unique to it alone and which, thus, have no equivalents in other languages. Valéry, more than most poets, depended on the genius of his mother tongue for his poetic effects, and these effects can be known only if the poems are read (and heard) in French. The basic situation of "The Cemetery Beside the Sea" is all that can be described here; this description must not be confused with the poem itself. They can be only distantly related.

The theme of the piece is Valéry's own dilemma. The poet always was torn between the desire to participate in the active life and the desire to withdraw into pure contemplation; contemplation, indeed, of contemplation itself. The poet goes in imagination to the cemetery beside the sea in his home town. He had dreamed there in his youth. At high noon among the graves and tombs he contemplates the sea, which seems to him to be the essence of changelessness. He is at peace and is motionless. He is existing in perfect thought, yet he is anxious and uneasy; he sees signs that he in fact exists in change, that things do not hold eternal perfection but that they change. One flaw in perfection that the poet sees is his own doubt of perfection—this is his proof. Even doubt must die; even the thought of imperfection cannot be perfect. The poet sees that he must live, that he cannot escape into pure abstraction and thought.

THE POETRY OF VAUGHAN

Author: Henry Vaughan (1622-1695)
Principal published works: Poems, 1646; *Olor Iscanus,* 1651; *Silex Scintillans,* 1650, 1655;
Thalia Rediviva, 1678

Henry Vaughan is best known as a religious poet, a follower of the metaphysical tradition of John Donne and George Herbert, and a precursor of Wordsworth in his interest in the ideas of the seventeenth century Platonists, philosophers who emphasized man's innate good, the innocent wisdom of childhood, and the possibility of mystical union with God. Like John Donne, Vaughan turned to religious poetry relatively late in his career; he was a law student in London during the years just before the Civil Wars, and his first volume of verse, *Poems,* reveals his close reading of the popular court poets of the age of Charles I.

A number of his early poems are love lyrics addressed to Amoret, probably an imaginary lady. They show little originality, though they are competent, pleasant, polished works. Even at this stage in his development Vaughan was a skillful metrist, able to create many different effects through a variety of verse forms. His sentiments and images are typical of the age; his passion is strictly "platonic." It is the lady's soul he loves, though he complains that she is as heartless and unyielding as the ladies addressed by the other Cavalier poets. Cupid, the cruel god of love, plays a major part in many of Vaughan's lyrics, as he does in the works of writers like Ben Jonson and Thomas Randolph, to whom the poet acknowledges his debt.

There are, among the imitative and undistinguished lines of these poems, flashes of that gift of language which makes some of Vaughan's later lyrics rank high among the verses of his century:

If, Amoret, that glorious Eye,
  In the first birth of light,
    And death of Night,
Had with those elder fires you spy
    Scatter'd so high
   Received form, and sight;

We might suspect in the vast Ring,
  Amidst these golden glories,
    And fierie stories;
Whether the Sun had been the King,
    And guide of Day,
  Or your brighter eye should sway.

The comparison of the lady's brightness to that of the sun is commonplace, but the poet's vision of the night sky is his own.

Poems included, in addition to the typically Caroline love lyrics, an amusing description of London night life that ended with a drinking song and a translation of Juvenal's tenth satire. Vaughan's translation reads smoothly, but it suffers greatly by comparison with Samuel Johnson's "The Vanity of Human Wishes," an adaptation of the same Latin poem. Though both English poets used iambic pentameter rhyming couplets, Vaughan's extended verse paragraphs have little of the pointed conciseness that the eighteenth century poet gave to the form. Satire was, in any case, quite foreign to Vaughan's temperament, and he wisely turned his attention to other subjects in his later works.

Most of the poems in *Olor Iscanus,* published in 1651, were written in the mid-1640's; they also show the influence of poets of the preceding generation. Most of the poems are epistles to Vaughan's acquaintances on a variety of occasions: the publication of a volume of plays, an invitation to dinner, or the marriage of friends. The influence of Ben Jonson's poetry is clear in these works, as well as in the two elegies on Vaughan's friends who met their deaths in the Civil War. There are echoes of Jonson's famous poem on the death of Sir Henry Morison in "An Elegy on the Death of Mr. R. W. slain in the late unfortunate differences at Routon Heath, near Chester":

Though in so short a span
His riper thoughts had purchas'd more
    of man
Than all those worthless livers, which
    yet quick,
Have quite outgone their own Arithme-
    tick.
He seiz'd perfections, and without a
    dull
And mossy gray possess'd a solid skull.

Vaughan's limitations as an elegiac poet are clear when one compares Jonson's lines on a similar subject:

It is not growing like a tree
In bulk doth make man better be;
Or standing long an oak, three hundred
    year,
To fall a log at last, dry, bald, and sere;
A lily of a day
Is fairer far in May,
Although it fall and die that night,
It was the plant and flower of light.
In small proportions we just beauties
    see;
And in short measures, life may perfect
    be.

One of the most pleasant poems in *Olor Iscanus* is the one addressed "To the River Isca," from which the volume takes its name. This pastoral, reflective lyric, filled with the traditional images of "gentle swains," "beauteous nymphs," "bubbling springs and gliding streams," promises fame to the river through the poetry it inspired in Vaughan.

Had Vaughan's career ended with *Olar Iscanus,* he would probably have ranked with the very minor Cavalier poets. However, some event, or combination of events, perhaps the death of a beloved younger brother, brought about his religious conversion, and he found his true poetic voice in the works that appeared in the first part of *Silex Scintillans* in 1650. Vaughan's debt to George Herbert is evident in many of the poems; he followed Herbert's example in experimenting with various stanza forms and unusual patterns of syntax. Vaughan's "Sundays," like Herbert's "Prayer," consists exclusively of phrases describing the title word; neither poem contains a verb:

Bright shadows of true Rest! some
    shoots of bliss,
        Heaven once a week;
The next world's gladness prepossessed
    in this;
        A day to seek;
Eternity in time; the steps by which
We Climb above all ages; Lamps that
    light
Man through his heap of dark days;
    and the rich,
And full redemption of the whole
    weeks flight.

A number of Vaughan's themes also seem to have been drawn from Herbert's poetry, among them the ceremonies of the church, the celebration of important days in the Christian year, and the constantly emphasized relationship of man's repentance and God's grace. What stands out as uniquely Vaughan's is the sense of innocence and joy that pervades much of his work. Although at some times he seems strongly aware of sin and the need for penitence, at others his Platonism seems to obliterate his consciousness of evil and he writes simple, joyous lyrics like the following:

My Soul, there is a Country
    Far beyond the stars,
Where stands a winged Sentry
    All skillful in the wars,
There above noise, and danger
    Sweet peace sits crown'd with smiles,
And one born in a Manger
    Commands the Beauteous files,
He is thy gracious friend,
    And (O my Soul awake!)
Did in pure love descend
    To die here for thy sake.

A poem often discussed in connection with Wordsworth's Immortality Ode is "The Retreat," in which Vaughan's Platonism is particularly evident. He refers to the glorious vision of God he preserved in his childhood and to his closeness to nature, which seemed to take him back to that heaven he inhabited before his birth:

Happy those early dayes! when I
Shin'd in my Angel-infancy.
Before I understood this place

Appointed for my second race,
Or taught my soul to fancy ought
But a white, Celestial thought,
When yet I had not walked above
A mile, or two, from my first love,
And looking back (at that short space,)
Could see a glimpse of his bright-face;
When on some gilded Cloud, or flower
My gazing soul would dwell an hour,
And in those weaker glories spy
Some shadows of eternity.

Some of Vaughan's other poems are far less sanguine about the human condition. "The World," whose opening lines, "I saw Eternity the other night like a great Ring of pure and endless light," are among the poet's most famous, pictures man as greedy and self-seeking: "the darksome statesman hung with weights and woe," "the fearful miser on a heap of rust," "the downright Epicure." The poet comments on the folly of those who reject salvation, who "prefer dark night before true light."

Another theme that seems to have fascinated Vaughan was the relationship of body and soul. Unlike the medieval poets who presented two forces pulling in opposite directions, the soul toward God and the body toward the gratification of physical desires, Vaughan sees them as harmonious, concerned chiefly about that period of separation between death and the resurrection. In "Resurrection and Immortality" the soul reassures the body, as if it were a frightened child, that all will be well:

> Like some spruce Bride,
> Shall one day rise, and cloth'd with
> shining light
> All pure, and bright
> Re-marry to the soul, for 'tis most
> plain
> Thou [the body] only fall'st to be
> refin'd again.

It is difficult to pinpoint characteristic images in Vaughan's poetry as a whole, for he varies his language with his theme. However, his use of light, brightness, the sun, and the stars, to reflect his sense of the glory of God is especially memorable. There is a particularly interesting

variation on this typically Platonic use of light in the poem entitled "Night":

> There is in God (some say)
> A deep, but dazzling darkness; As men
> here
> Say it is late and dusky, because they
> See not all clear;
> O for that night! where I in him
> Might live invisible and dim.

Vaughan makes effective use of commonplace images in a number of his poems. He builds one around the analogy between the root, lying dormant in the ground before it can appear clothed in new loveliness in the spring, and the buried body, preparing in death for the resurrection. In a lyric entitled "Man" Vaughan describes the human condition in the language of weaving:

> He knocks at all doors, strays and
> roams,
> Nay hath not so much wit as some
> stones have
> Which in the darkest nights point to
> their homes,
> By some hid sense their Maker gave;
> Man is the shuttle, to whose winding
> quest
> And passage through these looms
> God order'd motion, but ordain'd no
> rest.

Vaughan never entirely abandoned the poetic diction of some of the poems in *Olor Iscanus,* and his last volume, *Thalia Rediviva,* published in 1678, contains several works approaching the neo-classical manner of Waller and Denham. It should be noted, however, that many of these "late" poems were actually written many years before their publication, before Vaughan had done his best work.

Vaughan's religious poems are seldom brilliant throughout; he was a writer whose genius showed itself more fully in single fine lines than in sustained thoughts. However, his ability to convey a sense of personal feeling in his meditations, which sometimes reflect his moods of ecstasy, sometimes his melancholy view of man's rejection of salvation, makes his works moving as wholes, as well as beautiful groups of lines. His natural bent seems to have been more toward an exalted, visionary state than toward depression, for it is in the poems describing his joy that he is generally at his best. His sense of sin and struggle seems more often imitated from Herbert's poetry than drawn from his own feelings. Vaughan's work provides an interesting bridge between the intense struggle for personal faith that fills the poetry of Donne and Herbert and the ecstatic paeans of Crashaw and Traherne.

THE POETRY OF VIGNY

Author: Alfred de Vigny (1799-1863)
First published: Poèmes, 1822; *Éloa, ou la soeur des anges*, 1824; *Poèmes antiques et modernes*, 1826, 1829, 1837; *Les Destinées*, 1864

Alfred de Vigny's place in the mainstream of French poetry seems assured. In his life, he made few concessions to popular tastes and did not therefore attract the same adulation as his contemporaries Lamartine and Hugo. For a period of voluble Muses, his output was not great. Nonetheless, the esteem in which Vigny is held has remained constant since his death.

Until about 1830, it seemed that Vigny might rival Victor Hugo as the leader of the Romantic school; however, it became evident that his true position was outside the turmoil of the Romantic Cenacle. For Vigny was essentially a thinker, distrustful of lyrical effusions, who had a sense of moderation and discipline more characteristic of a previous generation than of his own. Eventually, he saw himself as having a social mission, but this he fulfilled from a distance, in the seclusion of his manor at the Le Maine Giraud, to which he retired in 1837.

The collection titled *Poèmes antiques et modernes,* though of uneven quality, shows that as early as 1826, Vigny was capable of treating serious problems in verse. Moreover, his use of the symbol, although hesitant, marks a major development in French poetry; for it allows Vigny to bring his ideas to life, to suggest more than he actually says, while retaining an impersonal form.

The first book, the "Livre mystique," of the *Poèmes antiques et modernes* is made up of three pieces: "Moise," "Eloa" and "Le Deluge." In "Moise," Moses is given a sense of discouragement he does not possess in the Old Testament. He feels all the weight of his age and experience; having led the Jews to within sight of the Promised Land, he now seeks only to die, to throw off the burden of wisdom and responsibility which alienates him from other men:

> O Lord! I have lived powerful and alone,
> Let me fall into the deep sleep of the earth!

The dominant idea of this poem is that of the moral solitude, the alienation, of the man of genius. So powerful, so convincing, is the portrait of Moses, that it takes on all the qualities of a myth. As Vigny himself pointed out in a letter to Mlle. Maunoir in December, 1838, Moses' name serves as a mask to suggest the weariness of the superior man of any century.

In "Moise," the wrath and even the injustice of God are stressed: Moses does not seek immortality, but has it thrust upon him. This theme is developed in "Eloa." Eloa, an angel born of a tear shed by Christ, attempts to save an archangel fallen from Heaven. At first, Satan, the fallen archangel, seems to repent. If God had intervened at that moment, writes Vigny, perhaps evil would have ceased to exist. But God abandons Eloa, and she is dragged off by Satan as his victim.

"La Fille de Jephte," which is to be found in the "Livre antique" of *Poèmes antiques et modernes,* may have been inspired by a reading of Chateaubriand, while its form was possibly borrowed from Byron. Nonetheless, the poem bears the unmistakable imprint of Alfred de Vigny, and is probably, after "Moise," one of the finest in the collection of 1826. The form, alexandrines in four-line stanzas, with couplet rhymes, is an innovation in French poetry, admirably suited to the rigor and sense of tragic inevitability implicit in the theme. Vigny tells the story of Jephtah, one of the judges of Israel, who, before attacking the Ammonites, promised to sacrifice to

God, after his victory, the first person to come to meet his army. Jephtah's daughter, his only child, was that person, and the poem describes the tragic meeting of the two.

The "Livre antique" of *Poèmes antiques et modernes* draws on classical and Biblical antiquity, while the third and final book, the "Livre moderne," is inspired by the Middle Ages, episodes in Spain, or happenings in France. Of the poems represented here, mention must be made of "Le Cor." The latter describes the plight of Roland, trapped in the pass of Roncevaux, summoning help by means of his horn, his oliphant. The poem is outstanding for its economy of word and syllable, the sense of urgency it communicates.

The importance of *Poèmes antiques et modernes* resides in Vigny's success in expressing in verse some of the problems at the center of his philosophic position. The poet's interpretation of man's condition seems to be summed up in the "Why?" and "Alas!" uttered by Moses in the first poem discussed here. In exposing his ideas, Vigny managed to give his verses an impersonal quality, a general value, through a clever, if timid, use of the symbol.

Twenty to thirty years of experience and meditation separate the *Poèmes antiques et modernes* from *Les Destinées*. The latter collection, having as its subtitle *Poèmes philosophiques,* was published in 1864, a few months after Vigny's death. It is the fruit of an attempt to clothe philosophical reflection in verse. The undoubted success of this venture is due in large measure to Vigny's consistent and conscientious use of the symbol. The publication of *Les Destinèes* marks a new development in the history of French poetry.

Les Destinées owes its title to the first poem of the collection. Here the poet poses the basic problem of man's condition on earth: since man was created, says Vigny, he has lived in uncertainty and unhappiness, the slave and victim of fate. The coming of Christ brought some relief, for the collar around man's neck was slackened. But, Vigny continues, the chain is still held from above, and though mankind may accomplish great deeds, there is still no real freedom or certainty about God's works.

After the extreme pessimism of "Les Destinées," Vigny, in "La Maison du Berger" ("The Shepherd's House"), announces the ideal after which he strives. The title expresses the symbol inspiring the poet's meditation; the poet, a thinker and social apostle who guides the people towards the ideal life, here resembles the shepherd in his caravan. For the poet should live ideally far from the tumult of an industrial society. Alluding no doubt to Lamartine, Vigny claims that poetry has been cheapened by writers who seek the plaudits of the crowd. On the other hand, nature is insensible. So the poet, turning to Eva, probably an ideal abstraction, not a single figure, whom he has led to the caravan, will prefer to the harshness of nature and the corruption of society the compassion and pity only woman can offer.

In "La Maison du Berger," Vigny proposes an ideal. In "La Mort du Loup" ("The Death of the Wolf") and "Le Mont des Oliviers" ("The Mount of Olives"), he suggests an attitude. The mood of these two poems is pessimistic. In the former, the courage of the wolf, as it dies, is held up as an example to man. This creature, its body wracked with pain after it has been mortally wounded, utters no sound. Man's duty, according to the poet, is to display the same courage: he must complete his tasks and prepare to meet misfortune and death uncomplainingly.

The somber stoicism of "La Mort du Loup" is also advocated in "Le Mont des Oliviers," another outstanding poem. First published in 1844, this work depicts Christ, a Christ perhaps more human than divine, in the garden of Gethsemane, where His sufferings began. Christ asks of God that His sufferings be used to explain to mankind the reasons for the apparent injustice of the Divinity and the presence of evil in the world. His plea goes unanswered:

> But the sky remains black,
> and God does not answer

In a final stanza, added in 1862, Vigny says that in the face of God's silence, man can only remain silent and aloof also.

In these two poems the image evoked is admirably appropriate. Yet their appeal lies essentially in Vigny's ability to develop and fill out the image, to give it a life of its own, while translating his thought faithfully. The thought, in a sense, feeds the image, and where the thought is strong and consistent, as is the case here, the image stands out in sharp relief.

Were *Les Destinées* to end here, one must conclude that Vigny's message was purely pessimistic: to exist is to suffer, to exist as a superior being requires a religion of honor to meet more suffering, a readiness to remain uncomplaining, stoical, and even unenthusiastic. In fact, this religion of honor, this stoicism, is for the poet only a beginning, not an end.

"La Bouteile a la Mer" ("The Bottle in the Sea") and the final poem of *Les Destinées*, "L'Esprit pur" ("The Pure Spirit"), indicate an evolution in Vigny's thought. In the former, an intrepid sea captain casts a bottle containing vital information about reefs and currents into the sea, just before his death. The poet's message is clear. Just as the bottle was later recovered, so might a work of art guide future generations; therefore the writer must ignore present adversity and look toward the future. A poem is a bottle cast into the sea.

"L'Esprit pur" may be considered Vigny's moral and literary testament. In this poem, written some months before his death, he affirms that the reign of the "Pure Spirit," of the written word, has come. The poet has a mission; he must serve as a guide for future generations and write for posterity; he will acquire nobility through his ability to join the past to the future by his writings.

Vigny's place in literature is inside no single school. Several of his themes are characteristically Romantic, while his restraint and respect for his art are reminiscent of Classical French poets. Moreover, his use of the symbol reminds the reader of the debt owed him by the Symbolist movement of the late nineteenth century. Alfred de Vigny's most outstanding trait, reflected in his poetry, was probably the esteem in which he held the Idea throughout his life. While a poet, he was always a thinker, a fact that explains much of the force as well as the occasional stiffness of his verse.

THE POETRY OF WALLER

Author: Edmund Waller (1606-1687)
Principal published works: Poems, 1645 and 1664; *Divine Love,* 1685

The poems of Edmund Waller were at one time famous, and from the time they were written until the middle of the eighteenth century he had the reputation of being England's best lyric poet. The poems were admired for several reasons: they seemed to recall the poetry of those Greek and Roman writers who were so greatly admired during the Renaissance, and they marked the use of a new poetic diction or vocabulary by English authors. Also, Waller's poetry represented a turning-away from the obscure (if brilliant) poetry of the Metaphysicals. Instead of difficult words and ideas he used the simplest expression; instead of the broken rhythms of this highly intellectual poetry he popularized the smoothness of the heroic couplet.

Waller's early poetry was amatory and pastoral. It contains the customary numbers of allusions to Flavia, Chloris, and other fictional ladies of this type of poetry. The poems are written in praise of the woman admired and of the idea of love itself. These works do not attempt to give a direct and literal idea of their subject; instead, they refer to the goddesses of myth and the beauty of nature. Thus the subject of "On Her Coming to London" is never really given the form of an actual person, but is described as Juno, Athena, Aurora, and other famous names of myth. The method of this kind of poem is comparison and exaggeration: after the invocation of these goddesses the poet says of his beloved that she is "one that shall / Compare, perhaps exceed them all."

The themes of Waller's love poems are not original, nor is their intention to describe a new way of expressing emotion. They attempt to reinvigorate the lyrics of classical times, and their themes are old and familiar. "To Phyllis" is the kind of *carpe diem* verse we find in Marvell's "To His Coy Mistress," and like that

poem it can be traced at least as far back as Catullus. The whole burden may perhaps be summed up by the first line: "Why should we delay?" Other poems utilize the ancient convention of love as a mortal illness, or a war between man and woman. "Of Love" exemplifies the use of the latter theme; it goes through the whole familiar canon of love's despair. Love makes the lover

> lament, and sigh, and weep,
> Disordered, tremble, fawn and creep.

The woman is the conventional tyrant of Renaissance love poetry, the lover her equally conventional slave. The struggle is in vain; like the hunted stag, the lover is outmatched by the forces against him.

Much of Waller's poetry is "occasional," the kind of writing that commemorates some event. He writes of the sentimental qualities of a riband that a woman has bound around her hair; of a painting which has caused him to fall in love; of a lady he has seen in a garden. In each of these Waller follows the convention of love at first sight. The lover, who is always pictured as the man of great sensibility, immediately responds to the beauty of the person or object he sees before him. His "On the Discovery of A Lady's Painting" invokes the Pygmalion myth and states that he has been seized by a passion unlike any "mortal flame" simply by seeing the representation of beauty. The most explicit statement of this kind of feeling is expressed in Waller's "Of Loving at First Sight," in which the poet conceives of himself as a seaman captured by a tempest and driven to his fate.

Waller did not confine himself solely to lyric poetry. His single best-known poem is about Oliver Cromwell, "A Panegyric to My Lord Protector." This poem was written in the decade when Cromwell ruled England, and its evident admiration for Cromwell was the cause of some embarrassment for Waller after Charles II became King in 1660. It reveals an admiration based on respect for power; the beginning is an apologia for the man who must use force in order to subdue "faction" and "civil hate." There are many historical references in the poem, notably to the strife between the various splinter sects of Puritanism and to that between Parliament and King. With a good deal of pride and exultation Waller praises the new strength of England, which allows its navy to dominate the seas of Europe. The power of the country extends, Waller writes, "as far as winds can blow." Like Milton, who also praised the power of the Puritan state, Waller writes of its new position in the European community, a position more powerful than it ever enjoyed under the Stuart kings. Yet the poem is about more than political and military power, for it praises especially the religious toleration of the new state, to which "the oppressed shall henceforth resort." Waller writes that this is a new nation which has captured something far more honorable than mere wealth or power. It has shown that England can once more breed things of the "noblest kind," for it has enjoyed a moral resurrection.

The culmination of the poem is the section on the personal achievement of Cromwell. Waller writes in praise not only of Cromwell's courage and generalship, but also of the sense of "proportion" which enabled him to build a state after tearing one down. He uses language from the Bible to describe the patriarchal nature of his hero, who has acted like the great figures from the Book of Kings. Cromwell first taught the English "to subdue their foes," but his greater accomplishment was to "order, teach, and their high spirits compose."

With prudent, if not exactly admirable flexibility, Waller wrote soon after "To the King, Upon his Majesty's Happy Return." This poem sings the praises of Cromwell's rival and is motivated by either a sincere change of heart or simple self-preservation. Like the rising sun, Charles II appears to dispel the clouds of rebellion and to bring forth "full majesty" to the land that has suffered from war and dictatorship. The qualities for which Charles is praised are not to be found in any biography of that king; they derive from the poetry of praise. He is compared to the sun and to Jove, to nature and to heaven. He is praised even more extensively as a Joshua and a Job. Finally, the poem culminates with a pious wish for the return of all those virtues that had departed with the king from England:

Faith, law, and piety, (that banished train!)
Justice and truth, with you return again.

After the Restoration, Waller continued in the vein of panegyric. His "Instructions to a Painter" is a long poem of praise for the nation; it celebrates one of the rare English victories over the Dutch in 1665. Waller conceives of this great event as the subject for an enormous canvas and he advises the hypothetical painter of this picture how best to give an idea of the heroic stature of the combatants. Pre-eminent among them is the "great monarch," who is described as Augustus himself. "To the King" also celebrates the king and his accomplishments and returns to the mode of myth and exaggerated, full-throated praise. There is the favorite comparison to Jove, and other allusions to heroes of the Western World who are like Charles in his "high wisdom" and "power."

Waller had a wide range of poetry. It should be noted that he tried his hand with success at religious poems. His "Divine Poems" begin with an argument for the authority of the Bible and discuss the nature and condition of man in the present. Their great theme is love; they move from the love of God for man to the love of man for his own kind. Their first statement is that only by this love can we "reform mankind" and their last is that we must retain the "image in our thought" of that love which made life possible. Waller writes in these poems that the classical and Christian traditions must eventually be opposed to each other, for the former have only philosophical falsehoods to offer to scriptural truths. After establishing this point of faith, the poet attempts to account for the Creation in terms of "love of creatures yet unmade": man exists only because the love of God permits this existence. Thereafter these religious poems move to descriptions of fallen man in "this Iron Age." These poems are typical of the Augustan attitude towards human history; they continually balance a sense of progress and aspiration by reminders of the human limitation.

Throughout these poems, no matter how varied their subjects Waller employed the rhyming couplet. He brought to technical excellence this form of verse and began what was to be a great change —his admirers called it a "reform"—in English poetry. The couplet became the favorite mode of verse in the century after Waller's first experiments with it. Waller's smoothness of expression and rhythm were widely imitated, and the diction he compiled became familiar in the poems of the eighteenth century. In essence, Waller brought back harmonics to English verse and began the great change from the poetry of Donne to that of Dryden.

THE POETRY OF WARREN

Author: Robert Penn Warren (1905-   )
First published: Thirty-six Poems, 1935; *Eleven Poems on the Same Theme*, 1942; *Selected Poems, 1923-1943*, 1944; *Brother to Dragons: A Tale in Verse and Voices*, 1953; *Promises: Poems 1954-1956*, 1957; *You, Emperors, and Others: Poems 1957-1960*, 1960; *Selected Poems New and Old, 1923-1966*, 1966

Robert Penn Warren's reputation as a novelist and critic has tended to overshadow his achievements and distinction as a poet. Like many of our best fiction writers, he was published as a poet before he gained recognition as a novelist; but, unlike most, he has continued to write poetry throughout his career. This fact would make him stand out even among the poets of his generation, most of whom, after achieving some measure of recognition, a niche in the pantheon of the establishment, have at best settled for the care and preservation of the "image" rather than the risky and perhaps unrewarding business of writing more poems. Both factors may help to explain the undeniable fact that Warren's poetry is not as well known as it might be and ought to be. The divorce between the audience for poetry and the audience for fiction has not been settled. The poetry-reading public remains inconsequentially small compared to the larger public for fiction. And within the poetic establishment there remains a lingering suspicion of the poet who also writes fiction.

In Warren's case this suspicion has without doubt been compounded by the fact that his novels have been extremely well received. Part of this suspicion can be written off as professional pride at best and, at worst, simple envy; but in a larger sense it is also the result of the specialization so characteristic of our culture as to be inevitably reflected by its artists and, indeed, strongly protected by them. Warren does not fit neatly and nicely. He is clearly, from the present point of view, not only out of date as a man of letters in the grand style, but a threat by his existence and creativity to the *status quo.*

Not that he has been ignored or unrecognized as a poet in the usual way. He has generally received excellent reviews and notices for his poetry and he has won many honors and awards. He has received the Pulitzer Prize, the National Book Award, the Shelley Memorial Award, and he has served as Consultant in Poetry at the Library of Congress. Some of his poems, particularly the earlier ones, are widely anthologized. But ironically, in spite of his honors, his influence by criticism and example, in spite of his innovation and, above all, his sustained and genuine productivity, he is not often considered critically as a poet.

There is a kind of double irony at work here, for had he continued to write in the manner of his earliest and best-known poems, the manner of *Thirty-six Poems* and *Eleven Poems on the Same Theme*, he might have been more acceptable. The early poems, chiefly distinguished by an elegant combination of form and deliberate artifice, deeply influenced by the rules and guidelines of the first generation, the elders, of "The Fugitives," are quite sharply distinct from his prose. At least at that state his prose and poetry seem to be separate concerns. But through the years of his own change and growth he has managed to bring the two into a closer kinship, to integrate his concerns and manners in prose and verse so that they are clearly part of the same body of work, clearly the voice of one man. Though most modern poets pay brief lip service to Ezra Pound's fiat, that poetry should be as well written as prose, major energy has been spent in cultivating what is special and singular about poetry as if to segregate forever the prosaic from the lyric precincts. It is in this sense that Warren's development as poet has gone against the grain.

In some of his early poems Warren

showed that he could turn the modern "metaphysical" lyric to perfection. The final, familiar quatrain of "Bearded Oaks" is a marvelous example, the manner of Andrew Marvell gracefully translated into twentieth century English. And in the frequently anthologized "Love's Parable" we see the influence of John Donne, its origins proudly shown in the syntax, in the archaisms and inversions, and even in the imagery.

Warren might have continued in that vein, and not without distinction; but he was at once a gifted storyteller and deeply involved in the living Southern tradition. Scattered among the early poems which were brought together in *Selected Poems, 1923-1943,* there are various examples of poems which break the pattern and have a very different kind of grace, life, and vigor. "The Ballad of Billie Potts" is a real story, a sustained narrative poem which is at once particular and concrete, precisely local in color and allusion, and laced with homely imagery, some of it directly out of the folk tradition and some contrived to be a close approximation of the original and source. And in a small group of poems set in Mexico he demonstrated an ease and ability to handle concrete scene and action in verse which could rival his abilities in prose.

The effects are the effects available in verse lines, strengthened by the surplus power of verbs and the rugged texture, a texture like some Mexican painting, but above all it is an achievement in presented *action.* Few of our poets could create a wild gallop like that one.

In 1953, Warren presented *Brother to Dragons: A Tale in Verse and Voices,* a book-length narrative poem which seems to combine in one work all his interests. It has the story line of a novel; much of it is dramatic in form; and by introducing himself as a character and commentator in the action Warren is, in effect, a critic as well. But the form is verse; and thus it is in Warren's poetry that we find the unity of his various interests, techniques, and concerns. On the immediate and dramatic level he tells the story of a particularly brutal and gruesome crime, the literal butchering of a Negro slave by Lilburn Lewis, the nephew of Thomas Jefferson. The background and pyschological complexity of the crime is as thoroughly explored as in any novel. Then by adding Thomas Jefferson, whose brave new world did not seem to take account of the potential for evil even in his family blood lines, Warren creates a dimension of dramatic conflict, in this case the conflict of ideas, on another level than the presented action. Finally there is Warren himself, literally visiting the site of the crime and imaginatively summoning up the ghosts, conversing with Jefferson, arguing too; thus modern man, in the form of the author, is brought directly into the drama as well. In a work of this size and scope all the demonstrated ability of Warren to use verse for scene, action, and psychological and metaphysical speculation had to be employed. What was needed as well, required by the length if nothing else, was a rhetorical line which could contain with simplicity and dignity the burden of thought without calling attention to itself and breaking the spell of the whole poem and without being so complex as to lose the meaning. This was for Warren a new kind of simplicity and power. To achieve it he returned to the roots of poetry, to the clear and sustained and unsurprising metaphor, to cadence. to repetition, to menomic power.

In one sense *Brother to Dragons* was a peak, a culmination of all Warren's work to date. Where he might go from there, in what direction, would have been difficult to imagine. *Promises: Poems 1954-1956* offered an answer. It was evident that *Brother to Dragons* had been a liberating experience for the poet, had, even as the new title implies, opened up new possibilities for him. On the surface the book is technically different from anything he had done before. There is a newly devised long line, based often on stress rhythms and speech cadences.

There are new variations on stanzaic form. The language itself, though clearly in his recognizable voice, seems different too. Its singularity is the simultaneous ability to join both the "poetic" and the prosaic to create a total effect of poetry. Something of the virtuoso's mastery of the modes of apparent simplicity, so evident in *Brother to Dragons,* is now focused on the genre of the contemporary lyric. And there is now, by implication, a declaration of independence. No subject, no word, no notion is to be segregated by definition from the realm of poetry.

The real breakthrough in *Promises* is in language. For a very long time, and still to a degree, the Southern literary tradition of which Warren's work is an important modern example had been founded upon a very clear and present distinction between poetry and prose. Though Southern poets and critics in this century have exercised great influence, it has been the Southern prose writers, the novelists and short story writers, who exploited most fully the richness and variety of the regional vernacular and public rhetorical language. Other poets—William Carlos Williams, Pound, Eliot, Stevens, each in a different way—worried with extending the limits of the language of poetry. But Warren, growing and developing as a novelist, had clearly seen the possibilities largely unexplored by other Southern poets. With *Promises,* after a brief period of silence, he returned with new forms, wider and richer language and subject matter, and a bold assault on the limits of poetry at a time when poetry seemed to have dwindled to two not completely dissimilar voices—the "academic" and the "beat." *Promises* won all the prizes for 1957.

Yet it is in his 1960 collection called *You, Emperors, and Others: Poems 1957-1960* that the new territory claimed and won in *Promises* is consolidated and settled. Bookjackets are not celebrated for their veracity, but the jacket of this book is quite simply accurate when it states:

"You, Emperors, and Others is an extension of the lyric voice which made *Promises* such an important literary event." There is consolidation as well as extension. There are examples of poems which could easily have been a part of *Promises,* but there is more variety in form and, if anything, more ease in the range and kinds of language the poet can employ. Perhaps the earlier poet would not have added the ironic dimension of mocking his own technique with the bravado of rhyming "supper" and "tup her," but the means and concerns are not essentially different from Warren's first poems. His dramatic ability and use of the folk vernacular are eloquently demonstrated. Remarkably, with his new freedom, his new toughness, even wisdom, the poet has not lost the thing that young poets are said to lose to time and experience, the purely lyric note. In truth, he is more at ease with the lyric voice than he has ever been before.

Warren's achievement over many years is an important part of the American literary scene. With a very few exceptions, there have been almost no examples in this century of the continued development and growth of an American poet from youth to age, to an age characterized by wisdom without loss of impulse, by technical ease without rigidity and habitual gestures. Yeats was such an example in our language. Warren is another. His "late" poems can bear the analogy. And he is still young enough to continue, to prove by and through his work that it is possible to be a poet here and now and for a lifetime. The promise of the future is implied clearly in one of the final poems of *You, Emperors, and Others,* one of a virtuoso sequence of "nursery rhymes." The subject is "history," in all the rich complexity that Warren's use of the word in his works suggests; but, in one sense, it may be conceived of as personal history, the history of the working poet, as well.

THE POETRY OF WHITTIER

Author: John Greenleaf Whittier (1807-1892)
Principal published works: Legends of New England, 1831; Moll Pitcher, 1832; Mogg
  Megone, 1836; Lays of My Home, 1843; Ballads and Other Poems, 1844; Voices of
  Freedom, 1846; Songs of Labor, 1850; The Chapel of the Hermits, 1853; The Panorama,
  1856; The Sycamores, 1857; Home Ballads, 1860; In War-Time, 1864; Snow-Bound,
  1866; The Tent on the Beach, 1867; Among the Hills, 1869; Miriam, 1871; The
  Pennsylvania Pilgrim, 1872; Hazel-Blossoms, 1875; The Bay of Seven Islands, 1883;
  St. Gregory's Guest, 1886; At Sundown, 1890

In the "Proem," a poem chosen to introduce his collected works, Whittier scrutinized his poetic achievement and noted that he had never been able to emulate the great lyric beauty and deep philosophic insight of poets like Milton and Spenser. With characteristic honesty he analyzed his inability to echo their marvelous music:

> The rigor of a frozen clime,
> The harshness of an untaught ear,
>   The jarring words of one whose
>   rhyme
>   Beat often Labor's hurried time,
> Or Duty's rugged march through storm
>   and strife, are here.

These sparse lines provide an outline for Whittier's life. Reared in a nonconformist Quaker faith, he always retained the Quaker concept of the presence of the Inner Light in each individual and the belief in special brotherhood and equality. From his earliest years he experienced the "rigors" of exacting farm work, where only the strictest economy and frugality kept the Whittier farm above poverty. This was his education, for he had little formal schooling beyond two terms at a local academy. In these years Whittier was primarily a sectional romantic, a journalist poet who was nourished on the strange literary diet of the Bible, Burns, and Byron. His poetry was blatantly derivative, though his first book, *Legends of New England*, handled native superstitions and folklore. Whittier's second main phase, from 1833 to the 1860's, was a period of reform activity and humanitarian interest. The intensity of his single-minded dedication to the Abolitionist cause effectively vetoed poetry and converted the aspiring young lyricist into a radical propagandist, politician, and part-time editor whose verses championed the rights of slaves and democratic principles. These years drew Whittier away from a love of poetry for its own sake, reforged his vapid sentimental lyricism into a powerful weapon for the oppressed, and strengthened his regard for moral action.

The remainder of Whittier's life is aptly summed up in these autobiographical lines from "The Tent on the Beach":

> For while he wrought with strenuous
>   will
>   The work his hands had found to
>   do,
> He heard the fitful music still
>   Of winds that out of dream-land
>   blew.
>   . . . . . .
> The common air was thick with
>   dreams,—
>   He told them to the toiling crowd;
> Such music as the woods and streams
>   Sang in his ear he sang aloud;
> In still, shut bays, on windy capes,
>   He heard the call of beckoning
>   shapes,
> And, as the gray old shadows prompted
>   him,
> To homely moulds of rhyme he shaped
>   their legends grim.

As his Abolitionist activities lessened, Whittier devoted more time to reworking the familiar ground of native legends and versifying the pent-up memories of his youth. By the 1850's the poet again dominated and Whittier entered into his final years as a religious humanist, striving for moral perfection and inner spirituality rather than for social and political reform.

His work as an Abolitionist nurtured his passionate concern for the principles of liberty, while through study and reading he had steeped his mind in the history and customs of New England until he understood the past as he had experienced the present.

Like most of the schoolroom poets, Longfellow, Lowell, Holmes, and others, Whittier's themes were few and limited: the value of domestic emotions, the innocence of childhood, the necessity of social equality, and the nobility of ethical action. However, unlike these other popular poets, Whittier drew upon his native roots for inspiration. In his best poems Whittier displayed a mastery of local color techniques, a competent use of rural imagery, and the everyday language of the Merrimack farmer. His instinctive handling of native materials conveyed his inner love for the environment that molded and his understanding of the traditions that inspired him. His technique was old-fashioned, even in his own day, while his poetry suffered from the diffusion and sentimentality inherent in the tradition of public rhetoric in which he wrote. He composed far too many poems and when imagination lagged he fell back on stock phrases, repetitive images, and imitative themes. Perhaps no other established nineteenth century American poet wrote so much poor verse, but the miracle is that by the most exacting poetical standards his best remains so good.

Aside from a few nature poems like "The Last Walk in Autumn" and an occasional Abolitionist poem like "Ichabod," Whittier's ballads and genre pieces represent his finest poetical achievement and contain some of the best examples of native folklore written in America. His ballads, especially, express his lifelong interest in colonial history, the Quakers, local legends, and folk superstitions. Unlike Longfellow's conscious literary ballads which emphasized the dream world of European romance, Whittier's ballads remain remarkably true to the graphic realism and dramatic intensity of traditional folk balladry. His earliest ballads in the 1840's—"The Exiles," "Cassandra Southwick," and "Barclay of Ury"—though over long and marred by didactic passages, show Whittier handling his proper subject matter and approaching surety of presentation that the ballad "Kathleen" demonstrated. His mature ballads took incidents like a skipper who had betrayed his own townspeople, a witch who prophesied death, or the terrifying actions of specter warriors, bedrocked them with exact physical detail, and then concentrated on the dramatic moment of conflict. "Telling the Bees" skillfully handles a local superstition with childlike detail to hide the chilling reality of nature's destruction; "The Garrison of Cape Ann," "The Palatine," and "The King's Missive" rework historical incidents; "Amy Wentworth," "The Countess," and "The Witch of Wenham" narrate pastoral romances; while the often parodied "Barbara Frietchie" was accepted by a war-wearied nation as an expression of their personal conviction that the Union must be preserved. Whittier's finest ballad, "Skipper Ireson's Ride," was based on an old Marblehead song about women tarring and feathering a fishing-boat captain. The ballad opens *in medias res*, plunging directly into the wild tumult and chaos of mob action as the skipper is pushed through Marblehead:

Body of turkey, head of owl,
Wings a-droop like a rained-on fowl,
Feathered and ruffled in every part,
Skipper Ireson stood in the cart.
Scores of women, old and young,
Strong of muscle, and glib of tongue.
Pushed and pulled up the rocky lane,
Shouting and singing the shrill refrain:
"Here's Flud Oirson, fur his horrd
    horrt,
Torr'd an futherr'd an' corr'd in a
    corrt
By the women o' Morble'ead!"

Finally Ireson cries out his remorse and with "half scorn, half pity" the women free him. The final refrain changes "Old" Floyd Ireson to "Poor" Floyd Ireson and becomes a mournful dirge forever accusing and dooming Ireson besides emphasizing the hollowness of the women's revenge.

Similarly, Whittier's genre poems elevated the ordinary details of Essex County life into a universal expression of boyhood innocence, agrarian simplicity, and pastoral romance that caught the pathos and beauty of a dying rural tradition. In poems like "Maud Muller," "In School-Days," "Among the Hills," and "Memories," Whittier idealized and typified the district school days, the harvest-filled autumn days, and the barefoot-boy days to capture the romantic aspirations of a responsive American public. "Cobbler Keezar's Vision," "Abraham Davenport," "To My Old Schoolmaster," and others contain some of Whittier's best rustic anecdotes as well as realistic and humorous sketches of the Yankee character. His satire of Cotton Mather in "The Double-Headed Snake of Newbury" reaches its climax in these lines:

> Cotton Mather came galloping down
> All the way to Newbury town,
> With his eyes agog and his ears set
> wide,
> And his marvellous inkhorn at his side;
> Stirring the while in the shallow pool
> Of his brains, for the lore he learned
> at school,

> To garnish the story, with here a streak
> Of Latin and there another of Greek.

Whittier's particular skill in re-creating the past is seen most fully in the contemplative poem, "The Pennsylvannia Pilgrim." In his genre poems Whittier captures the essence of the New England mind, while his selected use of picturesque detail and down-East humor place him in the direct line of American expression that stretches from Anne Bradstreet to Robert Frost. His one sustained triumph, "Snow-Bound," expresses the value of family affections by the symbolic development of a fire-storm contrast and remains the minor masterpiece of nineteenth century American poetry.

Although Whittier's poems fall far short of the poetic imagination and philosophical depth of major American poets such as Whitman, Poe, Dickinson, and Emerson, his verses exhibit more spiritual illumination and downright "grit" than the polished verses of Longfellow and the other minor poets. Despite the severe criticism of his poetry in the twentieth century, Whittier's place in American literature seems secure. He will continue to be read and enjoyed as long as people respond to their traditions and demand honest expression of their fundamental democratic and religious feelings.

THE POETRY OF WILBUR

Author: Richard Wilbur (1921-   )
Principal published works: The Beautiful Changes, 1947; *Ceremony and Other Poems,*
1950; *Things of This World,* 1956; *Poems, 1943-1956,* 1957; *Advice to a Prophet,* 1961

It is difficult to assess Richard Wilbur's lyric poetry in terms of a developing career, a linear working-out and discarding of certain ideas, in the way in which we organize the production of Chaucer's or Wordsworth's poetry. He has said that he turned from playful writing to serious poetry because of the experience of potential chaos in the war; but the war is not overpoweringly present in his first book, *The Beautiful Changes,* although the European Theater seems to loom in the background of many of these poems and the possibility of war remains behind some of his later work.

A comparison of two of the best poems may reveal another kind of development, not of ideas but of poetic power. "On the Eyes of an SS Officer" is one of the few poems in the 1947 volume directly related to the war. The poem is a syllogism in shape; its first two stanzas compare the eyes to ice and glaciers, then to fire and the sun. Clever things happen within the poem. In the first stanza a metaphor within a metaphor refers to fresh snows at the frozen end of the earth's spit. "Spit" is first a reference to barbecuing, a link to the fire stanza, then to sputum: it is a clue to the tone of disgust. The second stanza tells of one blinded by the sun. The blind saint is glorified, for he has seen the Platonic truth, but the SS Officer is called mindless. The last stanza concludes the statement and is filled with ambiguity with references to ice, fire, and eyes. The eyes are oases in a wilderness face. The eyes devise *their* fire, but the poet asks his God to consign the eyes to hell. This type of ambiguity is not exactly the kind Empson admires; first of all it is too rapid, too quickly understood; again it is not finally ambiguous, only ambiguous as we read.

One of Wilbur's best poems is "Advice to a Prophet," the title poem of his 1961 volume. Where in the earlier poem we see a concern with the problems of tone, problems resolved by apparent syntactic ambiguity and puns, here we see much larger problems being handled. The advice is offered to a prophet of doom, of the Bomb. The prophet's problem is to find a language by which he can communicate his message. He is evoking God's name to cause us to feel self-pity. The advice is not to speak of the military power of weapons nor of the end of the people, for these ideas are inconceivable. Rather, he speaks of the changing world. The loss of nature would destroy humanity; animals and trees are things in which we ourselves are mirrored. They are the ground of our perception, our self-knowledge, as well as the elements of our language. Language and knowledge have merged; consequently the poet asks how we can communicate with nature when we can no longer speak. Wilbur's use of concrete image and abstract noun is different. Finally adjectives themselves, bereft of nouns, must function in a bombed or otherwise emptied world.

The first poem solves the problem of how to express hatred in a poem by pressing language to its limits to equate and disequate traditional poetic subjects: ice, fire, eyes. In the second poem the language of association and the objects of the language are themselves examined. These are the poles of Wilbur's poetry. This is not to say that language in itself is a new interest for Wilbur. His translations reveal him an expert in French. The poem "Junk" in *Advice to a Prophet* is written in the style of Old English poetry, in two-stressed half-lines linked by alliteration: the theme is that of the "Lay of the Last Survivor" in *Beowulf* —the transience of artifacts. In Wilbur's volume, *Ceremony,* there is a poem "Beowulf" which interprets the old epic.

Unlike the Anglo-Saxon shaper of the poem, Wilbur has momentarily shifted the viewpoint, at the end of the fourth stanza, to inside Beowulf's head, and has confused the tenses of verbs, in order to comprehend heroism.

A study of the use of word play in the volumes shows one aspect of Wilbur's poetic maturing. In *The Beautiful Changes*, besides the complex business in "On the Eyes of an SS Officer," there are two poems selected by Wilbur in his collaboration for the Untermeyer anthology of 1955. In one, "Potato," the pun "blind" occurs twice, referring to the potatoes' eyes. The first line of "Bell Speech," a poem which may have been suggested by the name of the bell being that of St. Paul, has a phrase playing on the tongue-like clapper. Both of these puns are based on physiological and colloquial association; neither has a powerfully serious function. The puns are inefficient.

In *Ceremony* the case alters. For example, "Juggler" contains four puns which bear a good deal of meaning. The poem is about a juggler who is like God and who balances balls like the solar system, then hauls his heaven in and returns to earth to balance normal objects, such as tables, brooms, or plates. The problem is that the world falls from our hearts and is forgotten.

The three puns in this poem are "gravity," "lightness," and "sole." Gravity suggests our prejugglerian humorlessness as well as the state of the Newtonian world: lightness becomes that of objects, of the space around the sun, and of hearts: sole, is the juggler's loneliness and the soul of worlds, the Neo-Platonic, Lucretian soul. The fall of the earth, "fall" being the fourth pun, is overcome by a light-hearted language. In "Still, Citizen Sparrow" there is a picture of a vulture rising over the office described as "rotten." "Office" is both his function as a carrion-eater and a suggestion of the modern office building, leading to the edge of the sky—a skyscraper. The poem is an anti-flyting, taking up the owl's side in the ancient controversy of owl and nightingale, and the inversion is complete: contrary to Keats's vision of his nightingale, it is the owl of this poem, the vulture, who eats death and derides mutability. The world of the grind, of Noah, will out. In the title poem "Ceremony" there is the line in which those who are familiar with Old or Middle English will recognize a complex series of etymological puns. Another poem, "In the Elegy Season," reverses clichés in the same way that "Advice to a Prophet" does, but this time the cliché is a modern one, the idea of a summer being unremembered in winter.

In Wilbur's next volume, *Things of This World*, there is more play with words. "A Black November Turkey" contains word play of the sort we expect in the newer poems: the hens about the doomed turkey are "clocking," not clucking. They remind us of the bell Great Paul, the ticking of mutability, the wingèd chariot of Time.

Advice to a Prophet contains few puns in the better poems. In "Shame," a satiric poem, there is a pun which furthers the satire: "Scusi" is the capital city of the humble country, and its name reminds one of "Excuse me" in Romance languages. One of the best poems is "The Aspen and the Stream," in which the characters are the self-effacing, Faustian stream and the aspiring, Shelleyan aspen. Their languages help express their natures, for the aspen makes puns. The aspen tells the stream that he has lost the drift of what was being said. The language of word play has been transferred to the peripheries—satire, dialogue—of Wilbur's vision.

Such attention to language on the part of the reader raises the question of why one should pay so much attention to the poem. Analysis too close, too deep, will make anything seem profound. There must be a surface brilliance to attract the attention, to make the reader want to go deeper. Wilbur's method in his best poems is to force the reader's admiration by his sounds. These tonal effects give qualities of excellence to "Tywater," "After the Last Bulletins," "Piazza de Spagna, Early Morning," and "The Un-dead." The sounds of poems such as these evoke the sense, assuring that such poetry will endure.

THE POETRY OF WILDE

Author: Oscar Wilde (1854-1900)

First published: *Poems*, 1881; *The Sphinx*, 1894; *The Ballad of Reading Gaol*, by "C.3.3," 1898; *The Poems of Oscar Wilde*, 1906

Oscar Wilde's first literary reputation was made by his poems; the later success of his lectures, essays, stories, and plays obscured his reputation as a poet until the notoriety surrounding his last poem and last piece of writing, *The Ballad of Reading Gaol*. The most important volume is his *Poems* of 1881, the others being the Newdigate Prize poem, "Ravenna"; *The Sphinx*, published in 1894, and *The Ballad of Reading Gaol*, which appeared in 1898. The poems collected from periodicals by Robert Ross were added to the unpublished works to make up the modest collected edition of 1906. Wilde's poetry may be divided by form into long and short poems or by content into those which spiritualize bodily sensations and those which represent spiritual matters in terms of physical sensation.

The long poems of Oscar Wilde cover the twenty years between "Ravenna" and *The Ballad of Reading Gaol*. Their chief use is not to tell a simple fable like those found in Wilde's short stories, but chiefly to celebrate a situation. There is a similar static quality in the short poems where the lack of argument induces a hortatory opening and a fading or frenzied close. "Ravenna," as is proper in a poem intended to win a prize in late nineteenth century Oxford, is written in modified early eighteenth century couplets, in which the favorite words seem to be "O," "yon" and "adieu," giving the poet a declamatory stance to excite energy, a post from which he can observe Ravenna's scenery, and a pathetic resolution. The success of the poem is the succession of enameled portraits of flowers and other pastoral properties needed to construct the contrast between the Italian and English landscapes which is the matter of the poem, all expressed without one false note in the verse or a sincere one in the expression:

So runs the perfect cycle of the year.
And so from youth to manhood do we go,
And fall to weary days and locks of snow.

It is something of a shock to find Oscar Wilde and Rudyard Kipling publishing short poems entitled "Ave Imperatrix" within a year of each other. Kipling's seven stanzas were "Written on the Occasion of the Attempt to Assassinate Queen Victoria in March 1882"; the "Queen" in his poem is obviously Victoria; Wilde's "Queen" is England, but his tone expresses similar jingoistic rejoicing in imperial power and some of the geographical references are identical, particularly when Wilde brings in Afghanistan (strictly Kipling territory) as evidence of imperial might. After many apostrophes ("O wasted dust! O senseless clay!") Wilde shoulders the White Man's Burden and grants that heavy losses in the Pathan wars are necessary to the destiny of his "Imperatrix": "Up the steep road must England go." But he cannot help regretting the loss of many fine young men. A similar public stance is held in poems like "To Milton" and "Louis Napoleon." But Wilde soon tired of these Miltonic and Wordsworthian imitations and imitated instead Rossetti in his Roman Catholic sonnets and Swinburne in his nature pieces.

Wilde's ear was remarkably true; like those of Swinburne his lines have melody but lack sense, particularly if poem is placed against poem, when the inconsistencies typical of Wilde become obnoxious. Not that such placing is a fair test, but when "the Holy One . . . shepherd of the Church of God" of "Urbs Sacra Aeterna" in the section entitled "Rosa Mystica" becomes a "Fra Giovanni bawling at the mass" of "The Burden of Itys," one questions the sincerity of both the public poems and the private ones. Wilde's sincerity or his most deeply felt pose is contained in the long poems which glorify a naked pantheism that seems to place the sunny Italian body in the fresh fields of England. In that respect all but the last of his poems is a refinement of the first, "Ravenna," and the last, *The Ballad of Reading Gaol*, is a contradiction of such pieces as "Ave Imperatrix." His best known short poem is "Helas," which prefaces the 1881 volume and is usually regarded, like *The Picture of Dorian Gray*, as a form of Wilde's artistic credo; it begins with an anticipation of Lord Henry Wotton's training of Dorian:

> To drift with every passion till my soul
> Is a stringed lute on which all winds
>   can play . . .

and ends with the unanswered question that haunts all Wilde's work:

>   . . . lo! with a little rod
> I did but touch the honey of romance
> And must I lose a soul's inheritance?

Of the sonnets which make up the bulk of the short poems, those at the graves of Shelley and Keats are effective memorials, but the more characteristic and interesting are the "Impressions" and similar poems in the three sections titled "Wind Flowers," "Flowers of Gold," and "The Fourth Movement," in which Wilde is painting in clear, rich, and sophisticated color combinations. The best known of these "etudes in color" is "Symphony in Yellow," among the previously uncollected poems in the 1906 volume.

There are five long poems in the 1881 volume: "The Garden of Eros," "The Burden of Itys," "Charmides," "Panthea," and "Humanitad." Each is written in approximately the same stanza form of six lines, a quatrain plus a couplet, of varying pentameter and quadrameter meter: all five poems have the flowers, colors, and classical allusions and material of Tennyson's "Œnone," and many echoes of a golden treasury of English verse;

but their most characteristic feature is the length to which Wilde could prolong the combined bookish and natural sensations, as he was later to prolong sensation and sensibility in *The Ballad of Reading Gaol*. The easiest to follow is "Charmides" because it tells the legend of the Athenian youth who made love to the naked statue of Athena one long night and was drowned by the goddess the next day for his presumption; in the second section his body is washed ashore on the Greek coast and an Oread, who falls in love with the dead youth, is also slain by Athena; in the third section the girl and the youth are revived by Proserpine and consummate their love in a passionate scene in Hades.

"The Garden of Eros" begins with English flowers, passes to classical myth, surveys English poetry as culminating in Dante Gabriel Rossetti, and concludes the June night of the poem with a return to the beauty of the flowers, all described in fresh images of striking sensuality:

> Mark how the yellow iris wearily
>   Leans back its throat, as though it
>   would be kissed
> By its false chamberer, the dragon-fly.

"The Burden of Itys" follows the same pattern, an invocation to the classic gods of field and forest to visit English fields and repeat their bacchanals:

> O that some antique statue for one hour
>   Might wake to passion . . .

But the dream passes with the dawn. "Panthea" begins in the usual English pastoral setting, enumerates such attractive myths as those of Ganymede and Endymion, contrasts the lot of the poet's race to the gods'—"O we are born too late"—and reaches at last the consolation that in the end death will unite the past in "passions Hymeneal" with the earth which then becomes the "Kosmic Soul" of the conclusion. "Humanitad" is as personal a poem in its way as *The Ballad of Reading Gaol*: beginning in winter the poem laments the poet's inability to respond to the approaching spring as he used to because he is now too experienced in passion and wise to the ways of the world. In the search for a meaning to life—

> O for one grand unselfish life
>   To teach us what is Wisdom! . . .
> To make the Body and the Spirit
>   one . . .

he looks past modern Italy to ancient Greece, to Wordsworth, and finally to Christ, at which point he resolves the dilemma by deciding to come down from his own Cross: "That which is purely human, that is Godlike, that is God."

The sexual fantasies of "Charmides" are more evident in "The Sphinx" and in *Salome*. "The Sphinx" is a sequence of thirteen short poems in four-line stanzas which begin and end with an invocation to the Sphinx imagined by the poet to be brooding at him from a corner of his room. He asks the Sphinx about her lovers and supplies a long catalogue of possibilities before he decides that Ammon filled the role; then he remembers the present state of the Sphinx and tells her to assemble the ruins of her old lovers and to leave him, as the dawn enters, because she awakens in him "each bestial sense . . . foul dreams of sensual life." This effect is certainly borne out in the poem, where Wilde's sense of color and form becomes fully tactile, passionate, and ultimately preposterous. One doubts whether in Wilde's time poetry could go further without becoming obscene. His jail sentence put a stop to this kind of poetry and produced his last work.

The Ballad of Reading Gaol like "Charmides," tells a narrative of the hanging of a murderer for killing the woman he loved; the paradox of his fate and the correspondence Wilde saw to his own is, together with the realism, the source of the energy which carries the poem through six sections and contains more than one hundred six-line stanzas. In spite of repetitions induced by the stanzas Wilde kept adding to the poem, the ballad rhythm is rarely monotonous and the use of color even more startling than it was in Wilde's earlier verse: "little tent of blue," "scarlet coat," "yellow hole," "purple throat," "teeth of flame."

The first three sections narrate the six weeks spent by the subject of the elegy waiting to "swing"; the fourth describes the execution and in intimate and graphic detail shows its effect on the prisoners; the fifth section contains Wilde's reflection on the execution and on the meaning of prison as a place for repentance, a subject he covered more fully but equally indefinitely in *De Profundis;* the sixth section is a brief envoi or epilogue which repeats the central line of the poem: "all men kill the thing they love." This may be in accord with modern psychology; if Wilde was as utterly self-centered as he seems to have been, there could have been no truer epitaph for his own grave.

THE POETRY OF WILLIAMS

Author: William Carlos Williams (1883-1963)
Principal published works: Poems, 1909; *The Tempers,* 1913; *Al Que Quiere!,* 1917; *Kora in Hell: Improvisations,* 1920; *Sour Grapes,* 1921; *Spring and All,* 1922; *Collected Poems, 1921-1931,* 1934; *An Early Martyr and Other Poems,* 1935; *Adam and Eve & the City,* 1936; *The Complete Collected Poems of William Carlos Williams, 1906-1938,* 1938; *The Broken Span,* 1941; *The Wedge,* 1944; *Paterson* (Book One, 1946; Book Two, 1948; Book Three, 1949; Book Four, 1951; Book Five, 1958); *The Pink Church,* 1948; *The Collected Later Poems,* 1950; *The Collected Earlier Poems,* 1951; *The Desert Music and Other Poems,* 1954; *Journey to Love,* 1955; *Pictures from Brueghel and Other Poems,* 1962

In the headnote to *Paterson,* William Carlos Williams described his view of the function of poetry as a bare-handed answer to Greek and Latin. The deliberate rejection of a received tradition, and reliance on crude native energy of intelligence, are characteristic of a poet who has from the start been aggressively American in his poetic themes and techniques. It is not going too far to state that Williams has in fact defined himself in his poetic identity by a series of rejections: as early as 1910 he had thrown over the sonnet and the iamb as dead molds from an English and not an American tradition, and set out in search of what he would later call the "measure" of the indigenous "American idiom." Inevitably this search meant the development of new themes and approaches, an intensive reliance on personal sensibility, and the justification of seemingly unpoetic and arbitrary materials—lists of ice-cream prices, the sounds of the sea-elephant and of trees in rain — the whole human barnyard Williams observed daily in his practice as a busy pediatrician in a New Jersey suburb.

A characteristic early poem, "Between Walls," demonstrates Williams' relentlessness in the process of taking up slack, of concentrating his poetic materials. In this short piece the absence of punctuation, the title entering the very syntax of the poem, and the remarkable pressure exerted on single words all tend to reify language and to de-emphasize the distinctions between words and things in poetic description. Ideas are in *things* is the informal refrain of *Paterson,* the long epic poem in five books in which Williams extends the early discontinuous imagism of a poem like "Between Walls" into a large discourse revolving around the single figure of a man as a city. Late in his career, image and discourse finally come together supremely in this poem on personal and national history, and in the splendid old man's love poem, "Asphodel, That Greeny Flower," in the late volume, *Journey to Love.* And even in his famous early poem on a red wheelbarrow Williams had affirmed that much depends on the object under scrutiny, using emotional as well as descriptive language and exploding the restrictions of the Imagist school by attempting to unite concepts and objects in a single discourse.

Paterson develops and makes explicit another, related cluster of speculations on the importance of place. This emphasis is implied in such poems as "Dedication for a Plot of Ground," "Franklin Square," and "Nantucket," and indeed it is implied in the anxious descriptive bent of all the early poems, but only in *Paterson* does it become a compelling argument against T. S. Eliot's contention that "place is only place." Like Wallace Stevens, Williams believes that place is all we have: there is no other place, no other experience, and so the poem will celebrate things for being and happening in themselves, just as it will praise the mind for now and then lighting on something significant. The point is that any man's experience, however seemingly unpoetic, is universal and valuable to the degree that it is understood in all its relevant detail. Williams accordingly states at the outset of *Paterson,* his long place-poem, that the attempt is to begin with particulars and then make them general. Following this method the poet is obliged to be a noticer, someone whose vision is at once accurate and clairvoyant.

A detailed sense of place, of community and connection, is all the more important amidst the violence and deracination which Williams observed in the lives of his patients, in the state of the country ("Impromptu: The Suckers" is a bitter attack on the injustice done to Sacco and Vanzetti), in our two world wars and a depression. Anticipating the extended metaphor of divorce in *Paterson,* divorce between lovers, friends, poets and their readers, mind and world, thing and thought, certain earlier poems like "It Is a Living Coral" and the collection titled *Spring and All* convey an acute sense of debasement.

The need for accurate observation is at one with the need for love in a world without theological sanctions: energy and the release of energy, the analogies between sexual experience and other modes of knowing such as vision, are at once themes and techniques in Williams, who is one of those post-romantic poets for whom truth can lie only in the search for truth. In such a scheme no subject is too low, no juxtaposition too extravagant; the poem "Pastoral" looks, as do so many of the poems early and late, at sparrows, taking their unconscious ingenuousness as emblematic.

"Pastoral" is constructed as a haphazard montage, according to principles Williams may well have absorbed from his painter friends in Greenwich Village and Paris. According to this technique the position of images is almost as important as their content. Consecutive images are pulled ahead or back according to the lines of force of the surrounding images. Often Williams enforces a contrast of different orders of experience by such placement, setting emotional statements against descriptive ones, kinetic against static, honesty against pomposity. While

Williams' themes remain fairly constant throughout his writing career, these techniques of concentration-by-omission, and of working for speed in the movement of poems, undergo continual change. The effect of simultaneity, analogous to the all but instant impact of a painting on a canvas, is something he early achieves by the montage construction, by forcing attention to new linguistic clusters in the line taken as a unit, by making extensive use of elipse, and run-on lines.

In working as it were within the space created by the overarching metaphor of a man as a city, *Paterson* represents a development of the same method of calculated juxtaposition, naturalizing as it does blocks of prose in a poetic setting so as to suggest that the sources of all writing are the same.

Williams abolishes the capital letters at the beginning of each line. This gives the desired effect of placing enormous weight on the punctuation that remains, and the dash, the parenthesis, even the white spacing between words and lines carry a heavy freight of meaning. Thus every poem discovers its own form, a "measure" determined both by the subject at hand and by the breath-rhythm of the poet.

In the process of writing *Paterson* Williams discovered the three-tier line which he considered his own contribution to an American measure (he would not call it a formal metric, though he would say it possesses form). His 1955 volume, *Journey to Love,* draws upon and endlessly varies this line, as in "Asphodel, That Greeny Flower."

The vituperation and anger of the early poems turns often, in these later books, to gentleness, a celebration of a small circle of loved people and things; and in general Williams moves from his early concern with objects to a concern with actions, virtues, and broad scenes.

As a strictly secular poet, as a writer who has created genuine poems outside traditional metrics, as a theorist of "measure" and a detailed observer (especially in *Paterson*) of the debasement of the

American scene, Williams has been widely influential: poets as diverse as Robert Lowell, Charles Olson, and Theodore Roethke have gone to school to Williams and pursued his lines of inquiry and technique. The art of immediacy, it seems, is more imitable and available than the hieratic, allusive poetry of a more sophisticated poet like T. S. Eliot. Future literary historians may well decide that this less "intelligent" poet is in fact more significantly influential than Eliot in directing the course of American poetry.

THE POETRY OF WITHER

Author: George Wither (1588-1667)
Principal published works: Abuses Stript and Whipt, 1611; *Fidelia,* 1615; *Wither's Motto; Nec habeo, nec careo, nec curo,* 1621; *Faire-Virtue, The Mistresse of Philarete,* 1622; *Britain's Remembrancer,* 1628; *Collection of Emblemes, Ancient and Moderne,* 1635; *Heleluiah; or Britain's Second Remembrancer,* 1641

There is a story that when George Wither, an officer in the parliamentary forces during the English Civil War, was captured by the Royalists, he was in danger of being executed. But the Royalist and poet Sir John Denham is said to have interceded successfully for Wither on the ground that as long as Wither lived, Denham could not be accounted the worst poet in England. This story and the overwhelming quantity of his literary production—Wither claimed to have written eighty-six separate works by 1660 —have done much over the ages to damage the poet's reputation. The truth is that at his best Wither is a fine poet.

After two years at Oxford, Wither was in London in 1605 studying law. Among his first publications was a group of poems, mostly sonnets in the Shakespearean form, titled *Prince Henry's Obsequies,* published in 1612. This collection, occasioned by the death of Prince Henry, was largely courtly in tone, as was *Epithalamia,* which appeared in the next year, a volume of gratulatory poems on the wedding of Princess Elizabeth. However, Wither's most sincere feelings were not with the life of the court and the city, which, it appears, he had learned to loathe. This is the burden of his first important and successful volume, *Abuses Stript and Whipt,* a collection of scathing satires.

The book went through four editions in the year it was published. Wither's purpose he says, was to "teach my rough satiric rimes/To be as mad and idle as the times." He divided the volume into two parts, the first containing sixteen satires which in safe general terms denounced such depraving passions as Revenge, Ambition, Lust. The second part contained four satires "Of the Vanity, In-constancy, Weakness and presumption of Men." These poems were rather more specific. Among other things the poet condemned in strong words the new knights, vain preachers, and dishonest lawyers of the universities. He also attacked the court and the courtiers, and in a poem called "The Scourge" he attacked the Lord Chancellor. Moreover, Wither managed to disagree with a recent policy of truce with Spain. On the positive side, Wither fulsomely praised contemporary poets and drama. The style of the satires is witty and biting, and they are written in pleasingly fluid rhyming couplets. The major result of the book as far as Wither was concerned, however, was several months imprisonment in Marshalsea.

During his imprisonment, the poet wrote, among his less important works, *The Sheperd's Hunting,* a collection of five pastorals. The fourth of these poems contains a well-known passage in praise of poetry. One of the major purposes of this volume, however, was to justify allegorically his *Abuses Stript and Whipt.* Wither's technique was to use the traditional pastoral, the allegorical dialogue form best known in English in Spenser's *The Shepheardes Calendar.* Adopting the name of Philarete ("lover of virtue") a name he used for himself in some of his later poetry also, Wither pleaded his case to another Shepherd, Willy.

After his release from prison, primarily due to the intervention of Princess Elizabeth, Wither published his *Fidelia.* This book is made up largely of a lengthy Ovidian elegy in the form of a letter in which the languishing heroine complains to her unfaithful lover. *Fidelia* is important chiefly because it contains the first of several publications of Wither's best known lyric. This poem, based on the traditional topic, "Shall I, wasting in despair,/Die because a woman's fair," has an untraditional twist. Instead of developing the old Petrarchan idea of the hopeless lover, or the bitter, spurned lover, Wither speaks of love as a reciprocal matter: he will love as he is loved, no matter who the woman is. The poem concludes:

> Great, or good, or kind, or fair,
> I will ne'er the more despair;
> If she love me, this believe,
> I will die, ere she shall grieve:
> If she slight me when I woo
> I can scorn and let her go,
>   For if she be not for me
>   What care I for whom she be?

The best single volume of love poetry by Wither is his *Fair-Virtue, The Mistress of Philarete.* Besides reprinting "Shall I, wasting," this volume contains a number of other excellent lyrics which have carried Wither's reputation down to our time and which have had much to do with establishing him, not at all correctly, as being essentially a poet of "Sweet and open pastorals" who lived in a poetic land of enchantment peopled by dairy maids as fresh as strawberries. There is some truth in this idea, but considering Wither's biting moralistic satire and his later Puritan religious poetry, it is an insufficient definition for the reader who would understand the poet's overall accomplishment.

At any rate, among the best poems in *Fair-Virtue* is "I wandered out awhile agone," a skillful bit of good-humored cynicism in which the poet plays, in several stanzas, on his own name. The poet has wandered to a place inhabited by two lovely young ladies who move him to less than virtuous thoughts:

> Such equal sweet Venus gave,
> That I preferr'd not either,
> And when for love I thought to crave
> I know not well of whether . . .

In "A Christmas Carol" we find a poem full of vivid detail and the joy of the Christmas season:

> Now all our neighbours' chimneys smoke,
>   And Christmas blocks are burning;
> Their ovens they with baked meats choke,
>   And all their spits are turning.

But even in this poem, Wither does not forget his Puritanical will to satire: "Good farmers in the country nurse/the poor," but "Some landlords spend their money worse,/On lust and pride in London." Finally must be mentioned the arch little "Sonnet upon a stolen kiss," in which the lover worries that if he steals a kiss from his sleeping lover she will wake and grow angry. He concludes, "Well, if she do, I'll back restore that one,/and twenty hundred thousand more for loan."

A year before he had published *Fair-Virtue,* Wither had published another long satire that once again put him in prison. Once again the poem was a tremendous success, selling thirty thousand copies, as Wither tells us. This satire, written in over a thousand pentameter couplets, was called *Wither's Motto; nec habeo, nec careo, nec curo* ("Neither Have I, nor Want I, Nor Care I"). The poem develops a statement of the attitude to life expressed in the title. With this poem and *Fair-Virtue* ended the period of what Wither later called his Juvenilia. The rest of his poetry is essentially religious in intent and subject, for the poet, though he was an aristocrat and was at first a loyal subject of the king, became increasingly involved in affairs of the Puritan party.

In 1622-1623 appeared his *Hymnes and Songs of the Church.* More important was his *Britain's Remembrancer,* a long poem of some historical value in which Wither recounts his experiences during the plague time in London in 1625. Interspersed with the vivid descriptions are denunciations of the wickedness of the times and prophecies of the disasters about to fall on England.

Then in 1635 the poet was asked to write a series of emblems (moralized caption poems) for a volume of allegorical prints to be put out by a London publisher. The book was published as a *Collection of Emblemes, Ancient and Moderne;* among the more memorable of the emblem poems is "When with a serious musing I behold."

Finally, Wither's finest religious poetry was published in *Heleluiah; or Britain's Second Remembrancer* (1641). Among the best of these poems are the lullaby "Sleep, baby, sleep, what ails my dear"; "Song for Lovers" ("Come, sweet heart, come, let us prove"); "Song for the Happily married" ("Since they in singing take delight"); and "Song for the Shepherd" ("Renowned men their herds to keep").

THE POETRY OF WORDSWORTH

Author: William Wordsworth (1770-1850)
Principal published works: An Evening Walk and *Descriptive Sketches,* 1793; *Lyrical Ballads,* 1798, 1800; *Poems in Two Volumes,* 1807; *The Excursion,* 1814; *Poems* and *The White Doe of Rylstone,* 1815; *Peter Bell* and *The Waggoner,* 1819; *The River Duddon,* 1820; *Ecclesiastical Sketches,* 1822; *Yarrow Revisited, and Other Poems,* 1835; *Poems Chiefly of Early and Late Years,* 1842; *The Prelude,* 1850

The most original genius of his age, William Wordsworth attacked the poetic diction and mannerisms fashionable in the mediocre poetry of the late eighteenth century, but his earliest poetry abounds in the personifications, hackneyed expressions, and apostrophes that he came to dislike most. His earliest poems, contained in *An Evening Walk* and *Descriptive Sketches,* reveal the careful observation of nature that he excelled in during his most productive and most creative years between 1797 and 1807. He lacked only the discipline and the vision that came to him after he discarded Godwinism and the revolutionary fervor of his youth.

In 1797 he met Samuel Taylor Coleridge, the strongest influence on his maturing style and philosophy, and entered the period of his greatest work. Through Coleridge he discovered the associational psychology of David Hartley and discarded William Godwin's rationalism. As a result of his new interest in psychology, he chose peasants, children, and mental defectives as subjects for his poetry. This choice marked a break with the decadent neo-classicism of his minor contemporaries. Many of the poems in *Lyrical Ballads,* written in conjunction with Coleridge, thus dealt with subjects from common life in order to reveal the unsophisticated operations of the human mind. For this publication Colderidge was to have written poems in the manner of "The Ancient Mariner," in which the supernatural was made believable, while Wordsworth agreed to write on basic human emotions directly and sincerely expressed in ordinary life. The volume was dominated by Wordsworth, however, and when the public encountered such poems as "We Are Seven," "The Idiot Boy," and "The Thorn," it was shocked. The reviewers were simply unable to accept such passages as the opening lines of "The Thorn":

> There is a Thorn—it looks so old,
> In truth, you'd find it hard to say
> How it could ever have been young,
> It looks so old and grey.

But much more important in *Lyrical Ballads* was Wordsworth's famous group of poems on nature, the first truly "Wordsworthian" poems. Everywhere in nature he found harmony and an active force that he identified with God. He felt no separation between Man and nature, all things joining in harmony. In "Tintern Abbey," for example, he gave full and lasting expression to the Romantic concept of nature as divinity:

> . . . I have learned
> To look on nature, not as in the hour
> Of thoughtless youth; but hearing often-
> times
> The still, sad music of humanity,
> Nor harsh nor grating, though of ample
> power
> To chasten and subdue. And I have felt
> A presence that disturbs me with the
> joy
> Of elevated thoughts. . . .

Nature was to him alive, powerful, and healthy; it was the panacea for man's mechanical urban life. Only the man who turned to nature, who felt the joy of nature, could find health in escape from the stagnation of contemporary life.

During the bitterly cold winter of 1798-1799, Wordsworth and his sister were isolated in Goslar, Germany, without books and friends. There he discovered a new type of poetry. Because of his circumstances, he fell back on his inner resources; he fed his imagination upon recollections of England until he was seized by emotions similar to those he had felt years before when the experience was immediate. These newly created emotions seemed to him to overflow, and from this artificially induced emotional experience he created poetry. He described this discovery in the Preface to the second edition of *Lyrical Ballads,* where he wrote that "poetry is the spontaneous overflow of powerful feelings: it takes its origin from emotion recollected in tranquillity: the emotion is contemplated till, by a species of reaction, the tranquillity gradually disappears, and an emotion, kindred to that which was before the subject of contemplation, is gradually produced, and does itself actually exist in the mind. In this mood successful composition generally begins, and in a mood similar to this it is carried on. . . ." In such a mood he composed many of his finest poems; for example, "There Was a Boy," "Lucy Grey," "I Wandered Lonely as a Cloud," and "My Heart Leaps Up."

The famous Preface in which he described his newly derived theory of poetry was meant to be an answer to the critical opposition to the first edition of *Lyrical Ballads,* but it was much more. Here Wordsworth stated the doctrines upon which he built his greatest (and his worst) poetry. Negatively, he wanted to end "the deluge of idle and extravagant stories in verse." Positively, he attempted to choose incidents and situations from common life, to relate them in simple language, to give poetry a worthy purpose, and to emphasize genuine feeling. Although Coleridge (a little piqued because Wordsworth attributed these doctrines to him) unmercifully attacked these doctrines in *Biographia Literaria* in 1817, they were essentially sound and readily acceptable to the English public. Much of Wordsworth's poetry, like "Michael" and "Lines Written in Early Spring," is grounded in these doctrines

and gave them additional popularity. But these doctrines, when followed too mechanically, led to dullness and flatness, the two faults most often found in Wordsworth's poetry.

The year 1802 was a landmark in Wordsworth's career. Momentous events both in his personal life (a trip to France to see his illegitimate daughter) and in European politics (Napoleon's absolute rule in France and the beginning of the Napoleonic War) widened his creative horizons. Also, his discovery of Milton's sonnets inspired him, and he began to compose in a more majestic and musical style. His visit to Calais to visit Annette Vallon and his daughter made him intimately aware of the dangers of Napoleon's tyranny, and with renewed faith in the causes of liberty he began a series of sonnets. He now believed that Nature worked through man in an unending struggle for freedom. Several of these sonnets—"London, 1802," "The World Is Too Much With Us," "To Toussaint L'Ouverture," "It Is a Beauteous Evening Calm and Free"—are among his most famous poems. His plea to return to moral virtue and to establish ordered liberty is nowhere better expresssed than in these lines from "London, 1802":

> We are selfish men;
> Oh! raise us up, return to us again;
> And give us manners, virtue, freedom,
>   power.

These sonnets established Wordsworth as the pre-eminent poet of English patriotism.

In the spring of 1802, Wordsworth began to fear that his imaginative vision might be failing. Because to him the imagination was the supreme guide to freedom and to morality, his fear led him to re-examine his concept of the role of the human imagination. This he does in the famous, "Ode: Intimations of Immortality as Recollected from Early Childhood." From Plato and the Neo-Platonists he received the notion that the child's dreamlike moments were actually carry-overs from a pre-natal spiritual existence and that maturation gradually caused the ecstatic vision to fade completely away. But the doctrine of pre-existence led him to the pessimistic conclusion that maturity was a time of inevitable grief. He left the poem unfinished until 1804, when he added the last three stanzas. In the addition he re-affirmed the child's loss of vision, but he added that the adult has wisdom, "the philosophic mind," which gives to man "thoughts that do often lie too deep for tears." This resolution, though not the most optimistic, promised some hope to the poet who felt his own powers dwindling. Still, it marked a profound change in his view of nature, as is apparent from his revisions made in *The Prelude* during 1839, for now he placed the joyful contemplation of nature in the past, forever lost to him.

The "Ode to Duty," also written in 1804, clarified his new position. Duty replaced the rapturous visions and freedom of youth to the extent that he thought of the supreme power as moral law, not nature. In this poem Wordsworth accepted the stoic creed of Seneca and Kant according to which peace of mind is self-imposed inner control. The tragic death of his brother in 1805 brought Wordsworth's earlier and later moods into sharp antagonism. In "Elegiac Stanzas" he re-nounced the visions of his youth and faced the harsh reality of experience, and in "The Happy Warrior" he confirmed his newly adopted stoicism. With these two poems Wordsworth passed into the final phase of his career.

The major work of his decline was *The Excursion*. With the gradual loss of his inspiration, he became more and more conservative, accepted Christian orthodoxy, and developed the tendency to be dogmatic and sententious. He became a sage rather than a poet. These changes were marked by a change in his poetic technique, to the extent that his later poetry not only lacked inspiration but was often dull and unnecessarily heavy.

These characteristics are reflected in *The Excursion*. This long poem, second in length only to *The Prelude,* was intended to be the second and middle part of a long work to be called *The Recluse: or Views on Man, on Nature, and on Human Life,* a great philosophical poem which he never finished. Despite the inferiority of the majority of *The Excursion,* there are some admirable flashes such as the moving story of Margaret in Book I, but the poem as a whole is a marked decline from the great poetry of 1797-1807. After this poem Wordsworth wrote little that was truly great, although he reached a peak of artistic and metrical virtuosity in the Ecclesiastical Sonnets. But the radical young men who had defended him in his youth had become more conservative adults or, like Coleridge, Shelley, Keats, and Byron, had died years before, and the new generation of young poets thought of him as a "lost leader." He remained popular and was buried in Westminster Abbey when he died, but even when he received the laureateship in 1843, his popularity was primarily based on the poems of his earlier greatness.

The problem that Wordsworth's poetry presents to a modern reader is relatively simple: he wrote too much when he was not inspired and threw too little in the fire. Too often his verse is pedestrian and prosy, even dull. A sense of humor might have saved some of his poetry, but he showed little humor, especially in the poetry after *The Excursion*. Still he presents us with a formidable canon, and few people would deny the greatness of his early poems. His best work has a calm dignity that best expresses itself in the unadorned beauty of a cleanly chiseled line, in such lines as the following stanza from the "Lucy Poems":

> A violet by a mossy stone
> Half hidden from the eye!
> —Fair as a star, when only one
> Is shining in the sky.

His worst work is marred by bathos. His

view of nature was stimulating enough to save the young John Stuart Mill from committing suicide and continues to speak to the problems of a mechanical age; his observations on the human mind —though outdated by the development of depth psychology—remain vital and revealing. Matthew Arnold's praise of Wordsworth in his famous reply to Leslie Stephen's criticism is still the most judicious:

"To exhibit this body of Wordsworth's best work, to clear away obstructions from around it, and to let it speak for itself, is what every lover of Wordsworth should desire. Until this has been done, Wordsworth . . . has not had a fair chance before the world. When once it has been done, he will make his way best, not by our advocacy of him, but by his own worth and power."

THE POETRY OF WYATT AND SURREY

Authors: Sir Thomas Wyatt (1503-1542) and Henry Howard, Earl of Surrey (1517?-1547)
First published: Poems included in Richard Tottel's *Songes and Sonettes,* 1557

Sir Thomas Wyatt and Henry Howard, Earl of Surrey, are generally considered the inaugurators of the golden age of English poetry in the reign of Elizabeth I. Both men were educated in the humanistic tradition, and they early became familiar with the polished lyric poetry of the Italians and the French. They attempted to demonstrate in their own works that English, too, was a language flexible and elegant enough for court poetry. Skillful experimenters with metrics, they imitated a number of the verse forms popular on the Continent, including the sonnet, ottava rima, terza rima, and the rondeau. Many of the lyrics of both poets are based upon the Petrarchan conventions of the cruel, scornful lady and her forlorn, rejected lover; a number of the sonnets are, in fact, either translations or close adaptations of Petrarch's works.

While Wyatt and Surrey are most often mentioned as precursors of Elizabethan poetry, students of their works have pointed out that their poetry is, in fact, quite different from that of Sidney, Spenser, and their followers. Typical "golden" poetry makes its effect through rich language and imagery, while in the work of Wyatt and Surrey there is a directness, a simplicity, and an awareness of the natural world that seems closer to Chaucer and his contemporaries than to the Renaissance poets. They form, in a sense, a bridge between the medieval world and the Elizabethan Age.

Surrey was for generations considered the more accomplished poet, but Wyatt, who was almost fifteen years older, is for many modern readers the more rewarding. His meters are less polished than Surrey's, but the human voice speaks through this very lack of smoothness. The best lines in his characteristically rugged, dramatic style have been compared with the poetry of John Donne.

One sonnet begins forcefully:

Farewell Love and all thy laws for
ever:
Thy baited hooks shall tangle me no
more.

Like Donne, Wyatt often conveys a strong sense of personal emotion in his works, even in those which are translated from the Italian and full of the conventional poses of the sonneteer.

In several of the sonnets the power comes from aburptly stated paradoxes. The monosyllables of the following lines are especially effective:

I find no peace, and all my war is
done;
I fear and hope; I burn, and freeze
like ice;
I fly above the wind, yet can I not
arise;
And nought I have, and all the world
I season.

The personal voice sounds most strongly in Wyatt's three satires on the materialism and folly of his times. These poems are, like the sonnets, adaptations of Italian and classical models, but they are not often marred by the awkward inversions of some of the shorter poems. The diction of the satires is direct; Wyatt, the disillusioned courtier speaks, emphasizing the ultimate futility of man's quest for wealth and earthly power.

In "Of the mean and sure estate," Wyatt uses the beast fable in the manner of medieval poets like Chaucer and Langland, recounting the familiar tale of the poor country mouse who visits her city-dwelling sister, expecting to spend the rest of her days feasting on rich food in comfortable lodgings. She has not, however, reckoned with the presence of the household cat, and after one encounter she returns terrified to her frugal but secure existence at home. Wyatt draws his moral in the concluding passage:

> O wretched minds, there is no gold that may
> Grant that you seek, no war, no peace, no strife.
> No, no, although thy head were hooped with gold,
> Sergeant with mace, with hauberk, sword, nor knife
> Cannot repulse the care that follow should.
> Each kind of life hath with him his disease.

The satire on court life is still more scathing. Wyatt, protesting passionately the hypocrisy of the society in which he had spent much of his life, gives his reasons for finally withdrawing from it:

> I cannot frame my tune to feign,
> To cloak the truth, for praise without desert
> Of them that list all vice for to retain.
>
> I cannot speak and look like as a saint,
> Use wiles for wit, and make deceit a pleasure;
> Call craft counsel, for lucre still to paint;
> I cannot wrest the law to fill the coffer
> With innocent blood to feed myself fat,
> And do most hurt where that most help I offer.

The third satire is a dialogue between a practical-minded narrator and a lively courtier who "trots still up and down, and never rests, but running day and night." When the courtier defends this way of life, saying that inactivity would be death to him, the narrator notes that his greatest problem will be finding money for his activities, and he makes several suggestions that show Wyatt's contempt for the values of his society. The courtier may profitably lie, steal, deceive an old man in his dotage and marry his wealthy widow, however old and ugly she may be; comfort may be found elsewhere. Or he may play Pandarus for the suitors of pretty relatives—for a price. The courtier here interrupts to say that he would not exchange his honest name for any amount of gold, and the narrator, incredulous, predicts the future of all who care for reputation:

> Nay, then, farewell! And if thou care for shame,
> Content thee then with honest poverty,
> With free tongue what thee mislikes to blame,
> And for thy truth sometime adversitie:
> And there withall this thing I shall thee give—
> In this world now little prosperity,
> And coin to keep as water in a sieve.

Wyatt's greatest poetic gift revealed itself neither in the Petrarchan sonnet nor in the satires, but in the charming lyrics he wrote to be sung before courtly audiences. His brief stanzas and simple refrains have the fluency that many of his sonnets lack, and his temperament seems to have lent itself admirably to both the melancholy complaints and the cynical wit of the forsaken lover. The grace and dignity of such poems as the following can be very moving.

> Forget not yet the tried intent,
> Of such a truth as I have meant,
> My great travail, so gladly spent,
> Forget not yet.
>
> Forget not yet when first began
> The weary life ye know, since when
> The suit, the service, none can tell,
> Forget not yet.

In a similar mood is another frequently anthologized lyric, where again the simplicity of the language and even the lack of regularity in the meter convey emotion. The first stanza, which begins "They flee from me that sometime did me seek," pictures birds fluttering about the poet's chamber, while a second verse transforms one of these wild creatures into a beautiful woman who embraces him. Almost as if he were awaking from deep sleep the poet muses:

> It was no dream; I lay broad waking.
> But all is turned thorough my gentleness,

Into a strange fashion of forsaking;
And I have leave to go, of her goodeness,
And she also to use newfangleness.
But since that I so kindely am served,
I would fain know what she hath deserved.

Wyatt's lyrics encompass a variety of meters and tones, and many others could be quoted to illustrate the many ways he treated his favorite theme, the sorrows of unrequited love.

Surrey followed Wyatt in using both Continental and classical models, increasing the flexibility of the language as he mastered various poetic meters. Perhaps his greatest contribution to the succeeding age was the blank verse which he adapted from the Italian for his translation of parts of Vergil's *Aeneid;* his unrhymed iambic pentameter lines do not have the majestic flow of Marlowe's or Shakespeare's dramatic poetry, but in attempting to create a smooth narrative meter Surrey made a real step forward. His version of Book II begins:

They whisted all, with fixed face attent,
When Prince Aeneas from the royal seat
Thus gan to speak: "O Queen, it is thy will
I should renew a woe cannot be told,
How that the Greeks did spoil and overthrow
The Phrygian wealth and wailful realm of Troy:
Those ruthfull things that I my self beheld,
And whereof no small part fell to my share.

Surrey's second major contribution was his modification of the Italian sonnet form with its division into octave and sestet and its extremely demanding rhyme scheme. He developed a pattern very close to the three quatrains and couplet of the Shakespearian sonnet. Typical of his treatment of this verse form is a poem that reveals his sensitivity to nature, a quality that distinguishes him from Wyatt:

The soote season that bud and bloom forth brings
With green hath clad the hill and eke the vale,
The nightingale with feathers new she sings,
The turtle to her make hath told her tale.
Summer is come, for every spray now springs,
The hart hath hung his old head on the pale,
The buck in brake his winter coat he flings,
The fishes float with new repaired scale,
The adder all her slough away she slings,
The swift swallow pursueth the flyes small,
The busy bee her honey now she mings,—
Winter is worn, that was the flowers' bale:
And thus I see, among these pleasant things
Each care decays—and yet my sorrow springs.

Most of Surrey's sonnets are typical laments of forsaken lovers, smoother in meter and language than Wyatt's, but generally less moving.

While modern readers have focused their attention on the sonnets, lyrics, and satires of both Wyatt and Surrey, it must be noted that one of the verse forms Surrey often and Wyatt occasionally used was the jog-trot meter, the poulter's measure, a twelve-syllable line followed by a fourteen-syllable one. Surrey handled it as skillfully as possible, varying stresses and pauses to keep the singsong rhythm from becoming oppressive, but no matter how well handled, this was not a verse form for great poetry. One of the most appealing examples of Surrey's work in this meter is "Lady Surrey's Lament for Her Absent Lord," written by the poet while he was serving with the English army in Boulogne. He imagines his wife dreaming that he has returned.

Another time, the same doth tell me he is come,

And playing, where I shall him find,
  with T., his little son.
  So forth I go apace, to see that life-
    some sight,
And with a kiss, me thinks I say,
  "Now welcome home, my knight;
  Welcome, my sweet, alas! the stay
    of my welfare;
Thy presence bringeth forth a truce
  betwixt me and my care."

Two of Surrey's poems show his particular talents clearly. "Prisoned in Windsor, He Recounteth His Pleasure There Passed," written in the iambic pentameter quatrains of Wyatt's satires, is a poignant reminiscence of the happy days of the poet's youth, spent at Windsor Castle as the companion of the Earl of Richmond, the illegitimate son of King Henry VIII. Surrey draws a vivid picture of the life of the two boys, recalling

The gravel ground, with sleeves tied
  on the helm,
On foaming horse, with swords and
  friendly hearts,
With cheer, as though one should another whelm,
Where we have fought, and chased oft
  with darts;
With silver drops the mead yet spread
  for ruth,
In active games of nimbleness and
  strength,
Where we did strain, trained with
  swarms of youth,
Our tender limbs that yet shot up in
  length.

The poem concludes with Surrey's lament for his boyhood friend, now dead; his grief at his imprisonment is lessened by the memory of his greater loss.

Another of Surrey's outstanding works is his elegy "Of the death of Sir Thomas Wyatt the Elder," a tribute to the character of a man whom he certainly admired, whether or not he knew him well. Many phrases stand out as particularly apt, characterizing the older poet both as a fine individual and as the pattern of the Renaissance courtier. Surrey's estimate of Wyatt as a poet is doubtless hyperbolic, but it reveals his sense of debt to him:

A hand that taught what might be
  said in rhyme,
That reft Chaucer the glory of his wit,
A mark the which (unparfited, for
  time)
Some may approach, but never none
  shall hit.

The devoutly Christian conclusion follows the typical elegiac pattern, revealing both grief for personal loss and joy in the elevation of the dead man for all eternity:

But to the heavens that simple soul is
  fled,
Which left with such as covet Christ
  to know
Witness of faith that never shall be
  dead;
Sent for our health, but not received
  so.
Thus for our guilt this jewel have we
  lost:
The earth, his bones; the heavens possess his ghost.

Both poets composed metrical versions of parts of the Bible. Surrey, in particular, adapted passages to apply to his own desperate situation. Many of his Biblical poems were written while he was in the tower awaiting trial and the execution he gradually realized was inevitable. The recurrent theme of these works is the futility of his lifelong search for happiness in worldly pleasures and success and his present resignation to his fate and reconciliation with God.

Surrey's many love lyrics show a facility that approaches Wyatt's in the use of varied stanza forms. His poems in this manner lack some of the emotional power of his predecessor's work, but they are nonetheless pleasing:

Give place, ye lovers here before
That spent your boasts and brags in
  vain,
My lady's beauty passeth more
The best of yours, I dare well sayn,
Than doth the sun the candle-light,
Or brightest day the darkest night.

It is difficult to assess the contributions of Wyatt and Surrey to succeeding generations, but they certainly encouraged the vogue for court poetry, and they paved the way for the development of English as a poetic language by men like Sidney and Spenser. However, the two poets should be read today not for their historical significance, but rather for the dignity and the quiet appeal of their own work. While they rank among the near-great English poets rather than among the supreme masters, each has his own strength and lasting appeal.

THE POETRY OF YEATS

Type of work: Poetry
Author: William Butler Yeats (1865-1939)
Principal published works: Mosada: A Dramatic Poem, 1886; *The Wanderings of Oisin,*
1889; *Poems,* 1895; *The Wind Among the Reeds,* 1899; *In the Seven Woods,* 1903;
The Green Helmet and Other Poems, 1910; *Responsibilities,* 1914; *The Wild Swans at
Coole,* 1917; *Michael Robartes and the Dancer,* 1920; *Later Poems,* 1922; *The Cat and
the Moon and Certain Poems,* 1924; *The Tower,* 1928; *The Winding Stair,* 1933;
Collected Poems, 1933; *The King of the Great Clock Tower,* 1934; *A Full Moon in
March,* 1935; *New Poems,* 1938; *Last Poems and Plays,* 1940; *Collected Poems,* 1949

The conflict that the antimonies between dream and action caused in the mind of William Butler Yeats could not be resolved in the verse tradition of the Pre-Raphaelites. This was the poetry, together with that of Shelley and Keats and the plays of Shakespeare, with which he was most familiar. It was also the tradition to which he was closest in time. As he did not have a background of coherent culture on which to base his poetry, nor a personally satisfying faith, Yeats throughout his life had to create his own systems of thought—create, in fact, the convention in which he was to write.

In the introduction to *A Vision,* he said: "I wished for a system of thought that would leave my imagination free to create as it chose and yet make all it created, or could create, part of the one history, and that the soul's." His search for reality in belief and feeling was aided by his knowledge that the Romantic poets expressed faith in the power of the imagination. This knowledge also strengthened his conviction that the problems of human existence would never be solved by science and that answers would have to come from quite different disciplines: therefore, both his philosophy and his actions were of paramount importance to him in the writing of poetry.

Yeats spent many years in the study of the occult: spiritualism, magic, mysticism, and theosophy. His feelings for Ireland and for the Pre-Raphaelites led him, early in his life, to the study and use of ancient Irish myths. His hopes of independence for Ireland and his periodic identification with Irish nationalism, also a part of the fabric of his verse, were influenced by his passion for Maud Gonne and his friendship with his patron, Lady Gregory. He believed the system expounded in *A Vision* was revealed to him by his wife's power as a medium. Thus for Yeats, as for all poets, the pattern of his relationships, interests, beliefs, and loyalties was the material of his poetry. However, great poetry is always the expression of one man's personality in such a way that it is generally or universally meaningful. Magic, nationalism, and myth partly formed Yeats's complex personality, and his prose writings in these areas are undoubtedly esoteric. Although it was through these studies that Yeats was able to write as he did, it is not through them that the reader appreciates his poetry. All Yeats's poetry can be enjoyed and understood when carefully read, without reference to any of his prose. Yeats, in fact, took care to make his work understandable, and one of the most interesting aspects in the study of his poetry is his lifelong preoccupation with clarity, simplicity, and exactness.

This clarity was the goal toward which he worked throughout his career. For Yeats, symbol was the means by which the natural and the supernatural could be fused and the antimonies be resolved. Writing in many *personae,* he worked toward this unified expression of reality, with the result that the continuous development of his powers and his ultimate success are both rare and exciting achievements. Yeats's dedication to his art was such that to the end of his life his conscious goals were always in advance of the poems he had completed.

Yeats was a lyric poet, but his belief in and practice of "active virtue"—that is, following a discipline that one has forged oneself—makes his verse essentially dramatic. His first volumes of poetry express the sensibility of the Pre-Raphaelites; the lyrics are slight and the emotion, incompletely realized, often expresses his indecision between the life of dream and that of action. Twilight and longing predominate in these poems.

In his fourth volume, *In the Seven Woods,* published in 1903, Yeats began to find his true voice. Emotion is particularized and he has started to speak with authority. His technique is more sure and his tone more varied. In "Adam's Curse," in which the poet discusses the labor of writing poetry with a woman whom he loves, he uses common words and speech idioms which firmly link the poem to reality:

Better go down upon your marrow-bones
And scrub a kitchen pavement or break
   stones
Like an old pauper, in all kinds of
   weather;
For to articulate sweet sounds together
Is to work harder than all these.

In his verse plays of this period Yeats was beginning deliberately to eschew abstraction and to introduce more direct and bold speech into his work. His 1910 volume, *The Green Helmet and Other Poems,* shows this technique in his lyric verse, which is becoming more dramatic and assertive. In "No Second Troy" the use of Greek myth approximates a reconciliation between dream and reality.

The 1914 volume, *Responsibilities,* shows an increase in force. Here Yeats uses other voices, or *personae,* of beggars, fools, and hermits to present his ideas. At that time he was encouraged further in his progress toward exactness of expression and the use of only the most mean-

ingful images by his contact with Ezra Pound, who insisted that Yeats remove all abstractions from his verse. He appears to have learned quickly and well from the younger poet, and in subsequent poems he is able to integrate completely his theories of history and personality, and his feelings of despair for Ireland. He also learned to pare his images so that they are totally relevant to his emotion:

Things fall apart, the centre cannot
   hold;
Mere anarchy is loosed upon the world,
The blood-dimmed tide is loosed, and
   everywhere
The ceremony of innocence is drowned.

The Tower, published in 1928, contains several of Yeats's finest poems. The most brilliant and complex of these is "Sailing to Byzantium." The dazzling civilization of Byzantium which had successfully withstood the power of Rome as Yeats would probably have liked Ireland to withstand that of England, became for him the symbol of eternal art and of the fusion of the creator with the work of art. The reconciliation of youth and age, passion and intellect, is effected by the symbolic representation of the wisdom of the inspired soul in a supernatural form. In this poem, natural birds sing of the cycle of human life and the created birds of Byzantium, of the cycle of history. The glory of the old and of the young is here presented with a single steady vision, and the conflict between them has been resolved:

This is no country for old men. The
   young
In one another's arms, birds in the trees
—Those dying generations—at their
   song,
The salmon-falls, the mackerel-crowded
   seas,
Fish, flesh, or fowl, commend all sum-
   mer long
Whatever is begotten, born, and dies.
He continues:
An aged man is but a paltry thing,
A tattered coat upon a stick, unless
Soul clap its hands and sing, and louder
   sing. . . .

The poet has sailed to Byzantium that he may thus sing. His soul after death will not take "bodily form from any natural thing" but will be one of the singing birds of metal and enamel that the goldsmiths make to amuse the Emperor,

> Or set upon a golden bough to sing
> To lords and ladies of Byzantium
> Of what is past, or passing, or to come.

Another unified vision of life which is not dependent upon the supernatural is communicated in the poem "Among School Children." The mastery of technique which gives "Sailing to Byzantium" its *tour de force* brilliance, enables Yeats in this poem to communicate the feeling of peace after storm. The poet visits a convent school where the children see him as an old man, and as the children stare in mild curiosity, he is reminded of the "Ledaean body" of a woman he had loved, and this vision causes him to feel so joined in sympathy with her that he can visualize her as she must have been as a child:

> For even daughters of the swan share
> Something of every paddler's heritage.

The vision of the childhood of the woman who caused him much pain leads him to the thought that women would not think motherhood worth while if they could see their progeny at sixty. His suggestion that mothers as well as nuns worship images returns the poem to the convent school setting. In the last stanza of the poem Yeats, by a unifying image of continuity and completeness, reconciles the opposing forces of age and youth at the level of reality.

The poems written in the three years before Yeats's death at seventy-four show no diminution of power. He was still intent on his search for unity and reality of expression. In "The Circus Animals' Desertion," he reviews his poetic output and says that until he was an old man the machinery of his poetry was still in evidence:

> My circus animals were still on show,
> Those stilted boys, that gilded chariot.

He lists his old themes: the Irish myths, his lost love, and his preoccupation with the theater, and he tells how he dramatized his love in his plays. He faces his own delight in dreams which he feared would inhibit him from reality: "This dream itself had all my thought and love." He speaks of the *personae* in which he wrote and of the characters of Irish history:

> Players and painted stage took all my
> love
> And not those things they were the
> emblems of.

The reversal and resolution of these ideas comes in the last verse where he evaluates the use of images in his poetry, by questioning their origin and finding that they indeed had their bases in reality.

Thus his adolescent faith in the imagination had been justified and he could join the ranks of those whom he admired and who had fused the subjective and objective self into a meaningful whole: "The antithetical self comes to those who are no longer deceived, whose passion is reality."

The philosophy that Yeats so carefully constructed was the basis for a personal vision of life, which by unswerving dedication to craftsmanship and constantly renewed emotional and intellectual vitality he presented in his poetry in all its varied facets, and with always increasing significance.

POINT COUNTER POINT

Type of work: Novel
Author: Aldous Huxley (1894- 1963)
Type of plot: Social criticism
Time of plot: 1920's
Locale: England
First published: 1928

Principal characters:
> PHILIP QUARLES, a novelist
> ELINOR, Philip's wife
> SIDNEY QUARLES, Philip's father
> RACHEL, Philip's mother
> JOHN BIDLAKE, Elinor's father
> MRS. BIDLAKE, her mother
> LITTLE PHILIP, Philip's and Elinor's son
> BURLAP, editor of *Literary World*
> BEATRICE GILRAY, his mistress
> SPANDRELL, a cynic
> EVERARD WEBLEY, a disciple of force
> WALTER BIDLAKE, Elinor's brother
> MARJORIE CARLING, Walter's mistress
> LUCY TANTAMOUNT, Walter's infatuation

Critique:

Point Counter Point contains a novel within a novel. Within the framework of the outer novel, Huxley places a novelist who observes the activities of his own world of fictional characters and then plots a novel that is constructed exactly as Huxley has written *Point Counter Point*. From one set of individuals to another the focus of the novel moves, balancing each life against its counterpoint. The lives of these people repeat the same patterns in different forms, while Philip Quarles plots a novel based on their lives. It is apparent that Quarles is Huxley himself plotting *Point Counter Point*. Huxley would have us believe that the theme of this novel is one of variations on a single theme, the struggle of natural sexual desire and escapism against the bond of marriage.

The Story:

John Bidlake was an artist with an artist's temperament. He had been married three times. The first marriage had ended in bitter resentment. The second marriage had been idyllic for him, but

Isabelle had died two years later, leaving her husband with a void that he had tried to erase by pretending that he had never known a woman named Isabelle. His third marriage had lasted, although John had not lived with his wife for many years. He merely maintained a home where he went whenever he became ill enough to need his wife's nursing skill.

The children of his third marriage, Walter and Elinor, had not been too successful in their own experiments with marriage as a social institution. Walter had been living with a married woman named Marjorie Carling for a year and a half, and he was growing tired of her. Worse than his moral ties to Marjorie was the fact that she tenaciously tried to possess him, rejecting his proposal that they live together as close friends, each going his own free direction with whomever he pleased. Now Marjorie was going to have a baby, and her whining jealousy toward his latest infatuation, Lucy Tantamount, was pricking Walter's conscience. It annoyed him immensely that he was making Marjorie unhappy by going to a party at Tantamount House without her.

Elinor and Philip Quarles were traveling abroad, having left little Philip behind under the care of a governess and his grandmother, Mrs. Bidlake. Philip was a novelist. As he traveled through life, he jotted down in his notebook incidents and thoughts that might make rich material for his next novel. His mind was turned inward, introspective, and his self-centered interests gave him little time for emotional experience. Elinor, wishing that he could love her as much as she loved him, resigned herself to the unhappy dilemma of being loved as much as Philip could possibly love any woman.

Denis Burlap, editor of the *Literary World*, flattered himself with the just conceit that although his magazine was not a financial success, it as least contributed to the intellectual life of his time. When Walter, who was one of his chief contributors, asked for more pay, Burlap hedged until Walter felt ashamed of his demands. Burlap was attracted to Beatrice Gilray, a pathetic figure who had feared the very touch of a man ever since she had been attacked by her uncle while riding in a taxicab. Burlap hoped eventually to seduce Beatrice. Meanwhile they were living together.

Another significant member of this set was Spandrell, an indolent son of a doting mother who supported him. There was also Everard Webley, a friend of Elinor and an active political figure.

Philip's parents still lived together. Sidney Quarles pretended that he was writing a long history, but he had not progressed far beyond the purchase of office equipment. Rachel Quarles, assuming the burden of managing their affairs, endured with patience Sidney's whims and mild flirtations. Now it was someone in London, for Sidney made frequent trips to the British Museum to gather material for his history. The girl

in London with whom Sidney had been having an affair appeared one day at his country house and in loud and furious language informed her paramour that she was going to have a baby. When Mrs. Quarles appeared, Sidney quietly left the room. The girl threatened Rachel and then returned to London. Later the affair was settled quietly.

Marjorie appealed to Walter's pity enough to cause him some degree of anguish because of his association with Lucy Tantamount. Lucy herself was not much interested in Walter. Becoming tired of London, she went to Paris.

Elinor and Philip returned from abroad to find little Philip faring well under the care of his governess and his grandmother. John Bidlake, having learned that he was dying of cancer, had returned to his wife's home. He had become a cantankerous patient and treated little Philip with alternate kindness and harshness.

With Lucy in Paris, Philip had persuaded Walter to take Marjorie to the Quarles home in the country, in the hope that some sort of reconciliation would come about from this association. Rachel Quarles began to like Marjorie, and the pregnant woman found herself gaining cheer under this new affection. Shortly after she and Walter had come to the Quarles estate, Walter received a letter from Lucy in Paris, telling him that she had found a new lover who had seduced her in a shabby Parisian studio. With her newly-acquired content, Marjorie felt sympathetic toward Walter, who was crestfallen at the cruel rejection he had received from Lucy.

Everard Webley had long been in love with Elinor. Sometimes she wondered whether Philip would care if she went to another man, and she decided that it would be Philip's own fault if she turned to Everard. She felt that a breach was forming between herself and Philip, but she could not seem to gain enough attention or concern from him to make him realize what was happening.

She arranged a rendezvous with Everard.

Behind the scenes of love-making and unfaithfulness lurked the political enmity of Spandrell and Everard. Perhaps it was the lack of a useful purpose in his life that allowed Spandrell's plan to grow in his mind. Elinor Quarles was home alone awaiting Everard's call when Spandrell and a telegram arrived simultaneously. The telegram urged Elinor to come to her father's home, for little Philip was ill. Elinor asked Spandrell to wait and tell Everard that she could not keep her appointment with him. Spandrell agreed. When Everard arrived at Elinor's home, Spandrell attacked him and killed him. Spandrell lugged the dead body into an automobile and drove it away. Later that evening he met Philip and told him his son was ill.

Philip arrived at the Bidlake estate the next day in time to hear the doctor say that young Philip had meningitis.

For days Elinor stayed by the child's side, waiting for the crisis to pass. One night the sick boy opened his eyes and told his parents that he was hungry. They were overjoyed at his apparent recovery, but later that night he died suddenly. As they had done in the past, Elinor and Philip escaped their unpleasant world by going abroad.

For a long while the Webley murder baffled the police. Spandrell, haunted by his own conscience, sent the police a note which stated that Everard's murderer would be found at a certain address at a certain hour. On their arrival, the police found Spandrell dead with a letter of confession in his hands.

Burlap was the only happy man among these sensualists and intellectuals. One night he and Beatrice pretended they were children and splashed merrily taking their bath together. Happiness was like misery in the modern world, it seemed—lustful, dull, selfish.

Further Critical Evaluation of the Work:

Point Counter Point can be seen as the culmination of Aldous Huxley's early works. In each of his previous novels, *Crome Yellow* (1921), *Antic Hay* (1923), and *Those Barren Leaves* (1925), Huxley had tried to develop a form through which he could present his satirical vision of, and philosophical ideas about, the intellectual, moral, and spiritual condition of upper middle-class English society shortly after World War I. Although each of these earlier books contains biting satire and provocative ideas, they are relatively static and formless. But, in *Point Counter Point,* Huxley hit upon the organizing principle which offered both the formal control and the flexibility he needed to realize his artistic intentions—a structural analogy between prose fiction and music.

This "musicalization of fiction" involves a counterpointing of various character types against each other in various "parallel, contrapuntal plots." Since Huxley was writing what he termed "novels of ideas" in these early works, he seldom presents well-rounded "realistic" characters. They are, rather, satirical embodiments of twentieth century "types" that Huxley wished to examine by showing what happens when their one-sided behavior is pushed to its extreme. To cite a few of the novel's many examples: Everard Webley, the fascistic apostle of violence, is murdered. John Bidlake, the painter, has "devoured" people and things all of his life; he is, in turn, devoured by the cancer growing in his stomach. Spandrell, a cynic who cannot accept his own nihilism, drives himself to increasingly "evil" experiences in order to "affirm" negatively, but succeeds only in destroying himself needlessly and pointlessly. Burlap, who sees himself as a grieving widower and religious leader, turns his "spirituality" into childish sensuality. And Quarles, Huxley's fictional alter-ego, is so much the intellectual that he only writes about the lives of others instead of living his own.

As an alternative to this gross one-sidedness, Huxley pleads for "balance" in life and "wholeness" in living. But his spokesman, Mark Rampion, a character modeled on D. H. Lawrence, is only a querulous voice (Lawrence called his fictional counterpart a "gasbag"). Since this society is incapable of utilizing positive values, there is no dramatic function for Rampion in the novel, aside from sardonic commentaries on the other characters.

Thus, Rampion's positive statements cannot offset the negative vision projected by Huxley's large cast of grotesque "perverts" (Rampion's term). What remains is a brilliant, vivid picture of an overly sophisticated, sex-obsessed, self-devouring society. In *Point Counter Point,* Aldous Huxley presented one of the definitive portraits of the age that provoked it.

POLYEUCTE

Type of work: Drama
Author: Pierre Corneille (1606-1684)
Type of plot: Religious tragedy
Time of plot: Third century
Locale: Mélitène, the capital of Armenia
First presented: c. 1643

Principal characters:
   FÉLIX, Roman governor of Armenia
   PAULINE, his daughter
   POLYEUCTE, his son-in-law, an Armenian nobleman
   NÉARQUE, Polyeucte's friend
   STRATONICE, Pauline's friend
   ALBIN, Félix' friend
   SÉVÈRE, a Roman warrior, in love with Pauline

Critique:

Polyeucte, although a favorite of the general public in Corneille's time, was not considered his best play, that distinction being reserved for *The Cid* (1636). Modern criticism, however, has reversed this judgment. Despite its somewhat improbable plot, climaxed by miraculous conversions, the play holds for today's public particular religious interest, since it deals with the working of divine grace in the human soul. It is, however, the strong delineation of the main characters that has won for this work its present universal acclaim.

The Story:

Pauline, daughter of Félix, the Roman governor in Mélitène, had been married fourteen days to Polyeucte, an Armenian nobleman. Terrified by dreams which seemed to portend her husband's death, she vainly sought to delay his departure on a secret mission, the nature of which was known only to his friend Néarque. She related her fears to her friend Stratonice and told her of her earlier love for Sévère, a Roman of high birth whom her father would not allow her to marry because of Sévère's lack of fortune. When the Emperor Décie had appointed Félix governor of Armenia, she had accompanied him and dutifully married an Armenian nobleman of her father's selec-

tion. Meanwhile, they had heard that Sévère had met a hero's death while aiding the emperor in battle against the Persians. According to the report, the young Roman's body had never been found.

Now Pauline had dreamed that Sévère was not dead, but threatened her husband's life; that a band of impious Christians had thrown Polyeucte at the feet of Sévère, and that she, Pauline, crying out for aid from her father, had seen him raise a dagger to pierce Polyeucte's breast.

Her fears were further stirred when her father approached and said that Sévère was alive and was at that moment entering the city. It seemed that the King of Persia, struck by his gallantry, had reclaimed the body from the battlefield in order to gain the Roman honorable burial. But miraculously life had been restored to Sévère and the Persians had sent him to Rome in exchange for royal prisoners. Thereafter his greater deeds in war had bound him closer to the emperor, who had sent him to Armenia to proclaim the good news of his victories and to make sacrifices of thanksgiving to the gods.

Because his love for Pauline had really brought Sévère to Armenia, that Roman, informed by his servant that Pauline was

---

POLYEUCTE by Pierre Corneille, from CHIEF PLAYS OF CORNEILLE. Translated by Lacy Lockert. By permission of the publishers, Princeton University Press. Copyright, 1952, 1957, by Princeton University Press.

wedded, decided that life was not worth living and that he would rather die in battle. But first he would see Pauline. When they met, she told him that if hers alone had been the choice she would, despite his poverty, have chosen him; but that now she was married she would remain loyal to the husband whom she had learned to love. They bade each other farewell, he ready to die in battle, she to pray for him in secret.

Polyeucte returned from his mission, on which he had been secretly baptized a Christian. Ordered by a messenger from Félix to attend the sacrifices in the temple, he and Néarque planned to defy the idolatry of the worshipers there. Pauline told him of Sévère's visit but added that she had obtained his promise not to see her again.

Stratonice, a witness at the temple sacrifices, hurried to Pauline with the news that Polyeucte had become a Christian, a traitor to the Roman gods; he had mocked the sacred mysteries and, with Néarque, had declared that their god alone was the almighty king of earth and heaven. This defilement, Félix declared, would cost Néarque his life, but he hoped Polyeucte might come to his senses and recant after witnessing the punishment and death of his friend.

When Albin, the friend of Félix, brought news that Néarque was dead, he added that Polyeucte had witnessed his execution undismayed. Pauline, reminding her father that Polyeucte was his choice and that in marrying him she had but fulfilled her filial duty, begged him to spare his life. But Félix, fearing the thunderbolts of his gods and Sévère as well, refused to listen when Albin urged that Polyeucte's sentence be left to the emperor. Besides, he was tempted by the thought that Polyeucte's death would allow Sévère to wed his daughter and thus he would gain for himself a far more powerful protector than he now had. Meanwhile, Pauline visited Polyeucte in jail with the plea that if he must worship his chosen god he should do so silently and secretly, and thus give Félix

grounds for mercy. To her importunings Polyeucte replied that he was done with mortal ties, that he loved her, but loved his God more.

Polyeucte called for Sévère and told him that even as his wedding had parted the true love of Sévère and Pauline, so now by dying he hoped to bring them happily together. He hoped also that they would die Christians. Declaring himself ready for death, he was marched off by his guards.

Sévère was amazed at this example of magnanimity, but his hopes were shattered when Pauline told him she could never marry him, that it would stain her honor to wed anyone who, even innocently, had brought Polyeucte to his sad fate. She begged him, however, to try to save her husband from the death her father had ordered. He consented, if for no other reason than to prove to Pauline that he could equal her in nobility and thus be worthy of her. Félix, although he regarded this intervention on behalf of a rival as a trick to expose him to the full strength of the emperor's wrath, made one last effort to sway his son-in-law. He told Polyeucte that only on Sévère's account had he publicly taken his rigid stand and that he himself would adopt Christianity if Polyeucte would only pretend to follow the old gods until after Sévère had left the city. But Polyeucte saw through this wile and refused. Angered, Félix said he would avenge his gods and himself. When Pauline entered, Polyeucte commanded her to wed Sévère or die with him a Christian.

Again Pauline pleaded for Polyeucte's life, and again Félix was moved to make another attempt to persuade Polyeucte to abjure his new faith, but to no avail. Bidding farewell to Pauline, Polyeucte was marched out to death by Félix' order. Pauline rushed out after him, lamenting that she too would die if he were to die. Félix ordered Albin to deter her but issued his order too late; Pauline had seen her husband executed. Seeing him die, she felt that his death had unsealed her own eyes, acting as a divine visitation of grace. She declared herself a Christian, ready for death.

Sévère upbraided Félix for Polyeucte's death and threatened retaliation. Félix, suddenly yielding to a strange feeling that overcame him, declared that his son-in-law's death had made him a Christian.

This sudden conversion struck Sévère as miraculous. He ordered Félix to retain his position of authority, and promised to use all his persuasion to urge Emperor Décie to revoke his cruel commands and to let all worship the gods of their choice without fear of punishment.

Further Critical Evaluation of the Work:

Pierre Corneille's *Polyeucte* is based on a pious legend which contains a kernel of historical fact—the execution of Polyeucte and Néarque, two Armenian soldiers of Rome's Twelfth "Thundering" Legion, for their devotion to Christianity, in 251 A.D. Corneille took only minor liberties with the legend, according to which Polyeuctus (Polyeucte in French) was a son-in-law of the Governor, Félix, who ordered his execution. The martyr was, according to the legend, reluctant to die because of his love for his pagan wife, the Governor's daughter, Pauline.

Corneille shocked many of his contemporaries by making this Christian legend into a "tragedy" or, as he later called it, a "Christian tragedy." Since *Polyeucte* was written, literary critics have argued whether the Christian doctrine of salvation is compatible with the Greek concept of tragedy. Perhaps it is not, but there is a sad irony that approaches tragedy in the situation of Félix at the end of the play. Although he has found eternal salvation, he must live the rest of his life on earth knowing that he had to execute Polyeucte and Pauline in order to find it.

The plot outline of *Polyeucte* resembles somewhat that of Sophocles' *Antigone*. Félix, like Creon, is torn between duty to the state, which requires him to execute his own child's spouse, and duty to the family, which forbids this. But the conflict in *Polyeucte* is not strictly that of family against state. Polyeucte's motive for defying his father-in-law, unlike Antigone's for defying hers, has nothing to do with the family; his duty is to the Christian God, who transcends everything. Polyeucte's love for Pauline, unlike Antigone's for Haemon, is not a comfort on the way to the grave, but the one source of discomfort on the way to Heaven. The climax—the sudden conversions of Pauline and Félix—is not the expected result of human nature; it is a dramatized miracle. By using Greek forms and devices, Corneille comes as close as possible to demonstrating on stage the Christian miracle of God's work in human hearts.

THE PONDER HEART

Type of work: Novella
Author: Eudora Welty (1909-   )
Time: The present
Locale: Clay, a small town in Mississippi
First published: 1953

Principal characters:
> MISS EDNA EARL PONDER, the proprietor of a small family hotel
> UNCLE DANIEL PONDER, her uncle who loves to give things away
> BONNIE DEE PEACOCK PONDER, his "trial" wife

Reading any of Miss Welty's books, one is always tempted to contrast her treatment of her material with the treatment accorded the same sort of material by her fellow Mississippian, William Faulkner. Such a contrast is never to the disadvantage of either author, since their viewpoints are diametrically opposed. Each is legitimate; each is unique. Both put their characters in a locale that is easily distinguishable as the slightly seedy, much ingrown, certainly picturesque country of the Deep South. Both concentrate on characters that are slightly off the norm, the kind that are excused by their fellow townsmen because they are familiar and loved. But where Faulkner was likely to find tragedy, Eudora Welty can find a gentle comedy.

Miss Welty has a splendid knack of drawing her people and her towns so that the reader is tempted to fit names to them from his own knowledge and experience. Her people, her towns, her country really are Mississippi, but the tales she tells of them are not necessarily limited by the locale. In *The Ponder Heart,* for instance, her story of the largesse of the slightly simple-minded Uncle Daniel Ponder, the loving kindness of his townsmen, and the simplicity of his "trial" wife, Bonnie Dee, is not strictly limited to Southern characters. It might just as well be the tale of people in any small town. Basically, it is the story of the unfortunates in this world who have no clear way of understanding one another.

Most of Eudora Welty's work has been with the short story. *The Ponder Heart* might be called a novella, a very short

novel. Actually, it is a breathless monologue throughout, done by Miss Edna Earl Ponder, proprietor of a small family hotel and niece to Uncle Daniel, whose protector against the world she has become.

Uncle Daniel, rich as Croesus and correspondingly generous, was not very bright as the world rates people, but he was impressive-looking and neat as a pin. He invariably wore spotless white suits, a red bow tie, and carried a huge Stetson hat just swept off his head. Held under his father's thumb until he was mature, he had little chance to be as generous, as his conscience dictated. He had given Edna Earl the hotel she ran, but his father had been glad to get rid of that. The cattle and fields he gave away were easily retrieved. People liked him because he always gave something away, even if it was only small change; but he always felt alone.

After his father's death, Edna Earl was responsible for him. She felt fairly safe about his giving things away as long as he was unconcerned about money. His father had always given him an allowance of three dollars a week. She continued that practice with no objection from Uncle Daniel because he was happy to have a little change in his pocket. His desire to give things to people made a wonderful topic of conversation for Edna Earl to discourse on with the traveling salesmen. Stories of Uncle Daniel involved the whole town and most of the surrounding countryside.

One day Uncle Daniel escaped Edna Earl long enough to take a new little salesgirl at the 5 & 10 as his second bride. Edna Earl was rather reticent about his first wife's leaving him, though there seemed to be no rancor on either side. Since Uncle Daniel assured her that his second wife was just "on trial," Edna Earl had to sit back and see what would happen. Bonnie Dee Peacock Ponder, a little piece of white trash, held Uncle Daniel enthralled for five years before she disappeared. He always claimed she looked good enough to eat and she could cut his hair better than anyone had ever done before.

Edna Earl, in telling this story of *The Ponder Heart,* prepared her listener, a traveling salesman guest in her hotel, for the change in Uncle Daniel since the salesman last saw him. As headlong as the tale is, the reader is not too hard pressed to believe that Edna Earl might have crammed it all in just before dinner. There is the picture of Uncle Daniel as he was, of his married life, and of his most recent experiences. In the telling, Edna Earl becomes as clear as Uncle Daniel. She is the last respectable member of a family disintegrating; she is conscious of her dignity and jealous of the position she wishes for Uncle Daniel. She feels responsible for making things run, whether it is the rummage sale every week for the Negroes or Uncle Daniel's life. She wants things to run her way, however, and is not shy in demanding her way from the servants, the lawyers, the shopkeepers, or even the judge. She deplores the fact that the town is no longer on a through route, but she loves it. She despises the Peacock family as trash, but she does her duty by them because Uncle Daniel married one of them. Miss Welty brings in everyone and everything in town, every accent, every eccentricity, until the reader feels perfectly at home in Clay. If one begins to doubt that anyone in Clay is perfectly normal, that seems natural too.

Edna Earl's monologue covers the hunt for Bonnie Dee, her return, her turning Uncle Daniel out of his own house, her wholesale purchase of useless things (like the washer she put on the front porch before the house was wired for electricity), her sudden death, and the trial of Uncle Daniel for her murder.

As a bribe to bring Bonnie Dee back home after her disappearance, Edna Earl told Uncle Daniel that Bonnie Dee would have to have an allowance. No one had thought to give her one during her five-year "trial" marriage. Uncle Daniel reacted slowly to the thought of money, but he reacted surely. Not until the day of the trial did he think of the wealth he had in the bank. Apparently, it was a passing thought which that day prompted him to go to the bank early when only a clerk, who had never been warned to withhold money from Uncle Daniel, was the only person there. He withdrew every cent he had, padded his pockets with the money, and went to the trial.

The murder trial brought together the whole town and all of Bonnie Dee's huge family from the country. Edna Earl and a lawyer intended to take care of the case themselves without letting Uncle Daniel speak in his own defense. They relied too much on the obedience he had always paid them and neglected to take into account the feeling he would naturally have at being, for once, the focal point in a big situation. Uncle Daniel listened carefully to all the witnesses and then, without warning, took over the trial. Throwing bills right and left, pressing them upon all the people, he immediately convinced the jury of his innocence and even softened the hearts of Bonnie Dee's family.

But afterwards he was more alone than ever, isolated as he always would be because people never had understood him and because now he had nothing more to give them.

Miss Welty has the happy faculty of presenting her characters sympathetically, but she loses no sense of realism in doing so. She looks fondly upon her townspeople, and with a sense of humor, but she sees them plainly. Her pen, her eyes, and her ears are all bent to the same task, so that she writes of what she has seen and heard, using a fine sense of discrimination in detail. As a result, she writes what the reader can see and hear too. This visit to Clay, home of Uncle Daniel Ponder, is like a return to a place long remembered.

POOR PEOPLE

Type of work: Novel
Author: Fyodor Mikhailovich Dostoevski (1821-1881)
Type of plot: Impressionistic realism
Time of plot: First half of nineteenth century
Locale: St. Petersburg, Russia
First published: 1846

Principal characters:
MAKAR DIEVUSHKIN, a destitute government clerk
BARBARA DOBROSELOVA, his friend
POKROVSKI, a young tutor
THE ELDER POKROVSKI, the tutor's father
BWIKOV, a wealthy landowner

Critique:

Poor People, Dostoevski's first published work, appeared serially in 1846 in a literary periodical, *Recueil de Saint Petersbourg*. In this work, Dostoevski established a theme, the miseries of Russia's downtrodden masses, from which he never wandered far during his literary career. In *Poor People*, however, one can detect a sly humor that never appeared again in his work. Indeed, the already somewhat morbid and sick artist could hardly have seen anything but black despair in life after his sojourn in Siberia, where he was sent in 1849 for revolutionary political activities. Dostoevski's ruthless and unexpected manipulation of his characters' motives and personalities is foreshadowed in Makar's farewell letter to Barbara, in which Dostoevski has Makar admit that he had not been entirely sincere in his friendship with her.

The Story:

Makar Dievushkin, an impoverished government clerk, lived in an alcove in a rooming-house kitchen. Even though his accommodations were unpleasant, he consoled himself that he could see from his window the windows of Barbara Dobroselova, an unhappy young woman whom he supported in her shabby rooms across the street. Makar and Barbara corresponded; occasionally they walked together when Barbara felt well. Makar, poor but honorable, maintained the gravest dignity in his relationship and in his correspondence with Barbara. In their poverty and loneliness, each had warm sympathy and understanding for the other.

Among the boarders was a public relations man of literary pretentions, whose style Makar greatly admired. He was also interested in a former government clerk, Goshkov, and his family of four. Goshkov had lost his job through a legal suit; he was deeply in debt to the homely, shrewish landlady.

Across the street, Barbara's cousin Sasha appeared for the purpose of resolving a difference which had long existed between the cousins. Sasha questioned Barbara's acceptance of Makar's bounty.

Meanwhile Makar sent gifts to Barbara and became poorer with each passing day. He pawned his uniform and, in his poverty, became the butt of jokes. Barbara, protesting somewhat weakly his sacrifices for her, sent him, in return, her life's story, which she had written.

Barbara was the daughter of the steward of a prince in the province of Tula. Her family moved to St. Petersburg when she was twelve. She did not like the city and she detested the boarding school she attended. When Barbara was fourteen, her father died, debt-ridden. Her mother was consumptive. Creditors took all their possessions, and Barbara and her mother moved to the house of a distant relative, Anna Thedorovna, whose source of income was a mystery to them. There Barbara, with her cousin Sasha, an orphan, was tutored by a sick young student, Pokrovski, who was intelligent but irritable. The young girls teased Pokrovski remorselessly. Barbara, however, soon regretted her behavior and vowed to redeem herself in his eyes.

Pokrovski was visited from time to time by his father, a wizened, obsequious little man who worshiped his son. Because the old man was inquisitive and talkative, Pokrovski had limited the number of his visits to two a week. Old Pokrovski would do anything for his son.

Barbara outgrew the tutoring, but she still had not redeemed herself with Pokrovski. Bent upon wide reading, she sneaked into his room and accidentally upset his bookshelf. Pokrovski entered, and while the pair were replacing the books they realized that they were in love.

As Pokrovski's birthday approached, Barbara joined forces with the elder Pokrovski to buy the young tutor the works of Pushkin; they would give the set to him together. At the birthday party Barbara magnanimously let the doting old father give the books to his son. Pokrovski died soon afterward. Grief apparently weakened the old man's mind. He took his son's books and, following the funeral procession on foot, dropped a pathetic trail of books in the mud of the streets leading to the cemetery. Barbara had stopped writing her life story at the point where her mother was dying of tuberculosis.

The friendship between Makar and Barbara continued. Barbara became concerned with Makar's indulgences, which he could not afford, in her behalf; she urged him to get himself a decent uniform.

At the rooming house Makar, utterly destitute, felt deep pity for Goshkov in his poverty. He sent Barbara a volume of the writings of the public relations man; Barbara declared the book was trash. When the possibility of her becoming a governess in a wealthy household presented itself to Barbara, Makar, in spite of his own poverty, proudly told her that he could continue to care for her.

Hearing that Barbara had been insulted by an importunate suitor, Makar got drunk and was brought home by the police. In desperation he borrowed money everywhere, even from Barbara. His penury seemed to affect his mind. Meanwhile the friendship between the two had become the source of laughter to the other boarders. Makar even suspected the public relations man of maliciously gossiping in civil service circles about his having been brought home by the police. He feared for his reputation, all that he had left. Barbara invited him to come live with her and her cook, Thedora; she urged him to stop borrowing and to stop copying the public relations man's style in his letters.

A lecherous old man, sent by Anna Thedorovna, called on Barbara. After Barbara and Thedora got rid of him, Barbara, in alarm, told Makar that she would have to move immediately. Lack of money, however, prevented her removal. Because he could offer no security, Makar was refused a loan by a rich usurer. Everything went wrong; Makar's position at the rooming house became impossible. Barbara burned her hand and could not sew for a living. She sent Makar money, which he spent on drink. But even in his abject condition Makar gave coins to Goshkov that he might feed his family.

Makar made a mistake in his official work and was ordered before his superior, who was so affected at the sight of Makar's wretched person that he gave the poor clerk one hundred roubles and took his hand. These gestures saved Makar physically and morally. He regained his self-respect and faced life with a new vigor. All went well at the office and at the rooming house.

Bwikov, a wealthy landowner who had once courted Barbara and had deserted her in her misfortune, came to St. Petersburg and offered her money, which she refused.

Goshkov, meanwhile, was officially absolved of guilt in a case involving misappropriation of funds and was awarded substantial damages. Moved deeply by his freedom and solvency, the man broke in mind and body and died of shock.

Bwikov returned to Barbara and offered marriage to atone for his desertion. He planned to take her to his country estate for her health. After much debate Barbara and Makar agreed that she must marry Bwikov. Makar could not help remarking, however, that Bwikov would probably be happier married to a certain merchant's daughter in Moscow.

Barbara, preparing excitedly for a magnificent wedding, employed Makar to run countless petty errands for her. Makar planned to move into Barbara's rooms and to retain Thedora as his cook. It saddened him to think of Barbara's leaving him, of her going to the steppes to become the lady of a great estate. In a last letter he implored her to stay but admitted that his passionate turns of phrase were to some extent only a literary exercise.

Further Critical Evaluation of the Work:

"Honor and glory to the young poet whose Muse loves people in garrets and basements and tells the inhabitants of gilded palaces: 'look, they are also men, they are also your brethren.' " With these words, the great critic Belinsky hailed the arrival of Dostoevski on the Russian literary scene. The epistolary novel *Poor People* is a remarkably perceptive account of the multifarious humiliations which torment "poor folk." In depicting the victimized and the eccentric, Dostoevski proved himself the equal of Dickens, by whom he was much influenced. His portrayal of life in "garrets and basements" is entirely devoid of sentimentality; both the dignity and the wretchedness of Makar and Barbara come to light simultaneously.

Makar's persistent generosity is what finally distinguishes him, while a poetic sensitivity to life ennobles Barbara. Both characters maintain these virtues in the face of impossible circumstances. To support Barbara, Makar must acept the chaos and stench of the three-to-a-room boarding house whose walls are "so greasy that your hand sticks when you lean against them." His increasing poverty turns the smallest economic reverse into disaster. The deterioration of his wardrobe is humiliating, yet it deepens his sympathy for those in similar straits. IIis aroused compassion for other victims induces him not only to give Goshkov twenty kopecks, but also to add sugar to the poor man's tea. As her response to Pokrovski's father shows, Barbara is also capable of great generosity. But more impressive are her lyrical descriptions of her childhood and her feeling for nature. Despite Makar's literary pretentions, Barbara is by far the superior "stylist," though she never boasts about her talent.

But Dostoevski's main characters are far from perfect human beings. Makar's love for Barbara is tainted by a desire to extract from her gratitude and praise. Barbara, in turn, reveals a shocking capacity for transforming Makar into her servant once she becomes engaged to the rich Bwikov. Both are too involved in private dream worlds and excessively preoccupied with their reputations. Yet these faults, suggests Dostoevski, must be seen partially as exaggerated attempts to maintain a modicum of dignity in an uncomprehending world. When one is absolutely vulnerable, certain defenses must be erected, or, as Makar explains, "Poor people are touchy—that's in the nature of things."

POOR WHITE

Type of work: Novel
Author: Sherwood Anderson (1876-1941)
Type of plot: Psychological realism
Time of plot: 1880-1900
Locale: Missouri and Ohio
First published: 1920

Principal characters:
HUGH MCVEY, an inventor and manufacturer
SARAH SHEPARD, his foster mother
STEVE HUNTER, his partner
TOM BUTTERWORTH, his father-in-law
CLARA BUTTERWORTH, his wife

Critique:

Poor White is a significant novel, an early study of pioneer rural America invaded by industrialism. It is also the story of one man's rise from decadent, poor white folk to a life of creation and self-realization. Anderson graphically described, not only the growth of America, but also the conflicts and frustrations between man and the machine, a conflict that is today one of the major problems in our culture.

The Story:

As a young boy in Missouri, Hugh McVey was incredibly lazy. Hour after hour he would lie on the grass by the river doing absolutely nothing. Not having gone to school, he was ignorant and his manners were rude.

When the railroad came to town, Hugh got work sweeping the platform and doing odd jobs. His boss, Henry Shepard, took an interest in him, and bought him clothes. Soon Hugh went to live with Henry and his wife Sarah. Sarah, who was from New England, always preserved her memory of quiet Eastern villages and large industrial cities. Determined to educate Hugh, she lavished on him the discipline and affection she would have given her own child.

The situation was difficult, at first, for both of them. But Sarah Shepard was a determined woman. She taught Hugh to read, to write, to wonder about the world beyond the little town. She in-

stilled within him the belief that his family had been of no account, so that he grew to have a repulsion toward the poor white farmers and workers. Always she held out before him the promise of the East, the progress and growth of that region. Gradually, Hugh began to win his fight against natural indolence and to adjust himself to his new way of life. When the Shepards left town, Hugh was appointed station agent for the railroad.

He kept the job for a year. During that time the dream of Eastern cities grew more and more vivid for Hugh. He gave up his job and traveled east, working wherever he could. Always lonely, always apart from people, he felt an impenetrable wall between him and the rest of the world. He kept on, through Illinois, Indiana, Ohio.

Hugh was twenty-three when he settled down in Ohio. By accident, he got the job of a telegraph operator, just a mile from the town of Bidwell. There he lived alone, a familiar and puzzling figure to the people of the town. The rumor began to spread that he was an inventor working on a new device. Others suggested that he was looking over the town for a possible factory site. But Hugh was doing neither as yet. Then during his walks around the farmlands, he became fascinated by the motions of the farmers planting their seeds and their crops. Slowly there grew in his mind an idea for a crop-setting machine that would save the labor of the farmers and their families.

Steve Hunter, who had just come back from school in Buffalo, was another dreamer. He dreamed of being a manufacturer, the wealthiest in Bidwell. He succeeded in convincing the town's important people that Hugh was his man, and that he was working on an invention that would make them both rich. He persuaded them to invest in a new company which would build a factory and promote Hugh's invention. Steve went to see Hugh, who had progressed so that the blueprint for a plant-setting machine was complete. The two young men came to an agreement.

The town idiot, who had skill in woodworking, made models of the machine, and the machine itself was finally constructed in an old building carefully guarded from the curious. When the machine was not successful, Hugh invented another, his mind more and more preoccupied with the planning of devices and machines. A factory was then built and many workers were hired. With the factory, Bidwell's industrialization began.

What was happening in Bidwell was the same growth of industrialism that was changing the entire structure of the nation. It was a period of transition. Bidwell, being a small town, felt the effects of the new development keenly. Workers became part of the community, in which there had been only farmers and merchants.

Joe Wainsworth, the harness-maker, had invested his life-savings in Hugh's invention, and he had lost them. An independent man, a craftsman, he came to resent the factory, the very idea of the machine. People came into his shop less often. They were buying machine-made harness. Joe became a broken man. His employee, Jim Gibson, a spiritual bully, really ran the business, and Joe submitted meekly.

Meanwhile, Clara Butterworth came back to Bidwell after three years at the university in Columbus. She too was lonely, unhappy. When she returned, she saw that the old Bidwell was gone, that her father, Tom Butterworth, was wealthier than before, that the growth of the town was due primarily to one person, Hugh McVey. A week after she met Hugh, he walked up to the farm and asked her to marry him. They eloped and were married that night.

For four years they lived together in a strange, strained relationship. During those four years Joe Wainsworth's fury against Steve Hunter, against the new age of industry which had taken his savings, increased. One day he heard Jim Gibson brag about his hold over his employer. That night Joe Wainsworth killed Jim Gibson. As he fled from the scene, he met Steve Hunter and shot him.

Clara, Hugh, and Tom Butterworth were returning from a drive in the family's first automobile when they learned what had happened. Two men had captured Joe, and when they tried to put him into the automobile to take him back to town, Joe jumped toward Hugh and sank his fingers into his neck. It was Clara who broke his grip upon her husband. Somehow the incident brought Hugh and Clara closer together.

Hugh's career as an inventor no longer satisfied him. Joe Wainsworth's attack had unnerved him, made him doubt the worth of his work. It did not matter so much if someone in Iowa had invented a machine exactly like his, and he did not intend to dispute the rights of the Iowan. Clara was bearing his child, an individual who would struggle just as he had. Clara told him of the child one night as they stood listening to the noises of the farm and the snoring of the hired hand. As they walked into the house side by side, the factory whistles blew in the night. Hugh hardly heard them. The dark Midwestern nights, men and women, the land itself —the full, deep life current would go on in spite of factories and machines.

Further Critical Evaluation of the Work:

The intent of *Poor White* is, first of all, to describe the opening stages of industrialization in the great Ohio Valley; but this description, rather than being merely social or statistical, is set in profoundly human terms. That is, the birth and development of American industry are made specific and concrete through the individual lives of the people who invent the machines, who finance the enterprises, and who run the factories. Thus, *Poor White* is as much a historical novel as a novel dealing with the dramas of love and hate and individual psychology. Anderson catches a particular historical moment, and, almost in the manner of Tolstoy, explores individual reactions and contributions.

The two most significant human dramas are Hugh McVey's development on the one hand, and Clara Butterworth's relationship to him on the other. McVey, an inventor, and prototype of a creative personality—a genius of sorts—is shown by Anderson to have been influenced by the various regions of the United States. McVey is a product of "poor whites" dreaming near the banks of the Mississippi River and of discipline imposed on that dreaminess by a tough New England lady. If Anderson's attribution of innate characteristics to various regions of the country seems thin and stereotyped, Anderson does succeed in capturing the strengths and weaknesses of this individual and in exploring why this man in particular could play the historical role assigned to him in the novel.

The character of Clara Butterworth is mainly explored in terms of her sexual relationship with men, and this characterizaton lacks the force and focus of Hugh McVey's. Part of her vagueness may have resulted from Anderson's trying to describe her subjective confusion. Another reason may be that Anderson has made certain naturalist assumptions about her. Sexual urges that move her, and that drive the men around her, are heavily stressed by Anderson; and these urges, biologically irresistible, external and abstract, tend to rob her of her personality.

A final note should be added on the appearance of a socialist agitator near the end of the novel. The period Anderson describes is one in which the ideas of socialism, first introduced into this country, assumed vast popularity, especially in the farming regions of the midwest. Anderson suggests at the end of the novel that this agitator, and the ideas he supports, embody the next historical stage, the new society brought about by industrialization.

THE POORHOUSE FAIR

Type of work: Novel
Author: John Updike (1932-   )
Time: The 1980's
Locale: The Diamond County Home for the Aged, in New Jersey
First published: 1959

Principal characters:
JOHN HOOK,
BILLY GREGG,
GEORGE LUCAS,
MARTHA, his wife
ELIZABETH HEINEMAN, and
MRS. MORTIS, inmates in a home for the aged
MR. CONNER, the prefect
BUDDY, his assistant
TED, a teen-age delivery boy

At a time when literary excellence is too frequently measured by bulk and most first novels testify to little more than the immaturity of their writers, *The Poorhouse Fair* stands out as a work of great delicacy and precision in its blending of substance and structure. The point for praise is not the fact that John Updike has deliberately chosen to write a short first novel but that his beautifully realized insights and the brevity of the book testify to his imaginative self-sufficiency and his control over material that would set many writers to page after page of furious prose. Where another novelist might have tried to achieve similar effects in the mass and weight of some sprawling, documented design, John Updike presents a single animate image of a small complex of lives against a background in which implication, symbol, paradox, and irony gradually transform the mere lifelikeness of more naturalistic fiction into a vision of life rearranged to significant form and charged with moral meaning.

The book is short but far from slight in its resonance and depth. Readers tired of the affectedly tough, the oversensitive, or romantic escapism through personality in modern fiction sometimes ask this question: Why don't writers try to show what is really going on in the world about them—things like the corruption of power, the perversion of idealism, the conflict between individual will and social pattern, the loss of understanding, or identity, of belief? In his imaginatively conceived and poetically styled novel the author takes the indirect course of fable and symbolism to do exactly that. The story he tells is a ruefully perceptive parable on the cold comforts of a planned society and stubborn humanity's saving grace of individuality.

Like all good novels, *The Poorhouse Fair* is a metaphor of life. That is, what is here dramatically presented in terms of character and scene and what is figuratively implied in the confrontation of the cranky innocence, tested wisdom, and moral rigor of the aged by the impersonal benevolence of bureaucratic statism is contained in a single image which is both a picture of the world and the configuration of the novel itself. The meaning of John Updike's fable is plain. To be human is to possess a moral vision which makes the human effort seem worth while, and to be a man is to accept the responsibility for one's thoughts and deeds.

The time of the novel is projected, with sly subtlety, into the future, during the administration of President Lowenstein, and the action unfolds in the events of one day in the lives of the inmates of the Diamond County Home for the Aged, in New Jersey. It is the day of the annual fair, when these elderly men and women set up stands and sell such homemade products as quilts, candy, and peach-stone carvings to the visitors from nearby communities. But this year the great day gets off to a bad start. John Hook, a ninety-four-year-old ex-schoolteacher, and Billy Gregg, a seventy-year-old retired electrician, discover that the porch chairs have been given name tags so that hereafter each inmate will occupy only the chair assigned to him. This latest action by Conner, the prefect of the institution, provides an opportunity for protest.

As the morning passes, misunderstandings and misadventures add to Conner's burden of do-gooding humanitarianism. When Gregg introduces a diseased stray cat into the grounds, the prefect orders Buddy, his adoring assistant, to shoot the animal. Ted, a teen-age truck driver delivering cases of Pepsi-Cola for the fair, knocks down part of a stone wall. A pet parakeet belonging to Mrs. Lucas, the wife of George Lucas, a former real-estate salesman, gets loose in the infirmary. When rain threatens to ruin the fair, and the inmates take refuge in the community sitting room, Hook and Conner argue the ideals of an older America of faith and idealism against the theories of scientific determinism and social perfectibility.

Without losing their identities as very real people Hook and Conner drift almost imperceptibly into their roles as spokesmen for meaningful opposites in man's conception of the good life. Hook is a gentle, meditative man who can look back to the days of Taft and Mark Hanna in a period of greater political freedom, economic uncertainty, pride of craftsmanship, and, in times of private or public calamity, trust in God. Filled with that sense of repletion which is time's final gift to the old, he believes in the possible virtue of man, a quality of manliness that is both physical and spiritual. To Hook this quality of virtue redeems

the human animal's capacity for folly and evil because it brings man close to the idea of God. But in Conner's brave new world there is no more place for God than there is for error. Fanatical in his belief in progress, order, hygiene, and the elimination of superstition and pain, he possesses the inhuman energy of a machine. The truth is that he does not think of the inmates under him as people; they are his charges, and it is his job to confer on them the good they often cannot understand and sometimes do not want. In his view all life should be regulated and institutionalized, as passionless as the antics of tomorrow's adolescents, who satisfy their emotional needs by undressing and then staring in curiosity but without desire at one another's nude bodies. Conner is a citizen of a planned society, and the institution is his spiritual home.

The tensions of the day finally break when the inmates turn on Conner and stone him with the rubble from the damaged wall. Then the skies clear and the fair is held after all, but under circumstances which have allowed the old people to save some remnants of their pride and self-respect. Asking only the bread of understanding, they have been offered the cold stone of charity, and they have rejected it along with a world they never made. John Updike's home for the aged and the poor becomes an image of some future world of social planning and the regimentation it implies. Even so, the futile anarchy of the old, like Hook's compassion for man's frailty and respect for human dignity, suggests a more meaningful existence than that offered by the outside world whose citizens come to the fair to have refreshened their dimming memories of an older, more individualistic, less "planned" and regimented America.

If this brief outline makes *The Poorhouse Fair* sound like a social polemic or a sentimentalized fantasy, nothing could be farther from the truth. The novel is a story of real people; its tensions are those created by man's moral urgencies and spiritual needs. It is only on a secondary plane that it takes on historical and social implications as a picture of a country and an age caught uneasily between the values of the past and fears for the future. It is a serious work, but not a solemn one, for Updike is a novelist of wry humor which gives to his novel a coloring of astringent, unillusioned comedy that is perfectly in keeping with his picture of the stubborn, life-grasping qualities of the old in conflict with the dehumanized humanitarianism of their prefect.

Where so much is unpretentiously eloquent and everything is clear, it is carping criticism, perhaps, to say that John Updike writes with too tight a rein. There is considerable intensity here, but he seems determined to hold it in check.

What is needed is a less muted tone of voice to give greater effect to the emotional impact of his material. For the rest, *The Poorhouse Fair* is a novel of art in the true sense of that abused term. Among other things, this writer is the master of a wonderfully poetic style, and his descriptions are evocative and sensuous, filled with imaginative details yet always rooted firmly in the immediacy of things seen and heard. These qualities give to his prose the density and precision of poetry in a first novel in which the human need for understanding and to be one's self clash meaningfully with the impersonal authority of benevolent statism.

PORGY

Type of work: Novel
Author: DuBose Heyward (1885-1940)
Type of plot: Regional romance
Time of plot: Early twentieth century
Locale: Charleston, South Carolina
First published: 1925

Principal characters:
PORGY, a crippled Negro beggar
CROWN, a stevedore
BESS, his woman

Critique:

Porgy tells of Negroes living in a society dominated by whites, and the Negroes are presented as being elemental, emotional, amoral, and occasionally violent. Heyward develops in the reader a sympathy not only for the crippled Porgy, whose goatcart excites so much amusement among the whites, but also for Bess, who comes to live with him. Bess honestly tries to be true to Porgy, but she knows the weakness of her will and flesh when the brutal Crown touches her or when she has had liquor or dope. The story was dramatized in 1927 by Heyward and his wife Dorothy. The novel was also the basis for the opera *Porgy and Bess* (1935), for which Heyward wrote the book and, with Ira Gershwin, the lyrics.

The Story:

Porgy, a crippled Negro beggar, lived in a brick tenement called Catfish Row, once a fine old Southern mansion in Charleston, South Carolina. Different from the eager, voluble beggars of his race, Porgy sat silent day by day, acknowledging only by lifting his eyes the coins dropped in his cup. No one knew how old he was, and his large, powerful hands were in strange contrast to his frail body. His single vice was gambling. In a gambling session one evening in April he witnessed the brutal murder of Robbins by Crown, a stevedore who thought he had been cheated.

In May Porgy made his first trip by homemade goatcart through the city streets, to the mocking amusement of the white folks. The goatcart gave Porgy a new freedom. He no longer had to stay at one stand all day; but he could roam at will and take in more money than before.

In June Crown's woman, Bess, came to live with Porgy, and the cripple became a new man. He seemed less an impassive observer of life and he developed a tender affection for children. Bess left off her evil ways and became in truth Porgy's woman.

On the day of the grand parade and picnic of "The Sons and Daughters of Repent Ye Saith the Lord," Crown came upon Bess cutting palmetto leaves for the picnic on Kittiwar Island. He took her to his hut. At the end of the day he let her return to Porgy with the promise that in the fall, when cotton shipments would provide stevedoring work in Savannah, she would again be Crown's Bess.

In September, while the "Mosquito Fleet" was at the fishing banks, the hurricane flag was up over the custom house. Jake's wife, Clara, shuddered with fear for her husband whom she had warned not to go out that day in his boat, the *Seagull*. After an ominous calm the hurricane struck the city. The water of the bay, driven by the shrieking wind, rose above the sea wall, crossed the street, and invaded the ground floor of Catfish Row. Forty frightened Negroes huddled in the great second-story ballroom of the old mansion. During a lull in the storm Clara saw the wreck of her husband's boat near the wharf. Leaving her baby with Bess, Clara went out into the flood. A few minutes later she was overwhelmed during a sudden return of the storm's great fury. Bess and Porgy kept Clara's baby.

In October drays loaded with heavy bales of cotton came rumbling down the street. In Catfish Row there was excitement and happiness, for stevedoring jobs and money would be plentiful again. But the coming of the cotton seemed to Porgy to portend disaster. He asked Bess whether she was his woman or Crown's. His, she answered, unless Crown put his hot hands on her again as he did that day of the picnic. She could not answer for herself if that happened again. Porgy assured her he would not let Crown take her away from him. When Crown broke into their room one midnight not long afterward, Porgy stabbed him. Next day the body was found in the river nearby. The police got nowhere in their questioning of the occupants of Catfish Row, and there was a kind of communal sigh of relief when the officers left without having made any arrests. But when one of the buzzards that had fed upon Crown's body

lighted on the parapet above Porgy's room, the frightened little cripple felt that doom was in store for him. The next day Porgy, having been asked to identify Crown's body at the morgue, fled in terror in his goatcart, hotly pursued by a patrol wagon full of officers. Passersby laughed uproariously at the ridiculously one-sided race. Porgy was caught at the edge of town, but by the time he had been brought downtown he was no longer needed since another Negro had identified the body. Crown was declared to have come to his death at the hands of a person or persons unknown. Porgy was jailed for five days for contempt of court.

When he returned from jail and found Serena Robbins holding Jake's and Clara's orphan baby, Porgy suspected the worst. From a neighbor he learned that some stevedores had gotten Bess drunk and taken her off to Savannah. Porgy knew she would never return. Serena had adopted the baby. Porgy had for one brief summer known the joys that come to other people. Now he was just a pitiful old man sitting sadly in a goatcart with the morning sunlight shining upon him.

Further Critical Evaluation of the Work:

DuBose Heyward is one of the best examples of an American one-book author. Although he wrote three books of poems, six novels, a short story, and three plays, he is remembered now only for his first novel, *Porgy,* and for the folk opera developed from it. The story of Porgy first caught the attention of George Gershwin in 1926, but it was not until 1935 that the opera *Porgy and Bess* reached the stage. Gershwin wrote the music, DuBose and Dorothy Heyward the libretto, and the Heywards and Ira Gershwin the lyrics of this first and most successful serious American folk opera, which achieved international fame through a four-year world tour climaxed by performances in Leningrad and Moscow in 1955.

Porgy tells of blacks living in a society dominated by whites; the blacks are presented as being elemental, emotional, amoral, and occasionally violent. Heyward develops in the reader a sympathy not only for the crippled Porgy, whose goat cart excites so much amusement among the whites, but also for Bess, who comes to live with him. Bess honestly tries to be true to Porgy, but she knows the weakness of her will and flesh when the brutal Crown touches her or when she has had liquor or dope. Porgy's brief happiness with Bess is doomed despite the efforts of both to hold on to it.

Heyward's portrayal of both character and scene contains the perceptive observation of detail found in the best local color fiction. Heyward may seem at times to romanticize his men and women, yet his style transforms the sordidness and bitterness of their lives into a sad, enduring beauty. Crippled Porgy, weak-willed Bess, and cruel Crown live on in one's mind long after the book has been closed.

THE PORTRAIT OF A LADY

Type of work: Novel
Author: Henry James (1843-1916)
Type of plot: Psychological realism
Time of plot: About 1875
Locale: England, France, Italy
First published: 1881

> *Principal characters:*
> ISABEL ARCHER, an American heiress
> GILBERT OSMOND, her husband
> RALPH TOUCHETT, her cousin
> MADAME MERLE, her friend and Osmond's former mistress
> PANSY OSMOND, Osmond's daughter
> LORD WARBURTON, Isabel's English suitor
> CASPAR GOODWOOD, Isabel's American suitor
> HENRIETTA STACKPOLE, American newspaper correspondent, Isabel's friend

Critique:

With the exception of the English Lord Warburton, *The Portrait of a Lady* contains a gallery of Americans who work out their destinies against a European background. The influence of European culture is seen most closely as it affects the heroine, high-minded Isabel Archer. By means of careful penetration into her mental processes, the steps which lead to her marriage with the dilettante, Gilbert Osmond, are delineated, as well as the consequent problems which arise from this marriage. The novel is an excellent example of the Jamesian method of refracting life through an individual temperament.

The Story:

Isabel Archer, upon the death of her father, had been visited by her aunt, Mrs. Touchett. She proved so attractive to the older woman that Mrs. Touchett decided to give her the advantage of more cosmopolitan experience, and Isabel was quickly carried off to Europe so she might see something of the world of culture and fashion.

On the day the women arrived at the Touchett home in England, Isabel's sickly young cousin, Ralph Touchett, and his father were taking tea in the garden with their friend, Lord Warburton. When Isabel appeared, Warburton had been confessing to the two men his boredom and his distaste for his routine existence. The young nobleman was much taken with the American girl's grace and lively manner.

Isabel had barely settled at Gardencourt, her aunt's home, before she received a letter from an American friend, Henrietta Stackpole, a newspaper woman who was writing a series of articles on the sights of Europe. At Ralph's invitation, Henrietta went to Gardencourt to spend some time with Isabel and to obtain material for her writing.

Soon after Henrietta's arrival, Isabel heard from another American friend. Caspar Goodwood, a would-be suitor, had followed her abroad. Learning her whereabouts from Henrietta, he wrote to ask if he might see her. Isabel was much irked by his aggressiveness, and she decided not to answer his letter.

On the day she received the letter from Goodwood, Lord Warburton proposed to her. Not wishing to seem indifferent to the honor of his proposal, she asked for time to consider it. At last she decided she could not marry the young Englishman, for she wished to see considerably more of the world before she married. She was afraid that marriage to Warburton, although he was a model of kindness and thoughtfulness, would prove stifling.

Because Isabel had not seen London on her journey with Mrs. Touchett and since it was on Henrietta Stackpole's itinerary, the two young women, accompanied by Ralph Touchett, went to the capital. Henrietta quickly made the acquaintance of a Mr. Bantling, who undertook to squire her around. When Caspar Goodwood visited Isabel at her hotel, she again refused him, though his persistence made her agree that if he still wished to ask for her hand he might visit her again after two years had passed.

While the party was in London a telegram came from Gardencourt. Old Mr. Touchett was seriously ill of the gout, and his wife was much alarmed. Isabel and Ralph left on the afternoon train. Henrietta remained under the escort of her new friend.

During the time Mr. Touchett lay dying and his family was preoccupied, Isabel was forced to amuse herself with a new companion. Madame Merle, an old friend of Mrs. Touchett, had come to Gardencourt to spend a few days. She and Isabel, thrown together a great deal, exchanged many confidences. Isabel admired the older woman for her ability to amuse herself, for her skill at needlework, at painting, at the piano, and for her ability to accommodate herself to any social situation. On the other hand, Madame Merle spoke enviously of Isabel's youth and intelligence, lamenting the life which had left her, at middle age, a widow with no children and no visible success in life.

When her uncle died, he left Isabel, at her cousin's instigation, one-half of his fortune. Ralph, greatly impressed with his young kinswoman's brilliance, had persuaded his father that she should be given an opportunity to fly as far and as high as she might. For himself, he knew he could not live long because of his pulmonary illness, and his legacy was enough to let him live in comfort.

As quickly as she could, Mrs. Touchett sold her London house and took Isabel to Paris with her. Ralph went south for the winter to preserve what was left of his health. In Paris the new heiress was introduced to many of her aunt's friends among American expatriates, but she was not impressed. She thought their indolent lives worthy only of contempt. Meanwhile Henrietta and Mr. Bantling had arrived in Paris, and Isabel spent much time with them and Edward Rosier. She had known Rosier when both were children and she was traveling abroad with her father. Rosier was another dilettante, living on the income from his inheritance. He explained to Isabel that he could not return to his own country because there was no occupation there worthy of a gentleman.

In February Mrs. Touchett and her niece went to the Palazzo Crescentini, the Touchett house in Florence. They stopped on the way to see Ralph, who was staying in San Remo. In Florence they were joined once more by Madame Merle.

Unknown to Isabel or her aunt, Madame Merle also visited her friend, Gilbert Osmond, another American who lived in voluntary exile outside Florence with his art collection and his young, convent-bred daughter, Pansy. Madame Merle told Osmond of Isabel's arrival in Florence saying that as the heir to a fortune, Isabel would be a valuable addition to Osmond's collection.

The heiress who had rejected two worthy suitors did not refuse the third. She was quickly captivated by the charm of the sheltered life Gilbert Osmond had created for himself. Her friends were against the match. Henrietta Stackpole, who was inclined to favor Caspar Goodwood, was convinced that Osmond was interested only in Isabel's money, as was Isabel's aunt. Mrs. Touchett had requested Madame Merle, the good friend of both parties, to discover the state of their affections; she was convinced that Madame Merle could have prevented the match. Ralph Touchett was disappointed that his cousin should have fallen to the ground from her flight so quickly. Caspar Goodwood, learning of Isabel's intended marriage when he revisited her after the passage of the two years agreed upon, could not persuade her to reconsider her step. Isabel was indignant when he commented on the fact that she did not even know her intended husband's antecedents.

After her marriage to Gilbert Osmond,

Isabel and her husband established their home in Rome, in a setting completely expressive of Osmond's tastes. Before three years had passed, Isabel began to realize that her friends had not been completely wrong in their objections to her marriage. Osmond's exquisite taste had made their home one of the most popular in Rome, but his ceaseless effort to press his wife into a mold, to make her a reflection of his own ideas, had not made their marriage one of the happiest.

He had succeeded in destroying a romance between Pansy and Edward Rosier, who had visited the girl's stepmother and found the daughter attractive. He had not succeeded, however, in contracting the match he desired between Pansy and Lord Warburton. Warburton had found Pansy as pleasing as Isabel had once been, but he had dropped his suit when he saw that the girl's affections lay with Rosier.

Ralph Touchett, his health growing steadily worse, gave up his wanderings on the continent and returned to Gardencourt to die. When Isabel received a telegram from his mother telling her that Ralph would like to see her before his death, she felt it her duty to go to Gardencourt at once. Osmond reacted to her wish as if it were a personal insult. He expected that, as his wife, Isabel would want to remain at his side, and that she would not disobey any wish of his. He also made it plain that he disliked Ralph.

In a state of turmoil after her conversation with her husband, Isabel met the Countess Gemini, Osmond's sister.

The countess, visiting the Osmonds, had seen how matters lay between her brother and Isabel. An honest soul, she had felt more sympathy for her sister-in-law than for her brother. To comfort Isabel, she told her the story of Gilbert's past. After his first wife had died, he and Madame Merle had an affair that lasted six or seven years. During that time Madame Merle, a widow, had borne him a child, Pansy. Changing his residence, Osmond had been able to pretend to his new circle of friends that the original Mrs. Osmond had died in giving birth to the child.

With this news fresh in her mind, and still determined to go to England, Isabel stopped to say goodbye to Pansy, who was staying in a convent where her father had sent her to recuperate from her affair with Rosier. There, too, she met Madame Merle. Madame Merle, with her keen perception, had no difficulty realizing that Isabel knew her secret. When she remarked that Isabel would never need to see her again, that she would go to America, Isabel was certain Madame Merle would also find in America much to her own advantage.

Isabel was in time to see her cousin before his death. She stayed on briefly at Gardencourt after the funeral, long enough to bid goodbye to Lord Warburton, who had come to offer condolences to her aunt, and to reject a third offer from Caspar Goodwood, who knew of her husband's treatment. When she left to start her journey back to Italy, Isabel knew what she must do. Her first duty was not to herself, but to put her house in order.

Further Critical Evaluation of the Work:

The Portrait of a Lady first appeared serially in England and America (*Macmillan's Magazine,* Oct., 1880-Nov., 1881; *Atlantic,* Nov., 1880-Dec., 1881); it was published as a book in 1881. Usually regarded as the major achievement of James's early period of fiction writing, *The Portrait of a Lady* is one of the great novels of modern literature. In it James demonstrates that he has learned well from two European masters of the novel. Turgenev had taught him how to use a single character who shapes the work and is seen throughout in relationship to various other characters. From George Eliot he had learned the importance of tightening the structure of the novel and giving the story an architectural or organic form which develops logically from the given materials. He advances in *The Portrait of a Lady* beyond George Eliot in minimizing his own authorial comments and analysis and permitting his heroine to be seen through her own tardily awakening self-realization and also through the consciousness of the men and women who are closest to her. Thus his "portrait" of a lady is one which slowly grows stroke by stroke as touches are added which bring out both highlights and shadows, until Isabel Archer stands before us at the end a woman whose experiences have brought her excitement, joy, pain, and knowledge and have given her an enduring beauty and dignity.

Isabel is one of James's finest creations and one of the most memorable women in the history of the novel. A number of sources have been suggested for her. She may have been partly drawn from James's cousin Mary ("Minny") Temple, whom he was later to immortalize as Milly Theale in *The Wings of the Dove*. She has been compared to two of George Eliot's heroines, Dorothea Brooke in *Middlemarch* and Gwendolen Harleth in *Daniel Deronda;* to Diana Belfield in an early romantic tale by James entitled "Longstaff's Marriage"; to Bathsheba Everdene in Thomas Hardy's *Far from the Madding Crowd;* and even to Henry James himself, some of whose early experiences closely parallel those of Isabel. Yet, though James may have drawn from both real and fictional people in portraying Isabel Archer, she possesses her own identity; she grew from James's original "conception of a certain young woman affronting her destiny," as he later wrote in his Preface to the novel. He visualized her as "an intelligent but presumptuous girl" who would yet be "complex" and who would be offered a series of opportunities for free choice in the affronting of that destiny. Because of her presumption that she knew more than she did about herself and the world, Isabel was to make mistakes, including the tragic error of misjudging the nature of Gilbert Osmond. But her intelligence, though it was not sufficient to save her from suffering, would enable her to achieve a moral triumph in the end.

Of the four men in Isabel's life, three love her and one uses her innocence to gain for himself what he would not otherwise have had. She refuses marriage to Lord Warburton because, though he offers her a great fortune, a title, an entry into English society, and an agreeable and entertaining personality, she believes she can do better. She turns down Caspar Goodwood, who also offers wealth, because she finds him stiff and she is frightened by his aggressiveness. Her cousin, Ralph Touchett, does not propose because he does not wish her to be tied to a man who daily faces death. She does not even suspect the extent of his love and adoration until she is almost overwhelmed by learning it just as death takes him from her. She accepts Gilbert Osmond because she is deceived by his calculated charm and because she believes that he deserves what she can offer him: first, a fortune that will make it possible for him to live in idleness but surrounded by the objects of the "culture" she believes he represents; and second, a mother's love and care for his supposedly motherless daughter. Half of the novel is given over to Isabel's living with, adjusting to, and, finally, triumphing over the disastrous choice she has made.

In his Preface, James uses an architectural figure to describe *The Portrait of a Lady*. He says the "large building" of the novel "came to be a square and spacious house." Much of what occurs in the novel does so in or near a series of houses each of which relates significantly to Isabel or to other characters. The action begins at Gardencourt, the Tudor English country house of Daniel Touchett which Isabel finds more beautiful than anything she has ever seen. The charm of the house is enhanced by its age and its natural setting beside the Thames above London. It contrasts greatly with the "old house at Albany, a large, square, double house" belonging to her grandmother which Isabel in her childhood had found romantic and in which she had indulged in dreams stimulated by her reading. Mrs. Touchett's taking Isabel from the Albany house to Gardencourt is a first step in her plan to "introduce her to the world." When Isabel visits Lockleigh, Lord Warburton's home, she sees it from the gardens as resembling "a castle in a legend," though inside it has been modernized. She does not view it as a home for herself, or its titled owner as her husband, despite the many advantages he offers. The front of Gilbert Osmond's house in Florence is "imposing" but of "a somewhat uncommunicative character," a "mask." It symbolizes Osmond whose mask Isabel does not see through until she has married him. The last of the houses in *The Portrait of a Lady* is the Palazzo Roccanera, the Roman home of the Osmonds, which James first describes as "a kind of domestic fortress . . . which smelt of historic deeds, of crime and craft and violence." When Isabel later broods over it during her night-long meditation in Chapter 42, it is "the house of darkness, the house of dumbness, the house of suffocation."

We first see Isabel at Gardencourt on her visit with Mrs. Touchett, and it is here that she turns down the first of three proposals of marriage. It is fitting that also we should last see her here and by turns with each of the three men who have loved her. Asserting the independence on which she has so long prided herself, she has defied her imperious husband by going to England to see the dying Ralph, whose last words tell her that if she has been hated by Osmond she has been adored by her cousin. In a brief conversation with Lord Warburton after Ralph's death, Isabel turns down an invitation to visit him and his sisters at Lockleigh. Shortly afterward a scene six years earlier is reversed. Then she had sat on a rustic bench at Gardencourt and looked up from reading Caspar Goodwood's letter implying that he would come to England and propose to her—only to see and hear Warburton preparing to offer his own proposal. Now Caspar surprises her by appearing just after she has dismissed Warburton. There follows the one sexually passionate scene in the novel. In it Isabel has "an immense desire to appear to resist" the force of Caspar's argument that she should leave Osmond and turn to him. She pleads with streaming tears, "As you love me, as you pity me, leave me alone!" Defying her plea, Caspar kisses her:

> His kiss was like white lightning, a flash that spread, and spread again, and stayed; and it was extraordinarily as if, while she took it, she felt each thing in his hard manhood that had least pleased her, each aggressive fact of his face, his figure, his presence, justified of its intense identity and made one with this act of possession.

Caspar has possessed her for a moment only. "But when darkness returned she was free" and she flees into the house—and thence to Rome, as Caspar learns in the brief scene in London with Henrietta Stackpole which closes the novel.

James leaves the reader to conclude that Isabel's love for Pansy Osmond has principally determined her decision to continue enduring a marriage that she had freely—though so ignorantly and foolishly—chosen.

Henderson Kincheloe

PORTRAIT OF THE ARTIST AS A YOUNG DOG

Type of work: Short stories
Author: Dylan Thomas (1914-1953)
First published: 1940

Recent biographical studies of Dylan Thomas record a change in our appreciation of him only to be expected now that his death makes reassessment possible. We would have made the change earlier if his prose had been justly recognized as it is now beginning to be in anthologies. But during his lifetime Dylan Thomas was regarded in this country as a great English poet and reciter. Beginning now to see his work as a many-faceted whole, including poetry, fiction, dramas, essays, and impressionistic sketches, we recognize the prime importance of his first collection of short stories, which is also a mock-autobiography, mockingly titled in imitation of James Joyce.

If his critics are right in concluding that most of Thomas' best poetry was written in Swansea before he left Wales for London at the age of twenty, it may also be suggested that this collection of short stories set in Swansea and environs laid the foundations for much of the work that was to follow. "One Warm Saturday," the final story in the collection, seems to anticipate the events of Thomas' next book of prose, the unfinished novel, *Adventures in the Skin Trade,* and to use the same surrealistic style. In both the story and the novel the ever-pursued eludes capture by the hero as reality dissolves around him, which may well be the theme of *Portrait of the Artist as a Young Dog.*

But the relationship of these stories to the Thomas canon is not so straightforward. *Adventures in the Skin Trade* is his first prose work; Thomas called it his "Welsh book." It was commissioned by a London publisher and the first chapter appeared in the periodical *Wales* in 1937. The previous year Richard Church had suggested that Thomas write some autobiographical prose tales, and after his marriage in July, 1937, he set to work in

a very different style and produced "A Visit to Grandpa's," in which the surrealism is muted and the lyrical tone sustained by the young narrator; this story, standing second in *Portrait of the Artist as a Young Dog,* became Thomas' favorite broadcast and reading material. The most interesting feature of the new style of story is the rapid succession of apparently logical but often haphazardly related events, the whole ending in a diminuendo that seems anticlimactic.

The intention of the play of event on the diminutive observer is to record, by means of an episode that largely concerns or happens to others, a stage in the observer's growth, in his development as a "young dog."

The development of the "Dylan Thomas" of the *Portrait* stories into the "young dog" of the final tales is related to the development of the real Thomas as a writer, principally in the latter's use of autobiographical material for prose, poetry, and drama. Thomas delivered the typescript of *Portrait of the Artist as a Young Dog* to his publisher, in lieu of the "Welsh book" in December, 1939. Nine days later, talking to Richard Hughes, he remarked that the people of Laugharne, where he was then living, needed a play of their own. This remark is usually recognized as the origin of *Under Milk Wood.* Some years earlier Thomas had toyed with the notion of another imitation of Joyce, a sort of Welsh *Ulysses* that would cover twenty-four hours in the life of a Welsh village. Thus, from the notions of imitating Joyce and the suggestions of Church and Hughes, together with his development of a distinct prose style (instead of a prose extension of his verse, as in *Adventures in the Skin Trade*) came his best-known prose and drama. The autobiographical base is common to both works and to his poetry.

In real life Fern Hill and Ann Jones provided Gorsehill and Auntie Ann of the first story, "The Peaches," and also the poems "Fern Hill" and "Ann Jones." The fourth story, "The Fight," is a version of Thomas' first meeting with Daniel Jones, the Welsh composer, when they were boys in Swansea. Likewise, Trevor Hughes, his first genuine admirer, became the central character of the eighth story, "Who Do You Wish Was with Us?" and some of Thomas' experiences on the *South Wales Daily Post* are recorded in four of the stories, especially the last two.

The book, although composed of short stories, is given a sense of direction by careful ordering of the sequence and by repeated and cumulative details inside the stories. The ten stories fall into three periods of life: childhood, boyhood, and young manhood. The central character is called "Dylan Thomas," and although this fact is not stressed in each story it is obliquely indicated in most. Other characters reappear in some of the tales, such as his cousin Gwilym Jones and his older colleagues in journalism. But the chief cohesive factor in the collection is not the central character so much as the fact that each story celebrates a visit or an excursion either within the provincial town or just beyond it. Thus the town and its environs become a character in the book, elaborated in the names of its houses, its shops and pubs, and its weather from the warmth of summer evenings on the beach to its wet wintry nights. The locales of the stories, like the seasons of the year, change from story to story and help create the image of the region as a setting for the gallery of minor characters who dominate each story. The hero remains, as he says in "Just Like Little Dogs," a lonely and late-night observer of the odd doings of the townsfolk. The landmarks of the locale become associated with the stories of chance or temporary acquaintances met on his excursions, and these stories generally say that everyone has a

skeleton in the kitchen cupboard, as is certainly true of *Under Milk Wood*.

The skeleton is generally a private vice which is not too vicious and may be both comic and pathetic. From the first three stories, "The Peaches," "A Visit To Grandpa's," and "Patricia, Edith and Arnold," we learn that Dylan's Uncle Jim is drinking his pigs away; Cousin Gwilym has his own makeshift chapel and rehearses there his coming ministry; Grandfather Dan dreams he is driving a team of demon horses and has delusions about being buried; the Thomases' maid, Patricia, is involved with the sweetheart of the maid next door.

In the next pair of stories, "The Fight" and "Extraordinary Little Cough," the pains and pleasures of boyhood begin to affect the hero, chiefly in finding a soulmate, a fellow artist, and also in coming up against the horror of plain viciousness in his companions. The remainder of the stories deal with young manhood and are varied in subject and treatment, from the recital of a tale told to the narrator to the final story in which the narrator for the first time becomes the protagonist, although an ineffectual one.

Most of the stories include an episode set at night, and it seems a pity that the best of Thomas' night stories, the ghostly "The Followers," could not somehow be included now in the present collection.

The stories are arranged in roughly chronological order, culminating in "One Warm Saturday" and "Old Garbo," which show Dylan Thomas' inner way of escape from his home town as reality disappears in a wash of beer and a montage of what-might-have-been. In real life Thomas took to London and drinking to get out of Swansea; by the time he arrived in London he had already discovered how to blur the concrete outlines of provincial life and make its mores jump as he was to do best in *Under Milk Wood*. There is another possible explanation for his ability to see events under the conditions of dream, and that is his Welshness; there is a hint of that in the sorty, "Where Tawe Flows," titled after the "Great Welsh Novel" which a character named "Mr. Thomas" and three older friends are writing in weekly installments. "Mr. Thomas" is about to leave for London and a career as a freelance journalist. The novel is supposed to be a study of provincial life but the collaborators are only at the second chapter. We do not hear the contribution of "Mr. Thomas" because he has spent the week writing the story of a dead governess turned into a vampire because a cat jumped over her at the moment of her death. One of the foursome offers, instead, the biography of a character named Mary, an account supposed to be realistic but as fantastic as anything the real Mr. Thomas ever wrote.

Portrait of the Artist as a Young Dog accumulates the tensions of provincial life to the breaking point, as does Joyce's *A Portrait of the Artist as a Young Man.* At the end of both books the hero breaks from home as the style becomes distinctly broken. The increasingly nonrealistic style at the end of both books, a formal expression of the whirling thoughts of each young man, could be somehow symptomatic of the breaking of ties with Dublin and Swansea. Since it occurs in both books, and elsewhere, it cannot be explained as Joyce's Irishness or Thomas' Welshness; both are provincials heading for what they consider to be a literary center, Paris or London. In both books the break is long prepared for in the tensions built up, but more obviously in Joyce, from a highly imaginative childhood in the case of both author and hero through the pains of adolescence to the frustrations of university study or journalism on a provincial daily. The tensions recorded in both works are so strong that they expel their subjects far from their place of origin. If we want to know why Joyce died in Zurich or Thomas in New York, the answer is in their own autobiographies of provincial life.

A PORTRAIT OF THE ARTIST AS A YOUNG MAN

Type of work: Novel
Author: James Joyce (1882-1941)
Type of plot: Psychological realism
Time of plot: 1882-1903
Locale: Ireland
First published: 1916

Principal characters:
STEPHEN DEDALUS, an Irish student
SIMON DEDALUS, his father
EMMA, his friend

Critique:

In telling the story of his own youth under a thin disguise of fiction, Joyce has written one of the most compelling and forceful of recent autobiographies. He tried to show the beginnings of his artistic compulsion, and the events that led him to think and to act as he did. Highly descriptive, the book moves from incident to incident in an unhurried way, sketching in all the important moments and thoughts of Joyce's youth as he remembered them. This novel is a forerunner of Joyce's more significant and experimental *Ulysses*.

The Story:

When Stephen Dedalus went to school for the first time, his last name soon got him into trouble. It sounded too Latin, and the boys teased him about it. Seeing that he was sensitive and shy, the other boys began to bully him. School was filled with unfortunate incidents for Stephen. He was happy when he became sick and was put in the infirmary away from the other boys. Once, when he was there just before the Christmas holidays, he worried about dying and death. As he lay on the bed thinking, he heard the news of Parnell's death. The death of the great Irish leader was the first date he remembered—October 6, 1891.

At home during the vacation he learned more of Parnell. His father, Simon Dedalus, worshiped the dead man's memory and defended him on every count. Stephen's aunt, Dante Rior-

dan, despised Parnell as a heretic and a rabble-rouser. The fierce arguments that they got into every day burned themselves into Stephen's memory. He worshiped his father, and his father said that Parnell had tried to free Ireland, to rid it of the priests who were ruining the country. Dante insisted that just the opposite was true. A violent defender of the priests, she leveled every kind of abuse against Simon and his ideas. The disagreement between them became a problem which, in due time, Stephen would have to solve for himself.

Returning to school after the holidays, Stephen got in trouble with Father Dolan, one of the administrators of the church school he attended. Because he had broken his glasses, Stephen could not study until a new pair arrived. Father Dolan saw that Stephen was not working, and thinking that his excuse about the glasses was false he gave the boy a beating. The rest of the boys for once were on Stephen's side, and they urged him to complain to the head of the school. With fear and trembling, Stephen went to the head and presented his case. The head understood, and promised to speak to Father Dolan about the matter. When Stephen told the boys about his conversation, they hoisted him in their arms like a victorious fighter, and called him a hero.

Afterward life was much easier for Stephen. Only one unfortunate incident marked the term. In a spirit of fun, one of his professors announced in class that Stephen had expressed heresy in one of his essays. Stephen quickly changed the offending phrase and hoped that the mistake would be forgotten. After class, however, several of the boys accused him not only of being a heretic but also of liking Byron, whom they considered an immoral man and therefore no good as a poet. In replying to their charges, Stephen had his first real encounter with the problems of art and morality. They were to follow him throughout his life.

On a trip to Cork with his father, Stephen was forced to listen to the often-told tales of his father's youth. They visited the places his father had loved as a boy. Each night Stephen was forced to cover up his father's drunkenness and sentimental outbursts. The trip was an education in everything Stephen disliked.

At the end of the school year Stephen won several prizes. He bought presents for everyone, started to do over his room, and began an ill-fated loan service. As long as the money lasted, life was wonderful. Then one night, when his money was almost gone, he was enticed into a house by a woman wearing a long pink gown. At sixteen he learned what love was.

Not until the school held a retreat in honor of Saint Francis Xavier did Stephen realize how deeply conscious he was of the sins he had committed with women. The sermons of the priests about heaven and hell, especially about hell, ate into his mind. At night his dreams were of nothing but the eternal torture which he felt he must endure after death. He could not bear to make confession in school. At last he went into the city, to a church where he was unknown. There he opened his unhappy mind and heart to an understanding and wise old priest, who advised him and comforted his soul. After the confession Stephen promised to sin no more, and he felt sure that he would keep his promise.

For a time Stephen's life followed a model course. He studied Aquinas and Aristotle and won acclaim from his teachers. One day the director of the school called Stephen into his office and, after a long conversation, asked him if he had ever thought of joining the order of the Jesuits. Stephen was deeply flattered. Priesthood became his life's goal.

When Stephen entered the university, however, a change came over his thinking. He began to doubt, and the longer he studied, the more confused and doubtful he became.

His problems drew him closer to two of his fellow students, Davin and Lynch and farther away from Emma, a girl for whom he had felt affection since childhood. With Davin and Lynch he discussed his ideas about beauty and the working of the mind. Because he would not sign a petition for world peace, Stephen won the enmity of many of the fellows. They called him anti-social and egotistic. Finally neither the peace movement, the Irish Revival, nor the Church itself could claim his support.

Davin was the first to question Stephen about his ideas. When he suggested to Stephen that in everything Ireland should come first, Stephen answered that to him Ireland was an old sow that ate her offspring.

One day Stephen met Emma at a carnival, and she asked him why he had stopped coming to see her. He answered that he had been born to be a monk. When Emma said that she thought him a heretic instead of a monk, his last link with Ireland seemed to be broken. At least he was not afraid to be alone. If he wanted to find beauty, and to understand beauty, he had to leave Ireland, where there was nothing in which he believed. The prayers of his friends asking that he return to the faith went unanswered. Stephen got together his things, packed, and left Ireland, intending never to return. He did intend, some day, to write a book that would make clear his views on Ireland and the Irish.

Further Critical Evaluation of the Work:

A Portrait of the Artist as a Young Man by James Joyce is possibly the greatest example in the English language of the *bildüngsroman,* a novel tracing the growth and education of a young man, physically, mentally, and spiritually. Other examples of this genre range from Goethe's *The Sorrows of Young Werther* and Flaubert's *A Sentimental Education* to D. H. Lawrence's *Sons and Lovers.* Published in 1916, the work stands stylistically between the fusion of highly condensed naturalism and symbolism found in *Dubliners* (1914) and the elaborate mythological structure, interior monologues, and stream of consciousness of *Ulysses* (1922). In all three of these works there is a consistent concern for entrapment, isolation, rebellion from home, Church, and nation.

The novel is basically autobiographical, but in the final analysis the variants from, rather than the parallels with, Joyce's own life are of utmost artistic significance. The events of Stephen Dedalus' life are taken from the lives of Joyce, his brother Stanislaus, and his friend Byrne, covering the period between 1885 and 1902. The book begins with the earliest memories of his childhood, recounted in childlike language, and ends when Stephen is twenty-two with his decision to leave his native Dublin in search of artistic development to forge the conscience of his race. In the intervening years, like Joyce, Stephen attends the Jesuit Clongowes Wood School which he must leave because of family financial difficulties, attends a day school in Dublin, has his first sexual experience, his first religious crisis, and finally attends University College where he decides on his vocation as a writer. The dedication to pure art involves for Stephen, and Joyce, a rejection of the claims on him of duty to family, to the Catholic Church, and to Irish nationalism, either of the political type or of the literary type espoused by the writers of the Irish Renaissance. In his characterization of Stephen, however, Joyce eliminates much of himself: his sense of humor; his love of sport; his own graduation from the University before leaving Dublin; his desire to attend medical school in France; his deep concern for his mother's health; his affection for his father; and the life-long liaison he established with Nora Barnacle, who left Ireland with Joyce in 1904. The effect of these omissions is to make a narrower, more isolated character of Stephen than Joyce himself.

Portrait of the Artist as a Young Man is, on one level, an initiation story in which an innocent, idealistic youth with a sense of trust in his elders, slowly is brought to the recognition that this is a flawed, imperfect world, characterized by injustice and disharmony. Stephen finds this fact at home, at school, at church, in relationships with women and friends, and in the past and present history of his nation. Yet his pride prevents him from seeing any shortcomings in himself. In the second portion of the novel he becomes involved in the excesses of carnal lust; in the third portion, in the excesses of penitent piety, which also eventually disgust him. In the fourth section, in which he assumes the motto, *non servinum,* although he sees himself as a pagan worshiper of beauty, he becomes involved in excessive intellectual pride. In the final portion of the novel, Stephen develops his aesthetic theory of the epiphany—the sudden revelation of truth and beauty—through the artistic goals of "wholeness, harmony, and radiance." Thus his final flight from his real home—family, Church, nation—is still part of an almost adolescent rejection of the imperfections of this world and an attempt to replace it with the perfection of form, justice, and harmony of artistic creation.

Stephen Dedalus' very name is chosen to underline his character. His first name links him to Saint Stephen, the first martyr to Christianity and Stephen Dedalus sees himslf as a martyr, willing to give up all to the service of art. His last name, Dedalus, is famous from classical antiquity. It was Daedalus, the Athenian exile, who designed the great caste for King Minos of Crete and later designed the famous labyrinth in which the monstrous Minotaur was kept captive. Later, longing to return to his own land, but imprisoned in his labyrinth, Daedalus invented wings for himself and his son, Icarus, to fly from the labyrinth. Stephen, the artist, sees Dublin as the labyrinth from which he must fly in order to become the great artificer Daedalus was. It is important to remember, however, that Daedalus' son, Icarus, ignored his father's instructions on how to use the wings and because of pride and desire to exceed, flew too close to the sun, melting his wings. He plunged into the ocean and drowned. It is only later, in *Ulysses,* that Stephen recognizes himself as "lap-winged Icarus" rather than as Daedalus.

Joyce's technical skill is obvious in the series of interwoven recurrent symbols of the novel. The rose, for instance, which is associated with women, chivalric love, and creativity, appears throughout the novel. Water, also, is found in almost every chapter of the novel: it can be the water which drowns and brings death; it can also be the water which gives life, symbolic of renewal as in baptism and the final choice of escape by sea.

The central themes of *A Portrait of the Artist as a Young Man*—alienation, isolation, rejection, betrayal, the Fall, the search for the father—are developed with amazing virtuosity. This development is the second, following *Dubliners,* of the four major parts in Joyce's cyclical treatment of the life of man which moves, as the great medieval cyclical plays, from Fall to Redemption, from isolation and alienation to acceptance. The later development of Joyce's analysis of the human condition and of the relationship of art to life can be found in *Ulysses* and *Finnegan's Wake.* Joyce himself has emphasized the importance of the word "young" in the title of this work, and his conclusion, in the form of Stephen's diary which illustrates Stephen's own perceptions, words, and style, forces the reader to become more objective and detached in his judgment of Stephen. Knowing that all of Stephen's previous epiphanies have failed, the reader recognizes in these final pages, the human complexity of Stephen's important triumph in escaping from the nets of

Ireland but realizes that his triumph is complicated by important losses and sacrifices.

Ann E. Reynolds

THE POSSESSED

Type of work: Novel
Author: Fyodor Mikhailovich Dostoevski (1821-1881)
Type of plot: Psychological realism
Time of plot: Mid-nineteenth century
Locale: Russia
First published: 1871-1872

Principal characters:

STEPAN VERHOVENSKY, a provincial patriot and mild progressive
PYOTR, his nihilist son
VARVARA STAVROGIN, a provincial lady and employer of Stepan
NIKOLAY, her son, a victim of materialism
MARYA, his idiot wife
SHATOV, the independent son of one of Varvara's serfs

Critique:

The Possessed is Dostoevski's answer to Turgenev's treatment of Russian nihilism in *Fathers and Sons*. By means of a large number of characters representing all classes of Russian society, Dostoevski shows how an idle interest in nihilism brought on robbery, arson, and murder in one Russian community. The plot is exceedingly complex, but this very complexity tends to emphasize a similar quality in nineteenth-century Russian life, which convulsed violently when it concerned itself with denial of an ordering principle in the universe.

The Story:

Stepan Verhovensky, a self-styled progressive patriot and erstwhile university lecturer, was footloose in a provincial Russian town until Varvara Stavrogin hired him to tutor her only son, Nikolay. Although Stepan's radicalism, which was largely a pose, shocked Varvara, the two became friends. When Varvara's husband died, Stepan even looked forward to marrying the widow. They went together to St. Petersburg, where they moved daringly in radical circles. After attempting without success to start a literary journal, they left St. Petersburg, Varvara returning to the province and Stepan, in an attempt to assert his independence, going to Berlin. After four months in Germany, Stepan, realizing that he was Varvara's thrall emotionally and financially, returned to the province in order to be near her.

Stepan became the leader of a small group that met to discuss progressive ideas. Among the group were Shatov, the independent son of one of Varvara's serfs, a liberal named Virginsky, and Liputin, a man who made everyone's business his business.

Nikolay Stavrogin, whom Stepan had introduced to progressivism, went on to school in St. Petersburg and from there into the army as an officer. He resigned his commission, however, returned to St. Petersburg, and went to live in the slums. When he returned home, at Varvara's request, he proceeded to insult the members of Stepan's group. He bit the ear of the provincial governor during an interview with that dignitary. Obviously mentally unbalanced, Nikolay was committed to bed. Three months later, apparently recovered, he apologized for his actions and again left the province.

Months later Varvara was invited to visit a childhood friend in Switzerland, where Nikolay was paying court to her friend's daughter, Lizaveta. Before the party returned to Russia, however, Lizaveta and Nikolay broke their engagement because of Nikolay's interest in Dasha, Varvara's servant woman. In Switzerland, Nikolay and Stepan's son, Pyotr, met and found themselves in sympathy on political matters.

THE POSSESSED by Fyodor Mikhailovich Dostoevich. Published by The Modern Library, Inc.

In the province, meanwhile, there was a new governor, one von Lembke. Stepan, lost without Varvara, visibly deteriorated during her absence. Varvara arranged with Dasha, who was twenty, to marry Stepan, who was fifty-three. Dasha, who was the sister of Shatov, submitted quietly to her mistress' wishes. Stepan reluctantly consented to the marriage, but he balked when he discovered from a member of his group that he was being used to cover up Nikolay's relations with the girl.

New arrivals in the province were Captain Lebyadkin and his idiot, crippled sister, Marya. One day Marya attracted the attention of Varvara in front of the cathedral, and Varvara took the cripple home with her. Nikolay, she learned, had known the Lebyadkins in St. Petersburg. Pyotr assured Varvara, who was suspicious, that Nikolay and Marya Lebyadkin were not married.

By his personal charm and a representation of himself as a mysterious revolutionary agent returned from exile, Pyotr began to dominate Stepan's liberal friends and became, for his own scheming purposes, the protégé of Yulia, the governor's wife. Nikolay at first followed Pyotr in his political activities, but he turned against the revolutionary movement and warned Shatov that Pyotr's group was plotting to kill Shatov because of information he possessed. Nikolay confessed to Shatov that on a bet he had married Marya Lebyadkin in St. Petersburg.

As a result of a duel between Nikolay and a local aristocrat who hated him, a duel in which Nikolay emerged victorious without killing his opponent, Nikolay became a local hero. He continued intimate with Dasha, Lizaveta having announced her engagement to another man. Pyotr, meanwhile, sowed seeds of dissension among all classes in the town; he disclosed von Lembke's possession of a collection of radical manifestoes; he caused a break between his father and Varvara, and he secretly incited the working people to rebel against their masters.

Yulia led the leaders of the town in preparations for a grand fête. Pyotr saw in the fête the opportunity to bring chaos into an otherwise orderly community. He brought about friction between von Lembke, who was an inept governor, and Yulia, who actually governed the province through her salon.

At a meeting of the revolutionary group, despair and confusion prevailed until Pyotr welded it together with mysterious talk of orders from higher revolutionary leaders. He talked of many other such groups engaged in like activities. Shatov, who attended the meeting, denounced Pyotr as a spy and a scoundrel and walked out. Pyotr disclosed to Nikolay his nihilistic beliefs and proposed that Nikolay be brought forward as the Pretender when the revolution had been accomplished.

Blum, von Lembke's secretary, raided Stepan's quarters and confiscated all of Stepan's private papers, among them some political manifestoes. Stepan went to the governor to demand his rights under the law and witnessed in front of the governor's mansion the lashing of dissident workers who had been quietly demonstrating for redress of their grievances. Von Lembke appeased Stepan by saying that the raid on his room was a mistake.

The fête was doomed beforehand. Many agitators without tickets were admitted. Liputin read a comic and seditious poem. Karmazinov, a great novelist, made a fool of himself by recalling the follies of his youth. Stepan insulted the agitators by championing the higher culture. When an unidentified agitator arose to speak, the afternoon session of the fête became a bedlam, so that it was doubtful whether the ball would take place that night. Abetted by Pyotr, Nikolay and Lizaveta eloped in the afternoon to the country house of Varvara.

The ball was not canceled, but few of the landowners of the town or countryside appeared. Drunkenness and brawling soon reduced the ball to a rout which came to a sorry end when fire was discovered raging through some houses along the river. Captain Lebyadkin, Marya, and their servant were discovered murdered in their house, which remained unburned in the path of the fire. When Pyotr informed Nikolay of the murders, Nikolay confessed that he had known of the possibility that violence would take place, but that he had done nothing to prevent it. Horrified, Lizaveta went to see the murdered pair; she was beaten to death by the enraged townspeople because of her connections with Nikolay. Nikolay left town quickly and quietly.

When the revolutionary group met again, all mistrusted one another. Pyotr explained to them that Fedka, an ex-convict, had murdered the Lebyadkins for robbery, but he failed to mention that Nikolay had all but paid Fedka to commit the crime. He warned the group against Shatov and said that a fanatic named Kirillov had agreed to cover up the proposed murder of Shatov. After Fedka denounced Pyotr as an atheistic scoundrel, Fedka was found dead on a road outside the town.

At the same time, Marie, Shatov's wife, returned to the town. The couple had been separated for three years; Marie was ill and pregnant. When she began her labor, Shatov procured Virginsky's wife as midwife. The couple were reconciled after Marie gave birth to a baby boy, for the child served to regenerate Shatov and make him happy once more.

Shatov left his wife and baby alone in order to keep an appointment with the revolutionary group, an appointment made for the purpose of separating himself from the plotters. Attacked and shot by Pyotr, his body was weighted with stones and thrown into a pond. After the murder Pyotr went to Kirillov to get Kirillov's promised confession for the murder of Shatov. Kirillov, who was Shatov's neighbor and who had seen Shatov's happiness at the return of his wife, at first refused to sign, but Pyotr finally prevailed upon him to put his name to the false confession. Kirillov, morally bound to end his life, shot himself. Pyotr left the province.

Stepan, meanwhile, left the town to seek a new life. He wandered for a time among peasants and at last became dangerously ill. Varvara went to him, and the two friends were reconciled before the old scholar died. Varvara disowned her son. Marie and the baby died of exposure and neglect when Shatov failed to return home. One of the radical group broke down and confessed to the violence that had been committed in the town at the instigation of the completely unmoral Pyotr. Liputin escaped to St. Petersburg, where he was apprehended in a drunken stupor in a brothel.

Nikolay wrote to Dasha, the servant, suggesting that the two of them go to Switzerland and begin a new life. Before Dasha could pack her things, however, Nikolay returned home secretly and hanged himself in his room.

Further Critical Evaluation of the Work:

Dostoevski was nearly fifty years old when the final version of *The Possessed* (also translated as *The Devils*) appeared. (His poverty had forced him to write the book first in serial form for a Moscow literary review.) Because the novel rages so wildly against liberalism and "atheistic" socialism, many readers decided that its once-progressive author had now become a confirmed reactionary. Dostoevski himself lent credibility to this notion by his public statements. In a famous letter to Alexander III, Dostoevski characterized *The Possessed* as a historical study of that perverse radicalism which results when the intelligentsia detaches itself from the Russian masses. In another letter he proclaimed that "He who loses his people and his nationality loses his faith in his country and in God. This is the theme of my novel."

Further, given the nature of Dostoevski's personal history, a movement towards thorough-going conservatism could seem almost predictable. An aristocrat by birth, Dostoevski involved himself deeply in the Petrashevski Circle, a St. Petersburg discussion group interested in utopian socialism. Part of this group formed a clandestine revolutionary cadre, and for his participation in the conspiracy, Dostoevski was arrested. There followed a mock execution, four years of imprisonment and another four years of enforced service as a private in the Siberian army. Although freed in 1858, Dostoevski remained under surveillance, and his right to publish was always in jeopardy. He thus had every inducement to prove to government censors his utter fidelity to the *ancien regime* and "safe" principles.

But in fact *The Possessed* is not a reactionary novel. Dostoevski does not defend the institutions of monarchy, aristocracy, or censorship. He upholds Russian orthodoxy in a way that suggests a theocratic challenge to the *status quo*. His exaltation of the peasantry affords no comfort for capitalism or imperialism. And while appearing to embrace Russian nationalism, he presents an image of small-town culture which, to say the least, does not inspire Russophilia. His portrait of the ruling class is as devastating as any essay on the subject by Marx or Engels. Thus, Dostoevski's critique of radical political ideas proceeds from a basis other than that of extremist conservatism. But what is that basis?

The answer is partially revealed in Shatov's statement that half-truth is uniquely despotic. *The Possessed* is at once a criticism of a variety of political and philosophical half-truths and a searching toward a principle of Wholeness, a truth which will reunite and compose man's fragmented psyche, his divided social and political order, and his shattered relationship with God. Dostoevski does not describe that truth, partly because *the* truth is too mysterious and grand to be expressed in human language. Rather, he merely points to it by showing the defects and incompleteness in positions which pretend to be the truth.

It is through the enigmatic character of Stavrogin that Dostoevski most fully carries out his quest for Wholeness. For Stavrogin has embraced and discarded all the philosophies which Dostoevski deems inadequate. As a result, Stavrogin is the embodiment of pure negativity and pure emptiness. He is also pure evil, more evil still than Pyotr, who at least has his absolute devotion to Stavrogin as a ruling principle in his life. From Stepan Verhovensky, Stavrogin learned skepticism and the tolerant principles of "higher liberalism." In St. Petersburg, he advances to utopian socialism and a more passionate faith in salvation-through-science. But the elitism and shallow rationalism of this faith cause Stavrogin to take up messianic Russian populism. Yet he is led even beyond this stage to an investigation of orthodox theology. Unable to commit himself to the Christian faith, he perpetrates the hideous crime he later confesses to Father Tihon.

At each step in his development, Stavrogin trains disciples who both propagate his teachings and carry them out to their logical extremes. Pyotr belongs partly to Nikolay's "socialist period," while Shatov embraces the populist creed and Kirillov elaborates the themes of the theological phase. In Pyotr, socialist criticism of traditional society has produced a monomaniacal fascination with the revolutionary destruction and violence by which the new order shall emerge. Modeling this character after the infamous Russian terrorist, Sergey Nechayev, Dostoevski suggests that Pyotr is the natural outcome of socialism's faith in the power of reason to establish absolute values. Shigolov's "rational" defense of a socialist tyranny shows how thoroughly rational structures rely on nonrational premises. For Pyotr, then, the absence of rational certainties means that all behavior is permissible and all social orders are equally valid. He thus chooses to fight for a society based on men's hunger for submission, their fear of death, their longing for a Messiah. Like Machiavelli, he decides that only by founding society on the most wretched aspects of human nature can anything really lasting and dependable be built. As his Messiah, Pyotr has chosen Stavrogin, whose awesome and arbitrary will could be the source of order in a new society.

Kirillov elevates Pyotr Verhovensky's fascination with strength of will into a theological principle. Kirillov is not content with man's limited transcendence of the determinisms of nature. He aspires to the total freedom of God. Paradoxically, this freedom can only be achieved through suicide, that act which overcomes the natural fear of death by which God holds man in thrall. Not until all men are prepared at every moment to commit suicide can humanity take full responsibility for its own destiny. The great drawback in Kirillov's view is that it causes him to suppress his feelings of love and relatedness to his fellow man. Shatov's nationalistic theology is an attempt to do justice to these feelings. Rebelling against Kirillov's isolated quest for godhood, Shatov wishes to achieve the same goal by submerging himself in the life of a "God-bearing people." Yet Shatov's creed remains abstract and sentimental until Marya returns, providing him with a real person to love.

The birth of Marya's child, together with Stepan Verhovensky's "discovery" of the Russian people, are the symbols by which Dostoevski reveals his own answer to Nikolay Stavrogin. The child is for Shatov an unimaginable act of grace. Significantly, Kirillov experiences a sudden serenity and a confirmation of his mystical insight that "everything is good." For Dostoevski, the source of this grace is God, who brings exquisite order to the most corrupted human situations. Shatov's rapturous love stands in utter contradiction to Stavrogin's empty indifference. In that the child's real father is Stavrogin, Shatov's love is all the more wondrous. Stavrogin's final inability to respond to Liza's love is the logical result of his long struggle to free himself of dependency on his family, his people, his church. He boasts that he does not need anyone; from that claim comes spiritual and moral death. All that Stavrogin has touched is, in the end, dead—even Shatov.

The magnificence of Dostoevski's artistry is nowhere more apparent than in the conclusion to *The Possessed*. For he does not finally embody his great theme—human Wholeness through human dependence—in a titanic character like Stavrogin or Kirillov, but in the all-too-human Stepan. This quixotic buffoon, whom we laugh at and pity, ultimately attains the dignity he seeks. But he himself is surprised by it all, for it comes in a way he least expected it: through an encounter with his people, reunion with Varvara, and the administration of the sacrament.

Leslie E. Gerber

THE POSTMAN ALWAYS RINGS TWICE

Type of work: Novel
Author: James M. Cain (1892-1966)
Time: 1933
Locale: Southern California
First published: 1934

> Principal characters:
> FRANK CHAMBERS, a young drifter
> NICK PAPADAKIS, proprietor of the Twin Oaks Tavern
> CORA PAPADAKIS, Nick's young wife
> MR. SACKETT, the District Attorney
> MR. KATZ, a lawyer
> MADGE ALLEN, the keeper of an animal farm

Three related genres that developed in the novel form during the 1930's were the hard-boiled private detective (which departed from the genteel English novel of detection), the proletarian (which derived from European naturalism and American selective realism), and the tough guy (which derived from the former two). But perhaps for the best and most influential work of all three genres "the tough-guy novel" is a good term: Dashiell Hammett's *The Maltese Falcon,* published in 1929, and Raymond Chandler's *The Big Sleep,* published in 1939, in the private detective realm; B. Traven's *The Death Ship,* which appeared in an American edition in 1934, among proletarian novels; and Horace McCoy's *They Shoot Horses, Don't They?* published in 1935, among the pure tough-guy books are all minor classics in American literature. These and similar novels expressed the mood of American society during the depression, influenced action in motion pictures, affected the tone and attitude of more serious writers, and inspired certain European novelists during the 1940's. The quintessence of all these is James M. Cain's *The Postman Always Rings Twice.*

Although Frank Chambers, the twenty-four-year-old narrator of Cain's novel, belongs to that legion of unemployed who became tramps of the road, hoboes of the rails, and migrant workers, Cain is not deliberately interested in depicting the social ills of his time; if there is an attack on conditions that produced a man like

Frank, it is only implicit. Frank is an easy-going fellow, remarkably free of bitterness, even when given cause; although he commits murder and pistol whips a blackmailer, he is not willfully vicious. A spontaneous creature of action whose psychological nature readily accomodates ambivalent attitudes, he can be fond of Nick Papadakis and weep at his funeral, yet seduce his young wife Cora, and attempt to kill him twice.

And although this novel is concerned, as many of Cain's are, with murder and other forms of violence, and although it satisfies momentarily the average American's inexhaustible craving for details of crime and punishment, it cannot be classified as a detective tale. Cain, like the readers he has in mind, is fascinated by the intricacies of the law and of insurance claims, but his primary interest is in presenting an inside view of the criminal act. However, Frank is no gangster and Cora is no moll; they are not far removed in status or aspiration from the average anticipated reader of Cain.

For Frank and Cora lie down in the great American dreambed of the 1920's, only to wake up in a living nightmare in the 1930's. A lurid decade produced such a lurid relationship and such a lurid tale. When they meet at Nick's Twin Oaks Tavern on a highway outside Los Angeles, Frank has just been thrown off a truck, having sneaked into the back for a ride up from Tiajuana, and Cora is washing dishes in the restaurant. To demonstrate the animal impact of their encounter, Cain has them meet on page 5, make love on page 15, and decide to murder the obese, middle-aged Greek on page 23. Sharing the dream of getting drunk and making love without hiding, they go on what Cain calls "the Love-Rack." He regards the concept of "the wish that comes true" as a terrifying thing. This terror becomes palpable as soon as Frank and Cora believe that they have gotten away with murder and have acquired money, property, and freedom.

But in the background each has another dream which mocks the shared realization of the immediate wish. Cora came to Hollywood from a small town in Iowa bemused by the dream most girls of the Thirties cherished: to become a movie star. She failed, and Nick rescued her from a hash house. But basically her values are middle-class, and above all she wants respectability, even if murder is the prerequisite. An anachronism in the age of technology, though he has a certain skill as a garage mechanic, Frank desires to be always on the move, compelled by something of the spirit of the open road that Whitman celebrated. For a moment, but only for a moment, he shares this romantic, idyllic vision with Cora. After the failure of their first attempt to murder Nick, they set out together for a life of wandering. Thus, in the criminal affair of these lovers, these deliberate outsiders, two central dreams of the American experience—unrestrained mobility and respectable sedentariness—and two views of the American landscape—the open road and the mortgaged house—collide. As the dreams finally betray them, they begin, ironically, to turn on each other, for basically what Frank wants is Cora, the sexual dynamo, and what Cora wants is an instrument to be used to gain her ends—money and respectability. Though she may convince herself that the right man, instead of a fat foreigner, is a necessary part of her aspirations, this man would soon wake up in the wrong dream.

While the novel's larger thematic di-

mensions exist in the background, as a kind of fable of the American experience, giving it a lasting value in our literature, Cain is more immediately concerned with the lovers and with the action that results from their wish. This action keeps in motion certain elements that almost guarantee the reader's interest: illicit love; murder; the smell of tainted money; sexual violence that verges on the abnormal; and the strong characterizations of such men as Sackett, the district attorney; Katz, the eccentric lawyer; and Madge, the pick-up who takes Frank to South America to capture jaguars. Cain plays upon the universal wishes of the average American male.

What fascinates serious readers of literature is Cain's technique for manipulating reader response. Not only does he almost automatically achieve certain thematic ironies inherent in his raw material, but the ironies of action are stunningly executed. For instance, Frank cons Nick out of a free meal, but the con backfires in a way when Nick cons Frank into staying on to operate the service station; thus Frank becomes involved in a situation that will leave three people dead. After recovering from what he took to be an accident in the bathtub, Nick searches for Frank and persuades him to return to the roadside restaurant, thus helping to bring about his own death. Cleared of killing the Greek, Frank and Cora collect the insurance. Later, when she is waiting for a taxi to leave Frank, Cora sticks a note for him in the cash register; it refers to their having killed the Greek for his money. But Frank catches her and insists that he loves her; to test his love, Cora, who is now pregnant, swims so far out to sea that Frank will have to help her back; he does help her, but driving back from the beach, they have a wreck and she is killed. The police find the note in the cash register and conclude that Frank has engineered the wreck so that he can have all the money. Because he cannot be tried twice for killing the Greek, they execute him for murdering Cora. A careful pattern of minor ironies contributes to the impact of the major ones.

Cain's structural techniques are impressive. The swift execution of the basic situation in the first twenty-three pages has been noted, and each development, each scene, is controlled with the same narrative skill; inherent in each episode is the inevitability of the next. Everything is kept strictly to the essentials; the characters, for instance, exist only for the immediate action; there is almost no exposition as such. Cain is the acknowledged master of pace. Violence and sexual passion are thrust forward at a rate that is itself part of the reader's vicarious experience. Contributing to this sense of pace is the swift rhythm of the dialogue, which also manages to keep certain undercurrents flowing. Frank's character justifies the economy of style, the nerve-end adherence to the spine of the action. Albert Camus modeled the style of *The Stranger* on Cain's novel, and Meursault is cut to the pattern of Frank Chambers. But Cain has written what has been called a pure novel, for his deliberate intentions go no further than the immediate experience, brief as a movie is, as unified in its impression as a poem usually is. Though Frank writes his story on the eve of his execution, Cain does not even suggest the simplest moral: crime does not pay. An intense experience, which a man tells in such a way as to make it, briefly, our experience, it is its own reason for being. Camus' novel, however, operates on this premise only in the first half; in the second, he begins to develop a philosophical point of view that affects man in every phase of life.

For Cain, the postman, whose custom is always to ring twice, rang thrice. This first novel is one of America's all-time best sellers and has gone through a great many editions; Cain adapted it to the stage; and it was made into a famous motion picture. After thirty years it is still being read widely, both as popular entertainment and as a work of art of a very peculiar sort, respected, with severe qualifications, by students of literature.

THE POT OF GOLD

Type of work: Drama
Author: Titus Maccius Plautus (c. 254-184 B.C.)
Type of plot: Comedy
Time of plot: Second century B.C.
Locale: Athens
First presented: c. 195 B.C.

Principal characters:
EUCLIO, a miser
MEGADORUS, Euclio's rich neighbor, who wished to marry Euclio's daughter
EUNOMIA, Megadorus' sister
LYCONIDES, Eunomia's son, in love with Euclio's daughter
STAPHYLA, a slave belonging to Euclio

Critique:

Although the miser is unusual in Roman comedy, Plautus was not the first dramatist to use such a character, and he had as his models the older Greek dramatists who had made use of various kinds of misers in their plays. Menander, for instance, wrote three or possibly four plays which might have been Plautus' source or inspiration for his *The Pot of Gold*. Dating the Plautine play is difficult. Internal evidence indicates that the violation of Euclio's daughter occurred in August and that the play was produced for the Megalensian games, which were first held in 194 B.C. Like most Plautine comedies, this play had considerable influence on European drama. In the seventeenth century, versions by Ben Jonson, Molière, Thomas Shadwell, and Hooft appeared. Fielding's *The Miser*, written in the eighteenth century, also was based in part on this Plautine comedy.

The Story:

The grandfather of Euclio, an Athenian miser, had entrusted a pot of gold to his household deity after burying the pot within the hearth. The god, angered in turn at the grandfather, the father, and Euclio himself, had kept the secret of the treasure from all, until finally the daughter of Euclio had endeared herself to the god. In an effort to help the girl, the deity then showed Euclio where the gold was hidden, so that the miser, by using the money as a dower, might marry his daughter to Lyconides, the young man who had seduced her.

Euclio, miserly and distrustful by nature, was thrown into a feverish excitement by the discovery of the gold. He feared that someone would learn of its existence and either steal or gull it from him. After carefully hiding the gold in his house once more, he was afraid that even his old female slave, Staphyla, might learn of its whereabouts. Staphyla, in her turn, was worried by her master's strange behavior and by the fact that her young mistress was pregnant.

Meanwhile Megadorus, a wealthy neighbor and uncle of Lyconides, planned to marry Euclio's daughter, and he enlisted the aid of his sister Eunomia in his suit. Megadorus said that he was so pleased with the girl's character that he would marry her, contrary to the Athenian custom, without a dowry.

Seeing Euclio in the street, Megadorus went out to ask the old miser for his daughter's hand. Euclio, distrustful because of his new-found gold, thought Megadorus was actually plotting to take the gold from him. But Megadorus assured him that all he wanted was to marry the girl, with or without a dowry; he even offered to pay the expenses of the wedding. Upon these terms Euclio agreed to marry his daughter to Megadorus. After Megadorus left, however, Euclio could not convince himself that the prospective bridegroom was not after the pot of gold.

Euclio informed Staphyla of the proposed marriage, which was to take place the same day. Staphyla, knowing that

5273

when Euclio's daughter was married she could not conceal her pregnancy, immediately began to wory about her mistress. Staphyla had little time to worry, however, for very shortly a caterer, bringing cooks, entertainers, and food, arrived at Euclio's house to prepare the wedding feast. The caterer had been hired by Megadorus, as he had promised.

Returning from the market place with some incense and flowers to place on the altar of his household god, Euclio was horrified to see all the strangers bustling about his house, for he immediately thought they were seeking his pot of gold and would steal it from him. Euclio first drove all the caterer's people from the house in a fury and then removed his pot of gold from its hiding place. After he had removed it from the house he told them to return to their work.

Euclio decided to take the gold and hide it in the nearby temple of Faith. On the way he met Megadorus, who asked Euclio to join him in drinking a bottle or two of wine. Euclio refused, suspecting that Megadorus wanted to get him drunk and then steal the pot of gold. Going on to the temple of Faith, Euclio hid the money. Although he did not know it, a slave belonging to Lyconides, the young man who had violated Euclio's daughter, observed where the money was placed. The slave took the money from its hiding place, but Euclio, rushing back to see if it was still safe, prevented the theft.

In an effort to find a safe hiding place for his gold, Euclio took it to the grove of Silvanus. The slave, anxious to please his master and repay Euclio for a beating, watched where Euclio hid the gold in the grove.

In the meantime, Lyconides, having learned of Megadorus' plans to marry Euclio's daughter, went to Eunomia, his mother, and told her that he himself wanted to marry the girl. Pressed by Eunomia for his reasons, Lyconides revealed that he had violated the girl while he

was drunk and wished to make amends by marrying her. Even as they spoke, the excitement in Euclio's house among the women told Eunomia and Lyconides that the baby had been born to Euclio's daughter. Eunomia then agreed to help her son marry the girl.

Lyconides went to Euclio to tell of his guilt in violating the miser's daughter. He found Euclio greatly upset, for the miser had just discovered the theft of his gold from Silvanus' grove. Lyconides believed that Euclio was angry with him because he had fathered the daughter's child. Euclio, on the other hand, thought that the crime to which Lyconides was confessing was the theft of the gold. Finally the young man convinced Euclio that he had not stolen the miser's gold. He then told Euclio about his violation of the girl and the birth of the child Megadorus, in the meantime, had renounced the girl. Euclio, who had looked forward to the marriage of his daughter and the rich Megadorus, felt that he was utterly betrayed by the world.

After Euclio and Lyconides parted, the slave appeared and told Lyconides about the pot of gold he had stolen. Lyconides insisted that the slave bring the gold to him. After a lengthy argument the slave reluctantly obeyed; he hated to think that the gold would be returned to miserly Euclio.

When the slave brought the gold to Lyconides, the young man went to the house of Euclio and returned the treasure. The miser, glad to have the pot of gold once more in his hands, was so happy that he readily agreed to a marriage between his daughter and Lyconides, in spite of the fact that Lyconides had violated the girl and caused her to bear a child out of wedlock.

Strangely enough, after the wedding Euclio had a change of heart and gave the entire pot of gold to the newly wedded couple.

Further Critical Evaluation of the Work:

The Pot of Gold (Aulularia) is an excellent example of Plautus' dramaturgy at its best. The plot has two strands of action: Euclio's frantic attempts to keep his pot of gold safe from thieves, and Phaedria's offers of marriage on the very day she gives birth to Lyconides' illegitimate baby. Both lines of action are skillfully interwoven; the dramatic pace is swift and purposeful; and one scene arises from another with no digressions. This farce also exhibits Plautus' verbal exuberance to good effect—his punning, his comic alliteration, his idiomatic language, his metrical variety, and his keen sense of timing. Few playwrights knew how to handle a joke with such deftness, but merely reading them is tiresome, especially in translation. It is necessary to visualize the action taking place on a stage to get some idea of Plautus' ability.

Plautine drama was quite similar to our musical comedy. It used song and dance as part of the action; it required considerable theatrical experience; and it was based on adapted works. Plautus borrowed heavily from the Greek writers of the New Comedy, and it is often conjectured that *The Pot of Gold* was taken from a play by Menander, although it is impossible to determine which one. The miser has been a stock figure of farce almost from its inception.

Of Plautus' life little is known for certain. According to tradition he began writing his comedies after he lost a large sum in business and was forced to work in a flour mill. He wrote at least forty plays, some say over a hundred, but of these only twenty now exist. He was very popular and achieved wide fame. From his plays one can see that he knew theatrical technique inside and out, and he was attuned to his audiences in a way that only practical experience can give. From the name he took, Titus Maccius Plautus, one gathers that he played a clown, since *maccus* means clown and *plautus* means flatfoot.

The text of *The Pot of Gold* as we have it is not complete, since the conclusion is missing. However, on the basis of the two Arguments summarizing the plot—verses that preface the play and which were added by later Roman editors—one can reconstruct the ending. The translator, E. F. Watling, has composed an adequate and plausible finale on the information given in the Arguments. Plautus must have been about sixty when he wrote this play, because it was produced for the Megalensian games, which were first held in 194 B.C. The theme of money seems to fascinate playwrights as they grow older. One thinks of Aristophanes' *Plutus,* Shakespeare's *Timon of Athens,* and Molière's *L'Avare,* all of which were written in the authors' later years. The raciness of Plautus' earlier works is greatly subdued, although he could have introduced it easily considering Phaedria's unwed pregnancy.

The main interest of this play lies in the character of Euclio. Three generations of poverty, hard toil, and thrift have taken their toll on his personality. Euclio is so stingy that the neighbor's servants make jokes about it, and when he uncovers a pot of gold in his house, his only thought is to keep it from being stolen. The gold acts as a curse for him. It makes him suspicious of every kind word, of every good deed, of every person entering or leaving his house. He even suspects that the cooks are using a rooster to locate his gold. He acts like a madman in his apprehension, distractedly dashing in and out of his home. The gold is a burden that has cut him off from everyone. He does not realize that his daughter is pregnant, and learns of it only after she has given birth. Such a person invites the very thing he fears. Ironically, in trying to find the safest hiding place of all, he unwittingly gives himself away and the gold is stolen. But that only increases his frenzy. In the best scene in the play, where Lyconides tries to tell him he drunkenly made love to Phaedria, Euclio is so preoccupied with the theft that he thinks Lyconides is confessing to having taken the gold. And when he learns of Phaedria's pregnancy and birthing, it is a minor concern to him. Clearly, something dramatic must take place to induce a change of heart in him, and to make him realize that his daughter could use the gold as a dowry. What happened to transform Euclio is part of the missing conclusion. However, we do know that he gives the gold away, as a marriage gift to Phaedria, at the end.

The subplot by which Phaedria is at last married off to a man who loves her seems perfunctory, but it ties in nicely with Euclio's obsession. Megadorus is elderly, rich, innocent of Phaedria's condition, and willing to take her without a dowry. He sends his cooks to prepare the wedding feast at Euclio's, which prompts Euclio to remove the gold. And after it is stolen, Lyconides becomes the instrument by which it is returned, which establishes him as the successful suitor. Presumably Megadorus withdrew on learning that Phaedria was not a virgin. From the beginning of the play we know that Megadorus is simply the means of getting Lyconides to propose.

Like most Plautine comedies, this play had considerable influence on European drama. In the seventeenth century versions by Ben Jonson, Molière, Thomas Shadwell, and Hooft appeared. Fielding's *The Miser,* written in the eighteenth century, was also based in part on the Plautine comedy. But certainly the finest re-creation of Euclio was Molière's Harpagon in *L'Avare.*

James Weigel, Jr.

POWER

Type of work: Novel
Author: Lion Feuchtwanger (1884-1959)
Type of plot: Historical novel
Time of plot: Mid-eighteenth century
Locale: Germany
First published: 1925

Principal characters:
JOSEF Süss OPPENHEIMER, a court favorite
RABBI GABRIEL, his uncle
NAEMI, his daughter
KARL ALEXANDER, the Duke
MARIE AUGUSTE, the Duchess
WEISSENSEE, a politician
MAGDALEN SIBYLLE, his daughter

Critique:

What is a Jew? What causes a Jew, in the midst of disdain, antipathy, and persecution, to remain a Jew? Feuchtwanger deals with this problem through his fictional minister, Josef Süss Oppenheimer, the half-Christian Jew who chose to remain a Jew until his death. Subtly, Feuchtwanger shows us the metamorphosis of a rank materialist. At first Süss chose to remain a Jew because he wanted to be the greatest Jew in Germany. As a Christian he could never be at the top. At the end, he chose Judaism because he found inspiration in its teachings. The outer Süss was no more than a moneymonger, but the inner man was sensitive and human.

The Story:

All of Prussia rejoiced, and European courts lost their best topic of scandal when Duke Eberhard Ludwig broke with the countess who had been his mistress and returned to his wife to beget another heir to the throne. The countess had been his mistress for thirty years, bleeding the country with her extravagant demands for wealth and jewels. Ludwig was too vain, however, to remain her lover when she grew fat and middle-aged.

The countess sent for Isaac Landauer, the wealthy international banker who was her financial agent. Unable to advise her as to the means by which she could keep her hold on the duke, he offered to liquidate her possessions and send them to another province. But the countess, who had a strong belief in black magic, insisted that Landauer must bring to her the Wandering Jew to help cast a spell on Ludwig.

Landauer went to his young friend, Joseph Süss Oppenheimer, and offered half of what his dealings with the countess would bring him, if the young man would aid Landauer in the countess' scheme. The so-called Wandering Jew was an uncle of Süss, Rabbi Gabriel, whose melancholy demeanor and mystic ways had caused people to think that he was the legendary Wandering Jew. Süss considered the offer. It was tempting, but for some unknown reason the young man was half afraid of his uncle, whose presence always instilled in his nephew a feeling of inferiority. Furthermore, Rabbi Gabriel was rearing motherless, fourteen-year-old Naemi, the daughter whom Süss wished to conceal from the rest of the world. But at last he sent for Rabbi Gabriel.

Penniless Prince Karl Alexander came to Wildbad in hopes of gaining the grant of a substantial income from the duke. Süss, discovering the poverty of the prince, made himself the financial adviser of that destitute nobleman. Al-

POWER by Lion Feuchtwanger. Translated by Willa and Edwin Muir. By permission of the publishers, The Viking Press, Inc. Copyright, 1926, by The Viking Press, Inc.

though Landauer warned him that Karl Alexander was a poor risk, Süss continued his association with the prince merely because he hoped to ingratiate himself with the nobility. Half in gratitude, half in jest, the prince granted Süss admission to his levees.

On his arrival in Wildbad, Rabbi Gabriel told Süss that he intended to bring Naemi to his nephew. But Landauer no longer needed Gabriel to help carry out the countess' scheme, and the rabbi returned to his home. The countess had been banished from the duchy, taking with her the money procured by Landauer.

Süss became the favorite of Prince Karl Alexander. To Wildbad also came Prince Anselm Franz of Thurn and Taxis and his daughter, Princess Marie Auguste. Their mission was to urge Prince Karl Alexander to marry the princess and turn Catholic. Angry because the duke had refused to give him a pension, the prince consented.

Duke Eberhard Ludwig died suddenly, and Karl Alexander, now a Catholic, inherited the duchy. Süss became a court favorite, appointed by the new duchess to be keeper of her privy purse. Although Jews were forbidden to live in the duchy, the people had to acknowledge that the duke should be allowed his private court Jew.

Rabbi Gabriel had bought a little white house where he lived with Naemi and a servant. For three days, while the uncle was away, Süss went to Hirsau to visit his daughter. Then he returned to his duke. Since Karl Alexander's succession Süss had slyly directed him in measures which were resulting in a complete control of Swabia by the duke himself. The Constitution and the Parliament were powerless. Great noblemen had been ruined. Although his income was enormous, Süss himself refrained from holding any office. Süss had picked one former cabinet member, Weissensee, as President of the Ecclesiastical Council. One night he gave a party to which Weissensee brought his daughter, Magdalen Sibylle. Süss, noting the duke's attentiveness toward the girl, enticed her into his bedroom, where the duke followed. After that evening, the duke sent gifts to Magdalen Sibylle, his declared mistress, and Weissensee was promoted to a high office. Hating Süss, Weissensee secretly hoped to bring the favorite into disfavor at court. Learning that Süss had a daughter, he planned to place the Jew in the same position that Süss had placed him on the night Karl Alexander had taken Magdalen Sibylle.

The murder of a child revived the old legend that Jews sacrificed a Christian child at the Passover feast, and a Jew, Reb Jecheskel Seligmann, was arrested for the crime. Pressure was put on Süss to use his power to save the innocent man, but he refused because of the danger to his position at court. Then Rabbi Gabriel sent word to Süss that Naemi had heard rumors of his wickedness. At last Süss decided that he would help the arrested man. In rescuing Seligmann, he felt anew his power as the court Jew. Soon afterward, at the request of Rabbi Gabriel, he went to visit his mother. From her he learned that his real father had been a great Christian marshal in the German army. Confused, Süss finally decided that he was a Jew and would remain so.

Convinced at last that Süss was a swindler, the duke threatened to dismiss and dishonor him. But when Süss offered his own fortune in exchange for proof of any financial trickery, the duke changed his mind and roared his anger at the enemies of Süss. Realizing that the favorite now had more power than ever, Weissensee continued to plot his revenge. Arranging for the duke to spend some time at his home in Hirsau while Rabbi Gabriel was not at home, Weissensee took the duke to Süss' daughter. With visions of a heavenly rescue, the quiet, lonely child climbed to the roof of the house to escape from her attacker. She fell from the roof to her death.

Outwardly Süss professed forgiveness

toward the duke, but he pocketed more and more funds from the ducal treasury. His personality altered. Instead of ingratiating himself at court, he criticized and ridiculed his acquaintances. Filling the duke's head with dreams of conquest, Süss inveigled him into leading a new military coup. At the same time he planned the duke's destruction. While Karl Alexander lay dying at the scene of his defeat, Süss rained over his head a torrent of pent-up abuse. His enemies ordered his arrest.

For many months the case against Süss dragged on. Finally he was put into a stinking, rat-infested hole, where every day the authorities plied him for a confession, but he remained stubbornly alive and sane. Sentenced to hang, he assailed the court with icy, cutting words. He could have freed himself by declaring his Christian birth. He kept silent.

On the day of the hanging Süss died with the name "Adonai," the Hebrew name for God, on his lips, and the word was echoed by all the Jews who had gathered to watch him die.

Further Critical Evaluation of the Work:

The focus of *Power* is the issue of anti-Semitism. The central thought which Feuchtwanger wishes to communicate is that no Jew can ever be safe, whether or not he trusts the political and social system, and whether or not he achieves power in that system. In the end, Feuchtwanger says, the Jew will be murdered—and there will only be other Jews to mourn his passing.

Feuchtwanger himself was an important literary figure in pre-World War II Germany who was forced to flee the Nazis; he was a friend of playwright Bertolt Brecht and was at the center of much of the significant literary activity of the Weimar Republic. The flavor of the cultural life of Weimar is evident in *Power*. The density of the prose, the brutality, the sensuality and perversion, the breakdown of values, minds, and political institutions, have all been taken by Feuchtwanger and transposed to eighteenth century Germany, where they become the perfect medium for tracing the development of anti-Semitism.

In the 1920's, when *Power* was first published, anti-Semitism had not yet reached genocidal proportions. There were a few groups, right wing nationalists for the most part, who denounced the Jews as the cause of Germany's defeat; but at the same time, there were still Jews in positions of prominence in German social, cultural, and political life. It is to Feuchtwanger's special credit that he had the historical and dramatic insight to understand the embryonic stirrings of homicidal racism in Europe and especially in Germany, and to develop this theme in a novel. Additionally, the use of a minority group as a scapegoat, and the casual indifference (or outright collaboration) of officialdom in the violence committed against it, are phenomena which retain their significance for the contemporary reader. *Power* is incredibly and horribly prophetic.

THE POWER AND THE GLORY

Type of work: Novel
Author: Graham Greene (1904-   )
Type of plot: Psychological realism
Time of plot: The 1930's
Locale: Mexico
First published: 1940

> Principal characters:
> FATHER MONTEZ, a fugitive priest
> MARCÍA, the mother of his child
> FATHER JOSÉ, a renegade priest
> A LIEUTENANT OF POLICE
> A POOR MESTIZO

Critique:

This novel reflects the author's interest in Mexico and his experience as a resident of that country. It is not surprising that he should write a sympathetic novel about the persecution of priests in Mexico, since Greene himself is a convert and his serious novels are in keeping with Catholic idiom and doctrine. In this book he deals, as usual, with the psychology of the individual. *The Power and the Glory* was published in the United States in 1940 under the title *The Labyrinthine Ways*. It proved unpopular. A new edition, with the original title restored, has increased the body of readers familiar with the novel. In particular, Greene is a master of suspense.

The Story:

In a particular Mexican state the Church had been outlawed and the priests driven underground by the threat of being shot. After several months, word went out from the governor's office that there was still one priest, Father Montez, who was moving from village to village carrying on the work of the Church by administering the sacraments and saying masses. A young lieutenant of police, an ardent revolutionist and an anti-clerical, persuaded his chief to let him search for the priest who, as the authorities saw it, was guilty of treason.

Two photographs were pasted up together in the police station. One was the picture of an American bank robber who had killed several police officers in Texas; the other was that of the priest. No one noticed the irony, least of all the young lieutenant, who was far more interested in arresting the clergyman. While the officer was receiving permission to make a search for Father Montez, the priest was already in the village, having come there in order to get aboard a boat that would take him to the city of Vera Cruz and safety.

Before Father Montez could board the boat word came to him that an Indian woman was dying several miles inland. True to his calling, the priest mounted a mule and set out to administer the last rites to the dying woman, even though he realized that he might not find another ship to carry him to safety. There was one other priest in the vicinity, Father José. But Father José had been cowardly enough to renounce the Church, even to the point of taking a wife, a shrewish old woman. The authorities paid no attention to him at all, for they felt, and rightly so, that the priest who had renounced his vows was a detriment and a shame to the Church.

After completing his mission, Father Montez came back to the coast, where he spent the night in a banana warehouse. The English manager on the plantation allowed him to hide there.

The following day, hoping to find refuge from the police and from the revolutionary party of Red Shirts, he set out on muleback for the interior. As he traveled, he thought of his own past and of himself as a poor example of the priesthood. For Father Montez was a whiskey priest, a cleric who would do almost anything for a drink of spirits. In addition, he had in a moment of weakness fathered a child by a woman in an inland village. Thinking himself a weak man and a poor priest, he was still determined to carry on the work of the Church as long as he could, not because he wanted to be a martyr but because he knew nothing else to do.

After twelve hours of travel he reached the village where his one-time mistress and his child lived. The woman took him in overnight, and the following morning he said a mass for the villagers. Before he could escape the police entered the village. Marcía claimed him as her husband, and his child, a little grown girl of seven, named him as her father. In that manner, because of his earlier sins, he escaped. Meanwhile the police had decided on a new tactic in uncovering the fugitive. As they passed through each village they took a hostage. When a certain length of time had passed without the apprehension of Father Montez, a hostage was shot. In that manner the lieutenant of police in charge of the hunt hoped to persuade the people to betray their priest.

After the police had left the village without discovering him, Father Montez mounted his mule and went on his way. He traveled northward in an effort to escape the police and, if possible, to make his way temporarily into another state.

Some hours after leaving the village, Father Montez met with a mestizo who fell in with him. Before long the halfbreed discovered that Father Montez was the priest for whom the police were searching. He promised that he, a good Catholic, would not betray the secret, but Father Montez was afraid that the promised reward of seven hundred pesos would be too much of a temptation for the poor man.

When they reached a town, however, it was Father Montez' own weakness which put him into the hands of the police. He had to have some liquor, the sale of which was against the law. He managed to buy some illegally, but his possession of the contraband was discovered by one of the revolutionary Red Shirts, who raised a cry after him. Tracked down by a posse, the priest was caught and placed in jail. Fortunately, he was not recognized by the police, but since he had no money he was kept in jail to work out the fine.

The lieutenant of police who was searching feverishly for him unexpectedly did Father Montez a good turn. Seeing the ragged old man working about the jail, the lieutenant stopped to talk with him. The priest claimed to be a vagrant who had no home of his own. The lieutenant, feeling sorry for the old fellow, released him and gave him a present of five pesos. Leaving town, Father Montez started out across the country to find a place of temporary safety. After traveling for some time, he met an Indian woman who could speak only a few words of Spanish. She managed to make him understand that something was wrong with her child. He went with her and found that the baby had been shot; his immediate guess was that the American bandit had done the deed.

After performing rites over the child, Father Montez continued his flight. He eventually made his way into the next state, where he was given sanctuary by a German plantation owner. After resting a few days, he planned to go to a city and there present his problems to his bishop. Before he could leave, however, he was found by the mestizo, who said that the American bandit, a Catholic, was dying and needed the priest. Father Montez answered the call, even though he was sure he was being led into a trap. The bandit was really dying, but he lay in the state from which Father Montez had just escaped. With him was a party of police, waiting for the priest's appearance in order to arrest him.

Immediately after the bandit's death the police closed in and Father Montez was captured. Taken back to the capital of the state and tried for treason, he was found guilty and sentenced to be shot. The lieutenant of police, who felt sorry in a way for the old priest, tried to persuade the renegade Father José to hear Father Montez' last confession, but Father José, who feared the authorities, refused. Father Montez was led out and shot without the benefit of the Church's grace. Yet the lieutenant of police had not succeeded in removing the Church's influence; in the evening of the day on which Father Montez died another priest made his way, in secret, into the town where the execution had taken place.

Further Critical Evaluation of the Work:

Although in all of Greene's fiction published between the late thirties and the late fifties, he is concerned with the moral and spiritual struggle of man caught between the Devil and God—indeed one might say Greene's setting is man's soul—he is also preoccupied with politics. Perhaps more than any of the so-called political writers of the thirties and forties, he handled topical matters: big business, revolution, war, international spy rings and diplomacy. One must take care not to think of these situations as mere "stages" on which his heroes work out their salvation or damnation. They are rather integral to the novels themselves, contributing significantly to the total meaning. They also point up Greene's continual awareness of actual events in culture and of their importance to his dramatization of contemporary man.

It is pertinent, for example, that the spiritual odyssey of Father Montez should take place in Mexico whose reactionary political and religious heritage is being assaulted by a radical ideology. The priest's temptation is not only of the flesh or of doubt in God's existence; he is also tempted by the honest humanitarianism of the lieutenant of police.

Specifically, the lieutenant attempts to persuade the priest that man does not have his sources in the supernatural but in the exclusively natural. Therefore, he goes on to argue, the Church, in its failure to mitigate the people's poverty in favor of ministering to their spiritual needs, has actually betrayed them.

It is a cogent argument—one which is frequently made by modern revolutionaries—and one which the priest can only respond to by dying. Still the priest's self-sacrifice remains a powerful political statement that man at times will assert his faith in all its irrationality against the State and its rationality.

THE POWER OF DARKNESS

Type of work: Drama
Author: Count Leo Tolstoy (1828-1910)
Type of plot: Domestic tragedy
Time of plot: Nineteenth century
Locale: Russia
First presented: 1886

> *Principal characters:*
> Nikíta Akímitch Tchilíkin, a laborer
> Anísya, his mistress
> Peter Ignátitch, Anísya's husband, a well-to-do peasant
> Matryóna, Nikíta's mother
> Akím, Nikíta's father
> Akoulína, Peter's daughter by his first marriage
> Marína, an orphan girl

Critique:

This play on a theme of sin and redemption is embodied in the traditional Russian conflict of father against son, of the natural against the artificial life. Nikíta finds himself led into adultery and murder almost unknowingly, the implication being that evil is a state into which anyone can fall unless he is diligently wary of it. The plot may seem unexciting because of the didactic way in which Tolstoy deals with the evils of idleness, greed, and luxury, but his ability to depict the triumph of spiritual humility over materialistic arrogance must still be admired.

The Story:

Peter Ignátitch, a well-to-do peasant, was forty-two years old and sickly. His second wife, Anísya, was only thirty-two. She still felt young and had started an affair with Nikíta, their hired man. Peter, who considered Nikíta a loafer, had thought of dismissing him. As he was explaining his intention to his wife they learned that Nikíta was talking about getting married and leaving their farm. Anísya complained to Peter that Nikíta's departure would leave her with more work than she could handle.

When Anísya and Nikíta were alone, he told her that in spite of his marriage plans he would always come back to her. Anísya threatened to do violence to herself if Nikíta went away, adding that when her husband died Nikíta could marry her and become master of the farm. Nikíta declared, however, that he was satisfied with his lot. Then Matryóna, Nikíta's mother, came in and said that Nikíta's marriage was his father's plan, not her own, and that he need not worry about it. She then asked Nikíta to leave the room.

Left alone with Matryóna, Anísya confessed her love for Nikíta. Matryóna, who said that she had known of their affair all along, gave Anísya some poison and advised her to bury her husband before spring; she suggested also that Nikíta would make a good master on the farm. Concerning the marriage, she explained that Nikíta had had an affair with Marína, an orphan girl, and that when Akím, his father, learned about it he had insisted that Nikíta marry her. Matryóna had suggested that they talk the matter over with Peter, who was Nikíta's master. Having explained the situation, Matryóna again urged Anísya to use the poison on Peter, who was near death anyway.

At that point Peter and Akím came in, discussing Nikíta's proposed marriage.

THE POWER OF DARKNESS by Count Leo Tolstoy, from THE PLAYS OF LEO TOLSTOY. Translated by Louise and Aylmer Maude. By permission of the publishers, Amen House. Copyright, 1910, by Constable & Co. Copyright, 1923, by Oxford University Press, Inc. Renewed. All rights reserved.

Peter seemed to approve of the match until Matryóna told him that Marína was promiscuous and so had no claim on Nikíta. To determine the truth of this charge, Peter sent for Nikíta, who falsely swore that there had been nothing between him and Marína. As a result, the marriage was called off. Nikíta was then visited by Marína, who pleaded her love and said that she had always been faithful to him. Nikíta sent her away, saying that he was no longer interested in her.

Six months later Anísya and Matryóna were worried because Peter was about to die but had not told anyone where his money pouch was hidden. Anísya also told Matryóna that she had put the poison into Peter's tea. As they stood talking in the courtyard, Peter appeared on the porch of his house, saw Nikíta, who was happening by, and asked his forgiveness, a formal request made by the dying. Nikíta was temporarily struck with remorse. Matryóna, who then helped Peter back into the house, discovered that the money pouch was hanging by a cord around the sick man's neck. Anísya went into the house and came out again with the money pouch, which she gave to Nikíta. She then returned to the house, only to reappear a short time later, wailing a formal lament for Peter, who had just died.

Nine months after Peter's death, Nikíta, who had married Anísya and become the master of the farm, grew tired of his wife and began an affair with Akoulína, Peter's daughter by his first marriage. Anísya was afraid to say anything for fear that her murder of Peter would be discovered.

In the following autumn, Matryóna arranged a marriage for Akoulína, who had become pregnant by Nikíta. Matryóna told the father of the suitor that Akoulína herself could not be seen because she was sickly; at that moment, in fact, Akoulína was delivering her child in the barn. Nikíta could not decide what to do about the child, but Anísya gave him a spade and told him to dig a hole in the cellar.

Nikíta balked at the suggestion, feeling that he was not to blame for all his troubles. Anísya, happy that she could force Nikíta into sharing her own guilt, told him that he was already guilty because he knew that she had poisoned Peter and because he had accepted Peter's money pouch. At last Nikíta went to the cellar and dug the hole.

When Anísya brought the baby to him, covered with rags, Nikíta was horrified to discover that the infant was still alive. Anísya and Matryóna pushed Nikíta into the cellar, where he murdered the baby. After he had completed the deed he reappeared in a frenzy, threatening to kill his mother and claiming that he could still hear the baby whimpering. He then went off to forget his troubles in drink.

Some time after that Akoulína's wedding feast was held at Nikíta's farm. Nikíta saw Marína, who had been able to marry respectably and who was now a wedding guest. Alone and troubled, he told Marína that his only happiness had been with her. Distraught, Marína left Nikíta to himself. Then Matryóna and Anísya came to tell him that the bridal pair awaited his formal blessing. Feeling that it would be impossible to give his blessing, Nikíta thought of committing suicide until Mítritch, a drunken ex-soldier, appeared and began to talk of his experiences, concluding with the thought that a person should never be afraid of anyone. With this thought in mind, Nikíta decided to join the wedding feast.

When Nikíta appeared before the guests he was holding Akím by the hand. Suddenly, instead of blessing the bridal pair, he fell on his knees before his father. Proclaiming that he was guilty and wished to make his confession, he begged forgiveness of Marína, whom he had misused, and of Akoulína, saying that he had poisoned Peter. Although Akoulína said that she knew who had poisoned her father, a police officer, who happened to be a guest at the wedding, wanted to arrest Nikíta immediately. Akím prevented him by saying that his son must attend to God's business first. Nikíta then confessed that he had seduced Akoulína and murdered her child.

Finally, turning again to his father, Nikíta asked for his forgiveness. Akím told him that God would forgive him and show him mercy. Nikíta was then bound and led away.

Further Critical Evaluation of the Work:

Count Leo Tolstoy came to playwriting relatively late in his career, after he had completed his prose masterpieces, *War and Peace* (1869) and *Anna Karenina* (1877), and at a time when his religious "conversion" prompted him to view his writing in moralistic, rather than artistic, terms. Hence, the works of this period are heavily didactic and lack much of the balance, scope, and humanity of this previous efforts. Nevertheless, *The Power of Darkness* is a potent realistic play, one of the most intense and moving dramas of the period, and perhaps the outstanding realistic play of the pre-Chekhovian Russian theater.

Although there was no direct influence, *The Power of Darkness* resembles the powerful naturalistic dramas which were, at that time, rejuvenating Western theater. As in a typical naturalistic play, *The Power of Darkness* shows a group of weak, ordinary people who, after committing petty crimes out of greed, sexual jealousy, and self-deception, find themselves caught up by forces they cannot understand or control, driven to newer, greater crimes, and ultimately destroyed by the momentum of the evil they so easily unloosed. Small sins automatically lead to bigger ones; lesser crimes require more extreme deeds to maintain concealment; casual observers or passive accomplices are drawn into active conspiracy, and so on. Each evil deed, the participants believe, will be the last one and lead them, finally, to "happiness." The opposite is the case; they bind themselves tighter and tighter in a "net" of their own making.

Tolstoy's chronicling of this disintegration is fascinating in its realistic accuracy. Even in the midst of their depravity, the characters retain a certain sympathy; they are trapped and drawn to their destruction almost unconsciously. The catalyst is Nikíta's mother, Matryóna, the one character who seems consciously and deliberately evil, and she is one of the most fascinating creations of the modern stage. She plays on the others like a musician on instruments and seems to enjoy intrigue for its own sake. And she is the consummate hypocrite, acting the role of pious matron, while engineering the diabolical schemes. For example, as Peter dies from the poison she supplied, Matryóna offers him religious consolation.

However, if the process of disintegration and self-destruction described in *The Power of Darkness* causes it to resemble the naturalistic plays, its resolution is quite different. To the naturalists, man was the helpless victim of biological and economic circumstances. Their plays and novels were intended to illustrate man's hopeless situation in the face of an impersonal "scientific" universe. Tolstoy's vision was quite the opposite. To him, the "power of darkness" was more than balanced by the "power of Light," and his play is, above all, not a story of damnation, but one of redemption.

The focus of redemption is on Nikíta. From the beginning of the play his sin is clearly the product of arrogance and sensuality, rather than any positive inclination to evil. When circumstances force him to the most vicious of the crimes, the murder of the baby, he is too weak to withstand the pressure of his mother, and commits the act in a half-conscious frenzy. Immediately he is overwhelmed by guilt and remorse. He hears the breaking bones, the cries of the dying child, and seems on the edge of madness—but he is not granted that escape. He prepares to commit suicide, but that, too, is denied him.

Nikíta's insight comes when, in the midst of his suicide attempt, he is accosted by Mítritch, a drunken laborer, who tells him a parable about the "devil's power," concluding with the statement that: "when you begin to be afraid of people, then the devil, with his cloven hoof, will snatch you up right away and stick you wherever he wants to."

Nikíta thus realizes that his descent into evil has been the result of this "fear" of the opinion of men and his own foolish desire for the transitory pleasures of the material world. Shorn of that fear he gains his resolve and goes to the wedding party to confess. He accepts all of the blame for the crimes, which is, in a spiritual sense, true: all the conspirators are responsible for all the crimes. But, in spite of the totality of his guilt, he is redeemed.

PRAGMATISM

Type of work: Philosophical essays
Author: William James (1842-1910)
First published: 1907

No more illuminating or entertaining account of pragmatism has ever been written than James's *Pragmatism: A New Name for Some Old Ways of Thinking.* But this is more than a popular exposition prepared for the academic audiences of Lowell Institute and Columbia University during the winter of 1906-1907 it is historic philosophy in the making. Although James was profoundly influenced by Charles Sanders Peirce, who invented the basic statement and name of pragmatism, he was an independent thinker with a distinctive creative direction of his own.

Peirce's essay, "How to Make Our Ideas Clear," introduced the pragmatic notion that ideas are clarified by considering what we would expect in the way of experience if we were to act in a certain manner. The whole of our conception of the "sensible effects" of an object is the whole of our conception of the objects, according to Peirce. This essay, clear, radical, entertaining, appeared in the *Popular Science Monthly* in January, 1878. But professional philosophers were not interested in theory advanced by a mathematician, particularly when the theory went against the prevailing idealism of American philosophers. It was not until James revived the idea in 1898 with a talk on "Philosophical Conceptions and Practical Results" that the pragmatic philosophy began to stir up controversy. With the lectures on meaning and truth which were published under the titles *Pragmatism* and *The Meaning of Truth,* the former in 1907 and the latter in 1909, James brought pragmatism into the forefront of American thought.

In his first lecture on "The Present Dilemma in Philosophy," James distinguished between the "tender-minded" and the "tough-minded" in temperament, the former inclining toward a philosophy that is rational, religious, dogmatic, idealistic, and optimistic, and the latter, the tough-minded, inclining toward a philosophy that is empirical, irreligious, skeptical, materialistic, and pessimistic. He then went on to state his conviction that philosophy can satisfy both temperaments by becoming pragmatic.

His lecture on the pragmatic method begins with one of the most entertaining anecdotes in philosophical discourse. James describes a discussion by a group of philosophers on this question: Does a man go around a squirrel that is on a tree trunk if the squirrel keeps moving on the tree so that the trunk is always between himself and the man? Some of the philosophers claimed that the man did not go around the squirrel, while others claimed that he did. James settled the matter by saying, "Which party is right depends on what you *practically mean* by 'going round' the squirrel." It could be said that the man goes around the squirrel since he passes from the north of the squirrel to the east, south, and west of the squirrel. On the other hand, the man could be said not to go around the squirrel since he is never able to get on the various sides of the squirrel—on the right of him, then behind him, and so forth. "Make the distinction," James said, "and there is no occasion for any further dispute."

James then applied the method to a number of perennial philosophical problems, but only after a careful exposition of the meaning of pragmatism. He described the pragmatic method as a way of interpreting ideas by discovering their practical consequences—that is, the difference the idea's truth would make in our experience. He asks, "What difference would it practically make to anyone if this notion rather than that notion were true?" and he replies, "If no practical difference whatever can be traced, then the alternatives mean practically the same thing, and all dispute is idle."

In his lecture James argued that the pragmatic method was not new: Socrates, Aristotle, Locke, Berkeley, and Hume had used it. But what was new was the explicit formulation of the method and a new faith in its power. Pragmatism is to be understood, however, not as a set of grand theories but as a method which turns attention away from first principles and absolutes and directs it to facts, consequences, and results in our experience.

A bare declaration would hardly have been enough to make pragmatism famous. James devoted a considerable part of his lectures to brief examples of the application of the pragmatic method. He cited with approval Berkeley's analysis of matter as made up of sensations. Sensations, he said, "are the cash-value of the term. The difference matter makes to us by truly being is that we then get such sensations. . . ." Similarly, Locke applied the pragmatic method, James claimed, when he discovered that unless by "spirit" we mean consciousness, we mean nothing by the term.

Is materialism or theism true? Is the universe simply matter acting and interacting, or is God involved? James considers this problem pragmatically and reaches a curious result. As far as the past is concerned, he says, it makes no difference. If rival theories are meant to explain what is the case and if it makes no difference in our experience which theory is true, then the theories do not differ in meaning. If one considers the difference now and in the future, however, the case is different: "Materialism means simply the denial that the moral order is eternal . . . spiritualism means the affirmation of an eternal moral order and the letting loose of hope."

To this kind of analysis some critics have answered with the charge that James is one of the "tender-minded" philosophers he spoke harshly of in his earlier lectures. But throughout the course of this series of lectures and in subsequent books James continued to use pragmatism as a way of combining the tough and tender temperaments. He extended the use of the term "difference" so that the meaning of an idea or term was no longer to be understood merely in terms of sense experiences, as Peirce had urged, but also in terms of passionate differences, of effects upon human hopes and fears. The essays in *Pragmatism* show this liberalizing tendency hard at work.

The temperate tone of James's suggestions concerning the religious hypothesis is clear in one of his later lectures in the book, "Pragmatism and Religion," in which he writes that "Pragmatism has to postpone dogmatic answer, for we do not yet know certainly which type of religion is going to work best in the long run." He states again that the tough-minded can be satisfied with "the hurly-burly of the sensible facts of nature," and that the tender-minded can take up a monistic form of religion; but for those who mix temperaments, as James does, a religious synthesis that is moralistic and pluralistic, allowing for human development and creativity in various directions, is to be preferred.

Pragmatism is important not only as a clear statement of the pragmatic method and as an illustration of its application to certain central problems, but also as an exposition, although introductory, of James's pragmatic theory of truth. His ideas were developed more fully two years later in *The Meaning of Truth*.

Beginning with the common notion that truth is a property of ideas that agree with reality, James proceeded to ask what was meant by the term "agreement." He decided that the conception of truth as a static relation between an idea and reality was in error, that pragmatic analysis shows that true ideas are those which can eventually be verified, and that an idea is said to be verified when it leads us usefully to an anticipated conclusion. Since verification is a process, it becomes appropriate to say that truth "happens to" an idea, and that an idea *"becomes true, is made true by events."* A revealing summary statement is this: " 'The true,' to put it very briefly, is only the expedient in the way of our thinking, just as 'the right' is only the expedient in the way of our behaving."

The ambiguity of James's account, an ambiguity which he did not succeed in removing, allows extremes of interpretation. On the one hand, a reader might take the tender-minded route, something in the manner of James himself, and argue that all kinds of beliefs about God, freedom, and immortality are true in so far as they lead a man usefully in the course of his life. On the other hand, a tough-minded reader might be inclined to agree with James that an idea is true if the expectations in terms of which the idea makes sense are expectations that would be met, if one acted—but he might reject James's suggestions that this means that a great many ideas which would ordinarily be regarded as doubtful "become true" when they satisfy the emotional needs of a believer.

One difficulty with which James was forced to deal because of his theory of truth resulted, it might be argued, not from his idea of truth as the "workableness" of an idea, but from his inadequate analyses of the meanings of certain terms such as "God," "freedom" and "design." James maintained that, pragmatically speaking, these terms all meant the same thing, *viz.*, the presence of "promise" in the world. If this were so, then it would be plausible to suppose that if the idea that the world is promising works out, the idea is true. But if James's analysis is mistaken, if "God" means more than the possibility of things working out for the better, James's claim that beliefs about God are true if they work loses its plausibility.

Whatever its philosophic faults, *Pragmatism* is saved by its philosophic virtues. For the general reader it offers the rare experience of confronting first-rate ideas by way of a clear and entertaining, even informal, style.

THE PRAIRIE

Type of work: Novel
Author: James Fenimore Cooper (1789-1851)
Type of plot: Historical romance
Time of plot: 1804
Locale: Western Plains of the United States
First published: 1827

Principal characters:
NATTY BUMPPO, an old frontiersman
ISHMAEL BUSH, a desperado
ESTHER BUSH, his wife
ELLEN WADE, Esther's niece
ABIRAM WHITE, Esther's brother
DR. BATTIUS, a naturalist
PAUL HOVER, Ellen's lover
CAPTAIN MIDDLETON, of the United States Army
INEZ, Middleton's wife
HARD-HEART, a Pawnee chief

Critique:

This novel, the fifth and last volume of Cooper's familiar Leatherstocking series, closes the career of his famous frontiersman and scout, Natty Bumppo. The plot is full of incident, but it depends too much on coincidence to seem realistic to many modern readers. The character portrayal is not vivid; the women, especially, seem dull and unreal. Much of the action is slowed down by the stilted dialogue. Yet, in spite of these defects, *The Prairie* catches much of the spirit of the old West.

The Story:

Shortly after the time of the Louisiana Purchase the family of Ishmael Bush traveled westward from the Mississippi River. Ishmael was accompanied by his wife, Esther, and their sons and daughters. Also in the caravan were Ellen Wade, a niece of Esther; Abiram White, Esther's brother; and Dr. Battius, a physician and naturalist. As this company searched for a camping place one evening, they met an aged trapper, Natty Bumppo, and his dog. The trapper directed them to a nearby stream.

After night had fallen, Bumppo discovered Ellen in a secret meeting with her lover, Paul Hover, a wandering bee hunter. The three were captured by a band of Sioux. While the Indian raiders stole all the horses and cattle from Ishmael's party, the captives made their escape. Unable to proceed across the prairie, the emigrant family occupied a naturally fortified hilltop shown to them by Bumppo.

A week later, Paul, Bumpoo, and Dr. Battius were gathered at Bumppo's camping ground. They were soon joined by a stranger, who introduced himself as Captain Middleton of the United States Army. Bumppo was delighted to find that Middleton was the grandson of an old friend whom he had known in the days of the French and Indian wars. The young officer had come to find his wife, Inez, who had been kidnaped by Abiram White shortly after her marriage. She was now a captive in Ishmael's camp. Paul, Bumppo, and Dr. Battius agreed to help Middleton rescue her.

On the same day Ishmael and his sons left their camp to hunt buffalo. That evening they returned with meat, but Asa, the oldest son, did not return with the rest of the hunters. In the morning the entire family set out to search for him. At last his dead body was found in a thicket; he had been shot in the back with one of Bumppo's bullets. His family buried him and returned to camp. There they found that both Ellen and Inez were gone.

The girls, who had been rescued by Middleton and his friends, were rapidly making their escape across the prairie, when their progress was interrupted by a meeting with a Pawnee warrior, Hard-Heart. After the Indian had galloped away on his horse, the travelers found themselves in the path of a stampeding herd of buffalo. The group was saved from being trampled to death at the last moment by the braying of Dr. Battius' donkey, for at the strange sound the buffalo turned aside. However, Middleton's party was soon captured by a band of Sioux pursuing the buffalo herd. They were the same Indians who had captured Bumppo, Paul, and Ellen once before. At the same time Ishmael and his sons approached on foot in search of the two girls. The Indians remounted and gave horses to their captives so that all could ride to Ishmael's camp while he and his sons were away. During the Indian raid on the camp, Bumppo helped his friends escape on horseback.

They rode as far as possible before making camp for the night. But in the morning they found that the Sioux had followed them and had set fire to the prairie in order to drive them into the open. Bumppo rescued the party by burning off the nearby prairie before the larger fire reached it. As they started off, they met the lone Hard-Heart again. From him they learned that the Sioux and Ishmael's family had joined forces in order to search for them. Since Hard-Heart and the little band had a common enemy in the Sioux, he agreed to take them to his Pawnee village for protection.

In order to evade their pursuers, the fugitives crossed a nearby river. As they reached the far bank the Sioux appeared on the opposite shore. That night the fugitives remained free, but snow fell and made it impossible for them to escape without being tracked. They were captured and taken to the Sioux village.

Hard-Heart, Paul, and Middleton were bound by their savage captors. Out of respect for his age, Bumppo was allowed to roam freely, but he declined to leave his friends. The women were placed in the lodge of the Sioux chief.

Using Bumppo as an interpreter, the Sioux chief asked Inez to be his wife. At the same time Ishmael asked the chief to hand over to him Inez, Ellen, and Bumppo, as had been previously agreed. When the chief refused, Ishmael departed angrily.

The Indians then gathered in council to decide the fate of Hard-Heart, and many wished to torture him to death. But an old warrior stepped forward and declared that he wished to make the Pawnee his adopted son. Hard-Heart, however, refused to become a member of the Sioux tribe. The Sioux began their torture, but in the midst of it Hard-Heart escaped and joined a war party of his own Pawnees, who arrived on the scene at that moment.

Leaving their women to guard the prisoners, the Sioux prepared to fight. The braves of the two tribes gathered on the opposite banks of a river, neither side daring to make the first move. Then Hard-Heart challenged the Sioux chief to single combat.

Meanwhile, Bumppo helped the rest of the captives to escape. Shortly afterward they fell once more into the hands of Ishmael.

Hard-Heart was victorious in the single-handed combat, and his warriors put the Sioux to flight in the battle which followed.

The next morning Ishmael held a court of justice in order to deal with his captives. He realized his mistake in carrying Inez away from her husband and allowed the couple their freedom. He gave Ellen her choice of remaining with his family or going with Paul. She chose to go with her lover. Ishmael allowed Dr. Battius his freedom because he did not think the scientist worth bothering about. Then Bumppo came up for judgment.

Ishmael still believed that Bumppo had shot his son, Asa. Bumppo, however, revealed that it was really Abiram who had done the cowardly deed. Abiram confessed his crime and then fainted. Ishmael was reluctant to pronounce judgment on his brother-in-law, but he felt it his duty to do so. That evening he gave Abiram the choice of starving to death or hanging himself. Late that night Ishmael and Esther returned to find that Abiram had hanged himself. They buried him and continued on their way back to the frontier settlements.

Middleton, Paul, and the girls invited Bumppo to return to the settlements with them, where they would make comfortable his last days. He refused, giving as his reason his desire to die away from civilization. He chose to remain in the Pawnee village with Hard-Heart.

A year later, when Middleton's duties as an army officer brought him near the Pawnee village, he determined to pay Bumppo a visit. Arriving at the camp, Middleton found the old trapper near death. It was late afternoon. Bumppo revived enough to greet his old friend. At sundown, however, he seemed to be breathing his last. As the sun sank beneath the horizon, he made one last tremendous effort. He rose to his feet and, as if answering a roll call, he uttered a loud and firm "Here" — then fell back dead into the arms of his friends.

Further Critical Evaluation of the Work:

The Prairie is the third title published in the Leatherstocking Tales. When the series of five tales was published together in 1850, *The Prairie* became the last. Since Cooper had never seen the Great Plains area in which the action of the tale occurs, he drew from descriptions and additional information in accounts by Lewis, Clark, and other explorers. Beyond this he used his imagination.

The Prairie is related in several ways to the two earlier Leatherstocking Tales. Two themes in *The Pioneers*—the wasting of America's natural resources and the vanishing of the American Indian as a race—continue in *The Prairie*. Leatherstocking in *The Pioneers* had condemned the wasteful cutting and burning of trees, the greater slaughter of passenger pigeons, and the seining of fish that were left to rot on the lake shore. In *The Prairie* the old trapper complains: "What the world of America is coming to, and where the machinations and inventions of its people are to have an end, the Lord, He only knows. . . . How much has the beauty of the wilderness been deformed. . . ." The theme of the "vanishing American" had been touched on with the death of Chingachgook in *The Pioneers*. It became a leading theme in *The Last of the Mohicans* and it returns in *The Prairie* with the Pawnees and the Sioux warring as the Delawares and the Mingoes had fought in *The Last of the Mohicans,* making it easier for such white settlers as Ishmael Bush and his large family finally to take over what had been the Indians' ancient homeland.

Certain resemblances between characters and character relationships in *The Last of the Mohicans* and *The Prairie* may also be seen. The genteel Captain Duncan Uncas Middleton is a grandson of Duncan Heyward and Alice Munro, who represented gentility in *The Last of the Mohicans*. The love of the old trapper for his adopted son Hard-Heart parallels the feeling that Hawkeye had for young Uncas. The enmity of Hard-Heart and Mahtoree is as fierce as that of Uncas and Magua (but the good Indian kills the bad one in *The Prairie,* whereas the bad Indian killed the good one in *The Last of the Mohicans.*) The pedantic wordiness of Dr. Obed Battius surpasses in comic absurdity the talk and the psalm singing of David Gamut.

One may object to the complexity and many improbabilities of plot in *The Prairie,* to the old trapper's long-windedness, or to Dr. Battius' ridiculous vocabulary and views, but Ishmael Bush is one of Cooper's best-drawn characters, and the old trapper is both pathetic and noble as he approaches his death. The death scene itself so impressed the English novelist Thackeray that he imitated it with the death of Colonel Newcome in *The Newcomes* (1853-1855).

THE PRAISE OF FOLLY

Type of work: Essay
Author: Desiderius Erasmus (1466?-1536)
First published: 1511

Although written some four hundred and fifty years ago, *The Praise of Folly* is still an effective analytic examination of man's abilities and vanities. It not only gives the modern reader an idea of the struggle of the early humanists in their effort to rid the world of the conventions and forms of the Middle Ages, but it also gives him some insight into those problems of living with which we are still faced today.

Erasmus himself never thought very highly of this work which, even though written quickly and as something of a jest, is the one for which he is best remembered. He wrote it in about seven days in 1509 while he was recovering from an illness at the home of his English friend, Sir Thomas More. And it was not until two years after its writing that he had the book secretly printed in France. However, the fact that there were at least seven editions within a few months proves its immediate success and popularity.

Because of this work and several others Erasmus became one of the most popular men of letters of his time, and, consequently, he became one of the most influential. He was of prime importance in the spread of humanism throughout the northern part of Europe and was instrumental in many aspects of both the Reformation and the later phase of the Renaissance. Everything he did was to aid man in tearing away the veils of foolish traditions and customs and to help him find the road back to the true God and to his true self.

The form itself is an immediate indication of the type of work that the book is to be. Written as a parody of a classical oration, the essay sets Folly as the orator. Her subject is society and she quickly becomes a many-sided symbol which stands for all that is natural in man, for all his misdirected effort, and for all of his attempts to get the wrong things out of life. She discusses the problem of man's wisdom and tells how it can be united with man's action to gain success in a world of folly; she is concerned with the way in which reason and simple Christian advice can be presented to mankind; she wonders what the Christian humanist can do for himself and the world. Parody, irony, and satire are used throughout the essay to show man what he does and what he should do. And no one is spared. Neither king nor prince, pope nor priest, aristocrat nor working man escapes the indignation which Erasmus feels toward society.

At the beginning of her oration Folly declares that she is giving a eulogy of herself, and she justifies the impertinence by saying that she knows herself better than anyone else and that no one else will do it for her. Her father, she says, is Plutus. the real father of all men and gods. and she was born out of his passion for Youth. Significantly, her birth took place in the Fortunate Isles, and she lists among her followers Drunkenness, Ignorance, Self-love, Flattery, Forgetfulness, Laziness, Pleasure, Madness. Sensuality, Intemperance, and Sound Sleep—all of whom help her to gain control of all things.

It is Folly, for instance, who leads man to marriage and the conception of life, thus prolonging this life that is so foolish. It is Pleasure, one of her followers, who makes life bearable at all. It is Forgetfulness who makes youth such a carefree time, and who restores this same characteristic to old age, thereby bringing about a second childhood. By throwing off care and avoiding wisdom, we are told, one can achieve perpetual youth.

Folly goes on to say that she is the source of all that is pleasurable in life.

Man will never be completely divorced from Folly because he is ruled more by passion than by reason, and the two most important aspects of passion are anger and lust. One of the chief sources of man's pleasure, of course, is women, who are even more subject to folly than men. Men's coarser looks are a result of the infection of wisdom.

Friendship also derives from Folly because it makes us ignore the faults and defects of other people. Marriage itself is held together with compromise, infatuation, and duplicity. Without Folly man could not get along with others; he would soon begin to hate himself and everything would seem sordid and loathsome.

Folly praises herself under the guise of Prudence because she allows man to have first-hand experience with the world. She frees us from the shame and fear which cloud our minds and inhibit our actions, thus preventing any real experience. Because of Prudence we go along with the crowd, which is Folly. Indeed, it is Folly who has caused all the great achievements of mankind, wisdom and learning are no great help. Everything that man does is motivated by self-love, vainglory, flattery, or other followers.

To lead such a life of folly, error, and ignorance is to be human; it is to express one's true nature. All other forms of life are content with limitations but man is vainly ambitious. The most ignorant men are the happiest and some of the most deluded men are those who delight in telling lies. As an example, we are asked to consider the priests—those who propose to gain happiness by relying on magic charms and prayers, saints and particular rites. One cannot find happiness, we are told, without Folly, since all our emotions belong to Folly, and happiness depends on expressing our human nature which is full of Folly.

One of the most foolish of men, therefore, is that person who tries to deny his true nature and find happiness through the Christian religion. Folly proves that this religion has more to do with her own nature than with wisdom by showing that children, women, old people and fools take more delight in it than anyone else. It is they who are always nearest the altars. In the way that Christianity is most often taught and practiced, man must deny his true nature by disdaining life and preferring death. He must overlook injuries, avoid pleasure, and feast on hunger, vigils, tears, and labors. He must give up and scorn all physical pleasures, or at least he must take them more lightly than he does spiritual pleasures.

Folly is at her most serious when she tells us that this is the most foolish way, and the only sure way, to true happiness. Only by forgetting our bodies and everything physical can we approach this goal. We must give ourselves up completely to the spiritual aspects of life in order to achieve it. Only a very few men are able to accomplish this task completely enough while in this world, in order to approach an experience which she tells us is very close to madness. This madness, in turn, is similar to the heavenly joys that one will experience after death when the spirit has completely left the body.

PRECIOUS BANE

Type of work: Novel
Author: Mary Webb (1881-1927)
Type of plot: Regional romance
Time of plot: Mid-nineteenth century
Locale: England
First published: 1924

Principal characters:
PRUDENCE SARN, a harelipped girl
GIDEON, her brother
WIZARD BEGUILDY, an evil neighbor
JANCIS BEGUILDY, his daughter
KESTER WOODSEAVES, the weaver

Critique:

Just as Prudence Sarn seemed to view the past events of her life through a veil, so she tells her story. The story is not autobiographical, but into it Mrs. Webb put many experiences of her own youth. In this novel man seems to be controlled by forces of nature. The Bane, the poison that was in Gideon Sarn, moved him even to murder, for powers outside him drove him beyond his will. But when nature was satisfied, the Bane was exorcised; and peace came to the Sarns.

The Story:

The country people said there had been something queer about the Sarn family ever since old Timothy Sarn was struck by forked lightning. The lightning seemed to have gone into Timothy and into all the Sarns. In Prue's father the lightning took the form of a raving temper, and in Prue's brother Gideon the lightning was the more frightening because it was quiet but deadly. Dogs and horses turned away from Gideon's gray eyes. Prue understood her brother better than most, but even she was frightened when Gideon offered to be the sin-eater at their father's funeral. For a sin-eater took the sins of the dead person and sold his soul for a price. Gideon's price was the farm which would have been his mother's. Mrs. Sarn feared to accept the terms, for a sin-eater's

destiny was dreadful; but she feared more to let her husband go to his grave with all his sins, and so she gave Gideon the farm.

On the night after the funeral, Gideon told Prue his plans. They were going to become rich, own a house in town, and have fine clothes and beautiful furniture. Gideon promised Prue that for her help he would give her fifty pounds to get her harelip cured. He warned her, however, that he would work her as he would an animal. Because Prue had hated her harelip for many years, she consented to his terms. They signed an agreement and took an oath on the Bible that Gideon would be the master and Prue his servant.

Prue was also to learn to read and write and do sums so that she could keep the farm accounts. Her teacher would be Wizard Beguildy, a neighbor who was preached against in church because he earned his living by working spells and charms. Wizard was the father of Jancis Beguildy, a childhood friend of Prue and Gideon.

During the next four years Prue and Gideon slaved long hours in the field. Prue grew thinner and thinner and their mother became quite feeble. She was compelled to watch the pigs, for Gideon would let no one be idle. The farm prospered.

One part of Gideon's plan did not

work out, however, as he had arranged. In love with Jancis Beguildy, he decided that he would make his fortune and then marry her. Jancis did not want to wait that long, but Gideon would not change his mind.

Gideon and Jancis were handfasted and Jancis had a love-spinning, even though her father swore that she could never marry Gideon. At the love-spinning Prue first saw Kester Woodseaves, the weaver. When Kester came into the room, it seemed to Prue that a beautiful mist surrounded her. Then she turned sadly away. Gideon had told her often enough that no man would love a girl with a harelip.

A few days after the spinning Jancis went to tell Gideon that her father threatened either to sell her to a rich squire for his pleasure or to hire her out for three years as a dairymaid. Her only salvation was immediate marriage to Gideon. But Gideon told her that he had not made enough money, that she must be bound over for three years. Even Jancis' tears would not move him. Jancis was sent to work for Mr. and Mrs. Grimble.

After several months Jancis ran away from the Grimble farm. Because Gideon had a good crop of grain coming up, he promised to marry her after the harvest. Wizard Beguildy still swore that there would be no wedding, and Prue was afraid.

One day, as Prue was walking through the fields, Kester met her. When she tried to hide her face, Kester took her by the shoulders and looked straight into her eyes. He did not laugh, but talked to Prue as a man talks to a woman who is beautiful and attractive. His words were almost more than Prue could bear.

Never had there been such a harvest. Gideon's crop was piled in high ricks, and all the neighbor folks who had helped with the harvest came to the house to dance and feast. As soon as the grain buyer came to buy the crop, Jancis and Gideon would be married. But Gideon, unable to wait until their wedding, went to Jancis' home to be with her. Mrs. Beguildy tricked her husband into leaving so that the lovers could be together. Wizard Beguildy, arriving home early, found Jancis and Gideon in bed together, and the two men quarreled. Prue was more frightened than ever.

Prue had reason for her premonition of danger, for that night Wizard set the ricks on fire and everything burned except the house and the barn. Gideon was like a madman. When Jancis tried to comfort him, he said she was cursed by her father's blood, and he drove her away. He tried to get to Wizard to kill him, but Prue prevented this deed by having Wizard arrested. Gideon cursed the Beguildy family, even Jancis. Jancis swooned and lay for days in a trance. She and her mother were put off their farm, for no landowner would have the family of an arsonist on his land.

Gideon began to rebuild his dream, but Jancis was no longer a part of it. He worked himself and Prue and their mother almost to death. When the mother became too weak to work, Gideon put poison into her tea, for he would feed no one who could not earn her way. Prue knew that her brother's mind was deranged after the fire, but she had not known that he would kill for money.

Jancis returned with Gideon's baby. When Gideon drove her out of the house, Jancis took her baby to the pond and drowned herself and her child. Gideon began to see visions. He told Prue often that he had seen Jancis or his mother, and sometimes he heard Jancis singing. He talked queerly about the past, about his love for Jancis. He no longer wanted the money that had been his whole life. One day he rowed out on the pond and threw himself into the water and drowned. Prue was left alone.

Her vow to Gideon ended, Prue decided to leave the farm. When she rounded up the livestock and went into the village to sell them, the people called her a witch and blamed all the trouble on her harelip. They said that the forked lightning was in her worse than in all the other Sarns, and they put her in the ducking chair and ducked her in the pond until she was senseless. When she awakened, Kester was beside her, to lift her upon his horse and take her away to be his wife. Prue knew then that the forked lightning was not in her; the curse of the Sarns had been lifted.

Further Critical Evaluation of the Work:

The hero of Mary Webb's novel is Nature. Yet, it is a cruel force acting in a Darwinian universe that is only mollified when man acquiesces in its operation. Like a jealous owner, it brands him at his birth. The Sarn family is marked when Old Timothy, the grandfather, is struck by forked lightning. Prudence, the heroine, bears the scar, a disfiguring harelip. The main action of the novel is an account of Prue's and her brother's struggle with Nature to rise above the ordinary rhythms of life and gain the "precious bane."

By unlawfully assuming the Sarn land at his father's death, Gideon Sarn brings down Nature's curse. In his desire for money and status, he ignores his own passions; he rejects the love of Jancis Beguildy. Ultimately he pays for his avarice and his denial of his instincts by the loss of his soul and his life. He has dared to assert his superiority to Nature and in revenge it crushes him.

Initially he is abetted by Prudence. She binds herself to him under the promise that when their wealth is assured, he will pay for the removal of her disfigurement. Prudence, however, is saved from the curse by her realization of the corruption that wealth entails and her love for Kester Woodseaves, an enigmatic man of compassion and magnetic sexuality.

The final scene in which Woodseaves swoops down on his charger to save Prue from a mob which believes her to be a witch is primitive in its appeal, and the townspeople's dunking of Prue is a superstitious ritual designed to appease outraged Nature. The union of Kester and Prue itself is a ritual; it is one which signifies man's subordination to forces beyond him, unconscious forces that pull toward the rhythms of Nature and away from those of society.

PREFACE TO SHAKESPEARE

Type of work: Literary Criticism
Author: Samuel Johnson (1709-1784)
First published: 1765

Samuel Johnson's Preface to his edition of Shakespeare's plays has long been considered a classic document of English literary criticism. In it Johnson sets forth his editorial principles and gives an appreciative analysis of the "excellences" and "defects" of the work of the great Elizabethan dramatist. Many of his points have become fundamental tenets of modern criticism; others give greater insight into Johnson's prejudice than into Shakespeare's genius. The majestic, resonant prose of the preface adds authority to the views of its author.

Characteristically, Johnson makes his Shakespearian criticism the foundation for general statements about man, nature, and literature. He is a true neo-classicist in his concern with the universal rather than with the particular; the highest praise he can bestow upon Shakespeare is to say that his plays are "just representations of general nature." The dramatist has relied upon his knowledge of human nature, rather than on bizarre effects, for his success. "The pleasures of sudden wonder are soon exhausted, and the mind can only repose on the stability of truth," Johnson concludes. It is for this reason that Shakespeare has outlived his century and reached the point at which his works can be judged solely on their own merits, without the interference of personal interests and prejudices that make criticism of one's contemporaries difficult.

Johnson feels that the readers of his time can often understand the universality of Shakespeare's vision better than the audiences of Elizabethan England could, for the intervening centuries have freed the plays of their topicality. The characters in the plays are not limited by time or nationality; they are rather "the genuine progeny of common humanity, such as the world will always supply, and observation will always find."

Implicitly criticizing earlier editors of Shakespeare, who had dotted their pages with asterisks marking particularly fine passages, Johnson contends that the greatness of the plays lies primarily in their total effect, in the naturalness of the action, the dialogue, and the characterization. Again and again Johnson stresses the same point: "This, therefore, is the praise of Shakespeare, that his drama is the mirrour of life." His personages are drawn from the world familiar to everyone: "Shakespeare has no heroes; his scenes are occupied only by men, who act and speak as the reader thinks that he should himself have spoken or acted on the same occasion."

That Shakespeare wrote "contrary to the rules of criticism" was, for Johnson, no argument. Aside from the fact that Aristotle's rules were not widely known during Shakespeare's time, Johnson notes: "There is always an appeal open from criticism to nature." Life itself justifies the mingling of comedy and tragedy on the stage; together they exhibit "the real state of sublunary nature, which partakes of good and evil, joy and sorrow, mingled with endless variety of proportion and innumerable modes of combination."

While Johnson is aware of Shakespeare's skills in both comedy and tragedy, he suggests that his natural forte was the former: "In tragedy he is always struggling after some occasion to be comick; but in comedy he seems to repose, or to luxuriate, as in a mode of thinking congenial to his nature." Johnson later criticizes some of the tragic speeches as bombast, forced, unnatural emotion, and he complains that all too often scenes of pathos are marred by "idle conceits," and those inspiring terror and pity by "sudden frigidity." Yet the critic later confesses that in spite of these flaws each man finds his mind seized more strongly by Shakespeare's tragedies than by those of any other writer.

Johnson praises Shakespeare's language as that of the "common intercourse of life," used among those who speak only to be understood, without ambition or elegance." His comment is particularly interesting in the light of Wordsworth's insistence, in his Preface to *Lyrical Ballads,* written almost fifty years later, that poetry should be written in the "real language of men," not in the artificial diction that seemed to him to have enslaved the poets of the eighteenth century.

One of Johnson's most stringent objections to Shakespeare's work arises from his strong conviction that literature is essentially didactic. He is disturbed by Shakespeare's disregard of "poetic justice." Johnson was convinced that the writer should show the virtuous rewarded and the evil punished, and he finds that Shakespeare, by ignoring this premise, "sacrifices virtue to convenience." The fact that in life evil often triumphs over good is no excuse in Johnson's eyes: "It is always a writer's duty to make the world better."

Shakespeare's careless plotting and his "disregard for distinctions of time and place" are also noted as flaws; "we need not wonder to find Hector quoting Aristotle, when we see the loves of Theseus and Hippolyta combined with the Gothick mythology of fairies." Although Johnson dislikes Shakespeare's bawdry, he is willing to concede that that fault, at least, might have rested with the indelicacy of the ladies and gentlemen at the courts of Elizabeth I and James I, rather than with the playwright. These minor "errors" are far less irritating to Johnson than Shakespeare's use of puns: "A quibble was to him the fatal Cleopatra for which he lost the world, and was content to lose it."

Johnson's contemporaries often condemned Shakespeare for his lack of attention to the Aristotelian unities of time, place, and action, which were assiduously observed by the French classical dramatists and their English imitators. Johnson notes that Shakespeare did observe the unity of action, giving his plays a beginning, a middle, and an end, and developing his plot by cause and effect. Moreover, he sees no harm in Shakespeare's failure in most cases to limit his action to one place and one day. Most strict neo-classical critics maintained that such limitations of time and space were necessary for dramatic credibility. Johnson finds this assertion ridiculous, for every member of the audience knows that all drama is illusion: "He that can take the stage at one time for the palace of the Ptolemies, may take it in half an hour for the promontory of Actium. Delusion, if delusion be admitted, has no certain limitation." Real dramatic credibility comes from the validity of the emotions presented: "The reflection that strikes the heart is not, that the evils before us are real evils, but that they are evils to which we ourselves may be exposed."

Anticipating the historical critics of the nineteenth and twentieth centuries, Johnson assesses some of the aspects of Elizabethan England that probably influenced Shakespeare. He stresses the fact that the dramatist was in many ways a pioneer, for he had few truly outstanding English works of drama or poetry to build on. Shakespeare's complicated plots can be traced to the popularity of the elaborate pastoral romances read by his audiences and occasionally used as sources for the plays.

Johnson does not emphasize Shakespeare's learning; he notes that he could have read in translation the classical works he mentions. The playwright's greatest knowledge came not from books, but from life: "Mankind was not then to be studied in the closet; he that would know the world, was under the necessity of gleaning his own remarks, by mingling as he could in its business and amusements.

Concluding his general commentary, Johnson summarizes Shakespeare's gifts to English literature: "The form, the characters, the language, and the shows of the English drama are his. . . . To him we must ascribe the praise, unless Spenser may divide it with him, of having first discovered to how much smoothness and harmony the English language could be softened."

In the remainder of the Preface Johnson delineates his editorial standards, rejecting the temptation to follow the practices of his predecessors, who had emended, essentially rewritten, the plays where they could not understand or did not like what they found in the earliest texts of Shakespeare's works. Johnson followed Pope in basing his edition on the original quarto versions of the plays and on the First Folio, and he attempted, he says, to leave them as nearly as possible what he found them. His explanatory notes are to contain not only his own ideas, but also the views of earlier critics. He quotes others more often to refute them than to praise them, believing that "the first care of the builder of a new system, is to demolish the fabricks which are standing."

In a final exhortation to the reader Johnson places his efforts in perspective; notes are often necessary, but they are necessary evils. The reader who has not yet experienced Shakespeare's genius must first ignore the editor's aids and simply read for "the highest pleasure that the drama can give." Johnson's modesty is in itself a tribute to Shakespeare; his whole task as editor and critic was to make the great plays more accessible to the public, and his criticism still gives valuable insights to the modern lover of Shakespeare.

PREJUDICES: SIX SERIES

Type of work: Essays on social and literary themes
Author: H. L. Mencken (1880-1956)
First published: 1919-1927

During the fantastic decade of the 1920's, few literary events were so eagerly awaited as the appearance of a new volume of Mencken's *Prejudices,* so that one might enjoy the spectacle of the Sage of Baltimore as he pulled yet another popular idol down from its moss-covered pedestal and gloated over the fragments. This iconoclasm was accomplished with so much gusto and with such vigorous and picturesque language as to enchant a whole generation that had grown weary of the solemnity of much American writing. And the decade badly needed an iconoclast, for it must be remembered that what is now thought of as "the jazz age" was also the era of the Ku Klux Klan and the Anti-Saloon League, of Babbittry and Boosterism.

The essays in these volumes can be divided into two categories: literary criticism and criticism of the American scene as it appeared at that time. Literary criticism Mencken defined as a "catalytic process," with the critic serving as the catalyst. Actually, as a critic Mencken derived mainly from James Huneker, whom he enormously admired and had known personally. Huneker had been familiar with Continental writers, then not too well known in America; his criticism was essentially impressionistic, often written in breezy, epigrammatic language. Mencken carried certain of these characteristics much further; indeed, his verbal acrobatics became his hallmark. It was a racy, pungent style, very effective for the "debunking" then so popular and deliberately calculated to drive conservative readers into frenzies. His chief target, at which he never grew tired of heaving bricks, was the Puritan tradition in American literature with its consequent timidity, stuffiness, and narrowmindedness. As he saw it, the Puritan was afraid of aesthetic emotion and thus could neither create nor enjoy art. This fear had inhibited American literature, he claimed, and had made American criticism equally timid and conventional. Further, criticism had fallen into the hands of the professors, and there was nothing—not even a prohibition agent—that Mencken detested so much as the average American university professor. Hence, such men as Paul Elmer More, Irving Babbitt, Stuart P. Sherman, and William Lyon Phelps had scorn poured over them for years.

It is ironic that the critical writings of some of these men have withstood the passage of time more successfully than have those of Mencken. For though less a geographical provincial than they, he was more provincial in time and was interested mainly in the contemporary. Of the older native writers, he really admired only Poe, Twain, and Whitman—the nonconformists. Even among the moderns his preferences were curiously limited. He had great regard for Conrad and Dreiser, but he overlooked much of the talent that was budding during the 1920's. That he should have overpraised some of his contemporaries, Cabell, for example, should not be held against him; few critics are sufficiently detached to escape this fault. Dreiser was an important writer but not the "colossal phenomenon" that Mencken called him. But his greatest failure as a critic was his blindness to poetry. In the Third Series of *Prejudices* he included an essay, "The Poet and His Art," a study so full of false assumptions, logical fallacies, and plain misstatements of fact that it is a gruesome relic for a critic to have left behind him. And his remarks on Dante stagger belief: Dante's theology was unacceptable to Mencken; therefore, Dante could not *really* have believed it, and *The Divine Comedy* was, he said, a satire on the whole Christian doctrine of heaven and hell. Surely no gem that Mencken garnered from the Bible Belt could equal this statement in absurdity.

The essays dealing with the national scene were written in the same slashing manner and naturally infuriated far more readers, since Mencken attacked men, institutions, and ideas more familiar to them. Obviously, many of these pieces have little significance now, for they dealt with situations peculiar to that decade. But some of them are still valid: "The Sahara of the Bozart" (Second Series) is in some ways almost as true of the South today as it was in 1920; his comments on the farmer ("The Husbandman," Fourth Series) are even more appropriate. And his dissections of such eminent figures as Theodore Roosevelt and Thorstein Veblen are still funny.

Of Americans in general, Mencken had a low opinion, considering them a mongrel people incapable of high spiritual aspiration. His opinion of democracy was equally low. It was, he felt, merely a scheme to hearten the have-nots in their unending battle with the haves. The inferiority of Americans Mencken attributed to the lack of a genuine aristocracy and to Puritanism. Without an aristocracy, there could be no real leadership in America, and the vacuum would inevitably be filled by politicians, whom he detested. Nor did he have any faith in reform or reformers.

As for Puritanism, Mencken believed that it had always been the dominant force in our history and had left Americans the narrow-minded victims of religious bigotry. The predominance during the 1920's of the more extreme forms of Fundamentalism gave some support to his argument. But in his attacks on religion he made the mistake of throwing the baby out with the bath water; since he was himself a complete skeptic, he simply could not conceive of such a creature as a sincere and yet intelligent Christian. The terms were to him incompatible; quite genuinely, he could see no difference between Billy Sunday and Archbishop Temple.

Mencken's enemies were always urging him, in anguished tones, to leave this country if he found it so distasteful. His reply was that nowhere else could so much entertainment be had so cheaply. According to his calculations, it cost him personally only eighty cents a year to maintain Harding in the White House. Where could a better show be found for the money?

In spite of his exaggerations, crudities, and often bad taste, Mencken performed a valuable service. America always needs a gadfly, and his cynical wit provided the sting at just the right moment. Unfortunately, he has had no successor.

THE PRELUDE

Type of work: Poem
Author: William Wordsworth (1770-1850)
First published: 1850

Planned as the introductory portion of a long autobiographical and philosophical poem that was never finished, *The Prelude, or, Growth of a Poet's Mind,* was not published until shortly after Wordsworth's death in 1850. The projected, long poem, *The Recluse,* was to present a comprehensive development of the poet's views on man, society, and nature, but of the projected three parts, only the second, *The Excursion* (1814) was ever completed and published.

The Prelude was to provide the autobiographical introduction to *The Recluse,* tracing the development of the poet and his mind to the point where he was ready to formulate his beliefs and philosophy. Written between 1799 and 1805 and addressed to Coleridge as the important "Friend," the poem is a long and ambitious work, an attempt in blank verse to trace the history and development of the poet's feelings, ideas, and convictions.

Since Wordsworth so strongly advocated the use of poetry for individual emotions and insights, it is appropriate that we should have such a thorough description of the development of his mind. In addition, *The Prelude* contains some fine passages that illustrate the clarity and force of Wordsworth's use of language to convey both a precise description and a sense of the meaning of nature. Although the poem suffers from long prosaic stretches, it also contains much of the sense of the calm beauty and power of nature which distinguishes Wordsworth's verse.

The poem begins with an account of the poet's childhood in the English Lake Country, and Wordsworth, with many digressions addressed to nature and its power, wisdom, and infusing spirit, tells of the influence of nature on his solitary childhood. Some of the sense of awe and pleasure that he found in nature, as well as some of his clearest and most pene-trating use of diction, is evident in the following passage. Young Wordsworth has found a boat in a cave, unchained the boat, and rowed out into the center of a lake. He continues:

> . . . lustily
> I dipped my oars into the silent lake,
> And, as I rose upon the stroke, my boat
> Went heaving through the water like a
>   swan;
> When, from behind that craggy steep
>   till then
> The horizon's bound, a huge peak,
>   black and huge,
> As if with voluntary power instinct
> Upreared its head. I struck and struck
>   again,
> And growing still in stature the grim
>   shape
> Towered up between me and the stars,
>   and still,
> For so it seemed, with purpose of its
>   own
> And measured motion like a living
>   thing,
> Strode after me.

The image of the peak is invested with such simplicity and power that it is transformed into a kind of force holding terror and beauty for the guilty boy who has stolen a ride in a boat.

In describing his early years, the poet speaks of his youthful love of freedom and liberty. He found this sense of freedom in his rambles through the woods and on mountain paths where he did not feel fettered by the claims of society and school work. But, he reassures the reader, he was docile and obedient externally, keeping his rebellion and sense of freedom as a matter of the spirit. This mixture of the calm and docile exterior with the independent and rebellious interior seems part of the origin of Wordsworth's ability to control highly individualistic thought in calm, dignified, unostentatious verse forms and diction. It is not that, in *The Prelude,* Wordsworth uses the speech of common man. His speech is often abstract, speculative, pervaded with a sense of the mystery and meaning of nature. Rather, Wordsworth's diction, at its best, has a dignity and calm control, a lack of pretense, through which the force of his inner meaning gently radiates.

Wordsworth continues his journey through Cambridge, telling of experiences there, discussing the fact that he neither was nor cared to be a scholar. He still, despite his studies, concentrates inwardly on the spirit of things, the power of nature and the impetus nature gives to his feelings. At this point, Wordsworth begins to speculate on the differences between reason and emotion or passion, to equate the reason with the scholars and the emotion with his own apprehension of the world of nature:

> But all the meditations of mankind,
> Yea, all the adamantine holds of truth
> By reason built, or passion, which itself
> Is highest reason in a soul sublime;

Throughout the poem, Wordsworth makes the distinction between reason and passion, attributing an ultimate sterility to the quality of reason, while glorifying the element of passion or imagination.

Wordsworth tells next of his journey to the Alps after leaving Cambridge. The mountains there reminded him of the mountains familiar in his childhood, and he felt again, even more keenly, the majesty and awe of the scenery reflected in his spirit. He begins, more strongly, to feel his kinship with nature. In perhaps the dullest section of the poem, he describes his life among the crowds and industries of London, along with his tours of the historical monuments, after his return from Europe. Dissatisfied with life in London, he then went to France during the early stages of the French Revolution. In this section he expresses his feeling that he had not cared for man sufficiently, that, in his devotion to nature, he has neglected his feeling for his fellow creatures. Recalling his early love for freedom and liberty and adding his

new conviction of the importance of political liberty for man, Wordsworth became strongly attracted to the cause of the French Revolution, feeling, as he said in *The Prelude*, that he was tied emotionally and spiritually to the popular struggle against the monarchy. But the bloodiness of the revolution, popular ingratitude and popular refusal to acknowledge the heroes who championed its cause with greatest fervor and sincerity, soon disillusioned Wordsworth. Beginning to feel that blood had poisoned the cause of liberty, he returned to England.

Wordsworth relates how, disillusioned and alone, he sought to bring meaning back into his life. The penultimate section of *The Prelude* is titled "Imagination and Taste, How Impaired and Restored." At that period of his life he turned back to nature, finding there not solace alone but a sense of law and order that was lacking in man. He began to realize the difference in scale between nature and man, the range and effect of nature in comparison to the tiny ineffectuality of man. His sections of resolution frequently include passages like the following interpolation in the midst of a narrative section:

> O Soul of Nature! that, by laws divine
> Sustained and governed, still dost overflow
> With an impassioned life, what feeble ones
> Walk on this earth!

In his view, nature provides not only awe and spiritual impetus for man, but also order, rules of conduct, and the means of man's molding his behavior on this planet. In the final sections of the poem, Wordsworth uses nature as the authority for his new morality and assumes a much more overtly moral tone. He didactically advocates the importance of faith, of obedience, of not relying on man's unaided reason in human affairs. What was, in the earlier sections, the praise of emotion and freedom in opposition to rational restraint becomes the praise of the restraint of faith and spirit in opposition to rational license. This change is illustrative of the change in Wordsworth's whole career from the poet advocating the simple joy and freedom of nature to the sage defending abstract and conventional truths. His attitude is demonstrated in the following passage from the conclusion of the poem:

> . . . but, the dawn beginning now
> To re-appear, 'twas proved that not in vain
> I had been taught to reverence a Power
> That is the visible quality and shape
> And image of right reason; that matures
> Her processes by steadfast laws; gives birth
> To no impatient or fallacious hopes,
> No heat of passion or excessive zeal,
> No vain conceits; provokes to no quick turns
> Of self-applauding intellect; but trains
> To meekness, and exalts by humble faith.

As *The Prelude* shows Wordsworth's changing attitudes toward nature and man, both relating and illustrating the changes and development in his mind, so the poem also shows the different characteristics of Wordsworth's diction and poetic power. No other single poem has so much of his clear reverence for nature expressed with greater power and simplicity along with so much of his moralizing expressed with repetitive flatness. *The Prelude* is truly an autobiographical poem, a monument to the career, the changing ideas, and the changing use of poetry of and by William Wordsworth.

PRIDE AND PREJUDICE

Type of work: Novel
Author: Jane Austen (1775-1817)
Type of plot: Comedy of manners
Time of plot: Early nineteenth century
Locale: Rural England
First published: 1813

Principal characters:
MR. BENNET, father of five daughters
MRS. BENNET, his wife
ELIZABETH BENNET, her father's favorite
JANE BENNET, the family beauty
MARY,
CATHERINE (KITTY), and
LYDIA BENNET, younger sisters
MR. BINGLEY, an eligible bachelor
CAROLINE BINGLEY, his sister
MR. DARCY, a proud gentleman, Bingley's friend
MR. COLLINS, a conceited bore
LADY CATHERINE DE BOURGH, Collins' arrogant patroness

Critique:

Elizabeth Bennet, one of the most delightful heroines of all time, would be enough to make *Pride and Prejudice* outstanding among English novels. In addition, the book has a beautifully symmetrical plot in which the action rises and falls as inevitably as does an ocean wave. Many of the other characters besides Elizabeth are superbly drawn. Jane Austen's delicate but telling satire of the English country gentlefolk of her day— and indeed of her neighborhood—remains a delightful commentary upon the little foibles of human nature.

The Story:

The chief business of Mrs. Bennet's life was to find suitable husbands for her five daughters. Consequently she heard with elation that Netherfield Park, one of the area's great houses, had been let to Mr. Bingley, a gentleman from the north of England. Gossip such as Mrs. Bennet loved reported him a rich and altogether eligible young bachelor. Mr. Bennet heard the news with his usual dry calmness, suggesting in his mild way that perhaps Bingley was not moving into the county for the single purpose of marrying one of the Bennet daughters.

Mr. Bingley's first public appearance in the neighborhood was at a ball. With him were his two sisters, the husband of the older, and Mr. Darcy, Bingley's friend. Bingley was an immediate success in local society, and he and Jane, the oldest Bennet daughter, a pretty girl of sweet and gentle disposition, were attracted to each other at once. His friend, Darcy, however, created a bad impression, seeming cold and extremely proud. In particular, he insulted Elizabeth Bennet, a girl of spirit and intelligence and her father's favorite. He refused to dance with her when she was sitting down for lack of a partner, and he said in her hearing that he was in no mood to prefer young ladies slighted by other men. On future occasions, however, he began to admire Elizabeth in spite of himself. At a later ball she had the satisfaction of refusing him a dance.

Jane's romance with Bingley flourished quietly, aided by family calls, dinners, and balls. His sisters pretended great fondness for Jane, who believed them completely sincere. The more critical and discerning Elizabeth suspected them of hypocrisy, and quite rightly, for they made great fun of Jane's relations, especially her vulgar, garrulous mother and her two ill-bred officer-mad younger sisters. Miss Caroline Bingley, who was eager to marry Darcy and shrewdly aware of his growing admiration for Elizabeth, was especially loud in her ridicule of the Bennet family. Elizabeth herself became Caroline's particular target when she walked three muddy miles to visit Jane, who was sick with a cold at Netherfield Park after a ride through the rain to accept an invitation from the Bingley sisters. Until Jane was able to be moved home, Elizabeth stayed to nurse her. During her visit Elizabeth received enough attention from Darcy to make Caroline Bingley long sincerely for Jane's recovery. Nor were her fears ill-founded. Darcy admitted to himself that he would be in some danger from the charm of Elizabeth, if it were not for her inferior family connections.

Elizabeth now acquired a new admirer in the person of Mr. Collins, a ridiculously pompous clergyman and a distant cousin of the Bennets, who would some day inherit Mr. Bennet's property because that gentleman had no male heir. Mr. Collins' patroness, Lady Catherine de Bourgh, had urged him to marry, and he, always obsequiously obedient to her wishes, hastened to comply. Thinking to alleviate the hardship caused the Bennet sisters by the entail which gave their father's property to him, Mr. Collins first proposed to Elizabeth. Much to her mother's displeasure and her father's joy she firmly and promptly rejected him. He almost immediately transferred his affections to Elizabeth's best friend, Charlotte Lucas, who, twenty-seven and somewhat homely, accepted at once his offer of marriage.

During Mr. Collins' visit, the younger Bennet sisters, Kitty and Lydia, on one of their many walks to Meryton, met a fascinating new officer, Mr. Wickham, stationed with the regiment there. Outwardly charming, he became a favorite among the ladies, even with Elizabeth. She was willing to believe the story that he had been cheated out of an inheritance left him by his godfather, Darcy's father. Her suspicions of Darcy's arrogant and grasping nature deepened when Wickham did not come to a ball given by the Bingleys, a dance at which Darcy was present.

Soon after the ball, the entire Bingley party suddenly left Netherfield Park. They departed with no intention of returning, as Caroline wrote Jane in a short farewell note which hinted that Bingley might soon become engaged to Darcy's sister. Jane accepted this news at face value and believed that her friend Caroline was telling her gently that her brother loved elsewhere, and that she must cease to hope. Elizabeth, however, was sure of a plot by Darcy and Bingley's sisters to separate him and Jane. She persuaded Jane that Bingley did love her and that he would return to Hertfordshire before the winter was over. Jane almost believed her until she received a letter from Caroline assuring her that they were all settled in London for the winter. Even after Jane told her this news, Elizabeth remained convinced of Bingley's affection for her sister, and deplored the lack of resolution which made him putty in the hands of his designing friend.

About that time Mrs. Bennet's sister, Mrs. Gardiner, an amiable and intelligent woman with a great deal of affection for her two oldest nieces, arrived for a Christmas visit. She suggested to the Bennets that Jane return to London with her for a rest and change of scene and — so it was understood between Mrs. Gardiner and Elizabeth — to renew her acquaintance with Bingley. Elizabeth, not too hopeful for the success of the plan, pointed out that proud Darcy would never let his friend call on Jane in the unfashionable London street on which the Gardiners lived. Jane accepted the invitation, however, and she and Mrs. Gardiner set out for London.

The time drew near for the wedding of Elizabeth's friend, Charlotte Lucas, to the obnoxious Mr. Collins. Charlotte asked Elizabeth to visit her in Kent. In spite of her feeling that there could be little pleasure in such a visit, Elizabeth promised to do so. She felt that in taking such a husband Charlotte was marrying simply for the sake of an establishment, as was indeed the case. Since she herself could not sympathize with her friend's action, Elizabeth thought their days of real intimacy were over. As March approached, however, she found herself eager to see her friend, and she set out with pleasure on the journey with Charlotte's father and sister. On their way, the party stopped in London to see the Gardiners and Jane, Elizabeth found her sister well and outwardly happy, though she had not seen Bingley and his sisters had paid only one call. Elizabeth was sure Bingley had not been told of Jane's presence in London and blamed Darcy for keeping it from him.

Soon after arriving at the Collins' home, the whole party was honored, as Mr. Collins repeatedly assured them, by a dinner invitation from Lady Catherine de Bourgh, Darcy's aunt and Mr. Collins' patroness. Elizabeth found Lady Catherine a haughty, ill-mannered woman and her daughter thin, sickly, and shy. Lady Catherine was extremely fond of inquiring into the affairs of others and giving them unasked advice. Elizabeth turned off the meddling old woman's questions with cool indirectness, and saw from the effect that she was probably the first who had dared to do so.

Soon after Elizabeth's arrival, Darcy came to visit his aunt and cousin. He called frequently at the parsonage, and he and Elizabeth resumed their conversational fencing matches. His rather stilted attentions were suddenly climaxed by a proposal of marriage, but one couched in such proud and condescending terms that Elizabeth indignantly refused him. When he requested her reason for such an emphatic rejection, she mentioned his part in separating Bingley and Jane, and also his mistreatment of Wickham. Angry, he left abruptly, but the next day brought a letter answering her charges. He did not deny his part in separating Jane and Bingley, but he gave as his reasons the improprieties of Mrs. Bennet and her younger daughters, and

also his sincere belief that Jane did not love Bingley. As for his alleged mistreatment of Wickham, he proved that he had in reality acted most generously toward the unprincipled Wickham, who had repaid his kindness by attempting to elope with Darcy's young sister. Elizabeth, at first incensed at the proud tones in which he wrote, was at length forced to acknowledge the justice of all he said, and her prejudice against him began to weaken. Without seeing him again, she returned home.

She found her younger sisters clamoring to go to Brighton, where the regiment formerly stationed at Meryton had been ordered. When an invitation came to Lydia from a young officer's wife, Lydia was allowed to accept it over Elizabeth's protests. Elizabeth herself was asked by the Gardiners to go with them on a tour which would take them into Derbyshire, Darcy's home county. She accepted, reasoning that she was not very likely to meet Darcy merely by going into the same county with him. While they were there, however, Mrs. Gardiner decided they should visit Pemberly, Darcy's home. Elizabeth made several excuses, but her aunt was insistent. Then, learning that the Darcy family was not at home, Elizabeth consented to go.

At Pemberly, an unexpected and most embarrassing meeting took place between Elizabeth and Darcy. He was more polite than Elizabeth had ever known him to be, and asked permission for his sister to call upon her. The call was duly paid and returned, but the pleasant intercourse between the Darcys and Elizabeth's party was suddenly cut short when a letter came from Jane telling Elizabeth that Lydia had run away with Wickham. Elizabeth told Darcy what had happened, and she and the Gardiners left for home at once. After several days the runaway couple was located and a marriage arranged between them. When Lydia came home as heedless as ever, she told Elizabeth that Darcy had attended her wedding. Elizabeth, suspecting the truth, learned from Mrs. Gardiner that it was indeed Darcy who brought about the marriage by giving Wickham money.

Soon after Lydia and Wickham left, Bingley came back to Netherfield Park, and with him came Darcy. Elizabeth, now more favorably inclined to him than ever before, hoped his coming meant that he still loved her, but he gave no sign. Bingley and Jane, on the other hand, were still obviously in love with each other, and became engaged, to the great satisfaction of Mrs. Bennet. Soon afterward Lady Catherine paid the Bennets an unexpected call. She had heard it rumored that Darcy was engaged to Elizabeth. Hoping to marry her own daughter to Darcy, she had charged down with characteristic bad manners to order Elizabeth not to accept his proposal. The spirited girl was not to be intimidated by the bullying Lady Catherine and coolly refused to promise not to marry Darcy. She was far from certain she would have another chance, but she had not long to wonder. Lady Catherine, unluckily for her own purpose, repeated to Darcy the substance of her conversation with Elizabeth, and he knew Elizabeth well enough to surmise that her feelings toward him had greatly changed. He returned to Netherfield Park, and he and Elizabeth became engaged. Pride had been humbled and prejudice dissolved.

Further Critical Evaluation of the Work:

In 1813, her thirty-eighth year, Jane Austen became a published novelist for the second time with *Pride and Prejudice*. She had begun this work in 1796, her twenty-first year, calling it *First Impressions*. It had so delighted her family that her father had tried, without success, to have it published. Eventually putting it aside, she returned to it probably at about the time that her first published novel, *Sense and Sensibility,* appeared in 1811. No longer extant, *First Impressions* must have been radically altered; for *Pride and Prejudice* is not an apprenticeship novel, but a mature work, which continues to be the author's most popular novel, perhaps because its readers share Darcy's admiration for the "liveliness" of Elizabeth Bennet's mind.

The original title, *First Impressions,* focuses upon the initial errors of judgment from which the story develops, whereas the title *Pride and Prejudice,* besides suggesting the kind of antithetical topic which delighted rationalistic eighteenth century readers, indicates the central conflict involving the kinds of pride and prejudice which bar the marriages of Elizabeth Bennet and Darcy and Jane Bennet and Bingley, but bring about the marriages of Charlotte Lucas and Collins and Lydia Bennet and Wickham.

As in all of Jane Austen's novels, individual conflicts are defined and resolved within a rigidly delimiting social context, in which human relationships are determined by wealth and rank. Thus the much admired opening sentence establishes the societal values which underlie the main conflict: "It is a truth universally acknowledged, that a single man in possession of a good fortune, must be in want of a wife." Mr. and Mrs. Bennet's opening dialog concerning the eligible Bingley explores this truth. Devoid of individuality, Mrs. Bennet is nevertheless well attuned to society's edicts and therefore regards Bingley only in the light of society's "truth." Mr. Bennet, an individualist to the point of eccentricity, represents neither personal conviction nor social conviction. He lightheartedly views with equal indifference both Bingley's right to his own reason for settling there and society's right to see him primarily as a potential husband. Having repudiated society, Mr. Bennet cannot take seriously either the claims of the individual or the social order.

As the central character, Elizabeth, her father's favorite child and her mother's least favorite, must come to terms with the conflicting values implicit in her parents' antithetical characters. She is like her father in her scorn of society's conventional judgments, but she champions the concept of individual merit independent of money and rank. She is, indeed, prejudiced against the prejudices of society. From this premise she attacks Darcy's pride, assuming that it derives from the causes that Charlotte Lucas identifies: " . . . with family, fortune, every thing in his favour . . . he has a *right* to be proud."

Flaunting her contempt for money, Elizabeth indignantly spurns as mere strategy to get a rich husband or any husband Charlotte's advice that Jane ought to make a calculated play for Bingley's affections. She loftily argues, while under the spell of Wickham's charm, that young people who are truly in love are unconcerned about each other's financial standing.

As a champion of the individual, Elizabeth prides herself on her discriminating judgment, boasting that she is a student of character. Significantly, it is Darcy who warns her against prejudiced conclusions, reminding her that her experience is quite limited. For Darcy is not simply the representative of a society which primarily values wealth and consequence—as Elizabeth initially views him—but he is also a citizen of a larger society than the village to which Elizabeth is confined by circumstance. Consequently, it is only when she begins to move into Darcy's world that she can judge with true discrimination both individual merit and the dictates of the society which she has rejected. Fundamentally honest, she revises her conclusions as new experiences warrant, in the case of Darcy and Wickham radically altering her opinion.

More significant than the obviously ironic reversals, however, is the growing revelation of Elizabeth's unconscious commitment to society. For example, her original condemnation of Darcy's pride coincides with the verdict of Meryton society. Moreover, she always shares society's regard for wealth. Even while denying the importance of Wickham's poverty, she countenances his pursuit of the ugly Miss King's fortune, discerning her own inconsistency only after she learns of his bad character. Most revealing, when Lydia Bennet runs off with Wickham, Elizabeth instinctively pronounces the judgment of society when she states that Wickham would never marry a woman without money.

Almost unconsciously Elizabeth acknowledges a connection between wealth and human values at the crucial moment when she first looks upon Pemberley, the Darcy estate:

> She had never seen a place for which nature had done more, or where natural beauty had been so little counteracted by an awkward taste. They were all of them warm in their admiration; and at that moment she felt that to be mistress of Pemberley might be something!

She is not entirely joking when she tells Jane that her love for Darcy began when she first saw his beautiful estate.

Elizabeth's experiences, especially her discoveries of the well-ordered Pemberley and Darcy's tactful generosity to Lydia and Wickham, lead her to differentiate between Charlotte's theory that family and fortune bestow a *"right* to be proud" and Darcy's position that the intelligent person does not indulge in false pride. Darcy's pride is real, but it is regulated by responsibility. Unlike his aunt, Lady Catherine de Bourgh, who relishes the distinction of rank, he disapproves less of the Bennets' undistinguished family and fortune than he does of the lack of propriety displayed by most of the family. Thus Elizabeth scarcely overstates her case when, at the end, she assures her father that Darcy has no improper pride.

Elizabeth begins by rejecting the values and restraints of society, as represented by such people as her mother, the Lucases, Miss Bingley, and Lady Catherine, upholding instead the claims of the individual, represented only by her whimsical father. By the end of the novel, the heart of her conflict appears in the contrast between her father and Darcy. Loving her father, she has tried to overlook his lack of decorum in conjugal matters. But she has been forced to see that his freedom is really irresponsibility, the essential cause of Jane's misery as well as Lydia's amorality. The implicit comparison between Mr. Bennet's and Darcy's approach to matrimony points up their different methods of dealing with society's restraints. Unrestrained by society, having been captivated by the inferior Mrs. Bennet's youth and beauty, Mr. Bennet consulted only his personal desires and made a disastrous marriage. Darcy, in contrast, defies society only when he has made certain that Elizabeth is a woman worthy of his love and lifetime devotion.

When Elizabeth confronts Lady Catherine, her words are declarative, not of absolute defiance of society, but of the selective freedom which is her compromise, and very similar to Darcy's: "I am only resolved to act in that manner, which will, in my own opinion, constitute my happiness, without reference to *you,* or to any person so wholly unconnected with me." Jane Austen does not falsify the compromise. If Elizabeth dares with impunity to defy the society of Rosings, Longbourne, and Meryton, she does so only because Darcy is exactly the man for her and, further, because she can anticipate "with delight . . . the time when they should be removed from society so little pleasing to either, to all the comfort and elegance . . . at

Pemberley." Her marriage to Darcy is in a sense a triumph of the individual over society; but, paradoxically, Elizabeth achieves her most genuine conquest of pride and prejudice only after she has accepted the full social value of her judgment that "to be mistress of Pemberley might be something!"

Granting the full force of the snobbery, the exploitation, the inhumanity of all the evils which diminish the human spirit and which are inherent in a materialistic society, the novel clearly confirms the cynical "truth" of the opening sentence. Yet at the same time, without evading the degree of Elizabeth's capitulation to society, it affirms the vitality, the independent life which is possible at least to an Elizabeth Bennet. *Pride and Prejudice,* like its title, offers deceptively simple antitheses which yield up the complexity of life itself.

Catherine E. Moore

THE PRINCE

Type of work: Philosophy of politics
Author: Niccolò Machiavelli (1469-1527)
Time: Fifteenth and sixteenth centuries
Locale: Principally Italy
First published: 1532

Principal personages:
CESARE BORGIA, Duke of Valentinois and Romagna
FRANCESCO SFORZA, Duke of Milan
POPE ALEXANDER VI, Roderigo Borgia, father of Cesare and Lucrezia
    Borgia
POPE JULIUS II
CATERINA SFORZA, Countess of Forli
LOUIS XII, King of France

This is the book that gives meaning to the critical adjective "Machiavellian." It is an ingenious and fascinating study of the art of practical politics, composed by a man who never rose higher than the position of secretary to the Second Chancery in Florence. The success of his book is due partly to his wit and partly to his having known some of the most clever and powerful rogues of the Renaissance. His model for the "Prince" was Cesare Borgia, a man who used all means of conquest, including murder, to achieve and hold political position.

Machiavelli never pretended that his book was a guide to the virtuous. On the other hand, he did not set out to prescribe the way to wickedness. He meant his account to be a practical guide to political power, and through a combination of experience, logic, and imagination he constructed one of the most intriguing handbooks of Western civilization: a primer for princes.

In beginning a discussion concerned with the manners and attitudes of a prince—that is, a ruler of a state—Machiavelli writes:

Since . . . it has been my intention to write something which may be of use to the understanding reader, it has seemed wiser to me to follow the real truth of the matter rather than what we imagine it to be. For imagination has created many principalities and republics that have never been seen or known to have any real existence, for how we live is so different from how we ought to live that he who studies what ought to be done rather than what is done will learn the way to his downfall rather than to his preservation.

This passage makes it clear that Machiavelli intended to explain how successful politicians actually work rather than how they ought to work.

The Prince begins with a one paragraph chapter which illustrates Machiavelli's logical approach to the problem of advising prospective princes. He claims that all states are either republics or monarchies. Monarchies are either hereditary or new. New monarchies are either entirely new or acquired. Acquired states have either been dominated by a prince or been free; and they are acquired either by a prince's own arms or by those of others; and they fall to him either by fortune or because of his own character and ability.

Having outlined this inclusive logical bifurcation, Machiavelli first discusses the problems connected with governing a hereditary monarchy, and then goes on to discuss mixed monarchies.

In each case, as his argument develops, Machiavelli considers what the logical alternatives are, and what should be done in each case if the prince is to acquire and hold power. In writing of mixed monarchies, for example, having pointed out that acquired states are either culturally similar to the conquering state or not, he then considers each possibility. If the acquired state is culturally similar, it is no problem to keep it; but if the acquired state is different in its customs, laws, or language, then there is a problem to be solved. One solution might be to have the ruler go to the acquired territory and live there. As an example, Machiavelli refers to the presence of the Turkish ruler in Greece.

Another possibility for solving the problem which arises when an acquired territory differs culturally from the conquering state is the establishment of colonies. Colonies are inexpensive to acquire and maintain, he argues, because the land is acquired from a few landowners of the conquered territory and they are the only ones who complain. Such a plan is preferable to maintaining soldiers, for policing a new state is expensive and, in addition, offends the citizens being policed.

Thus, by the somewhat mechanical device of considering logical alternatives, Machiavelli uses his limited experience to build a guide to power. What he says, although refreshing in its direct approach to the hard facts of practical politics, is not entirely fanciful or naïve. Not only did Machiavelli, through his diplomatic missions, come to know intimately such leaders as Louis XII, Julius II, the Emperor Maximilian, and Cesare Borgia, but he also used his time to advantage, noting political tricks that actually worked and building up his store of psychological truths.

It is doubtful that any ruler or rebel ever succeeded simply because he followed Machiavelli to the letter, but it may well be that some political coups have been the result of inspiration from *The Prince*. (Indeed, shortly after Fidel Castro's overthrow of the Batista government in Cuba in 1959, a newspaper account reported that among the books on Castro's revolutionary reading list was Machiavelli's *The Prince*.)

What is inspiring for the politically ambitious in *The Prince* is not the substance but the attitude, not the prescription but the unabashed, calculating, and aggressive air with which the author analyzes the means to power.

For the reader without political ambition *The Prince* is a sometimes amusing and sometimes frightening reminder of the realities of political fortune. For example, Machiavelli writes that anyone who helps another to power is bound to fall himself because he has contributed to the success either by his cleverness or his power, and no prince can tolerate the existence of either in another person close to him. This is a lesson which would have been useful to some of the men close to the top in the U.S.S.R.

Machiavelli considers this question: Why did the kingdom of Darius, occupied by Alexander the Great, not rebel after Alexander's death? The answer is that monarchies are governed either by a prince and his staff or by a prince and a number of barons. A monarchy controlled by the prince through his representatives is very difficult to conquer, since the entire staff owes its existence to the prince and is, consequently, loyal. But once such a monarchy is captured, power is easily maintained. So it was in Alexander's case. But a nation like the France of Machiavelli's day is ruled by a king and barons. The barons are princes of a sort over their portions of the state, and they maintain control over their subjects. It is easy to conquer such a state because there are always unhappy barons willing to join a movement to overthrow the king. But once conquered, such a state is difficult to hold because the barons may regroup and overthrow the new prince.

Sometimes power is acquired through crime, Machiavelli admits, and he cites a violent example: the murder of Giovanni Fogliani of Fermo by his nephew Oliverotto. Machiavelli advises that the cruelty necessary to attain power be kept to a minimum and not be continued, for the purely practical reason that the prince will lose power otherwise. The best thing to do, says the author, is to commit one's acts of cruelty all at once, not over an extended period.

This cold practicality is echoed in such injunctions as those to the effect that if one cannot afford to be generous, accept with indifference the name of miser; it is safer to be feared than to be loved, if one must choose; a prince need not have a morally worth-while character, but he must *appear* to have it; if a prince's military support is good, he will always have good friends; to keep power one must be careful not to be hated by the people; it is always wiser for a prince to be a true friend or a true enemy than to be neutral; a prince should never listen to advice unless he asks for it; and it is better to be bold than cautious.

Machiavelli's prime examples are Francesco Sforza and Cesare Borgia, particularly the latter. The author writes that he is always able to find examples for his points by referring to the deeds of Borgia. Considering the value of using auxiliary arms, the military force of another state, Machiavelli refers to Borgia's unfortunate experience with auxiliaries in the capture of Romagna. Finding the auxiliaries untrustworthy, Borgia turned to mercenaries, but they were no better, so he finally used only his own troops. Machiavelli's conclusion in regard to auxiliary troops is that "If any one . . . wants to make sure of not winning he will avail himself of troops such as these."

After reviewing Cesare Borgia's rise to power (with the remark that "I could not suggest better precepts to a new prince than the examples of Cesare's actions"),

Machiavelli concludes that "I can find nothing with which to reproach him, rather it seems that I ought to point him out as an example . . . to all those who have risen to power by fortune or by the arms of others." This praise follows a description of such acts as Borgia's killing of as many of the hapless lords he had despoiled "as he could lay hands on."

Machiavelli praises the actions of other leaders, such as Francesco Sforza and Popes Alexander VI and Julius II, but only Cesare Borgia wins unqualified praise. Sforza, for example, is recognized as having become Duke of Milan "by the proper means and through his own ability," but later on he is criticized because of a castle he built when he should have been trying to win the good will of the people.

The Prince concludes with a plea to the Medici family to free Italy from the "barbarians" who ruled the republic of Florence and kept Italy in bondage. Machiavelli makes a plea for liberation, expresses his disappointment that Borgia is not available because of a turn of fortune, and closes with the capitalized cry that "THIS BARBARIAN OCCUPATION STINKS IN THE NOSTRILS OF ALL OF US."

Unfortunately for the author, his plea to the Medici family did him no good, and he died with the Republic still in power. Perhaps he himself was not bold enough; perhaps he was not cruel enough. In any case, he left behind a work to be used by any leader willing to be both.

THE PRINCE AND THE PAUPER

Type of work: Novel
Author: Mark Twain (Samuel L. Clemens, 1835-1910)
Type of plot: Social criticism
Time of plot: Sixteenth century
Locale: England
First published: 1882

Principal characters:
TOM CANTY, a London street beggar
JOHN CANTY, his father
EDWARD, Prince of Wales
MILES HENDON, a disinherited knight
HUGH HENDON, his brother
HUGO, a thief

Critique:

In many ways, *The Prince and the Pauper* is a companion piece to *A Connecticut Yankee at King Arthur's Court.* Both are historical satires; both deplore the lack of democracy and cleanliness of early England; both scrutinize the past from a viewpoint of modern morality. Lastly, both exhibit humor derived from ludicrous situations. In its compactness and relative brevity *The Prince and the Pauper* is in some ways superior to *A Connecticut Yankee.* But the denouement of the novel is disappointing. It is as if the fantasy got away from the author and overwhelmed him. The outstanding quality of this novel is the beloved simplicity of the prince himself, his unswerving tenacity to his royal training throughout all his difficulties, and his final act of clemency.

The Story:

On the same day, in London, Tom Canty and the Prince of Wales were born, the first unwanted and the second long awaited. While the prince, Edward Tudor, lay robed in silks, Tom Canty wallowed in the filth of Offal Court.

Tom's father forced him to beg during the day and he beat the boy at night; but Tom had private dreams of his own. Pretending that he was a prince, he gathered his ragtaggle court of street urchins around him. One day, hoping to see Prince Edward of England, he invaded the royal precincts, but when he tried to approach the prince he was cuffed by a guard and ordered away. Edward, witnessing the incident, protected Tom and took the young beggar into the palace. There, in the privacy of Edward's chamber, Tom confessed his longing to be a prince. When the two boys exchanged garments they discovered that they were identical in appearance. Unrecognized as the real prince and mistaken for the beggar boy, Edward was promptly thrown into the streets of London, where he wandered helplessly, mocked by people whom he approached with pleas that they pay homage to him as their rightful prince.

Meanwhile, in the palace, it was thought that the prince had gone mad because he could recall none of the royal matters which he was supposed to know. King Henry issued an edict that no one should discuss the royal lapse of memory, and the Princesses Mary and Elizabeth mercifully tried to aid their supposed brother, who by that time was too frightened to confess that he was Tom Canty, a beggar dressed in the prince's clothing.

King Henry VIII, sick in bed, had given the Great Seal of the kingdom to Prince Edward for safekeeping. When Henry demanded the return of his seal, Tom reported that he did not know where it was.

While the Prince of Wales, a homeless waif, wandered the streets under the crowd's mocking raillery, King Henry died. Edward was found by John Canty, Tom's father, and brought to Offal Court; but during the wild celebration of Tom's ascension to the throne Edward escaped from John Canty. Again tormented by skeptical crowds who laughed at his protests that he was now King of England, Edward was rescued by Miles Hendon, the disinherited son of a baronet. Thinking Edward was mad, Miles pitied the little waif and pretended to pay him the homage due to a monarch.

Miles had loved a girl named Edith, who was coveted by Miles' brother Hugh. By trickery, Hugh had gained his father's confidence and Miles was turned away from home. Edward declared that Miles had suffered unjustly and promised the adventurer any boon he might ask. Recalling the story of De Courcy, who, given a similar opportunity by King John, requested that he and all his descendants might be permitted to wear hats in the presence of the King of England, Miles wisely asked that he be permitted to sit down in Edward's presence, for the young king had been ordering Miles about like any other personal servant.

In the role of King of England, Tom was slowly learning to conduct himself royally. Regarded by his attendants as mad, he was able to display his lack of training, and his failure to recall events familiar to Edward, with no calamitous results. At the same time his gradual improvement offered hope that his derangement was only temporary.

John Canty lured Edward away from Miles' protection and took the boy to Southwark, there to join a pack of thieves. Still vainly declaring himself king, Edward was again the center of ridicule. One of the thieves, Hugo, undertook to teach Edward the tricks of his trade. Making his escape, Edward wandered to a farmhouse where a kind woman, pitying the poor, insane beggar boy who declared himself King of England, fed him. Edward wandered on to the hut of a hermit who accepted naïvely Edward's claim to

royalty. In turn, the hermit revealed to Edward that he was an archangel; the hermit was really mad. While Edward slept, the hermit brooded over the wrongs done him by King Henry. Believing Edward really to be the king, and planning to murder him, the hermit managed to tie up the boy while he slept. John Canty and Hugo, following the trail of the escaped waif, rescued him and forced him to rejoin the band of rogues. Again he was compelled to aid Hugo in his dishonest trade. At last Miles found the boy and saved him.

Miles was on his way back to Hendon Hall to claim his heritage and Edith for a wife. Arriving at their destination, they learned that Miles' father was dead and Hugh, married to Edith, was master of Hendon Hall. Only five of the old servants were still living, and all of them, in addition to Hugh and Edith, pretended not to recognize Miles. Denounced as a pretender, Miles was sentenced to the stocks, where the abuse showered upon him by the mob so enraged Edward that he protested loudly. When the guards decided to whip the boy, Miles offered to bear the flogging instead. Grateful to his friend, Edward dubbed Miles an earl, but the imprisoned man sorrowed at the boy's display of insanity. Upon Miles' release from the stocks the two set out for London, where they arrived on the day before the coronation of King Edward VI.

In regal splendor, enjoying the adulation of his subjects, Tom Canty rode through the streets of London toward Westminster Abbey. There, just as the crown was about to be set on his head, a voice rang out demanding that the ceremony cease, and the real king, clothed in rags, stepped forth. As the guards moved to seize the troublemaker, Tom, recognizing Edward, ordered them to halt. The Lord Protector solved the mystery by asking the ragged king to locate the Great Seal that had been lost since King Henry's death. Edward, after much dramatic hesitation, managed to remember the exact location of the Seal. Tom admitted that he had innocently used it to crack nuts.

When Miles was brought before the rightful King Edward, he exercised his privilege of sitting in the king's presence. At first he had doubted that the waif was really the king, but when Edward ordered his outraged guards to permit that disrespectful act, Miles knew that his young friend had not been insane after all. Furthermore, Edward confirmed Miles' title of earl. Hugh was stripped of his titles and land. Later he died, whereupon Miles married Edith, whose earlier refusal to acknowledge his identity had been the result of Hugh's threat to kill his brother.

Tom returned to Offal Court with Edward's promise that he and his family would be honored for the rest of their lives. Edward righted many wrongs he had encountered during his adventures. John Canty, whom he wanted to hang, was never heard from again.

Further Critical Evaluation of the Work:

The Prince and the Pauper was Mark Twain's earliest attempt to join his recent fascination for the romantic past of Europe with his natural bent for satirizing the injustices and social conventions of his own age. He was to do the same later, with far better effect, in *A Connecticut Yankee in King Arthur's Court* (1889), and with less success in *Personal Recollections of Joan of Arc* (1896). It is generally agreed that *The Prince and the Pauper* is a story mainly for children—though if that is wholly true, it must also be said that it is a children's story very rewarding for adults.

Twain employs in this novel many of the themes and devices which he may have exercised to better effect in other works, but which are nonetheless used well here also. There are, for example, all the usual techniques he learned so expertly as a teller of tall-tales—tongue-in-cheek irony, ridiculous understatement, and exaggeration, to name a few. Miles Hendon's separation from Edward gives Twain the opportunity for soliloquy, a favorite literary device used with great success in *Huckleberry Finn*. The exchange of identities—as in *Huckleberry Finn* and *Pudd'nhead Wilson*—is another common occurrence in Twain's works, as is his use of coincidence.

Twain was also able in *The Prince and the Pauper* to underscore some of the social follies and injustices of his own age without actually having to attack them directly in the novel. He did this by satirically treating the social and legal conventions of Tudor England, and then assuming his readers would recognize for themselves the parallels with their own times. Hence, religious intolerance is the target of "In Prison," a chapter in which two women, who have kindly befriended Edward and Miles, are mercilessly burned at the stake because they are Baptists. Tom Canty, as king, labors to change laws which are unduly harsh or blatantly unjust; and Edward himself learns of the unnecessary cruelty of prisons, as well as the nature of the kind of life poor people must endure as a result of their poverty.

However, Twain's major criticism of society, both Tudor and his own, is of its mistaking the outward appearances of men or their circumstances as a final gauge of their true worth. The novel suggests that, under different circumstances, any man *could* be a king—just as Tom Canty, given the opportunity, learns to be one. Tom and Edward are equally intelligent and virtuous young boys, but each is born to a different kind of "court." Chance and circumstances alone determine much of our outward behavior and appearance. For Twain, this was as true for his own times as he felt it had been for Tudor England.

THE PRINCE OF HOMBURG

Type of work: Drama
Author: Heinrich von Kleist (1777-1811)
Type of plot: Historical tragedy
Time of plot: 1675
Locale: Prussia
First presented: 1821

Principal characters:
FREDERICK WILLIAM, Elector of Brandenburg
THE ELECTRESS
PRINCESS NATALIE OF ORANGE, niece of the elector
FIELD MARSHAL DÖRFLING
PRINCE FREDERICK ARTHUR OF HOMBURG
COLONEL KOTTWITZ, of the regiment of the Princess of Orange
COUNT HOHENZOLLERN, of the elector's suite

Critique:

Heinrich von Kleist led a short, turbulent life as a poet and died by his own hand at the age of thirty-four. Predestined by family tradition to spend a life of service to his own country, he entered the army at the age of fourteen. However, constant yearnings toward creativeness led him to secure a discharge. He then embarked on a course of study which included Kant's philosophy and the theories of Rousseau. He began to pour all of his creative powers, which were singular for a man in his mid-twenties, into a series of plays. One of these was the farcical *The Broken Jug*, the only light piece he was to compose. His early works met with little success, for he had a limited knowledge of the techniques of writing for the stage. He was essentially a romanticist. *The Prince of Homburg*, his last dramatic work, employs romantic poetic imagery, but its subject presupposes a vital, realistic framework. The play contains rich characterizations which convey the Prussian virtues of discipline and obedience. Its chief fault lies in the lack of stage techniques; it is episodic, lacking in action, and cluttered with a number of secondary characters.

The Story:

After three days of heading a cavalry charge in pursuit of the Swedes, Prince Frederick Arthur of Homburg had returned to Fehrbellin. Exhausted and battle weary, the prince fell into a dreamlike sleep, weaving a laurel wreath as he half dozed. The Elector Frederick William was informed by Count Hohenzollern of the prince's strange condition, and as the elector, the electress, and their niece, Princess Natalie, appeared in the garden where he slept, a strange thing occurred. The elector took the wreath from the prince, entwined it in his neckchain and gave it to Natalie. They backed away as the somnambulistic prince followed murmuring incoherently, and as they retreated inside, the prince snatched a glove from Natalie's hand.

When the prince awoke, he told Count Hohenzollern about the occurrence, which he thought had been a dream. Hohenzollern reproved him for his romantic fantasies and urged him to make ready for the coming battle with the Swedes.

The field marshal of Brandenburg was dictating the orders of battle to his officers; but the prince, who was to play an important role in the battle, was absorbed with his thoughts. Hoping to remember from whom he had got the glove, he wore it in his collar. The electress and Natalie were present, and plans were being formed to send them to a place of safety. As the field marshal reached the section of the orders which pertained to the prince, Natalie, preparing to depart, suddenly realized that she had but one glove. The prince, who loved Natalie, quickly became aware that he held the missing glove. In order to be sure it was hers, he dropped it on the floor in front of him. Natalie claimed it, and the prince, in a fit of ecstasy, did not hear his battle orders clearly though his mission was to be a key one.

The battlefield of Fehrbellin resounded with cannon and the elector's forces were sure of victory. As the rout of the Swedes became apparent, the prince precipitously gave orders to advance. His colleagues made an effort to dissuade him from this impetuous action, insisting that he hear the order of battle again; he was definitely supposed to remain in his position until a given signal. However, when the arduous prince rebuked Kottwitz, an elderly colonel, for lack of fervency, Kottwitz, rather than appear unpatriotic, joined the prince in the advance.

The electress and Natalie had paused during their journey to safety at a house in a nearby village, where news reached them that the elector had died in battle; both he and his great white horse were reported killed during the bombardment. The prince sought out the women and took the opportunity to tell the distraught Natalie of his love for her, and to offer her his protection. The elector was her last relative; now that he was dead she had no one to turn to.

But the elector was not dead. He had changed horses with one of his officers, and the officer astride the white horse had been mistakenly identified as the elector. The same messenger who brought word that the elector was still alive had further news for rejoicing. The war was over for the time being, and the elector had returned to Berlin.

It became apparent to the elector that Prince Frederick was responsible for ignoring the battle order, and although terms for peace with the Swedes were being discussed, the strong military spirit of the elector prompted him to punish the prince for failing to follow orders. The prince was sentenced to die and placed in prison to await the day of his execution.

The prince, given permission to visit the electress, begged clemency through her. She was touched by his plea, as was Natalie, who threw herself at the feet of the elector to beg for the prince's life. In addition to Natalie's plea, the officers of the elector's army circulated a petition asking that the prince's life be spared. At last the elector agreed to pardon him.

Natalie took the letter of pardon from the elector to the prince's cell. But upon his reading the pardon, events took a different turn. In his letter the elector had specified that the prince's sword would be returned if the young man thought the elector had been unjust in his sentence. The prince then refused the pardon; his military training and nationalistic spirit prompted him to realize that the sentence was just.

The officers of the army visited the elector to plead on the prince's behalf. Count Hohenzollern made the strongest case. Had the elector not deceived the young prince by snatching the laurel wreath and entwining it with his neckchain, the prince would not have felt an uncontrollable destiny forcing him into battle. Therefore, it was the elector's own fault that the prince's mind had been clouded by what he thought was a vision foretelling valorous deeds. The elector countered by blaming Count Hohenzollern himself for the whole affair, for he was the one who had led the elector to the sleeping prince.

When the prince appeared before the assembled officers and the elector, he was ready to die; nevertheless, he made such a strong plea to the elector that he was able to save himself. Meanwhile, peace with Gustaf Karl of Sweden had been effected by promising Natalie's hand to a Swedish nobleman. The prince begged the elector to revoke the agreement and to attack the Swedes instead. The elector, ordering his troops to resume battle, tore up the death warrant. Prince Frederick Arthur was hailed as the hero of the field of Fehrbellin.

Further Critical Evaluation of the Work:

Kleist's last drama, *The Prince of Homburg,* was banned in his own time by censors who objected to seeing a Prussian officer show cowardice in the face of death. It was not published until 1821 and even in 1828, when it was produced in Berlin, the scene of Frederick's terror had to be altered. Modern critics, however, see in the work Kleist's most mature drama, a coming to terms with the demands of the state and its laws, while acknowledging the role of the individual and his spirit, including even the force of the irrational.

Kleist's earlier tragedies tended to the excessive, with extravagant emotions and a certain wild quality, notably in *Penthesilea.* With the defeat of Prussia by Napoleon, however, his work took a patriotic turn and though the censors saw in Frederick's character a slur on Prussian heroism, Kleist's drama is actually one of the finest embodiments of the Prussian ideal, created through the resolution of the initial conflict between the emotional power—moving as if in a dream—of the prince and the recognition of the validity of the law which governs the social community.

The two poles of the drama are Frederick, the Romantic, sleepwalking hero, who moves according to his own inner law, achieving success, but without taking his place in a structured society, and the Elector, who represents the demands of the state, yet tempers them with wisdom and a gentle humor. In Kleist's generally tragic view of the world, men are most often destroyed by the irreconcilable conflicts into which they are cast by an almost hostile fate. That Kleist here could avoid the potential tragedy and bring his hero to a recognition of his true role seems to be a personal as well as a dramatic development. Unfortunately, the drama failed and Kleist himself, in a mood of despair, ended his own life.

THE PRINCESS

Type of work: Narrative poem
Author: Alfred, Lord Tennyson (1809-1892)
First published: 1847

> *Principal characters:*
> WALTER VIVIAN, the heir to Vivianplace, an English estate
> THE POET
> LILIA, Walter Vivian's sister
> FIVE COLLEGE STUDENTS, friends of Walter and the Poet
> THE PRINCE,
> THE KING, his father,
> CYRIL and
> FLORIAN, two friends of the Prince,
> PRINCESS IDA, ruler of a women's college
> KING GAMA, her father,
> ARAC, her brother,
> PSYCHE and
> BLANCHE, her tutors,
> AGLAÏA, the daughter of Psyche, and
> MELISSA, the daughter of Blanche, characters in a story told by Walter
> Vivian and his friends

First published in 1847, *The Princess* underwent numerous major changes in its later editions; in the third edition of 1850, the poet added the six intercalary songs in addition to partial revisions of the "Prologue" and "Epilogue." The fourth edition, published in 1851, saw the introduction of the passages relating to the "weird seizures" of the Prince. Reasons for these changes may be Tennyson's almost immediate dissatisfaction with the work and his desire to clarify public misunderstandings of it or his reaction to the rather unfavorable reception of the poem by contemporary critics. Indeed, the poem today is generally regarded as one of Tennyson's ambitious but lesser works, owing chiefly to the mixed style and the shifting tone of the poem, as well as the somewhat transitory nature of his subject, women's rights.

The Princess begins as a light mock-heroic work and ends with a "serious message"; it begins seemingly not seriously concerned with women's rights and ends equivocally with the poet almost avoiding the issue. Tennyson himself sensed this apparent disunity of the poem and writes in the "Conclusion": "I moved as in a strange diagonal,/And maybe neither pleased myself nor them." Tennyson's ambivalence about his subject and his failure to sustain the comic approach constitute a major blemish for some modern critics, but though the narrative itself is disparaged, few critics deny the power, beauty, and simplicity of the intercalary lyrics of this poem. Several of these are judged among the finest of his poems, and for grace and precision and music, only a small number of English lyrics may favorably compare.

In the "Prologue" the poet and five other college companions join their friend, Walter Vivian, on his father's estate where they view the exhibition of the neighboring Institute, of which Walter's father is patron. A book of family history relating the courage of a female ancestor inspires Lilia, Walter's sister, to speak out for women's rights, particularly their education. Walter tells how at college the seven friends told chain-stories to pass away the time; Lilia suggests that they tell such a story now. Walter agrees and adds that Lilia be the heroine, "Grand, epic, homicidal," and the poet, who will begin the story, be the hero. The seven-part story which follows is narrated by each of the seven friends; between each part the ladies present sing one of the six songs.

The young Prince, whose family suffers from a curse laid down by a sorcerer, finds that the Princess to whom he was once betrothed as a child now rejects him and wishes to "live alone/Among her women." He begs the King, his father, to be allowed to investigate this puzzle, but the King, of a warlike masculine nature, replies that they will settle this dispute by war. Driven by an inner voice, the Prince rides off to the southern kingdom of the Princess, accompanied by his two friends Cyril and Florian. At a town near the palace where the girls had established their women's college the Prince obtains women's clothes for Cyril, Florian, and himself, and together they enter the college disguised, bearing a letter of introduction from Gama, the King and father of the Princess.

In the second narrative the college portress leads the still disguised males to Princess Ida, who greets them as new students and explains the rules to them: they must not for three years correspond with home, leave the boundaries of the college grounds, or converse with men. Ida tells them they must give up "convention" and work now for the freedom of women. She seems surprised that the males praise so highly the Prince, her former suitor. Next they encounter Psyche, Florian's sister, and Ida's favorite tutor. They admire Aglaïa, Psyche's daughter, while Psyche lectures them on the history of feminine slavery. Finally Psyche recognizes her brother beneath his disguise, and nearly betrays them until her natural affection overcomes her duty to Ida. Melissa, the daughter of Blanche, who is Ida's other favorite, also learns their identity but refuses to reveal their secret.

In the third section Ida invites the men to travel with her, but before their departure the Prince has his first seizure, the curse-inflicted malady of his family. Recovering, the Prince as his own mock-ambassador tries to acquaint Ida with his passion for her and with her unnatural attitude toward men; he alludes to her missing "what every woman counts her due,/'Love, children, happiness.'" Ida reiterates her dedication to her ideals, claiming that while children may die, "great deeds" cannot.

In the fourth section a maid sings "Tears, idle tears," but Ida is unmoved by its sentiment of love. The Prince replies with his song, "O Swallow," a love song; Ida, however, spurns his "mere love poem," saying she admires only art addressed to "great ends." At this point Cyril sings a bawdy song which discloses their true identity. The women flee in panic, and Ida in her haste falls into the river. The Prince rescues her but is captured by her retinue and experiences his second seizure.

In the fifth section, the Prince and his companions, released by the Princess out of gratitude, stumble into the camp of the Prince's father. Gama, the Prince, and the King argue how to win Ida's hand; the King favors aggression, but Gama and the Prince suggest peaceful means. Taunted as a coward, the Prince agrees to a tournament where he will face Arac, Ida's brother, who champions women's rights. Again he falls into a trance and is unable to distinguish shadow and substance. Awakening, he find the tournament ready to begin; fighting Arac, he is wounded and falls into a deep coma.

The sixth part opens with the Prince in a mystic trance. Ida in her triumph sings "Our enemies have fallen," then opens the palace as a hospital for the wounded. Her foolish insistence upon ascetic withdrawal and her unnatural contempt for men is evident; as she gazes upon the wounded Prince, however, she begs the King to allow her to care for his son. She embraces Psyche, whom she had dismissed as a traitor, and disbands the college despite Blanche's objections.

In the final part the palace has become a hospital with the maidens nursing the sick. Ida is heartsick because of the frustration of her ideals, but she finds "peace" aiding the wounded men. The Prince lies in a delirious state tended by Ida; as she cares for him she begins to love him, casts off her "falser self," and kisses the Prince. He succumbs to his love for her and falls into a blissful sleep. That night he awakes to find her reading poems to him; these are two of the best lyrics of the poem, "Now sleeps the crimson petal," and "Come down, O Maid." In the latter poem love is described as being of the "valley," not of mountain heights where Ida's idealism had carried her.

Ida admits her lack of humility, her desire to achieve "power" more than "truth," yet she still regrets the collapse of her idealistic plans to help women achieve status. The Prince, respecting her idealism, replies that they will work to-gether for her goal. He says that women are not "undevelopt" men, that they should join with man in love; from this union the man gains "sweetness" and "moral height," the woman "mental breadth," without losing "the childlike in the larger mind." Either sex alone is "half itself," and together in marriage each "fulfils/Defect in each." The Prince attributes to Ida his rebirth into a better life, his losing doubt and "haunting sense of hollow shows."

The narrative closes and the framework returns with the poet's explanation of the feud which arose between the mockers (the men) and the realists (the women). To satisfy both he proposed his "strange diagonal" and perhaps pleased neither.

THE PRINCESS CASAMASSIMA

Type of work: Novel
Author: Henry James (1843-1916)
Type of plot: Social criticism
Time of plot: Late nineteenth century
Locale: London
First published: 1886

Principal characters:

HYACINTH ROBINSON, an orphan, apprenticed bookbinder, and revolutionary

MISS AMANDA PYNSENT, the dressmaker who brought up Hyacinth

PRINCESS CASAMASSIMA, an Italian princess with "modern" ideas

ANASTASIUS VETCH, a musician and a friend of Miss Pynsent

PAUL MUNIMENT, the chemist who leads Hyacinth into revolutionary work

LADY AURORA LANGRISH, a noblewoman who works for the good of the poor

MILLICENT HENNING, Hyacinth's childhood playmate

Critique:

In the novel *Roderick Hudson*, the beautiful Christina Light allows herself to be married to the powerful Italian family of Prince Casamassima. Some ten years later James depicts the Princess Casamassima, now separated from her husband, determined to reject her empty social life and to work with the proletariat to destroy oppression. James thus examine critically not only the evils of the social and economic systems which demand reform, but also the motives and methods of the people who propose to carry out those reforms. In many novels James studies the interaction of characters from two widely separated continents, but in this work he examines the interaction of characters from two widely separated social classes as the world of princes and dukes encounters the world of bookbinders and chemists. Every character changes as a result of this contact across class lines. Whether these changes in character are for the better or for the worse, James leaves to his readers to decide.

The Story:

Florentine Vivier, a French dressmaker, gave birth to an illegitimate son and accused an Englishman, Lord Frederick Purvis, of being the boy's father. Because Lord Frederick and his family refused to recognize the baby, Florentine Vivier stabbed Lord Frederick to death, a crime for which she received the maximum prison sentence. Her son, called Hyacinth Robinson, she entrusted to another poor dressmaker, Miss Amanda Pynsent, who brought him up without telling him the unfortunate circumstances surrounding his birth.

Years later Mrs. Bowerbank, a prison matron, visited Miss Pynsent to tell her that Florentine Vivier was dying in the prison hospital and had asked to see her son, now ten years of age. Miss Pynsent consults Mr. Vetch, a violinist in a Bloomsbury theater, who was her closest friend. On his advice she took Hyacinth to the prison. He did not know that the woman was his mother. The grim prison frightened him, and at first his mother spoke only in French, saying that she feared he was ashamed of her. She embraced him pitifully before the matron bustled the visitors away.

Years again passed. In the interval the rowdy family of Millicent Henning, the childhood friend of Hyacinth, had been ejected from their quarters next to Miss Pynsent's shop in Lomax Place. Mr. Vetch had a copy of Lord Bacon's *Essays* bound as a gift for Hyacinth and thus had met the master bookbinder Eustache Poupin, exiled from France after the Commune of 1871. Mr. Vetch learned that he and Poupin had a common bond of hate for the existing social and political fabric. Poupin secured for Hyacinth an apprenticeship with Crookenden's bookbindery and taught him French and socialism.

Millicent Henning, grown to a bold, handsome young woman, unexpectedly appeared once more in Lomax Place to renew her friendship with Hyacinth. Poupin introduced Paul Muniment to Hyacinth. Paul took him to visit his crippled sister, Rose Muniment, and there they met Lady Aurora Langrish, who devoted her time to caring for the poor and who admired Paul a great deal. She was a spinster much neglected by her large and wealthy family. Paul led Hyacinth more deeply into revolutionary activity. In the meantime Hyacinth had looked up the newspaper reports of his mother's trial, and he considered himself the aggrieved son of Lord Frederick Purvis.

Mr. Vetch got for Hyacinth tickets to take Millicent to see the play, *The Pearl of Paraguay*. Captain Godfrey Sholto, whom Hyacinth had met at a revolutionists' discussion group at "The Sun and Moon" public house, came from his box at the theater to invite Hyacinth to meet his companions, the Princess Casamassima and her old companion, Madame Grandoni.

Prince Casamassima tried to see the princess to beg her to return to living with him, but she refused to see him. As the prince was leaving her house, he saw Hyacinth ushered in, at the princess' invitation, to tea. Later, Hyacinth bound a copy of Tennyson as a gift for the princess, but when he tried to deliver his gift he learned that she had left London for a series of visits in the country. Hyacinth also encountered Captain Sholto

in a bar and, as Sholto hurried him strangely along, they encountered Millicent. Hyacinth suspected that Millicent had arranged to meet Sholto.

Paul Muniment announced at a meeting at "The Sun and Moon" that the revolutionary organizer, Hoffendahl, who had spent twelve years in Prussian prisons, was in London. After Hyacinth declared his readiness to give his life for the cause, Paul took him to see Hoffendahl. There he swore an oath to perform an act of violence whenever Hoffendahl should send the order. Meanwhile, the princess had invited Hyacinth to stay at her country house, Medley. The princess was extremely pleasant and Hyacinth stayed on in the country. One day Captain Sholto rode up to Hyacinth as he was walking on the estate and asked Hyacinth to obtain an invitation to dinner for him. Clearly, Hyacinth had replaced Sholto as the princess' favorite.

He returned from Medley to find Miss Pynsent dying. In her will she left a small sum of money to him. Mr. Vetch added to this sum and advised Hyacinth to travel on the Continent. On his return, he heard that the princess had sold all her beautiful furnishings, moved to a tawdry, lower middle-class house in Madeira Crescent, and become friendly with Paul Muniment, who was now deeply involved in revolutionary activities. In the meantime Hyacinth's own contact with wealth and leisure had made life seem more valuable and the society which produces and appreciates art more tolerable.

The prince followed the princess and observed her going out with Paul Muniment. He demanded that Madame Grandoni tell him what she was doing. As the prince left Madame Grandoni, he met Hyacinth. While they were walking away from the house they saw Paul and the princess return and enter together. Madame Grandoni abandoned the princess. The prince wrote to Paul saying that he would send no more money to his wife.

At Poupin's Hyacinth found the German worker Schinkel with sealed orders for him. He was to go to a grand party and there assassinate a duke. Mr. Vetch tried to keep Hyacinth from doing some desperate action. Hyacinth went to the store where Millicent worked, only to find her talking to Captain Sholto. The princess, going to Hyacinth's room, found Schinkel waiting. She demanded that he break in. Inside, they find that Hyacinth had shot himself in the heart.

Further Critical Evaluation of the Work:

The Princess Casamassima is James's most concerted effort to catch the revolutionary atmosphere of the London during the 1870's and 1880's. In his Preface to the novel he speaks of his awareness of political forces brewing beneath the vast surface of society. He did not know these forces in any intimate detail, however, and the novel shows it. His portraits of lower-class characters are solid enough (Hyacinth Robinson, Miss Pynsent, Mr. Vetch) and even brilliant (Millicent Henning).

The trouble lies in the portrayal of the revolutionaries. Paul Muniment, who introduces Hyacinth into revolutionary work is vague at the center. The famous revolutionary leader Hoffendahl does not even appear on stage; his "potency" is merely a felt presence. Nevertheless, James's political fable has its finenesses. The drama of Hyacinth's gradual awareness of what revolutionary behavior amounts to is superbly done. The little bookbinder finds that he has been used by Muniment and the Princess, and at the same time he discovers that he has become deeply attached to those objects of art possessed by the class he has been working to overturn. In his youthful idealism, he has been working against all he now respects and wishes to preserve. The irony here is compounded by the case of the Princess herself. Under the influence of Muniment and her own idealism she comes to repudiate her wealth and position at the very time Hyacinth aspires to the finer things to which she has introduced him. In the Princess, James gives us a vivid picture of the upper-class revolutionary—a person in full-fledged rebellion from her class. In contrast to Lady Aurora Langrish whose enthusiasm for the revolution fades when she discovers she cannot catch Paul Muniment, the Princess' revolutionary sympathies are not so easily dissipated. There is something about her seriousness which is cold and inhuman. She is a good portrait of a revolutionary fanatic and reactionary. Needless to say, for James revolutionary politics was not a pleasing spectacle.

THE PRINCESS OF CLÈVES

Type of work: Novel
Author: Madame de La Fayette (1634-1693)
Type of plot: Sentimental romance
Time of plot: Sixteenth century
Locale: France
First published: 1678

Principal characters:

THE PRINCESS DE CLÈVES, née Chartres, a beautiful young noblewoman
THE PRINCE DE CLÈVES, her husband
THE DUKE DE NEMOURS, in love with the princess
THE VIDAME DE CHARTRES, uncle of the princess
THE QUEEN DAUPHINE, Mary, Queen of Scots, friend of the princess

Critique:

Because *The Princess of Clèves* is superior to any of the other romances written by Madame de La Fayette some literary historians and critics have hesitated to credit her with the authorship of a book so simple in outline but elegant in detail. There seems no reason to doubt the authenticity of the work, however, if we remember that during its composition the novel was discussed and criticized by the brilliant men and women who attended the salon over which Madame de La Fayette presided. These included the Duke de Rochefoucauld, Madame de Sévigné, Huet, the royal tutor, Segrais, the poet, Cardinal de Retz, and many others. The writer undoubtedly profited by the suggestions and advice of her friends. Certainly, out of their personal memories of an earlier time, they aided in reconstructing the historical background and details of the book. More important, this early novel defined areas of experience which later writers have charted more completely. The careful analyses of emotion, the atmosphere of intrigue, the conflict between duty and desire, and the subjective portrayal of character, as presented here, have made the romance one of the landmarks of French literature. The influence of the book can be traced through two distinct literary trends: the psychological novel and the *roman à clef*, which presents real people and events under a thin fictional disguise.

The Story:

The court of Henri II of France was filled with many intrigues, as much of the heart as of anything else. The court itself was divided into several groups. One group was partial to the queen, who was at odds with Henri II because he chose to be guided in his personal life and in his government by Diane de Poitiers, the Duchess de Valentinois, who had been his father's mistress and was now a grandmother in her own right. A second group was that which surrounded the Duchess de Valentinois. A third group was that which had as its center Princess Mary, wife of the dauphin, the beautiful and brilliant young woman who was also Queen of Scotland.

Into this scene of rivalry came Madame de Chartres, with her very beautiful daughter, to be married to a nobleman with rank as high as possible; Madame de Chartres hoped even for a prince of the blood. Unfortunately for the mother's hopes, the intrigues of the court kept her from arranging a match so brilliant or advantageous. A marriage with either M. de Monpensier, the Chevalier de Guise, or the Prince de Clèves seemed the best that could be made, and there were obstacles to a marriage with either of those, as Mme. de Chartres discovered. Each of the groups at the court was afraid that such a marriage would upset the status of the powers as they stood.

Finally the arrangements were made for a marriage to the Prince de Clèves.

The gentleman was perturbed, however, by the attitude of his bride. He loved her greatly, and she seemed to love him dutifully but without the abandon he wished for. He tried to be satisfied when she told him that she would do her best to love him, but that she felt no real passion for him or any man. The marriage was celebrated in grand style, and a fine dinner party, attended by the king and queen, was given at the Louvre.

For many months no one at the court, where extramarital attachments were the rule rather than the exception, dared to say anything about the young wife. Thanks to her mother's solicitude and her own lack of passion where men were concerned, the Princess de Clèves kept a spotless reputation. Her mother, who soon was on her deathbed, knew from various conferences the princess had had with her—unusual conferences for a married woman to have with her mother, for in reality they were confessions—that the princess had no inclinations to stray from her marital vows.

One evening, however, there was a court ball given in honor of one of the king's daughters, whose marriage was impending. A late arrival at the ball was the Duke de Nemours, the handsomest, most gallant courtier in France. At his entrance the Princess de Clèves who had never seen the duke before, was ordered by the king to dance with him.

In spite of the fact that Queen Elizabeth of England had taken an interest in the Duke de Nemours and had expressed the wish that the young man would visit her court, he remained where he could be near the Princess de Clèves. Even the repeated requests of the French king, who saw in de Nemours a possible consort for Queen Elizabeth, could not remove the duke from her side. Meanwhile the Princess de Clèves did everything she could to conceal her love for the duke from everyone, even from her lover himself. She was determined to remain a faithful and dutiful wife.

One day, while the princess and the duke were in the apartments of the Queen Dauphine, the princess saw de Nemours steal a miniature portrait of herself. Although she had ample opportunity, the princess said nothing to stop him from taking her picture. Some time later the duke was injured by a horse in a tournament, and several people noted the look of distress on the face of the Princess de Clèves. The court was beginning to realize that love was blossoming between the two.

As soon as she realized what was happening in her heart, the Princess de Clèves went to her husband and asked him to take her away from Paris for a time. They went to an estate in the country. While they were there, the princess confessed to her husband that she was falling in love with someone. Admiring her candor, he promised to help her overcome the passion. Although she refused to name the man she loved, the Prince de Clèves guessed that it was one of three men, a trio which included the Duke de Nemours. But he had no proof.

Although neither knew it, while the princess was confessing her love, the Duke de Nemours was hiding so close to them that he could overhear what was said.

Months went by, and gradually, despite her efforts to keep away from him, the princess indicated to her husband that the Duke de Nemours was the man she loved. The prince was torn by jealousy, but his wife's confession and her obvious efforts to curb her love prevented him from taking any action in the matter. His only recourse was to accuse her at intervals of not being fair to him in loving another.

The strain becoming too much for the Princess de Clèves, she asked her husband's permission to retire to a country estate near Paris. He yielded graciously but sent one of his own retainers to make sure of her conduct while she was away. The retainer returned to report that twice, at night, the Duke de Nemours had entered the garden where the princess was; the retainer did not know, and so could not report, that his mistress had refused to see the man who loved her.

After the retainer had made his report, the prince fell ill of a fever. When the princess returned, she was unable to convince him that she had not been unfaithful, even though he wanted to believe her. Rather than stand in the way of her happiness, he languished and died.

Some months after her husband's death the Duke de Nemours prevailed upon the princess' uncle, the Vidame de Char-tres, to intercede for him with the princess. The uncle did, even to arranging for an interview between the two. At that time the princess told the duke that, in spite of her love for him, she could never marry him. Soon afterward she entered a convent for a time. Later she retired to an estate some distance from Paris. Shortly after her arrival at the country estate she fell ill and died within a matter of days.

Further Critical Evaluation of the Work:

This novel, sometimes called the first modern novel, combines aspects of the chronicle and romance, as well as aspects of Racinian and Corneillian tragedy.

The background depicts, with the authenticity of a chronicle, the court of Henri II, although the values are those of the court of Louis XIV. Rather than supporting those values, however, the novel seems to implicitly criticize them. There is a marked discrepancy between the values of the court and those of the heroine. The Princess perceives the discrepancy between appearance and reality at court because "things are seldom what they seem." The novel depicts with lucidity and tedious repetition the intrigues, love quarrels, and petty disturbances that fill out the round of days at court. The seeming magnificence of the court is shown to be superficial, and, in addition, is devalued by the obvious burdensome routine of court life.

In the manner of the romance, the novel describes the ideal qualities of all the ladies and gentlemen. Each lady is the most beautiful; each lover is the most handsome. Their clothing, jewels, hair, eyes, and so on are all without equal. The analysis of the passions, however, is not ideal and serves in still another way to undercut the values of the court. The novel reveals the transitory quality of passion, and the ultimate awareness of this is one of the reasons that the Princess refuses the Duke's offer of marriage. All of the supposed "digressions" in the novel relating the multiple loves, shifts of affection, and duplicity of the King and others only serve to reinforce the view that passion is not of lasting value.

Like the tragedies of Racine, the novel depicts the overwhelming passion that comes upon one without any warning, a passion that completely absorbs one's being. Yet unlike the heroines of Racine's tragedies, and similar to the heroes of Corneille's tragedies, the Princess is able, through her will, to triumph over her passion.

The novel is thus part of a literary tradition (the chronicle and romance) and reflects values of the court while implicitly criticizing these values. But it is unique (in conjunction with the tragedies of Racine) in analyzing the passions, that is, the inner life of the individual. By undercutting the traditional social values, new emphasis is placed upon the need for the individual to construct values for himself, rather than accept those of the social body.

PRINCIPLES OF LITERARY CRITICISM

Type of work: Critical treatise
Author: I. A. Richards (1893-   )
First published: 1924

Ivor Armstrong Richards was born in Sandbach, England, on February 26, 1893. He received his formal education at Magdalene College of Cambridge University, where he received the degree of M.A. He became a teaching Fellow of Magdalene in 1926 and has also held positions as visiting professor at Tsing Hua University, Peking, from 1929 to 1930, visiting lecturer at Harvard in 1931, and Director of The Orthological Institute of China from 1936 to 1938. Throughout his life, he has been vitally interested in the Orient. While teaching in China, he studied Chinese philosophy and worked on his book *Mencius on the Mind.* He has had a special interest in the thought of Confucius. In 1964 he was made an Honorary Fellow of Magdalene College.

Although he has written poetry and drama, his major contributions have been in the fields of literary criticism and philology. His first book, *The Foundations of Aesthetics,* published in 1922 and written in collaboration with psychologist C. K. Ogden and art authority James Wood, examined the whole area of aesthetics in an attempt to arrive at the nature of beauty and to offer the authors' own definition of aesthetics. In 1923, Richards and Ogden published *The Meaning of Meaning,* a psychologically oriented pursuit of "meaning" in the arts. But more significant critical pronouncements were made in the next three books: *Principles of Literary Criticism* in 1924, *Science and Poetry* in 1926, and *Practical Criticism* in 1929. All three books treat the question of value in the arts, primarily poetry, and all are concerned with the problem of correct interpretation of art. Their aims are different, however: *Principles of Literary Criticism* spells out the theory; *Science and Poetry* discusses the role and future of literature in life; and *Practical Criticism* applies

theory to individual literary works. Richards' last major critical book, *Coleridge on Imagination,* published in 1935, explores several meanings of the concept of imagination and singles out Coleridge's definition as the one most accurate and applicable to twentieth century criticism.

From the early 1930's, as the solution to problems in education and general communication, Richards has been interested in Basic English. In writing *The Meaning of Meaning,* he and Ogden realized that they repeatedly used certain key words which, they discovered, could form a basic language that would permit the expression of any idea. While it was Ogden who published the first Basic word list, Richards has actively pursued his own linguistic research in *Basic in Teaching: East and West, Interpretation in Teaching, How to Read a Page,* and *Basic English and Its Uses.*

Among his critical books, *Principles of Literary Criticism* most directly concerns the deriving of value from the arts, especially the art of poetry. In many ways the basis of all Richards' pronouncements on criticism, it sets forth his fundamental critical and artistic theories.

He begins this complex study by indicating several difficulties which often preclude valid criticism. First of all, there is too much of what Richards calls "experimental aesthetics" in the arts: futile attempts to make human tastes and actions amenable to laboratory examination. Moreover, criticism tends to concentrate on secondary aspects of the arts and thereby ignores the all-important subject of value. And at other times, the very language of criticism causes misunderstandings because of its vague, often deceiving vocabulary. For example, critics often speak of objects of art as if the objects themselves possess qualities, whereas what they should say is that the objects evoke effects in us.

To offset these impediments, Richards insists that valid criticism is contingent upon an understanding of the nature of experience and the formulating of an acceptable theory of valuation and communication in the arts. The first of these topics, experience, is approached purely psychologically. In fact, much of *Principles of Literary Criticism* is comprised of chapters which give the psychological background to particular facets of aesthetic appreciation and communication. In Chapter XI, "A Sketch for a Psychology," Richards reminds us that the mind is the nervous system and is thus a system of impulses which are influenced by various stimuli. Our response to certain stimuli depends upon the needs of the body at a given moment. The basis of aesthetic experience, then, also lies in the impulses which arise in the mind as a result of various stimuli. These stimuli may be either new and independent or associated with former experiences.

Other aspects of experience are discussed throughout the book; for example, the role of memory, of emotion and coenesthesia, and of attitudes. The fine line between the "pleasure-unpleasure" of a sensation is also considered. An important adjunct to the discussion of experience is treated in Chapter XXII, "The Poet's Experience." The difference between the artist and the ordinary man, points out Richards, is first of all in the "range, delicacy, and freedom" of the relationships he can make among facets of his experience. Secondly, it is in the "availability" of the artist's experience: the ability to have a particular state of mind available when needed. Moreover, the artist has a higher degree of what Richards terms vigilance: a more complete, satisfactory organization of the impulses within him. Thus, though we all have experiences and, except for the insane, can organize them to some extent, the poet is more capable of making use of his experience.

After attempting to suggest succinctly the causation, nature, and effect of expe-

rience, Richards moves on to the two topics with which he is most concerned, valuation and communication. The arts, he says, are our "storehouses" of recorded values. He admonishes the critic to be concerned with value and morality. His definition of value is explained in Chapter VII, "A Psychological Theory of Value," in which he asserts that anything is valuable that satisfies a desire within us without thwarting an equal or more important desire. Additional value is achieved when any desire is sacrificed to another. Value, then, is defined as the exercise of impulses and the fulfilling of their desires.

Though all men are concerned with values, he who is most concerned is the artist. He is the one preoccupied with recording and perpetuating the experiences he deems most valuable; he is also the one most likely to have valuable experiences to record; finally, he is the one most able to organize or systematize the significant and trivial impulses which are a part of experience. The poet, moreover, lays the basis of morality, for the problem of morality is the problem of obtaining the most value from life. Thus, Richards is opposed to the "Art for Art's sake" theory of poetry, a theory which denies external values in art. He urges the similarity between the world of poetry and the real world and fears that any separation of poetic experience from life results in imbalance, narrowness, and incompleteness in advocators of the aesthetic theory. Value can even determine whether a poem is good or bad. In Chapter XXV, "Badness in Poetry," Richards asserts that art can fail if (1) communication is defective or (2) if the experience communicated is not valuable.

For value in the arts to be perceived by the spectator there must, of course, be effective communication. In Chapter IV, "Communication and the Artist," Richards states that not only are the arts communicative, but they are the "supreme form" of communication, even though the artist may not have communication as his primary goal; he is usually concerned foremost with making the work correct.

By communication, Richards means that under certain conditions individual minds are able to are quite similar experiences. Never is there an actual transference of or participation in the shared experiences, however. Communication, a complicated process, occurs when one mind acting upon its environment influences another mind, and that other mind undergoes an experience that is similar to the experience in the first mind.

If the arts are the supreme form of communication, the artist is faced with the challenge of transmitting his experiences to the reader effectively. To do he must maintain a state of normality. For no matter how available his past experience is, the artist must be normal enough to communicate it. Since communication requires responses which are uniform and are initiated by stimuli which can be handled physically, any eccentricity in the artist will be disastrous if it interferes with his responses. His expression in the arts means nothing to his spectators if he is unable to organize his responses.

After probing the nature of experience, the essence of value, and the importance of communication in the arts, Richards turns his attention more specifically to the practicing critic of poetry. The good critic must meet three qualifications: he must be able to experience without eccentricity the state of mind of the work he is criticizing; he must be able to differentiate between experiences by discerning their more subtle features; and he must be adept at judging values. But given these capabilities, the critic is still unable to pass sound judgments on poetry if he is unsure of exactly what poetry is. One of the reasons for so much backward criticism, Richards believes, is that

the critic simply does not know what he is judging. He needs a workable definition of poetry, and Richards offers one by defining poetry as a group of experiences which differ only very slightly from a standard experience. Such a definition, he says, is far more meaningful than calling poetry the artist's experience, for the latter implies that only the artist has the experience. In Richards' view the reader's involvement is necessary for completion of the poetic experience.

These four topics,—experience, value, communication, and poetry and the critic —are the major concerns of *Principles of Literary Criticism*. Many other related topics are discussed. Among the most significant for poetry and literary criticism are his treatments of analyzing a poem (XVI), of rhythm and meter in verse (XVII), of allusiveness in modern poetry (XXVIII), and of the creative imagination (XXXII). The book closes with a brief essay on "The Poetry of T. S. Eliot," an appendix which was added to the second edition of the book in 1926.

In his discussion of the imagination, Richards shows his allegiance to Coleridgean theory. He accepts the concept of the imagination as being the synthesizing or balancing of dissimilar qualities. This concept, he concludes, is the heart of poetry and the other arts.

It would be futile to attempt to estimate the influence that *Principles* has had on the field of criticism. Let it suffice to say that the book is credited with beginning the whole era of modern criticism. Practically every modern critic, from a traditionalist like Lionel Trilling to a new critic such as Cleanth Brooks, has been influenced by this work because of its penetrating study of experience, value, and communication and its clarification of the definition of poetry.

PRINCIPLES OF POLITICAL ECONOMY

Type of work: Economic treatise
Author: John Stuart Mill (1806-1873)
First published: 1848

John Stuart Mills' central concern in *Principles of Political Economy* is the production and distribution of wealth, which he defines as everything that serves human desires and which is not provided gratuitously by nature. The most important elements in wealth are goods currently produced

Production requires labor and appropriate natural objects. The labor devoted to a product is rewarded out of its sale proceeds, but before these are realized, advances to workers are required, which come from capital. "Productive" labor is that which yields an increase in material wealth.

Capital consists of wealth used for productive activity. Capital provides the tools and materials needed to carry on production, as well as subsistence for the laborers while the production process is going on. The quantity of a nation's industry is limited by its stock of capital. Increased capital means increased ability to hire workers, and thus increased output and employment. The accumulation of capital results from saving. It is not from demand for commodities, but from capital, that demand for labor arises, although the demand for commodities determines in what productive activities workers can find employment.

Differences in the productivity of nations may arise from geographic factors such as climate and fertility of soil. There are also important differences in labor quality—in physical vigor, in ability to persevere in pursuit of distant objectives, in skill, knowledge, and trustworthiness. Productivity is enhanced by legal and social institutions favoring security of person and property, and by effective cooperation as manifested in division of labor. Because of greater specialization of men and equipment, large-scale productive establishments are often more efficient than small ones.

The rate at which production grows depends on the rate of growth of labor, capital, and land, and on improvements in productive technique. Increases in population tend to raise the total quantity of production by increasing the labor supply but may, by increasing the number of consumers, keep down the living standards of the working class. Unless birth rates are limited, increases in population and labor supply must continually tend to force wages to low levels.

The rate at which capital increases reflects the flow of saving, which depends on the level of income and the desire to accumulate rather than to consume. Willingness to save is encouraged when the expected profits of investment are high and when uncertainty and insecurity are at a minimum. Whether a society is progressive or backward depends in large degree on the level of saving it achieves.

The real limits to production growth arise from the limited quantity and limited productiveness of land. Cultivation of land is subject to diminishing returns —that is, increased application of labor and capital by any given proportion will increase total output only in some lesser proportion. Fortunately, tendencies toward diminishing return can be counteracted by improvements in methods of production, but these are more likely to produce decreasing costs in industry than in agriculture. The pressure of population growth against diminishing returns is the principal cause of widespread poverty.

While the laws of production are essentially physical, the principles of distribution are social; once the goods are produced, they can be distributed as men wish. An important determinant of income distribution is the nature and distribution of private property. Critics currently find much fault with the institution of private property and propose socialist systems involving democratic management of productive operations and equal division of the product. Such schemes cannot be dismissed as impracticable. Admittedly some people might shirk their responsibilities to work, but this is also a serious defect of existing property and wage arrangements. A communitarian society would have to guard against an excessive birth rate and might encounter problems in determining who should perform which tasks. As an ideal, the communist society is far more attractive than the unjust pattern of the present, but the reason is that practices relating to private property have not conformed to the ideal of assuring to each person the fruits of his labor or abstinence. The best system will be that which is consistent with the greatest amount of human liberty and spontaneity.

The produce of society is divided among the three classes who provide productive agents: labor, capital, and land. Wages are determined by the proportion between population (supply) and capital (demand); thus high birth rates tend to inhibit increases in wage rates. Limitation of births by the working class would be promoted by the extension of education and by any sudden, rapid improvement in their condition.

The profits of the capitalist are the reward for abstinence, for risk-taking, and for the effort of superintendence. Profits arise from the fact that labor produces more than is required for its subsistence; workers depend on the relationship between the productivity of labor and the wage rate.

The rent of land is determined by the demand for it (and its produce), the suppy of land being fixed. Differences in rent reflect differences in productivity on lands of different quality. Growth of population and capital tends to increase rents, as demand for food increases.

As economic systems expand through growth of labor and capital, the rate of profit tends to decline because higher food prices force up wage costs. The declining rate of profit may in turn halt the increase of capital and produce a stationary state. This state of affairs would not necessarily be bad, provided no one were poor, and provided the unseemly struggle for wealth and power were replaced by more elevated pursuits. Social improvement would also result from improvement of the relationship between employer and worker, perhaps through profit-sharing or through co-operatives of producers or consumers.

The value of any article means the amounts of other things for which it will exchange in the market. To possess value, an article must possess utility (be desired), and be subject to some difficulty of attainment. Value tends to that level at which the quantity which buyers will take (demand) is equal to the quantity which sellers will offer (supply). Since cost of production is a chief determinant of supply, value tends to equal cost (plus a normal profit for capital), unless monopoly conditions prevail. Although labor is the chief element of cost, capital must also be rewarded or it will not be forthcoming. The longer the waiting between the application of labor and the emergence of the finished product, the greater the capital cost.

Money provides a common measure of value and facilitates specialization and exchange. Variations in the general price level tend to be proportional to changes in the quantity of money, or in its rapidity of circulation, assuming the quantity of goods remains unchanged. Since credit may serve as a substitute for (metal) money, it can also influence the level of prices. Expansion or contraction of credit, in such forms as promissory notes or bank deposits, are principal elements accounting for periodic commercial crises. A paper currency not convertible into precious metal is liable to depreciate through excessive issue.

Although the supply of any individual commodity may exceed the demand for it, it is not possible for the supply of all commodities to be excessive. Each person's willingness to work and produce reflects his desire to acquire goods for consumption or investment.

In international exchanges, value depends not on the absolute levels of labor and capital required to produce an item. but on the comparative costs. A country may be able to import cloth more cheaply than to produce it, by paying for it with exports of another product in which its labor and capital are highly efficient, even though it could produce cloth with less labor and capital than the country from which it imports. Both participants in such trade tend to benefit from it, and total world output may be increased by the more efficient use of resources through specialization.

Should a country's imports be excessive in relation to its exports, it will tend to export gold and silver to pay the difference. The outflow of money will tend to reduce the price level in that country (and raise it elsewhere), until the trade imbalance is rectified.

The proper functions of government extend, at the very least, to defining and determining the rights of property and contract, the rules of partnerships and corporations, the regulation of insolvency, the monetary system, weights and measures. In addition, government activity may be necessary where the consumer cannot judge or achieve his own interest (e.g., children's education), or in cases where each person's desire can be effectuated only if all conform (e.g. limiting work hours). It may undertake activities beneficial to the public from which no private person could realize a profit (e.g., lighthouses, scientific research). And since charity will be offered by private persons in any case, it may be better to have it provided by the government so as to minimize possible harmful effects. However, it is necessary to avoid government activities based on fallacious doctrines—policies of tariff protection, price-fixing, restricting entry into a business or occupation, prohibiting trade-union activity.

Limitation of government activity is desirable to avoid undue enhancement of central power or the use of coercive authority in ways which infringe on important individual freedoms. Enlargement of government may also impair the efficiency of its operations.

Taxation should be imposed so as to exact equal sacrifice from each person. This result could be achieved by an income tax taking a fixed proportion of income beyond a minimum exemption. Taxation of inheritance and of unearned increases in land rent is highly desirable, but current saving should be excluded in calculating taxable income.

All things considered, there is a presumption in favor of laissez faire; that is, the burden of proof is on those who favor extension of the role of government.

THE PRISONER OF ZENDA

Type of work: Novel
Author: Anthony Hope (Sir Anthony Hope Hawkins, 1863-1933)
Type of plot: Adventure romance
Time of plot: 1880's
Locale: "Ruritania"
First published: 1894

Principal characters:
RUDOLF RASSENDYLL, an English gentleman
LADY ROSE BURLESDON, his sister-in-law
RUDOLF, King of Ruritania
MICHAEL, DUKE OF STRELSAU, King Rudolf's half-brother
ANTOINETTE DE MAUBAN, in love with Michael
PRINCESS FLAVIA, betrothed to King Rudolf
FRITZ VON TARLENHEIM, a loyal subject of the king
COLONEL SAPT, another loyal subject

Critique:

Many novels have been written about the intrigues and plots of royalty, but few hold the reader's attention as does *The Prisoner of Zenda*. In its pages we meet kings and would-be kings, beautiful ladies, loyal subjects, and those who would sell out their leader for the promise of gold or power. There are thrills and excitement enough for all: murder, duels at midnight, trysts, daring rescues. If Anthony Hope's desire was to give his readers a few hours of pure enjoyment, and it seems to have been his sole purpose in writing this novel, he was successful. His success is confirmed by the fact that the story is almost as popular today as it was when first published.

The Story:

To his sister-in-law, Lady Rose Burlesdon, Rudolf Rassendyll was a great disappointment. In the first place, he was twenty-nine years old and had no useful occupation. Secondly, he bore such a striking resemblance to the Elphbergs, ruling house of Ruritania, that Rose thought him a constant reminder of an old scandal in which her husband's family had been involved. More than a hundred years before, a prince of the country of Ruritania had visited England and had become involved with the wife of one of the Rassendyll men. There was a child, who had the red hair and the large straight nose of the Elphbergs. Since that unfortunate event, five or six descendants of the English lady and the Ruritanian prince had had the characteristic nose and red hair of their royal ancestor. Rose thought Rudolph's red hair and large nose a disgrace for that reason.

Rassendyll himself, however, had no concern over his resemblance to the Ruritanian royal family. A new king was to be crowned in that country within a few weeks, and he decided to travel to Ruritania for the coronation, in order to get a close view of his unclaimed relatives. Knowing that his brother and sister-in-law would try to prevent his journey, he told them that he was going to take a tour of the Tyrol. After he left England, his first stop was Paris, where he learned something more about affairs in the country he was to visit. The new king, also called Rudolf, had a half-brother, Michael, Duke of Strelsau. Michael would have liked to become king, and it was hinted that he would try to prevent the coronation of Rudolf. Rassendyll also learned that there was a beautiful lady, Antoinette de Mauban, who loved Michael and had his favor. She, too, was traveling to Ruritania for the coronation.

When he reached Ruritania and found the capital city crowded, Rassendyll took lodging in Zenda, a small town some fifty miles from the capital, and prepared to go by train for the coronation. Zenda was part of Michael's domain, his hunting lodge being only a few miles from the inn where Rassendyll stopped. Rassendyll learned also that King Rudolf was a guest at his half-brother's hunting lodge while waiting for the coronation. There were more rumors of a plot against the king and talk that Black Michael, as he was called, planned to seize the throne.

Rassendyll walked every day through the woods near the hunting lodge. One day he heard two men discussing how much he resembled the king. The men introduced themselves as Fritz von Tarlenheim and Colonel Sapt, faithful friends of King Rudolf. While they talked, the king himself appeared. The king had shaved his beard, but otherwise he and Rassendyll were identical. Pleased to meet his distant cousin, the king invited Rassendyll to the lodge. There the king drank so much that Fritz and Sapt could not wake him the next morning.

This was the day of the coronation, and as the king slept in his stupor Fritz and Sapt proposed a daring plan to Rassendyll. They knew that if the king did not appear for the coronation Black Michael would seize the throne. Their plan was to shave Rassendyll's beard and dress him in the king's clothes and have him crowned in the king's place. By the time the ceremonies were over, the king would have recovered, would take his rightful place, and no one would be the wiser. It was a dangerous gamble, for exposure would mean death, but Rassendyll agreed to the plot.

Fritz and Sapt locked the king in the wine cellar and left a servant to tell him of the plan when he awoke. Rassendyll, with Fritz and Sapt, proceeded to the palace. With the two men to help him, he carried off the deception, even convincing the Princess Flavia that he was the real king. His role with Flavia was the most difficult for Rassendyll, for he must be gracious and yet not commit the king too far.

The success of the conspirators was not to last. When they returned that night to the lodge, they found the servant murdered and the real king gone. Black Michael's men had worked well. Black Michael knew that the supposed king was an impostor, and Rassendyll, Fritz, and Sapt knew that Black Michael had the real king. But neither group dared call the other's hand. Rassendyll's only chance was to rescue the rightful king. Black Michael's hope was to kill both Rassendyll and the king and thus seize the throne and Princess Flavia for himself. Rassendyll was attacked and almost killed many times. Once he was saved by a warning from Antoinette de Mauban, for although she loved Michael she would not be a party to murder. Also, she did not want Michael to be successful, for his coup would mean his marriage to Flavia. Michael learned of her aid to Rassendyll and held her a semi-prisoner in the hunting lodge where he had hidden the king.

Playing the part of the king, Rassendyll was forced to spend much time with Flavia. He wanted to tell her his real identity, but Fritz and Sapt appealed to his honor and persuaded him that all would be ruined if Flavia learned that he was not the true king.

When they learned that King Rudolf was dying, Rassendyll, Fritz, and Sapt knew that they must take a daring chance to rescue him. They and part of the king's army attacked the lodge. Those not aware of the deception were told that Black Michael had imprisoned a friend of the king. There was a bloody battle both outside and inside the lodge. Black Michael was killed and King Rudolf wounded before the rescue was completed. When he knew that the king would live, Rassendyll realized that his part in the deception was over. The king sent for him and thanked him for his brave work in saving the throne. Princess Flavia also sent for him. She had been told the whole story, but her only concern was to learn whether Rassendyll had spoken for himself or the king when he had given her his love. He told her that he would always love only her and begged her to go away with him. But she was too honorable to leave her people and her king, and she remained in Ruritania, later to marry the king and rule with him.

Rassendyll left Ruritania and spent a few weeks in the Tyrol before returning to England. His sister-in-law, still trying to get him to lead a more useful life, arranged through a friend to get him a diplomatic post. When he learned the post would be in Ruritania, he declined it. Rassendyll resumed his former idle life, with one break in his monotonous routine. Each year Fritz and Rassendyll met in Dresden, and Fritz always brought with him a box containing a rose, a token from Flavia.

Further Critical Evaluation of the Work:

Despite its severe brevity and occasional plot weaknesses, *The Prisoner of Zenda* is among the most enduring of adventure romances. In part the reasons for this are predictable: mystery, intrigue, suspense, and love are integrated neatly in the tale; there is plenty of adventure, much of it framed as a conflict between evident Good and Evil; lastly, there is a strong central character—Rudolf Rassendyll—to hold the book together. It is, then, a highly formulaic romance, hence a popular one, yet it is also much more than this: in its touches of ethical ambiguity and in its clever use of "disguise" (both thematically and dramatically), *The Prisoner of Zenda* takes up the complex matter of defining, then judging, man's moral nature.

Early branded a wastrel by his sister-in-law, Rassendyll in time proves his sincerity and honor. What he learns, simply, is value—a theme which Anthony Hope explores not only in his major character, but also socially in his excoriations of kings and gentry. What the reader learns, as the sister-in-law does not, is the difference between real and apparent nobility. We come to judge Rassendyll not by his complexion or his attitude of indifference, but by his courageous, constant actions. In the same way, his "kingliness" is evidenced not in borrowed robes and crowns, but in a quality of spirit which cannot be counterfeited.

Yet Rassendyll's character is also qualified throughout the novel. He is genuinely tempted by the throne and by Flavia's attendant charms. Too often he ignores the morality of his actions: once when he backstabs a guard; again when, madly vengeful, he destroys two of Black Michael's hirelings. With bold strokes Anthony Hope defines Rassendyll's identity through two character foils—the dissipated real king (significantly, a namesake and distant relative), and the brash knave, Rupert Hentzau. The former reinforces Rassendyll's worst qualities even as he illustrates, by contrast, the best. On the other hand, Hentzau appears at a glance to be thoroughly different from Rassendyll, yet Rudolf's fascination with Rupert's attractive evil clearly suggests an affinity between them. When Rassendyll spares his enemy, then later tries desperately to slay him, the psychological overtones are plain: regretfully, he has let escape the evil in himself.

The themes of moral ambiguity ("if it were a sin may it be forgiven me," says Rudolf at one point) and political chicanery in the novel fit well with the idea of individual honor. What is to be gained by acting honorably in a world without principle? This is a penetrating question, especially toward the end of the adventure when Rudolf and Flavia must elect honorable self-sacrifice or selfish love. Their choice of the former, it seems, points out the novel's answer: the world becomes a measure better and an individual a measure greater only as there are those ready to prefer honor over happiness.

THE PRIVATE LIFE OF THE MASTER RACE

Type of work: Drama
Author: Bertolt Brecht (1898-1956)
Type of plot: Social chronicle
Time of plot: 1933-1938
Locale: Germany
Partial presentation: 1938; first published: 1944
Principal characters:
VARIOUS CITIZENS OF THE THIRD REICH

Critique:

The Private Life of the Master Race, an exposé of the Nazi regime, is composed of seventeen scenes or one-act plays taken from a longer work, *The Fears and Miseries of the Third Reich.* The scenes form a pageant of the first five years of Hitler's reign. In the usual sense these scenes do not make a play, for there are no characters who appear in more than one scene; the unity of the work is maintained only by the historical sequence and by a fragmentary narration. Brecht here aims at an epic drama, and he does achieve by documentary presentation a vivid sweep in time. He is highly regarded as a poet. The worth of the play lies in the poetry and in the cumulative details of a reign of terror under National Socialism.

The Story:

During the first years of the Nazi regime, techniques for suppressing opposition were rapidly perfected. One object of suppression was any radio capable of receiving broadcasts from Russia. The Nazis relied on the German distrust of Communism to aid in harsh enforcement of the law. Soon neighbors were betraying neighbors. Sets were confiscated and the owners beaten.

In Berlin, in 1933, a storm trooper came to visit his sweetheart who was a maid in a wealthy home. While she was feeding him in the kitchen, the cook's brother came in with a tube to repair the family radio. Since the brother, a common worker, did not give the Heil Hitler greeting plainly enough, the trooper put on a demonstration to show the Nazi power. He pretended to explain the current methods of exposure by staging a scene at the welfare office. He was the more anxious to scare the worker because he had drunk the Nazi's beer.

The trooper, ostensibly in mufti, pretended that he was in a welfare line discussing the things wrong in Germany. The worker answered him by imitating the common complaints heard from non-Nazis. Simulating camaraderie, the trooper clapped the worker on the shoulder. On arriving at the office, the man would be closely interrogated, for there was a chalk cross on his shoulder. The trooper had drawn the cross on his hand and transferred it to the worker's shoulder with a friendly pat. After that bit of dramatizing the worker left abruptly.

In the concentration camps the Socialists, the Communists, and the non-political liberals realized too late that they should have been united before Hitler came to power. Now they were impotent. In the factories there were broadcasts by happy workers who had been carefully coached in what they were to say. In private homes a member of the family would be returned in a zinc box; the official explanation was always that death had come from natural causes.

By 1935 even the scientists were afraid. Spied on by their Nazi employees, they were often handicapped in their laboratories by the prohibition against correspondence with foreign scientists. It was forbidden even to mention the name of Einstein, for he was a Jew.

In Frankfort a Jewish wife was packing. Her husband was a prominent physician and an Aryan. She had stood her racial stigma as long as she dared, but now their friends were beginning to cut them socially. Carefully tending to her wifely duties, she telephoned to friends, asking them to look after things in her absence. After she had finished calling, she prudently burned the notebook containing the telephone numbers. Then she began rehearsing the speech she would make to her husband.

She would be brave. She would go to Amsterdam for a few weeks until the persecution died down. Really, the only reason she was leaving was to relieve her husband from embarrassment. As she went through the carefully thought-out speech, her husband came in. At once she broke down. The husband pretended to believe that she would be gone only a short while, and when things were better he would come to Amsterdam for her. He would like a few days outside of Germany himself. Surely the Nazis could not for long shackle the intellectuals.

Even the judges were confused. They had come to the point where they gave decisions the way the party wanted them, but sometimes it was difficult to know just what the party desired. In Augsburg three storm troopers broke into a store run by a Jew and took some valuable jewelry after wounding the Jew. To the judge the case looked like a simple one; the Jew had offered great provocation, the storm troopers had acted rightly in defending the honor of the party. But after talking with the prosecutor the judge was not sure how he should decide.

There was race pollution mixed in the case. The Jewish store manager had a nineteen-year-old daughter about whom there had been rumors. The father also had an Aryan partner who had access to party headquarters. The owner of the building had changed his testimony. Perhaps the case was clear cut; the judge would decide against the storm troopers, for German justice was honorable even for Jews.

But the inspector in the case confused him again. He said the prosecutor was inducing the judge to give the wrong decision because he wanted the judge's post for himself. The harassed judge asked an older colleague for advice, but the other man could give him little help. With a heavy heart the judge prepared to go into his courtroom, where ribald storm troopers occupied every seat.

Perhaps one of the most effective devices of the regime was to teach the children in the youth organizations to inform on their parents.

In 1936 a man who had been released from a concentration camp came to call on a man and a wife with whom he had worked in the resistance movement. The couple were afraid to take him into their confidence again, for the pressure in the concentration camps was great. The meeting was an embarrassing one. The couple tried not to notice the released man's shrunken hand with the missing fingers, and he in turn pretended not to notice their lack of confidence in him.

As food became scarcer in the stores, the waiting lines were longer in the mornings. Butter was sacrificed to cannons and prices rose beyond the ability of the people to pay. The store owners themselves led a precarious existence, for they never knew when they would be arrested for infractions of rules. A butcher, who had been a Nazi before 1933, forced his son to join the storm troopers, but his loyalty did him little good. When he refused to put cardboard hams in his window, the Nazis began to persecute him. In despair the butcher hanged himself in his shop window over a card which announced to the world that he had voted for Hitler.

There were faint signs of resistance to the all-powerful regime. Farmers were supposed to hand over their grain to the government and buy feed at a fixed price.

Here and there, however, a farmer would take the precaution of having his wife and children stand guard. While they watched he would feed grain to his hungry pigs.

In Lübeck, in 1937, a fisherman lay dying. He had argued long hours with his storm trooper son over Hitler's evident determination to start a war. Now as the dying man talked with his pastor he dared to mention the life to come. The son left his father's bedside without speaking. The pastor had referred to the Sermon on the Mount; no good Nazi could be taken in by Jewish superstition.

In Hamburg, in 1938, just after the union with Austria, a small group discussed ways and means of getting out an opposition leaflet. Such a project was almost impossible. A woman in the group read a letter from an executed father to his small son, a letter in which the father declared that his hard fate would not have been in vain if his son remained true to the common people.

Further Critical Evaluation of the Work:

Perhaps Brecht's most important work, *The Private Life of the Master Race* marks a clean break from the Ibsen tradition. With seventeen locales over a seven-year period, the writer's demand on the propmen might seem absurd. Fortunately, props are unimportant to Brecht, as simple signs and bleak settings suffice; he depends on the talents of the actors to depict the tensions that existed between the responsibilities of morality and the expectations of a fascist state. Individuals are not the focus here, but society. Brecht asks a great deal from his audience or readers, who are assumed to be curious about the play's content, but not awed; it is a play to be viewed, not read.

The reader is moved from Breslau in 1933, through many scenes, and finally to Hamburg in 1938, all the while receiving information about the hidden atrocities of Hitler's Germany. The vocabulary recreates vividly such hideous Nazi practices as kidnaping women and "promising children" from occupied areas, and impregnating captive women with the semen of S. A. Nazi "ideal" men. From the Nazi Youth Movement-produced child informant, through scenarios of anti-Semitism, to the activity of the S. A., the reader with each new scene is bombarded by threatening illusions, especially the apparition of the Panzer. The Panzer, or armored personnel carrier, is loaded with various personality types in the guise of soldiers—"the pupils of the notorious Einstein, yet trained in the iron school of the Führer, and taught the truth about Aryan science." The Panzer symbolizes both merciless army strikes, and the constant oppression of Nazi S. A. activists.

In *The Private Life of the Master Race,* the reader confronts the perils of a controlled social attitude of optimism in the face of the realities of boredom and repression; Brecht offers an intelligent study of how intellectuals—doctors, judges, and scientists—could have allowed themselves to be "bossed by half-savages." Brecht dedicated this work to the "other Germany," not to the nostalgia of the Weimar Republic but into the future, the bright future of post-Nazi Germany.

PRIVATE LIVES

Type of work: Drama
Author: Noel Coward (1899-1973)
Type of plot: Comedy of manners
Time of plot: 1930
Locale: France
First presented: 1930

> Principal characters:
> SIBYL CHASE, a bride
> ELYOT CHASE, her husband
> AMANDA PRYNNE, Elyot's first wife
> VICTOR PRYNNE, her husband

Critique:

One of the most popular of the plays of Noel Coward, *Private Lives* is sophisticated high comedy at its best, a story of misadventures created by an exchange of husbands and wives. Originally performed by Coward himself and the late Gertrude Lawrence, it won immediate success. There is little plot, but the brilliant dialogue and unconventionality of theme more than sustain the play and place it among the best brittle farces of the modern stage.

The Story:

Sibyl Chase loved being married. She was as much in love with the idea of being a bride as she was with her husband Elyot, perhaps more so. On her honeymoon night Sibyl went into raptures over Elyot, but she did not forget, or let him forget, that she knew he had loved his first wife Amanda madly. She was certain that their breakup had been Amanda's fault, that she had been a mean-tempered and probably a wanton woman. When Sibyl told him that she knew how to handle a husband, how to make him happy, Elyot feared that she meant she knew how to manage a husband. He was a trifle disturbed.

Unknown at first to the Chases, Amanda was honeymooning at the same hotel with her new husband, Victor Prynne. Victor had much the same ideas about marriage as Sibyl had. He would take care of Amanda, make her forget that dreadful brute to whom she had been married. The fact that Amanda never asked to be taken care of was unimportant. Victor would teach her to be a suitable wife.

When Amanda and Elyot saw each other again, each wanted to move out of the hotel before their respective mates knew about the presence of the other couple. But Sibyl and Victor were not accustomed to making abrupt changes without reason, and so they refused to leave. Thus Amanda and Elyot thought they were not responsible when they talked together again and found that they still loved each other passionately after five years of separation. Recalling their happy times together, each tried for a time to avoid the issue uppermost in their hearts and minds. At last Elyot broke the polite conversation by saying that he still loved Amanda. They fell into each other's arms.

Amanda tried for a time to make them consider Sibyl and Victor, but Elyot easily convinced her that those two would suffer more if they all lived a lie. After making their plans to go to Paris, Amanda left without telling her husband, Elyot without telling his wife.

Because they had fought so violently and so often in their married days, Amanda made Elyot promise that whenever they started to bicker they would use a password and each keep quiet for two minutes. In Amanda's flat in Paris they were often forced into quick use of the magic password, for they were torn equally between love and hate. Amanda's conscience bothered her a little, but Elyot could easily soothe that nagging little voice with love, logic, or a flippant remark. Sorry that they had wasted five years of separation after their divorce, they agreed to marry each other again as soon as Sibyl and Victor would divorce them. Elyot was annoyed when he learned that Amanda had spent those five years in having little affairs with various men, but he saw no reason for her being annoyed at his own transgressions.

Their quarrels occurred over nonsensical things for the most part. At the root was often Amanda's concern for the moral questions involved in their past and present relationship. When Elyot brushed these aside with worldly and flippant comment, Amanda came back to him more passionately than before.

The last explosion occurred as a result of Amanda's mention of another man of whom Elyot had always been jealous. Without knowing quite how the quarrel got out of hand, they found themselves throwing things at each other and slapping each other viciously. The magic password failed to work during their quarrel. As each slammed into a different bedroom, neither was aware that Sibyl and Victor had come into the room at the height of the rumpus and settled themselves quietly on the sofa.

The next morning Sibyl and Victor had a very sensible discussion concerning the situation they had found the night before. Sibyl wept copiously, not so much from sorrow as from custom; it was the right thing for an injured wife to do. Each blamed the other's mate for the sordid scene in Amanda's apartment. When Amanda and Elyot joined them, they were very polite with each other and with Sibyl and Victor. At first the situation was like a cozy morning call for coffee. When Amanda and Elyot admitted that they were sorry, that it was all a mess and a mistake, Sibyl and Victor agreed that the culprits were not contrite enough. Elyot, in particular, seemed crass about the whole thing, particularly to Victor, who wanted to thrash him. But Elyot could see no use in heroics; he honestly admitted that his flippancy was only an attempt to cover real embarrassment.

At the beginning of the unpleasant scene Amanda and Elyot had refused to speak to each other, but as Sibyl and Victor continued to do the proper thing, mouthing little platitudes about morals and the sanctity of marriage, Elyot winked at Amanda. While the injured spouses made and reversed plans for divorces, the sinners paid less and less attention. At last Sibyl and Victor began to quarrel, each accusing the other of weakness in still loving such a wicked and worldly person as Amanda or Elyot. When Sibyl gave Victor a resounding slap, he in turn shook her soundly. In the midst of the quarrel Amanda and Elyot picked up their suitcases and tiptoed out the door together.

Further Critical Evaluation of the Work:

That old combination of irresistible force and immovable object makes Coward's *Private Lives,* allegedly written in five days, one of his most popular and enduring plays. Elyot and Amanda (originally portrayed by Coward and Gertrude Lawrence) are the modern equivalent of the ever-dueling couples found in Restoration drama, and the constant battle between two such evenly matched foes makes the play sophisticated high comedy at its best. In the second act, usually considered the play's peak, the duo is alone on stage most of the time and head for their inevitable collision with all the finesse and flair of two tipsy diplomats who have designs on each other's territory. Neither can submit, for both must have the final word, and blasé as they are about most things, they fiercely maintain their independence. Ironically, considering its prickly partners, the play contains one of Coward's few effective love scenes.

Yet in this sparkling misadventure based on the then daring idea of an exchange of husbands and wives, it is not character, nor theme, nor plot (of which there is precious little) which sustains the play. Rather it is the brilliant dialogue and the atmosphere of magic playfulness which holds our attention. Coward creates a brittle farce and appeals to the audience's desire to vicariously identify with the casual superiority of his heroes. He gives us a smart and sassy world and does not permit us time to quibble over why we are so attracted. He makes us feel that anything two such charming, if selfish, people want must be acceptable; the morality and standards of life outside the play are absent from our minds. It is Coward's special talent that for a brief time he makes us use his ruler alone to take the measure of events.

THE PRIVATE PAPERS OF HENRY RYECROFT

Type of work: Novel
Author: George Gissing (1857-1903)
Type of plot: Reflective romance
Time of plot: Late nineteenth century
Locale: England
First published: 1903

Principal character:
HENRY RYECROFT, a thoughtful man

Critique:

This work, sometimes called a novel, is a kind of biography of the reflections of a thoughtful, literate man. It is held together by the person of Henry Ryecroft, but there is little structure for the book as a whole. Rather, the episodes and sketches give Ryecroft's views on the widest variety of subjects from Xenophon to berries. The character of Ryecroft himself is revealed with scrupulous minuteness. Essentially a withdrawn humanist, he is gentle and remote but aware of his England.

The Story:

For many years Henry Ryecroft had toiled unceasingly at all kinds of writing. He did straight hack work, translating, and editing. At first he knew the bitterest of poverty, but at long intervals a book appeared under his name and at last he gained a somewhat less precarious livelihood. At rare intervals some modest affluence enabled him to take a short trip abroad. By the time he was fifty his health was failing; his wife had been dead for years, and his married daughter had a home of her own.

By a stroke of luck he inherited a legacy from an acquaintance, a sufficient income for his modest needs. He lost no time in leasing for twenty years a cottage in rural Devon and in bidding goodbye to his writing. In Devon he settled down contentedly with a quiet housekeeper. After his death his private papers, written during his few years in Devon, were arranged by a friend and published.

It was spring. For more than a week Ryecroft had done no writing. His house was perfect, with just enough room, a completely rustic setting, an interminable quiet. His housekeeper, who rarely spoke more than a word or two at a time, kept the house shining and cheerful. Ryecroft walked about the countryside in the pleasant weather. He was no botanist, but before long he knew the names of most of the common plants he saw.

One day he came upon a boy crying bitterly. The child had been given sixpence and sent to repay a debt, but he had lost the money and for hours he had been weeping in the wood. He did not fear his parents' wrath; rather, he was aware of how much a sixpence meant to them. Ryecroft gave him a sixpence. Not long before he could not have afforded such a sum.

Ryecroft remembered the many years when he was bound to the pavements of London. He lived in a mean room, ate irregularly, begrudged time away from his hack writing. The beds he slept in so soundly would now seem an abomination. He had been young in those days, but not for anything, not even for a regained youth, would he go through those lean years again.

Ryecroft had always purchased books, even when he was poor. Once he got a complete Gibbon at a bargain and carried it home in two trips. To look at booksellers' windows and at advertisements one might think that the English were literary or at least book lovers. But the daily newspaper was a better measuring rod. It was devoted to horse racing, scandal, war, and threats of war; books got very little space.

In the summer Ryecroft sat reading one day in his garden. A chance breeze carried a perfume that reminded him of his boyhood. His wise father had seen to it that his family was seldom in crowds. In those days it was still possible to find spots along the English coast where crowds were unknown, and the Ryecrofts always spent tranquil vacations at the seaside. It always seemed that their keenest pleasure came on the trip home when the train stopped at their station.

At one period of his life Ryecroft, with little respect for the Sabbath, had reserved his best satire for the day of sanctified rest. Now Sunday had become the culmination of a quiet week; its deeper quiet made a perfect day. The housekeeper, doing only necessary work, went to church twice. Surely it did her good. Ryecroft arose later than usual and dressed in different clothes. While the housekeeper was gone, he looked into rooms he seldom saw during the week. In London Sunday had always meant cacophonous church bells. When he was a boy, Sunday had been the day he was permitted to look at expensive adult books.

One thing about contemporary England was the decline of taste in food. Faddists vaunted the delights of vegetarianism, but lentils were a poor foreign substitute for good, honest English meat. Ryecroft had even met a man who boasted of eating only apples for breakfast.

A friend, a successful author, came to visit for two days. The friend, working only two or three hours a day, made two thousand pounds a year. He and Ryecroft, poor scriveners together in London, had never dreamed that they both should know prosperous times. His friend's visit recalled London more sharply; the only things he really missed in the metropolis were concerts and picture galleries.

In autumn Ryecroft was busy learning to distinguish the hawkweeds. He had no notion of a scientific classification; common names were more fitting. At dusk, as he was walking past a farmhouse, he saw the doctor's rig at the gate. After he had passed by he turned back to see the chimney silhouetted in the sunset afterglow. The scene was irresistible; he hurried home to read *Tristram Shandy* again after twenty years. Such impulses came fairly often. One morning he awoke an hour early, in great impatience to read the correspondence of Goethe and Schiller.

The triumph of Darwinism and the spread of positivism had many consequences. Agnosticism was an early result, too reasonable to last. Oriental magic, Buddhism, hypnotism were all the rage for a while, as psychical phenomena and telepathy were now, but Ryecroft was equally indifferent to esoteric fads and to the discoveries of Marconi and Edison. Boasts about triumphs of human knowledge were childish. He agreed somewhat with Spinoza, who said that the free man thinks of death only rarely, although he was not free in Spinoza's sense. Thinking of death very often, he found the stoics a comfort.

During his first winter in Devon, Ryecroft tried to keep a wood fire. Now he had a comfortable coal grate. A storm recalled the days when he would gladly have tramped far in the wind and rain, but such an exploit would kill him now. His room seemed the most comfortable in all England. Comfortable also because he was able to spend money, he sent fifty pounds to an indigent friend and passed a pleasant hour thinking of his friend's delight at the windfall.

In those days it was the fashion to condemn the English kitchen. Cooks were called gross and unimaginative, but Ryecroft believed that English cooking was the best in the world. The beef tasted like beef, and the mutton was decidedly mutton. Rather than being a nation with one sauce, only England knew the virtues of meat gravy. However, English cooking had been better before the oven became the cook's friend and refuge; a spitted joint was incomparably better than a modern oven roast.

The strength of England probably came from two sources. First there had been Puritanism, which set moral standards. Also, the English read the Old Testament; they were the chosen people. Perhaps the last thirty years had seen the decline of conventional religion and the growth of materialism. The old prudishness, however, had given way to new strength.

Further Critical Evaluation of the Work:

Not really a novel at all, Gissing's long reflective essay is a prose poem, an elegiac celebration of true rest after enervating toil. The author, a persona for Gissing, mourns his past life of poverty, starvation, and loneliness but takes infinite consolation from the simple comforts of his cottage, savory meals, spring flowers, and good books. Walter Allen (*The English Novel,* 1954) finds Ryecroft "repellent" in his irresponsible rejection of life, but concedes that Gissing's cruel struggle to achieve literary success, in the hostile London of hack writer and journalist, explains Ryecroft's glorification of hermit-like peace.

Gissing's book is a philosophical meditation very much in the tradition of Thoreau's *Walden.* Unlike the American transcendentalist, Ryecroft does not go into isolation in order to return to the world a wiser man than he left it. His cottage in Devon is more comfortable than Thoreau's primitive cabin precisely because he plans to stay until the end. *Walden* celebrates withdrawal as a resting place in the journey of living and being; *The Private Papers of Henry Ryecroft* is stoical and resigned, and it is content to shore up associations and impressions that will prepare for death. It has a tragic dimension, whereas *Walden* is an idyl and a mental epic.

Ryecroft's stoicism gives him the courage to live without illusions. "Sympathetic understanding" strikes him as a largely illusory hope; his splendid isolation is far more satisfying: "The mind which renounces, once and for ever, a futile hope, has its compensation in ever-growing calm." Although still committed to the life of the mind and human values, Ryecroft is skeptical of democracy and contemptuous of science:

> I see it (science) restoring barbarism under a mask of civilization; I see it darkening men's minds and hardening their hearts; I see it bringing a time of vast conflicts, which will pale into significance "the thousand wars of old" . . . .

There are many today who would call Ryecroft's bias prophetic.

THE PROFESSOR

Type of work: Novel
Author: Charlotte Brontë (1816-1855)
Type of plot: Psychological romance
Time of plot: Nineteenth century
Locale: Belgium and England
First published: 1857

Principal characters:
>WILLIAM CRIMSWORTH, the narrator, a young teacher
>EDWARD CRIMSWORTH, his brother
>MR. HUNSDEN, a wealthy mill owner
>M. PELET, master of a boys' school
>MLLE. ZORAÏDE REUTER, mistress of a girls' school
>MLLE. FRANCES EVANS HENRI, a student

Critique:

The Professor, Charlotte Brontë's first completed novel, was not published until after her death. Simplified in plot and free from the atmosphere of mysticism and mystery contained in *Villette, The Professor* reads like an early study for that later novel. The story of an English teacher who seeks fortune in Europe, the book presents a rather touching love story and deals with certain problems which seem to have disturbed the young author: Catholicism, marriage, continental culture. The brief picture of Hunsden suggests an embryonic Rochester, and the characterization of Zoraïde Reuter is quite well drawn. Much of the material in this novel was drawn from Charlotte Brontë's own experience; the location of the girls' school in Brussels, for example, is that of the institution attended by the Brontë sisters in 1842.

The Story:

Orphaned in infancy, William Crimsworth had been meagerly supported by his mother's brothers, Lord Tynedale and the Hon. John Seacombe. William's brother Edward, ten years his senior, had taken over his deceased father's mill and prospered.

Upon his graduation from Eton, William, refusing to accept further aid from the uncles who had treated his mother so coldly, asked his brother for employment. When he arrived at Bigben Close, where the mill was located, Edward censured his young brother for having submitted to Tynedale and Seacombe for so many years. Edward was harsh and cold in speech and act, and his pretty young wife, although inclined at first toward warmth, began to treat William in much the same way. Edward hired William as a clerk at ninety pounds a year and requested that the young man live away from Crimsworth Hall.

A grudging brother and a harsh master, Edward invited William to his house only once, along with some other mill workers, to attend a party. That evening William met Mr. Hunsden, a flippant, wealthy mill owner who, judging Edward a false brother and a tyrant, publicly denounced him. As a result Edward furiously dismissed William. Hearing of William's decision to go to the continent, Mr. Hunsden gave him a letter of introduction to a Mr. Brown in Brussels.

When William presented his letter, Mr. Brown suggested teaching as a possible career. Through his influence William became a teacher of English and Latin in the pension of M. Pelet. Next door to M. Pelet's day school was a seminary for girls headed by Mlle. Reuter. Shortly afterward Mlle. Reuter asked William to give lessons to her girls during part of each week.

Having met Madame Reuter, a gross and droll woman, William was surprised to find her daughter, Zoraïde Reuter, young and charming. Teaching young ladies, William discovered, was not the same as teaching young boys. Mademoiselles Eulalie, Hortense, and Caroline proved to be haughtily disdainful but at the same time coquettish. M. Pelet, taking deep interest in William's personal relationships at Mlle. Reuter's school, questioned him about his impressions of Mlle. Reuter and the three young coquettes of the classroom.

William admired Mlle. Reuter. When he made a weak attempt at flirtation, she did not discourage him. But one night he overheard M. Pelet and Mlle. Reuter talking in the park about their forthcoming marriage, which M. Pelet wished to hasten and she wished to delay. M. Pelet then accused her of encouraging William, who was obviously in love with her, and he described the affair as ludicrous, since she was ten years William's senior. Mlle. Reuter, laughing pleasantly at M. Pelet's disclosure, denied interest in William.

Although William knew M. Pelet to be insincere in his friendship, he did not reveal his knowledge. He did, however, attempt to overcome his attraction toward Mlle. Reuter. William sensed that she was trying to regain his favor when she appealed to him to treat kindly a new pupil, Mlle. Frances Henri, who was also a teacher at the seminary. William, not disposed to please Mlle. Reuter, harshly criticized Frances on her first appearance. Later he was surprised at the girl's fine accent in reading English, and his interest turned from Mlle. Reuter to Frances, who was an enigma to him. Once, taking time for private and encouraging discourse with his apt pupil, he found that the schoolmistress had been eavesdropping. William learned that the girl's mother had been English, that she had been reared by an aunt, and that she was trying to educate herself in the hope of teaching French in England, where her present profession as a teacher of sewing would not be a stigma upon her dignity if she were also a teacher of language.

William, watching Frances grow in poise and wit, made special efforts to encourage her, until Mlle. Reuter warned him that he gave Frances too much of his time. The directress seemed to hover over him constantly in an attempt to recapture his affections; but he found her deceitful, artful, cruel. After she abruptly dismissed Frances from the seminary, she innocently pleaded that she did not know the young woman's address.

Frances returned to the seminary to find William, but the directress kept them from meeting. Instead, William received a note of thanks from his pupil and twenty francs in payment for his teaching. William gave Mlle. Reuter notice that he intended to quit the seminary.

After a month's futile search for Frances he accidentally came upon her mourning over the grave of her father. When it began to rain, Frances took William to her rooms, where the pair drank tea and read from an English book. Frances was earning a living by lace mending. She could not seek another position as a teacher because she feared that Mlle. Reuter would not give her satisfactory references. Bitterly resenting Mlle. Reuter's treachery, William took his leave. He managed to return the twenty francs before he departed.

Drawn to William by his coolness, Mlle. Reuter had repulsed M. Pelet with hints that she favored the English schoolmaster. After William's resignation, perceiving that she had overplayed her hand, she returned her favor to M. Pelet. Smirking with victory, he informed William of his forthcoming marriage. William, deciding that the school would be intolerable with Mme. Pelet under the same roof, resigned his position.

Frances wrote that she had been employed by a Mrs. D. to teach in an English school in Brussels. Along with this communication came a letter from Hunsden announcing his arrival. Hunsden, after berating William for his failure to forge ahead, casually announced that Edward's mill had failed. He had sold Crimsworth Hall and abused his wife until she left him, but he had managed to renew his credit, start another business, and regain his wife. William's one concern over the matter was the whereabouts of his mother's portrait, which had hung in Crimsworth Hall. The next morning William received from Hunsden, as a gift, the missing portrait.

Within a few weeks William was fortunate enough to be appointed professor of English in a college in Brussels. Cheered by the promise of his new position, William went to Frances, whom he had not seen since the night he had met her in the cemetery, and asked her to marry him. She accepted on the condition that she retain her teaching post. Although William's income was large enough for both,

she pleaded that she did not wish to marry him merely to be supported.

William and Frances were married. Within a few months Mrs. Crimsworth proposed that she elevate her position by starting a school, and William agreed to her plan.

When they had been married ten years, a period in which Frances' school flourished and a son had been born, the Crimsworths went to England to live. They settled near Hunsden, who during the years that followed became their close friend. Young Victor Crimsworth, reflecting in character many of the attributes of each parent, grew up in the atmosphere of a tranquil and loving home.

Further Critical Evaluation of the Work:

Charlotte Brontë's first novel, *The Professor,* if compared to her mature, well structured works like *Jane Eyre, Shirley* and *Villette,* does fall short in many respects. It fails in balance, character motivation, dynamic moral testing of its hero, and an unskillful author intrusion.

Its length, neither that of a novel nor a short story, may account for some of these defects. In a full-length novel Brontë might have worked out better proportion in both the English and Belgian episodes, and had time to lengthen or shorten other episodes, such as Crimsworth's meetings with Mlle. Henri. Often the reader feels oppressed by prolonged set descriptions, such as the narrator's extensive delineation of his three students—Eulalie, Hortense, and Caroline—and the conference with M. Pelet and Mlle. Reuter. These might not seem so awkward and irrelevant had the work been longer and contained more characters. Often Brontë spends care on such scenes which have no great bearing on the plot at all. After she makes a close drawing of Edward Crimsworth and his wife, they practically drop from sight; only are they briefly reported on by Yorke Hunsden on his first visit to Brussels.

In fact, Crimsworth's two entirely different experiences in England and Belgium have little connection, united merely by the slender thread of Hunsden's friendship. Hunsden, without rational motivation and after months of silence, suddenly writes and appears at Crimsworth's door. The quite contrived introduction of M. Vandenhuten and his son (rescued earlier from drowning by Crimsworth) are used only as a means of Crimsworth's getting a job after his leaving M. Pelet's school. They function not at all before or afterward.

The hero himself meets with no impossible choices or tragedies. All is low-key, purposefully drawn so by Miss Brontë. Crimsworth, her narrator, retains a balanced, even interpretation of himself and others. But one wishes for a hero who would develop. One longs for dynamic situations, exciting dialogue.

Brontë attains the latter only in exchanges between Hunsden and Crimsworth; the former is her most striking achievement in *The Professor,* although she makes Zoraïde Reuter, the schoolmistress, a second fascinating and well developed character. Unfortunately, hero Crimsworth and heroine Mlle. Henri are quite lackluster.

It is customary for critics to read *The Professor* as a forerunner to the later novels, a work in which Charlotte Brontë experiments with plot structure and character, both of which she skillfully handles in *Jane Eyre* and *Shirley*. However, *The Professor* has story interest of its own and the novel tells a great deal about the author's values from the many asides to the reader. Brontë reveals her ideas of marriage, her intolerance toward the Belgian character, and her deep suspicion of Roman Catholicism. And much of her personality is richly exhibited by the bold choice of a male first person narrator.

THE PROFESSOR'S HOUSE

Type of work: Novel
Author: Willa Cather (1873-1947)
Type of plot: Psychological realism
Time of plot: A few years after World War I
Locale: Hamilton, a Midwestern university town
First published: 1925

Principal characters:
>GODFREY ST. PETER, a middle-aged teacher and historian
>LILLIAN ST. PETER, his wife
>ROSAMOND, and
>KATHLEEN, their daughters
>LOUIE MARCELLUS, Rosamond's husband
>SCOTT McGREGOR, Kathleen's husband
>TOM OUTLAND, a former student at Hamilton
>AUGUSTA, a seamstress

Critique:

Although Willa Cather uses a minimum of lively incident in *The Professor's House,* the novel is intricate in both its character portrayal and its plot structure. Godfrey St. Peter is one of the author's most sensitive and sympathetic creations, and it is the mirror of his nostalgic but discerning mind which reflects the tensions of shifting relationships in the St. Peter family. The story does not move in straightforward fashion; flashbacks and indirect revelation of past events are used to throw light on a baffling and complicated personal problem. There is little surface drama in what happens to Godfrey St. Peter, but his inward struggle is unfolded with uncommon directness and illumination.

The Story:

The Oxford prize for history brought Professor Godfrey St. Peter not only a certain international reputation but also the sum of five thousand pounds. The five thousand pounds, in turn, built the St. Peter family a new house, into which the Professor had been frankly reluctant to move.

For half a lifetime the attic of the old house had been his favorite spot—it was there that he had done his best writing, with his daughters' dress forms for his only company—and it was in this workroom that Augusta, the family sewing-woman, found him when she came to transfer the dress forms to the new house. To her astonishment, the Professor declared quizzically that she could not have them; he intended to retain the old house in order to preserve his workroom intact, and everything must be left as it was.

Nevertheless, the new house made its own claims. That same evening found the Professor host at a small dinner party for a visiting Englishman. The Professor's daughters and their husbands were present, and during dinner the conversation turned to the new country house being built by Rosamond and Louie. Louie explained to the visitor why the name Outland had been selected for the estate. Tom Outland had been a brilliant scientific student at Hamilton, as well as The Professor's protégé. Before being killed in the war, he had been engaged to Rosamond. His will had left everything to her, including control of his revolutionary invention, the Outland vacuum. Later, Louie Marcellus himself had married Rosamond and successfully marketed Tom's invention. The new house, Louie concluded, would serve in some measure as a memorial to

Outland.

Louie's lack of reserve visibly irritated the McGregors, and the Professor himself maintained a cool silence. The next morning his wife took him to task for it. Lillian had been fiercely jealous of her husband's interest in Tom Outland. The Professor found himself reflecting that people who fall in love, and who go on being in love, always meet with something which suddenly or gradually makes a difference. Oddly enough, in the case of Lillian and her husband, it had seemed to be his pupil, Tom Outland.

More and more the Professor sought the refuge of his study in the old house, where he could insulate himself against increasing family strain. Even here, however, interruptions came. Once it was Rosamond, self-conscious about accepting all the benefits of the Outland invention. Her father refused to share her good fortune but suggested that she aid cancer-ridden Professor Crane, who had collaborated with Tom in his experiments. Rosamond stiffened immediately, for outside the family she recognized no obligations.

Soon there was more evidence that the family was drifting apart. Kathleen confessed to her father her violent reaction to Rosamond's arrogance. It became known that Louie, attempting to join the Arts and Letters Club, had been blackballed by his brother-in-law. The Professor was distressed by the rift between his daughters, both of whom he loved, although he had a special affection for Kathleen.

Louie Marcellus' real fondness for the St. Peters was demonstrated when the time came for the Professor to fill a lecture date in Chicago. He and Rosamond, paying all bills, took them to Chicago, installed them in a luxurious hotel suite, and tempted them with diversions. During a performance of *Mignon*, Lillian, softened by memories aroused by the opera, confirmed the Professor's impression that her resentment of Tom Outland had affected their marriage.

Louie's next plan was even more elaborate: he and Rosamond would take the Professor and Lillian to France for the summer. The Professor loved France, but he recognized the futility of trying to compromise his and Louie's ideas of a European vacation. He begged off, pleading the pressure of work, and eventually the others departed without him.

The Professor moved back into the old house and luxuriated in independence. He decided to edit for publication Tom Outland's youthful diary, and constantly he turned over in his mind the events in Tom's dramatic history.

Years before, Tom had appeared on the Professor's doorstep as a sunburned young man who was obviously unaccustomed to the ways of society. Tom wanted to go to college, although his only previous instruction had come from a priest in New Mexico. Interested and curious, the Professor saw to it that Tom had a chance to make up his deficiencies and enter the university. The St. Peter house became the boy's second home, and the little girls were endlessly fascinated by his tales of the Southwest. To them he confided that his parents had died during their wagon journey westward and that he had been adopted by a kindly worker on the Sante Fé Railroad.

Tom's diary was chiefly concerned with his strangest boyhood adventure. To regain his strength after an attack of pneumonia, he became a herd rider on the summer range. With him went his closest friend, Roddie Blake. On the range Tom and Roddie were challenged by the nearness of the mysterious Blue Mesa, hitherto unclimbed and unexplored. They saved their wages and made plans; when their job was finished, they set out to conquer Blue Mesa.

They made a striking discovery. In the remote canyons of the mesa were Indian rock villages, undisturbed for three hundred years and in a miraculous state of preservation. This gift of history stirred Tom to a strong decision. His find should be presented to his country; the relics must not be exploited for profit. With Roddie's consent he took six hundred dollars, boarded a train, and left for Washington.

Weeks later he returned, worn out by red tape and indifference, only to learn that Roddie had finally weakened and sold the Indian treasures to a foreign scientist. In a climax of bitterness he quarreled with Roddie. A year later he walked into the Professor's garden.

Recalling Tom Outland had always brought the Professor a kind of second youth. Tom was the kind of person the Professor had started out to be—vigorous, unspoiled, ambitious. Marrying Lillian had brought happiness, none the less real for having now faded; but it had chained him, he felt, and diverted the true course of his life. Now, reviewing the past, the Professor suddenly felt tired and old. At the news that the travelers would soon return, he thought he could not again assume a family role that had become meaningless.

When Augusta came for the keys to re-open the new house, she found the Professor lying unconscious on the floor of his den. Its one window had blown shut, and the unvented gas stove had done the rest. Augusta sent for the doctor, and the Professor was revived. He found that his temporary release from consciousness had cleared his mind. He was not only ready to face his family, but he was ready to face himself and a problem that came too late for him to flee.

Further Critical Evaluation of the Work:

Critical estimates of *The Professor's House* always are forced to deal with Willa Cather's insertion of "Tom Outland's Story" into the middle of the novel. Cather once remarked that in writing this novel she was attempting to experiment with form by "inserting the *Nouvelle* into the *Roman*" and loosely arranging the novel's structure into the three-part form of a sonata. Nonetheless, many critics have argued that Outland's story is too much of a digression from that of Professor St. Peter, and that the lengthy inclusion seriously detracts from the novel's unity.

In many ways, however, Outland's story can be viewed as integral to that of the Professor. The Professor, in fact, recognizes a great deal of himself, especially when young, in Outland. Outland's enthusiasm for life rekindles in the Professor his own flagging interest in his work, as well as his zest for living. Idealistic, creative, intelligent, and altruistic—as well as sensitive and appreciative of the simpler values in life—both men are basically the same. Their characters are complementary, so that by knowing about the one, we gain a more complete understanding of the other. In one sense, Outland's "Story" is a metaphor for the Professor's: the kinds of fundamental values and meaning Outland discovers on the mesa are the same the Professor had experienced in finding the form for and eventually completing his work on the Spanish explorers.

Other characters in the novel lack the generous spirit for life which typify Outland and the Professor. Louie Marcellus comes the closest to such spirit, but like his wife, he is more concerned with spending money than discovering other values for living. The rest of the family are severely caught up in jealousies: Mrs. St. Peter of the Professor's friendship with Tom Outland, Kathleen and Scott of the wealth Rosamond inherited from Outland.

St. Peter feels great disappointment in his family's shortcomings, made all the more obvious by their contrast to his own and Outland's larger natures. He feels his family has stifled his better nature; without Tom Outland he has no one from whom he can draw a sense of delight of living. Having lost, momentarily, the will to live, he makes no effort to save himself from the leaking gas of the stove. He is doubly saved by Augusta, from both the gas and his sense of defeat in life, for he wakes with a new determination to survive even without the broad values in living which he had shared unspoken with Tom Outland.

PROMETHEUS BOUND

Type of work: Drama
Author: Aeschylus (525-456 B.C.)
Type of plot: Classical tragedy
Time of plot: Remote antiquity
Locale: A barren cliff in Scythia
First presented: Date unknown

Principal characters:
PROMETHEUS, a Titan
HEPHAESTUS, his kinsman and the god of fire
KRATOS, Might
BIA, Force
OCEANUS, god of the sea
Io, daughter of Inachus, a river god
HERMES, the winged messenger of the gods

Critique:

Displaying perfectly the Aeschylean pattern, *Prometheus Bound* is a dramatic treatment of the legend of Prometheus, the Fire-Bearer. The spectacle of a demigod in conflict with his destiny, defiant in the face of severe punishment, makes for compelling drama. The mood is one of sharp irony and deep reflection, for the suffering of Prometheus is a symbol of man's inhumanity to man.

The Story:

Condemned by Zeus for giving fire to mere mortals, the Titan Prometheus was brought to a barren cliff in Scythia by Hephaestus, the god of fire, and two guards, Kratos and Bia. There he was to be bound to the jagged cliffs with bonds as strong as adamant. Kratos and Bia obeyed willingly the commands of Zeus, but Hephaestus experienced pangs of sorrow and was reluctant to bind his kinsman to the storm-beaten cliff in that waste region where no man came, where Prometheus would never hear the voice or see the form of a human being. He grieved that the Titan was doomed forever to be guardian of the desolate cliff. But he was powerless against the commands of Zeus, and so at last he chained Prometheus to the cliff by riveting his arms beyond release, thrusting a bitin wedge of adamant straight through his heart, and putting iron girths on both his sides with shackles around his legs. After

Hephaestus and Bia departed, Kratos remained to hurl one last taunt at Prometheus, asking him what possible aid mankind might now offer their benefactor. The gods who gave Prometheus his name, Forethinker, were foolish, Kratos pointed out, for Prometheus required a higher intelligence to do his thinking for him.

Alone and chained, Prometheus called upon the winds, the waters, mother earth, and the sun, to look on him and see how the gods tortured a god. Admitting that he must bear his lot as best he could because the power of fate was invincible, he was still defiant. He had committed no crime, he insisted; he had merely loved mankind. He remembered how the gods first conceived the plan to revolt against the rule of Kronos and seat Zeus on the throne. At first Prometheus did his best to bring about a reasonable peace between the ancient Titans and the gods. Failing, and to avoid further violence, he had ranged himself on the side of Zeus, who through the counsel of Prometheus overthrew Kronos. Once on the throne, Zeus parceled out to the lesser gods their share of power, but ignored mortal man with the ultimate plan in mind of destroying him completely and creating instead another race which would cringe and be servile to Zeus' every word. Among all the gods, only Prometheus objected to this heartless proposal, and it was Prometheus' courage, his act alone, which saved man from burial in the deepest black of Hades. It was he who taught blind hopes to spring within man's heart, and gave him the gift of fire. Understanding the significance of these deeds, he had sinned willingly.

Oceanus, brother of Prometheus, came to offer aid out of love and kinship, but he first offered Prometheus advice and preached humility in the face of Zeus' wrath. Prometheus remained proud, defiant, and refused his offer of help on the grounds that Oceanus himself would be punished were it discovered that he sympathized with a rebel. Convinced by Prometheus' argument, Oceanus took sorrowful leave of his brother.

Once more Prometheus recalled that man was a creature without language, ignorant of everything before Prometheus came and told him of the rising and setting of stars, of numbers, of letters, of the function of beasts of burden, of the utility of ships, of curing diseases, of happiness and lurking evil, of methods to bring wealth in iron, silver, copper, and gold out of the earth. In spite of his torment, he rejoiced that he had taught all arts to humankind.

Io, a young girl changed into a heifer and tormented by a stinging gadfly, came

to the place where Prometheus was chained. Daughter of Inachus, a river god, she was beloved by Zeus. His wife, Hera, out of jealousy, had turned Io into a cow and set Argus, the hundred-eyed monster, to watch her. When Zeus had Argus put to death, Hera sent a gadfly to sting Io and drive her all over the earth. Prometheus prophesied her future wanderings to the end of the earth, predicting that the day would come when Zeus would restore her to human form and together they would conceive a son named Epaphus. Before Io left, Prometheus also named his own rescuer, Hercules, who with his bow and arrow would kill the eagle devouring his vital parts.

Hermes, messenger of Zeus, came to see Prometheus and threatened him with more awful terrors at the hands of angry Zeus. Prometheus, still defiant, belittled Hermes' position among the gods and called him a mere menial. Suddenly there was a turbulent rumbling of the earth, accompanied by lightning, thunder, and blasts of wind, as angry Zeus shattered the rock with a thunderbolt and hurled Prometheus into an abysmal dungeon within the earth. Such was the terrible fate of the Fire-Bearer who defied the gods.

Further Critical Evaluation of the Work:

In several ways *Prometheus Bound* is something of a puzzle. We do not know the date of its production, although we can safely assume it came rather late in Aeschylus' career, possibly between 466 B.C. and 456 B.C., which was the year of his death. Nor do we know its exact order in the Aeschylean trilogy on Prometheus, because this is the only surviving play. But we know it was followed by *Prometheus Unbound*. Further, it is the one extant play by Aeschylus to deal directly with a metaphysical problem by means of supernatural characters. But even the questions it raises are unresolved. This drama is a mystery centering on a mystery.

The situation of the play is static: Prometheus is fastened to a Scythian crag for enabling mankind to live when Zeus intended to destroy this ephemeral creature. Once Hephaestus wedges and binds him down, Prometheus is immobile. Thereafter the theatrical movement lies in his visitors—the chorus of nymphs, Oceanus, Io, and Hermes. Essentially this is a drama of ideas, and those ideas probe the nature of the cosmos. We may forget that the characters are mainly extinct Greek gods. The issues that Aeschylus raises are still very much alive today.

The Greeks loved a contest, and *Prometheus Bound* is about a contest of wills. On the one side is Zeus, who is omnipotent in this world, while on the other is Prometheus, who has divine intelligence. Neither will give an inch, for each feels he is perfectly justified. Zeus rules by right of conquest, and Prometheus resists by right of moral superiority. On Zeus' side are Might and Force, the powers of compulsion and tyranny. But Prometheus has knowledge and prescience. The play consists of a strange debate between the two. Zeus in his inscrutability and majesty does not appear, but we see his agents enforcing his will.

The drama begins and ends with the exercise of Zeus' almighty power. That power is used simply to make Prometheus suffer. At first it binds him to a crag and finally it envelops him in a cataclysm. Zeus has a fearsome capacity to inflict pain, not merely on Prometheus but on Io as well. In both instances it seems due to disobedience. If Prometheus opposed Zeus by giving man the fire and skills he needed to survive, Io resisted Zeus love. Because of this Zeus exiled her from her home and changed her into a cow, while jealous Hera forced her to flee from land to land, bitten by a gadfly. Thus Prometheus shows rebellion on the divine plane (he being a Titan), while Io rebels on the human level. The price of their rebellion is written in their flesh, and both regard Zeus as their persecutor. Aeschylus certainly disliked political tyranny, but it is a mistake to read this play merely as a parable of man's inhumanity to man. The issues go far deeper.

Prometheus has omniscience and therefore knew what would come of his revolt. He made a great personal sacrifice when he supported mankind out of compassion. In a real sense he is a savior and a tremendous hero. His knowledge does not keep him from suffering like man, nor does it make him accept his pain calmly. He knows why he suffers but still defies his fate. He feels that he is right and Zeus is wrong. Moreover, he claims that Zeus is not the ultimate power, that Zeus is subservient to the Fates and the Furies.

Yet Prometheus holds the winning hand in this play and he knows it, for he possesses a secret that Zeus needs to retain his power. No matter how much suffering Zeus may caused him, one day Zeus will have to come begging. That is his only consolation in torment. Every counsel to moderation or humility is superficial and vain, for why should Prometheus give up the joy of seeing Zeus humbled just to alleviate his own agony? This motivation comes through clearly in the bitter dialogue with Hermes.

Thus Prometheus is not only self-righteous and vengeful, he is full of arrogant pride. He chooses his pain; perhaps he even deserves it. No one justifies Zeus, for he is beyond any notion of justice. But Prometheus exults in justifying himself to any divinity who will listen. Yet we remember his services to man and feel compassion for him. He is an authentic tragic hero, arousing both pity and fear.

As a dramatic character Io represents the human condition. The daughter of a god, she is shut out of her home by Zeus' command. Io is given a bestial body and made to run over the face of the earth in pain, stung by the ghost of many-eyed Argus (conscience). But in the distant future she and Zeus will be reconciled.

We can only guess at the resolution of the Zeus-Prometheus conflict in *Prometheus Unbound* by Aeschylus. Possibly Zeus gained in maturity after centuries of rule and decided to release the Titan freely, after which Prometheus gave him the secret. Just as man evolved through the gifts of Prometheus into a civilized creature, perhaps Zeus changed and made his reign one of wisdom and force. It is hard to believe that Prometheus would alter unless such a change did come about in Zeus. But this is pure speculation. The debate between Prometheus and Zeus remains open. Is Prometheus a rebel because God is unjust? Or is it that he places himself above God, doing what pleases him in the knowledge that he must suffer for it. Aeschylus never solves this dilemma in the play—he merely shows it to us in the strongest dramatic terms. Tautly written, *Prometheus Bound* is profound precisely because it remains an enigma. In judging the debate we judge ourselves.

James Weigel, Jr.

PROMETHEUS UNBOUND

Type of work: Poem
Author: Percy Bysshe Shelley (1792-1822)
Type of plot: Lyric drama
Time of plot: Remote antiquity
Locale: Asia
First published: 1820

Principal characters:
PROMETHEUS, a Titan
EARTH, his mother
ASIA, Prometheus' wife
JUPITER, king of the gods
DEMOGORGON, supreme power, ruling the gods
MERCURY, messenger of the gods
HERAKLES, hero of virtue and strength
PANTHEA, and
IONE, the Oceanides

Critique:

This poem, called a lyric drama by the author, is more lyric than dramatic. The poem owes its form to Shelley's study of Greek drama, however, and the characters are drawn from Greek mythology. Through the combined mediums of drama and poetry Shelley expounds his idea that universal love is the one solution to mankind's ills. *Prometheus Unbound* is valuable as a key to Shelley's philosophy; it is also enjoyable as a work of art.

The Story:

Prometheus, the benefactor of mankind, was bound to a rocky cliff by order of Jupiter, who was jealous of the Titan's power. Three thousand years of torture Prometheus suffered there, while heat and cold and many torments afflicted him. An eagle continually ate at his heart. But Prometheus still defied the power of Jupiter.

At last Prometheus asked Panthea and Ione, the two Oceanides, to repeat to him the curse he had pronounced upon Jupiter when Jupiter had first begun to torture him. But neither Earth, his mother, nor the Oceanides would answer him. At last the Phantasm of Jupiter appeared and repeated the curse. When Prometheus heard the words, he repudiated them. Now that he had suffered tortures and found that his spirit remained

unconquered, he wished pain to no living thing. Earth and the Oceanides mourned that the curse had been withdrawn, for they thought Jupiter had at last conquered Prometheus' spirit.

Then Mercury approached with the Furies. Mercury told the captive that he would suffer even greater tortures if he did not reveal the secret which Prometheus alone knew — the future fate of Jupiter. Jupiter, afraid, wished to avert catastrophe by learning the secret, and Mercury promised that Prometheus would be released if he revealed it. But Prometheus refused. He admitted only that he knew Jupiter's reign would come to an end, that he would not be king of the gods for all eternity. Prometheus said that he was willing to suffer torture until Jupiter's reign ended. Although the Furies tried to frighten him by describing the pains they could inflict, they knew they had no power over his soul.

The Furies mocked Prometheus and mankind. They showed him visions of blood and despair on earth; they showed the Passion of Christ and men's disregard for His message of love. Fear and hypocrisy ruled; tyrants took the thrones of the world.

A group of spirits appeared and prophesied that Love would cure the ills of mankind. They prophesied also that Prometheus would be able to bring Love to earth and halt the reign of evil and grief.

When the spirits had gone, Prometheus acknowledged the power of Love, for his love for Asia, his wife, had enabled him to suffer pain without surrendering.

While Asia mourned alone in a lovely valley for her lost husband, Panthea appeared to tell of two dreams she had had. In one, she saw Prometheus released from bondage and all the world filled with sweetness. In the other dream she had received only a command to follow. Just then the echoes in the valley broke their silence. They called Asia and Panthea to follow them. The listeners obeyed.

Asia and Panthea followed the echoes to the realm of Demogorgon, the supreme power ruling the gods. They stopped on a pinnacle of rock, but spirits beckoned them down into Demogorgon's cave. There he told them that he would answer any question they put to him. When they asked who had made the living world, he replied that God had created it. Then they asked who had made pain and evil. Prometheus had given knowledge to mankind, but mankind had not eradicated evil with all the gifts of science. They asked whether Jupiter was the source of these ills, the evil master over man.

Demogorgon answered that nothing which served evil could be master, for only eternal Love ruled all. Asia asked when Prometheus would gain his freedom and bring Love into the world to conquer Jupiter. Demogorgon then showed his guests the passage of the Hours. A dreadful Hour passed, marking Jupiter's fall; the next hour was beautiful, marking Prometheus' release. Asia and Panthea accompanied this spirit of the Hour in her chariot and passed by Age, Manhood, Youth, Infancy, and Death into a new paradise.

Meanwhile, Jupiter, who had just married Thetis, celebrated his omnipotence over all but the soul of man. Then Demogorgon appeared and pronounced judgment on Jupiter. Jupiter cried for mercy, but his power was gone. He sank downward through darkness and ruin.

At the same time Herakles approached Prometheus. In the presence of Asia Panthea, the Spirit of the Hour, and Earth, the captive was set free. Joyfully, Prometheus told Asia how they would spend the rest of their days together with Love. Then he sent the Spirit of the Hour to announce his release to all mankind. He kissed Earth, and Love infused all of her animal, vegetable, and mineral parts.

The Spirit of Earth came to the cave where Asia and Prometheus lived and told them of the transformation that had come over mankind. Anger, pride, insincerity, and all the other ills of man had passed away. The Spirit of the Hour reported other wonders that took place. Thrones were empty, and each man was king over himself, free from guilt or pain. But he was still subject to chance, death, and mutability, without which he would oversoar his destined place in the world.

Later in a vision Panthea and Ione saw how all the evil things of the world lay dead and decayed. Earth's happiness was boundless, and even the moon felt the beams of Love from Earth as snow melted on its bleak lunar mountains. Earth rejoiced that hate, fear, and pain had left mankind forever. Man was now master of his fate and of all the secrets of Earth.

Further Critical Evaluation of the Work:

Regardless of the difficulty in deciphering a concrete meaning from this "lyrical drama," one is nevertheless immediately struck by a considerable display of artistic ability in handling all the possible variations of the lyric form and verse patterns. (Bennett Weaver's *Prometheus Unbound*, 1957, deals with the many facets of this work in detail.) The work as a whole is unique in form and in tone, and it ignores blatantly Keats's famous admonition to Shelley: "load every rift of your subject with ore." Shelley fortunately clung to his own distinctive mode, however, letting himself project his style with such liquidity that he challenges music for comparison. Many of the songs in *Prometheus Unbound* are a remarkable lyrical flowering—nearly two dozen are in forms original with him. To a great extent these lyrical passages, providing melodic and variegated rhythms, account for Raymond D. Havens' remarks in "Shelley the Artist" that the entire work is "vital, rich, fresh, varied, alive." Newman Ivey White, whose biography of Shelley is the most accurate, complete, and judicious, goes even further in his laudatory comments, claiming that many of the passages in the work, if considered only as separate poems, would place Shelley among the greatest of English poets.

Numerous studies have been made of the various meanings of the drama; it is perhaps equally valuable to understand in what ways the poem may be considered a "remarkable lyrical flowering." From Prometheus' opening oration to the paean-like ending, the reader is carried along with the delicacy, vivacity, thunder, or choric effect of the lines. The spacelessness of the work is its virtue, and its muted, ethereal effect is lyrically matchless.

This work, worthy of the name "lyrical drama," illustrates supremely how Shelley has fashioned not only his individual lyric patterns but also the Pindaric ode, the "Fourteeners," the Spenserian stanza, couplets, and infinite variations of the Greek choral effects into a distinctively Shelleyan image. Every conceivable meter can be detected; the inversions, the intricately developed rhythm patterns are numerous. A "lyrical flowering" seems an appropriate phrase for the entire work, perhaps Shelley's greatest.

THE PROMISED LAND

Type of work: Novel
Author: Henrik Pontoppidan (1857-1943)
Type of plot: Social criticism
Time of plot: Late nineteenth century
Locale: Denmark
First published: 1891-1895

Principal characters:
EMANUEL HANSTED, a clergyman and reformer
HANSINE, his wife
MISS TONNESEN, his former fiancée
DR. HASSING, a physician

Critique:

Pontoppidan's novel reflects the class distinctions and the division between town and country folk in nineteenth-century Denmark, at a time when the peasants were struggling for a greater voice in the affairs of that country. As in the case of so many European novels dealing with social problems, the characterization, the plot, and the happenings are secondary to the social meaning and the tone of the work. As a result, the characters are types rather than individuals, and in a plot subordinate to theme the happenings are not skillfully tied together. Quite obviously these items were relatively unimportant to the author; he was intent upon giving a picture of the struggle between the People's Party and the Conservatives, and the effects of that struggle on individuals. Sympathetic to the less-favored group, Pontoppidan, like so many problem novelists, told only one side of the story; one result is that his upper-class characters, like those of the American novelist Theodore Dreiser, are often overdrawn.

The Story:

Emanuel Hansted, son of a wealthy Copenhagen family, and a minister, had left his home city years before to take over a pastorate in the country. Somewhat of a reformer, he had become addicted to the socialism rife in Europe in the second half of the nineteenth century, and to prove his fellowship with the peasants whom he served he had married a peasant girl and undertaken to farm the land on which the rectory was situated.

As the years passed Hansted's wife, Hansine, presented him with three children; his land, however, repaid him only with debts. Although he tried experiment after experiment, Emanuel's fields did not produce enough to support his family. Stubbornly, Emanuel refused to acknowledge that he was no farmer; he even continued to refuse any payment from his parishioners and gave away the money he received for the benefit of the poor.

In spite of his sacrifices, despite his never-flagging efforts to share their lives, and his ties with them through marriage, the peasants did not accept him as one of themselves. The fact that he had come among them as an outlander was too strong for them to forget, even in the times of stress that came when the newly-formed People's Party of Denmark, representing chiefly the peasantry, was trying to control the government, in order to provide for the education of the masses and to improve the lot of the common people generally.

To the casual eye Emanuel might have seemed a peasant, for he had nothing to do with the few gentry who lived in the vicinity. He even distrusted the doctor, whom he had to call in occasionally to treat a member of his family. Indeed, Emanuel summoned Doctor Hassing only when an emergency existed. As for his family, Emanuel had put his father and his sister entirely out of his mind; only his wife and children, who tied him to the peasantry, were acknowledged as kin.

One summer all of nature and mankind seemed determined to show that Emanuel was a misfit in the rural area he had adopted. His crops were even poorer than usual. He had borrowed the seed he put into the ground, and, after it was in, nature refused to send the weather he needed to produce successful yields in the fields. In Copenhagen the Conservative Party gained in strength and defeated the People's Party, first in small items, then in large. As the peasants lost their political power, the people of Emanuel's parish began to look upon him as one who belonged on the other side.

As if that were not enough, Emanuel's oldest child, a son, began to suffer from an ear inflammation that had gone untended for two years. At last, upon Hansine's insistence, Emanuel sent for Dr. Hassing. The physician could not believe that Emanuel had permitted the child's health to fall into such a dangerous state; Emanuel, on his part, could not understand that the child was really ill. Failing to follow the doctor's advice, he treated his son as if he were well and healthy. Because of his father's failure to face reality, the boy died.

Before long Emanuel and Hansine began to drift apart, for their son's death had erected a barrier between them that had been years in the making. Hansine felt that her husband really was unhappy, and she believed that he actually wanted to escape from the dismal, unappreciative rural parish.

Quite by chance, while out walking alone to prepare his Sunday sermon, Emanuel came upon Dr. Hassing and a small party of picnickers. Prevailed upon to join the group, he found among them Miss Tonnesen, his former fiancée from Copenhagen. Emanuel walked back to Dr. Hassing's home with the picnickers and, because it was growing dark, remained for supper. The genteel conversation, the quiet wealth of the home, the very food on the table, the music after supper—all of these things reminded Emanuel of what he had lost when he had refused Miss Tonnesen's love, rejected the family warmth of his parents' home, and turned instead toward the simple, rude life of the peasants. In the days following he ridiculed the people with whom he had spent a few hours, but Hansine saw that he was merely trying to convince himself that he had chosen the right path in his life's work.

A few weeks later Miss Tonnesen, who had gone out into the rural area to prove to herself that her former suitor had sunk beneath her, visited the rectory. Her father had been the former rector of the parish; under his care the rectory had been a place of beauty, both within and without. His daughter, seeing it for the first time in many years, was amazed to see how Emanuel had let it fall into disrepair. Only a few of the rooms, equipped with the barest of essentials, were in use. The gardens and lawns were overgrown; even the outbuildings and fields had been years without proper care. Miss Tonnesen could scarcely believe that the man she had loved could have permitted the grounds in his charge, and himself as well, to slip into the state in which she found them.

Miss Tonnesen's visit bothered Hansine. She saw in the other woman all that her husband had given up when he had married her instead of a woman from his own social class. Even Hansine's children asked if they could go to Copenhagen to visit the beautiful lady. Emanuel himself realized that Miss Tonnesen represented something he had lost, but could still regain. He became dissatisfied with the peasantry, and they quickly sensed his unrest. His farm workers left him when, angry because the rains ruined any chance he had of harvesting a crop of rye, he abused them for their laziness.

The climax came when the director of the district high school, a man who as head of the institution had done much for the peasants, died. Everyone in the region went to the funeral. After it was over a political meeting formed of its own accord. Emanuel, when asked to address the meeting, spoke out against the sloth and narrow prejudices of the peasants. As he spoke, murmurings arose; he finally had to stop speaking when the crowd began to shout insults and ridicule. As he slowly left the meeting, he could hear a new speaker declaring that the pastor should return to his own people.

He met Hansine at the edge of the crowd; slowly they started home. On the way back Hansine told Emanuel that he ought to return to Copenhagen and she to her former life. He sadly agreed. The children, it was decided, would go with their father. To Emanuel's delight, his father and sister wrote him to return as soon as possible. As a result, one morning he and his remaining two children climbed into a carriage and drove away, while Hansine turned to walk to her parents' cottage.

Further Critical Evaluation of the Work:

Nobel Prize-winer Henrik Pontoppidan attempted in *The Promised Land* to illustrate the conflicts that overtake a human being who attempts to submerge his instincts to his intellectual beliefs. Emanuel Hansted is a complicated, tormented individual, divided between theory and instinct, duty and passion. He is not entirely sympathetic, but he is understandable and pitiable. A dreamer, he tries unsuccessfully to gain the confidence of the peasants, but, despite his efforts to make himself one with the soil and the peasant life, his urban background ultimately betrays his ambitions.

Pontoppidan writes with a deceptively aloof, almost cold, style, but his characters are warm-blooded, many-faceted human beings. Hansine, Emanuel's wife, speaks little, but it is clear that she feels deeply. He married her because she was a peasant, because he felt that she would help him to forget his past, but gradually she comes to realize that they are wrong for each other. With great artistry, the author subtly suggests her feelings, implying much with few words. Her sacrifice at the end of the book is both inevitable and touching.

Emanuel's past in Copenhagen is only revealed in pieces, through allusions in conversation. His former relationship with the attractive, sophisticated Ragnhild Tonnesen is disclosed bit by bit; the reader discovers the realities behind the appearances slowly. This technique requires great control on the part of the author, but it builds with relentless inevitability to the emotional crisis at the heart of the book. Politics and religion play an important part in the novel, but primarily it is a story of human beings.

Emanuel saw everything evil in the sophistication of his past life in the city, and made the mistake of seeing only good in the crude life of the peasants. He craved truth and justice, and saw a moral earnestness in the peasant faces which touched him deeply. So completely did he reject the city and its ways, including science and progress, that he refused to let a doctor see his son until it was too late to save the boy's life. There was a dormant power in the people, he believed, and he wanted to be the one to raise it.

But, as one of the other characters comments, he only sacrificed himself—and his family—to his opinions. Niels, on the other hand, is his exact opposite, a young upward-mobile peasant, writing for the local newspapers in his spare time, ambitious, hopeful for the future. Everywhere, signs of change are in the air, but Emanuel cannot understand where they are leading. His vague dreams and misplaced ideals only lead him astray. His doubts and struggles are vividly portrayed by the author in this important novel of the birth of the modern age in Denmark.

THE PROPHET

Type of work: Poetry
Author: Kahlil Gibran (Gibran Khalil Gibran, 1883-1931)
Time: Ielool, the month of reaping
Locale: The city of Orphalese
First published: 1923

Principal characters:
ALMUSTAFA, a mystic and prophet
ALMITRA, a seeress

Kahlil Gibran's *The Prophet* belongs to that group of unique publishing events which includes Edward FitzGerald's *The Rubáiyát of Omar Khayyám* and certain of the works of William Blake, to whom Gibran was compared by the sculptor Rodin. There is, for example, an indefinable quality about FitzGerald's translation which causes even the insensitive to pause and ponder, and its admirers have become a cult. It is a work that appeals especially to the impressionable young adult, and a generation ago the poem was sometimes bound in leather in a miniature edition and used as a prom favor at college dances. Similarly, *The Prophet* owes much to the young of a generation ago, who found in Gibran's poetry a quality that approached the elusive flame center of the word "sincerity." Word of mouth recommendations rather than the publisher's promotions have pushed hardcover sales of this thin volume to more than two million copies—a truly remarkable sales record for a book of poetry.

In order to understand the power of Gibran's poetry it is necessary to know something of his life, of the agonies of remorse that burned within him, of the loneliness of spirit that heightened his senses and enabled him to see the travail of all mankind. The ingredients of his message surpass the mere arrangement of words, even "the *best* words in the best order," for Gibran seemed to say that all men spring from the dust of the cosmos, that the universe is in us and we are of it. In this idea lies the essence of his appeal to the mystic and especially to the youthful mystic.

Christened Gibran Khalil Gibran, the poet was born in Bechari (Basharri), anon, the son of a poor shepherd family. When he was twelve, his mother took the family to Boston, hoping, like many immigrants of the day, to gain wealth quickly and then return to the homeland, where the easy-going father had remained to care for the family's small holdings. Soon the opportunities in the new world were apparent and the mother decided that the sensitive Kahlil must be educated so that he could become a great man. The older son and the two daughters joined the mother at unskilled labor in order to earn the money with which Kahlil might gain an education. But within a few years the family had been decimated by tuberculosis and only Kahlil and his sister Mariana remained. Kahlil never completely recovered from his grief and his sense of guilt over the fact that his family must have died for him.

Bolstered by the loyalty and industry of Mariana, Kahlil began to write and draw, illustrating his own writings in the manner of William Blake. Financial success was elusive, but Gibran gained a patron who prevailed upon him to go abroad for study. He spent two years in Paris, then returned to the United States and soon set up a studio in Greenwich Village, where he worked for the remainder of his life. He began to publish in 1918 with *The Madman*, and in 1923 appeared his masterpiece, *The Prophet*, which has been translated into more than a dozen languages.

The illustrations which accompanied most of the poetry Gibran produced were often as striking as his words, and his works now hang in some of America's finest art museums. Always frail, he was driven beyond endurance by an inner force which would not let him rest, and death overtook him in 1931 in the full flower of his productivity. His body was returned to Lebanon and buried with great honors in the village of his birth.

The Prophet consists of twenty-six poetic essays on various aspects of life, preceded by an introduction and followed by a Farewell, wherein the Prophet promises to return to his people, borne by another woman after a momentary rest upon the wind. Thus, the continuity of life is implied, the circle of birth and death and rebirth.

The introduction, called "The Coming of the Ship," tells how the Prophet is now about to board the ship that has arrived to take him back to his native land after twelve years among the people of the city of Orphalese. During these twelve years the people of the city have come to love and revere the Prophet for his wisdom and gentle spirit, and they gather in the great square before the temple and beseech him not to leave but to remain forever in their midst. As the multitude weeps and pleads, Almitra, the seeress who had first befriended the Prophet on his arrival in the city, comes out of the sanctuary and asks him to speak to them of life before he departs.

She asks first that he speak of Love, whereupon the Prophet admonishes the hushed audience to follow love when he beckons even though he may wound as he caresses, even though he may destroy dreams as he entices. For love demands complete commitment, a testing in the sacred fires, if one is to see into his own heart and have knowledge of Life's heart. The cowardly should cover themselves and flee from love, for those who can never be possessed by love can never know fulfillment.

The Prophet is then asked in turn to speak of Marriage, Children, Giving, Eating and Drinking, Work, Joy and Sorrow, Houses, Clothes, Buying and Selling, and, by a judge of the city, to talk of Crime and Punishment. In response to the latter request the Prophet speaks at length, pointing out that whereas the most righteous cannot rise above the highest which is in each of us, so the weak and wicked cannot fall below the lowest in each of us; therefore, we must condemn lightly, for we, the whole, are not entirely blameless for the evil done by one of our parts.

Then a lawyer in the crowd asks for comment on Laws, an orator on Freedom, and a priestess on Reason and Passion, whereupon the Prophet compares reason to a ship's rudder and passion to its sails. Without both, the ship is useless. Without the rudder it will toss aimlessly; without the sails it will lie becalmed like a wingless bird.

The Prophet then speaks of Pain, Self-Knowledge—wherein he likens the self to a limitless, an immeasurable, sea—Teaching, Friendship, Talking, Time, Good and Evil, Prayer, Pleasure, Beauty —which he finds too elusive for definition—Religion, and Death. Of the last he urges mature acceptance, for, like the brook and the lake, life and death are one.

By the time the Prophet has finished speaking twilight had fallen, and he goes straightway to his ship, there to bid a final farewell to his followers. As the ship lifts anchor the sorrowful crowd disperses until only Almitra remains upon the sea wall, watching his ship recede into the dusk and remembering his promise to return in another way at another time.

The Prophet is a work to be experienced, not described. Gibran's insistent subjectivity, shrouded in a religious-like mysticism, swirls the reader inexorably inward toward the center of a vortex where evil has been flung aside and the soul of man stands revealed in all its nobility and goodness.

PROSERPINE AND CERES

Type of work: Classical myth
Source: Unknown
Type of plot: Allegory of fertility and death
Time of plot: Remote antiquity
Locale: Mediterranean region
First transcribed: Unknown

Principal characters:
CERES, goddess of fertility
PROSERPINE, her daughter
HADES, king of the underworld
VENUS, goddess of love
CUPID, her son
TRIPTOLEMUS, builder of a temple to Ceres
ARETHUSA, a fountain nymph
ALPHEUS, a river god
DIANA, goddess of the hunt
JUPITER, king of the gods
MERCURY, messenger of the gods

Critique:

Prominent in popularity among the legends created by the Greeks and the Romans is the story of Proserpine and Ceres. As a fable which identifies itself with the simplest explanation of the seasons, it has lived by being transferred in oral legend, in poetry, and in prose from generation to generation. Although the story has changed in certain details, its basic structure remains. Its hold upon the imagination of the Western world lies in its appeal as a record of man's search for a beautiful interpretation of grief.

The Story:

One of the Titans, Typhoeus, long imprisoned for his part in the rebellion against Jupiter, lay in agony beneath Mount Aetna on the island of Sicily in the Mediterranean Sea. When Typhoeus groaned and stirred, he shook the sea and the island of Sicily so much that the god of the underworld, Hades, became frightened lest his kingdom be revealed to the light of day.

Rising to the upper world to make entrance to his kingdom, Hades was discovered by Venus, who ordered her son Cupid to aim one of his love darts into the breast of Hades and so cause him to fall in love with Proserpine, daughter of Ceres, goddess of fertility.

Proserpine had gone with her companions to gather flowers by the banks of a stream in the beautiful vale of Enna. There Hades, stricken by Cupid's dart, saw Proserpine, seized her, and lashed his fiery horses to greater speed as he carried her away. In her fright the girl dropped her apron, full of flowers she had gathered. At the River Cyane, Hades struck the earth with his scepter, causing a passageway to appear through which he drove his chariot and took his captive to the underworld.

Ceres sought her daughter everywhere. At last, sad and tired, she sat down to rest. A peasant and his daughter found her in her disguise as an old woman, took pity on her, and urged her to go with them to their rude home. When they arrived at the house they found that their only son, Triptolemus, was dying. Ceres first gathered some poppies. Then, kissing the child, she restored it to health. The happy family bade her join them in their simple meal of honey, cream, apples, and curds. Ceres put some of the poppy juice in the boy's milk and that night when he was sleeping she placed the child in the fire. The mother, awakening, seized her child from the flames. Ceres assumed her proper form and told the parents that it had been her plan to make the boy immortal. Since the mother had hindered that plan, she would teach him the use of the plow.

Then the goddess mother continued her search for Proserpine until she returned to Sicily. There, at the very spot Hades had entered the underworld, she asked the river nymph if she had seen anything of her daughter. Fearful of being punished, the river nymph refused to tell what she had seen but gave to Ceres the belt of Proserpine, which the girl had lost in her struggles.

Ceres decided to take revenge upon the land, to deny it further gift of her favors so that herbage and grain would not grow. In an effort to save the land which Ceres was intent upon cursing, the fountain Arethusa told the following story to Ceres. Arethusa had been hunting in the forest, where she was formerly a woodland nymph. Finding a stream, she decided to bathe. As she sported in the water, the river god Alpheus began to call her. Frightened, the nymph ran, the god pursuing.

The goddess Diana, seeing her plight, changed Arethusa into a fountain which ran through the underworld and emerged in Sicily. While passing through the underworld, Arethusa saw Proserpine, now queen of the dead, sad at the separation from her mother but at the same time bearing the dignity and power of the bride of Hades.

Ceres immediately demanded help from Jupiter, ruler of the gods. The king of the gods said that Proserpine should be allowed to return to the valley of Enna from which she had been abducted only if in the underworld she had taken no food.

Mercury was sent to demand Proserpine for her mother. But Proserpine had eaten of a pomegranate. Because she had eaten only part of the fruit, a compromise was made. Half of the time she was to pass with her mother and the rest with Hades. Ceres, happy over the return of Proserpine during one half of each year, caused the earth to be fertile again during the time Proserpine lived with her.

Ceres remembered her promise to the peasant boy, Triptolemus. She taught him to plow and to plant seed, and he gathered with her all the valuable seeds of the earth. In gratitude the peasant's son built a temple to Ceres in Eleusis where priests administered rites called the Eleusinian mysteries. Those rites surpassed all other Greek religious celebrations because in the mysteries of nature, men saw symbolized the death of man and the promise of his revival in future life.

Further Critical Evaluation of the Work:

This fertility myth seems to have Mycenaean (pre-Homeric) origins, but the earliest and in many ways the most perfect version survives from the late seventh century B.C. in the Homeric Hymn to Demeter, that is, Ceres. Demeter (either "earth mother" or "grain mother") and her daughter Persephone (corrupted by the Romans into Proserpina) were originally two aspects of one mythic personality: the mother was associated with the harvest, the daughter with the sprouting grain. The Greeks, fearfully avoiding mention of the daughter's name, called her simply Kore, that is, (grain) maiden. This practice was usual with the powerful and mysterious chthonian (underworld) deities whom the Greeks wished not to risk offending.

The literary history of the myth is extensive, including two appearances in Ovid (*Metamorphoses* 5.341 ff. and *Fasti* 4.417 ff.), but there are only minor variations, such as where the rape occurred, who Triptolemus was, how many pomegranate seeds Proserpine ate, and how much of the year she remains with Hades. The above synopsis, which is a conflation of Ovid's accounts, differs from the Homeric Hymn in the Triptolemus episode. In the Hymn, Ceres' hosts, Celeus and Metanira, are not peasants but the rulers of Eleusis, near Athens. In her old age, Metanira has borne a child, Demopho(o)n, whom she gives to Ceres, disguised as Doso, to suckle. Triptolemus was one of Eleusis' youthful nobility, and was among the first to participate in Ceres' mysteries, or secret rites, in the temple built by Celeus. The hymn also has Proserpine spend one-third of the year with her husband below the earth; this reflects a tripartite seasonal year of spring, summer, winter. Despite mention in the Hymn that Proserpine emerges to the upperworld in the spring, reputable scholars argue that her four months' absence is associated with the summer-long storage of harvested grain in June (the grain was put in jars in the cool earth till planting in the winter). The traditional interpretation is that the fresh seed grain is planted in the winter and the maiden shoots emerge in the early spring.

The so-called Eleusinian mysteries most closely resembled what we might call a universal religion. Its objective was preparation for eternal peace through understanding the mystery of cyclic growth. Although great numbers of Greek-speaking persons were initiated into the mysteries, little authoritative information about them survives. Clement of Alexandria (fl. A.D., second century), a convert to Christianity, reveals that votaries dramatized the myth of Ceres and Proserpine, fasted, handled sacred objects, and partook of the sacramental porridge of water, flour, and mint which Ceres was offered at Eleusis. The so-called Lesser Mysteries were celebrated in Athens in the early spring; they consisted of prayers, purifications, and the like. The Greater Mysteries were performed in September/October; nine days of grand procession from Athens to Eleusis and back featured numerous rituals, at the height of which priests and priestesses were consecrated. Certainly the mysteries relied heavily on symbolic ritual and mythic reënactment. The nine days of the Greater Mysteries correspond to the nine days of Ceres' fasting as she searched for her daughter; the pomegranate with its many "bloody" seeds symbolizes fertility; Proserpine's marriage to Hades metaphorically explains the mystery of fertilization and growth within the earth. It is even theorized that the secret dramas included ritualistic sexuality, imitating the *hieros gamos* ("sacred union") of the underworld deities to bring fertility to the fields. (Such a ritual was common to a number of cults, and within the myth of Ceres herself is her union with her brother Jupiter, the sky god, which produced Proserpine.)

The basic structure of the myth is simple: peaceful innocence, sudden violence, misguided revenge, and finally reconciliation; within this dramatic structure the myth-makers have woven origins of the Eleusinian cult. (Ovid's insertion of the Arethusa myth is forced, since it is merely preparation for its lengthier telling immediately following in the *Metamorphoses*.) But there are also some excellent descriptive sequences: the gathering of flowers by Proserpine, the sudden dark violence of Hades, the awesome burning of Metanira's child in the fire. Finally, the characterizations of both in Ovid's versions and in the Hymn are classic: Proserpine as the innocent virgin, carefully protected; Demeter, the doting mother, the prototype of *mater dolorosa*; Hades, the lustful villain who brings havoc when he makes an unprecedented appearance in the upperworld; Jupiter, the supreme administrator and magistrate who must act to prevent the extinction of men (the gods' sacrificers) and who must strike a compromise between equally powerful forces. The resolution is no doubt necessary to explain why in other myths Proserpine seems quite at ease in her role as queen of the dead. (It is likely that this character is a further confusion of the witch goddess, Hecate, and a primitive earth goddess.) In fact, excepting her rape, she is virtually always found in the underworld, ruling with authority. There she appears in the various heroic *katabaseis*—descents by Orpheus, Aeneas, and others; there also is she the object of an attempted rape by Theseus and Pirithous.

The most significant modern adaptation of the myth is the musical drama *Persephone* (1934) by Igor Stravinsky and André Gide, in which the heroine willingly sacrifices herself to bring joy and youth to the gloomy realm below.

E. N. Genovese

PURPLE DUST

Type of work: Drama
Author: Sean O'Casey (1884-1964)
Type of plot: Satiric comedy
Time of plot: The present
Locale: Clune na Geera, Ireland
First presented: 1940

Principal characters:
CYRIL POGES, a pompous English businessman
O'KILLIGAIN, a foreman stonemason
BASIL STOKE, Poges' colleague
SOUHAUN, Poges' mistress
AVRIL, Stoke's mistress
THREE IRISH WORKMEN

Critique:

In *Purple Dust,* Sean O'Casey returned to certain stylistic aspects of his earlier plays: the mixture of moving poetry with extravagant comedy. However, though the occasional poetic passages of the Irish workmen concerning their noble past are indeed beautiful, the emphasis of the play is on the profoundly comic aspects of two stuffy Englishmen trying to adjust to the rigors of the bucolic life. O'Casey, as usual, is extolling the hardy Irish, and quite disapproves of men who cling to the past without partly looking to the future. When men venerate the past without a true sense of understanding and appreciation, as do Poges and Stoke, the result is especially disastrous.

The Story:

Three workmen were standing languidly in a large, gloomy room that obviously was once the living room of a ruined Elizabethan mansion. The three pondered on the wisdom of two English gentlemen, Cyril Poges and Basil Stoke, in coming to live in such a decaying old house. Though the fresh paint had brightened things up a bit, it covered, for the most part, rotting wood. The sudden appearance of the sixty-five-year-old Poges and the thirtyish, serious Basil followed by their mistresses, Souhaun and Avril, confirmed the workmen's suspi- cions that the owners were slightly awry in their thinking; the group danced in, boisterously singing of the joys of country living. The handsome foreman, O'Killigain, explained to the workmen that these were people who saw historical loveliness in decaying ruins, and who took foolish delight in any locale with a story behind it. With the reappearance of the pretty Avril, O'Killigain exerted his poetic Irish charm to entice her into a rendezvous later that night.

Poges, Basil, and Souhaun returned from a tramp in the fields. Poges and Basil talked excitedly about the glories of past history and its better times, much to the disgust of O'Killigain, who firmly believed that life in its present state was far more worth living. His philosophy was lost on the other two, who went about their comic business of hanging pictures and discovering new aspects of country living—new business for them, but common enjoyment for the hardy Irish workmen.

Although Poges wanted to forget the outside world and its ways, his reverie was constantly interrupted by prosaic occurrences: arguments with Basil and the girls, altercations with his butler over men outside who wished to know if he desired roosters and hens, and interruptions by one of the workmen, who informed him of an excellent buy in a cow. Poges raged that he would get in touch with the Department of Agriculture. At Poges' displeasure over the disconnected telephone, another workman lost his temper. Poges heard himself scorned as a man who thought that the glory of the world could be stuffed into a purse, a man who was patronizing toward the Irish, a mighty race a thousand years older than his own. Basil and Avril left for a horseback ride, in spite of warnings that Irish horses were true horses, instead of English animals. The predictions were accurate; a battered Basil appeared shortly afterward and announced that his horse indeed had become a wild animal, and that, when last seen, Avril was riding away quite naked with O'Killigain.

The next day brought a cold dawn. Though Poges and Basil had spent the night fully clothed, they had almost frozen to death in the old house, along with the rest of the household. Poges still tried to rationalize; the cold air would revitalize them and exhilarate them. Barney, the butler, and Cloyne, the maid, were none the less disgusted with the whole situation; they thought the place an unlighted dungeon. As Barney struggled to light a damp fire, Cloyne rushed back into the room to scream that there was a wild bull in the entrance hall. This announcement caused a great panic among the transplanted city dwellers. Basil reëntered with a gun, then ran for his life as Poges roared for help and Cloyne fainted. A workman saved them all by shooing out a harmless cow which had innocently wandered into the hallway.

Later Poges thought he had found a friend in the same workman, who reminisced with him over glorious days in the past. Once again Poges expressed his philosophy that all the greats had gone with their glory, their finery turned to purple dust, and that today's man was shallow by comparison. However, O'Killigain and another workman later transfixed Poges by their poetic visions of the glorious Irish past and the fight for independence. Although Poges was momentarily surprised to find that these country workers had such depth, his spirit of English nationalism soon reasserted itself.

Poges' calamities continued. His next misadventure was with an oversized, heavy garden roller. Though his friends warned him, Poges persisted in his efforts to operate the machine. The result was a wrecked wall, as Poges let the roller get away from him to roll into and through the side of the house. Following closely on this incident, a terrified Basil shot and killed the indolent cow which had earlier invaded the hallway.

An interview with the local canon lifted Poges' spirits when the churchman praised Poges for restoring a portion of the past to slow down the reckless speed of the present. As the workmen continued to bring in furniture, Souhaun, like Avril to O'Killigain, almost succumbed to one of the workmen and his poetic charm. The moving into the room of a gilded desk-bureau proved to be another disaster. The top was first scarred by a workman's boot; then the bureau and the entrance were both damaged as the piece of furniture was pushed and pried through the door.

Because the wind was rising and storm clouds were brewing ominously, the workmen were sent away, but not before O'Killigain and the workman had entreated Avril and Souhaun to accompany them. The beautiful picture of Irish life conjured quickly by the man left the girls quite unsettled, but Poges and Basil made great fun of the workmen's poetic proposals. As the day grew darker and the rain fell, Poges found still other troubles; the postmaster arrived to complain about Poges' midnight phone calls to him. Suddenly the sound of a galloping horse was heard over the howl of the wind.

Warned that the river was rising, the terrified group in the darkened room made plans to climb to the roof before the house was flooded. Souhaun was nowhere to be found; she was with the workman on the galloping horse. O'Killigain, who had said that he would come for Avril when the river rose, appeared as he had promised. Avril left, renouncing Basil as a gilded monkey. Basil ran for the roof and a defeated Poges followed slowly, longing, once more, for dear England.

Further Critical Evaluation of the Work:

Purple Dust may not be Sean O'Casey's greatest play, but it is probably his funniest. He begins with a potentially hilarious situation, the attempt by two stuffy Englishmen to "restore" an ancient, ramshackled Tudor mansion in the Irish countryside in the face of opposition from the local citizenry. To this beginning he adds a cast of broad, colorful, and sometimes poetic types, and, utilizing a thin but completely functional plot line, presents a sequence of zany scenes that would have fit nicely into a Marx Brothers movie.

But that is not to say that *Purple Dust* is without serious content. Eschewing the kind of abstract symbolism and forced rhetoric that damaged such earlier "idea" plays as *Within the Gates* (1933), *The Star Turns Red* (1940), and *Oak Leaves and Lavender* (1946), O'Casey mixes comedy with message so adroitly in *Purple Dust* that he is able to present some strident satire and provocative ideas without losing any humor or theatrical effectiveness.

Cyril Poges and Basil Stoke are two brilliant comedic and satiric creations. Poges is the self-made man, the blustery pragmatic tycoon who has bullied his way to the top and believes he can impose his will on any one and any thing. At the same time, he feels his lack of background and tries to compensate by consuming large amounts of "culture"; he fancies himself an instant expert on art, history, poetry, and literature because he has bought and paid for great quantities of it. Stoke, on the other hand, represents inherited wealth, position, and formal education. He considers himself a thinker and speaks in long, abstract, convoluted sentences that turn the simplest thing into a complex metaphysical problem. Their hilarious debate over the nature of a "primrose" would not be out of place in an "Absurd" play by Eugene Ionesco.

But, regardless of their differences, both men are embodiments of the British Capitalist. Their various pretensions and blind spots set them up as perfect dupes for the canny rural Irish workmen. The chief symbol of the play is, of course, the absurd Tudor house they mean to refurbish as a way of making a connection with the historical grandeur of the past (Tudor England restored in rural Ireland!) as well as finding pastoral simplicity in the present. They add any object to the house that seems vaguely historical, regardless of its authenticity or its appropriateness—a "Jacobean" table, "Cambodian" bowl (out of Woolworth's), a set of medieval armor, a "quattrocento" bureau—while at the same time denying themselves such "luxuries" as modern indoor plumbing and electricity on the grounds that they are historically inauthentic.

Their pseudo-culture soon turns to disaster—the bowls are smashed, the bureau is broken to pieces, and finally the house itself is submerged. Their dream of bucolic simplicity likewise turns into a nightmare; the animals keep them awake at night, a cow wanders into the house and they flee in terror from the "wild beast," and the gentle autumn rain grows into a flood that inundates them all.

But O'Casey is not attacking tradition as such—only a false, pretentious, and ignorant use of it. Opposed to the Old English Capitalists are the Young Irish Workers and two of them, Jack O'Killigain and Philip O'Dempsey, articulate O'Casey's positive vision of man, tradition, and Ireland. Poges' ignorance of history is contrasted with O'Dempsey's profound grasp of his heroic historical and cultural background. He divorces himself from most of his contemporaries and aligns himself with the Irish heroes of the past. These visions are put into action when, as the flood waters start pouring in on Poges and Stoke, O'Killigain and O'Dempsey spirit their women, Avril and Souhaun, off to a mountain sanctuary. The survivors of the new flood will be the young, the passionate, and the truly Irish.

THE PURPLE LAND

Type of work: Novel
Author: W. H. Hudson (1841-1922)
Type of plot: Adventure romance
Time of plot: Nineteenth century
Locale: Uruguay and Argentina
First published: 1885

Principal characters:
RICHARD LAMB, an English adventurer
PAQUITA, his wife
DOÑA ISIDORA, her aunt
LUCERO, a horse tamer
MARCOS MARCO, General Coloma
MARGARITA, his daughter
DON PERALTA, a mad landowner
DEMETRIA PERALTA, his daughter

Critique:

The Purple Land is a story of romantic adventure, perhaps not quite so entertaining as *Green Mansions*, but with merits of its own. The reader gets an insight into the lives and environment of the people of an unhappy far-off purple land in revolutionary South America. Hudson is one of the great masters of sensuous prose. Perhaps the reason for this stylistic skill is the fact that he was a botanist and the keenness of observation required in scientific writing is reflected in his choice of adjectives and verbs.

The Story:

Richard Lamb married Paquita without her father's consent and eloped with her to Montevideo. There they went to see Doña Isidora, a relative of Paquita, and stayed with her for some time. Doña Isidora gave Lamb a letter to the overseer of the *Estancia de la Virgen de los Desamparados,* a ranch called in English Vagabond's Rest.

Lamb departed with the letter, and in the Florida department he began to learn the history of the unhappy land of Uruguay. The Argentines and Brazilians interfered in the country's politics, and, as if the foreign influences were not enough to cause trouble, there was constant friction between the country and the town districts. At a pulpería, or tavern, he met Lucero, a horse tamer, and went to stay at his house; but he soon left Lucero and continued his journey to the estancia.

Lamb took advantage of rustic hospitality throughout his journey. One night he stayed at a house in which lived a family with many children. The children were all named after particular Christian concepts, such as Conception and Ascension. However, there were far too many insects infesting the house for his comfort, and he departed early the next day. Lamb continued his journey through Lucuarembó department and then entered the county of his destination. There he discovered that Doña Isidora's letter meant nothing; there was no employment for him.

During his stay at the estancia he had a fight with a man called Barbudo and gained a reputation for being a great fighter. When he discovered that his reputation as a fighter would only lead to more and bloodier fights, he decided to return to Montevideo.

At Toloso, Lamb met a group of English expatriates in a pulpería, and he remained with his fellow countrymen for a time. Finally he found them to be quite worthless and quarreled with them. Then he headed once more for Montevideo. In the Florida department he met a lovely girl named Margarita and helped her get her doves from a branch in a tree.

THE PURPLE LAND by W. H. Hudson. Published by E. P. Dutton & Co., Inc.

Margarita was so different from the rest of her family that Lamb could not help wondering how she came to be born into such a rough, coarse family. There he met Anselmo, who was an indefatigable talker and teller of pointless tales. There, too, he met Marcos Marco.

Lamb and Marcos started out to go to Montevideo together, but on the way they were captured by an army detail and taken prisoners because Lamb had neglected to get a passport. They were taken before a justice of the peace at Las Cuevas. Through the machinations of the justice's fat wife, Lamb was free to move about until his trial. Marcos, however, was imprisoned. Lamb talked the fat wife into giving him the key to the fetters which bound his friend Marcos. Lamb freed his friend so that Marcos would be able to sleep comfortably in his captivity, but Marcos took advantage of his opportunity and escaped during the night. Lamb, being a lover of nature, captured a small snake and used it as a means to ward off the attentions of the justice's wife. He was finally released.

Later, at the estate of Alday, he first heard of General Santa Coloma, who in reality was Marcos Marco. He told Anita, an orphan living with the Aldays, the story of Alma, who wanted a playmate, and Little Niebla. Anita wanted a playmate too and the next morning she ran off to find one. Monica, the daughter of the household, searched for and found Anita. Monica then asked Lamb to tell her a story out of the great store of anecdotes he knew.

Lamb was taken to see General Colo-

ma, whom he recognized as his friend Marcos. He joined the general and fought in the battle of San Paulo. The general explained to Lamb the mystery of Margarita; she was Coloma's daughter.

When the battle of San Paulo ended badly for the general's army, Lamb escaped. At a pulpería he met Gandara, who wanted to take him prisoner because he had been a member of General Coloma's army. Lamb shot Gandara and escaped. He stayed for a time at the home of an expatriate Scotsman named John Carrickfergus, but soon he continued his journey to Montevideo.

His next important stop was at the home of Don Peralta, who was demented. Don Peralta had lost a son, Calixto, who had been killed in battle several years before. Demetria Peralta, the daughter, was the heir to the estate, but she and everyone else were under the thumb of Don Hilario, the supervisor of the estate. When Lamb rode away, he left with Santos, a servant, who told him the history of the Peralta family. Demetria wished to marry Lamb and thus be able to take over and administer the property which was really hers. Lamb could not marry her, but he arranged to abduct her and take her to Montevideo, where she would be safe from Hilario. When they arrived safely in Montevideo, Paquita looked after Demetria as if she were her own sister. From Montevideo they went to Buenos Aires, where the unsanctioned marriage of Lamb and Paquita promised to give still more trouble for the young couple.

Further Critical Evaluation of the Work:

Curiously, William Henry Hudson is not as famous for the two books (*The Purple Land* and *Far Away and Long Ago*) that he wrote about an area that he knew well (the pampa of Uruguay and Argentina), but for *Green Mansions,* a book written about an area that he did not know well (the Venezuelan jungle). Part of *The Purple Land*'s true worth has thus escaped critics, who have not fully appreciated its worth as a socio-historical documentary about an interesting part of the world during the embryonic decades of its history. Hudson knew and loved the pampa well. He had the unusual experience of being a talented Anglo-Saxon bred in the pampa during wild times. His powers of observation and description were notable, and we are indebted to him for colorful vignettes of pampa life during the middle of the nineteenth century.

Many social types of Uruguay are clearly drawn in the pages of *The Purple Land*. The confusion of the times is also mirrored, when a wild, loosely-knit society was taking control of the rolling, green pampa of Uruguay, a place blessed with deep top soil, green grass, and ample water. Armies of gaucho cavalry flying white pennants from their lance tips (the *Blancos,* or Whites) battled armies of gaucho cavalry flying red pennants from their lance tips (the *Colorados,* or Reds). They initiated the traditional struggle between these two political factions for dominance of the Republic of the Left Bank (*Banda Oriental,* or East Bank) of the Uruguay River. Richard Lamb's adventures are therefore more meaningful than they may seem at first glance, for through them we gain insights into the Uruguayan life of the times. Many rural types, customs, and above all the terrible political drawbacks of the times are depicted.

Lamb's apparently aimless travels are also typical of the life of the times, and Hudson enriches his narrative with many details of sociology and natural science. The interesting and adventurous phases of life on the rolling pampa, with its purple tints at twilight, are also given us. Therefore, even though Uruguayan literature has produced some of the best works from South America in the novel and poetry, this novel written by a foreigner occupies a position of merit in the letters of Uruguay.

PYGMALION

Type of work: Drama
Author: Bernard Shaw (1856-1950)
Time: c. 1900
Locale: London
First presented: 1913

Principal characters:
  HENRY HIGGINS, a phonetician
  ELIZA DOOLITTLE, a flower girl
  ALFRED DOOLITTLE, her father, a dustman
  COLONEL PICKERING, another phonetician
  FREDDY EYNSFORD HILL, a poor young gentleman

Throughout his career Shaw agitated for the reform of the vagaries of English spelling and pronunciation; nevertheless his assertion is immaterial that *Pygmalion* was written to impress upon the public the importance of phoneticians in modern society. *Pygmalion,* like all of Shaw's best plays, transcends its author's didactic intent. The play will continue to be performed and read, not for indoctrination into one of Shaw's pet theories, but for the laughter its characters provoke.

The play is a modern adaptation of the Pygmalion myth (though some have claimed that it is a plagiarism of Tobias Smollett's *Peregrine Pickle),* in which the sculptor-king Pygmalion falls in love with a creature of his making, a statue which Aphrodite, pitying him, brings to life. The Pygmalion of Shaw's play turns up as Henry Higgins, a teacher of English speech; his Galatea, Eliza Doolittle, a cockney flower girl whom Higgins transforms into a seeming English lady, mainly by teaching her to speak cultivated English. In the process of transforming a poor girl into a lady, Higgins irrevocably changes a human life. By lifting Eliza above her own class and providing her with only the appurtenances of another, Higgins makes her unfit for both. On this change and Higgins' stubborn refusal to accept its reality and its consequences, Shaw builds his play.

From the beginning, when Higgins first observes her dialectal monstrosities, Eliza is characterized as a proud, stubborn girl, even though educated only by the cru-

dities of poverty and the gutter. Brassy enough to ask Higgins to make good his boast that he can pass her off as a duchess within three months, she calls on him and offers to pay him for elocution lessons which will take her off the streets and into a position as saleswoman in a flower shop. Like all the proud, she is also sensitive, and she tries to break off the interview when Higgins persists in treating her as his social inferior. Little wonder, then, that months later, when Higgins has indeed proved his boast, she resents his indifference toward her and her future, and, after telling him what a cad he is, runs away to his mother, who has befriended her.

Higgins can best be understood in contrast to Colonel Pickering, his foil, who finances the transformation. As a fellow phonetician, Pickering approves of the project as a scientific experiment, but as a gentleman he sympathizes with Eliza as a sensitive human being. It is Higgins' uproariously tragic flaw that he, like all of Shaw's heroes, is not a gentleman. He is brilliant and cultured, but he lacks manners and refuses to learn or even affect any, believing himself to be superior to the conventions and civilities of polite society and preferring to treat everyone with bluntness and candor. He is, or so he thinks until Eliza leaves him, a self-sufficient man. When he discovers that she has made herself an indispensable part of his life, he goes to her and in one of the most remarkable courtship scenes in the history of the theater pleads with her to live with Pickering and himself as three dedicated bachelors. At the end of the play he is confident that she will accept his unorthodox proposition, even when she bids him goodbye forever.

As a matter of fact, Shaw himself was never able to convince anyone that Eliza and Higgins did not marry and live happily ever after. The first producer of the play, Sir Herbert Beerbohm Tree, insisted on leaving the impression that the two were reconciled in the end as lovers, and this tradition has persisted. Enraged as always by any liberties taken with his work, Shaw wrote an essay which he attached to the play as a sequel denouncing any sentimental interpretation of *Pygmalion*.

He concedes that *Pygmalion* is a romance in that its heroine undergoes an almost miraculous change, but he argues that the logic of the characterization does not permit a conventional happy ending. Higgins is, after all, a god and Eliza only his creation, so that an abyss separates them. Furthermore, Shaw contends, their personalities, backgrounds, and philosophies are irreconcilable. Higgins is an inveterate bachelor and likely to remain one because he will never find a woman who can meet the standards he has set for ideal womanhood—those set by his mother. Eliza, on the other hand, being young and pretty, can always find a husband whose demands on a woman would not be impossible to meet. Therefore, Shaw insists, Eliza marries Freddy Eynsford Hill, a penniless but devoted young man who played only an insignificant role in the play itself. Stubbornly, Shaw would not even permit them the luxury of living happily ever after: they have financial problems which are gradually solved by opening a flower shop subsidized by Colonel Pickering. Shaw's Pyg-

malion is too awe-inspiring for his Galatea ever to presume to love him.

Even with the addition of such an unconventional ending to the play, *Pygmalion* would be highly atypical of Shavian drama were it not for the presence of Alfred Doolittle, Eliza's father. Through Doolittle, Shaw is able to indulge in economic and social moralizing, an ingredient Shaw could not dispense with. Like Eliza, Doolittle undergoes a transformation as a result of Higgins' meddling, a transformation that is unpremeditated, however, in his case. Early in the play Doolittle fascinates Higgins and Pickering by his successful attempt to capitalize on Eliza's good fortune. He literally charms Higgins out of five pounds by declaring himself an implacable foe of middle-class morality and insisting that he will use the money for a drunken spree. Delighted with the old scoundrel, Higgins mentions him in jest to a crackpot American millionaire who subsequently bequeathes Doolittle a yearly allowance of three thousand pounds if he will lecture on morality. Thus he becomes a dustman transformed into a lion of London society, a reprobate changed into a victim of bourgeois morality. Although he appears only twice in the play, Doolittle is so vigorous and funny that he is almost as memorable a comic character as Higgins.

The truth of the matter is that the play itself is memorable because of its vigor and fun, notwithstanding Shaw's protestations about its didacticism. The reason why Shaw did protest so much in his insistence on the serious intent of the play may lie in his realization that *Pygmalion* was his least serious, least didactic, play.

QUALITY STREET

Type of work: Drama
Author: James M. Barrie (1860-1937)
Type of plot: Comedy of manners
Time of plot: Napoleonic wars
Locale: English provincial village
First presented: 1902

Principal characters:
    Miss Phoebe Throssel, a spinster
    Miss Susan Throssel, her sister
    Valentine Brown, loved by Phoebe

Critique:

This play contains acute if not very penetrating observations on the problem of a wartime love affair in which the lovers are apart for ten years, during which time both change superficially. Most of the action is based on the heroine's successful attempt to bring her lover to his senses. Barrie employs dramatic irony quite effectively throughout and the minimum of privacy in the lives of people in a small village is brought out with good comic effect.

The Story:

In the days of the Napoleonic wars, two sisters, Phoebe and Susan Throssel, lived in a little house in Quality Street, the main thoroughfare of a provincial English village. Both were single, both were pretty. One day they entertained a needlework party in their charming blue and white parlor. One of the ladies present repeated a rumor that a gentleman of the village had enlisted to go to the wars. All wondered who the gentleman could be.

Phoebe told her sister that Valentine Brown, a dashing doctor who had come to the village two years before, had walked with her in the street, and had said that he wanted to tell her something important. The retiring Phoebe had asked Brown to come to the house to tell her. Both sisters assumed that Brown was coming to propose marriage to Phoebe, a likely conclusion since a venture in which Brown had invested their savings had

failed and he would naturally feel responsible for their welfare. In anticipation of his proposal, Susan gave Phoebe a wedding dress which she had made for her own marriage, a wedding which had never materialized.

But to Phoebe's disappointment and humiliation, Brown said nothing of marriage. Instead, he told them that he was the man who had enlisted. He declared his friendship for both sisters and his liking for the little blue and white parlor, but he gave no indication of love for Phoebe, who had given her heart to him. Ironically, Phoebe revealed her disappointment by telling Brown that she had thought he was going to announce his marriage and that they were curious to know the name of the fortunate young lady. The sisters, out of pride, did not mention that the loss of their investment left them all but destitute. They planned to set up a school in their house.

Ten years later Susan and Phoebe were still conducting their school, which had prospered in spite of their many shortcomings as teachers. They were loved, but hardly respected by the older children. Dancing and the more gentle acquirements they taught with pleasure, but they detested Latin, and would teach algebra only at the request of their pupils' parents. They could not bring themselves to whip the older boys, most of whom they feared.

The wars were over at last, and everywhere people were celebrating the victory at Waterloo. On Quality Street all but Susan and Phoebe were preparing for a village ball that night. While Phoebe was out of the house, Captain Valentine Brown, who had lost his left hand during a battle on the continent, came to call on his dear old friends. Disappointed at the disappearance of the delightful blue and white parlor, he paid his respects to Miss Susan and asked to see Phoebe of the ringlets and the dancing eyes. When Phoebe returned, Captain Brown could not hide his dismay at the way she had changed into a drab, mouselike spinster. Phoebe was hurt by his unconcealed feelings. She was further hurt later in the day when a former pupil, now Ensign Blades and a veteran, asked her, under duress, to attend the ball with him. Miserable, Phoebe declined. But Phoebe was only thirty and tired of teaching. Inspired by Susan and by Patty, the maid, she transformed herself into the Phoebe of ten years before. When Brown came again, he failed to recognize Phoebe, and he was told that she was the sisters' niece. Completely taken in and charmed by "Miss Livvy," he asked her to accompany him to the ball. "Livvy" teased him, to his discomfort, about his gray hairs.

At later balls and parties of the victory celebration, "Livvy" continued to capture the fancy of all the young men of the village. Difficulties posed by the dual existence of Phoebe-"Livvy" were met by the explanation that Phoebe or "Livvy" was either out or indisposed.

At one ball the swains hovered about "Livvy" constantly, but Captain Brown stoutly held his place as her escort. The sisters' gossipy spinster neighbors, who lived across the street and observed their comings and goings, began to suspect that something was not quite right. They were almost in a position to expose

Phoebe at the ball, but Susan saved the day by lending another young lady "Livvy's" coat. Captain Brown, alone with "Livvy," told her of his love for Phoebe, explaining that he had fallen in love with Phoebe during the balls because of "Livvy's" resemblance to the Phoebe of days gone by. "Livvy," the flirt, had made Captain Brown realize that he was no longer twenty-five and that he preferred, after all, the retiring, modest, quiet Phoebe.

School over, the parlor was redecorated with its blue and white frills for the summer holiday. Phoebe, tiring of her dual role, announced that "Livvy" had been taken sick, and became the tired schoolteacher again. The gossips who came to call were more suspicious than ever because no doctor had visited "Livvy." They almost discovered that there was no one in the sick room, but they prudently did not go beyond the partly opened door.

That day Captain Brown came to propose to Phoebe. When the sisters left the parlor for a moment, he entered the sick room and found it empty. Then he heard the entire story from Patty, the maid. Captain Brown was amused, but carried on the masquerade when "Livvy" came out of the sick room and announced her recovery. The sisters were stupefied when he offered to take "Livvy" to her home twenty miles away. They stepped out of the parlor to have a hurried consultation, but they knew that Captain Brown had found them out when they heard him talking to a "Livvy" he devised with pillows and a shawl and which he carried out to a waiting coach, to the satisfaction of the gossips who were watching from their windows.

Miss Susan Throssel announced the forthcoming marriage of her sister Phoebe to Captain Valentine Brown. The reopening of school was quite forgotten.

Further Critical Evaluation of the Work:

James Barrie's best plays are those in which he treads the thin line between "reality" and "fantasy" with the touches of fantasy adding a lively, imaginative dimension to the essentially realistic situations (except for *Peter Pan,* where touches of reality sharpen the meaning of the fantasy). *Quality Street* is a charming "realistic fantasy" about a prolonged love affair that finally succeeds against the obstacles of time, age, and human misunderstanding.

Even in 1902, the subject matter and attitudes present in the play would have seemed dated, had Barrie not taken the edge off of the play's realism with a number of adroit theatrical devices. His touch is light, sentimental, and gently ironic so that one is moved by the plight of the spinster sisters, but does not take them too seriously. By placing his story in an English provincial village during the Napoleonic wars and emphasizing period settings and costumes, Barrie further distances his action from the modern world and so justifies actions and speeches for his characters that would be excessive and trite in a modern context. But the appeal of the play can probably best be accounted for by the fact that in mood and feeling it is close to a fairy tale.

The specific fairy tale is "Cinderella." Phoebe Throssel is the girl kept from her Prince Charming, Valentine Brown, not by conniving stepsisters, but by her intended's perversity in enlisting in the army rather than proposing to her. Upon his return ten years later, it is age, exaggerated by Phoebe's spinsterly role as schoolmarm, that keeps them apart. The transformation is occasioned not by magical intervention, but by Phoebe's own frustration.

So she effects her change—into her own niece Livvy—and goes off to the ball. There, like her prototype, she charms everyone including the object of her affections, but must keep her true identity a secret. The "glass slipper" which reveals the heroine and resolves the hero to marry her is replaced by the more conventional device of a talkative maid. Valentine Brown is converted by his flirtation with Livvy to the idea that it is Phoebe he really wants because she is mature and lady-like. They will live, as in all fairy tales, happily ever after, with Phoebe getting her Prince Charming and Valentine getting both the lady-like Phoebe and the flirtatious "Livvy" in one woman.

Whether or not such a conclusion would be acceptable in the modern world—either Barrie's or our own—is very doubtful. But "Quality Street" is no more real than "Never Land," and, while not so obviously a "wish-fulfillment" play, *Quality Street* is as much a fairy tale for adults as *Peter Pan* is for youngsters.

QUEEN VICTORIA

Type of work: Biography
Author: Lytton Strachey (1880-1932)
Time: 1819-1901
Locale: England and Germany
First published: 1921

Principal personages:

GEORGE IV, King of England, whose death brought Victoria to the
throne

THE DUKE OF KENT, Victoria's father

THE PRINCESS OF SAXE-COBURG, Victoria's mother

ALEXANDRINA VICTORIA, Queen Victoria of England

FRÄULEIN LEHZEN, Victoria's influencial governess

BARON STOCKMAR, King Leopold's physician and adviser, later Victoria's and Prince Albert's

KING LEOPOLD OF BELGIUM, Victoria's uncle

PRINCE ALBERT OF SAXE-COBURG, Victoria's cousin and influencial,
beloved husband

VICTORIA, THE PRINCESS ROYAL,

EDWARD, PRINCE OF WALES,

PRINCESS ALICE,

PRINCE ALFRED,

PRINCESS HELENA,

PRINCESS LOUISE,

PRINCE ARTHUR,

PRINCE LEOPOLD, and

PRINCESS BEATRICE, the nine royal children

LORD MELBOURNE,

WILLIAM LAMB,

SIR ROBERT PEEL,

LORD PALMERSTON,

HENRY JOHN TEMPLE,

BENJAMIN DISRAELI, and

WILLIAM EWART GLADSTONE, influencial Prime Ministers

Objecting to the standard "life" of the nineteenth century biographer, Lytton Strachey founded a significant new school of biography. He transformed the ideal biography from a long, redundant eulogy to a concise, clear, and factual account of the subject's life. With the publication of *Queen Victoria* he graphically illustrated that biography could be an art without following the "classical models" of Boswell's *Johnson* or Lockhart's *Scott*. The small biography is restrained; the author is detached; the tone is ironic; and the style is polished. *Queen Victoria* presents a woman as well as a queen, a woman who comes alive as we share Strachey's impressions of her long life.

Strachey opens the biography with an inevitably complicated résumé of the future queen's disreputable—indeed scandalous—uncles, especially of the notorious Prince Regent, who became George IV, and the Duke of Clarence, later King William IV. Victoria's father, the Duke of Kent, the fourth son of George III, married only when he thought that he and his children might succeed to the English throne. Victoria's mother, the Princess of Saxe-Coburg, discovered after her marriage that her husband was impoverished, but she also knew that if she could bear a child before her sisters-in-law, that child would be ruler of England. On May 24, 1819, she gave birth, but the child was a girl, later to be christened Alexandrina Victoria against her father's wishes. This birth was practically ignored; the English were waiting for the birth of a boy.

The child, reared in obscurity at Kensington, was placed under the governance of Fräulein Lehzen, daughter of a Hanoverian clergyman and the only person who could control the little "Drina's" outbursts of temper. Under the influence of this governess the future queen was taught to be horrified at the shameless behavior of her uncles, and always to be mindful of the virtues of simplicity, regularity, propriety, and devotion. Victoria never forgot her lessons. The Duchess of Kent had decided that her daughter would become a "Christian queen," regardless of the child's happiness. When Victoria was eleven, her mother invited the Bishops of London and Lincoln and the Archbishop of Canterbury to examine her; she passed, displaying a great variety of Christian knowledge. Still she was not told that she was, in fact, to be Queen of England. When she finally learned of the responsibility eventually to be thrust upon her, she calmly accepted her duty.

But before the day when she would actually become Queen of England, two things happened to the young girl: she met and fell madly in love with her cousin, Prince Albert of Saxe-Coburg, and she discovered that her mother was having an affair with Sir John Conroy. When Victoria became queen, she entirely separated herself from her mother and momentarily forgot the "beautiful" German prince. She fell under the rigid influence of Fräulein Lehzen and of the Prime Minister, William Lamb, Viscount Melbourne, and she thought that she was happy. She thought that she was free to do as she pleased without her mother's prying eyes, but the eyes and advice of Lehzen and Melbourne were as prying and confining as her mother had been. For example, Victoria was led by her advisers to believe the groundless rumors against Lady Flora Hastings and, as a result, lost the support of the English public. Also she interfered with the government more than many of her subjects thought she should, and thereby she turned the English against her.

In 1840 she married Prince Albert, with whom she was still madly in love. Albert, however, had a will of his own and was not in love with his doting bride. Although he was his wife's intellectual superior and interested in the arts, she let him entertain no scholars or literary men. He had a much better mind for politics, but she was so influenced by Fräulein Lehzen that she would not discuss politics with him. In short, Prince Albert was a miserably unhappy young man who felt that fate had tricked him into an unpleasant marriage. But the prince was advised by clever Baron Stockmar, one of the best political advisers in Europe, and Stockmar taught him the way to make his will known. Victoria worshiped her husband, and he used her feelings for his own ends. Very slowly Fräulein Lehzen was pushed into the background and Prince Albert became the leading power behind the throne. In fact, he finally exerted so much influence over Victoria that he was King of England in everything but name. He was still bored, without sympathy for the English whom he considered either too frivolous or too gloomy and unhappy.

Despite Prince Albert's unhappiness, Queen Victoria was happy. Her family was growing; she thought that she was married to the wisest and most perfect man in the world, to the extent that she despised her subjects when they did not agree; and she was untroubled by political intrigue. Prince Albert discovered a way to forget his misery; he lost himself in his work. First, he reformed the organization of the royal household, overcoming abuses and saving much money. Second, he became Victoria's private secretary, had a full voice in politics, and was respected for his well-conceived opinions on political matters. Third, he organized the Great Exhibition of 1851, symbol of

English ingenuity and of the full bloom of the Victorian Age. The Great Exhibition took two years to complete and cost so much that popularity turned against Albert. But when it closed, over six million people had visited it and England had been recognized as the first industrial power in Europe.

But the Great Exhibition was followed by trouble from one man, especially hated by the royal couple: Lord Palmerston. Palmerston was ambitious, crude, and impatient; he played the game of international politics cynically, much to Prince Albert's horror, and aided revolutionists, republican movements, and the overthrows of the monarchies throughout Europe, much to Victoria's horror. In fact, he seemed to be a fanatic who did not realize the consequences of his behavior. The dispute between the royal couple and the ambitious politician involved England in one of the most senseless wars of her history, the Crimean War between Russia and Turkey. The issues of this war were not clear; the end of the war was mysterious. But Lord Palmerston became Prime Minister as a result of it.

Despite the political intrigue, Victoria was happy in her three-fold role of queen, wife, and mother, and she had become a symbol of the ideal, especially in the last two roles. Her nine children, her farms, and her dairies needed to be looked after with the same care that she employed in the affairs of her country. The Prince of Wales was a special problem for her because he refused to adhere to the "obligations" laid down by his mother and father. Her children began to marry into the royal houses of Europe, and she passed many days with her consort in almost idyllic happiness. But such happiness was not to last. In 1861 Prince Albert became sick and died, partly because Victoria had refused to believe the seriousness of his condition and call better doctors to his bedside.

This was the turning point of her life. From Prince Albert's death until her own, she was a mysterious figure to the English, a woman clothed in black and separated from the ordinary affairs of life. She felt her loss more deeply than most because she had become so dependent on her consort for advice; in fact, she felt that with his death England had lost a sovereign. Consequently, she was determined to spend the rest of her life convincing the English people that Albert had really been what she believed he was. She supervised the publication of massive biographies, intrigued to have statues of him erected in major cities, and finally planned and executed a magnificent memorial, Albert Hall. Still she was not cheerful. Her popularity had decreased so much that people openly questioned whether a royal family was worth the money and greatly curtailed the royal allowance. Victoria felt that she was surrounded by hostility, by people who refused to sympathize with her grief, and she came to hate her subjects more and more. But all was not so gloomy. Disraeli, now Prime Minister, won her respect and full support and lightened her unhappiness by such little things as calling her "Faery"—an allusion to Gloriana in *The Faerie Queene*—and giving her the title "Empress of India." She responded with such delightful trivia as gifts of primroses and a peerage. Also, Gladstone's adoration of her as a figure mysteriously and augustly set above and apart from others caused the public to begin to view her with increasing awe; few of her subjects could remember any other monarch. This adoration did two things: it strengthened the position of the crown but weakened the political power of the monarch. Also the seven frustrated attempts to assassinate her ennobled her in her subjects' eyes.

Toward the end of her long life, Victoria had become an institution and a symbol. Her manners and morals were impeccable: for example, she never allowed a divorced woman to enter court and she frowned on second marriages. She even kept Prince Albert's room as a shrine. Her strong sense of duty was an institution shared by her public. Also she was the symbol of the age that bears her name, especially of the imperialism that she so stanchly supported. When she died on January 22, 1901, an age died with her.

Lytton Strachey has not been always fair with the facts, but he has created his impressions in such a clear-cut and fascinating manner that he sweeps the reader into the life of Victoria, revealed as a woman, a great but intellectually limited queen, and a loving wife.

THE QUEEN'S NECKLACE

Type of work: Novel
Author: Alexandre Dumas, *père* (1802-1870)
Type of plot: Historical romance
Time of plot: Eighteenth century
Locale: France
First published: 1848

Principal characters:
MARIE ANTOINETTE, Queen of France
JEANNE DE LA MOTTE VALOIS, an impoverished noblewoman
CARDINAL DE ROHAN
PHILIPPE DE TAVERNEY, a courtier
ANDRÉE DE TAVERNEY, his sister
COUNT DE CHARNY, a naval officer
OLIVA, a girl resembling the queen
COUNT CAGLIOSTRO, an Italian adventurer and supposed magician

Critique:

Always a defender of the integrity of the monarchy, Dumas here presents a lively picture of court intrigue and royal passion. As a mystery story this novel presents not one loose thread or irrelevant detail. As historical fiction it attempts to describe the person of Marie Antoinette as a woman of extreme charm, intelligence, and honor. Count Cagliostro, a character in several romances by Dumas, is again in this book a sinister and mysterious figure motivating the action.

The Story:

The Countess Jeanne de La Motte Valois, a descendant of the fallen royal house of Valois, aspired to return to favor in the court of Louis XVI. Suffering extreme poverty, she was honored by a visit from the queen, who gave her money and promised her assistance.

The queen was always a victim of intrigues by her enemies. Even on the night when she had, with the assistance of Andrée de Taverney, made a charitable visit to the Countess de La Motte, one of her enemies had whispered into the king's ear that her majesty had gone on a nocturnal mission of doubtful purpose. Her honesty and proud demeanor put the king to shame, however, and as a conciliatory gesture he offered her a fabulously expensive necklace, which she refused on the grounds that France needed a new battleship more than the queen needed jewels.

Andrée's brother, Philippe de Taverney, was favored by Marie Antoinette for his courtesy and grace. He promptly fell in love with her. At a court reception Philippe was thwarted in his love by perceiving that Count de Charny had won the queen's favor. It was Andrée's fate to have fallen in love with de Charny also, and she watched with jealousy the queen's innocent flirtation.

While Jeanne de La Motte was plotting to gain entrance to the royal court, Cardinal de Rohan, disliked by the queen because of his former disapproval of her marriage to King Louis, was also hoping to win a place at court. These two hopefuls, combining talents, agreed to aid one another in their ambitious projects.

Count Cagliostro, a mystic and a malicious conspirator against the nobility of France, plotted to create a public scandal about the queen. To aid him he produced an unknown girl, Oliva, whose amazing resemblance to Marie Antoinette deceived even the queen's closest friends. First Count Cagliostro sent Oliva to the salon of M. Mesmer, where she exploited her emotions publicly, drawing attention to herself. Her witnesses mistook her for the queen. Next Count Cagliostro brought the girl to a masquerade ball attended by many of the nobility in disguise, but an affair beneath the dignity of the queen. Again it was said that Marie Antoinette had appeared in public in a most ungracious manner. At the salon and at the ball Jeanne de La Motte had seen the woman who was not really the queen at all. Cardinal de Rohan had been with Jeanne at the ball. Jeanne had perceived that he loved Marie Antoinette, whose disdain for him was well-known.

Widespread gossip about her conduct reached the queen, who, anxious to belie her accusers, brought Jeanne to the king and asked her to assure the monarch that the queen had not degraded herself in the salon of M. Mesmer. The king loyally asserted that he needed no assurance from an outsider that his queen did not lie. But the gossip about Marie Antoinette's presence at the masquerade ball was not so easily explained away. The queen denied having been there; Jeanne claimed that she had seen her. Others were called as witnesses. Both Philippe and de Charny said that they had recognized her when her mask dropped off. King Louis came to the queen's rescue by vowing that he had been with her in her apartment on the night of the ball.

Jeanne, guided by her intuition, knew that the queen coveted the beautiful necklace that the king had wanted to purchase for her from the jewelers, Boehmer and Bossange. When Jeanne assured de Rohan that the queen would be pleased to own the necklace, he, hoping to buy her royal favor, arranged to purchase it by delivering a down payment of five hundred thousand francs. Jeanne, at Versailles, promptly told Marie Antoinette of de Rohan's generous intention. Her reaction was to assume responsibility for the payment of the necklace herself; as queen, she could not accept so generous a favor from a subject. When de Rohan brought the necklace to her, she graciously dismissed the old enmity between them. Unfortunately, King Louis chose that time to be frugal and refused to grant the queen the sum of money she desired. With timely malice Count Cagliostro collected from de Rohan an old debt of five hundred thousand francs. Hearing of the transaction from Jeanne, the queen ordered her to take the necklace back to Boehmer and Bossange.

But Jeanne had her own plans. She forged a note from the jewelers to the queen acknowledging receipt of the necklace. Next she forged a note from the queen to the jewelers promising to pay the balance due them within three months. Meanwhile Jeanne kept the jewels. To safeguard her theft, she had to prevent de Rohan, who assumed that the queen had kept the necklace, from meeting Marie Antoinette. He had been told by the deceived jewelers that the queen would pay for the necklace.

Count Cagliostro assisted Jeanne in her plan by taking Oliva to live in a house close to that of Jeanne. When the two women met, Jeanne knew at once she was facing the woman who had compromised the queen by her conduct at M. Mesmer's salon and at the ball. She escorted Oliva to the park on three successive nights, and there de Rohan courted the woman he mistook for Marie Antoinette. De Charny, witnessing the amorous meeting, thought that he saw the queen. Angry and grieved, he reproached Marie Antoinette for her conduct. Again she realized that someone had been impersonating her.

When the day of payment for the necklace arrived, the jewelers petitioned the queen for their money. After an exchange of angry words, Marie Antoinette and the jewelers realized that they had been duped and that their respective notes were forgeries.

The scandal broke. De Rohan, believing that the queen was his mistress but wishing to conceal the fact for his own protection, still assumed that the queen would pay for the jewels. The jewelers thought that he would pay for them. The public thought that the queen retained the necklace so that de Rohan, for love of her, would be forced to pay, or that the king, to avert scandal, would satisfy the jewelers.

When de Charny came to offer the queen his money, she declared her intention to prove her innocence, and she placed de Charny in hiding while she conducted an interview with de Rohan.

When the deceived cardinal discreetly hinted at their secret love affair, the queen, outraged, sent for the king. De Rohan had no proof of his accusation. Still believing that he had possessed the queen and that she had kept the necklace, he was sentenced to the Bastille.

De Charny emerged from hiding to throw himself at the queen's feet just as the king returned. To explain de Charny's supplicating position, Marie Antoinette had to invent a lie. She said that he was begging for permission to marry Andrée de Taverney, who had entered a convent.

Brought before the queen, Jeanne de La Motte refused to divulge any enlightening evidence and followed de Rohan to the Bastille. Jeanne knew, however, that she controlled the situation. If pressed too hard, she could intimate that the queen and de Rohan had a reason for charging her with the theft of the necklace. Then the police discovered Oliva. Seeing her, the queen understood the intrigue that had been worked against her, but Jeanne was still able to connive and to lie about her association with Oliva so that, in the end, no one was convinced of the queen's innocence. The public, believing Marie Antoinette guilty of adultery and theft, assumed that the person known as Oliva had been invented to conceal the queen's guilt.

After the trial, Cardinal de Rohan and Count Cagliostro, also arrested, were freed. Jeanne de La Motte was publicly branded. The queen was still suspected of being involved in a scandal. No one in the palace realized all involved in the affair were themselves on the threshold of the Bastille and that the Revolution was impending.

Further Critical Evaluation of the Work:

The Queen's Necklace is a sequel to the *Memoirs of a Physician* and the second of the Marie-Antoinette series. It was written by Dumas in collaboration with Auguste Maquet. This is generally classed as the last of the most famous or great novels in which Maquet collaborated. The picturesque tragedy of the diamond necklace is narrated in Dumas' best style and is a very fine piece of work, usually considered to be a favorite with English and American readers because it moves steadily and uninterruptedly to its conclusion; there are fewer threads of plot to be followed than in some of Dumas' other novels.

In a brief introduction Dumas refers to the Revolution of 1848, just accomplished, and to his foretelling of it in 1832, in *Gaule et France.* The prologue is borrowed from La Harpe's *Prophétic de Cazotte,* but Dumas has instilled into it a great deal for spirit and life. The novel itself gives a thoroughly amusing and cleverly constructed picture of court intrigues and dissoluteness, and of the rumblings of the coming storm. It does, however, present Marie Antoinette as a sympathetic character of intelligence and charm amidst the decadence surrounding her. She is portrayed by Dumas as being victimized by her enemies, who try to cast doubts upon her honor. The queen shares with Count Cagliostro the distinction of being one of the most clearly defined characters in the novel and one who instigates most of the major action of the story—action that is lively and robust in the Dumas manner.

The novel first appeared as a serial in *La Presse in* 1849-1850 and was instrumental in helping Dumas out of some difficulties caused by a controversy surrounding the reissue of some of his earlier works in the Paris journals as new stories. The result of this controversy was a fine series of stories of which the most prominent was *The Queen's Necklace.*

QUENTIN DURWARD

Type of work: Novel
Author: Sir Walter Scott (1771-1832)
Type of plot: Historical romance
Time of plot: 1468
Locale: France and Flanders
First published: 1823

Principal characters:

QUENTIN DURWARD, a Scottish cadet
LUDOVIC LESLY (LE BALAFRÉ), his maternal uncle
ISABELLE, Countess of Croye, disguised as Jacqueline, a servant
LADY HAMELINE, her aunt
KING LOUIS XI
COUNT PHILIP DE CRÈVECŒUR, of Burgundy
CHARLES, Duke of Burgundy
WILLIAM DE LA MARCK, a Flemish outlaw
HAYRADDIN MAUGRABIN, a Bohemian

Critique:

Quentin Durward was one of the many Scotsmen who sought their fortunes abroad in the service of foreign kings, and the story of his adventures is the first of Scott's novels with a foreign setting. There is no doubt in the mind of the reader that Scott liked this Scotsman very much because the character of the hero is the idealized younger son who goes out to seek fortune with nothing but his own wit and bravery. *Quentin Durward* is among the best of Scott's novels, its authenticity little marred by some slight reorganization of actual events to implement the plot.

The Story:

When Quentin Durward, a young Scottish gentleman, approached the ford of a small river near the castle of Plessis-les-Tours, in France, he found the river in flood. Two people watched him from the opposite bank. They were King Louis XI in his common disguise of Maître Pierre, a merchant, and Tristan l'Hermite, marshal of France. Quentin entered the flood and nearly drowned. Arriving on the other side and mistaking the king and his companion for a respectable burgher and a butcher, he threatened the two with a drubbing because they had not warned him of the deep ford. Amused by the lad's spirit and daring, Maître Pierre took him to breakfast at a nearby inn to make amends. At the inn Quentin met a beautiful young peasant girl, Jacqueline. Actually, Jacqueline was Isabelle, Countess of Croye. Quentin tried to learn why the merchant, Maître Pierre, acted so much like a noble. He saw many other things which aroused his curiosity but for which he found no explanation.

Shortly afterward Quentin met Ludovic Lesly, known as Le Balafré, his maternal uncle, who was a member of King Louis' Scottish Archers. Le Balafré was exceedingly surprised to learn that Quentin could read and write, something which neither a Durward nor a Lesly had heretofore been able to do.

Quentin discovered the body of a man hanging from a tree. When he cut the man down, he was seized by two officers of Tristan l'Hermite. They were about to hang Quentin for his deed when he asked if there were a good Christian in the crowd who would inform Le Balafré of what was taking place. A Scottish archer heard him and cut his bonds. While they prepared to defend themselves from the mob, Le Balafré rode up with some of his men and took command of the situation, haughtily insisting that Quentin was a member of the Scottish Archers and beyond the reach of the marshal's men. Quentin had not joined the guards as yet, but the lie saved his life. Le Balafré took Quentin to see Lord Crawford, the commander of the guards, to enroll him. When the Scottish Archers were summoned to the royal presence, Quentin was amazed to see that Maître Pierre was King Louis.

Count Philip de Crèvecœur arrived at the castle to demand audience with the king in the name of his master, the Duke of Burgundy. When the king admitted De Crèvecœur, the messenger presented a list of wrongs and oppressions, committed on the frontier, for which the Duke of Burgundy demanded redress. The duke also requested that Louis cease his secret and underhand dealings in the towns of Ghent, Liège and Malines, and, further, that the king send back to Burgundy, under safeguard, the person of Isabelle, Countess of Croye, the duke's ward, whom he accused the king of harboring in secret. Dissatisfied with the king's replies to these demands, De Crèvecœur threw his gauntlet to the floor of the hall. Several of the king's attendants rushed to pick it up and to accept the challenge, but the king ordered the Bishop of Auxerre to lift the gauntlet and to remonstrate with De Crèvecœur for thus declaring war between Burgundy and France. The king and his courtiers then left to hunt wild boars.

During the chase Quentin Durward saved the king's life by spearing a wild boar when Louis slipped and fell before the infuriated beast. The king decided to reward Quentin with a special mission. He was ordered to stand guard in the room where the king entertained De Crèvecœur and others, and at a sign from the king Quentin was to shoot the Burgundian. But the king changed his mind; the signal was not given. Then the king made Quentin the personal bodyguard of Isabelle and her aunt, Lady Hameline, on their way to seek the protection of the Bishop of Liège.

En route to Liège the party was assaulted by the Count de Dunois and the Duke of Orleans. Quentin defended himself with great courage and received timely help from Lord Crawford, who arrived with a body of Scottish Archers. Lord Crawford made both men prisoners. The party's guide on the second half of

the journey was Hayraddin Maugrabin, a Bohemian, whose brother it was whom Quentin had cut down earlier. Nothing untoward occurred until the small party reached Flanders. There Quentin discovered, by following Hayraddin, that a plot had been hatched to attack his party and carry off the women to William de la Marck, the Wild Boar of Ardennes. Quentin frustrated these plans by going up the left bank of the Maes instead of the right. He proceeded safely to Liège, where he gave over the women into the protection of the bishop at his castle of Schonwaldt. Four days later William de la Marck attacked the castle and captured it during the night. Lady Hameline escaped. In the bishop's throne room in the castle William de la Marck murdered the churchman in front of his own episcopal throne. Quentin, aroused by the brutality of William, stepped to the side of Carl Eberson, William's son, and placed his dirk at the boy's throat, threatening to kill the lad if William did not cease his butchery. In the confusion Quentin found Isabelle and took her safely from the castle in the disguise of the daughter of the Syndic of Liège. They were pursued by William's men, but were rescued by a party under Count de Crèvecœur, who conducted them safely to the court of the Duke of Burgundy at Peroune.

The king came to the castle of the Duke of Burgundy, asserting the royal prerogative of visiting any of his vassals. Disregarding the laws of hospitality, the duke imprisoned Louis and then held a council to debate the difficulties between France and Burgundy. Hayraddin appeared as a herald from William de la Marck, who had married the Lady Hameline. But Toison d'Or, the duke's herald, unmasked Hayraddin because he knew nothing of the science of heraldry. The duke released Hayraddin and set his fierce boar hounds upon him, but ordered the dogs called off before they tore Hayraddin to shreds. Then he ordered that Hayraddin be hanged with the proper ceremony.

The king and the duke also debated

the disposal of Isabelle's hand and fortune. But she had fallen in love with Quentin and said that she preferred the cloister to any of the suggested alliances. The duke solved the problem, at least to his satisfaction, by declaring that Isabelle's hand would be given to the man who brought him the head of William de la Marck.

The king and the duke joined forces to assault Liège. Their combined forces gallantly besieged the city but were forced to go into bivouac at nightfall. That night William made a foray but was driven back into the city. Next day the forces of the king and the duke attacked once more, made breaches in the wall, and poured into the city. Quentin came face to face with William de la Marck, who rushed at him with all the fury of the wild boar for which he was named. Le Balafré stood by and roared out for fair play, indicating that this should be a duel of champions. At that moment Quentin saw a woman being forcibly dragged along by a French soldier. When he turned to rescue her, Le Balafré attacked de la Marck and killed him.

Le Balafré was announced as the man who had killed de la Marck, but he gave most of the credit to Quentin's valiant behavior and deferred to his nephew. While it was agreed that Quentin was responsible for de la Marck's death, there was still the question of his lineage, which the duke questioned. Indignant, Lord Crawford recited the pedigree of Quentin and thereby proved his gentility. Without more ado, Quentin and the Countess Isabelle were betrothed.

Further Critical Evaluation of the Work:

Quentin Durward appeared when Sir Walter Scott's career as a novelist was nearly a decade old. Although Scott was still signing his novels "By the Author of Waverley," his authorship was by no means unknown. The "Wizard of the North" touched the familiar formulas of his fiction with an undeniable magic. With *Waverley* (1814) he had invented the historical novel, a new genre. This fictional treatment of the last of the Stuart uprisings in 1745, manifesting genuine insight into events "Sixty Years Since," had been solidly founded upon his knowledge of Scotland, its history, and its people. The author had perceived in the Jacobite-Hanoverian conflict the clash of two cultures at the very moment when the former was passing away forever and the other was just coming into being. He had made figures from history a part of his fiction, through them creating the tensions in which his fictitious characters were caught. This first novel established the pattern and theme for the serious historical novel, not only Scott's "Waverley Novels," but those of later writers such as James Fenimore Cooper.

Abounding in wealth and fame, his energies given also to public service, business, an estate in Scotland, an active social life, and other kinds of writing, Scott worked too hard and wrote too fast—one novel a year, sometimes two. With his tenth novel, *Ivanhoe* (1820), he sagaciously determined that his English reading public, after so many Scottish novels, would welcome a foray into English history. *Ivanhoe* became the talk of London, and his career gained new impetus. However, by 1823, his publisher, conscious of a waning popularity, advised Scott to turn to other kinds of writing. But the author boldly moved into the foreign territory of fifteenth century France and once again created a literary sensation—the reception of his new novel in Paris rivaled that of *Ivanhoe* in London. After *Quentin Durward,* Scott was recognized as a great writer both at home and abroad.

Today, *Quentin Durward* stands as a milestone in Scott's career rather than as a significant novel. His own remarks on the work contain casual apologies for his license with historical facts; some critics charge him with the worse fault of allowing superficial knowledge to make of *Quentin Durward* a mere costume romance rather than a serious historical novel. Others rate it simply as a good tale of adventure.

Nonetheless, *Quentin Durward* provides a good example of the conflict at the heart of Scott's best historical novels—the thematic clash between the old order and the new. The order which is passing away is the age of chivalry with its feudal system and its chivalric code. The age which is coming into being takes its traits from the leader who, rather than the titular hero, is the central character of the novel—King Louis XI of France. Louis is the antithesis of the chivalric ideal. Honor is but a word to him; he studies the craft of dissimulation. His unceremonious manners express contempt rather than knightly humility. He exercises the virtues of generosity and courtesy only with ulterior motives. Crafty and false, committed to his own self-interest, he is a complete Machiavellian.

If Louis is the chief representative of the new age, no one is a genuine survival of the old, despite noblemen who cling to a narrow concept of honor or imitate medieval splendor. Although Louis' principal rival, Charles of Burgundy, is his direct opposite, he is an inadequate symbol of chivalry. When Quentin says that he can win more honor under Charles's banner than under those of the king, Le Balafré counters with a description more accurate: "The Duke of Burgundy is a hot-brained, impetuous, pudding-headed, iron-ribbed dare-all." The decay of chivalry is epitomized in the hopelessness of Quentin's search for a leader who would keep his honor bright, and is confirmed by his ultimate conclusion that none of these great leaders is any better than the other. During the dramatic episode at Charles's court, when the king, ironically, is prisoner of his own vassal, the court historian, Des Comines, reminds Louis—who knows better than anyone else—that strict interpretation of the feudal law is becoming outdated while opportunity and power drive men to compromise and alter the old codes of chivalry.

Quentin Durward himself is the standard-bearer of the old order. Desiring to follow a man who will never avoid a battle and will keep a generous state, with tournaments and feasting and dancing with ladies, he lives upon ideas of brave deeds and advancement.

However, Quentin's ideals are impossible from the start. His rootlessness is symptomatic of the dying culture he reveres. His only real ties are with the mercenary band of Scottish Archers. Their weather-beaten leader Lord Crawford, one of the last leaders of a brave band of Scottish lords and knights, as well as Quentin's kinsman, the hideously scarred, almost bestial Le Balafré, serve as evidence that the glorious past is irrevocably past.

Moreover, though Quentin is introduced as a simple and naïve youth, he is not a rare survival of perfect chivalry. Equipped only with a rude mountain chivalry, he has his fair share of shrewdness and cunning. Far more politic than his experienced kinsman Le Balafré, this simple youth counsels Isabelle on the ways of telling half-truths with a skill which would credit Louis himself. Though it offends his dignity as a gentleman to accept money from a wealthy plebeian—ironically, King Louis in disguise—he immediately discerns that the simple maid of the little turret is far more attractive after she is revealed as Isabelle, Countess of Croye, a high-born heiress. Presented by the king with an unpleasant crisis—an order to be prepared to kill the noble Crèvecoeur from ambush—in which it would be "destruction in refusing, while his honor told him there would be disgrace in complying," Quentin chooses compliance.

Yet as an emblem of the future, Quentin is neither as contemptible as his wily king nor as foolish as his older comrades deem him. The venerable Lord Crawford defends him well when he argues: "Quentin Durward is as much a gentleman as the King, only as the Spaniard says, not so rich. He is as noble as myself, and I am chief of my name." Furthermore, the youthful squire successfully endures the perilous journey, the chivalric testing of a man, bravely and skillfully evading the snares of the wicked, from the literal traps in and around Louis' castle to the treacherous ambush planned by the king and the more horrible fate threatening him during the sack of Schonwaldt. Thus only partially valid is Crèvecoeur's ironic description of Quentin's trials as a pleasant journey full of heroic adventure and high hope. Crèvecoeur's capitulation at the end is more just: "But why should I grudge this youth his preferment? Since, after all, it is sense, firmness, and gallantry which have put him in possession of Wealth, Rank, and Beauty!"

In the characterization of both Quentin and Louis, Scott dramatizes the ambiguities which afflict a time of transition. Louis, lacking any real sense of moral obligations, nevertheless understands the interests of France and faithfully pursues them. Detested as too cautious and crafty, he nonetheless exhibits a coolness before the wrath of Charles that far outshines the brave deeds of arms which Quentin values. If Quentin too passively drifts into the service of Louis, he can summon courage enough to defy the king, and principle enough to support the king in adversity—even at the cost of telling a little falsehood and the risk of sacrificing his life.

Scott in this novel, as in others, vividly depicts the various ways in which men cope with a world of changing values, where as Crèvecoeur's speech jocularly implies, sense and firmness have replaced gallantry, and wealth and rank have toppled beauty in the scale of things. It is this view of reality which seems most characteristic of the author: he is, like Quentin, most certainly a

Romantic, idealizing the glories of a legendary time; but he understands the practical demands of a present reality and the value of a Louis or of a shrewd and brave youth like Quentin Durward.

Catherine E. Moore

QUO VADIS?

Type of work: Novel
Author: Henryk Sienkiewicz (1846-1916)
Type of plot: Historical novel
Time of plot: c. A. D. 64
Locale: Rome
First published: 1895

Principal characters:
VINICIUS, a young Roman patrician
LYGIA, a foreign princess whom Vinicius loves
PETRONIUS, Vinicius' uncle, intimate friend of Nero
NERO, the Roman emperor
CHILO, a Greek sycophant
PETER, leader of the Christians
TIGELLINUS, Petronius' enemy, Nero's friend

Critique:

Quo Vadis? is a tremendous achievement, both as a historical re-creation and as a vivid and dramatic work of fiction. Those who enjoy learning history by reading novels will find it extremely satisfactory. Others who are willing to settle for a good story will be moved by its sharply depicted characters, its tremendous tensions and energy. No one has succeeded better than Sienkiewicz in portraying the broad panorama of Roman civilization in the last, degenerate days of the Empire, and no one else has so credibly presented the early Christians as real, live people.

The Story:

When Vinicius returned to Rome, after duty in the colonies, he called on his uncle, Petronius, who was one of the most influential men in Rome. A friend of the Emperor Nero, Petronius owned a beautiful home, choice slaves, and numerous objects of art. Petronius had no delusions about the emperor. He knew quite well that Nero was coarse, conceited, brutal, thoroughly evil.

Petronius was happy to see his handsome young nephew. Vinicius had fallen in love with Lygia, daughter of a foreign king, now living with Aulus, Plautius and Pomponia. He asked his uncle to help him get Lygia as his concubine. Petronius spoke to Nero, and Lygia was ordered brought to the palace. The giant Ursus was sent as Lygia's devoted servant by her foster parents.

At a wild orgy in the palace, Vinicius attempted to make love to Lygia. Through the watchfulness of Acte, who was a Christian and a former concubine of Nero, he did not succeed. Lygia herself was a Christian and she feared both the lust of Vinicius and that of the emperor himself. Then Acte received information that Lygia would be handed over to Vinicius. At the same time, the daughter of the Empress Augusta died. The empress and her circle believed that Lygia had bewitched the child. Alarmed at the dangers threatening the girl, Acte and Ursus planned Lygia's escape.

That night the servants of Vinicius came and led Lygia away from the palace. Meanwhile Vinicius waited at his house, where a great feast was to take place in honor of his success in securing Lygia. But Lygia never arrived, for on the way to his house a group of Christians had suddenly attacked the servants of Vinicius and rescued the girl. Her rescuers took Lygia outside the city walls to live in a Christian colony.

Vinicius was furious. Petronius sent some of his own men to watch the gates of the city. Day after day Vinicius

QUO VADIS? by Henryk Sienkiewicz. Translated by Jeremiah Curtin. By permission of Mr. J. C. Cardell and the publishers, Little, Brown & Co. Copyright, 1896, 1897, 1900, by Jeremiah Curtin. Renewed, 1924, 1925, 1927, by Alma Mary Curtin.

grew more and more upset. Finally, Chilo, a Greek who passed as a philosopher, offered for a sufficient reward to find Lygia. By pretending to be a convert, he learned where the Christians met in secret. He and Vinicius, together with a giant named Croton, went there, and then followed Lygia to the house where she was staying. When they attempted to seize the girl. Ursus killed Croton. Vinicius was injured in the scuffle. For a few days he stayed with the Christians who took care of him. Lygia herself nursed him until she became aware of her love for the pagan patrician. Afterward, rather than succumb to temptation, she left him to the attentions of others.

Vinicius had heard the Christians speaking at their meeting. While recuperating, he was amazed at their goodness, at their forgiveness, at their whole religious philosophy. He heard their leader, Peter, talk of Christ and of Christ's miracles, and his mind became filled with odd and disturbing thoughts. He realized that he must either hate the God who kept Lygia from him, or love Him. Strangely enough, he became convinced that he no longer had the desire to take Lygia by force. He maintained his contacts with the Christians. At last, after he had accepted their faith, Lygia agreed to marry him.

In the meantime Nero had gone to Antium. There the noble Tigellinus planted in his mind the idea that he should burn Rome in order to write and sing a poem about the tremendous catastrophe. Accordingly, Nero fired Rome, and almost all of the city was destroyed. Vinicius rushed from Antium to save Lygia. Luckily, she had left the city before the fire gained headway. The populace was angry and violent about the fire. Rebellion was in the air. The empress and the Jews at court persuaded Nero to blame the Christians for the fire. Chilo, who had been befriended by the Christians and whose abominable crimes had been wiped away by Christian for-

giveness, turned traitor. He gave the emperor all the information he had about the Christians and led the guards to the hiding places of the sect. Cruel persecutions began.

Petronius tried desperately to stop Nero and save Vinicius. Failing in his attempt, he knew that his own days were numbered. The Christians were crammed first into prisons and then brought into the arena for the entertainment of the populace. Virgins were raped by the gladiators and then fed to starving lions. Christians were crucified, burned alive. After Lygia had been seized and imprisoned, Vinicius failed in an attmept to rescue her.

At last her turn came to be led into the arena to amuse the brutal populace. Stripped, she was tied to the back of a raging bull. When the bull was sent running into the arena. Ursus rushed forward and locked his strong arms around the animal. To the astonishment of all, the bull yielded and died. Then the people demanded that Lygia and Ursus be set free, and the emperor had to obey the public clamor. Petronius advised Vinicius that they should all leave the city, for Nero had subtle ways of removing people who had offended him.

The persecutions continued, the spectacles in the arena growing more and more ghastly. At last the people sickened of the bestial tortures. One of the dying Christians looked straight at Nero and accused him of all his infamous crimes. While Glaucus, a martyr, was being burned alive, he looked at Chilo, the Greek who had betrayed them. Glaucus, who had been left for dead by Chilo, forgave the Greek who had caused the Christian's wife and children to be sold into slavery. Moved by the dying man's mercy. Chilo cried out in a loud voice that the Christians were innocent of the burning of Rome, that the guilty man was Nero. Despairing of his own fate, Chilo was on the point of complete collapse. But Paul of Tarsus took him aside and assured him that Christ was merciful to even the worst of sinners. Then he baptized the Greek. When Chilo went back home, he was sized by the emperor's guards and led away to his death in the arena.

Vinicius and Lygia escaped to Sicily. When Petronius heard that the emperor had ordered his own death, he invited some of the patricians to his house at Cumae, where he had gone with Nero and the court. There at a great feast he read an attack against Nero and astounded everyone by his foolhardiness. Then he and Eunice, a slave who loved him, stretched out their arms to a physician. While the party continued and the astonished guests looked on, Petronius and Eunice bled to death in each other's arms.

Nero returned to Rome. His subjects hated him more than ever. A rebellion broke out at last, and he was informed that his death had been decreed. He fled. With some of his slaves around him, he attempted to plunge a knife into his throat. But he was too timid to complete the deed. As some soldiers approached to arrest him, a slave thrust the fatal knife into his emperor's throat.

Further Critical Evaluation of the Work:

The name *Quo Vadis?* means "Where are you going?" In the title of Henryk Sienkiewicz's novel, it alludes to a legend concerning Simon Peter who asked that question of a vision of Christ, and was told, "I go to Rome to be crucified again." The novel begins where the legend ends, with the story of Vinicius, a Roman who was touched by the mission which Peter then undertook in Rome.

Vinicius' story is a love story. His love begins as lust for the beautiful body of Lygia, a Germanic hostage. It is transformed, by his contact with Lygia and with those who share her Christian faith, into a deep love for Lygia, for her God, and for all mankind. This love leads him away from the lustful, gory world of the Roman aristocracy, in which he has lived all his life, into the hidden world of the Christians, with life in the catacombs, occasional memories of Christ in sermons by Simon Peter and Paul of Tarsus, and the constant threat of the arena. Both of these worlds are presented vividly.

The sympathies of Sienkiewicz, himself a devout Christian, plainly lie with the Christians. But *Quo Vadis?* gives a balanced picture of pagan Rome. True, Nero is present to preside over bloody spectacles and dinner parties lit by living torches, and, true, Sienkiewicz, for the sake of the plot, takes liberties with history by making Nero responsible for the fire that burned Rome. But, alongside Nero, there are truly noble Romans, like Aulus Plautius and Petronius, who despise the debauched emperor. Petronius finds comfort in philosophy and in the worship of Thanatos, the goddess of death, in whose honor he poisons himself when life can hold no good for him. His comfort is not as great as that of the Christians, with their hope of Heaven and their deep love for one another. The point is plain, but by no means overwhelming. The reader, like the first century Roman, has his choice.

RABBIT, RUN

Type of work: Novel
Author: John Updike (1932-   )
Time: 1959
Locale: Mount Judge, Pennsylvania
First published: 1960

Principal characters:

> HARRY ANGSTROM, nicknamed "Rabbit," a former basketball star, now, at twenty-six, a salesman
> JANICE ANGSTROM, his wife
> NELSON, their son
> EARL ANGSTROM and
> MARY ANGSTROM, Rabbit's father and mother
> FRED SPRINGER, Janice's father
> MRS. SPRINGER, his wife, called Mom-Mom by her grandson
> JACK ECCLES, a young Episcopal minister
> LUCY ECCLES, his wife
> RUTH LEONARD, with whom Rabbit lives
> MARTY TOTHERO, Rabbit's former basketball coach
> MRS. HORACE SMITH, a wealthy widow for whom Rabbit works as a gardener

The quality distinguishing John Updike's fiction and putting him in the front rank of novelists at an unusually young age is his ability to "get into" his characters, to experience their palpable worlds as they experience them, and to convey these experiences in prose that is at once rich and translucent. He is in that stream of post-realism that conceives life as it is broadly and inclusively, that finds in the ordinary enough of the extraordinary to excite the poetic imagination without forsaking thorough grounding in quotidian reality. Beyond this, faint but perceptible, is a tough intellectual and religious concern for values, appearing in his fiction not so much as the assertion of one given value system or the other but rather as a constant probing of conflicts of evaluation as these arise in tangible experience.

So much is Updike a novelist of experience and its normative repercussions that a plot *précis* as such can be misleading; Updike is concerned with experience in its fullness, not events in their succession, and what happens in his fiction is not mirrored accurately by a historical timetable. This is not to say that his fiction is the fiction of pure sensibility. Updike—partly by means of a perspective maintained carefully by an empathizing yet detached narrator—is concerned with experience: not simply what happens or what a character feels, but with the whole complex of interactions among events, perception, emotion, and reflection that makes up experience.

With these qualifications of plot in mind, the action of *Rabbit, Run* can be summarized. Harry Angstrom, nicknamed "Rabbit," was once an extraordinary high school basketball player. He is now, at twenty-six, a salesman of a household gimmick, "Magipeel." He has a mousy, somewhat alcoholic, pregnant wife Janice and a small son, Nelson. On a spring afternoon Rabbit, full of the energy of the season, stops to play basketball with a group of teenage boys. In the game, in the memories it brings to him and in the air there is a promise of life. But at home he finds his wife drinking and watching a children's television program; she has made a stupid purchase; and she has left their son at his parents' house and their car at hers. Rabbit goes to collect these, but, when he gets to his parents' house, he gives in to a sudden impulse to run away. He picks up the car and begins to drive, feeling furtive, never quite free, even though he drives all the way into West Virginia; finally, for no special reason except that he does not feel the freedom he had hoped for, he turns back.

Instead of going home, he seeks out his former basketball coach, Marty Tothero, who, since Rabbit's high school days, has been fired for being involved in a scandal and now lives in a broken-down hotel. Rabbit goes to him, presumably, for advice; Tothero seems at first willing to give it but finally does nothing more than get him a bed for the day and, for the evening, a date with Ruth Leonard, a sometime prostitute. Rabbit pays her to take him home; they make love, and he decides to move in with her.

The next morning, Palm Sunday, he goes back to his apartment to pick up some clothes. Jack Eccles, a young Episcopalian minister, is there; he has been asked by Janice's family to help them. Rather than pressure Rabbit, however, Eccles, a progressive, "soft-sell" minister, merely talks to him and arranges a golf date for two days later.

Under the direction of Eccles, an interim arrangement is established. Rabbit works as a gardener for Mrs. Horace Smith, plays golf with the minister, and continues to live with Ruth. Eccles, on whom the novel now begins to focus, visits Rabbit's and Janice's parents, searching for the core of the problem, finding nothing but inertia. Rabbit pushes Ruth towards a kind of total intimacy that finally, ironically, comes to stand between them; he also gets her pregnant. When Janice's baby is born, Rabbit deserts Ruth, comes home, takes a new job in his father-in-law's used car lot, and, for a short while, feels wonderful. But when Janice comes home, he wants to make love; she, of course, cannot. He leaves looking for Ruth but finally spends the night in a hotel, and Janice begins to drink. Finally, completely drunk, she tries to give the baby, Rebecca, a bath and accidentally drowns her. Rabbit comes back once again. But at the burial, after pleading that he is innocent,

he cannot stand what he thinks are the accusing stares of the mourners and he runs again. He goes to Ruth, pleads with her to have their baby; she too rejects him. With his guilt and responsibilities crowding him, he begins once again to run.

Rabbit Angstrom embodies a vital principle; his name suggests animal and electrical energy, unhumanized. Running is the pure expression of this energy, whether it be toward or away from something, or, as in the end, just running. Once, as a high school basketball player, Rabbit had found an organized human use for that energy; now he finds only an occasional productive outlet for it—making love, working in Mrs. Smith's garden, hitting one good golf shot, taking care of his clothes. For the most part he finds that human involvements frustrate his natural energies and that his gracefulness and desire for the kind of beauty he found in basketball games are resented by others.

By making the minister and his wife Lucy important characters in the novel, Updike suggests that Rabbit presents not simply a social problem, but also a quasi-theological one. Eccles, foolish and often ridiculous, is nonetheless a minister trying to minister, and he points to a truth about Rabbit: that Rabbit (Updike suggests this very lightly) is suffering a religious crisis, even *the* religious crisis, of separation from God, and the concommitant modern crisis of a lack of faith in the presence of some Grace by which God will bridge this separation. Eccles is the last of a series of should-be guides for Rabbit, following his parents and his coach. From Eccles's point of view—and Eccles's point of view is included in the novel—Rabbit is a special case, for Rabbit has, or seems to have a physical and emotional, if not quite spiritual, "touch": Rabbit has experienced some of the things that Eccles must assume. He knows Grace, at least in its physical analogues; hence the enigmatic epigram from Pascal: "The motions of Grace, the hardness of the heart; external circumstances."

Rabbit is also the beginning of something special for Updike. In this novel, he begins to go beyond the bounds of realism, or rather to probe for a meaningful use of both realistic and mythic materials. Here he probes the living myths of contemporary America; the belief in physicality, the paradoxes of escape and movement, the image of the athlete as the cultural hero, the legends of love. He does so with considerable success. Indeed, it is arguable, though at this early date relatively unimportant, that *Rabbit, Run* is Updike's finest work in its picture of life lived on the edge of the abyss, of youth without spiritual resource, of a society which breeds emotional waste and squalor because of its disregard for the gap between fact and value in the lives of the unready and the immature.

THE RAINBOW

Type of work: Novel
Author: D. H. Lawrence (1885-1930)
Type of plot: Psychological realism
Time of plot: Nineteenth and early twentieth centuries
Locale: England
First published: 1915

Principal characters:
TOM BRANGWEN, a farmer
LYDIA LENSKY, his wife
ANNA LENSKY, Lydia's child by her first husband
WILL BRANGWEN, Anna's husband
URSULA BRANGWEN, Anna's and Will's daughter
ANTON SKREBENSKY, Ursula's lover

Critique:

The *Rainbow* has been the center of much controversy. The author used it as a lever to bring intelligent consideration of basic human relations into the open, where those relationships could be reviewed in a clear-eyed, objective manner, and in doing so he made use of the sexual aspects of marriage and love. The book is essentially a comparison of the matings of three successive generations. The book was not well received when it appeared. The author was ostracized and the novel was suppressed for a time by the police. That such a tempest was occasioned by *The Rainbow* is hard for the reader to understand today, for by present standards the book can be read and appreciated for what it is, an excellent psychological study.

The Story:

Tom Brangwen was descended from a long line of small landholders who had owned Marsh Farm in Nottinghamshire for many generations. Tom was a man of the soil, living alone on his farm with only an old woman for his company and housekeeper. Then a Polish widow, Lydia Lensky, became the housekeeper of the vicar of the local church. She brought her small daughter, Anna, with her. Within a few months Tom Brangwen found enough courage to present the widow with a bouquet of daffodils one evening in the vicar's kitchen and to ask the woman to be his wife.

Their marriage was a satisfactory one, judged by the standards of the world. Tom was kind to his stepdaughter. Later he had two sons by his wife. But knowing his stepdaughter was easier for him than knowing Lydia. The fact that they were of different nationalities, cultures, and even languages kept the couple from ever becoming intellectually intimate with one another. There were times when either one or both felt that the marriage was not what it should be for them, that they were not fulfilling the obligations which their mating had pressed upon them. On one occasion Lydia even suggested to her husband that he needed another woman.

Little Anna was a haughty young girl who spent many hours imagining herself a great lady or even a queen. In her eighteenth year a nephew of Tom Brangwen came to work in the lace factory in the nearby village of Ilkeston. He was only twenty years old; the Brangwens at Marsh Farm looked after him and made him welcome in their home.

Anna Lensky and young Will Brangwen fell in love, with a naïve, touching affection for each other. They soon announced to Tom and Lydia that they wished to be married. Tom leased a home in the village for the young couple and gave them a present of twenty-five hundred pounds so they would not want because of Will's small salary.

The wedding was celebrated with rural pomp and hilarity. After the ceremony the newly-married couple spent two weeks alone in their cottage, ignoring the world and existing only for themselves. Anna was the first to come back to the world of reality. Her decision to give a tea party both bewildered and angered her husband, who had not yet realized that they could not continue to live only for and by themselves. It took him almost a lifetime to come to that realization.

Shortly after the marriage Anna became pregnant, and the arrival of the child brought to Will the added shock that his wife was more a mother than she was a married lover. Each year a new baby came between Will and Anna. The oldest was Ursula, who was always her father's favorite. The love which Will wished to give his wife was given to Ursula, for Anna refused to have anything to do with him when she was expecting another child, and she was not satisfied unless she was pregnant.

In the second year of his marriage Will Brangwen tried to rebel. He met a girl at the theater and afterward took her out for supper and a walk. After that incident the intimate life of Will and Anna began to gain in passion, intense enough to carry Will through the daytime when he was not necessary to the house until the nighttime when he could rule his wife. Gradually he became free in his own mind from Anna's domination.

Since Ursula was her father's favorite child, she was sent to high school. That privilege was a rare thing for a girl of her circumstances in the last decade of the nineteenth century. She drank up knowledge in her study of Latin, French, and algebra. But before she had finished, her interest in her studies was shared by her interest in a young man. The son of a Polish friend of her grand-

mother's was introduced into the house, young, blond Anton Skrebensky, a lieutenant in the British Army. During a month's leave he fell in love with Ursula, who was already in love with him. On his next leave, however, she drove him away with the love she offered to him. He became afraid of her because of that love; it was too possessive.

After finishing high school, Ursula took an examination to enter the university. Having passed the examination, she decided to teach school for a time, for she wanted to accumulate money to carry her through her education without being a burden to her parents. Anna and Will were furious when she broached the subject of leaving home. They compromised with her, however, by securing for her a position in a school in Ilkeston. Ursula spent two friendless, ill-paid, and thankless years teaching at the village elementary school. At the end of that time she was more than ready to continue her education. She decided to become a botanist, for in botany she felt she was doing and learning for herself things which had an absolute truth.

Then one day, after the Boer War ended, Ursula received a letter which upset her completely. Anton Skrebensky had written that he wished to see her again while he was in England on leave. Within a week he arrived in Nottingham to visit her at school. Their love returned for each of them with greater intensity than they had known six years before. During the Easter holidays they went away for a weekend at a hotel, where they passed as husband and wife. They went to the continent as soon as Ursula had finished classes for the summer. Even then, however, Ursula did not want to marry Skrebensky; she wanted to return to college to take her degree. But Skrebensky continued to press increasingly for marriage. He wanted Ursula to leave England with him when he returned to service in India.

Meanwhile Ursula had so neglected her studies that she failed her final examinations for her degree and had to study to take them over again before the summer was finished. When Ursula failed her examinations a second time, Skrebensky urged her to marry him immediately. In India, he insisted, her degree would mean nothing anyway. In the meantime they went to a house party, where they realized that there was something wrong in their mating, that they could not agree enough to make a successful marriage. They left the party separately and a few weeks later Skrebensky was on his way to India as the husband of his regimental commander's daughter.

After he had gone, Ursula learned that she was pregnant. Not knowing that he was already married, she wrote to Skrebensky and promised to be a good wife if he still wished to marry her. Before his answer came from India, Ursula contracted pneumonia and lost the child. One day, as she was convalescing, she observed a rainbow in the sky. She hoped that it was the promise of better times to come.

Further Critical Evaluation of the Work:

When D. H. Lawrence was composing *The Rainbow,* he realized that the critics and the general reader would not accept the novel. During that time he wrote to Amy Lowell concerning the critical reception of a book of his short stories: "The critics really hate me. So they ought." It is a curious remark from any writer, but especially from one who was so intent upon working a moral change in his readers. Lawrence knew, however, that not only was his fiction "shocking"—and it was to become more so—in its treatment of sexuality, particularly that of women, but that he created character and experience that challenged the way the critics viewed the world. In his fiction, and it became fully apparent in *The Rainbow,* he dramatized experience as dynamic, shifting, and allusive. For him the world was neither stable, nor certain, nor finally rationally explicable; his vision undercut all the preconceptions of the Edwardian critics. So their "hatred" of Lawrence's fiction was actually a defense of themselves. The fact that *The Rainbow* appeared during the first years of World War I seems to have validated Lawrence's argument against those who saw civilization as stable, knowable, and controllable.

One question preoccupies Lawrence in this novel: is the self capable of expansion, of becoming an entity, of achieving freedom, especially in the modern age where the traditional supports of community, family, and religion have been weakened or eliminated? In Will and Anna Brangwen's generation, the first to enter the industrial world, the self does survive, if only at a minimum. If, unlike Tom and Lydia Brangwen, they fail to create the "Rainbow," an image of the fully realized self in passionate community, and if their love degenerates to lust, they at least endure. True freedom, however, is denied them.

For Ursula, their daughter and the novel's heroine, the question of freedom hardly pertains, at least at the beginning. It is simply a matter of her survival. Her vision of the "Rainbow" at the end must be taken as a promise of freedom—and for many readers an unconvincing one—rather than a fulfillment. Yet it is a perception she earns by surviving both the inner and the outer terrors created by the twentieth century.

Even though, then, *The Rainbow* is a psychological novel in which Lawrence is primarily concerned with states of feeling and being below the level of history, the social and political backgrounds are of utmost importance; indeed they are of central significance to an understanding of the question of self-realization. For if Lawrence explores the dialectic of the psyche, he does so in an understanding of the determining impact which history has on that psychological drama.

A novel of three generations, the time span of *The Rainbow* runs from 1840 to 1905. In the background yet always urging their attention on us are the major cultural changes of the age: the rapid expansion of industry; the diminuation of the arable land; the growth of society originally based on the hamlet and town to one centered in the city; the breakdown of the nuclear family and the spread of education. In short, Lawrence dramatizes the English revolution from a feudal to a democratic, capitalistic society. In the foreground of these radical changes are the relationships between Tom and Lydia, Will and Anna, and Ursula and Anton. And as the novel moves in time from the middle of the nineteenth to the beginning of the twentieth century and in space from Ilkeston, Beldover, and Nottingham to London and Paris, what becomes increasingly apparent is that both these relationships and the sanctity of the self are harder to sustain.

In the first generation Tom Brangwen and his wife, Lydia, are firmly rooted in the earth and their marriage, after an early crisis, flowers into a relationship of deep and lasting love under whose influence their daughter, Anna, also grows. Yet if their way of life moves according to the rhythms of nature, it is limited by its pure physicality and it is fated, moreover, to be overwhelmed by other rhythms, those created by the motion of the piston. In fact, Tom himself is drowned when a canal bursts and floods his farm. The symbolic significance of his death—the rural life killed off by the industrial—is emphasized by its appearance at the structural mid-point of the novel.

The second generation, Anna and Will, move from the farm at Ilkeston to the town Beldover, and finally to a major industrial city, Nottingham. Their escape from the limiting existence on the farm to the greater individual liberty of the town, however, exacts a great cost: their love and marriage, although bountiful, fails to fulfill them. Because of their insistence on the self, they cannot make the deep connection which Tom and Lydia achieved. They are sustained by the rich fecundity of their marriage, but are left without unity.

It is left to Ursula to carry out the quest which her parents abandoned: that search for the completely free self in unity. But the forces confronting her are even greater than those her parents faced. The new society, characterized by the machine, is not only hostile to the individual but it has successfully destroyed the community. Cut off as she is from the life of feeling, freed from the restraints imposed by the older society, Ursula wanders through London and Paris preyed on by all, especially by Anton Skrebensky who would swallow her if she allowed him. Yet she survives as an independent self, aided by the strength she has inherited from her grandmother. Still Ursula has not discovered the necessary relationship to the whole life of man. That she can only imagine in her final vision of the "Rainbow." It was precisely her vision, which was also D. H. Lawrence's, of man fully free, connected, and equal that challenged so effectively the world-view of the Edwardians and led to their "hatred" of him. Lawrence showed his critics that there was no hope for society based on what they themselves were.

David L. Kubal

RAINTREE COUNTY

Type of work: Novel
Author: Ross Lockridge, Jr. (1914-1948)
Type of plot: Regional chronicle
Time of plot: Nineteenth century
Locale: Raintree County, Indiana
First published: 1948

Principal characters:
JOHN WICKLIFF SHAWNESSY, a teacher
SUSANNA DRAKE, his first wife
ESTHER ROOT, his second wife
NELL GAITHER, his sweetheart
PROFESSOR JERUSALEM WEBSTER STILES, his friend
SENATOR GARWOOD B. JONES, a politician

Critique:

Raintree County is a long novel, panoramic in scope. The story deals with the events of a single day, but by a series of flashbacks it encompasses almost half a century of American history and life. Through the story pass statesmen, soldiers, prostitutes, gamblers, shoddy politicians, simple people of the soil, all fused into the picture that is America. Here are the men and women of the new Republic, struggling through greed, lust, and war to produce the freedom that had been promised one hundred years before.

The Story:

July 4, 1892: That was the day Raintree County, Indiana, had been waiting for. Her most illustrious son, Senator Garwood B. Jones, would make the main address of the day, introduced by his old friend, John Wickliff Shawnessy, teacher. And as John Shawnessy awoke on the morning of that fateful day, his life began to pass before his eyes. It was a fitful picture—events and people crossed each other without regard to time. Some of the pictures were symbolic, some real. But through them all John Shawnessy searched for the meaning of his life. Somewhere was the key to the secret of his existence. During the day he visited the graveyard, studied an old atlas of the county, talked with old friends. Pieced together, the events of that day told the story of John Wickliff Shawnessy, teacher.

Johnny's father was a preacher, a doctor, a teetotaler. His mother was a gentle woman whom he loved more than he was aware of. Johnny's childhood and adolescence were spent like those of most youths in Raintree County, in playing, working, and dreaming of greatness to come. Two people stood out above all others in those days. One was Garwood B. Jones, the other, Nell Gaither. Garwood, showing signs of becoming a politician, was a smooth talker, a shrewd judge of character, a man without principles. Nell was the girl Johnny had loved since he was old enough to know such feelings. She was a combination of lady and hoyden.

Life in Raintree County was brightened by the appearance of Professor Jerusalem Webster Stiles, who established an academy of higher learning. The "Perfessor," as he was affectionately called, was a cynic and a fraud. His training of the young men was devoted slightly to Greek and Latin and heavily to methods of seducing desirable women. His caustic tongue and vivid history drew young men like a magnet.

On the day he had his graduation picture taken, Johnny met Susanna Drake, a southern girl of wealth and sensuous beauty, but questionable reputation. She

was an orphan, lately moved to the village from New Orleans to occupy a house she had inherited. She spoke boldly to Johnny and filled him with desire. Although he desired Susanna's beauty, his heart remained true to Nell.

A picnic was held on graduation night. Nell went with Garwood, who escorted her most of the time, but she and Johnny slipped off together and confessed that they loved each other. In Paradise Lake the two went swimming, nude. Johnny never knew what might have happened next, for they were forced back to decency by the yells of their comrades. It seems that the "Perfessor" and the minister's wife had run off together, and a posse with a rope was hunting the scoundrel. They found the woman at home—the elopers had missed their train —and Johnny later helped the "Perfessor" to escape. Many years were to pass before the man and the boy met again.

On July Fourth of that same year, Johnny found himself again at Paradise Lake, this time with Susanna. As he yielded to his desire and possessed the girl, he knew that it was Nell he really loved.

Susanna returned to New Orleans. In October, Johnny received a letter saying she was coming back to him, pregnant. By the time Susanna arrived, Johnny had made his peace with himself and decided to marry her, although he still loved Nell. Even when Susanna confessed on the night before the wedding that she was not pregnant but only loved him so much that she must marry him, Johnny forgave her.

After the wedding Johnny and Susanna spent a long honeymoon in the South. The year was 1859 and war was fast approaching. Johnny was anti-slavery and Susanna violently pro-South. She seemed to be driven by some mad obsession about Negroes. In New Orleans, Johnny learned a little of her history. Her father had loved a slave and had installed the woman in his house, giving her equality with his insane wife. All three had died in a fire, but it was rumored that

the husband and slave had been shot first, locked in an embrace.

Home again, Susanna gave birth to a baby who soon became the greatest joy of his father. Susanna grew more and more withdrawn, alternately spitting out hate and melting in passion. She was driven by desperation, for what Johnny could only suspect. In one last frenzy, she set fire to their house and burned the baby to death. She was rescued, her mind completely gone, and Johnny sent her back to her people to be cared for. He knew at last what he had long suspected. Susanna was the daughter of the slave woman, reared as his own by her father because he loved the Negro woman above all else. Susanna had also known, but she had fought against the knowledge. Unable to escape it, she had tried to expiate the sin through fire, as her father's wife had done.

Johnny enlisted in the war and lived through many bloody campaigns. He ceased to be John Shawnessy, a human being, and became only John Shawnessy, a soldier. He was wounded, reported dead, present at the theater when Lincoln was shot. None of these events really touched Johnny. His soul was back in Raintree County, rooted in the soil of his homeland.

After the war he spent two years in New York with the "Perfessor," now a newspaperman. Johnny had planned through the war years to get his marriage annulled and return home to marry Nell. But he found that Nell had married Garwood after Johnny's reported death and had died in childbirth. There was nothing now to keep him in Raintree County. But New York provided nothing substantial to his life, and when he was called home by his mother's death, he put his roots down for good. He taught school and became the local philosopher. Susanna, he learned, had escaped her relatives; she was believed dead. On the strength of that information, Johnny married a former pupil, Esther Root. Esther's father, considering Johnny an atheist and a bigamist, would not give his consent. The couple eloped, and Mr. Root would never again receive his daughter. The years were good to Johnny and Esther. They had a fine family and a respected place in the community. There were people, however, who considered John Shawnessy evil and plotted to expose him to the world.

On the night of July 4, 1892, after the departure of Senator Garwood B. Jones, a delegation from the revival meeting accused Johnny and a local widow of immorality. But the "Perfessor," back to cover the celebration, showed the crowd instead that it was the minister, leader of the posse, who had seduced one of his flock. The "Perfessor" thought it a huge joke that he who had once been run out of town by a preacher could now turn the tables after so many years.

The day having ended, John Shawnessy walked the deserted streets of this village in Raintree County. He was thinking of the yesterdays and tomorrows that are America.

Further Critical Evalution of the Work:

In *Raintree County* the author attempted to weave the history of a continent and nation into his tumultuous narrative of the story of a man and the women in his life. Crosscutting between July 4, 1892, and the preceding decades, the story is refracted from many different points of view: from that of the major protagonist, John Shawnessy, and that of his second wife, Esther, his daughter, Eva, his father, and others. Professor Jerusalem Stiles, a unique comic character, acts in the capacity of the classic Greek chorus, participating in and commenting upon the action.

The prose flows like a river, an image itself which reappears frequently in the book. The chapters do not end as much as catapult into each other. Always, the book, although long, seems to be rushing forward. The style is a strange and vital mixture of Thomas Wolfe and James Joyce, the novel an attempt to create an American epic. The author obviously relished language and enjoyed playing with words; his rich prose, narrowly avoiding lushness, is finely descriptive and evocative of the variety and size of the American landscape.

The characters hurl from scene to scene and decade to decade, meaning well but seemingly fated to compromised destinies. It is not enough for them to mean well. Life is full of missed opportunities. John Shawnessy possessed all of the traits and talents to be a great man, but frustrated by his own passionate personality, he had to learn to be satisfied with slowly ripening wisdom instead of fame or power.

The Civil War sprawls through the center of the book, the dramatic heart of Lockridge's epic. The Battle of Chickamauga is vividly portrayed from the viewpoint of John Shawnessy. Sharp ironic contrasts are shown between true patriotism and verbose, windfilled sentiments.

RALPH ROISTER DOISTER

Type of work: Drama
Author: Nicholas Udall (1505-1556)
Type of plot: Farce
Time of plot: Sixteenth century
Locale: England
First presented: c. 1553

Principal characters:
RALPH ROISTER DOISTER, a well-to-do, cowardly braggart
MATHEW MERYGREEKE, Roister Doister's hanger-on
DAME CHRISTIAN CUSTANCE, a well-to-do widow
GAWIN GOODLUCK, Dame Custance's fiancé
SYM SURESBY, Gawin Goodluck's friend

Critique:

This drama is one of the early English plays acted by schoolboys and patterned after the Roman drama popular in the schools at the time. Neither the plot nor the characters demanded much subtlety from the youthful actors who originally played it. The humor is broad and the language at times very earthy. Some scenes are truly slapstick, as the scene in which grown men armed with swords are routed by a widow and her servants armed only with household utensils. Some of the characters in the play are modeled on the stock figures of Roman drama, and some are not. Merygreeke is quickly recognizable as the parasite of Roman drama, and Roister Doister himself is found to be the braggart so typical of classical comedy. Dame Christian, on the other hand, is an English addition to the drama, in her way a sixteenth-century version of Chaucer's Wife of Bath. Her humor can, in fact, be traced to the broad comedy of early mystery plays, as presented in the Towneley Cycle.

The Story:

Mathew Merygreeke, a gay young rascal who likened himself to the grasshopper of the fable, had often had fun and money at the expense of Ralph Roister Doister, a well-to-do, doltish young man who bragged long and loud of his bravery but failed to act anything but the coward when called to action.

In addition, Ralph Roister Doister imagined himself in love with every woman he met, and he swore each time he fell in love that he could not live without the woman who had most lately caught his eye. One day, meeting Merygreeke on the street, he asserted that he was now madly in love with Dame Christian Custance, a widow reported to be wealthy. She had captivated Roister Doister when he saw her at supper.

Merygreeke, anxious to please the man he constantly gulled, agreed to help Roister Doister pursue his suit. He assured the foolish braggart that the widow was certain to accept him and that Roister Doister ought really to try to marry someone of higher station and greater fortune.

Merygreeke went for musicians to serenade Dame Custance, while Roister Doister waited in front of the widow's home. As he waited, three of the widow's servant women came from the house and talked and sang. When they noticed Roister Doister, he came up, talked to them, and tried to kiss them. After talking with them for a time, Roister Doister gave them a love letter to deliver to their mistress. He boasted that he had written it himself.

Given the letter by her serving-woman, Dame Custance was furious. She reminded her servants that she was an honorable woman, affianced to Gawin Goodluck, who had been for some months on a sea voyage. Dame Custance refused to break the seal of the letter, much less read it.

Meanwhile, to further his suit, Roister Doister sent his servant to the widow's house with some love gifts, a ring and a token in a cloth. The young servant, after some trouble, convinced the widow's serving-women to take the gifts to their mistress, even though she had been angry at receiving the letter.

Handed the gifts, the widow became even angrier, lectured her servants on their conduct, and finally sent a boy to find the man who had delivered the gifts to her house.

Merygreeke, after many a laugh over what happened during Roister Doister's suit, finally went to Dame Custance and revealed his scheme for gulling Roister Doister. The widow said she would never marry such a doltish man, but agreed to join in the fun at the braggart's expense. She went so far as to read the letter he had written to her and said she would make a reply.

Rejoining Roister Doister, Merygreeke listened to the suitor's woeful tale and then told him in outrageous terms that the widow had refused his suit, called him vile names, and accused him of cowardice. Roister Doister immediately vowed that he would assault the widow's house with intent to kill her in combat, along with all her servants. Over Merygreeke's protests, Roister Doister set out to get his men together. Merygreeke laughed and waited, knowing that the cowardly braggart would never carry out his vow.

When they arrived at the widow's house, Merygreeke offered Roister Doister an excuse for not leading the assault. Instead, the braggart began once more to woo the widow with music and song. He sent Merygreeke to call the widow from her house.

Dame Custance went out to Roister Doister and repeated her refusal of his foolish proposal. Then she read his letter aloud, and by rephrasing it and repunctuating it she made the letter as insulting as Roister Doister had meant it to be loving. The result thoroughly confused the suitor, who vowed it was not the letter

he had sent to her. After she left, Roister Doister sent for the scrivener who had actually written the letter for him. The scrivener took the letter, read it aright, and convinced Roister Doister that someone had tricked him.

In the meantime Sym Suresby, friend of the widow's fiancé, arrived to tell Dame Custance that her affianced suitor, Gawin Goodluck, had returned from his voyage and would be with her shortly. Suresby saw and heard enough of the conversation between the widow and Roister Doister to think that the widow was unfaithful to Goodluck. He went off, leaving the widow furious at the tomfoolery of Roister Doister. When she chased Roister Doister off, he again vowed to have revenge on the widow and her servants. Gathering his men, he approached her house a second time.

The widow, meanwhile, had gone to a trusted friend to enlist his support in getting rid of the troublesome Roister Doister, who threatened to ruin her approaching marriage to Goodluck. The friend consented to aid her. They also enlisted Merygreeke, who agreed to help them and at the same time pull more tricks at the expense of Roister Doister.

The foolish suitor and his men were routed by the widow with household utensils used as weapons. Having proved himself a coward as well as a fool, Roister Doister renounced his suit for the widow's hand. When Goodluck appeared soon afterward, Dame Custance was able to assure him that the reports he had had from Sym Suresby were muddled and that she had never broken her vows to him. She did, however, berate Suresby for not making certain of the truth before repeating what he had heard.

Merygreeke returned on behalf of Roister Doister and asked forgiveness of the widow and Goodluck. When he promised them that they should have much fun at Roister Doister's expense if they would but agree, they assented heartily and invited Merygreeke and Roister Doister to have dinner with them that very day.

Further Critical Evaluation of the Work:

For the student of English drama the real significance of *Ralph Roister Doister* is its position as the first English comedy. Written by Udall, himself a schoolmaster, the play was probably first performed by his students. It is very much a literary reflection of the Renaissance and its "New Learning" in England, for on one level the play is a teaching device as an imitation of a classical pattern. In fact, since the study of Plautus and Terence was a part of the revival of classical studies during the Renaissance, some have seen *Ralph Roister Doister* as merely an adaptation of Plautus' *Miles Gloriosus*.

The play, however, is no mere translation from the Latin, but rather is a skillful combination of classical and native elements. Udall has carefully incorporated the classical rules of the Roman comedy into his dramatic structure. He follows, for example, the classical pattern of dividing the action into five acts, and further adds to its literary qualities by composing the entire play in rhymed couplets. By merging the recent classical influence with the older, native English drama of the morality plays and interludes, Udall makes this play an important stepping stone leading to the golden age of Elizabethan drama. In *Ralph Roister Doister,* not only does doggerel verse become smooth couplets and coarse language become witty conversation, but also the character types from the English and classical pattern merge. Merrygreeke, for example, shows similarities to both the flattering parasite of the classical tradition and the mischievous Vice of the native tradition. And further, within the classical framework, the setting is typically English.

The intricate plot of the play, too, is an important development in the English stage. As it unfolds, develops, and comes to a satisfactory conclusion it marks an important step in the movement of the English play from the medieval mysteries and moralities to the intricate unravelings of Shakespeare's *Twelfth Night.*

THE RAMAYANA

Type of work: Poem
Author: Valmiki (fl. fourth century B.C.)
Type of plot: Religious epic
Time of plot: Remote antiquity
Locale: India
First transcribed: c. 350 B.C.

Principal characters:
> RAMA, a prince and incarnation of Vishnu
> SITA, his wife
> LAKSHMAN, his brother and loyal follower
> DASA-RATHA, his father, King of the Kosalas
> RAVAN, Demon-king of Lanka (Ceylon)
> KAIKEYI, one of King Dasa-ratha's wives and enemy of Rama

Critique:

Although relatively unknown to Western readers, the story of Rama is one of the most popular tales among the people of India, where the story holds great religious significance. In India, where the tale has been recounted for untold generations, there are several versions of the story, but the main outlines remain the same, with Rama and Sita the idealized versions of Man and Woman. To the Western reader the characters may appear to be human beings with supernatural powers, roughly equivalent to certain figures in Greek legend and myth, but to Hindus the characters of the *Ramayana* (*The Fortunes of Rama*) are more than this; they are gods, to be reverenced today as they have been in ages past. Scholars disagree on the various versions of the *Ramayana,* and the problem of the original story and additions by later generations of storytellers will perhaps never be solved. The best approach for a general reader is probably to accept the story and enjoy it.

The Story:

King Dasa-ratha of the Kosalas, who kept his court at Ayodhya, had four sons, though not all by the same mother. According to legend, the god Vishnu, in answer to King Dasa-ratha's supplications, had given a divine liquor to each of the king's wives, so that they might bring forth sons, each of whom was partly an incarnation of Vishnu. Of the sons born, Rama was the handsomest and strongest of all, his mother having drunk more of the magic beverage than Dasa-ratha's other wives.

When Rama grew to manhood he heard of Sita, beautiful, talented, and virtuous daughter of King Janak and the Earth-mother. King Janak was the possessor of a wondrous bow, a mighty weapon that had belonged to the gods, and King Janak resolved that whoever could bend the bow should have Sita for his wife. The king knew, of course, that no ordinary mortal could possibly accomplish the feat.

Rama and his brothers traveled to the court of King Janak and were granted permission to try drawing the mighty bow. With ease Rama bent the bow, with such strength that the weapon snapped in two. King Janak promised that Sita should be Rama's bride and that each of his half-brothers, too, should have a noble bride from the people of Videha.

So Sita became the wife of Rama; her sister Urmila became the bride of Lakshman, Rama's favorite brother; Mandavi and Sruta-kriti, cousins of Sita, became the wives of Bharat and Satrughna, the other half-brothers of Rama. When all returned to Ayodhya, Dasa-ratha, fearing that rivalry between his children might create unhappiness and tragedy in his house, sent Bharat and Satrughna to live with their mothers' people.

Years passed, and King Dasa-ratha grew old. Wishing to have the time and opportunity to prepare himself for the next life, he proposed that Rama. his favorite son, should become regent. The king's council and the populace rejoiced in the proposal, and plans were made to invest Rama with the regency and place him on the Kosala throne. Before the preparations had been completed, however, Manthara, a maid to Queen Kaikeyi, one of King Dasa-ratha's wives, advised the queen that Rama's succession to the throne should be prevented and that Bharat, Queen Kaikeyi's son, should become regent. The ill advice was heard, and Queen Kaikeyi remembered that she had been promised two boons by her husband. So when King Dasa-ratha came to her she asked that Bharat should be made regent and that Rama should go into exile for fourteen years. King Dasa-ratha was sad, but he had given his word and he must fulfill his promises. Like a dutiful son, Rama heard his father's decision and prepared to go into exile. He expected to go alone, but his wife Sita and his brother Lakshman prepared to go with him to share his lonely and uncomfortable exile in the dismal Dandak forest. The Kosala people mourned his departure and accompanied him on the first day of his journey away from Ayodhya.

Leaving his native country, Rama journeyed south. He and his companions crossed the Ganges River and came to the hermitage of Bharad-vaja, a holy man. After visiting with him they went on to the hill of Chitrakuta, where stood the hermitage of Valmiki, a learned and holy man. There they learned that King Dasaratha had died the day after Rama's departure from Ayodhya, remembering in his hour of death a curse laid on him by a hermit whose son he had accidentally killed. Rama stayed with Valmiki for a time. Bharat returned to Ayodhya to become regent, as his mother had planned. However, he recognized Rama's claim and set out on a journey to find Rama

and to ask him to become King of the Kosalas. But Rama, having given his word, remained in exile as he had vowed to do. Bharat returned to Avodhya to place Rama's sandals on the throne as a symbol of Rama's right to the kingship.

In order that his kinsmen might not find him again, Rama left Valmiki's hermitage and after a long journey he established his own hermitage near the dwelling of Agastya, a holy and learned man. There Rama, Sita, and Lakshman lived in peace until they were disturbed by a demon-maiden, enamored of Rama, who had been repulsed in her addresses by both Rama and Lakshman. Spurned and seeking revenge, she went to her brother, Ravan, demon-king of Lanka (Ceylon) and asked his help. Ravan was a powerful being who through asceticism had achieved power even over the gods. His domination, according to legend, could be broken only by an alliance of men and the monkey people. Ravan sent a demon in the disguise of a deer to lead Rama astray while on the hunt. When Rama failed to return, Sita insisted that Lakshman go look for him. In the absence of the brothers, Ravan came and abducted Sita.

Rama, having learned what had happened, allied himself with the monkey people in order to make war upon the demons and win back his beloved wife. Hanuman, one of the monkey people's leaders, found Sita at Ravan's palace and led Rama and the forces of the monkey people to Ceylon. There Ravan's city was besieged and many battles were fought, with combat between the great leaders of both sides and pitched battles between the forces of good and evil. Finally Ravan and his demon forces were defeated, Ravan was killed, and Sita was rescued and restored to her husband. Sita, who had remained faithful to Rama throughout her captivity, proved in an ordeal by fire that she was still virtuous and worthy to be Rama's wife.

Rama, Sita, and Lakshman returned in triumph to Avodhya. where Rama was welcomed and became king of the Kosala people. Rumors were spread, however, that Sita had not been faithful to her husband, until at last Rama sent his wife away, and she went to live at the hermitage of Valmiki. Shortly after her arrival at the hermitage she gave birth to Rama's sons.

More years passed and the two sons grew up, tutored in their youth by the wise Valmiki, who took his charges eventually to Ayodhya. There Rama, recognizing them as his sons, sent for Sita and had her conducted to his court. Since her virtue had been in doubt she was asked for a token that she had been true to her marriage vows. The earth opened to a great chasm, and the Earth-mother herself rose up on her throne to speak on behalf of Sita and to take her to the land of the gods. Thus Sita was taken away from the husband and the people who had doubted her.

Further Critical Evaluation of the Work:

The *Ramayana* is one of the two Hindu epics, the other being the earlier *Mahabharata*. Whereas the *Mahabharata* is genuinely a heroic (or "folk") epic deriving from an oral tradition, the *Ramayana* is more nearly like a literary epic, written in conscious imitation of the heroic-folk tradition. But whatever the original may have been, the *Ramayana* has been altered many times by subsequent rewriting and recension. In its extant versions, the *Ramayana* contains about 24,000 couplets (less than one-fourth the length of the *Mahabharata*) and is divided into seven books, as against the eighteen books of *Mahabharata*. In terms of conventional Western epic form, the Greek heroic-folk epic contains twenty-four books; the English literary epic contains twelve. Of the seven books of the *Ramayana,* the central story covers books two through six. Book I is introductory. Book VII appears to be a species of appendix. It is called *Uttara,* or "Supplemental," and provides both epilogue to and critique of the foregoing six books. It also provides instruction for the recital of the *Ramayana* by minstrels in much the same way that medieval *enseignements* coached jongleurs in their repertoire and their performance. Yet the *Ramayana,* like most Western epics and unlike the *Mahabharata,* has unity, which stems from concentration on one main story.

One of the major themes in the central narrative is the relationship between destiny and volition, with the consequent consideration of personal responsibility or the lack of it. The key questions ultimately revolve around the power of the gods, for the obligatory nature of human promises hinges upon belief in the divine prerogative of retribution. Hence, King Dasa-ratha rescinds his proposal that Rama should succeed him as regent in order to honor his prior promise of Queen Kaikeyi. So, too, Rama dutifully accepts Bharat as regent and goes into exile, in deference to the King's expressed wishes (really, the gods' demands). Just as Rama accepts his fate, so also his brother Lakshman and his wife Sita accept theirs. But while Lakshman simply does his duty and perseveres, Sita is subjected to the most stringent of tests. After being kidnaped by Ravan, she is called upon to prove her virtue. The trial being so debilitating, Sita is finally rescued by her Earth-mother. All of these claims upon human endurance require intervention by the gods. The message of the

Ramayana thus seems to be that human volition is subservient to divine will. The corollary also appears to establish the social order as subject to the divine order.

Closely allied to the theme of free will versus fate is the theme of duty. One aspect of this theme of duty is Rama's behavior, often cited as a model for other men to emulate. Rama's submission to his father's decision, his acceptance of exile, and his fidelity to his promise to remain in exile all bespeak Rama's filial piety and deference to duty. This view of duty follows the pattern traditional for warriors, princes, and kings; as such, it is compatible with ideals presented in the *Mahabharata* as well as with Western ethical assumptions. The other, and more important, aspect of the theme of duty is less conventional as an issue proper to epic consideration, for it concerns not wars and the affairs of state, the usual epic grist, but human love and domestic matters. This aspect of duty, then, deals with Sita's story, which, all things considered, comprises the main plot line in the epic. Sita, like Rama, is held up as an exemplar of ideal behavior—for women. Her behavior is characterized by sweetness, tenderness, obedience, patient suffering, and, above all, faithfulness; her piety and self-sacrifice ultimately qualified her for relief from mortal travail by being resorbed into her Earth-mother. She endured all without complaint and thus became the model for the perfect woman, wife, and mother, her image of duty unalloyed.

The *Ramayana* also deals with typical Hindu motifs. There is, for example, the Brahman's curse which King Dasa-ratha remembered on his deathbed. Also, there is the asceticism, as exemplified in Valmiki's hermitage and in Rama's own abstemious life after leaving Valmiki's hermitage. In addition, this asceticism reflects another Hindu value; the emphasis on social order, which is manifested in the caste system. The orderly functioning of society, with all people acknowledging their proper places in it, is a high priority in the Hindu ethos. Furthermore, the concepts of truth and duty provide the definitive guidelines for action. Truth and duty go hand in hand to create twin obligations for Dasa-ratha and Bharat as well as Rama and Sita and every devout Hindu. And the didactic elements of the *Ramayana* reinforce these typical Hindu motifs. Most explicitly, the teachings of Valmiki convey the precepts. But the implicit message of the plot and of the human interaction conveys the ethical and moral substance even more clearly. Thus the Hindu ideals of faith and conduct are both taught and demonstrated in the *Ramayana*.

In addition to the Hindu motifs as well as the themes of duty and free will versus fate, the *Ramayana* also presents an interesting juxtaposition of the natural and the supernatural. The central narrative begins with the natural or "real-world" events: the political machinations at the court of King Dasa-ratha; the banishment of Rama, Sita, and Lakshman; and the death of King Dasa-ratha and the subsequent dilemma of Bharat when Rama refuses the throne. But the next half of the narrative deals with the supernatural: the intrusion of the demon-maiden; the intervention of Ravan; the alliance with the monkey people; the real and allegorical battle between the forces of good and the forces of evil; and the Earth-mother's absorption of Sita. This combination of natural and supernatural worlds synthesizes the ethical and spiritual concerns of Hinduism, incorporating the concepts of fatalism and duty. Through this synthesis, the *Ramayana* goes beyond the confines of a national cultural epic to become part of the sacred literature of Hinduism. As such, it joins company with the *Mahabharata,* the *Vedas,* the *Brahmanas,* the *Upanishads,* and the *Puranas.* The religious perspective has made the *Ramayana* one of the best known and best loved works in India.

Joanne G. Kashdan

THE RAMBLER

Type of work: Periodical essays
Author: Samuel Johnson (1709-1784)
First published: 1750-1752

Regularly every Tuesday and Saturday during the years 1750 to 1752 Samuel Johnson published one of the more than two hundred essays that make up the *Rambler*. He records in one of the later papers the difficulties a man with his procrastinating temperament had in meeting a regular deadline like this one, and he indicates that many of his brief moralizing works were hastily composed and sent off to the press unrevised. It is thus especially remarkable that his essays give such a uniformly polished, coherent effect. The style is throughout dignified, and balanced, and the arguments of the moral and philosophical dissertations are inevitably clear and logical.

Johnson departed in the *Rambler* from the typical pattern of the popular eighteenth century periodical essay as it was developed by Joseph Addison and Richard Steele in the *Tatler* and the *Spectator*. He considered his role as essayist to be that of teacher, rather than that of entertainer. While he included a number of amusing sketches in his collection, even the most humorous have moral overtones, and the majority of the papers are general comments on human faults and weaknesses. He indicates that some of his readers protested at the prevailing tone of seriousness in his work, but he did not yield to their criticism; it is only in his later groups of essays, the *Idler* and the *Adventurer,* that he allowed his mood to mellow and consented to discuss lighter topics in a less lofty style than that of the *Rambler*.

One philosophical theme runs throughout all of the *Rambler* essays, giving unity to the diverse topics Johnson treated, that of the "Vanity of Human Wishes," the futility of man's quest for happiness in riches, fame, beauty, success in business, society, marriage, or friendship. Johnson speaks with deep understanding of the way human beings tend to live always in the future, forever hoping for the improvement of their states, improvement that rarely comes. He begins his second essay by remarking that "the mind of man is never satisfied with the objects immediately before it, but is always breaking away from the present moment, and losing itself in schemes of future felicity; and that we forget the proper use of the time, now in our power, to provide for the enjoyment of that which, perhaps, may never be granted us has been frequently remarked. . . ."

Johnson treated this general theme in a number of different ways, sometimes speaking in the abstract about the nature of fame, hope, or the uses of time, sometimes implying the same conclusions by relating the histories of individuals. He many times created imaginary correspondents whose letters he reproduces without comment, leaving the reader to draw the obvious conclusions.

Cupidus, for example, whose name suggests greed, writes to the Rambler about his long, frustrating wait for riches. The estate that was to be his had been left to his three aunts during their lifetime, and he passed many years in anxious inquiries about the state of their health, fearing that they might marry and leave heirs of their own and despairing of ever gaining his fortune. When the third sister finally died at the age of ninety-four, Cupidus expected to find happiness at last. Yet he confesses at the end of his letter that his joy was short-lived. "I had formed schemes which I cannot execute, I had supposed events which did not come to pass, and the rest of my life must pass in craving solitude, unless you can find some remedy for a mind, corrupted with an inveterate disease of wishing, and unable to think on anything but wants, which reason tells me will never be supplied."

Another letter relates the tribulations of Victoria, who was raised by her mother to assume that beauty was the single goal to be achieved in life; she spent her childhood in learning the accomplishments of a lady of fashion and protecting her complexion and her figure, and she was duly introduced to society, where she was flattered and fussed over until she contracted smallpox. When she recovered, she found that her looks, and with them all the attention she had had in the past, had vanished. She writes that she now realizes the necessity for valuing more permanent qualities than beauty; time would have banished her fair appearance if disease had not.

In addition to numerous letters such as these, Johnson wrote several Oriental fables, similar to his *Rasselas*, to illustrate his moral themes. He tells of Obidah, a Near Eastern gentleman who set forth across a beautiful plain one morning, following those paths that seemed to him loveliest, confident that they led him in the direction of the main road toward his destination, and then discovered that he was hopelessly lost. This tale illustrates, as the hermit who rescued Obidah and sent him on his way, says: "Human life is the journey of a day. We rise in the morning of youth, full of vigour and full of expectation; we set forward with spirit and hope . . . and travel on a while in the straight road of piety towards the mansions of rest." Gradually we are drawn away from this road by our search for ease and pleasure, until "the darkness of old age begins to invade us, and disease and anxiety obstruct our way. We then look back upon our lives with horror, with sorrow, with repentance; and wish, but too often vainly wish, that we had not forsaken the ways of virtue." Other fables point up the folly of trusting in wealth to provide loyal friends or popularity, the advantages of moderate wants, and the impossibility of trusting absolutely in anyone but God.

Although such themes as these recur most often in the *Rambler,* Johnson dealt with a number of other subjects as well. He devotes several essays to marriage and the problems of those alliances based on wealth, social position, or even on affection that rested on insufficient knowledge of character. He also treats the follies of the housewife who has no interests but in her pies and her embroidery, of the mother who is so anxious to be the center of society that she is violently jealous of her own growing daughter, of the London belle who longs for the idyllic quiet of the countryside, then finds that she has no inner resources for amusing herself when she is removed from balls, card games, plays, and concerts. These brief, witty character sketches, in which Johnson most resembles Addison and Steele, provide welcome light intervals in otherwise serious volumes.

There is, interspersed throughout the *Rambler,* a considerable number of essays that contain serious literary criticism. One of the first of these works, a discussion of the writing of fiction, sets forth Johnson's conviction that literature has an important didactic function. He points out the dangers he sees in the modern novel, which is aimed primarily at impressionable young people. Since this kind of work is as true to life as its author can make it, its characters are apt to be taken as models by youthful readers. Johnson is particularly disturbed by the tendency to present characters who combine large measures of both virtue and vice: "There have been men, indeed, splendidly wicked, whose endowments threw a brightness on their crimes, and whom scarce any villainy made perfectly detestable, because they never could be wholly divested of their excellences; but such have been in all ages the great corrupters of the world, and their resemblance ought no more to be preserved, than the art of murdering without pain."

Johnson wrote several highly technical essays on Milton's versification in *Paradise Lost,* pointing out the genius and the flaws in the sounds of his words, the cadences of his lines, and his handling of technical problems of metrics. Of greater interest than these specialized discussions is Johnson's critical analysis of Milton's blank verse tragedy, *Samson Agonistes*. He praises the poem for its wisdom, its moral tone, and the beauty of many of the passages, but he feels that it fails to fulfill Aristotle's principle that the action of a drama must lead inevitably to the catastrophe. Johnson contends that the scenes with Manoa, Delilah, and Harapha that compose the body of Milton's play have no real bearing on the conclusion and that consequently, in spite of its virtues, the drama is a failure.

Johnson concluded the *Rambler* papers with a statement of what he felt he had accomplished in his essays, freely admitting that the nature of the publication made unevenness in the quality of vari-

ous selections inevitable. He expresses the hope that he has been able in his works to "refine our language to grammatical purity, and to clear it from colloquial barbarisms, licentious idioms, and irregular combinations," and that he has "added to the elegance of its construction, and something to the harmony of its cadence."

He makes no apology for the prevailing tone of seriousness; his "principal design," he states firmly, was "to inculcate wisdom or piety." He sees his papers on "the idle sports of imagination" and his literary criticism as distinctly subordinate to the moral essays, and he concludes with his desire that he may be "numbered among the writers who have given ardour to virtue, and confidence to truth."

RAMEAU'S NEPHEW

Type of work: Novel in the form of a dialogue
Author: Denis Diderot (1713-1784)
Time: 1761
Locale: Paris
First published: In German, translated by Goethe, 1805; in French, 1823

Principal characters:
> RAMEAU, nephew of Jean Philippe Rameau, a French composer
> DIDEROT, the author, French encyclopedist and writer

Rameau's Nephew could hardly have been other than the work of a French author: It submits to no simple classification: although fictional, the characters were actual persons and their ideas, in all probability, were their own. But there is the problem—for those who concern themselves about such matters—of deciding how much of Diderot can be found in the character Rameau, and how much of Rameau was in Diderot. On the one hand, the character Diderot is a mild champion of traditional values, and Rameau is a vivacious apologist for roguery. But the brilliant turns of this satirical dialogue suddenly force upon the reader the suspicion that Diderot the author is delighted with the convention-defying attitudes of his friend Rameau; perhaps Diderot believes Rameau more than Rameau believes himself.

The dialogue is a satirical critique of manners and morals. It makes particular reference to prominent writers, musicians, politicians, critics, and other leading figures of eighteenth-century France. Many of the comments are unkind, and some are painfully so—or would have been had the work been published at the time of its composition. But Diderot kept his lively satire under wraps, not only because of its references to living persons, but also because of a reluctance to stir up the censor and all others to whom Rameau's carefree morality might prove intolerable.

The character Rameau is marvelously wrought to suit Diderot's intention. Although Rameau is clearly an individual and is convincing, as witty rogues in literature usually are, he is not simply one thing or another. On the contrary, Diderot states that Rameau is his own opposite. Sometimes Rameau is thin, sometimes fat; sometimes he is filthy, sometimes powdered and curled. His physical vacillation is matched by a vacillation of mood. Sometimes he is gay, sometimes depressed; sometimes he is courageous, sometimes timid to the point of fear. Rameau is a sensualist, a lover of wine and wenches. But his passionate defense of an egoistic hedonism is a sign of his need to apologize for his manner; his morality is a device to prop up his manner. Underneath Rameau's abandon the reader perceives a poignant longing for depth and respectability.

Having created a character whose contrary traits reveal the human being at odds with himself—thus providing the motive for a discussion of morality—Diderot provides Rameau with a gentlemanly antagonist, the man of ideas, Diderot himself. Diderot's mild responses, ostensibly intended to counter Rameau's philosophy, actually prompt Rameau with the acuity of a Socrates, stimulating Rameau to a lively defense of the sense-gratifying life of a social parasite.

Rameau, who contradicts himself within himself, and Diderot, who contradicts Rameau, together bring out the difficulty of all moral problems and of morality itself. Man is neither merely intellectual nor merely sensual; his desire to understand is often in conflict with his desires, and his desires are in conflict with each other. Consequently, no one moral rule or set of principles will do. To be a good man, a person must have a kind of moral genius. For such a person, rules are instruments to be used only with ingenuity and sometimes to be discarded altogether. If a person is at war with himself, or with another, as Rameau is with himself, or with Diderot, a just victory is not always possible. Sometimes there is no such thing as the proper answer. For a good man, life is a creative struggle that must be judged as works of art are judged, without dogmatism and with respect for the impossible goals the human spirit sets for itself. Perhaps the theme of the dialogue is best understood dialectically: without the restraint of reason and human consideration, the human being becomes something worse than a fool, but without attention to the fact of human appetites the moralist becomes something less than a human being.

For Rameau is the fool and Diderot is the moralist. But Rameau fancies himself as something of the classic fool, the darling of the courts, the discerning jester who makes the bitter truth palatable. The fact is that he comes close to being a compromising sponger, a guest in great houses only because he is sometimes an amusing conversationalist. Although he comes close to being merely parasitical, he is saved by his own need for apology. A man who must speak to Diderot is already more than a professional guest.

The dialogue is presented against a background of chess. The narrator takes shelter in the Regency Café where the finest chess players of Paris compete with each other. When Rameau enters and engages Diderot in conversation, he begins a kind of verbal chess game that shows him to be the brilliant and erratic player while Diderot is slower but more canny. Rameau's attitude is revealed at once. In response to Diderot's expression of interest in the games, Rameau speaks scornfully of the players—although they are the best in Paris—and when Diderot remarks that Rameau forgives nothing but supreme genius, Rameau retorts that he has no use for mediocrity.

One must read carefully for, to continue the chess metaphor, the moves are deceptive. Rameau argues that evil comes from men of genius, that the genius—and he cites his uncle as an example—is so

absorbed in his own work that he neglects family and state, and he concludes that a child showing the mark of genius should be smothered or thrown to the dogs. Diderot asks whether it would have been better if Voltaire had been a "good soul" attending to his business and family and doing nothing more, or whether it was better that, though deceitful, ambitious, and mean, he wrote great plays. The implication is that Diderot prefers the latter. But when Rameau says it would have been better for Voltaire himself if he had been the former, Diderot acknowledges that this is true.

As the conversation continues, each man forces upon the other an appreciation of a perspective quite different from his own. Diderot is fascinated by the antics of Rameau, for Rameau is not only a rascal and a wit but also a great mime whose conversation is enlivened by spontaneous performances in which he shows, by the economy of caricature, the manners of those with whom he must associate.

Because Diderot responds to Rameau's zest for life, he is saved from unrealistic moralizing. Nevertheless, Rameau can go too far. When he applauds the behavior of an informer whose act resulted in the execution of the informer's friend, Diderot is quick to say that he finds such an attitude repulsive. He considers it almost unbearable to be in the presence of a man who regarded a great crime as something worthy of the same critical admiration one might give to a work of art. But although nothing more is said on the subject, the fact that Diderot admits to being pursued by "dark fancies" suggests that the moralist has caught something of Rameau's aesthetic attitude toward great acts, whether heroic or foul, and feels himself at grips with the problem of evil within himself.

Diderot and Rameau fall into a long critical discourse on music. Rameau is all for music which honestly expresses the passions. The true, the good, and the beautiful are his Father, Son, and Holy Ghost—but his truth and beauty are close to the earth, allied to the passions of men. Diderot admits that there is a great deal of sense in what Rameau says, but he regrets that Rameau talks of nothing but gold, wine, good food, and women.

The moralist must reconcile himself and his morality to the facts of human passion. Somehow Diderot must come to acknowledge Rameau's importance as the creative beast, but as a man of ideas he finds it almost intolerable that not everything about human action can be reduced to a categorical formula. For Diderot the problem was what it remains for contemporary man, the problem of reconciling Freud's view of man with Christ's conception. In fact, Diderot anticipates Freud twice, within two pages: once, by having Rameau envious of Diderot's literary talent, for in so doing, Rameau accords with Freud's theory of the artist's motive; again, when Rameau asserts that were his son to develop without interference, he would want good food and dress, fame, and the love of women, Diderot replies that if the child were left in his natural state, he would grow to manhood knowing no better than to murder his father as a rival and then seduce his own mother.

Like Dostoevski, Diderot appreciated the exceptional man who stepped beyond the bounds of conventional morality; unlike Nietzsche, he did not deify the immoralist. *Rameau's Nephew* is a skillful and satirical attempt to do justice to man the moralist and also to man the animal.

THE RAPE OF LUCRECE

Type of work: Poem
Author: William Shakespeare (1564-1616)
Type of plot: Tragedy
Time of plot: 500 B.C.
Locale: Ancient Rome
First published: 1594

Principal characters:
COLLATINE, a Roman general
LUCRECE, his wife
TARQUIN, Collatine's friend and son of the Roman king

Critique:

The story of Tarquin's violation of Lucrece is an ancient Roman legend which has been presented in many versions other than in this poem by Shakespeare. Because the Elizabethans were especially fond of this legend, Shakespeare had numerous sources upon which to draw. Compared with his other writings, this poem is far more conventionally Elizabethan, yet its passages of great emotion and its consistently beautiful poetry rank it above other interpretations of the story known in his day.

The Story:

At Ardea, where the Romans were fighting, two Roman leaders, Tarquin and Collatine, spoke together one evening. Collatine, in the course of the conversation, described his beautiful young wife Lucrece in such glowing terms that Tarquin's passions were aroused. The next morning Tarquin left the Roman host and journeyed to Collatium, where he was welcomed by the unsuspecting Lucrece as one of her husband's friends. As he told her many tales of Collatine's prowess on the battlefield, Tarquin looked admiringly at Lucrece and decided that she was indeed the most beautiful woman in Rome.

In the night, while the others of the household were asleep, Tarquin lay restless. Caught between desire for Lucrece and dread of being discovered, to the consequent loss of his honor, he wandered aimlessly about his chamber. On the one hand there was his position as a military man who should not be the slave of his emotions; on the other hand was his overwhelming desire.

But what dreadful consequences might be the result of his lustful deed! His disgrace would never be forgotten. Perhaps his own face would show the mark of his crimes and the advertisement linger on even after death.

He thought for a moment that he might try to woo Lucrece but decided that such a course would be to no avail. Since she was already married, she was not mistress of her own desires. Again he considered the possible consequences of his deed.

At last emotion conquered reason. As Tarquin made his way to Lucrece's chamber all sorts of petty annoyances deterred him. The locks on the doors had to be forced; the threshold beneath the door grated under his footstep; the wind threatened to blow out his torch; he pricked his finger on a needle. Tarquin ignored these omens of disaster. In fact, he misconstrued them as forms of trial which only made his prize more worth winning.

When he reached the chamber door, Tarquin began to pray for success. Realizing, however, that heaven would not countenance his sin, he declared that Love and Fortune would henceforth be his gods. Entering the room, he gazed at Lucrece in sleep. When he reached forward to touch her breast, she awoke with a cry of fear. He told her that her beauty had captured his heart and that she must submit to his will.

First he threatened Lucrece with force, telling her that if she refused to submit to him he would not only kill her but also dishonor her name. His intention was to murder one of her slaves, place him in her arms, and then swear that he killed them because he had seen Lucrece embracing the man. But, if she yielded, he promised to keep the whole affair secret. Lucrece began to weep and plead with Tarquin. For the sake of her hospitality, her husband's friendship, Tarquin's position as a warrior, he must pity her and refrain from this deed. Her tears serving only to increase his lust, Tarquin smothered her cries with the bed linen while he raped her.

Shame-ridden, he stole away, leaving Lucrece desolate. She, horrified and revolted, tore her nails and hoped the dawn would never come. In a desperate fury, she railed against the night; its darkness and secrecy that had ruined her. She was afraid of the day, for surely her sin would be revealed. Still worse, through her fall, Collatine would be forever shamed. It was Opportunity that was at fault, she claimed, working for the wicked and against the innocent. Time, the handmaiden of ugly Night, was hand-in-hand with Opportunity. But Time could work for Lucrece now. She implored Time to bring misery and pain to Tarquin. Exhausted from her emotional tirade, Lucrece fell back on her pillow. She longed for a suicide weapon; death alone could save her soul.

As the dawn broke she began to consider her death. Not until she had told Collatine the complete details of her fall would she take the step, however, for Collatine must revenge her on Tarquin.

Lucrece called her maid and asked for pen and paper. Writing to Collatine, she asked him to return immediately. When she gave the messenger the letter, she imagined that he knew of her sin, for he gave her a sly, side glance. Surely everyone must know by now, she thought. Her grief took new channels. Studying a picture of the fall of Troy, she tried to find the face showing greatest grief. Hecuba, who gazed mournfully at Priam in his dying moments, seemed the saddest. Lucrece grieved for those who died in the Trojan War, all because one man could not control his lust. Enraged, she tore the painting with her nails.

Collatine, returning home, found Lucrece robed in black. With weeping and lamentations she told him of her shame, but without naming her violator. After she had finished, Collatine, driven half-mad by rage and grief, demanded the name of the traitor. Before revealing it, Lucrece drew promises from the assembled soldiers that the loss of her honor would be avenged. Then, naming Tarquin, she drew a knife from her bosom and stabbed herself.

Heartbroken, Collatine cried that he would kill himself as well, but Brutus, his friend, stepped forward and argued that woe was no cure for woe; it was better to revenge Lucrece. The soldiers left the palace to carry the bleeding body of Lucrece through Rome. The indignant citizens banished Tarquin and all his family.

Further Critical Evaluation of the Work:

The Rape of Lucrece was entered at the Stationers' Register on May 9, 1594. Like *Venus and Adonis,* which had been published the previous year, it was finely printed by Richard Field and dedicated to the Earl of Southampton. Both of these narrative poems had been written while the theaters were closed because of the plague, but these companion pieces are not the idle products of a dramatist during a period of forced inactivity. Rather, as the dedications and the care in publication indicate, they are efforts at a more serious, more respectable type of composition than playwriting.

Longer and graver in tone than *Venus and Adonis, The Rape of Lucrece* was extremely popular, going through many editions, and was frequently quoted by contemporaries. The stern Gabriel Harvey, a Cambridge fellow and friend of Spenser, enthusiastically approved of the poem and paired it with *Hamlet* for seriousness of intent. The poem may be the "graver labor" which Shakespeare had promised Southampton in the dedication to *Venus and Adonis*. Whether or not Shakespeare intended to pair the poems, *The Rape of Lucrece* does provide a moralistic contrast to the view of love and sexuality expressed in the earlier poem.

The genre of *The Rape of Lucrece* is complaint, a form popular in the later Middle Ages and the Renaissance and particularly in vogue in the late 1590's. Strictly speaking, the complaint is a monologue in which the speaker bewails his fate or the sad state of the world. Shakespeare, however, following the example of many contemporaries, took advantage of the possibilities for variety afforded by dialogue. The poem includes the long set speeches and significant digressions which had become associated with the complaint. The poetic style is the highly ornamented sort approved by sophisticated Elizabethan audiences.

The story of the poem is a familiar one. It appears in Gower's *Confessio Amantis,* Lydgate's *Fall of Princes,* and Chaucer's *Legend of Good Women,* although Shakespeare seems to have relied more specifically on Livy's *History of Rome* (I, Chapters 57-59) and Ovid's *Fasti* (II, 721-852). The rhyme royal stanza may have been suggested by its traditional use in serious narrative or, more immediately, by Daniel's use of it in his popular *Complaint of Rosamond.* Certainly *The Rape of Lucrece* shares with Daniel's poem the Elizabethan literary fascination with the distress of noble ladies.

Despite the potentially erotic subject matter, the poem is not at all sensual, except in the lushness of its imagery. Even the passion of the rape scene is attenuated by a grotesquely extended description of Lucrece's breasts. The long, idealized description of the heroine is a rhetorical tour de force, not sexual stimulation. The theme of heroic chastity is always paramount and we are never distracted by action. Indeed, the prose "argument" which precedes the poem describes a story with enormous possibilities for action and adventure, but Shakespeare, consistent with his higher purpose, chose to focus, reflectively and analytically, on the moral and psychological issues. Although the result is sometimes boring, there are occasional signs of Shakespeare's dramatic ability, especially in the exchanges before the rape.

The characters are static and stylized, bu the revelation of the characters is skillfully done. As Tarquin's lust wrestles with his conscience, he is portrayed in an agony of indecision. The main medium of his internal conflict is the conventional theme of the antagonism of passion and reason. This section is a compendium of reflections on and rationalizations for the destructive power of lust. Moreover, Tarquin thinks in terms of conventional images. However, the contrasts and antitheses, as he is tossed back and forth between common-places, effectively represent his inner struggle. When he gives in, it is more a tribute to the potency of lust than a delineation or indictment of his character. When Lucrece appeals to the very concerns which have bedeviled Tarquin, there is a dramatic poignancy which most of the rest of the poem lacks. After the rape, the change in Tarquin's conventional thoughts is striking: his recognition of guilt and shame is a narrative exemplum of Shakespeare's Sonnet 129.

Lucrece's complaint is also wholly conventional in substance, but once again contrast and antithesis give a vitality to her grief as she rationalizes her suicide as not the destruction of her soul but the only way to restore her honor. The imagistic alternations from day to night, clear to cloudy, reflect her anguish and the difficulty of her decision.

The whole structure of the poem suggests that the exploration and decoration of conventional themes concerning lust and honor are the main intent. The poem centers on the mental states and moral attitudes of the characters immediately before and after the crucial action. The rape is a premise for the reflections, the suicide a logical result. The set speeches are reinforced by free authorial moralizing. Significant digressions, like the long physical description of Lucrece and her extended apostrophe to Opportunity, further elaborate the main themes. The longest and most effective digression is Lucrece's contemplation of the Troy painting. The opportunities for finding correlatives are fully exploited. The city of Troy is apt because it has been brought to destruction by a rape and Paris is the perfect example of the selfishness of lust. Sinon, whose honest exterior belies his treachery, reminds Lucrece of the contrast between appearance and reality, nobility and baseness, which she had noted in Tarquin. The whole digression, which repeats by means of allusion, is ornamental rather than explanatory.

The severe paring of the plot further reveals Shakespeare's main concern. For example, Collatine, the offended husband, appears only briefly, suffers silently, and does not even personally initiate the revenge. He does not intrude on the crucial issues. In addition, the bloodthirstiness of Lucrece's plea for revenge is another sign that elucidation of character is unimportant compared to the beautiful expression of moral imperatives. The revenge itself is, mysteriously, instigated by Brutus (an action which makes more sense in Livy) and is carried out perfunctorily in a few closing lines, because it is secondary to the main, conventional themes of the poem.

Regardless of its moral earnestness and occasional tedium, *The Rape of Lucrece* is gorgeously ornamented with figures of speech, especially alliteration and assonance, and with figures of thought which please rather for brilliance of execution than depth of conception. *The Rape of Lucrece* is, like *Venus and Adonis,* a rhetorical showpiece.

Edward E. Foster

THE RAPE OF THE LOCK

Type of work: Poem
Author: Alexander Pope (1688-1744)
Type of plot: Mock-heroic epic
Time of plot: Early eighteenth century
Locale: London
First published: 1712

Principal characters:
BELINDA, Miss Arabella Fermor
LORD PETRE, Belinda's suitor
THALESTRIS, Belinda's friend
ARIEL, a sprite
UMBRIEL, a gnome

Critique:

The Rape of the Lock, generally considered the most popular of Pope's writings as well as the finest satirical poem in the English language, was written at the suggestion of John Caryll, Pope's friend, ostensibly to heal a family row which resulted when an acquaintance of Pope, Lord Petre, playfully clipped a lock of hair from the head of Miss Arabella Fermor. Pope's larger purpose in writing the poem, however, was to ridicule the social vanity of his day and the importance that was attached to affected manners.

The Story:

At noon, when the sun was accustomed to awaken both lap dogs and lovers, Belinda was still asleep. She dreamed that Ariel appeared to whisper praises of her beauty in her ear. He said that he had been sent to protect her because something dreadful — what, he did not know — was about to befall her. He also warned her to beware of jealousy, pride, and, above all, men.

After Ariel had vanished, Shock, Belinda's lap dog, thought that his mistress had slept long enough, and he awakened her by lappings of his tongue. Rousing herself, Belinda spied a letter on her bed. After she had read it, she promptly forgot everything that Ariel had told her, including the warning to beware of men.

Belinda, aided by her maid, Betty, began to make her toilet. Preening before her mirror, she was guilty of the pride against which Ariel had cautioned her.

The sun, journeying across the sky, witnessed its brilliant rival, Belinda, boating on the Thames with her friends and suitors. All eyes were upon her, and like the true coquette she smiled at her swains but favored no one more than another.

Lord Petre, one of Belinda's suitors, admired a lock of her hair and vowed that he would have it by fair means or foul. So set was he on getting the lock that before the sun rose that morning he had built an altar to Love and had thrown on it all the trophies received from former sweethearts, meanwhile asking Love to give him soon the prize he wanted and to let him keep it for a long time. But Love granted him only half his prayer.

Everyone except Ariel seemed happy during the cruise on the Thames. That sprite summoned his aides, and reminded them that their duty was to watch over the fair Belinda, one sylph to guard her fan, another her watch, a third her favorite lock. Ariel himself was to guard Belinda's lap dog, Shock. Fifty sylphs were dispatched to watch over the maiden's petticoat, in order to protect her chastity. Any negligent sylphs, warned Ariel, would be punished severely.

After her cruise on the Thames, Belinda, accompanied by Lord Petre and the rest of the party, visited one of the palaces near London. There Belinda decided to play ombre, a Spanish card game, with two of her suitors, including Lord Petre. As she played, invisible sylphs sat on her important cards to protect them.

Coffee was served after the game. Sylphs guarded Belinda's dress to keep it from being spotted. The fumes from the coffee sharpened Lord Petre's wits to the point where he thought of new stratagems for stealing Belinda's lock. One of his cronies handed him a pair of scissors. The sylphs, aware of Belinda's danger, attempted to warn her before Lord Petre could act, but as the maid bent her head over her coffee cup he clipped the lock. Even Ariel was unable to warn Belinda in time.

At the rape of her lock, Belinda shrieked in horror. Lord Petre cried out in triumph. He praised the steel used in the scissors, comparing it with the metal of Greek swords that overcame the Trojans. Belinda's fury was as tempestuous as the rage of scornful virgins who have lost their charms. Ariel wept bitterly and flew away.

Umbriel, a melancholy gnome, took advantage of the human confusion and despair to fly down to the center of the earth to find the gloomy cave of Spleen, the queen of all bad tempers and the source of every detestable quality in human beings, including ill-nature and affectation. Umbriel asked the queen to touch Belinda with chagrin, for he knew that, if she were gloomy, melancholy and bad temper would spread to half the world. Spleen granted Umbriel's request and collected in a bag horrible noises such as those uttered by female lungs and tongues. In a vial she put tears, sorrows, and griefs. She gave both containers to Umbriel.

When the gnome returned to Belinda's world, he found the girl disheveled and dejected. Pouring the contents of the magic bag over her, Umbriel caused Belinda's wrath to be magnified many times. One of her friends, Thalestris, fanned the flames of the maiden's anger by telling her that her honor was at stake and that behind her back her friends were talking about the rape of her lock. Thalestris then went to her brother, Sir Plume, and demanded that he confront Lord Petre and secure the return of the precious lock. Sir Plume considered the whole episode much magnified from little, but he went to demand Belinda's lock. Lord Petre refused to give up his prize.

Next Umbriel broke the vial containing human sorrows, and Belinda was almost drowned in tears. She regretted the day that she ever entered society and also the day she learned to play ombre. She longed for simple country life. Suddenly she remembered, too late, that Ariel had warned her of impending evil.

In spite of Thalestris' pleas, Lord Petre was still adamant. Clarissa, another of Belinda's circle, wondered at the vanity of women and at the foolishness of men who fawn before them. Clarissa felt that both men and women need good sense, but in making her feelings known she exposed the tricks and deceits of women and caused Belinda to frown. Calling Clarissa a prude, Thalestris gathered her forces to battle with Belinda's enemies, including Clarissa and Lord Petre. Umbriel was delighted by this Homeric struggle of the teacups. Belinda pounced upon Lord Petre, who was subdued when a pinch of snuff caused him to sneeze violently. She demanded the lock, but it could not be found. Some thought that it had gone to the moon, where also go love letters and other tokens of tender passions. But the muse of poetry saw it ascend to heaven and become a star.

Further Critical Evaluation of the Work:

When Robert Lord Petre cut off a lock of Arabella Fermor's hair one fateful day early in the eighteenth century, he did not know that the deed would gain world-wide fame, attracting attention over several centuries. Nor did he perhaps foresee the ill feeling his act would create between the Petre and Fermor families. The story would probably have been soon lost among the trivia of family histories, had not John Caryll asked his good friend the poet Alexander Pope to write a little poem about the episode, one which would show the comic element of the family quarrel and thus help heal it.

What began as a trivial event in history, turns, under the masterly guidance of Pope's literary hand, into one of the most famous poems in the English language, and perhaps the most perfect example of burlesque we have. *The Rape of the Lock* was begun at Caryll's behest ("This verse, to Caryll, Muse! is due") in 1711; Pope spent about two weeks on it and produced a much shorter version than the one he wrote two years later; adding more additions in 1717, he then developed the final draft of the poem as it now stands.

The poem as we have it uses the essentially trivial story of the stolen lock of hair as a vehicle for making some thoroughly mature and sophisticated comments on society and man. Pope draws on his own classical background— he had translated the *Iliad* and the *Odyssey*—to combine epic literary conventions with his own keen, ironic sense of the values and societal structures shaping his age. The entire poem, divided into five Cantos, is written in heroic couplets. Pope makes the most of this popular eighteenth century verse form (rhymed iambic pentameter lines), filling each line with balance, antithesis, bathos, and puns.

The literary genre of "burlesque" typically takes trivial subjects and elevates them to seemingly great importance; the effect is comic, and Pope manages an unbroken sense of amusement as he relates "What dire offense from amorous causes springs,/ What mighty contests rise from trivial things."

From the opening lines of the poem, suggestions of the epic tradition are clear. Pope knew well not only the *Iliad* and the *Odyssey,* but also Milton's *Paradise Lost.* The narrator of *The Rape of the Lock* speaks like Homer, raising the "epic question" early in the poem: "Say what strange motive, goddess! could compel/ A well-bred lord t' assault a gentle belle?" Pope's elaborate description of Belinda's toilet in Canto I furthers comparison with the epic; it parodies the traditional epic passage describing warrior shields. Belinda's make-up routine is compared to the putting on of armor: "From each she nicely culls with curious toil,/ And decks the goddess with the glittering spoil."

The effect of using epic conventions is humorous, but it also helps establish a double set of values in the poem, making the world of Belinda and Sir Plume at the same time trivial and significant. Epic conventions contribute to this double sense in each Canto: (I) the epic dedication and invocation; (II) the conference of protective gods; (III) the games and the banquet; (IV) descent into the underworld; and (V) heroic encounters and apotheosis. The overall result is that, although we have a basically silly situation, we have characters such as Clarissa who utter the always sensible virtues of the eighteenth century:

Oh! if to dance all night, and dress all day,
Charmed the smallpox, or chased old age away;
Who would not scorn what housewife's cares produce,
Or who would learn one earthly thing of use? . . .

But since, alas, frail beauty must decay,

And she who scorns a man, must die a maid;
What then remains but well our power to use,
And keep good humor still what'er we lose?

Clarissa in these lines from Canto V expresses the norm of Pope's satire: the intelligent use of reason to control one's temperamental passions.

The heroic couplet merges perfectly with the epic devices in the poem, for as a verse form the heroic couplet naturally seems to express "larger than life" situations. It is therefore, profoundly to Pope's credit that he successfully applies such a stanzaic pattern to a subject which is anything but larger than life. The critic Maynard Mack has said that Pope "is a great poet because he has the gift of turning history into symbol, the miscellany of experience into meaning."

Pope, perhaps more than anyone else writing poetry in the eighteenth century, demonstrates the flexibility of the heroic couplet. Shaped by his pen, it contains pithy aphorisms, social commentary, challenging puns, and delightful bathos. (The last of these juxtaposes the serious with the small, as in the line, "wrapped in a gown for sickness and for show"). But the key, if there is a key, to the classic popularity of *The Rape of the Lock* is the use of the heroic couplet to include—sometimes in great catalogued lists—those little, precise, and most revealing details about the age and the characters that peopled it. The opening lines of Canto III illustrate Pope's expert use of detail. The passage describes court life at Hampton Court, outside London, and is a shrewd comment on the superficiality of the people there:

Hither the heroes and the nymphs resort,
To taste awhile the pleasures of a court;
In various talks th' instructive hours they passed,
Who gave the ball, or paid the visit last;
One speaks the glory of the British queen,
And one describes a charming Indian screen;
A third interprets motions, looks, and eyes;
At every word a reputation dies.
Snuff, or the fan, supply each pause of chat,
With singing, laughing, ogling, and all that.

The poet's criticism of such life is clear by the swift juxtaposition of Hampton Court life with a less pretty reality in the following lines:

Meanwhile, declining from the noon of day,
The sun obliquely shoots his burning ray;
The hungry judges soon the sentence sign,
And wretches hang that jurymen may dine.

Though always its critic, Pope held a keen interest in the life of London's aristocracy. A Catholic by birth, he was not always in favor with the crown, but before the queen's death in 1714 he enjoyed meeting with a group of Tories which included Swift, Arbuthnot, Atterbury, and Parnell. Steele and Addison, England's first newspaper editors, courted him on behalf of the Whig party, but he refused to become its advocate.

Forbidden by law from living within several miles of London, he lived much of his adult life at Twickenham, a village on the Thames not too far from London but far enough. He transformed his dwelling there into an eighteenth century symbol, with gardening and landscaping; he included vineyards and the house had a temple and an obelisk to his mother's memory. During the 1720's he built his grotto, an underpass connecting his property under a dividing road; it was a conversation piece, with, according to one contemporary, bits of mirror on the walls which reflected "all objects of the river, hills, woods, and boats, forming a moving picture in their visible radiations." For Pope, 4-feet-6-inches tall and sick all his life, it was a symbol of the philosophic life and mind. Although he never married, his biographers tell us he felt a warm, if not always happy, affection for Martha and Teresa Blount, neighbors during his youth. Pope enjoyed great literary fame even during his lifetime, and near the end of his life, when he entered a room, whispers of "Mr. Pope, Mr. Pope," would buzz among the occupants.

Jean Marlowe

RASSELAS

Type of work: Novel
Author: Samuel Johnson (1709-1794)
Type of plot: Philosophical romance
Time of plot: Eighteenth century
Locale: Abyssinia and Cairo
First published: 1759

Principal characters:
RASSELAS, Prince of Abyssinia
NEKAYAH, his sister
PEKUAH, her maid
IMLAC, a poet

Critique:

The History of Rasselas, Prince of Abyssinia, one of the most popular works of Samuel Johnson during his own lifetime, is still widely read. However, it is a weighty novel, ponderous in style and slow moving. There is almost no narrative, for the plot deals with the efforts of four people to find a working philosophy by which they can guide their lives. The age in which Johnson lived was characterized by superficial optimism, and this novel is an attack on that optimism. There is a popular theory that Johnson wrote Rasselas in one week, in order to pay his mother's funeral expenses, but many scholars refute this theory. The novel shows that Johnson hated pretense of any kind, and he used his pen to fight it at every opportunity.

The Story:

It was the custom in Abyssinia for the sons and daughters of the emperor to be confined in a remote place until the order of succession to the throne was established. The spot in which Rasselas and his brothers and sisters were confined was a beautiful and fertile valley situated between high mountains. In the valley was everything needed for a luxurious life. Entertainers were brought in from the outside world to help the royal children pass the time pleasantly. These entertainers were never allowed to leave, for the outside world was not to know how the royal children lived before they were called on to rule.

It was this perfection which caused Rasselas in the twenty-sixth year of his life to become melancholy and discontented. He was unhappy because he had everything to make him happy; he wanted more than anything else to desire something which could not be made available to him. When he talked of his longing with an old philosopher, he was told that he was foolish. The old man told him of the misery and suffering of the people outside the valley and cautioned him to be glad of his present station. But Rasselas knew that he could not be content until he had seen the suffering of the world.

For many months Rasselas pondered on his desire to escape from the valley. He took no action, however, for the valley was carefully guarded and there was no chance for anyone to leave. Once he met an inventor who promised to make some wings for him so that he could fly over the mountains, but the experiment was a failure. In his search for a way to escape, his labor was more mental than physical.

In the palace there was a poet, Imlac, whose lines pleased Rasselas by their intelligence. Imlac was also tired of the perfect life in the valley, for in the past he had traveled over much of the world. He had observed the evil ways of mankind and had learned that most wickedness stemmed from envy and jealousy. He had noticed that people envy others with more worldly goods and oppress those who are weak. As he talked, Rasselas longed more than ever to see the world and its misery. Imlac tried to discourage him, for he believed that

Rasselas would long for his present state should he ever see the violence and treachery which abounded in the lands beyond the mountains.

But when Imlac realized he could not deter the prince, he agreed to join him in his attempt to leave the perfect state. Together the two men contrived to hew a path through the side of a mountain. When they were almost ready to leave, Rasselas saw his sister Nekayah watching them. She begged to accompany the travelers for she too was bored with the valley and longed to see the rest of the world. Because she was the favorite sister of Rasselas, he gladly allowed her and her maid, Pekuah, to join them. The four made their way safely through the path in the mountainside. They took with them enough jewels to supply them with money when they reached a city of trade. They were simply dressed and no one recognized them as royalty.

In Cairo they sold some of their jewels and rented a magnificent dwelling. They entertained great men and began to learn the customs of people different from themselves. It was their object to observe all possible manners and customs so that they could make their own choices about the kind of life each wanted to pursue. But they found many drawbacks to every form of living.

Rasselas and Nekayah believed that it was only necessary to find the right pursuit to know perfect happiness and contentment. Imlac knew that few men lived by choice but rather by chance and the whims of fortune. But Rasselas and Nekayah believed that their chance birth had at least given them the advantage of being able to study all forms of living and thus to choose the one most suitable for them to pursue. So it was that the royal pair visited with men of every station. They went into the courts and into the fields. They visited sages of great fame and hermits who had isolated themselves to meditate. Nowhere did they find a man completely happy and satisfied, for each desired what the other had and thought his neighbor more fortunate than he.

Only once did Rasselas find a happy man. This man was a philosopher who preached the doctrine of reason. He stated that by reason man can conquer his passions and disappointments and thus find true happiness. But when Rasselas called on the sage the following day, he found the old man in a fit of despair. His daughter had died in the night, and the reason which he had urged others to use failed completely in his own life.

Imlac and Nekayah spent long hours discussing the advantages of one kind of life over another. They questioned the state of marriage as compared with celibacy and life at court as compared with pastoral pleasures, but at no time could they find satisfactory solutions for their questions. Nowhere could they find people living in happiness. Imlac suggested a visit to the pyramids so that they might learn of people of the past. While they were in a tomb, Pekuah was stolen by Arabs, and it was many months before she was returned to Nekayah. Pekuah told her mistress that she had spent some time in a monastery while she waited for her ransom, and she believed that the nuns had found the one truly happy way of life.

Their search continued for a long period. Often they thought they had found a happy man, but always they would find much sorrow in the life they thought so serene. Nekayah at one time decided that she would cease looking for happiness on earth and live so that she might find happiness in eternity. A visit to the catacombs and a discourse on the soul prompted her decision.

When the Nile flooded the valley, confining them to their home for a time, the four friends discussed the ways of life which promised each the greatest happiness. Pekuah wished to retire to a convent. Nekayah more than anything desired knowledge and wanted to found a woman's college, where she could both teach and learn. Rasselas thought he wanted a small kingdom where he could rule justly and wisely. Imlac said he would be content to drift through life, with no particular goal. Because all knew their desires would never be fulfilled, they began to look forward to their return to the Abyssinian valley where everyone seemed happy and there was nothing to desire.

Further Critical Evaluation of the Work:

According to his own statement, Johnson wrote *Rasselas* in the evenings of one week in 1759 to defray the expenses of his mother's funeral. But one should not assume either that the tale was completely spontaneous or that its mood was entirely determined by the illness and death of his parent. Johnson had very likely been considering the subject for some time. His translation of Father Lobo's *A Voyage to Abyssinia* in 1735, his use of an Oriental setting in his early play *Irene* in 1737, and his employing the device of the Oriental apologue in several *Rambler* papers all pointed the way. Moreover, two *Rambler* papers (Nos. 204 and 205) suggested part of the theme of *Rasselas* in telling how Seged, Lord of Ethiopia, decided to be happy for ten days by an act of will and how this quest for pleasure was vain. Even closer in theme was Johnson's finest poem, *The Vanity of Human Wishes,* in 1749.

Though the mood of *Rasselas* may seem to be predominantly gloomy, involving if not cynicism at least a tragic view of life, it is possible to see in it some of the qualities of an ironic apologue or a Menippean satire. The manuscript title of the book, "The Choice of Life," is a key both to its plan and to its philosophy. Human nature being what it is, Johnson indicates, happiness can be only illusory, accidental, and ephemeral, existing more in hope than in reality, and always being in the end nothing to be compared with life's miseries. Thus those who seek for happiness through "a choice of life" are destined to end in failure. This kind of reading of the story may seem pessimistic enough. But there is another aspect of it that recognizes the kind of multifariousness in life that resists and defeats facile theories about existence like those of the young travelers in the novel. Here is plainly opportunity for some comedy or satire.

Johnson skillfully begins with the conventional notion that perfect bliss exists in an earthly paradise. Rasselas, an Abyssinian prince, his sister, and two companions escape from what they have come to regard as the boredom of the perfect life in the Happy Valley to set out on a search for true happiness in the outside world. They try all kinds of life: pleasure-loving society, solitude, the pastoral life, life of high and middle estates, public and private life. But though Rasselas holds that happiness is surely to be found, they find it nowhere. The simple life of the country dweller so praised by Rousseau and his followers is full of discontent. Men of wealth and power cannot be happy because they fear the loss of both. The hermit, unable to answer the question about the advantages of solitude, returns to civilization. The philosopher who preaches the philosophic systems of happiness succumbs to grief over the death of his daughter. Another philosopher who thinks one can achieve happiness by "living according to nature" cannot explain what this phrase means. The abduction of the maid Pekuah injects an element of plot so that Rasselas' sister, Nekayah, is able to learn that one "who has no one to love or to trust has little to hope." And Pekuah reports on her return that the female "happy valley" of the harem is boring because the women talk of nothing but the tediousness of life.

In the final chapter, all the travelers decide on an ideal vocation. But, says the narrator, "they well knew that none could be obtained." So they resolve to return to Abyssinia. Was it in defeat? Not necessarily. All had achieved a valuable education and had lost their insularity. Moreover, as one contemporary critic has suggested, instead of ending in rationalistic despair, they had learned to ask an important question: that is, What activity is most appropriate to man and can best satisfy him and fulfill his destiny? In short, like Voltaire's famous hero, they could be expected in some way eventually to cultivate their own gardens.

By accident, it should be noted here, Voltaire's *Candide* and *Rasselas* were published within two months of each other. Both attacked the fashionable optimism of their day: Leibnitz's "best of all possible worlds" and Pope's "Whatever is, is right." Candide begins in the best of all possible castles; Rasselas, in the Happy Valley. Each has a philosopher-friend—Pangloss and Imlac. Each sets out to explore the world, though for different reasons. Each is disillusioned. But here the resemblance ends. Voltaire's wit is brilliant, slashing, and destructive and is exerted on a tangible and vivid world. Johnson's is deliberate and speculative, balanced, measured, and wise. His world is fanciful. And, if like Sir Thomas More in his *Utopia,* Johnson chose a setting for his story in a non-Christian part of the world, he did so because he wished to deal with man on a purely naturalistic level and discuss basic issues without involving other considerations. In the process, he does not allow his deeply religious nature, so unlike Voltaire's skepticism, to go entirely unperceived. One does not forget, for example, that after Imlac's discussion of the nature of the soul, the Princess Nekayah is moved to insist that the choice of life is no longer so important as the choice of eternity.

To many readers *Rasselas* has long seemed to be chiefly a series of essays, narrative and digressive, like those in the *Rambler,* loosely strung together with a narrative thread that could be described more nearly as plan than plot. Chapters like "A Dissertation on the Art of Flying," "A Dissertation on Poetry," "A Disquisition upon Greatness," and "The Dangerous Prevalence of Imagination" can be lifted out of their context to achieve all but complete independence as separate literary works. The characters are two-dimensional and the dialogue is far from life-like. The style is in places so rhythmic and sonorous as to suggest poetry rather than prose. For these and other reasons, the right of the narrative to be called a novel has frequently been questioned.

So far as the structure of *Rasselas* is concerned, recent critics have been able to suggest illuminating patterns. One of the most useful suggestions is that the novel can be regarded as having three sections or movements of sixteen chapters each, ending with a kind of coda. The first concerns the Happy Valley and the theme of the "choice of life," centered upon the restless prince and his determination to find happiness outside. The second section, in which the travelers make their comprehensive survey of mankind, is focused on Rasselas' "experiments upon life" and the discovery that no one fits his theory and possesses happiness. The section ends with Imlac's famous apostrophe to the pyramids. In the third section, the travelers, now no longer mere observers, find themselves actually involved in life as the victims of others. The chief incidents here concern Pekuah's abduction and return, the encounter with the astronomer, the brief meeting with the disillusioned old man, and final visit to the Catacombs, and the abandonment of the quest. To some critics the coda, "A Conclusion in Which Nothing Is Concluded," is an aesthetic defect. But in all fairness, it can probably be regarded as such only by those who would require Johnson to append more of a moral tag than he plainly thought wise. The discoveries of the travelers concerning life and the fallacy of their quest can be considered to have positive rather than merely negative value and can be regarded as conclusion enough.

Lodwick Hartley

RAVENSHOE

Type of work: Novel
Author: Henry Kingsley (1830-1876)
Type of plot: Domestic romance
Time of plot: Early nineteenth century
Locale: England
First published: 1862

Principal characters:
 CHARLES RAVENSHOE, of the old House of Ravenshoe
 FATHER MACKWORTH, a resident priest
 WILLIAM HORTON, a groom, friend of Charles
 ADELAIDE SUMMERS, a vain girl
 MARY CORBY, ward of the Ravenshoes
 CUTHBERT, older brother of Charles
 LORD SALTIRE, an atheist and dandy

Critique:

This very long novel is slow in pace, and to some modern tastes Kingsley may seem arch with his interminable asides and his painful foreshadowing. In summary form the novel attempts to cover several centuries in the story of an English family, but the bulk of the book is concerned with the affairs of one generation; rather than a panorama of a family, Kingsley gives the adventures of one son. Divested of its paraphernalia, the tale is a lively one in the Regency tradition. The malevolent priest is perhaps the outstanding character.

The Story:

The House of Ravenshoe had long been a bastion of Catholicism in England, and the Church of Rome had for generations assigned a resident priest to the household. Densil Ravenshoe, when he reached manhood, showed a rebellious spirit by going off to London and consorting with Lord Saltire, a notorious atheist. After he had been imprisoned for his debts, his father sent the resident priest to bail him out.

For a while Densil was reconciled to priestly rule, but the new Father Mackworth had his difficulties with him. Densil at last married a Protestant woman, to the consternation of the Church. Five years went by and Densil had no children. Father Mackworth was thinking of asking for another assignment, but he was eavesdropping one evening and what he heard caused him to stay on at Ravenshoe. Cuthbert, Densil's first son, was born, and the priest had the satisfaction of baptizing him in the true faith.

Five years later a second son, Charles, was born. Densil's wife died in childbirth, and shortly the terrible truth came out: Densil had promised to bring up his second son as a Protestant. Charles was given to a nurse, Norah, wife of James Horton, the gamekeeper. She had a boy, William, just a week older than Charles, and she gladly accepted her new charge. Father Mackworth, resolved that a Protestant should never own Ravenshoe, made his plans early.

Charles was a cheerful lad, well liked by all. When he was ten, he went to visit at Ranford, the estate of the Ascots, who were related to the Ravenshoes. Charles was immediately accepted by his Protestant relations; Cuthbert had never been able to win their love. At Ranford Charles met beautiful, imperious Adelaide Summers, a ward of Lady Ascot, and promptly fell in love with her. Another new friend was the famous Lord Saltire, who became fond of the boy.

There was a great storm at Ravenshoe. In the bay a ship went down, split on a rock. Only a few were saved, among them Mary Corby, the daughter of the captain. She was a lovely girl who was accepted as one of the family. She soon fell in love with Charles.

At Oxford, Charles had two intimate

friends, Lord Welter, his cousin from Ranford, and John Marston, a scholar. Marston was a good influence over Charles but Welter was a brutal, arrogant bully. Unfortunately Charles followed Welter's habits of drinking, brawling, and gaming. After a wild night of carousing, both Charles and Welter were sent down from the university. To delay his homecoming, Charles stopped off for a visit at Ranford. Lord Saltire helped him make his peace with his father. During his visit he became engaged to Adelaide.

Charles spent several months of enforced vacation at Ravenshoe. During that time Welter and Marston both came to see him. Marston proposed to Mary but she refused him. This period was marred by Father Mackworth, who seemed to Charles an evil genius. Ellen Horton, William's younger sister, ran away because of some trouble which seemed to be connected with Father Mackworth. At the beginning of the next term Charles went back to Oxford.

His stay was brief, for he was recalled by the death of his father. Father Mackworth was in possession of a ruinous secret which Cuthbert offered to buy for ten thousand pounds. Father Mackworth refused money, but to keep Charles from inheriting Ravenshoe he revealed that Norah had switched babies long ago; Charles was really her own son, and William Horton, the groom, was a Ravenshoe. William, a Catholic, became second in line to own Ravenshoe. Distraught, Charles rushed to Ranford to see Adelaide, only to learn that she had run away with Welter.

Calling himself Charles Horton, he took service with Lieutenant Hornby. As a servant he learned that Ellen, his own sister, had been Welter's mistress; now she was a maid in the same household with Adelaide, Welter's new mistress. Welter and Adelaide lived by gambling. Charles had an interview with Welter, who excused his villainy by saying that he had not known that Ellen was Charles' sister. In reality, Charles was

well rid of the scheming Adelaide. After seeing Mary, who had become a governess, from a distance, Charles enlisted in the army to fight against the Russians.

The Ascot family, heavily in debt, had put all their hopes on a horse they had entered in the Derby. In a desperate attempt to recoup his fortunes, Lord Ascot substituted a less famous jockey and bet against his own horse. The Ascot entry won and the family was ruined. At his father's death, Welter became Lord Ascot. Although he had married Adelaide by that time, society ignored her.

In the Crimea, Charles took part in the famous charge of the Six Hundred at Balaklava. Hornby was killed and Charles was wounded. Invalided home, he took service again as a groom under an officer with whom he had served. He hoped to remain and eventually to find his sister Ellen. His health remained poor.

When William made a trip to Sevastopol to look for Charles, a lying soldier had convinced him that Charles was dead. When he heard the news, Lord Saltire made a new will, bequeathing a large sum to Mary but leaving the bulk of his fortune to Welter and Adelaide.

Thinking themselves at last secure, Welter and his wife began to move freely in society. One night, to his horror, Welter recognized Charles in a tavern. Adelaide wanted Welter to keep still, but her husband, conscience-stricken, informed Lord Saltire, who prepared to make a new will immediately. But the great lord died before morning.

Charles was nursed back to health at Ranford after an operation to heal his war wound. When he returned to Ravenshoe, he was a guest of William, now in control of the estate since Cuthbert's death by drowning. But Lady Ascot had started a chain of inquiries which threatened Father Mackworth's design. Finally paralyzed after a stroke, he summoned Ellen, now a nun, and through a wedding certificate in her keeping the truth came out. James Horton, father of Charles and Ellen, had always been looked upon as the illegitimate son of

Densil's father, Petre Ravenshoe. But Petre had really married James' mother, and so Charles was the true heir of Ravenshoe after all. Father Mackworth had at one time possessed the marriage certificate, but Ellen had stolen it when she ran away. Her return with the certificate provided proof of Father Mackworth's duplicity.

Ellen returned to her nursing duties; Father Mackworth died after begging forgiveness of the heir he had dispossessed. Charles, the Protestant owner of Ravenshoe, made ample provision for his good friend William and the two were married in a double ceremony, Charles to the faithful Mary and William to his childhood sweetheart. At the celebration Welter acknowledged that Lord Saltire's estate really belonged to Charles. Adelaide had become a permanent invalid after a riding accident; hence they would never have children. In reparation, Welter had willed his entire fortune to Charles.

Further Critical Evaluation of the Work:

Appropriately, Henry Kingsley dedicated his second and best novel, *Ravenshoe,* to his older brother Charles; not only did the brothers hold each other in high esteem and affection, but their writing shared same common virtues and reflected similar interests and predilections. *Ravenshoe,* like *Westward Ho!,* is distinguished by typical Kingsley virtues: lively descriptions of noble, manly deeds; beautiful pictures of English sea and countryside; a good-humored joviality of tone; and an invigorating sense of the author's enthusiastic love of life. At the same time, Henry Kingsley's characteristic weaknesses are also evident in *Ravenshoe;* the plot is encumbered with too many incidents, the style is careless, the narrative flow is disrupted by too-frequent authorial intrusions, and the storyline is often melodramatic and implausible.

The most attractive feature of the novel is the characterization of Charles Ravenshoe. He hovers somewhere between obstinacy and determination, foolishness and whimsy, rebelliousness and independence; but in the end he always has the reader's affection and sympathy. The novel is essentially the story of the good-hearted, exuberant boy who must learn, through suffering and hardship, to accept the responsibilities of manhood. He needs to temper his boyish boisterousness with level-headed, adult patience and discipline; his animal energy and high spirits must eventually find constructive and worthy outlets. Kingsley shows us the external steps of this growth process in Charles, who at the close of the novel is a sober, dreamy, and even somewhat melancholy man, although he does not probe deeply into the hero's private thoughts, emotions, or motivations. In addition to Charles, *Ravenshoe* contains some memorable minor characters. The implacable enemies, Lady Ascot and Lady Hainault, are delightful comic creations; the villainous Jesuit, Father Mackworth, while he is a one-dimensional figure, nevertheless gains depth and life temporarily in scenes such as the moving description of Cuthbert's drowning. Lord Saltire, the atheist considered in his youth to be the devil incarnate, is an excellent example of the traditional type of the elderly and respectable reformed roué.

Ravenshoe is distinguished by its atmosphere of vitality and humor pervaded by a regretful sense of melancholy at the passing of the traditions of England's old rural houses. Although even the most avid admirers of Kingsley's fiction do not claim him as one of the great British novelists, they know the enjoyment that awaits readers of *Ravenshoe* in the form of spirited fun and excellent entertainment.

THE REAL LIFE OF SEBASTIAN KNIGHT

Type of work: Novel
Author: Vladimir Nabokov (1899-   )
Time: 1899-1938
Locale: England and Europe
First published: 1938

The Real Life of Sebastian Knight, written in Paris in 1938 but not published in the United States until 1941, is Vladimir Nabokov's first work in English; previously he had written in Russian. Although this earlier novel does not show quite the same ingenious conjuring with language as do *Lolita* and *Pale Fire,* it is, none the less, a brilliant, sometimes funny, and almost perversely complex book.

The novel is written as a biography of Sebastian Knight, a writer who has just died, by his younger half brother, who designates himself only as V. Beginning as an attempt to present the real Sebastian, V.'s biography becomes the quest of V. himself to understand the personality of the man revealed by his search. Two problems, therefore, run as concurrent themes through the novel: first, the problem of communication between a writer and his readers, the task of conveying reality with precision, and, secondly, the greater problem of what this reality is—the multiple views possible of the same thing and the necessarily unsuccessful attempt to capture anything so elusive as personal identity. The novel presents a dazzling series of masks, none of which may be removed completely because knowing more about Sebastian Knight does not help us to understand him but rather increases his complexity.

Within the novel are three different literary attempts to portray Sebastian. The first is V.'s own earnest, painstaking effort to portray his brother objectively. At the opposite extreme is a slick, superficial biography, already published, by Mr. Goodman, Sebastian's former secretary. But V. admits in quoting from it at length that even this book contains elements of truth. Somewhere in the middle are Sebastian's own novels, which reveal obliquely something of the man himself, even though we can never be sure of how much they disclose.

V.'s first-hand knowledge of Sebastian, colored by the adoration of a younger brother for the clever older one and by V.'s nostalgia for Russia, is confined to Sebastian's youth. Sebastian had been born in Russia; his English mother, a restless, romantic woman, deserted her husband and baby; his father remarried. Sebastian left Russia for Cambridge and remained in England, becoming almost a caricature of an Englishman and writing his novels in England. At this point in his biography, V. must search for people who knew Sebastian, for V. saw almost nothing of him after he left Russia, and their few meetings were cold and strained.

V.'s search for the truth becomes a kind of detective novel, but an enigmatic and paradoxical one. His elaborate quest is continually frustrated—by someone's inability to remember, by his own timidity, by his willingness to content himself with an intuitive impression, almost as if he does not wish to have any illusions shattered. One is reminded of Sebastian's own first novel, a parody of a detective story; indeed, the quotations from Sebastian's writing provide not only a glimpse of his real self but also an insight into this novel, for one might say of it that he employed parody as a means of achieving effects of serious thought and feeling. This novel of Sebastian's, called *The Prismatic Bezel,* also hints at the many-faceted obliquity of Nabokov's novel.

V.'s quest degenerates into a melodramatic farce. He finds the woman whom Sebastian loved and tricks her into an admission of her identity, but again he contents himself with his own impression of her and his own estimate of the effect she must have had on his brother. Nabokov weaves parallel situations from Sebastian's novels and from his and the narrator's life into a glittering web which conceals as much as it reveals. One cannot know another person because countless factors of which one is totally unaware intervene. His method is the juxtaposition of a series of glimpses, absurd and touching, like a series of sleight-of-hand tricks. One cannot tell what is the trickery of legerdemain and what is not.

Two incidents, one near the beginning, the other at the end of the book, illuminate its meaning. On one of his trips to Europe, Sebastian finds a village called Roquebrune, the town where his mother had died. He finds her house and sits for a long time in the garden, trying to find the mother whom he scarcely knew. At length, he can almost see her figure, like some pastel ghost, gliding up the stairs to the door. Much later, he discovers by accident that the Roquebrune he had found was not even the same town where his mother had lived, but another, many miles away. There is something funny and pathetic in his own deception, something which undercuts and transcends the experience. Its meaning is made clearer by the end of the book. V. had been in Marseilles when he received a telegram telling him Sebastian was seriously ill. After many delays he finds the hospital, has some difficulties in making the porter understand him, but is eventually shown into the room where the Englishman, still alive, is sleeping. He spends only a few minutes there, but he feels he can at last express the kinship he has always felt with his brother, that at last these mo-

ments listening to the sound of his breathing have crystallized a whole series of other moments as words could not have done. Yet, on leaving the room, he discovers by chance that this man was not his brother at all, for Sebastian had died the day before. But he says that later he found his life transformed by the short time he spent in the dying man's company. He now believed that the soul—any man's soul—is a way of being rather than a constant state; therefore souls are constantly in flux and interchangeable. V. feels that he is Sebastian Knight; he wears his mask. Sebastian may even be V., or both may be someone they never knew. In this mood he begins to write his brother's biography.

One cannot, of course, know another person completely, for one cannot know oneself. The fact that V. goes on to write Sebastian's biography proves that he has understood for only a moment. But the existence of a series of masks does not necessarily mean that nothing lies behind them, only that one can penetrate no further.

Nabokov's method is oblique, moving as does the chess knight who must leap in two directions and skip over intervening pieces, because our knowledge of identity must be reached obliquely. This novel is at once a fascinating puzzle and a profound statement, whose depths are disguised as absurdities. It is technically not the *tour de force* which *Lolita* and *Pale Fire* are, but its discussions of the relationship between the writer and his art reveal much about the author's own technique. Its themes are similar to those of his other works, as is its deliberate comic view, which approaches within a hair's-breadth of the tragic. This book is at once a witty bit of hocus-pocus and a fine and moving novel.

REBECCA

Type of work: Novel
Author: Daphne du Maurier (1907-   )
Type of plot: Mystery romance
Time of plot: 1930's
Locale: England
First published: 1938

Principal characters:
MAXIM DE WINTER, owner of Manderley
MRS. DE WINTER, Maxim's wife and the narrator
MRS. DANVERS, the housekeeper at Manderley
FRANK CRAWLEY, estate manager of Manderley
JACK FAVELL, Rebecca's cousin
COLONEL JULYAN, a magistrate

Critique:

Rebecca is an excellent example of the suspense novel. From the time the drab little companion marries Maxim de Winter, the reader is aware that there is something wrong with the situation at Manderley, the fine house where Rebecca was formerly the mistress. All through the novel there are hints that some startling disclosure about Rebecca is to come, a revelation which will explain many strange events. In development of situation and in character portrayal there is ample evidence of the author's technical skill.

The Story:

Manderley was gone. Since the fire which had destroyed their home, Mr. and Mrs. de Winter had lived in a secluded hotel away from England. Occasionally Mrs. de Winter recalled the circumstances which had brought Manderley and Maxim de Winter into her life.

A shy, sensitive orphan, she had been traveling about the continent as companion to an overbearing American social climber, Mrs. Van Hopper. At Monte Carlo Mrs. Van Hopper forced herself upon Maxim de Winter, owner of Manderley, one of the most famous estates in England. Before approaching him, Mrs. Van Hopper had informed her companion that Mr. de Winter was recovering from the shock of the tragic death of his wife, Rebecca, a few months previously.

During the following days the young girl and Mr. de Winter became well acquainted; when Mrs. Van Hopper decided to return to America, Maxim de Winter unexpectedly proposed to her companion. Already deeply in love with him, the girl accepted and they were married shortly afterward.

After a long honeymoon in Italy and southern France, Mr. and Mrs. de Winter returned to Manderley. Mrs. de Winter was extremely nervous, fearing that she would not fit into the life of a great estate like Manderley. The entire staff had gathered to meet the new mistress. Mrs. Danvers, the housekeeper, had been devoted to her former mistress and immediately began to show her resentment toward the new Mrs. de Winter.

Gradually Mrs. de Winter pieced together the picture of Rebecca. She learned that Rebecca had been a beautiful, vivacious woman, a charming hostess. As she became acquainted with the relatives and friends of her husband, she became convinced that they found her lacking in those qualities which had made Rebecca so attractive and gracious. One day she went secretly to the closed rooms Rebecca had occupied. Everything was as Rebecca had left it before her fatal sail in her boat. Mrs. Danvers suddenly appeared and forced her to view Rebecca's lovely clothes and other personal possessions.

When the bishop's wife suggested that the traditional Manderley fancy dress ball be revived, Mr. de Winter gave his consent. Mrs. de Winter announced her intention of surprising them all with her costume. At Mrs. Danvers' suggestion, she planned to dress as an ancestress whose portrait hung in the hall at Manderley. But as Mrs. de Winter descended the stairs that night a silence fell over the guests, and her husband turned angrily away without speaking. Realizing that something was wrong, Mrs. de Winter returned to her room. Beatrice, Mr. de Winter's sister, went to her immediately and explained that Rebecca had worn the identical costume to her last fancy dress ball. Again Mrs. Danvers had humiliated her new mistress. Although Mrs. de Winter reappeared at the ball in a simple dress, her husband did not speak to her all evening; and her belief that he had never ceased to love Rebecca became firmly established in her mind.

The next day a steamer ran aground in the bay near Manderley. A diver sent down to inspect the damaged steamer discovered Rebecca's boat and in its cabin the remains of a human body. Mr. de Winter had previously identified the body of a woman found in the river as that of Rebecca.

Unable to keep silent any longer, Mr. de Winter told his wife the whole story of Rebecca and her death. The world had believed their marriage a happy one, but Rebecca had been an immoral woman, incapable of love. To avoid the scandal of a divorce, they made a bargain; Rebecca was to be outwardly the fitting mistress of Manderley, but she would be allowed to go to London periodically to visit her dissolute friends. All went well until she began to be careless, inviting her friends to Manderley and receiving them in the boathouse. Then she began to plague Frank Crawley, the estate manager of Manderley, and Giles, Mr. de Winter's brother-in-law. There had been gossip after Frank

and others had seen Rebecca's cousin, Jack Favell, at the boathouse with her. One evening Mr. de Winter had followed her to the boathouse to tell her that their marriage was at an end. Rebecca taunted him, suggesting how difficult it would be to prove his case against her, asserting that should she have a child it would bear his name and inherit Manderley. She assured him with a smile that she would be the perfect mother as she had been the perfect wife.

She was still smiling when he shot her. Then he put her in the boat and sailed out on the river. There he opened the seacocks, drilled holes with a pike, and leaving the boat to sink, rowed back in the dinghy.

Mrs. de Winter was horrified, but at the same time she felt a happiness she had not known before. Her husband loved her; he had never loved Rebecca. With that discovery, her personality changed. She assured her husband that she would guard his secret.

A coroner's inquest was held, for the body in the boat was that of Rebecca. At the inquest it was established that a storm could not have sunk the boat; evidence of a bolted door, the holes, and the open seacocks pointed to the verdict of suicide which the coroner's jury returned.

That night Jack Favell, drunk, appeared at Manderley. Wildly expressing his love for Rebecca and revealing their intimate life, he tried to blackmail Mr. de Winter by threatening to prove that de Winter had killed his wife. Mr. de Winter called the magistrate, Colonel Julyan, to hear his case. Favell's theory was that Rebecca had asked her husband to free her so that she could marry Jack, and that de Winter, infuriated, had killed her.

From Rebecca's engagement book it was learned that she had visited a Doctor Baker in London on the last day of her life. Colonel Julyan and Mr. and Mrs. de Winter, with Jack Favell following in his car, drove to London to see Doctor Baker. On checking his records, the doctor found that he had examined a Mrs. Danvers on the day in question. They realized that Rebecca had assumed the housekeeper's name. Doctor Baker explained that he had diagnosed Rebecca's ailment as cancer in an advanced stage. The motive for suicide established, Colonel Julyan suggested that the matter be closed.

Driving back to Manderley after leaving Colonel Julyan at his sister's home, Mr. de Winter told his wife that he believed that Colonel Julyan had guessed the truth. He also realized that Rebecca had intimated that she was preg-nant because she had been sure that her husband would kill her; her last evil deed would be to ruin him and Manderley. Mr. de Winter telephoned Frank from the inn where they stopped for dinner, and the estate manager reported that Mrs. Danvers had disappeared. His news seemed to upset Mr. de Winter. At two o'clock in the morning they approached Manderley. Mrs. de Winter had been sleeping. Awaking, she thought by the blaze of light that it was dawn. A moment later she realized that she was looking at Manderley, going up in flames.

Further Critical Evaluation of the Work:

For nearly four decades Daphne du Maurier has excited and terrified readers with some of the best suspense novels of the twentieth century. She is one of a small group of writers who have, by their artistic ingenuity, insight into character and situation, and technical virtuosity, elevated popular "formula" fiction into serious literature. And there is no better example of her skill and power than her early suspense masterpiece, *Rebecca*.

The basic structure of *Rebecca* is that of the modern "Gothic Romance," but Miss du Maurier has utilized and transformed the rigid formula of this popular genre to create a very original and personal fiction. The unnamed narrator, at least for the first two-thirds of the novel, is the typical heroine of a Gothic Romance. Although her character is not deep, her qualities and desires are carefully chosen to provoke maximum interest and sympathy. Two narrative questions animate the rather leisurely early chapters of the novel: can the heroine, an orphan with little training or worldly experience, adjust to the unfamiliar, demanding social role as mistress of Manderley? And can she win and keep the love of her passionately desired, but enigmatic, even sinister husband, Maxim de Winter? These two elements—Manderley, the isolated, beautiful, but ultimately threatening setting, and de Winter, the charming, handsome, but moody, mysterious "hero-villain"—are standard essentials in the genre.

After they set up residence at Manderley, these two questions become fused as the dominating, almost spectral presence of Maxim's first wife, Rebecca, becomes increasingly felt. This presence is made concrete by Mrs. Danvers, the efficient, sinister, intimidating housekeeper, who still "serves" her original mistress, and Jack Favell, Rebecca's crudely handsome, lascivious cousin. They, along with the gradual revelation that Rebecca's death was not accidental, give the novel that sense of growing threat and conspiracy that is *de rigueur* in the Gothic Romance.

Approximately two-thirds of the way through the book, however, Miss du Maurier adds a special twist to the story that takes it out of the Gothic Romance category and establishes it as a unique suspense thriller. Maxim finally breaks down and confesses to the heroine that Rebecca was "vicious, damnable, rotten through and through," and that he murdered her when she tormented him about a "son and heir" that was not his. Thus, the focus shifts from the heroine's mysterious danger to her husband's legal fate. Instead of fearing for the physical safety of the narrator, the reader is placed in the ironic position of cheering for the criminal to escape detection and punishment. And the "villains," Mrs. Danvers and Jack Favell, become petty, pitiable creatures rather than serious conspirators..

Most importantly, the heroine is freed by this knowledge from Rebecca's "ghost." Knowing that Maxim loves and needs her, and faced with a threat that is real and specific, rather than undefined and pervasive, she can deal with her situation in a direct, forceful way as an emotionally whole, self-confident woman. Thus, the heroine grows from a pretty household decoration to the mistress of Manderley, from a girl to a woman, and from a child-bride to a mature lover and wife. It is, finally, Miss du Maurier's skill and sensitivity in describing her heroine's maturity in a manner that is psychologically believable and emotionally satisfying that qualifies *Rebecca* as a unique and serious work of art.

THE REBEL GENERATION

Type of work: Novel
Author: Johanna van Ammers-Küller (1884-1966)
Type of plot: Social chronicle
Time of plot: 1840-1923
Locale: Leyden, Holland
First published: 1925

Principal characters:
    LOUIS CORNVELT, an upper middle-class Hollander
    NICHOLAS, and
    DAVID CORNVELT, his sons
    SARAH, and
    KATIE CORNVELT, his daughters
    MARIE ELIZABETH SYLVAIN (LYSBETH, "SYLVIA"), his niece
    DR. WILLIAM WISEMAN, Katie Cornvelt's husband
    (DR.) ELIZA WISEMAN, daughter of William and Katie
    LOUIS CORNVELT, David's son
    CLARA CORNVELT, David's daughter
    MILLICENT CORNVELT, great-granddaughter of Louis Cornvelt, Sr.
    STEPHEN CORNVELT, Millicent's cousin, in love with her
    DOROTHY CORNVELT, Stephen's wife
    PUCK, and
    KITTY CORNVELT, daughters of Stephen and Dorothy

Critique:

The Rebel Generation is a sociological novel presenting the changes in middle-class Dutch culture through several generations of a single family. It demonstrates how the ethical standards and the mores of the people changed, especially the relationships between parents and children. The novel also presents the struggle by women for equality with men. The presentation of the attempts by women to achieve equality with men shows how seriously nineteenth-century women faced the problem and how the solution appeared to women of a later generation to be a mixed blessing. The Rebel Generation is usually considered Johanna van Ammers-Küller's greatest success. It has been translated into several languages and has had a successful production on the stage.

The Story:

In 1840, Louis Cornvelt was a prosperous owner of a weaving mill in Leyden. Strongly orthodox and conservative in every way, he was a stanch Calvinist whose beliefs colored his treatment of his family and his employees. His wife, his sons, and his daughters were expected to be completely submissive to his will and the way of life he represented.

Outwardly, at least, they were, until the arrival in the Cornvelt home of an orphaned niece, Marie Elizabeth Sylvain. Reared in a much more permissive atmosphere in the home of her French father, she brought new ideas and an air of rebellion into the Cornvelt home. Three of the sons fell in love with her, but she refused their overtures of love and marriage, for she could not stand the idea of placing herself under the domination of a man. Her rebellion extended so far as to cause her to run away to France when her uncle refused to allow her to earn a living for herself; he felt that such a course might demean him and his family in the eyes of their friends and neighbors.

Marie Elizabeth Sylvain's cousins, fired by her arguments and example, tried to rebel, too, but in the end each submissively accepted their father's domination. Katie Cornvelt married a young medical doctor, William Wiseman, as her father wished, although she found the man's profession and person repugnant to her. Nicholas Cornvelt ran his father's woolen mill in the old way, as his father dictated, even though the younger man realized that more progressive methods were needed if the mill were to compete with more progressive business houses. Sarah Cornvelt gave up the young man she loved when their fathers refused to countenance their marriage. David Cornvelt, in love with his French cousin, gave her up too when his father demanded that he do so. The young people had been so used to domination that they could not break from the habit of obedience, even after they were grown.

By 1872 the children of Louis Cornvelt were themselves middle-aged and had children of their own who were approaching maturity. Having been reared in a home completely dominated by their father, the children attempted to rule their families in much the same way and to require of the new generation absolute obedience to parents and loyalty to a harshly conservative code. In their time, however, the new generation was supported and encouraged to rebellion by changes in the life of the time. In Holland, as in other European countries, new liberality in politics, new theories in sociology, a breakdown of orthodox religion, and other changes contributed to an outlook that fostered rebellion against paternal domination of children and masculine domination of women.

Dr. William Wiseman and his wife were horrified when their daughter Eliza announced she wished to become a doctor, for such a career had previously been unheard of for a woman. Although her father wanted a son to be a doctor, he could not imagine his daughter becoming one, and he fought to check her interest in medical studies.

Eliza Wiseman found help and encouragement when her mother's cousin, Marie Elizabeth Sylvain, returned to Holland from France to work for the emancipation of women. Marie Elizabeth had received a considerable fortune which she devoted to the cause of equality of the sexes, using the money to assist capable young women to gain an education and to publish periodicals in support of feminine equality. Eliza Wiseman was not the only one in the Cornvelt clan to receive help from their cousin, who called herself Sylvia.

Sarah Cornvelt had married a retired army officer. When her husband died, leaving her with almost no income and several daughters almost grown, Sarah's brothers attempted to take over her affairs, offering her a small allowance from their pockets in return for their domination. Encouraged by her French cousin, Sarah refused to accept the men's proposals and established herself and her daughters as professional dressmakers. Sarah, like her sisters, had had too much domination under the rule of father and husband to accept the domination of her brothers.

David Cornvelt, a distinguished professor, found rebellion in other quarters than his sister Sarah's household. In his own home the younger generation refused to follow his dictates, even though rebellion hurt them and other members of the family. David's son Louis became a political radical and wrote pamphlets that kept his father from appointment to a post in the national cabinet. David's daughter Clara persisted in being a social worker among the lowest classes, even though she gave in to her father in matters of love.

In 1923 the senior members of the Cornvelt family found themselves in their turn faced with a generation of young people who were in rebellion against their parents. By this time even the older generation was dissatisfied. The changes in family relationships were unsatisfactory. So far as women were concerned, emancipation and equality with men had been achieved. Dorothy Cornvelt, married to Dr. Eliza Wiseman's nephew, was a lawyer and a member of Parliament. But her home life was empty, for both her husband and children were indifferent to her professional and political life. Her husband, Stephen Cornvelt, became infatuated with Millicent Cornvelt, a distant cousin from a branch of the family which had migrated to England. His infatuation with the girl was so great that he asked for a divorce, and neither he nor the young girl could see why his wife should deny the request.

The children of Stephen and Dorothy Cornvelt also felt that life was too loose for them. Although they were well educated and free from most parental restraints, they were unhappy. They felt a need for a return to the safety of a stable home and the guidance of older people, even though they disliked interference by their elders. When Stephen tried to dissuade his daughter Kitty from a career as a dancer, she rebelled as violently as any earlier Cornvelt had done. Her sister Puck, however, a successful businesswoman, indicated by her behavior the course that later generations might take. She gave up her career to marry the man she loved, expecting to find happiness in family life and the influence of her husband. She also rebelled, but her rebellion was against too much freedom, rather than too little.

Further Critical Evaluation of the Work:

The Rebel Generation, by Johanna van Ammers-Küller, was the first volume of one of the author's two trilogies dealing with Dutch family life in the nineteenth and twentieth centuries. Though not a success in its native country, this particular novel received world-wide attention and was a bestseller in several languages. What the reader sees in the novel is a series of portraits of strong-willed men and women who are related more by ideas and behavior than by the obvious familial connection. Ammers-Küller, though not a strictly feminist writer, has portrayed the struggle of women for equality in a way that blends in well with her overall picture of Dutch manners and morals of the era. She has perhaps not been listed with some of the great feminist writers of the early part of this century, however, for while she beautifully illustrates women's struggle for equality, she also shows how at least one generation of the Cornvelt family reversed the trend by their own desires.

One of the flaws of the book which strikes the modern reader is that the author has sacrificed imaginative writing for her "message." Plot, characterization, and even to some extent setting, are all subservient to the main theme of rebellion within three generations of one Dutch family. Her lack of subtlety will not bring her into the forefront of great writers of the twentieth century, and her faltering feminism will not allow her to be totally accepted as a champion of women's liberation either. What Ammers-Küller will be remembered for is her solid novel of Dutch middle-class life, something which has not been overdone and is little known outside The Netherlands.

THE RECRUITING OFFICER

Type of work: Drama
Author: George Farquhar (1678-1707)
Type of plot: Comedy of intrigue
Time of plot: Early eighteenth century
Locale: Shrewsbury, England
First presented: 1706

Principal characters:
 CAPTAIN PLUME, the recruiting officer, a gay blade
 SYLVIA BALANCE, Captain Plume's fiancée
 MR. WORTHY, Captain Plume's friend
 MELINDA, Mr. Worthy's fiancée and cousin of Sylvia Balance
 JUSTICE BALANCE, Sylvia's father
 ROSE, the pretty young daughter of a farmer
 SERGEANT KITE, Captain Plume's aide

Critique:

This is not Farquhar's best-known play —that honor goes to *The Beaux' Stratagem*—but it is superior to many of the other Restoration comedies. Perhaps the most richly comic soldier in English drama is to be found here in Sergeant Kite, who doubles as a fortune-teller and a pander for his master. It is a long step from the *Miles Gloriosus* of the Plautine comedy, through Captain Bobadil of Ben Jonson's comedy, to this grandly comic figure. In this play the reader is taken from London to Shrewsbury, a welcome change in comedies of this period, most of which were laid in London. In moving his scene from London, Farquhar followed the example of Thomas Shadwell, the poet and playwright who succeeded John Dryden as Poet Laureate. Indeed, the reader is constantly reminded of similarities of incident and tone between the plays of Shadwell and Farquhar. There is less of the elegant tone in this play, however, for it rather leans to the sentiment of later eighteenth-century drama.

The Story:

Captain Plume, commander of a company of grenadiers, and his aide, Sergeant Kite, went to Shrewsbury to enlist a number of recruits for Captain Plume's command. They went to Shrewsbury because of success in gaining recruits in that city some months before, and because of Captain Plume's amorous successes at the same time. Upon the arrival of the pair they were greeted with the news that a young woman who had just given birth to a child had named Captain Plume as the father. At the captain's request, Sergeant Kite married the woman and went on record as the father of the child. This was not the first time he had done as much for the captain; he had accumulated a list of six wives in the same manner.

Captain Plume also found his good friend, Mr. Worthy, at Shrewsbury. Mr. Worthy had been a happy-go-lucky chap, much like Captain Plume, until his fiancée had inherited a fortune. The girl, Melinda, had taken on airs after becoming a rich woman, and she proceeded to make life miserable for Worthy. His latest grievance was that another officer on recruiting duty, one Captain Brazen, had apparently become a successful rival for Melinda's hand and fortune. Captain Plume asked Worthy about Sylvia Balance, whom the captain loved but could not marry because his life was too uncertain and he had too little money. Worthy told Captain Plume that Sylvia Balance still thought very well of him.

While Worthy and Captain Plume talked, Melinda and Sylvia were having a conversation of their own, in which Sylvia told her cousin that she was determined that the captain should not leave Shrewsbury alone. The two women quarreled, and after Sylvia's departure Melinda wrote a letter to Sylvia's father telling him that Captain Plume intended to dishonor Sylvia.

That evening Captain Plume had dinner with Sylvia and her father, Justice Balance, who considered the captain a fine match for his daughter. During the evening news came from Germany by mail that Justice Balance's son and heir had died. Immediately the attitude of Justice Balance toward Captain Plume changed, for he did not like to think of the captain as the husband of his daughter if she were to have all his fortune. Calling Sylvia into private conference, he told her of the change in his attitude. Although the girl was very much in love with the captain, she promised that she would not marry without her father's consent. Captain Plume left the house without learning what had happened. A short time after his departure Melinda's spiteful letter to Sylvia's father arrived. In order to get her away from the captain, Justice Balance immediately sent Sylvia by coach to one of his country estates.

Both Worthy and Captain Plume interpreted Sylvia's departure erroneously. They thought that she believed herself too good for the captain after she had inherited a fortune of two thousand pounds a year. The captain, claiming that he would get along as well without her, proceeded to go about his business of recruiting. While doing so he met a farmer's pretty young daughter, named Rose. Rose and he immediately fancied one another, and the captain went so far as to give his half-promise that he would make the girl his wife. In return, she helped him to add almost a dozen more recruits to his company. These included her own brother and her former sweetheart.

One day Sylvia, disguised in some of her brother's clothes, returned to Shrewsbury, where she met the two recruiting officers, Captain Plume and Captain Brazen, in the company of Melinda. When she told them that she was Mr. Willful, a young man of good family who wished to enlist, they both bid for the new recruit, who finally agreed to join Captain Plume's company. The captain was so pleased with young Mr. Willful that he proffered his friendship, even though the recruit was to be an enlisted man in the company.

Saying that he would be censured for entering the army voluntarily, the recruit asked Captain Plume to have him impressed into service by the provisions of the acts of Parliament. The captain agreed to do so. To help her deception, and also to test the direction of Captain Plume's affections, Sylvia in her disguise pretended to be in love with Rose.

The fiancée of Worthy, meanwhile, had been to see a fortune-teller who was really Sergeant Kite in disguise. The fortune-teller told Melinda that she would die unmarried if she let a man who was to call on her at ten o'clock the following morning leave the country. He had also managed to secure a copy of her handwriting, which he showed her in an attempt to make her think the devil was his helper. Melinda was so impressed that she promised herself to follow the fortune-teller's advice.

Justice Balance decided that the best way to keep his daughter's honor and fortune from falling into the hands of Captain Plume was to provide the officer with the soldiers he needed and to draft them according to the provision made by Parliament. In order to do so, the justice opened his court and had the bailiff bring in a number of men who were eligible for the draft. Among the men was Sylvia in her disguise as Mr. Willful. She had been accused, as a man, of having taken Rose as a common-law wife. In the courtroom Mr. Willful behaved impudently, and the justice decided to punish the brash young man by sending him off as a private in Captain Plume's company of gendarmes. Thus Sylvia tricked her father into sending her away with the captain. In fact, the justice ordered Captain Plume not to discharge Mr. Willful for any reason.

After the hearing Justice Balance went to his home, where he learned that his daughter, dressed in her deceased brother's clothes, had disappeared from his country estate. The justice immediately realized that he had been tricked, that the Mr. Willful whom he had sent off with Captain Plume was really Sylvia. He also thought that Captain Plume had been a party to the deception. When the captain called at the justice's home a short time later, it was soon apparent that he knew nothing of the scheme, for he agreed to discharge the new soldier at Justice Balance's request.

Mr. Willful was called in and unmasked as Sylvia. Then the father, realizing how much his daughter loved the captain, gave them permission to marry. Immediately thereafter Worthy and Melinda arrived to say that they had also reached an agreement and were to be married shortly. Melinda also apologized for the spiteful letter she had sent to Justice Balance. Captain Plume, pleased over the prospect of a handsome fortune coming to him with his wife, announced that he was retiring from the army. He turned over all the recruits he had enlisted to Captain Brazen, who had been unsuccessful in finding any men for his company.

Further Critical Evaluation of the Work:

Farquhar is one of those transitional figures in the history of literature, like Chaucer and Blake, who straddle different ages or ideologies. Their work seems either unerringly current, as was the case with Chaucer and Farquhar, or as in Blake's case, strangely remote. Farquhar was no prophetic genius like Blake, but he did have a touch of Chaucer's social imagination; just as Chaucer dramatized the emergence of pre-Renaissance individualism in his studies of medieval character, Farquhar achieved a happy balance between Restoration licentiousness and early eighteenth century sentiment. Had he lived (he died at twenty-nine), Farquhar possibly could have saved comedy from indulging its preference for feeling over wit—a trend that eventually defused comedy of its satirical power and resulted in the triumph of the sentimental comedy championed by Cibber and Steele.

Farquhar's characters, even rakes like Captain Plume, are brothers to Etherege's and Wycherley's rakes of the early Restoration comedy, but they do not sacrifice their feelings to a cold wit. They are also less devious and manipulative in seduction and deception than their Restoration models. Plume enjoys the selfish victories of the rake, but he also admits to a tormented conscience: "The world is all a cheat; only I take mine, which is undesigned, to be more excusable than theirs, which is hypocritical. I hurt nobody but myself, but they abuse all mankind."

The sentiment in Farquhar is expressed mainly in his sympathy for his characters. He develops them so that even minor characters are not merely caricatures or stereotypes. Morally, like Captain Plume, he has few illusions. "The world is all a cheat," and although Farquhar may make his sinners sympathetic, sinners they remain. Sergeant Kite is as immoral as he is alive, but his immorality cannot dehumanize him to the point where he becomes a ridiculed fop or fool, as would have been the case in the earlier comedy. Like Falstaff, the notorious "recruiter" of *Henry the Fourth, Part One,* Kite is a comic creation greater than the laughs he receives.

THE RED AND THE BLACK

Type of work: Novel
Author: Stendhal (Marie-Henri Beyle, 1783-1842)
Type of plot: Psychological realism
Time of plot: Early nineteenth century
Locale: France
First published: 1830

Principal characters:
JULIEN SOREL, an opportunist
M. DE RÊNAL, mayor of Verrières
MADAME DE RÊNAL, his wife
MATHILDE DE LA MOLE, Julien's mistress
FOUQUÉ, Julien's friend

Critique:

This novel is unusual in that its chief character is a villain. He is an interesting villain, however, for Stendhal analyzes the psychological undercurrents of his nature in an attempt to show clearly how struggle and temptation shaped his energetic but morbidly introspective character. The author analyzes the actions of Julien's loves in the same way. This method of writing slows down the action of the plot considerably, but on the other hand it makes the characters real and understandable and shows much of the sordid conditions of French society at the end of the Napoleonic wars.

The Story:

Julien Sorel was the son of a carpenter in the little town of Verrières, France. Napoleon had fallen, but he still had many admirers, and Julien was one of these. Julien pretended to be deeply religious. Now that Napoleon had been defeated, he believed that the church rather than the army was the way to power. Because of his assumed piety and his intelligence, Julien was appointed as tutor to the children of M. de Rênal, the mayor of the village.

Madame de Rênal had done her duty all her life; she was a good wife and a good mother. But she had never been in love with her husband, a coarse man who would hardly inspire love in any woman. Madame de Rênal was attracted to the pale young tutor and fell completely in love with him. Julien, thinking it his

duty to himself, made love to her in order to gain power over her. He discovered after a time that he had really fallen in love with Madame de Rênal.

When Julien went on a holiday to visit Fouqué, a poor friend, Fouqué tried to persuade Julien to go into the lumber business with him. Julien declined; he enjoyed too much the power he held over his mistress.

The love affair was revealed to M. de Rênal by an anonymous letter written by M. Valenod, the local official in charge of the poorhouse. He had become rich on graft and he was jealous because M. de Rênal had hired Julien as a tutor. He had also made unsuccessful advances to Madame de Rênal at one time.

The lovers were able to smooth over the situation to some extent. M. de Rênal agreed to send Julien to the seminary at Besançon, principally to keep him from becoming tutor at M. Valenod's house. After Julien had departed, Madame de Rênal was filled with remorse. Her conscience suffered because of her adultery and she became extremely religious.

Julien did not get on well at the seminary, for he found it full of hypocrites. The students did not like him and feared his sharp intelligence. His only friend was the Abbé Pirard, a highly moral man.

One day Julien went to help decorate the cathedral and by chance found Madame de Rênal there. She fainted, but he could not help her because his duties

THE RED AND THE BLACK by Stendhal. Published by Liveright Publishing Corp.

called him elsewhere. The experience left him weak and shaken.

The Abbé Pirard lost his position at the seminary because he had supported the Marquis de La Mole, who was engaged in a lawsuit against M. de Frilair, Vicar General of Besancon. When the Abbé Pirard left the seminary, the marquis obtained a living for him in Paris. He also hired Julien as his secretary.

Julien was thankful for his chance to leave the seminary. On his way to Paris he called secretly upon Madame de Rênal. At first she repulsed his advances, conscious of her great sin. But at last she yielded once again to his pleadings. M. de Rênal became suspicious and decided to search his wife's room. To escape discovery, Julien jumped out the window, barely escaping with his life.

Finding Julien a good worker, the marquis entrusted him with many of the details of his business. Julien was also allowed to dine with the family and to mingle with the guests afterward. He found the Marquise de La Mole to be extremely proud of her nobility. Her daughter, Mathilde, seemed to be of the same type, a reserved girl with beautiful eyes. Her son, the Comte de La Mole, was an extremely polite and pleasant young man. However, Julien found Parisian high society boring. No one was allowed to discuss ideas.

Julien enjoyed stealing volumes of Voltaire from the marquis' library and reading them in his room. He was astonished when he discovered that Mathilde was doing the same thing. Before long they began to spend much of their time together, although Julien was always conscious of his position as servant and was quick to be insulted by Mathilde's pride. The girl fell in love with him because he was so different from the dull young men of her own class.

After Julien had spent two nights with her, Mathilde decided that it was degrading to be in love with a secretary. Her pride was an insult to Julien. Smarting,

he planned to gain power over her and, consequently, over the household.

Meanwhile the marquis had entrusted Julien with a diplomatic mission on behalf of the nobility and clergy who wanted the monarchy reestablished. On this mission Julien met an old friend who advised him how to win Mathilde again. Upon his return he put his friend's plan into effect.

He began to pay court to a virtuous lady who was often a visitor in the de La Mole home. He began a correspondence with her, at the same time neglecting Mathilde. Then Mathilde, thinking that Julien was lost to her, discovered how much she loved him. She threw herself at his feet. Julien had won. But this time he would not let her gain the upper hand. He continued to treat Mathilde coldly as her passion increased. In this way he maintained his power.

Mathilde became pregnant. She was joyful, for now, she thought, Julien would know how much she cared for him. She had made the supreme sacrifice; she would now have to marry Julien and give up her place in society. But Julien was not so happy as Mathilde over her condition, for he feared the results when Mathilde told her father.

At first the marquis was furious. Eventually, he saw only one way out of the difficulty; he would make Julien rich and respectable. He gave Julien a fortune, a title, and a commission in the army. Overwhelmed with his new wealth and power, Julien scarcely gave a thought to Mathilde.

Then the Marquis received a letter from Madame de Rênal, whom Julien had suggested to the marquis for a character recommendation. Madame de Rênal was again filled with religious fervor; she revealed to the marquis the whole story of Julien's villainy. The marquis immediately refused to let Julien marry his daughter.

Julien's plans for glory and power were ruined. In a fit of rage he rode to Verrières, where he found Madame de Rênal at church. He fired two shots at her before he was arrested and taken off to prison. There he promptly admitted his guilt, for he was ready to die. He had his revenge.

Mathilde, still madly in love with Julien, arrived in Verrières and tried to bribe the jury for the trial. Fouqué arrived and begged Julien to try to escape. But Julien paid no attention to the efforts his friends made to help him.

Tried, he was found guilty and given the death sentence, even though his bullets had not killed Madame de Rênal. In fact, his action had only rekindled her passion for him. She visited him and begged him to appeal his sentence. The two were as much in love as they had been before. When M. de Rênal ordered his wife to come home, Julien was left again to his dreams. He had lost his one great love — Madame de Rênal. The colorless Mathilde only bored and angered

him by her continued solicitude.

Julien went calmly to his death on the appointed day. The faithful Fouqué obtained the body in order to bury it in a cave in the mountains, where Julien had once been fond of going to indulge in his daydreams of power.

A woman had loved a famous ancestor of Mathilde with an extreme passion. When the ancestor was executed, the woman had taken his severed head and buried it. Mathilde, who had always admired this family legend, did the same for Julien. After the funeral ceremony at the cave, she buried Julien's head with her own hands. Later, she had the cave decorated with Italian marble.

Madame de Rênal did not go to the funeral. But three days after Julien's death she died in the act of embracing her children.

Further Critical Evaluation of the Work:

Stendhal's *The Red and the Black* is one of the most polished and refined artistic stones in the literary crown of European literature. While innovation and refinement are the binary supports of all literature, it is seldom that an author is able to combine these qualities in one work. Marie-Henri Beyle, better known by his *nom de plume* Stendhal, is just such an author, and *The Red and the Black* is just such a novel.

Stendhal took the French novel from the hands of romantic writers such as Chateaubriand and honed it into a rapier of social criticism and philosophical exposition. Although the French novel was the scion of other literary talents, Stendhal was its mentor. It is the content of Stendhal's novels that mark him as a harbinger, one who influenced a century of Continental literary *epigones*. He was the first French writer to battle with the social and philosophical implications inherent in the modern creed known as liberalism. Because liberalism was the prevailing philosophical buttress of the emergent French middle class, and because Stendhal sought to assess the social attitudes of that class, he must be considered as the first significant bourgeois novelist. *The Red and the Black* amalgamates the best of Stendhal's abilities as refiner and innovator.

Like each of Stendhal's novels, *The Red and the Black* is autobiographical. Published in 1830, the work reflects the author's ideas rather than the outer events of his life. Thus, to appreciate fully the novel, it is necessary to know the background of Stendhal's life and the broad social developments which determined the writer's complex and often contradictory *Weltanschauung*.

Stendhal was born into a provincial bourgeois family in Grenoble. His family background was a mixture of contradictions. The father was a middle-class businessman whose aggressive, pragmatic, Philistine habits the son professed to loathe. His mother's aristocratic family, however, attracted him. To Stendhal the family appeared to live a balanced, harmonious life with its social as well as cultural surroundings. It was a world of social hierarchy where all classes knew their place. Yet, despite his preference for the world of the provincial aristocrat, Stendhal followed a life which was markedly bourgeois in orientation and philosophy. He implicitly accepted the liberal ideas articulated in the French Revolution and became an avid supporter of Napoleon, the personification of French liberalism. Napoleon championed the notion of a French civil service staffed by men of talent rather than of high birth as had been the case in the pre-Napoleonic world. The writer launched his career with Napoleon's regime. He marched through Europe with Napoleon's armies and was present in the retreat from Moscow. Following Napoleon's defeat, Stendhal exiled himself to Milan, Italy. He returned to Paris in 1821 and compromised his values to the ultra-conservative political climate then existing in France. It was not a difficult compromise since the official values espoused in Paris were similar to those expressed by the maternal side of Stendhal's family. Stendhal's life in France between 1821 and 1830 was similar to that of the hero of *The Red and the Black,* Julien Sorel: he carried the social and intellectual baggage appropriate for survival in the intricate Parisian world.

Liberalism was the intellectual cloak of the French Revolution and Napoleon the child of the revolution. In Stendhal's France, the most important arrow in a liberal's quiver was his belief in self-determination. The liberal felt that man was basically reasonable and hence perfectible; he believed that man needed a society where talent could freely rise to its highest level of accomplishment and find expression in whatever political, economic, or intellectual manner deemed appropriate by the individual. This creed naturally appealed to those segments of French society which had been prevented by aristocratic privilege from assuming worthwhile positions in the French civil service. Stendhal aimed to make his mark in France by ascribing to this philosophy. Yet, however much he might have believed in French liberalism, or thought he believed in it, he was nonetheless troubled—aristocrat that he partly was—by the lack of parameters to this philosophy. Indeed, Julien's love affairs for Madame de Rênal, the wife of the provincial bourgeois mayor, and Mathilde de La Mole, the daughter of a French aristocrat, are symbolic of his own intellectual "affairs" with modern bourgeois liberalism and traditional aristocratic conservatism.

Was it possible to fuse such disparate social attitudes? Where were the limits on a person's right to individual self-determination? What were the social implications of such a philosophy? In an attempt to answer these questions, Stendhal wrote *The Red and the Black*. Julien Sorel was his litmus paper, recording the social concerns of Stendhal. Although Stendhal was a realist and recognized the inevitable triumph of the modern French bourgeoisie over the pre-modern aristocratic way of life, Stendhal's own confusion about his social values does not detract from the impact of his novel; in fact, it only enhances its historical value. For France, like Stendhal, was engrossed in precisely the identical dilemma and confusion of values. Like France, Stendhal knew that time was needed to assimilate contradictory social orientations. Yet societies, like creative individuals such as Stendhal, are capable of amalgamating the most diverse elements into a cohesive unit. *The Red and the Black* represents just such a creative fusion.

John G. Tomlinson, Jr.

THE RED BADGE OF COURAGE

Type of work: Novel
Author: Stephen Crane (1871-1900)
Type of plot: Impressionistic realism
Time of plot: Civil War
Locale: A Civil War battlefield
First published: 1895

Principal characters:
HENRY FLEMING, a young recruit
JIM CONKLIN, a veteran
WILSON, another veteran

Critique:

Most war stories are epic histories of generals and victories or defeats. In *The Red Badge of Courage* we follow only the personal reactions of a soldier; we do not even know what battle is being fought or who the leaders are. We know only that Henry Fleming was motivated, not by the unselfish heroism of more conventional and romantic stories, but first by cowardice, then by fear, and finally by egoism. The style of narrative of the novel belongs to a late period in English prose fiction. The stream of Henry's thought tells a story, and the reader must perceive the hero's environment through the subjective consciousness of the young man. This novel set the pattern for the treatment of war in modern fiction.

The Story:

The tall soldier, Jim Conklin, and the loud soldier, Wilson, argued bitterly over the rumor that the troops were about to move. Henry Fleming was impatient to experience his first battle, and as he listened to the quarreling of the seasoned soldiers he wondered if he would become frightened and run away under gunfire. He questioned Wilson and Conklin, and each man stated that he would stand and fight no matter what happened.

Henry had come from a farm, where he had dreamed of battles and longed for army life. His mother had held him back at first. When she saw that her son was bored with the farm, she packed his woolen clothing and with a warning that he must not associate with the wicked kind of men who were in the military camps sent him off to join the Yankee troops.

One gray morning Henry awoke to find that the regiment was about to move. With a hazy feeling that death would be a relief from dull and meaningless marching, Henry was again disappointed. The troops made only another march. He began to suspect that the generals were stupid fools, but the other men in his raw regiment scoffed at his idea and told him to shut up.

When the fighting suddenly began, there was very little action in it for Henry. He lay on the ground with the other men and watched for signs of the enemy. Some of the men around him were wounded. He could not see what was going on or what the battle was about. Then an attack came. Immediately Henry forgot all his former confused thoughts, and he could only fire his rifle over and over; around him men behaved in their strange individual manner as they were wounded. Henry felt a close comradeship with the men at his side who were firing at the enemy with him.

Suddenly the attack ended. To Henry, it seemed strange that the sky above should still be blue after the guns had stopped firing. While the men were recovering from the attack, binding wounds, and gathering equipment, another surprise attack was launched from the enemy line. Unprepared and tired from the first fighting, the men retreated in panic. Henry, sharing their sudden terror, ran, too.

When the fearful retreat had ended, the fleeing men learned that the enemy had lost the battle. Now Henry felt a surge of guilt. Dreading to rejoin his companions, he fled into the forest. There he saw a squirrel run away from him in fright. The fleeing animal seemed to vindicate in Henry's mind his own cowardly flight; he had acted according to nature whose own creatures ran from danger. Then, seeing a dead man lying in a clearing, Henry hurried back into the retreating column of wounded men. Most were staggering along in helpless bewilderment and some were being carried on stretchers. Henry realized that he had no wound and that he did not belong in that group of staggering men. There was one pitiful-looking man, covered with dirt and blood, wandering about dazed and alone. Everyone was staring at him and avoiding him. When Henry approached him, the young boy saw that the soldier was Jim Conklin. He was horrified at the sight of the tall soldier. He tried to help Jim, but with a wild motion of despair Jim fell to the ground dead. Once more Henry fled.

His conscience was paining him. He wanted to return to his regiment to finish the fight, but he thought that his fellow soldiers would point to him as a deserter. He envied the dead men who were lying all about him. They were already heroes; he was a coward. Ahead he could hear the rumbling of artillery. As he neared the lines of his regiment, a retreating line of men broke from the trees ahead of him. The men ran fiercely, ignoring him or waving frantically at him as they shouted something he could not comprehend. He stood among the flying men, not knowing what to do. One man hit him on the head with the butt of a rifle.

Henry went on carefully, the wound in his head paining him a great deal.

He walked for a long while until he met another soldier, who led Henry back to his regiment. The first familiar man Henry met was Wilson. Wilson, who had been a terrible braggart before the first battle, had given Henry a packet of letters to keep for him in case he were killed. Now Henry felt superior to Wilson. If the man asked him where he had been, Henry would remind him of the letters. Lost was Henry's feeling of guilt; he felt superior now, his deeds of cowardice almost forgotten. No one knew that he had run off in terror. Wilson had changed. He no longer was the swaggering, boastful man who had annoyed Henry in the beginning. The men in the regiment washed Henry's head wound and told him to get some sleep.

The next morning Wilson casually asked Henry for the letters. Half sorry that he had to yield them with no taunting remark, Henry returned the letters to his comrade. He felt sorry for Wilson's embarrassment. He felt himself a virtuous and heroic man.

Another battle started. This time Henry held his position doggedly and kept firing his rifle without thinking. Once he fell down, and for a panicky moment he thought that he had been shot, but he continued to fire his rifle blindly, loading and firing without even seeing the enemy. Finally someone shouted to him that he must stop shooting, that the battle was over. Then Henry looked up for the first time and saw that there were no enemy troops before him. Now he was a hero. Everyone stared at him when the lieutenant of the regiment complimented his fierce fighting. Henry realized that he had behaved like a demon.

Wilson and Henry, off in the woods looking for water, overheard two officers discussing the coming battle. They said that Henry's regiment fought like mule drivers, but that they would have to be used anyway. Then one officer said that probably not many of the regiment would live through the day's fighting. Soon after the attack started, the color bearer was killed and Henry took up the flag, with Wilson at his side. Although the regiment fought bravely, one of the commanding officers of the army said that the men had not gained the ground that they were expected to take. The same officer had complimented Henry for his courageous fighting. He began to feel that he knew the measure of his own courage and endurance.

His outfit fought one more engagement with the enemy. Henry was by that time a veteran, and the fighting held less meaning for him than had the earlier battles. When it was over, he and Wilson marched away with their victorious regiment.

Further Critical Evaluation of the Work:

The Red Badge of Courage, Stephen Crane's second novel (*Maggie: A Girl of the Streets* had appeared under a pseudonym in 1893) and his most famous work, has often been considered the first truly modern war novel. The war is the American Civil War and the battle is presumed to be the one fought at Chancellorsville, though neither the war nor the battle is named in the novel. Nor is there mention of Abraham Lincoln or the principal battle generals, Joseph Hooker (Union) and Robert E. Lee and "Stonewall" Jackson (Confederate). This is by design, since Crane was writing a different kind of war novel. He was not concerned with the causes of the war, the political and social implications of the prolonged and bloody conflict, the strategy and tactics of the commanding officers, or even the real outcome of the battle in which historically the combined losses were nearly thirty thousand men (including "Stonewall" Jackson, mistakenly shot in darkness by one of his own men).

From beginning to end the short novel focuses upon one Union Army volunteer. Though other characters enter the story and reappear intermittently, they are distinctly minor, and they are present primarily to show the relationship of Henry Fleming (usually called only "the youth") to one person, to a small group of soldiers, or to the complex war of which he is such an insignificant part.

Much of the story takes the reader into Henry's consciousness. We share his boyish dreams of glory, his excitement in anticipating battle action, his fear of showing fear, his cowardice and flight, his inner justification of what he has done, his wish for a wound to symbolize a courage he has not shown, the ironic gaining of his false "red badge," his secret knowledge of the badge's origin, his "earning" the badge as he later fights fiercely and instinctively, his joy in musing on his own bravery and valiant actions, his anger at an officer who fails to appreciate his soldiery, and his final feeling that "the great death" is, after all, not a thing to be feared so much. Now, he tells himself, he is a man. In centering the story within the consciousness of an inexperienced youth caught in a war situation whose meaning and complexities he cannot understand, Crane anticipates Ford Madox Ford, Ernest Hemingway, and other later novelists.

Crane has been called a realist, a naturalist, an impressionist, and a symbolist. He is all of these in *The Red Badge of Courage*. Though young Stephen Crane had never seen a battle when he wrote the novel, he had read about them; he had talked with veterans and had studied history under a Civil War general; and he had imagined what it would be like to be a frightened young man facing violent death amid the confusion, noise, and turmoil of a conflict which had no clear meaning to him. Intuitively he wrote so realistically that several early reviewers concluded that only an experienced soldier could have written the book. After Crane had later seen the Greeks and Turks fighting in 1897 (he was a journalist reporting the war), he told Joseph Conrad, "My picture of war was all right! I have found it as I imagined it."

Although naturalistic passages appear in the novel, Crane portrays in Henry Fleming not a helpless chip floating on the indifferent ocean of life but a youth sometimes impelled into action by society or by instinct yet also capable of consciously willed acts. Before the first skirmish Henry wishes he could escape from his regiment and considers his plight: " . . . there were iron laws of tradition and law on four sides. He was in a moving box." In the second skirmish he runs "like a rabbit." When a squirrel in the forest flees after Henry throws a pine cone at him, Henry justifies his own flight: "There was the law, he said. Nature had given him a sign." But he is not content to look upon himself as on the squirrel's level. He feels guilt over his cowardice. When he carries the flag in the later skirmishes, he is not a terrified chicken or rabbit or squirrel but a young man motivated by pride, by a sense of belonging to a group, and by a determination to show his courage to an officer who had scornfully called the soldiers in his group a lot of "mule drivers."

From the beginning, critics have both admired and complained about Crane's impressionistic writing and his use of imagery and symbols in *The Red Badge of Courage*. Edward Garnett in 1898 called Crane "the chief impressionist of our day" and praised his "wonderful fervour and freshness of style." Joseph Conrad (himself an impressionist) was struck by Crane's "genuine verbal felicity, welding analysis and description in a continuous fascination of individual style," and Conrad saw Henry as "the symbol of all untried men." By contrast, one American critic in 1898 described the novel as "a mere riot of words" and condemned "the violent straining after effect" and the "absurd similes." Though H. G. Wells liked the book as a whole, he commented on "those chromatic splashes that at times deafen and confuse in the *Red Badge,* those images that astonish rather than enlighten."

Yet judging by the continuing popularity of *The Red Badge of Courage,* most readers are not repelled by Crane's repeated use of color—"blue demonstration," "red eyes," "red animal—war," "red sun"—or by his use of images—"dark shadows that moved like monsters," "The dragons were coming," guns that "belched and howled like brass devils guarding a gate." Only in a few passages does Crane indulge in "arty" writing—"The guns squatted in a row like savage chiefs. They argued with abrupt violence"—or drop into the pathetic fallacy—"The flag suddenly sank down as if dying. Its motion as it fell was a gesture of despair." Usually the impressionistic phrasing is appropriate to the scene or to the emotional state of Henry Fleming at a particular moment, as when, after he has fought he feels heroically, the sun shines "now bright and gay in the blue, enameled sky."

A brilliant work of the imagination, *The Red Badge of Courage* will endure as what Crane afterward wrote a friend he had intended it to be, "a psychological portrayal of fear."

Henderson Kincheloe

THE RED ROOM

Type of work: Novel
Author: August Strindberg (1849-1912)
Type of plot: Realistic satire
Time of plot: 1870's
Locale: Stockholm and X-köping, a provincial town in Sweden
First published: 1879

Principal characters:

ARVID FALK, a writer
CHARLES NICHOLAS FALK, his brother, a businessman
MRS. CHARLES NICHOLAS FALK
SELLÉN, a painter
LUNDELL, a practical painter
OLLE MONTANUS, a philosopher and sculptor
YGBERG, a philosopher
REHNHJELM, a would-be actor
LEVIN, a post-office clerk
NYSTRÖM, a schoolmaster
SMITH, a publisher
FALANDER, an actor
AGNES (BEDA PETTERSON), a young actress
STRUVE, a journalist
BORG, a young doctor

Critique:

A biting satire leveled against contemporary Swedish society, *The Red Room* was Strindberg's first published novel. The story deals with the fortunes of a group of young Swedish intellectuals and artists trying to get along in Stockholm of the 1870's. The intellectuals and artists, dedicated to their tasks and to honest appraisals of the society about them, are constantly tricked, defeated, and victimized by the insensitive bourgeois world in which they live. They are constantly faced with poverty (although there are a few examples of unpredictable and temporary success when the artist happens, quite by chance, to catch the public fancy), scorn, or indifference. By the end of the novel, all the artists have either gone mad, committed suicide, or sold out to the commercial society. Various institutions are also satirized: the government agency where a large staff does no work, the newspaper that makes or breaks reputations to suit its purpose without regard to factual accuracy, the Parliament that endlessly debates inconsequential matters, the charitable organization out of touch with reality.

The Story:

Arvid Falk, a young government worker who wanted to be a poet, told Struve, a journalist, some facts concerning the waste and inadequacy of a government department where he, Arvid, had worked. Struve worked this material into an exposé for a newspaper that was looking for sensational stories. Arvid was discharged for giving out the information.

Arvid's brother, Charles Nicholas, a flax merchant, liked to feel that he was supporting Arvid by lending him money, offering him cigars, and inviting him to dinner. He could not believe that Arvid, despite certain unconventional opinions, would give out such information for publication. Charles Nicholas was a rising merchant, but his favorite cronies were a beaten clerk named Levin and an apathetic schoolmaster named Nyström. Levin and Nyström would flatter Charles Nicholas and write him fulsome verses of appreciation for the small sums of money he lent them. Charles Nicholas had a young wife who slept until noon every day and aspired to become a social and civic leader.

Arvid visited his friends: Sellén and Lundell, who were painters; Rehnhjelm, who ardently desired to be an actor, and Olle Montanus and Ygberg, who spent all day arguing the fine points of philosophy. All were serious about their art or their arguments, and all were poor. Although the practical Lundell made a living by doing magazine illustrations, the group had little money; frequently they were forced to combine their credit or pawn some of their clothes in order to scrape together enough money for dinner.

Out of a job, Arvid brought some of his verses to Smith, a successful publisher who offered Arvid the job of writing about Ulrica Eleonora, a Swedish historical personage, and doing hack work on other trite and uninteresting subjects. Arvid tried to do the work, in which he had no interest at all, but was unable to complete his dull assignments. He joined his friends in the Red Room, a café where they gathered, argued, and spent as little money as possible.

Arvid finally got a job on a newspaper. As a reporter on the affairs of Parliament he did his work successfully, although he was privately outraged at the time wasted in interminable and senseless discussions. Most of the Swedes, however, were proud of their new, more democratic Parliament.

About this time Sellén had succeeded in getting a picture hung in the Academy show. At first it was pointed out as an example of the new decadent, Bohemian art, and as such was criticized by one of the papers. For reasons having nothing to do with art, another paper defended Sellén's painting, and he became a hotly debated and highly successful young man. For the moment all the members of this Bohemian group were working; they were able to pay for their drinks at the Red Room and recover the overcoats they had pawned.

When a group of unscrupulous men organized a marine insurance company called Triton, Charles Nicholas Falk was pleased and flattered to be a member of their board. At the same time his wife was pleased to be on a committee organized to erect a large crèche for a church. Charles Nicholas helped to forward his wife's social ambitions by making a large donation for the crèche, but he made the donation with shares of the marine insurance company. When Mrs. Falk was accepted by society, she made visits to the homes of poor people and tried to convert them to believing in her church. She had little success and assumed that the poor people were simply ignorant and uncouth. Later, when the marine insurance company was proved to be a hoax and collapsed, the project for the crèche, along with Mrs. Falk's social aspirations, had to be abandoned.

In the meantime, Rehnhjelm had gone to the town of X-köping and joined a theatrical company. He played only minor parts and the theater manager took advantage of him, but he felt that he was learning the profession. He was impressed by Falander, a suave older actor, and he fell in love with Agnes, a sixteen-year-old ingénue. His love for Agnes was pure and idealistic; and he did not know that she had long been Falander's mistress. When he finally and belatedly discovered this fact, he thought he would commit suicide in his despair at the wickedness in the world. Instead, he returned to Stockholm and the security offered by his wealthy family.

Arvid became a successful journalist and his poems were published at last. He moved from paper to paper every so often in the hope that each would offer him the opportunity to report the news as honestly as he saw it, but the papers were interested only in versions of news or scandal that would fit their particular needs. Frustrated in his efforts, Arvid became friendly with Borg, a cynical and iconoclastic doctor, and he fell in love with Beda Petterson, a young girl who worked in a Stockholm café. The vogue for Sellén's work had ended and he was again poor. In the meantime Lundell had become a society portrait painter. One night Borg found Arvid in a low dive with two representatives of a paper even lower than the conventional papers Arvid had found so unprincipled. Arvid had gone raving mad. Borg took him on a ship voyage under treatment for his nervous breakdown.

When Arvid recovered and returned to Stockholm, he found that the old group at the Red Room had broken up. Olle Montanus, unable to work except as a stonemason, had finally committed suicide. Sellén's painting had again become fashionable. Charles Nicholas had, strangely enough, emerged unscathed from the Triton disaster and was about to establish a bank. Arvid discovered that Beda Petterson and Rehnhjelm's Agnes were really the same woman, a kind of symbol for the faithless woman whose only allegiance is a physical connection to some man. None of his living friends or associates retained any semblance of the idealism and honesty that had once motivated all their actions and conversations. Arvid himself became a conventional schoolmaster, married a schoolmistress, and studied numismatics in his spare time. Only Borg, the skeptic who expected nothing, remained unchanged.

Further Critical Evaluation of the Work:

August Strindberg's status as a giant of the modern theater has greatly overshadowed the fact that he was also a prolific novelist. To most non-Scandinavians, Strindberg's fiction is remembered—if at all—as quasi-auto-biographical adjuncts to such dramatic masterpieces as *The Father, Miss Julie, The Dance of Death, A Dream Play,* and *The Ghost Sonata.* But, to Scandinavian readers, Strindberg's reputation as a novelist almost equals his status as a playwright, and his first published novel, *The Red Room,* is frequently considered to be the first modern Swedish novel.

As in all of Strindberg's writings, there is a strong autobiographical flavor to *The Red Room.* The protagonist, Arvid Falk, in many ways resembles the young Strindberg and reflects his brief foray into journalism (1872-1874). Most of the characters who gather in the "red room" are modeled on artistic comrades acquired during those newspaper years. The financial manipulations and disasters, particularly the "Triton Insurance" affair, were suggested by Strindberg's own bankruptcy in the wake of the financial crisis of 1878.

But it is a mistake to read *The Red Room* as straight autobiography. Strindberg's tone throughout the novel is detached, ironic, and, although bitter at times, essentially comic. While Arvid Falk's experiences parallel many of Strindberg's own, the character is too naïve, foolish, and frivolous to be accepted as self-portraiture. The novel can be more easily understood as a skillful blending of comic *Bildüngsroman,* social satire, and "idea" novel.

Like all of Strindberg's novels, and, in a different way, his plays, *The Red Room* is basically a quest for identity. As the typical hero of a *Bildüngsroman,* or novel of education, initiation, and development, Arvid is personally bland

and learns through the examples and advice of "mentors" who surround him. Each mentor represents a particular social role and/or philosophical viewpoint. At the same time, these figures are used by Strindberg as satirical targets, enabling him to vent his anger on any and all social abuses in view— official indolence, creative exploitation, religious fakery, insurance swindle, feminine hypocrisy, journalistic distortion, parliamentary duplicity, and dishonest reformism. Thus, Strindberg is able to brilliantly combine his quest for identity theme with a satirical portrait of nineteenth century middle-class Swedish society.

Instead of equipping him to find psychological equilibrium and socially meaningful work, Arvid's search only confuses and demoralizes him. Each new mentor and every new learning experience only serve to further disillusion and depress him. His employers and business associates all exploit or disappoint him. His bohemian friends, who have committed their lives to art, all either starve, sell out, or commit suicide. Thus, Arvid's education brings him to the edge of madness and only the intervention of Borg, the cynical doctor, saves his sanity. In the end Arvid's only survival is in total conformity, suppression of all creative impulses, and escape into conventional marriage and esoteric scholarship.

Behind the personal psychology and social satire of *The Red Room,* Strindberg makes a number of philosophical speculations. Three attitudes toward life are offered: idealism, realism, and nihilism. Arvid is the idealist, first described as "a child; he still believed in everything, truth and fairy tales alike," and his is the one philosophy that is quickly and thoroughly discredited. Realism in this book means to accept the corruption of the system and attempt to turn it to personal advantage. The only characters in the novel who thrive are those realists—and they are also the most despicable.

Strindberg seems to side philosophically with the nihilists, Falander, the actor, and Olle Montanus, the sculptor. Both characters articulate their philosophies at length, but find them difficult to live with. Although externally successful, Falander is deeply disturbed by his painful vision and drowns his nihilism in absinthe. Montanus acts out the implications of the philosophy. Discouraged by his inability to make his contemporaries aware of the state of art and society in Sweden, as well as by his own limits as an artist—and the limitations of art itself—Olle commits suicide. Only Borg, whose cynicism is very close to nihilistic, but who emotionally detaches himself from the implications of his ideas, is able to survive both the corrupt materialism of his society and the metaphysical pointlessness of his existence.

Yet Strindberg does not rest easily with pessimism. There is too much energy and humor in his characterizations and too much lyrical beauty in his natural descriptions to support a completely bleak view. What remains is not a neat psychological, social, or philosophical statement, but a powerful and provocative vision of man in conflict with himself, his society, and his cosmos.

THE RED ROVER

Type of work: Novel
Author: James Fenimore Cooper (1789-1851)
Type of plot: Historical romance
Time of plot: Mid-eighteenth century
Locale: Newport, Rhode Island and the Atlantic Ocean
First published: 1827

> *Principal characters:*
> HARRY WILDER, formerly Henry Ark, actually Henry de Lacy
> THE RED ROVER, captain of the *Dolphin*
> DICK FID, and
> SCIPIO AFRICA, seamen, Harry Wilder's friends
> GERTRUDE GRAYSON, General Grayson's daughter
> MRS. WYLLYS, her governess

Critique:

Cooper, who knew the sea quite well, wrote this novel to repeat the success of *The Pilot.* His characters, as is customary with him, are types, and there is little character development. The plot is simple and plausible until the end of the story, when Cooper unravels the mystery surrounding Henry Ark and the Red Rover by proving improbable relationships among the characters. However, few novels of the sea contain a better record of life and work aboard a sailing ship.

The Story:

While in the town of Newport, Rhode Island, Harry Wilder saw in the outer harbor a ship, the *Dolphin*, which interested him greatly. He decided to try to secure a berth on her for himself and his two friends, Dick Fid and Scipio Africa, a Negro sailor. His determination was strengthened after meeting a stranger who in effect dared him to try to obtain a berth there. That night the three men rowed out to the ship lying at anchor, in order to give the vessel a closer inspection. Hailed by the watch on deck, Wilder went aboard her. There he learned that he had been expected and that if he were interested in sailing with her, he might go to see the captain. The captain was the mysterious, mocking stranger whom Wilder had met that afternoon in the town. But before Wilder signed on as a member of the ship's crew, the captain revealed the true nature of the ship and admitted that he himself was the Red Rover, the scourge of the sea. Wilder, who had formerly been an officer in the British Navy, was given the post of second in command. He persuaded the captain to sign on Dick and Scipio as well. He then returned to shore to settle his affairs in the town. The other two men remained aboard the *Dolphin*.

At the same time the *Royal Caroline*, a merchantman trading along the coast and between the colonies and England, lay in the inner harbor ready to embark on the following day. Two ladies, Gertrude Grayson and her governess, Mrs. Wyllys, were to take passage on her to Charleston, South Carolina, Gertrude's home. Wilder met the ladies as if by chance and tried to dissuade them from sailing aboard the *Royal Caroline*. He hinted that the *Royal Caroline* was unsafe, but his words were discredited by an old seaman who insisted that there was nothing wrong with the ship. The ladies decided to sail in spite of Wilder's warnings. Then the master of the *Royal Caroline* fell from a cask and broke his leg, and a new captain had to be found immediately. The Red Rover sent a message ordering Wilder to apply for the vacant position. He did, and was immediately hired.

The voyage of the *Royal Caroline* began with difficulties which continued as time went on. They were not long out of port when a ship was sighted on the horizon. It continued to keep its distance in approximately the same position, so that all aboard the *Royal Caroline* suspected that it was following them. In trying to outdistance the other ship, Wilder put on all sail possible, in spite of the threatening weather. A storm struck the ship and left her foundering in heavy seas. When Wilder commanded the crew to man the pumps, they refused and deserted the sinking ship in one of the boats. Only Wilder and the two women were left aboard the helpless *Royal Caroline*. Hoping to make land, they embarked in a longboat, but the wind blew them out to sea. They were sighted and picked up by the *Dolphin*.

Gertrude and Mrs. Wyllys were not long aboard the *Dolphin* before the true state of affairs became apparent to the women in spite of the kindly treatment afforded them. Mrs. Wyllys realized also that Roderick, the cabin boy, was in reality a woman. But this mystery was nothing when compared with that of Harry Wilder.

Dick Fid told the story of Harry Wilder's past history to the two ladies and the Red Rover, thus explaining the affection Wilder, Dick, and Scipio held for each other. Some twenty-four years earlier, Dick and Scipio had found a child and a dying woman, apparently a nurse, aboard an abandoned ship. After the woman died, the two seamen took care of the boy. They had only one clue to follow in their efforts to locate the child's relatives. This was the name Ark of Lynnhaven which had been painted on a ship's bucket and which Scipio had tattooed on Dick's arm. But there was no ship of that name in any port registry, and so the search for the child's relatives was abandoned.

As Dick finished his story, another ship was sighted. It was the *Dart*, a British naval vessel on which Wilder, Dick, and Scipio had previously sailed. Wilder wanted the Red Rover to flee, but the captain had another plan for dealing with the *Dart*. After showing British colors, the Red Rover was invited by Captain Bignall of the *Dart* to come aboard his ship. There the pirate captain learned that Henry Ark, alias Harry Wilder, was absent from the *Dart* on a dangerous secret mission. The Red Rover realized that he had betrayed himself to his enemy. He went back to the *Dolphin* and then sent Wilder, Dick, Scipio, and the two women to the *Dart*.

Wilder had informed the Red Rover that once aboard his own ship, the *Dart*, he would be duty bound to reveal the true nature of the *Dolphin*. But in telling Captain Bignall his story, Wilder begged for mercy for both the master and the crew of the pirate ship. Bignall agreed and sent Wilder back to the *Dolphin* with lenient terms of surrender. The Red Rover refused them and told Wilder that if there were to be a fight Captain Bignall would have to start it. As the *Dart* attacked the pirate ship, a sudden storm gave the *Dolphin* an unexpected advantage. Its crew boarded the *Dart*, killed Captain Bignall, and captured the ship. The crew of the *Dolphin* demanded the lives of Wilder, Dick, and Scipio as traitors, and the Red Rover handed them over to the crew. When the chaplain who was aboard the *Dart* came forward to plead for their lives, he saw the tattoo on Dick's arm. He told the story of the *Ark of Lynnhaven* and revealed that Harry Wilder must be the son of Paul de Lacy and Mrs. Wyllys, who had kept the marriage a secret because of parental disapproval and later because of Paul's death. Mrs. Wyllys then begged for the life of her son, whom she had thought dead all these years. The Red Rover dismissed his crew until the next morning, when he would announce his decision concerning the fate of the prisoners.

The next morning, the Red Rover put his crew and all the gold aboard the *Dolphin* into a coaster and sent them ashore. The crew of the *Dart*, Wilder, Dick, Scipio, and the women were put aboard the *Dart* and told to sail off. When they were some distance away, they saw the *Dolphin* catch fire and burn. None had been left aboard her but the Red Rover and Roderick. Some aboard the *Dart* thought they saw a small boat putting off from the burning ship, but none could be sure because of the billowing smoke.

Twenty years later, after the colonies had won their independence from England, the Red Rover, a veteran of the Revolutionary War, reappeared in New-port and made his way to the home of Captain Henry de Lacy, who had previously called himself Henry Wilder. Admitted, he identified himself as the long-lost brother of Mrs. Wyllys. Shortly thereafter the Red Rover, pirate and patriot, died.

Further Critical Evaluation of the Work:

Though *The Red Rover* has never been as popular with readers as Cooper's two greatest sea romances, *The Pilot* (1824) and *The Two Admirals* (1842), it has its own sturdy merits as a suspenseful tale of intrigue and adventure. Superficially, the early scenes of the novel bring to mind the classic American sea novel, Melville's *Moby Dick* (1851). Harry Wilder, like Ishmael, is drawn mysteriously to a ship anchored in the harbor. Aboard the ship, Wilder encounters the notorious Red Rover, just as Ishmael meets the enigmatic Captain Ahab. And just as Ahab violates metaphysical laws in his pursuit of the White Whale, so the Red Rover is a law unto himself as he plunders merchant vessels in the period before the Revolutionary War. Beyond this point the similarities between the novels are less clearly marked than the contrasts. Melville's novel is composed on an epic scale, with a profound sense of tragic drama. *The Sea Rover,* quite the opposite, is an entertaining melodramatic romance, written without any pretentions to examine deeply the mysteries of man's place in the universe.

Nevertheless, the novel is interesting from points of view other than simply those of a sea adventure story. Considered from a psychological perspective, *The Sea Rover* reveals Cooper's contradictory ideas about the structure and philosophical ideas of the work. In *Studies in Classic American Literature* (1923), D. H. Lawrence suggests that Cooper's "white novels," among which the sea stories may be included, betray the novelist's confusion about the superiority of democracy. Cooper, according to Lawrence, believes that the American is bound to assert his superior claims over other peoples, even if these claims are undeserved. But this forceful assertion is a form of aggression. And Cooper, at least philosophically, is disturbed by aggressiveness. One side of him prefers gentle action, another violent force. Without pressing Lawrence's suggestion too far, it is certainly true that in *The Red Rover* Cooper is both repelled by and attracted to the brutality of the captain of the *Dolphin,* just as he is ambivalent about his feelings concerning Wilder. For Wilder is at the same time the gentle, chivalrous comrade of the women, Gertrude Grayson and Mrs. Wyllys, and the tough-minded, rugged sailor-adventurer.

Cooper partially resolves the conflict between aggressive and gentle conduct through the mechanism of the Revolutionary War. The romantic rebel in the personage of the Red Rover emerges as the patriotic rebel, when the pirate reappears late in the book as a veteran and hero of the American Revolution. Now his violence has the sanction of patriotic duty. And Harry Wilder, formerly seaman, also changes roles. By the end of the novel he is Captain Henry de Lacy, gentleman. Thus, on a psychological level, Cooper justifies the intrepid, violent action of the story from the viewpoint of its satisfactory conclusion: both the Red Rover and Wilder are seen as American heroes who have advanced the cause of freedom.

REDBURN

Type of work: Novel
Author: Herman Melville (1819-1891)
Type of plot: Adventure romance
Time of plot: Mid-nineteenth century
Locale: New York, the Atlantic Ocean, and England
First published: 1849

Principal characters:
WELLINGBOROUGH REDBURN, a young lad on his first voyage
CAPTAIN RIGA, master of the *Highlander*
HARRY BOLTON, a young English prodigal

Critique:

Redburn, like much of Herman Melville's work, was based on his own life. The background of the Redburn family is very similar to that of the Melville family after the father's death. The trip on a merchant vessel is clearly based on a similar round trip to Liverpool which Melville himself had made while still in his teens. The incident of the guidebook, for instance, and the guidebook itself, are taken directly from Melville's own experience. Again, like other of Melville's books, *Redburn* is authentic in its treatment of sailors and sea life. Melville saw seafaring life through the eyes of a common sailor who learned his trade the hard way and wrote his novel from the seaman's point of view. Also, we find in *Redburn* the beginnings of the philosophical elements that made *Moby Dick,* Melville's masterpiece, one of the great novels of all time.

The Story:

Wellingborough Redburn's father had died, leaving the mother and children poorly provided for, even though the father had been a highly successful merchant and at one time a wealthy man. When Redburn was in his middle teens, he decided to take some of the burden off his mother by going to sea. Given an old gun and a hunting jacket by an older brother, young Redburn left his home along the Hudson River and went to New York to seek a berth on a ship.

A college friend of his older brother aided Redburn in finding a berth on a ship bound for Liverpool. Unfortunately the friend had emphasized the fact that Redburn came from a good family and had wealthy relatives; consequently, Captain Riga, master of the *Highlander,* was able to hire the young lad for three dollars a month. Having spent all his money, and unable to get an advance on his wages, Redburn had to pawn his gun for a shirt and cap to wear aboard ship.

During his first few days out of port Redburn thought that he had made a dreadful mistake in going to sea. His fellow sailors jeered at him as a greenhorn; he made many silly mistakes; he became violently seasick; and he discovered that he did not even have a spoon with which to take his portion of the food from the pots and pans in which it was sent to the forecastle. Most horrifying of all was the suicide of a sailor who dived over the side of the ship in a fit of delirium tremens.

As the thirty-day cruise to Liverpool from New York wore on, Redburn learned how to make himself useful and comfortable aboard the ship. When he went aloft alone to release the topmost sails, he earned a little respect from his fellow seamen, although they never did, throughout the voyage, let him forget that he was still a green hand and had signed on as a "boy." Redburn found the sea fascinating in many ways; he also found it terrifying, as when the *Highlander* passed a derelict schooner on which three corpses were still bound to the railing.

For Redburn one of the liveliest incidents of the voyage was the discovery of a little stowaway on board the *High-lander*. The small boy had been on board the vessel some months before, when the father had been a sailor signed on for a trip from Liverpool to New York. The father had since died, and the boy had stowed himself away in an effort to return to England. Everyone on the ship, including the usually irascible Captain Riga, took a liking to the homesick stowaway and made much of him.

Redburn had little in common with his fellow crew members, most of whom were rough fellows many years older than he. Through them, however, he received an education quite different from that which he had learned in school. At first he tried to talk about church and good books to them, but he soon discovered that such conversation only irritated them into more than their usual profanity and obscenity. Redburn thought they were not really very bad men; they had never had the chance to be good men. Most of all, he disliked them because they looked upon anyone who could not follow the seaman's trade as a fool.

A long, low skyline in the distance was Redburn's first glimpse of Ireland. He met his first true European when an Irish fisherman hailed the *Highlander* and asked for a line. When he had hauled fifteen or so fathoms of the line into his boat, the Irishman cut the line, laughed, and sailed away. Even though the rope was not Redburn's, he, boylike, felt that the man had played a scurvy trick.

When the *Highlander* arrived at Liverpool, Redburn decided that the English city was not a great deal different from New York. Sailors and ships, he found, were the same in one place as in another, with a few notable exceptions. His trips into the city, away from the waterfront, and excursions into the Lancashire countryside convinced him that he, as an alien, was not welcome. People distrusted him because of his ragged clothing, and he had no money to purchase a new outfit, even though Captain Riga had advanced him three dollars, one month's pay, upon the ship's arrival in port.

Redburn's greatest disappointment came when he tried to use for his excursions an old guidebook he had brought from his father's library. The guidebook, almost half a century old, was no longer reliable, for streets and structures it mentioned were no longer in existence. Redburn felt that the whole world must have changed since his father's time; he saw in the unreliable guidebook a hint that as the years passed the habits and ideals of youth had to be charted anew. Each generation, he learned, had to make its own guidebook through the world.

While in Liverpool, Redburn met Harry Bolton, a young Englishman of good family but a prodigal son. Bolton said that he had shipped on two voyages to the East Indies; now he wanted to emigrate to America. With Redburn's help Harry Bolton was enrolled as a "boy" on the *Highlander* for its return trip to New York. The two boys, traveling on Bolton's money, made a quick excursion to London before the ship sailed, but they were back in Liverpool within forty-eight hours. Redburn saw little of England beyond the port where he had arrived.

On the return trip to America the ship carried a load of Irish emigrants. Redburn quickly felt sorry for them but at the same time superior to the miserable wretches crowded between decks. The steerage passengers suffered a great deal during the voyage. Their quarters were cramped at best, and during heavy weather they could not remain on deck. For cooking they had a stove placed on one of the hatches, one stove for five hundred people. Worst of all, an epidemic of fever broke out, killing many of the emigrants and one of the sailors.

Bolton had a miserable trip, and Redburn was sorry for him, too. The English boy had lied in saying he had been at sea before. Because he could not bear to go aloft in the rigging, he, in place of Redburn, became the butt of all the jokes and horseplay that the crew devised.

After the ship reached America, however, the voyage seemed to both Redburn and Bolton to have been a good one. They discovered that they really hated to leave the vessel which had been home to them for several weeks. But their nostalgia for the vessel was soon dissipated by Captain Riga. The captain dismissed Redburn without any pay because the lad had left his duties for one day while the ship was at Liverpool. The captain even told Redburn that he owed the ship money for tools he had dropped into the sea. Bolton was given a dollar and a half for his work; the pittance made him so angry he threw it back on the captain's desk. The two boys then left the ship, glad to be back on land once more.

Further Critical Evaluation of the Work:

The best way to read *Redburn* is as a prologue to *Moby Dick.* The story of the white whale is anticipated by the tragic themes of the earlier novel: its relentless depiction of misery and cruelty on board Captain Riga's ship, as well as in Liverpool port, develops a universal consciousness of human suffering, of the crushing effect of experience on innocence. F. O. Matthiessen called *Redburn* "the most moving of its author's books before *Moby Dick.*" Redburn is abused by the other sailors for openly showing his fright when a man with delerium tremens throws himself over the side; the isolation makes him dread lest he become "a sort of Ishmael." He does, of course, become just that (and seems strengthened by the transformation) in *Moby Dick,* which was published two years after *Redburn* appeared.

Not only is Redburn similar to Melville's narrator in *Moby Dick,* but the whole novel is strewn with anticipations of the great novel's themes and characterizations. The mad sailor Jackson foreshadows Ahab: "He was a Cain afloat; branded on his yellow brow with some inscrutable curse; and going about corrupting and searing every heart that beat near him." The friendship between Harry Bolton and Redburn is curiously similar to that between the cannibal Queequeg and Ishmael: Harry is the prodigal son of a genteel family and Queequeg a royal personage; Harry introduces Redburn to London, Queequeg introduces Ishmael to the *Pequod*; Harry is finally killed when he is crushed between a ship and a whale, while Queequeg dives into the heart of a whale to rescue Tashtego.

All these similarities indicate the direction of Melville's art. He was moving from a fiction of initiation and adventure to one of philosophical depth. The symbolic action of Redburn is a cruder version of the same superstructure that supports Melville's masterpiece.

THE REDSKINS

Type of work: Novel
Author: James Fenimore Cooper (1789-1851)
Type of plot: Historical romance
Time of plot: 1842
Locale: Upstate New York
First published: 1846

Principal characters:
HUGH ROGER LITTLEPAGE, the narrator and the heir to Ravensnest
HUGH ROGER LITTLEPAGE, called Uncle Ro, his uncle
MARY WARREN, a friend of the Littlepage family
THE REVEREND MR. WARREN, her father
SENECA NEWCOME, an anti-renter
OPPORTUNITY NEWCOME, his sister
MRS. URSULA LITTLEPAGE, Hugh's grandmother
PATT LITTLEPAGE, Hugh's sister
JOSHUA BRIGHAM, another anti-renter
SUSQUESUS, an old Onondaga Indian living at Ravensnest
JAAP (JAAF), an old colored servant at Ravensnest
HALL, a mechanic

Critique:

The Redskins, or, Indian and Injin, is the final novel in Cooper's Littlepage series. Like many of Cooper's novels, this work deals with the conflict between a cultured upper class of high principles and an uncultured middle class with no principles except those of self-interest. Cooper's characters are drawn in keeping with their sympathies, according to whether they sympathize with the rights of the land-owning Littlepage family or with the grasping Newcome family. Cooper stacks the cards in favor of the landowners and makes the conflict one between the patroons and the poltroons. He tends to caricature his villains and to treat them with satire and irony. In spite of the rather restricted interest of the anti-rent controversy around which The Redskins centers, the novel has suspense, action, romance, villainy, conflict, and some sharp, if limited, insights into the structure of American society. Cooper saw clearly the perpetual struggle for power within America, and he described it with compelling logic.

The Story:

Hugh Littlepage and his Uncle Ro, the owner of Satanstoe and Lilacsbush, had been traveling through Europe and the East for five years, and they had not heard from their family in America for eighteen months. Upon arriving at their apartment in Paris they received a bundle of letters and packages from the family. Among other things the letters told them that the Littlepages' Ravensnest estate was in danger from tenants who had formed a terrorist party known as the "Injins." Since Hugh was now master of the estate and the rents were due in the fall, he and his uncle decided to return home early, even though they were not expected before autumn. They decided to travel under the name of Davidson in order to keep their return a secret.

Arriving in New York, they went to see the Littlepage agent, Jack Dunning, who informed them that the estate was threatened from two sides. On the one hand, there were the Ravensnest tenants led by the demagogue lawyer named Seneca Newcome; on the other there were the Albany politicians, who depended on the tenants for votes. The politicians had already raised the taxes on the estate, and the tenants were petitioning for a removal of the rents and a chance to buy the property at their own low prices. To speed up the process the tenants had resorted to terrorizing the landlords with tar buckets, rifles, and calico hoods. To mask their greed for land, they claimed that their activities were carried on in the name of liberty, equality, and justice.

Because it would be dangerous to visit Ravensnest openly Hugh and his uncle disguised themselves as a watch peddler and an organ grinder, acquired a broken German accent, and started for Ravensnest. On the boat to Albany they met Seneca Newcome, who, thinking that they might make good Injins. invited them to Ravensnest. They got off at Albany and went from there to Troy. In that city they made the acquaintance of the Rev. Mr. Warren and his daughter Mary. In his new role as an organ grinder Hugh invented a false history for himself and his uncle, a story accepted by the Warrens. Hugh soon learned that the Warrens lived at Ravensnest, where Mr. Warren was an Episcopal clergyman, and that Mary was a close friend of Hugh's sister Patt. Mary proved to be a charming, well-bred girl in striking contrast to Opportunity Newcome, who was also present at the inn. After Seneca Newcome joined the group the conversation turned from Opportunity's pretentious learning to anti-rentism. Mary and her father argued gracefully and well in marked contrast to Seneca's and Opportunity's ill-constructed logic.

After a journey by train and carriages Hugh and his uncle arrived in Ravensnest. Still in their new roles as a peddler and an organ grinder, they traveled about the area to see for themselves how matters stood. At the tavern where they stopped overnight, they heard two men arguing over anti-rentism. While a lawyer took a mild stand against it, Hall, a mechanic, stood firmly against it and the greed behind it.

After a day's walk the travelers arrived at Ravensnest manor. They decided, however, to retain their disguises and visit the two old men on the place, the Indian, Susquesus, and the colored servant, Jaap. While they were at the hut of these faithful old retainers, Hugh's grandmother, Mrs. Ursula Littlepage, his sister Patt, Mary Warren, and his uncle's two wards, Henrietta Coldbrook and Anne Marston, rode up. None penetrated the disguises. After the others had gone Susquesus revealed that he knew who Hugh and his uncle were, but he promised secrecy.

The two also visited the Miller farm where they learned that Tom Miller was hostile to anti-rentism and that a farmhand of his strongly favored it. The farmhand, Joshua Brigham, was extremely greedy, Miller pointed out. While they were at the Miller farm, the five women again rode up, and Uncle Ro showed them some watches. Mrs. Littlepage, who wished to buy a very expensive watch for Mary, told them that they could receive payment for the watch at the manor.

That evening, still dressed as peddlers, they went to the Littlepage home. Hugh, asked to play his flute, performed very well, but when the flute was passed around his grandmother recognized it. When she drew her grandson aside he confessed to the deception. Soon he and his uncle were reunited with Mrs. Littlepage and Patt, who also promised secrecy. Later that evening Hugh slept in the Miller house next to Joshua Brigham. Drawn into a discussion on anti-rentism, the farmhand, thinking Hugh shared his sentiments, told of his plans for robbing the Littlepages of their land. He also revealed that the Injins were to hold a meeting the next day.

On the following day Hugh and his uncle, riding in a wagon to the meeting at the town of Ravensnest, were stopped on the way by a gang of hooded Injins who wanted to know their business. Interrupted by the appearance of Mr. Warren and Mary, the hoodlums disappeared into the bushes. The Littlepages, trying to pacify the hiding Injins by expressing mild anti-rentist sentiments, provoked Mr. Warren to argue with them, whereupon the Injins came out of hiding. The Injins then drove Uncle Ro and Mr.

Warren to the meeting, leaving Hugh to drive Mary. On the way he disclosed to her his true identity and motives.

At the meeting house the imported lecturer began to rant about liberty, equality, and justice, accused the Littlepage family of standing for slavery, aristocracy, and injustice, and declared that they were no better than other folks. When he had finished, Hall, the mechanic, got up to speak. He said that the true aristocrats of America were demagogues and newspaper editors, that the Littlepages had as much right to their ways as he did to his, and that if the Littlepage property should be divided, that of the tenants should be too. His speech was interrupted by several Injins who came whooping into the meeting house. Most of the people fled, but Mary, Hall, and the Littlepages remained, comporting themselves with dignity.

The Injins ran wild stealing calico and wagons from their own sympathizers. After seeing the Warrens off, Hugh and his uncle got into their wagon and rode toward the manor. They could see a party of armed men following them. On the way they met some anti-renters who had been deprived of their wagon. They walked alongside, still talking about the virtues of anti-rentism. Suddenly a group of real Indians appeared in the road. Surprised, Uncle Ro forgot his German accent, and the anti-renters, realizing who their companions were, ran into the bushes. The Littlepages learned that the Indians had come from Washington and were seeking Susquesus, the old Onondaga who lived at Ravensnest manor. When the terrorist Injins appeared, the real Indians let out a war whoop and the Injins ran. Two, Joshua Brigham and Seneca Newcome, were captured but were soon released. The Littlepages invited the Indians to stay in an old farmhouse at the manor. When Hugh and his uncle arrived home, everyone knew who they really were, and there was great rejoicing.

That night the Indians held a conference on the lawn in which Susquesus was the center of attention. The Indians spoke about the old days, the coming of the white man, and the different types of men with force, eloquence, and reserve. Hugh felt that they were as much gentlemen in their own way as he and Uncle Ro were in theirs.

Later that night Hugh, looking from his bedroom window, saw Opportunity Newcome riding toward the house. The ostensible purpose of her visit was to tell him that the Injins were trying to get a legal charge against him and that they were planning arson. He immediately warned Mary to keep an eye out for trouble and then went to tell the Indians to do the same.

A short time later Mary signaled to him as he was patrolling the grounds. She said that two Injins were setting fire to the kitchen. Hugh rushed to the kitchen window and fired a shot into the air as the men came out. He clubbed one over the head and fell grappling with the other. Hugh might have been overpowered if Mary had not come to his aid. At that moment the Indians, attracted by the shot, arrived on the scene. The prisoners turned out to be Joshua Brigham and Seneca Newcome. A short time later a few Injins set fire to a load of hay and then ran off, the Indians close at their heels.

Sunday morning was peaceful. The Littlepages went to church and sat in the canopied pew that the tenants resented. After church, following a brief meeting down the road, three anti-renters presented Hugh with a petition to remove the canopy; he refused. On the way home Opportunity coyly asked Hugh to release her brother, but he was noncommittal. After leaving her he learned that the canopy had been torn down and placed over the Miller pigpen. On arriving home he was told that Seneca had tried to escape arson charges by proposing to each of the four young women at the manor.

Later that day a final ceremony was held in honor of Susquesus. The peace pipe was passed around, and Jaap, the colored companion of Susquesus, was invited to make a speech. He was interrupted, however, by the appearance of a large group of Injins. While the Littlepages waited to see what was intended, Opportunity rode up, drew Hugh into the house, and told him that these Injins were not afraid of Indians. She said that Hugh was standing over an earthquake if he did not release her brother. Hugh was called outside again when it was discovered that the Injins had surrounded the Warrens. Mr. Warren and Mary maintained their composure, however, and managed to go free. The Injins were duly warned about the ferocity of the Indians, and the ceremony was continued. The Indians told how the white men broke their laws for selfish reasons and hid their shame under calico hoods, while the red men upheld their laws even at great personal sacrifice. The Injins were humiliated by this speech. While they were listening, Jack Dunning, the business agent, arrived with the sheriff and a posse to drive off the Injins. But by this time the Injins had lost public support and were thoroughly disgraced. Taking advantage of the confusion, Opportunity released her brother and Joshua Brigham, and the two were never seen in that part of the country again. The Supreme Court upheld the rights of the landlords and the anti-rent wars ended.

Uncle Ro gave a good portion of his estate to Mary when she and Hugh were married. Hugh heard that Opportunity Newcome intended to sue him for breach of promise, but nothing ever came of that threat.

Further Critical Evaluation of the Work:

As entertainment, *The Redskins* offers suspense, action, romance, and villainy. From a social and political perspective, however, this work depicts a period when the American people were becoming increasingly aware of their power and influence. The reader will discern Cooper's belief that Jacksonian democracy had degenerated into an ill-conceived, leveling movement which threatened the genteel American ethic in the pre-Civil War period. Hugh Littlepage—gentleman, world traveler, and landowner—represented the ideal America which Cooper wanted to preserve from the opportunistic and materialistic self-interests of the middle class represented by Seneca Newcome.

The Redskins begins with an indirect approbation of the American leisure class and their values. The reader quickly learns that the Littlepage family had become wealthy in the course of two generations and were spending much of their leisure abroad. Their apartment in Paris and their recent return from far-away places set the tone for the Littlepages' adventurous spirit and cosmopolitan taste. At the same time, the news of trouble at Ravensnest serves as a means to depict Hugh and his Uncle Ro as representative American landowners who willingly accept their responsibilities as paternal but benevolent superiors.

However, while Hugh and his Uncle Ro are members of the landed class, they can also identify with the lesser classes as illustrated by the disguises they adopt when they return to New York to investigate Ravensnest's troubles. Incognito as immigrant artisans, the two members of Cooper's "natural" aristocracy learn about the real feelings, ideals, and fears of such individuals as: the Reverend Mr. Warren and his daughter, Mary, and the true nature of the anti-renter, Seneca Newcome, and his crass sister, Opportunity Newcome.

Cooper's message is clear. Jacksonian Democracy would work if America were a nation of Warrens who are basically honest, hardworking, and sensible. In reality, however, America also consisted of men like Newcome, who, under the guise of justice and reform, would tear down the American Republic and its noble principles and values. In *The Redskins,* these principles and values triumph at the ceremony where wise old Susquesus is reunited with the members of his tribe. Jaap, Susquesus's black companion, reveals the story behind the old prairie Indian's exile. This development illustrates Cooper's ideal values of benevolent paternalism and noble obligations as the anti-renter movement dissipates by the moral force of Jaap's tale—and the physical presence of Susquesus's braves.

THE REIVERS

Type of work: Novel
Author: William Faulkner (1897-1962)
Time: May, 1905
Locale: Yoknapatawpha County, Mississippi; Memphis and Parsham, Tennessee
First published: 1962

Principal characters:

LUCIUS PRIEST, the narrator, eleven years old at the time of the story

BOON HOGGANBECK, a part-Chickasaw Indian and the poorest shot in the county

NED WILLIAM MCCASLIN, the Priests' coachman, a colored member of the McCaslin and Priest families

LUCIUS QUINTUS PRIEST, called "Boss," young Lucius' grandfather, a Jefferson banker and owner of the stolen Winton Flyer

MISS SARAH, his wife

MAURY PRIEST, his son, young Lucius' father

MISS ALISON, Mrs. Maury Priest

MISS REBA RIVERS, the proprietress of a Memphis brothel

EVERBE CORINTHIA, called Miss Corrie, one of Miss Reba's girls, loved by Boon Hogganbeck

MR. BINFORD, Miss Reba's landlord and protector

MINNIE, Miss Reba's maid

OTIS, Miss Corrie's delinquent nephew from Arkansas

SAM CALDWELL, a railroad brakeman and Boon's rival, who aids in transporting the stolen racehorse

UNCLE PARSHAM HOOD, a dignified old colored man who befriends young Lucius Priest

LYCURGUS BRIGGINS, his grandson

BUTCH LOVEMAIDEN, a brutal deputy sheriff

MCWILLIE, the rider of Acheron

COLONEL LINSCOMB, the owner of Acheron

MR. VAN TOSCH, the owner of Coppermine, the stolen racehorse renamed Lightning

BOBO BEAUCHAMP, Mr. van Tosch's stableboy and Ned William McCaslin's cousin

DELPHINE, Ned's wife, the Priests' cook

Subtitled "A Reminiscence," *The Reivers* begins on a note of action recalled in memory, and about a fourth of the way through the novel, posthumously awarded the 1963 Pulitzer Prize for fiction, we come upon one of William Faulkner's most engaging yarns.

In 1905 eleven-year-old Lucius Priest, Boon Hogganbeck, tough, faithful, but completely unpredictable and unreliable part-Chickasaw Indian mad about machinery, and freeloading Ned William McCaslin, the Priests' colored coachman and handyman, are on their way to Memphis in the Winton Flyer owned by young Lucius' grandfather and "borrowed" for the excursion without the owner's permission or knowledge. Because of the condition of the roads the truants are forced to make an overnight stop at Miss Ballenbaugh's, a small country store with a loft above it containing shuck mattresses for the convenience of fishermen and fox or coon hunters. The next morning, after one of the breakfasts for which Miss Ballenbaugh is famous, they start out early and soon reach Hell Creek bottom, the deepest, miriest mudhole in all Mississippi. There is no way around it: started in one direction, the travelers would end up in Alabama; head in the other, and they would fall into the Mississippi. Of course the automobile becomes mired and remains stuck in spite of their labors with shovel, barbed wire, block and tackle, and piled branches. Meanwhile on the gallery of a paintless cabin nearby, his two mules already harnessed in plow gear, a barefooted redneck watches and waits. This backwoods opportunist remarks that mud is one of the best crops in the region when the three give up in exasperation and he appears to pull the car out of the slough. Then follows some stiff bargaining. Boon claims that six dollars is too much for the job, all the more so because one of his passengers is a boy and the other is black. The man's only answer is that his mules are color-blind.

This is the tall-story idiom and spirit of Huck Finn brought forward in time, but its presence in *The Reivers* is not so much a matter of imitation as of a common source. For there is a sense in which Faulkner stands at the end of a literary tradition rather than, as many of his admirers claim, at the beginning of a new one. Through all of his writing runs a strain of broad folk humor and comic invention going back through Mark Twain to A. B. Longstreet's *Georgia Scenes* and George W. Harris' *Sut Lovingood's Yarns*, and beyond them to the Davy Crockett almanacs and the anonymous masters of oral anecdote who flourished in the old Southwest. The early American was by nature a storyteller. The realities of frontier life and his own hard comic sense created a literature of tall men and tall deeds repeated in the trading post, the groggery, the rafters' camp, wherever men met on the edge of the wilderness. These stories, shaped by the common experience and imagination, had a geography, a mythology, and a lingo of their own. Some were streaked with ballad sentiment. Others guffawed with bawdy humor. But mostly these tales were comic elaborations of character, of fantastic misadventures in which the frontiersman dramatized himself with shrewd appraisal and salty enjoyment. Through them goes a raggle-taggle procession of hunters, peddlers, horse traders, horse thieves, eagle orators, prophets, backwoods swains, land speculators, settlers—a picture of the country and the times.

Faulkner's Yoknapatawpha County lies, after all, in the same geographical belt with the Mississippi River and the Natchez Trace, and these are regions of history, folklore, and fantasy revealed in tall-story humor. This humor came into Faulkner's fiction as early as *Mosquitoes*, in the account of Old Hickory's descendant who tried raising sheep in the Louisiana swamps and eventually became so much at home in the water that he turned into a shark. It contributes to effects of grotesque outrage and exaggeration in *As I Lay Dying*, gives *Light in August* a warming pastoral glow, adds three episodes of pure comedy to *The Hamlet*, and provides illuminating comment on the rise and fall of Flem Snopes. Faulkner's habit in the past, however, was to subordinate his racier effects to the more serious concerns of man's mortality and the disorder of his moral universe. Not until he wrote *The Reivers* did he give free play to his talent for comedy of character and situation and, like Mark Twain in *Huckleberry Finn*, make it the master bias of structure and theme.

Other parallels with Twain's novel are not lacking. One is the unmistakable flavor of a style derived from the drawled tones of reminiscence. If we turn back to the nineteenth chapter of *Huckleberry Finn* we see how this style was being shaped to reveal habits of thought and feeling in art, a truly colloquial style, marvelously tuned in pulse and improvisation, with the incorrectness of folk speech in its idiom as Lucius Priest tells his story to his grandson. In *The Reivers* it is made to support both a burden of feeling within a boy's range of response and an old man's accumulation of a lifetime's reflections; and it can record sensory impressions with poetic finality.

Like *Huckleberry Finn*, too, *The Reivers* is a story of initiation, of innocence corrupted and evil exorcised. Both show the world through the eyes of childhood, an effective device when employed as a freshener of experience or a corrective of judgment, but between the two novels there is this important difference: Huck is protected by the earthy nonchalance of his own native shrewdness and resourcefulness from the contamination of the shore. Young Lucius Priest lives by the code of his class, the code of a gentleman, and he brings its values to the bordello and the racetrack. The true test is not innocence itself but what lies behind the mask of innocence. Grandfather Priest claims that when adults speak of childish innocence, they really mean ignorance. Actually, children are neither, in his opinion, for an eleven-year-old can envision any crime. If he possesses innocence, it is probably lack of appetite, just as his ignorance may be a lack of opportunity or ability.

So young Lucius Priest had only the gentleman's code to protect him when his grandfather, the president of a Jefferson bank and the owner of the second automobile ever seen in the county, goes to Louisiana to attend a funeral and Boon Hogganbeck tempts the boy with a proposal that they drive the Winton Flyer to Memphis during its owner's absence. Lucius proves vulnerable to Boon's proposal and after considerable conniving they set out. On the way they discover Ned William McCaslin hidden under a tarpaulin on the back seat. Having passed Hell Creek bottom, they arrive in Memphis, but instead of going to the Gayoso Hotel, as Lucius expected (the McCaslins and Priests always stayed at the Gayoso because a distant member of the family had in Civil War times galloped into the lobby in an effort to capture a Yankee general), Boon drives his passengers to Miss Reba's house on Catalpa Street. (This is the same Miss Reba, grown older, who figures in *Sanctuary*.) Boon has his reasons; Miss Corrie, one of Miss Reba's girls, shares with the Winton Flyer the affections of his crude but open and innocent heart. That night Ned, a

master of indirection and a reckless gambling man, trades the stolen automobile for a stolen racehorse never known to run better than second. Before the three can return to Jefferson it is necessary for young Lucius to turn jockey and win a race against a better horse, Colonel Linscomb's Acheron. Meanwhile he has fought with Otis, the vicious nephew who slurred Miss Corrie, and his chivalric gesture restores her self-respect. Boon and Ned become involved in difficulties with the law as represented by Butch Lovemaiden, a corrupt deputy sheriff; it is discovered that Otis has stolen the gold tooth prized by Minnie, Miss Reba's maid; and Boon finds, and fights, rivals for Miss Corrie's charms. As the result of all this Lucius, forced to assume a gentleman's responsibilities of courage and conduct, has lost the innocence of childhood before his grandfather appears to set matters straight. At times the boy is close to despair but he realizes that he has come too far, that to turn back now would not be homesickness but shame.

Lucius survives his ordeal, but at considerable cost to his conscience and peace of mind. Grandfather Priest has the final word on his escapade. When the boy asks how he can forget his folly and guilt, his grandfather tells him that he can't because nothing in life is ever forgotten or lost. Lucius wants to know what he can do. His grandfather says that he must live with it. To the weeping boy's protests he replies that a gentleman can live through anything because he must always accept the responsibility of his actions and the weight of their consequences. Grandfather Priest ends by telling Lucius to go wash his face; a gentleman may cry, but he washes his face afterward.

From these examples it will be seen that under its surface of fantastic invention and tall-story humor *The Reivers* is another moral fable in the Faulknerian manner. Yet it is quite different in effect from the earlier, darker studies of manners and morals. In tragedy, and Faulkner was a great tragic artist, the soul of man stands naked before God, and He is not mocked. In comedy it is not the possible in man that is to be revealed but the probable in conduct or belief. Thus, man in comedy is viewed in relation to some aspect of his society. In *The Reivers*—the title means plunderers or freebooters—a master of comedy was at work testing young Lucius Priest by the behavior of a gentleman in a world of evasion and deceit where it is easier to run from one's responsibilities than to stand up and face them.

In setting these matters straight, the triumph of the novel is in the manner of the telling. *The Reivers* is a story about a boy, but it is told by a man grown old enough and wise enough through the years of accumulated experience to look back on his adventure, relish it in all its qualities of adventure and fantasy, and at the same time pass judgment on it. This judgment is never harsh. Lucius Priest, telling the story to *his* grandson, is revealed as a person of tolerance and understanding of much that is so deeply and irrevocably ingrained in the eternal condition of man, and his point of view gives the novel added depth and dimension.

Put beside the novels of his great period, *The Reivers* is minor Faulkner. At the same time it is a good yarn in the tall-story tradition, skillfully told, comic in effect, shrewd in observation on manners, morals, politics, and the general cussedness and downright foolishness of mankind. More to the point, it broadens even if it does not deepen our knowledge of Faulkner's legendary Mississippi county.

THE RELAPSE

Type of work: Drama
Author: Sir John Vanbrugh (1664-1726)
Type of plot: Social satire
Time of plot: Seventeenth century
Locale: England
First presented: 1696

Principal characters:
SIR NOVELTY FASHION, LORD FOPPINGTON, a London fop
YOUNG FASHION, his brother
LOVELESS, a gentleman
AMANDA, his wife
WORTHY, a gentleman of the town
SIR TUNBELLY CLUMSEY, a country squire
MISS HOYDEN, Sir Tunbelly's daughter
COUPLER, a matchmaker
BERINTHIA, a comely widow

Critique:

The Relapse, Or, Virtue in Danger was written as a sequel to Colley Cibber's Love's Last Shift because in Vanbrugh's opinion the latter play did not present an accurate picture of human nature. Lord Foppington is Cibber's Sir Novelty Fashion elevated to the peerage. The Relapse was a huge success, and for more than fifty years it held the London stage, sometimes running in more than one theater at a time. Historically, the play is important because it helped to break up the formulas followed in the artificial comedy of manners. Vanbrugh has been accused of irreligion, which is probably not wholly true, and of licentiousness, which is probably accurate.

The Story:

In the country Loveless and Amanda led a quiet life after a stormy period of marriage troubles. Because Loveless had to go to London rather frequently and because she had reason to doubt his fidelity, Amanda was apprehensive. But Loveless assured her he was temptation-proof; going to London provided a test of his reform.

Young Fashion and his servant Lory called on Sir Novelty Fashion, the new Lord Foppington, young Fashion's elder brother. Lord Foppington had recently bought a title. Since he was the eldest son, he had plenty of money, although he spent too much as it was. Young Fashion, on the contrary, was destitute. He was minded to join the army as a last resort, but at Lory's suggestion he resolved to humble himself to ask the new lord to pay his debts. But Lord Foppington was busy with the tailor and the shoemaker and hardly spared his brother a word. Although Lord Foppington was on the point of going out, he did invite his brother to stay and have a home dinner by himself.

Angered by his brother's attitude, young Fashion determined on revenge. Coupler, a matchmaker who providentially came in, had a plan. Coupler had arranged a marriage between Lord Foppington and Miss Hoyden, wealthy daughter of Sir Tunbelly Clumsey. Lord Foppington was to pay the matchmaker two thousand pounds, but he was afraid the new lord would evade the money agreement. It was decided that young Fashion was to go to Sir Tunbelly's house and, pretending to be his brother, marry Miss Hoyden. Coupler, in turn, was to receive a fee of five thousand pounds. Young Fashion agreed to the plan, after a hard time fighting off Coupler's amorous advances.

Loveless and Amanda were installed in their London lodgings and Loveless had already been to the theater. In a confidential mood he told his wife of seeing a beautiful woman in the audience, a woman so handsome he had been unable to keep his eyes off her. Amanda was alarmed, but he told her he admired the woman only in an aesthetic way. Berinthia, Amanda's widowed friend, came to call. To Loveless' surprise, she was the woman he had admired in the theater. Because he pretended to be indifferent to Berinthia's charms, Amanda invited her to stay with them while they were in London.

Lord Foppington also came to call and was quite smitten with Amanda's beauty. Resolving to make a conquest at once, he drew her aside and declared his love. Amanda slapped his face. Loveless, seeing the fracas, wounded Lord Foppington with his sword. Although the wound was not serious, the surgeon pretended that it was, in order to increase his fee. As Lord Foppington was being carried out, Worthy entered and was also attracted by Amanda's charms. After the men had all left, Berinthia had a long talk with Amanda about men and love.

Young Fashion determined to make one more attempt before taking revenge on his brother. Once again he told Lord Foppington of his debts and asked for money to settle them. Lord Foppington refused haughtily, and in the ensuing quarrel young Fashion tried to fight a duel with his brother. Lord Foppington contemptuously refused to fight and left. Resolved to do his worst, young Fashion set out for Coupler's house.

Loveless made love to Berinthia and finally seized her. He left, however, when they were interrupted by Worthy's arrival. Worthy was in love with Amanda. Because Berinthia had once been his mistress, he asked her help in his suit. Berinthia's plan was to let Amanda become jealous of her erring husband; in her anger she would be an easier prey. When Amanda returned, Berinthia told her that Loveless was pursuing a strange woman.

Armed with a letter from Coupler, young Fashion called at Sir Tunbelly's house. When he knocked, Sir Tunbelly quickly locked Miss Hoyden in her room with her old nurse and sent armed peasants to the gate. Young Fashion was cordially received, however, when he explained that he was Lord Foppington. Miss Hoyden, ripely nubile, was all atwitter.

Although the nurse was supposed to be a chaperone, she was an indulgent one, and she allowed young Fashion to talk privately with Miss Hoyden. Sir Tunbelly wanted to defer the wedding for a while to allow time to invite the guests, but young Fashion did not dare wait so long. For a small bribe, since Miss Hoyden was more than willing, the nurse made arrangements for Bull, the chaplain, to marry them secretly in the morning. And, since they were to be married so soon, she saw no harm in their staying together that night. The following morning the complaisant Bull performed the ceremony.

When Berinthia and Amanda again discussed the subject of love, Berinthia skillfully played on Amanda's doubts of Loveless' fidelity. According to plan, Worthy then arrived to say that Loveless would be out until very late, and that while waiting for Loveless he would play cards with the ladies. Artful Berinthia withdrew to her chamber and left Worthy and Amanda alone. In her bedroom, meanwhile, Berinthia received the erring Loveless. Putting out the candles, he seized Berinthia and dragged her into the closet. She shouted for help, but she was careful to scream very softly.

Lord Foppington arrived at Sir Tunbelly's house to claim his bride. Taken for an impostor, he was set upon and bound, and young Fashion declared he had never seen the man before. A neighbor identified Foppington, however, and young Fashion fled precipitately. Miss Hoyden decided to keep still about her marriage to young Fashion and to marry again, this time the real Lord Foppington.

Back in London, Coupler showed young Fashion a letter. Lord Foppington had married Miss Hoyden but would wait until they returned to Lord Foppington's own bed to consummate the marriage. Young Fashion had to wait until the couple came to town to regain his Miss Hoyden. Fortunately, the parson of Fat-goose Living had just died and young Fashion had the disposition of the post. By promising the living to Bull, young Fashion persuaded him that he should tell the truth about the secret marriage.

Meanwhile Berinthia, trying to arouse Amanda's jealousy to the point where she would accept Worthy as a lover, arranged to have Amanda present at a masquerade. Loveless was there in the company of Berinthia, who was masked. Convinced that her husband had a mistress, Amanda received Worthy in her home, but in spite of his best efforts she retained her virtue.

Lord Foppington invited the whole company to come and honor his new bride. Young Fashion appeared also and declared that Miss Hoyden was married to him. Sir Tunbelly was thunderstruck and Lord Foppington was contemptuous of his younger brother's story. True to their agreement, the nurse and Bull backed him up. When it was learned that young Fashion was Lord Foppington's brother, Sir Tunbelly withdrew his opposition and accepted his son-in-law. Lord Foppington met the new turn of events as gracefully as he could. Miss Hoyden, having learned that her first husband was Lord Foppington's brother, had no complaint to make, just so long as she was married to someone.

Further Critical Evaluation of the Work:

Although the earthiness and witty cynicism of Vanbrugh's play provide a healthy correction to Colley Cibber's sentimental tendencies, Vanbrugh lacked Cibber's sense of dramatic form. He may have been more accurate than Cibber in depicting human nature, but he was less adept at fashioning a well-constructed play. This is particularly odd because Vanbrugh eventually became one of England's greatest architects, the builder of Blenheim Palace for the Duke of Marlborough and the designer of the Haymarket Theatre, which he managed for two years. He was well aware of the indifferent plotting of his play, however, because he apologized for it in the "Prologue" where he attributed the play's lack of "plot or wit" to the haste of its composition: "It was got, conceived, and born in six weeks space."

If Vanbrugh was weak in plot and dialogue, his characters were nevertheless compelling creations and very popular with actors. Even Colley Cibber, whose work was the object of Vanbrugh's satire, admitted that Vanbrugh's lines were easier to memorize than those of any other playwright. Vanbrugh gave actors a great deal to do in the sense that action in his plays is broad and suggestive; even if the language is not rich in wit, it often has a dramatically effective force. In the opening scene, Amanda fears that if Loveless goes to town, he will be unfaithful. She expresses this in a series of direct statements ending with a bathetic conclusion:

> I know the weak defence of nature
> I know you are a man—and I—a wife.

Vanbrugh is one of those writers of Restoration Comedy who fed the arguments of its moralistic enemies. His husbands *are* corrupt sensualists, and because of Vanbrugh's crude dramaturgy there is little to redeem them in their wit. When they seduce, they do so with their bodies, not a *bon mot*. Loveless actually carries Berinthia off stage. The humor is salacious and broad. Her response is to cry "I'm ravished"—in a soft voice. One can easily understand the enthusiasm of Vanbrugh's audiences, and one can also appreciate the opportunities for farcical acting that his plays provide.

R. E. LEE

Type of work: Biography
Author: Douglas Southall Freeman (1886-1953)
Time: 1807-1870
Locale: Mostly the Confederate States of America
First published: 1934-1935

Principal personages:
GENERAL ROBERT E. LEE
MARY CUSTIS LEE, his wife
GENERAL WINFIELD SCOTT, U.S.A.
PRESIDENT JEFFERSON DAVIS, C.S.A.
THOMAS JONATHAN ("STONEWALL") JACKSON,
JAMES LONGSTREET,
JAMES EWELL BROWN STUART,
RICHARD STODDERT EWELL,
AMBROSE POWELL HILL, and
JUBAL ANDERSON EARLY, Generals of the Confederacy
GENERAL ULYSSES S. GRANT, U.S.A.

By heritage, education, profession, and talent Douglas Southall Freeman was ideally fitted to write the definitive biography of Robert Edward Lee. The son of a Confederate veteran, a Doctor of Philosophy in history from Johns Hopkins University, editor of the Richmond *News Leader,* whose "chief avocation" was "the study of military history" and whose prose style was fascinating, he accepted in 1915 a publisher's invitation to tell the life story of the South's best beloved hero. It seems that Douglas Freeman's ambition to compose such a book was born in 1903, when as a youth of seventeen he attended a reunion of Confederate veterans in Petersburg, Virginia, in the company of his father, who lived to see his son's work published. At first the biographer expected to write only a single volume, but a wealth of compelling material, much of it scarcely tapped, expanded his number to four; as a title for his monumental production, Dr. Freeman chose the general's autograph: *R. E. Lee.* Following this work, Freeman returned to the life of General Lee himself for a one-volume biography entitled *Lee of Virginia,* and intended for a young adult audience or for readers who found the four-volume work too formidable. The author then laid aside the manuscript — which was published posthumously — to begin work on his exhaustive biography of George Washington, which had reached six volumes at the time of his sudden death in 1953.

Volume I of *R. E. Lee,* containing thirty-six chapters, covers a period of fifty-five years, from Lee's birth on January 19, 1807, to the beginning of the War between the States in 1861 and the early months of 1862. It takes its reader with never flagging interest through the West Point years, marriage, gradual rise in the United States Army, the Mexican War, the capture of John Brown, "The Answer He Was Born to Make," and the early, unsuccessful operations in western Virginia. Concerning Lee's momentous decision, which has entailed much dispute by many persons, the author states: "The spirit of Virginia had been alive in his heart every hour of his life. . . . He was a United States officer who loved the army and had pride in the Union, but something very deep in his heart kept him mindful that he had been a Virginian before he had been a soldier."

Volume II, composed of thirty-five chapters, recounting the Seven Days' Battles east of Richmond against McClellan, Second Manassas against Pope, the Sharpsburg Campaign in Maryland with McClellan again the adversary, and the Battle of Fredericksburg against Burnside, all in 1862, concludes with the victory over Hooker at Chancellorsville and the death of Stonewall Jackson in May, 1863. In his Foreword to R. E. Lee, Freeman explains his belief that "... military biography, like military history in general, may fail to be instructive because, paradoxically, it is too informative." To avoid the problem of burdening his narrative with too many facts, therefore, the author adopts a technique related to the novelist's use of the limited point of view: events are presented to the reader only in the sequence and manner in which they were experienced by Lee himself. The result, apparent in Volume II, is a masterful narration, tense, powerful, and alive, and above all remarkable for its verisimilitude.

Volume III, twenty-nine chapters in length, proceeds from the beginning of the Gettysburg Campaign through that fateful conflict with the full power of Dr. Freeman's critical study. Then comes the "hammer and rapier" matching of Grant against Lee in 1864, with such battles as the Wilderness, Spotsylvania Courthouse, and Cold Harbor, the historian's expositions being precise but never tiresome. Grant crosses the James, and the long, encircling blue lines outside Petersburg are held in check by Lee's thin gray battalions for nearly ten months, with the unique Battle of the Crater furnishing a new, strange story for the history of war. The reader lives with freezing, starving Southern veterans to the end of the winter of 1864-1865.

The first eleven chapters of Volume IV relate the close of the war in Virginia with the surrender at Appomattox Courthouse. The next sixteen chapters picture General Lee—body, mind, and soul—as he turns to civilian pursuits and works sincerely and consistently for peace and reconciliation. He maintains his dignity and grandeur as college president at Lexington, until his death on October 12, 1870. The final chapter, "The Pattern of a Life," is Freeman's masterpiece. Epitomizing Lee's career and character, it can be designated properly by one term only: a classic.

R. E. Lee was a labor of love. For nineteen years, from its inception in 1915 to its publication in 1934-1935, the author, discarding apocryphal and legendary tales, scrupulously winnowed and used documented facts. Averring that he was "fully repaid by being privileged to live, as it were, for more than a decade in the company of a great gentleman," Dr. Freeman adds in his foreword: "There were no 'secrets' and no scandals to be exposed or explained. . . . Neither was there any occasion to attempt an 'interpretation' of a man who was his own clear interpreter." The reader enjoys the biography as he shares the author's uplift of spirit.

Though detailed, the narrative is never boring. Minor, no less than major, incidents are recorded delightfully; for instance, Lieutenant Lee's riding double on horseback with a brother officer along Pennsylvania Avenue in Washington; kissing a little boy whom he mistook for his own son; picking up under shellfire a small sparrow and putting it back in a tree from which it had fallen; smiling upon hearing a Negro attendant explain that he had not been shot because he stayed back where the generals stayed.

Dr. Freeman would have transcended human ability if he had never erred in his minutiae. Few and inconsequential, however, are such slips as entitling the Right Reverend John Johns "Bishop of Virginia" in 1853, whereas at that time he was Assistant Bishop, and calling Colonel David A. Weisiger "Daniel" Weisiger. Generally Freeman's accuracy of research and transcription equals his natural stylistic charm. Moreover, R. E. Lee retains freshness and vigor throughout its length. Nor have verbal mannerisms become so patent in it as the author's often repeated "doubtless" in his later *George Washington.*

Promptly upon the appearance of the first two volumes, *R. E. Lee* was awarded a Pulitzer Prize, and, in the years which have followed, neither the scholar nor the mere average reader has been prone to dispute the judges' logic. Definitely this life of an unspotted American hero is the *magnum opus* of an unexcelled American biographer.

REMEMBRANCE OF THINGS PAST

Type of work: Novel
Author: Marcel Proust (1871-1922)
Type of plot: Psychological realism
Time of plot: Late nineteenth, early twentieth centuries
Locale: France
First published: 1913-1927

    Principal characters:
        MARCEL, the narrator
        MARCEL'S GRANDMOTHER, a kind and wise old woman
        M. SWANN, a wealthy broker and esthete
        MME. SWANN, formerly a cocotte, Odette de Crécy
        GILBERTE, their daughter, later Mme. de Saint-Loup
        MME. DE VILLEPARISIS, a friend of Marcel's grandmother
        ROBERT DE SAINT-LOUP, her nephew, Marcel's friend
        BARON DE CHARLUS, another nephew, a Gomorrite
        MME. VERDURIN, a vulgar social climber
        THE PRINCE and PRINCESS DE GUERMANTES, and
        THE DUKE and DUCHESS DE GUERMANTES, members of the old aristocracy

Critique:

Remembrance of Things Past is not a novel of traditional form. Symphonic in design, it unfolds without plot or crisis as the writer reveals in retrospect the motifs of his experience, holds them for thematic effect, and drops them, only to return to them once more in the processes of recurrence and change. This varied pattern of experience brings together a series of involved relationships through the imagination and observation of a narrator engaged in tracing with painstaking detail his perceptions of people and places as he himself grows from childhood to disillusioned middle age. From the waking reverie in which he recalls the themes and characters of his novel to that closing paragraph with its slow, repeated echoes of the word *Time,* Proust's novel is great art distilled from memory itself, the structure determined entirely by moods and sensations evoked by the illusion of time passing, or seeming to pass, recurring, or seeming to recur. The title shows Proust's two-fold concern as a novelist: time lost and time recalled. To the discerning reader it is plain that for Proust the true realities of human experience were not con-tained in a reconstruction of remembered scenes and events but in the capture of physical sensations and moods re-created in memory. The seven novels which make up *Remembrance of Things Past* are *Swann's Way, Within a Budding Grove, The Guermantes Way, Cities of the Plain, The Captive, The Sweet Cheat Gone,* and *The Past Recaptured.*

The Story:

All his life Marcel found it difficult to go to sleep at night. After he had blown out the light, he would lie quietly in the darkness and think of the book he had been reading, of an event in history, of some memory from the past. Sometimes he would think of all the places in which he had slept—as a child in his great-aunt's house in the provincial town of Combray, in Balbec on a holiday with his grandmother, in the military town where his friend, Robert de Saint-Loup, had been stationed, in Paris, in Venice during a visit there with his mother.

He remembered always a night at Combray when he was a child. M. Swann, a family friend, had come to

REMEMBRANCE OF THINGS PAST by Marcel Proust. Translated by C. K. Scott-Moncrieff and Frederick A. Blossom. By permission of Brandt & Brandt and the publishers, Random House, Inc. Copyright, 1924, 1925, by Thomas Seltzer, 1927, 1929, 1930, 1932, by Random House, Inc., 1934, by The Modern Library, Inc.

dinner. Marcel had been sent to bed early, where he lay for hours nervous and unhappy until at last he heard M. Swann leave. Then his mother had come upstairs to comfort him.

For a long time the memory of that night was his chief recollection of Combray, where his family took him to spend a part of every summer with his grandparents and aunts. Years later, while drinking tea with his mother, the taste of a small sweet cake suddenly brought back all the impressions of his old days at Combray.

He remembered the two roads. One was Swann's way, a path that ran beside M. Swann's park where the lilacs and hawthorns bloomed. The other was the Guermantes way, along the river and past the chateau of the Duke and Duchess de Guermantes, the great family of Combray. He remembered the people he saw on his walks. There were familiar figures like the doctor and the priest. There was M. Vinteuil, an old composer who died broken-hearted and shamed because of his daughter's friendship with a woman of bad reputation. There were the neighbors and friends of his grandparents. But best of all he remembered M. Swann, whose story he pieced together slowly from family conversations and village gossip.

M. Swann was a wealthy Jew accepted in rich and fashionable society. His wife was not received, however, for she was his former mistress, Odette de Crécy, a cocotte with the fair, haunting beauty of a Botticelli painting. It was Odette who had first introduced Swann to the Verdurins, a vulgar family that pretended to despise the polite world of the Guermantes. At an evening party given by Mme. Verdurin, Swann heard played a movement of Vinteuil's sonata and identified his hopeless passion for Odette with that lovely music. Swann's love was an unhappy affair. Tortured by jealousy, aware of the vulgarity and pettiness of the Verdurins, determined to forget his unfaithful mistress, he went to Mme. de Saint-Euverte's reception. There he

heard Vinteuil's music again. Under its influence he decided, at whatever price, to marry Odette.

After their marriage Swann drifted more and more into the bourgeois circle of the Verdurins. When he went to see his old friends in Combray and in the fashionable Faubourg Saint-Germain, he went alone. Many people thought him both ridiculous and tragic.

On his walks Marcel sometimes saw Mme. Swann and her daughter, Gilberte, in the park at Combray. Later, in Paris, he met the little girl and became her playmate. That friendship, as they grew older, became an innocent love affair. Filled also with a schoolboyish passion for Mme. Swann, Marcel went to Swann's house as much to be in her company as in Gilberte's. But after a time his pampered habits and brooding, neurasthenic nature began to bore Gilberte. His pride hurt, he refused to see her for many years.

Marcel's family began to treat him as an invalid. With his grandmother, he went to Balbec, a seaside resort. There he met Albertine, a girl to whom he was immediately attracted. He met also Mme. de Villeparisis, an old friend of his grandmother and a connection of the Guermantes family. Mme. de Villeparisis introduced him to her two nephews, Robert de Saint-Loup and Baron de Charlus. Saint-Loup and Marcel became close friends. While visiting Saint-Loup in a nearby garrison town, Marcel met his friend's mistress, a young Jewish actress named Rachel. Marcel was both fascinated and repelled by Baron de Charlus; he was not to understand until later the baron's corrupt and depraved nature.

Through his friendship with Mme. de Villeparisis and Saint-Loup, Marcel was introduced into the smart world of the Guermantes when he returned to Paris.

One day, while he was walking with his grandmother, she suffered a stroke. The illness and death of that good and unselfish old woman made him realize for the first time the empty worldliness of his smart and wealthy friends. For comfort he turned to Albertine, who came to stay with him in Paris while his family was away. But his desire to be humored and indulged in all his whims, his suspicions of Albertine, and his petty jealousy, finally forced her to leave him and go back to Balbec. With her, he had been unhappy; without her, he was wretched. Then he learned that she had been accidentally killed in a fall from her horse. Later he received a letter, written before her death, in which she promised to return to him.

More miserable than ever, Marcel tried to find diversion among his old friends. They were changing with the times. Swann was ill and soon to die. Gilberte had married Robert de Saint-Loup. Mme. Verdurin, who had inherited a fortune, now entertained the old nobility. At one of her parties Marcel heard a Vinteuil composition played by a musician named Morel, the nephew of a former servant and now a protegé of the notorious Baron de Charlus.

His health breaking down at last, Marcel spent the war years in a sanitarium. When he returned to Paris, he found still greater changes. Robert de Saint-Loup had been killed in the war. Rachel, Saint-Loup's mistress, had become a famous actress. Swann was also dead, and his widow, remarried, was a fashionable hostess who received the Duchess de Guermantes. Prince de Guermantes, his fortune lost and his first wife dead, had married Mme. Verdurin for her money. Baron de Charlus had grown senile.

Marcel went to one last reception at the Princess de Guermantes' lavish house. Meeting there the daughter of Gilberte de Saint-Loup, he realized how time had passed, how old he had grown. In the Guermantes library, he happened to take down the novel by George Sand which his mother had read to him that remembered night in Combray, years before. Suddenly, in memory, he heard again the ringing of the bell that announced M. Swann's departure and knew that it would echo in his mind forever. He saw then that everything in his own futile, wasted life dated from that far night in his childhood, and in that moment of self-revelation he saw also the ravages of time among all the people he had ever known.

Further Critical Evaluation of the Work:

In *Remembrance of Things Past (A la récherche du temps perdu),* Marcel Proust, together with Leo Tolstoy (*War and Peace*), Fyodor Dostoevski (*The Brothers Karamazov*), Thomas Mann (*Joseph and His Brothers*), and James Joyce (*Ulysses*) transformed the novel from a linear account of events into a multi-dimensional art. The breakthrough was not into Freudian psychology, or existentialism, or scientific determinism, but into a realization that all things are, or may be, interwoven, bound by time, yet freed from time, open to every associational context.

What is reality? Certainly there is the reality of the sensory experience; yet any moment of sensory experience may have numerous successive or even simultaneous realities as it is relived in memory in different contexts, and perhaps the most significant reality—or realities—of a given act or moment may come long after the moment when the event first took place in time. Percy Shelley, in *A Defence of Poetry,* said, "All things exist as they are perceived: at least in relation to the percipient." And things which may have seemed inconsequential at the moment of their occurrence may take on richly multi-faceted meanings in relation to other events, other memories, other moments. The initial act is not as significant, not as real, as the perceptions of it which may come in new contexts, Reality *is* a context, made up of moods, of recollections joined by chance or design, sets of associations that have grown over the years. This concept of the notion of reality, one that had been taking shape with increased momentum since the Romantic Movement, opened the way to "those mysteries . . . the presentiment of which is the quality in life and art which moves us most deeply."

The elusive yet pervasively important nature of reality applies not only to events, such as the taste of the *Madeleine* (or small cake), but also to the absence of events, for the failure of Marcel's mother to give him his accustomed goodnight kiss proved to be an occasion which memory would recall again and again in a variety of relationships. Thus reality can and inevitably for all of us does sometimes include, if not indeed center on, the nonbeing of an event. That nonexistence can be placed in time and in successive times as surely as events that did happen; moreover 'it"—that nothing where something might or should have been—may become a significant part of the contexts which, both in time and freed from time, constitute reality.

Such thematic variations and turns of thought have led some to identify Proust as a "dilettante." Perhaps, in its literal sense, the term is justified, for his mind must have delighted in what, to the reader, may be unexpected turns of thought. In this he is most closely to be associated with Thomas Mann, whose consideration of time in the first volume of *Joseph and His Brothers* leads us into labyrinthine but essential paths; or whose speculations about the God-man relationship in Volume Two, in the section headed "Abraham Discovers God," lead us down a dizzying path of whimsical yet serious thought. But the fact remains that Mann and Proust have opened doors of contemplation that modern man cannot afford to ignore if he would increase his understanding of himself, the world in which he lives, and the tenuous nature of reality and of time.

What Proust does with time and reality he also does with character. Although he is a contemporary of Freud, and although Freudian interpretation could be applied to some of his characters in part, his concept of character is much too complex for reduction to ego, id, and the subconscious. Character, like reality, is a changing total context, not static and not a thing in itself to be held off and examined at arm's length. Baron de Charlus is at once a study of character in disintegration and a caricature, reduced in the end to a pitiable specimen, scarcely human. But it is Marcel, the *persona* of the story, who is seen in most depth and frequently in tortured self-analysis. His character is seen in direct statements, in his comments about others and about situations, in what others say to him or the way they say it, even in descriptive passages which would at first glance not seem to relate to character at all. "Only the exhaustive can be truly interesting," Thomas Mann said in the preface to *The Magic Mountain*. Proust surely agreed. His detail is not of the catalog variety, however; it works cumulatively, developmentally, with the thematic progression of symphonic music.

But finally the totality of the work is "the remembrance of things past," or as the title of the seventh, the final volume, has it, "the past recaptured." To undersand it in its full richness one must become and remain conscious of the author, isolated in his study, drawing upon his recollections, associating and reassociating moments, events, personalities (his own always central), both to recapture the past as it happened and to discover in it the transcendent reality which supersedes the time-bound moment of the initial occurrence. The total work is a story, a succession of stories, and a study of the life process, which, as we come to understand it, must greatly enrich our own sense of ourselves and of the lives which we live.

Kenneth Oliver

REMEMBRANCE ROCK

Type of work: Novel
Author: Carl Sandburg (1878-1967)
Type of plot: Historical chronicle
Time of plot: 1607-1945
Locale: England and America
First published: 1948

Principal characters:

ORVILLE BRAND WINDOM, former Justice of the United States Supreme Court
OLIVER BALL WINDROW, a woodcarver and philosopher
MARY WINDLING, a young Puritan
JOHN SPONG, whom she married
REMEMBER SPONG, their daughter
ORTON WINGATE, a sojourner in Plymouth
PETER LADD, a seaman and gambler
RESOLVED WAYFARE, a follower of Roger Williams
ORDWAY WINSHORE, a Philadelphia printer
ROBERT WINSHORE, his older son
JOHN LOCKE WINSHORE, his younger son
MARINTHA (MIM) WILMING, a dressmaker's assistant
OATES ELWOOD, friend of Robert and Locke
ANN, his sister, Locke's wife
OMRI WINWOLD, an ex-gambler
JOEL WIMBLER, an abolitionist
BROOKSANY, his wife
MILLICENT (MIBS), their daughter
RODNEY WAYMAN, Mibs' husband, a Confederate officer

Critique:

Remembrance Rock, a first novel published when its writer was 70, is a work almost as sprawling and formless as the land it celebrates. The pattern is simple: three stories dealing with the settling of Plymouth, the American Revolution, and the Civil War, set between a prologue and an epilogue which have for background Washington in the years of World War II. Imperfect as a novel, the book is nevertheless a great American document, presenting in human terms and in the idiom of Sandburg's "swift and furious people" the growth of the American dream through more than three centuries of our national history. Remembrance Rock has been called a saga, a chronicle, a sermon, a collection of Chaucerian tales, a miscellany on folk themes; and it is all of these. By means of fable, paean, symbol, and style that ranges from the grave, proud language of Bunyan and Defoe to the downright slangy and boisterous, Sandburg has projected a poet-historian's testament of American life. The result is a narrative as passionate and affirmative as the tough and mystic eloquence of his poetry. Unity of theme is provided by characters recurring in the major episodes and by the symbolic reappearances of a bronze plaque bearing an inscription of Roger Bacon's Four Stumbling Blocks to Truth: 1) The influence of fragile or unworthy authority. 2) Custom. 3) The imperfection of undisciplined senses. 4) Concealment of ignorance by ostentation of seeming wisdom.

The Stories:

The rock stood in the cedar-shaded garden of former Supreme Court Justice Orville Brand Windom, a giant boulder about which he had scattered earth from Plymouth, Valley Forge, Gettysburg, the Argonne. The justice was old, with a deep and brooding concern for the American land, its history, its people. Some of his ideas he spoke to the world in a radio broadcast he made in 1944. Others he recorded in three chronicles of the living past that his grandson, Captain Raymond Windom, veteran of Okinawa, found in a locked box after the old man's death. These tales, like the antique bronze plaque inscribed with Roger Bacon's Four Stumbling Blocks to Truth, were Justice Windom's legacy of wisdom and love to his grandson, his grandson's wife, and their son, Joseph Stilwell Windom.

I

Red-haired Oliver Ball Windrow, the woodcarver, had on one side of his face the look of a poet and dreamer, on the other a countenance of wrath and storm. A seeker and questioner, he loved Mary Windling, a girl only half his age and a member of the Separatist congregation that worshipped secretly at Scrooby, and for her he made a small plaque of bronze, on which he inscribed Roger Bacon's Four Stumbling Blocks to Truth, to wear on a silver cord around her neck.

Mary liked his sudden whims and strange humors, but in the end she married a young workman named John Spong. This happened in 1608, just before the Scrooby congregation escaped to Holland. For twelve years Mary Spong and her husband lived in Leyden. Infrequent news came from England. Windrow had wed Matilda Bracken, the devoted mute who kept his house. Then, in 1620, he and his two daughters died of smallpox. Mary's sadness for her old friend was lessened by promises and fears surrounding plans of the Puritans to try their fortunes in the new world.

The Spongs and their daughter Remember were passengers aboard the *Mayflower* when it sailed. Little Remember had only one memory of Plymouth. One day, while she was playing on the wharf, some boys began to torment her. Another boy came with an ax handle and beat them off. She forgot to ask his name.

Mary Spong, dying during that first terrible winter in the wilderness, gave her daughter the tarnished keepsake Windrow had made years before. Remember grew up in Plymouth, a cluster of houses between forest and sea, and those gaunt years of hardship and toil helped to shape her strong body, her resolute will, her sober decorum that hid deep passions. Her father grew grim and silent as time passed. He disliked Orton Wingate, a sojourner in Plymouth, a man whose face showed peace and calm on one side, turmoil on the other. But Wingate was Remember's friend and came to sit with her from time to time. She knew without his saying that she could have had him for her husband. Restless, uncertain of her own mind, she waited.

Sometimes she rebelled against the harsh Puritan laws, as when she concealed Hode Latch, a convicted drunkard for whom constables were searching, and then she was afraid that she was damned. Perhaps Peter Ladd sensed that wild streak in her when he came courting. He was a young seaman who drifted into Plymouth, steadied himself for a while, and then fell once more into dissolute ways. When Remember refused him, he went away to make his fortune in the slave trade. Two years later he was drowned in a wreck off the Virginia capes.

Roger Williams, free-thinking preacher, lived in Plymouth for a time. Several years later he was shaking the colonies with his liberal beliefs and teachings. A new age was beginning when Williams, a fugitive, built his own town beside Narragansett Bay, but Remember Spong could not know how far-reaching were to be his challenges to usages of authority and custom. She feared him most because he revealed the rebel in herself. For that reason she was of two minds about Resolved Wayfare, a newcomer to the colony in 1638. Wayfare had crossed the ocean to learn for himself the meaning of Roger Williams' message. He was also the boy, grown to manhood, who had defended Remember on the Plymouth wharf.

After he saved John Spong's life during a blizzard, Remember nursed the young man back to health. During that time there was a battle of wills between them. He wanted her to go with him to Providence, but she, like her father, held that the teachings of Roger Williams were of Satan. Although Wingate's wisdom and the cruel lashing of an unmarried mother finally convinced her of the folly and blindness of custom, she could not quite make up her mind to go with Wayfare on his journey. Yet she walked with him some distance into the forest, and before they parted she gave him the bronze keepsake she had from her mother. Knowing that they would meet again, they vowed to be true as long as grass would grow or water flow. That was the solemn promise between them.

II

In March, 1775, Ordway Winshore, master printer, left Philadelphia to visit his sons in New York and Boston. Below rusty hair, his face on one side promised peace, on the other wrath and doom—a face half serious, half comic, making him a man easy to confide in. Among his fellow travelers were two young British lieutenants, Francis and George Frame. During a tavern halt Francis Frame broke his hand by striking a blacksmith who had cursed King George. The Philadelphia printer felt that the war was beginning.

Winshore spent two days in New York with Locke, his younger son, a typesetter for Henry Tozzer, printer of Independence leaflets. Locke reported that his brother Robert was deep in the activities of Massachusetts patriots. He also hinted at Robert's romance with a dressmaker's assistant.

Another passenger in the coach to Boston was Marintha Wilming, to whom George Frame paid marked attention. Winshore liked her, not knowing, however, that she was the girl his older son loved.

Not far from Boston, Robert Winshore

helped some Sons of Liberty to tar and feather Hobart Reggs, a prosperous Tory who had informed on a British deserter. Sapphira, Reggs' daughter, accidentally saw his face during the tarring.

Boston, Winshore found, was a seething, sullen city filled with British troops, Tories, Rebels, and neutrals. At the dress shop where Marintha Wilming worked there was much talk of Ann Elwood, an innocent young girl who had been tricked into a false marriage by a Grenadier sergeant. Winshore met Marintha—Mim—again in Robert's company and visited the house where she lived with her aunt. He also encountered Isaiah Thomas, printer of the *Massachusetts Spy* and Robert's employer, and in Henry Knox's bookstore he met Mary Burton, whom he, a widower, was to marry a short time later. One day, at the dress shop, Sapphira Reggs recognized Robert. When Lieutenant George Frame attempted to arrest him at the home of Mim's aunt, Robert escaped. Fleeing, he lost the old bronze plaque which had come to him from a great-granduncle and which he wore on a chain under his shirt.

Robert was with the Minute Men when the British marched on Lexington. Darius, Mim's brother, was killed in the fighting, and Lieutenant George Frame was crippled for life. Robert ventured into Boston to tell Mim of her brother's death, but the girl, distracted by his news and George Frame's injuries, declared that she wanted to forget him and his rebel violence.

Locke became a military courier. In Philadelphia, Winshore and his new wife read Paine's *Common Sense*. Robert and Oates Elwood, Ann's brother, marched with Benedict Arnold toward Quebec until they became ill with fever and were forced to turn back. The British evacuated Boston. Robert was invalided home. Locke and Elwood, carrying messages from General Greene to General Washington, spent a night with the Winshores in Philadelphia. Robert was there, a messenger at the Continental Congress. There was no time for Locke to tell his family that he had secretly married Ann Elwood. The next night, while riding to New

York, Locke was shot by British scouts. Mim Wilming, working in a Philadelphia dress shop, delivered the shroud for his burial. Meeting Robert for the first time since the fighting at Lexington, she told him that she believed at last in the patriots' cause.

The years moved ahead with dates and names—July 4, 1776, and the Unanimous Declaration, Christmas night and Trenton, Valley Forge. Near Morristown, Ann Winshore gave birth to a son named after his dead father. Mim, nursing the sick and wounded at Bethlehem, became ill with putrid fever. Ordway Winshore drove through the British lines in Quaker clothes to take her back to his house and nurse her there. When word came that Robert had died at Valley Forge, she showed his father the plaque she had found after Robert's flight from arrest. Winshore told her it was hers to keep.

Summer came, and with it the British left Philadelphia. The Winshores hung out the flag which had been hidden under Mim's mattress during her illness. One day Oates Elwood arrived with his sister and her baby. Mim told Winshore that his grandson, born in 1777, the Year of the Three Gallows, would see many dawns. He was the future.

III

Omri Winwold had been many things —tavern chore-boy, mill worker, lawyer's clerk, gambler. He was a man of easy manners but deep reserves, his brick-dust beard covering a face peacefully calm on one side, seamed with turmoil on the other. The person who understood him best was a distant cousin, Brooksany Wimbler, whose husband Joel was an abolitionist harness-maker in Arpa, New York.

For years Omri had dreamed of a farm in Illinois, and in 1836 he headed west by wagon with his wife Bee and their infant son, Andrew Marvel. Near Arpa, where he stopped to say goodbye to the Wimblers, he deserted his sluttish wife, taking the child with him, after she had behaved shamelessly with a bachelor mover. The Wimblers knew nothing of his plans, but they believed that he had continued his journey west.

All America seemed moving westward by highway and canal. Millicent Wimbler was a baby in arms when her parents went with a large party of neighbors to found the antislavery community of New Era, Illinois. Her childish nickname, Mibs, stuck, even after she grew into a beautiful young woman with a will of her own. She had two admirers. One was Hornsby Meadows, instructor at New Era College and a crusading abolitionist. The other was Danny Hilton, a farmer and contractor. She went to church and to antislavery lectures with Hornsby, to dances and the Lincoln-Douglas debate in nearby Galesburg with Danny, but she would have neither. Hornsby finally married Fidelia Englehart, a village teacher. Danny went to Chicago. Then, in 1859, Rodney Wayman and his friend Nack Doss rode into New Era. Wayman was a cattle buyer from Atlas, Illinois. A Southerner, he had been a banjo player in a traveling minstrel show, a miner in California. Mibs married him without her parents' consent two weeks later.

In Pike County, meanwhile, Omri Winwold had prospered. Taking a gambler's chance on a charge of bigamy, he had married Sarah Prindle, a neighbor's daughter. After her death he married her sister, Anne Moore, a widow. By 1857 his roomy farmhouse held eight children, from Andrew Marvel, who was twenty-two, to Robert, who was seven—a good muster, Omri felt, after his unsettled early years. In 1852, during a business trip to St. Louis, he ran into Bee again and also met her husband, Henry Flack. The husband never knew the truth about Omri and Bee. After Bee ran away to San Francisco and Anne Winwold died, Omri and Flack, both lonely, became close friends. When Rodney Wayman brought his bride home to Atlas, and Mibs and Omri had established their kinship, letters passed once more between Omri and

Brooksany.

Storm clouds were gathering. John Brown raided Harper's Ferry. Clayborn Joel Wayman was born a few months before Lincoln was elected. Rodney was buying horses in Texas with Nack Doss when the war began. Both became captains in the Confederate Army. Doss was killed in a raid in Mississippi. Captured at Chickamauga, Rod was sent to the military prison at Camp Morton. Omri's boys who were old enough joined up. Rodney Wayman, Junior, was born that first year of the war, but his father never had word of him; he had escaped from Camp Morton and rejoined the troops. Joel Wimbler, commissioned in the commissary service, was furloughed home and lay dying in New Era. Brooksany died a few days after her husband. Going through their things, Mibs found in a trunk an ancient bronze plaque with Roger Bacon's Four Stumbling Blocks to Truth inscribed on it in antique script. She hung the keepsake around her neck, under her dress.

At Fredericksburg, Rod was again wounded and taken prisoner. While he lay in a barn hospital, Colonel Hornsby Meadows died on the floor next to him.

Rod lived in the filth and stench of Johnson's Island until Mibs came to get him, an exchanged prisoner. One night they went to have supper with Omri, and Rod lost some of his deep bitterness when he saw the younger Winwolds maimed and crippled in the war. Andrew Marvel, brevetted brigadier general, lacked an arm. Milton was paralyzed by a bullet in his spine. Holliday, starved in a prison camp, was dead.

The fighting ended, but deeper grief hung over the land when Lincoln's body was brought back to Springfield for burial. Mibs felt, however, that their days of storm and travail were almost over. Across the wide land the arch of union, strength, and love still held firm.

Captain Raymond Windom and his wife knew that they, too, had seen years of crisis and destiny. To them it seemed only fitting that other earths, symbols of hardship and storm and stars coming after the storm, should be buried at the base of Remembrance Rock—gravel from Anzio, sand from Utah Beach in Normandy, black volcanic ash from Okinawa.

Further Critical Evaluation of the Work:

Remembrance Rock is a long, complex, and occasionally rambling chronicle-romance that summarizes many of the poet's patriotic feelings about America. Sandburg devoted five years to writing the book, his only novel. With his accustomed diligence he researched the general social background of the Pilgrims, both in England and America; of the Revolutionary period from 1775-1777; and of the pre-Civil War era up to the death of Lincoln, roughly 1836-1865. But Sandburg's research was not intended to treat actual history, as he does in the Lincoln biographies; instead, he was concerned with the spiritual heritage of the people. To be sure, real historical figures and events crowd the pages of the novel; yet the major characters are clearly of heroic proportions—the creations of myth, not fact. To provide a "frame" for his narrative, Sandburg uses Justice Windom, a contemporary of the 1940's, as the mouthpiece for his own ideas. Thus, he examines four selective but crucial moments in the history of the nation to answer four significant questions: How did America come to be what it is now (in 1948)? When and where did it begin and develop? What is the "mysterious variable" that in moments seems to be a constant in the moral history of the people? And what is the "ever shifting and hazardous" principle that underlies the American Dream?

To answer these questions, Sandburg approaches American history as myth, symbol, and unified design. In each of the four narratives (really brief novels in themselves), he traces the lives of patriots who have inherited a 1607 medallion engraved with Roger Bacon's "Four Stumbling Blocks to Truth." Each Stumbling Block—or "Cause of Error"—corresponds to an adventure of the narrative; the moral lesson of the history parallels that of Bacon's warnings. For example, the Puritans in England oppose religious persecution, thereby avoiding the first error—"the influence of fragile or unworthy authority." In America, however, the Puritans practice their own form of intolerance. They fall prey to the second error, "custom." Fortunately, with the onset of the Revolutionary War, old customs are swept aside as the patriots establish a more humanistic morality. During the Civil War, patriots must overcome the third error, that of "the imperfection of undisciplined senses." For the fourth historical period, Sandburg's own, the patriot Justice Windom must avoid the error of "concealment of ignorance by ostentation of seeming wisdom." In effect, the poet satirizes his own "ostentation" in creating the bombastic rhetoric spoken by Windom. Thus, with gentle irony Sandburg concludes his panoramic history: even he, the author-patriot, has a Stumbling Block to overcome.

In addition to Roger Bacon's "Four Stumbling Blocks to Truth," Sandburg uses other unifying devices in the novel. The similarity of the names of his protagonists—Windom, Windling, Wingate, Winshore, Winwold—serves to remind the reader both of the continuity and variety that marks the American heritage. Windom (win-*doom,* the old word for *judgment*) is an appropriate name for the former Supreme Court Justice; just as Orton Wingate is a "gate" to the future, Ordway Winshore provides a shore-mooring for freedom, and Omri Winwold (*wold* as *forest*) helps to clear the wilderness and bring civilization to mid-America. Sandburg's women characters are alike in their patriotic devotion to the land; they, too, form a pattern of heroism. In each section of the novel a woman treasures the Roger Bacon medallion. Typically, the author develops his stories around the relationship between a young girl (representing the future) and an older man (the past), or between the girl and her fiancé or husband (the present). The characters, then, are treated both realistically and symbolically, as protagonists in stories and as heroic figures of a national myth. Because of the symbolic patterns of the novel, its ideas cannot be appreciated fully from the perspective of a conventional work of either fiction or chronicle. In spite of its sentimentality, repetitiousness, and grandiloquence, *Remembrance Rock* attempts to commemorate, in a form approaching folk poetry, the very spirit of the nation.

THE RENAISSANCE

Type of work: Essays in art appreciation and criticism
Author: Walter Pater (1839-1894)
First published: 1873

In the preface to *The Renaissance,* originally titled *Studies in the History of the Renaissance,* Pater writes, "The subjects of the following studies . . . touch what I think the chief points in that complex, many-sided movement." The subjects themselves are the French, Italian, and German writers, painters, and sculptors, ranging from the thirteenth to the eighteenth century, in whose lives and in whose works Pater finds represented the many sides, the divergent attitudes and aims, of the Renaissance.

Pater's method is impressionistic. The task of the aesthetic critic, he says, is first to realize distinctly the exact impression which a work of art makes upon him, then to determine the source and conditions—the "virtue"—of that impression, and finally to express that virtue so that the impression it has made on him may be shared by others. *The Renaissance* is largely the record of the impressions induced in the refined temperament of Walter Pater by the art he studies.

The Renaissance, for Pater, was "not merely the revival of classical antiquity which took place in the fifteenth century . . . but a whole complex movement, of which that revival of classical antiquity was but one element or symptom." Accordingly, in the first chapter, he finds the roots of the movement in thirteenth century France, illustrated in the prose romances, *Li Amitiez de Ami et Amile* and *Aucassin et Nicolette.* It is in their "spirit of rebellion and revolt against the moral and religious ideas of the time" that these tales prefigure that later "outbreak of the reason and the imagination," the high Renaissance of fifteenth century Italy.

One important part of that later Renaissance, says Pater, was the effort made by fifteenth century Italian scholars "to reconcile Christianity with the religion of ancient Greece." Pico della Mirandola typified that effort, both in his writings and in his life; he was "reconciled indeed to the new religion, but still [had] a tenderness for the earlier life." Lacking the historic sense, Pico and his contemporaries sought in vain, as Pater saw it, a reconciliation based on allegorical interpretations of religious belief; "the Renaissance of the fifteenth century was . . . great, rather by what it designed . . . than by what it actually achieved."

In discussing Boticelli, Pater acknowledges that he is a painter, of secondary rank, not great as Michelangelo and Leonardo are great. Nonetheless his work has a distinct quality, "the result of a blending in him of a sympathy for humanity in its uncertain condition . . . with his consciousness of the shadow upon it of the great things from which it shrinks." He is a forcible realist and a visionary painter as well. Part of his appeal to Pater is simply in this, that "he has the freshness, the uncertain and diffident promise which belong to the earlier Renaissance"—that age which Pater called "perhaps the most interesting period in the history of the mind."

The chapter titled "Luca della Robbia" is as much about sculpture in general as it is about Luca. The limitation of sculpture, says Pater, is that it tends toward "a hard realism, a one-sided presentment of mere form." The Greeks countered this tendency by depicting the type rather than the individual, by purging the accidental until "their works came to be like some subtle extract or essence, or almost like pure thoughts or ideas." But this sacrificed *expression.* Michelangelo "with a genius spiritualised by the reverie of the middle age," offset the tendency of sculpture towards realism by "leaving nearly all his sculpture in a puzzling sort of incompleteness, which suggests rather than realises actual form." Luca della Robbia and other fifteenth century Tuscan sculptors achieved "a profound expressiveness" by working in low relief earthenware, the subtle delineation of line serving as the means of overcoming the special limitation of sculpture.

In "The Poetry of Michelangelo" we find out less about the poetry itself than we do about Pater's impressions of it. No one, says Pater, need be reminded of the strength of Michelangelo's work. There is, however, another and equally important quality of his work, and that Pater refers to variously as "charm," "sweetness," and "a lovely strangeness." It is in a "brooding spirit of life," achieved only through an idealization of life's "vehement sentiments," that this quality of sweetness resides. There were, says Pater, two traditions of the ideal which Michelangelo might have followed: that of Dante, who idealized the material world, and that of Platonism. It was the Platonic tradition that molded Michelangelo's verse; "Michelangelo is always pressing forward from the outward beauty . . . to apprehend the unseen beauty . . . that abstract form of beauty, about which the Platonists reason." Yet the influence of Dante is there too, in the sentiment of imaginative love. To Pater, Michelangelo was "the last . . . of those on whom the peculiar sentiment of the Florence of Dante and Giotto descended: he is the consummate representative of the form that sentiment took in the fifteenth century." In this sentiment is another source of his "grave and temperate sweetness."

The fifteenth century witnessed two movements: the return to antiquity represented, says Pater, by Raphael and the return to nature represented by Leonardo da Vinci. In Leonardo the return to nature took on a special coloring, for Leonardo's genius was composed not only of a desire for beauty but also of a curiosity which gave to his paintings "a type of subtle and curious grace." His landscapes, as in the background of his masterpiece, *La Gioconda,* partake of the "*bizarre* of *recherché.*" One of the most famous passages in the book is Pater's description of *La Gioconda.* Pater sees in the Mona Lisa the image of archetypal woman: "All the thoughts and experience of the world have etched and moulded" her features.

In "The School of Giorgione" (which did not appear in the first edition), Pater propounds his famous dictum that "All art constantly aspires towards the condition of music." The "condition of music" is a complete fusing, an interpenetration, of matter and form. The other arts achieve perfection in the degree that they approach or approximate this condition. Giorgione and others of the Venetian school are representative of the aspiration towards perfect identification of matter and form in their realization that "painting must be before all things decorative." Their subjects are from life, but "mere subject" is subordinated to "pictorial design," so that matter is interpenetrated by form.

In the chapter on Joachim du Bellay, Pater turns from Italy to France, to the theories and the elegant verse of the *Pleiad.* Du Bellay wrote a tract in which he sought "to adjust the existing French culture to the rediscovered classical culture." In this tract, says Pater, the Renaissance became aware of itself as a systematic movement. The ambition of the *Pleiad* was to combine the "music of the measured, scanned verse of Latin and Greek poetry" with "the music of the rhymed, unscanned verse of Villon and the old French poets."

The longest chapter of *The Renaissance* is devoted to Johann Joachim Winckelmann, a German scholar in the study of antiquity. His importance, for Pater, is chiefly that he influenced Goethe: "Goethe illustrates a union of the Romantic spirit . . . with Hellenism . . . that marriage . . . of which the art of the nineteenth century is the child." The Hellenic element, characterized by "breadth, centrality, with blitheness and repose," was made known to Goethe by Winckelmann. Winckelmann stands, then, as a link between antiquity (and the Renaissance) and the modern, post-Enlightenment world.

The most celebrated part of the book —and indeed of Pater's entire body of writing—is the conclusion to *The Renaissance.* Here he utters the famous, and frequently misinterpreted, dicta: "Not the fruit of experience, but experience itself, is the end" and "To burn always with this hard, gemlike flame, to maintain this ecstasy, is success in life." These statements must be seen in the context of Pater's conception of the nature of human existence.

For Pater reality is human experience. It consists not in the objective, material world but in the impressions of color, odor, and texture which that world produces in the observer's mind. Each impression endures for but a single moment and then is gone. Life is made up of the succession of these momentary impressions, and life itself is brief.

Not to make the most of these moments, not to experience them fully, is to waste a lifetime. "What we have to do," says Pater, "is to be for ever curiously testing new opinions and courting new impressions." Given the brevity of our lives and given as well the brevity of the very impressions which constitute our lives, "we shall hardly have time to make theories about the things we see and touch." Hence, "not the fruit of experience, but experience itself, is the end."

This emphasis on experience also leads Pater to distinguish among kinds of experience, and the highest kind, he says, is the great passions (themselves a kind of wisdom) we gain from art. "For art comes to you proposing frankly to give nothing but the highest quality to your moments as they pass"—a life constituted of such moments will indeed "burn always" with a "hard, gemlike flame."

Pater omitted the conclusion from the second edition of the book, fearing "it might possibly mislead some of those young men into whose hands it might fall." Having explained his beliefs more fully in *Marius the Epicurean* and having altered the conclusion slightly, he restored it to later editions.

RENÉE MAUPERIN

Type of work: Novel
Authors: Edmond (1822-1896) and Jules (1830-1870) de Goncourt
Type of plot: Domestic tragedy
Time of plot: Nineteenth century
Locale: France
First published: 1864

Principal characters:
RENÉE MAUPERIN, a sensitive, talented girl in her late teens
HENRI MAUPERIN, her brother
MADAME DAVARANDE, her sister
MONSIEUR MAUPERIN, Renée's father
MADAME MAUPERIN, his wife
NAOMI BOURJOT, Renée's friend and fiancée of Henri Mauperin
MADAME BOURJOT, her mother and lover of Henri Mauperin
MONSIEUR DENOISEL, family friend of the Mauperins
DE VILLACOURT, shabby heir of an old French family

Critique:

For those readers who prefer the analysis of "a slice of life," this novel is the Goncourt brothers' best work of fiction. In it the authors have presented a detailed and careful study of a middle-class French family during the middle of the nineteenth century. The younger people are products of their parents' later lives, for we are told that older generation was one which had originally believed in the revolutionary movements of the late eighteenth century but had in mature years become conservative owners of property. Perhaps nowhere in literature has the lingering death of a victim of any disease been as carefully delineated as has the death of Renée Mauperin, whose slow and sad departure from this life consumes at least a fourth of the chapters of the novel and is, to the sensitive reader, almost excruciating.

The Story:

Renée Mauperin's father had served under the first Napoleon and had battled for the liberal forces until he had become a husband and father, with the responsibilities that such a position had forced upon him. After acquiring a family he had ceased being a scholar and political figure, in favor of the more financially reliable career of sugar refiner. His wife was a very proper woman, one who wished to see her children married

well and respectably, that she might enjoy her old age in satisfaction of a job well done.

The children of the Mauperins, at least the oldest two, were model children, so well disciplined and quiet that they failed to excite the interest of their father. Renée, the third child, born late in his life, was Mauperin's favorite. Renée was a lively youngster from the beginning, a lover of horses and action, a vivacious creature who was demonstrative in her affection, and an artistic but spirited personality. While these qualities endeared her to her father, they made her the bane of her mother's existence. The oldest daughter had dutifully married and become the respectable Madame Davarande, but Renée, who had already dismissed summarily a dozen suitors of good family and fortune, showed no inclination to accept any who came seeking her hand.

Almost as great a worry to Madame Mauperin was her son, on whom she doted. Henri Mauperin was a political economist and a lawyer; he was also a cold and calculating fellow, though his mother, in her excessive love for him, failed to realize just how selfish he was. She thought that he had never given a thought to marriage and chided him for his lack of interest. She felt that at the age of thirty he should have settled down.

Not knowing his plans, Madame Mauperin arranged to have him often in the company of Naomi Bourjot. Naomi was the only daughter of a very rich family known to the Mauperins for many years. The only difficulty lay in convincing her father that Henri, who had no title, was a suitable match for his daughter. Henri himself had seen that such was to be the great difficulty, and he had undertaken to gain the aid of Madame Bourjot in his suit. His method of securing her aid was to become her lover.

Through the medium of an amateur theatrical, Naomi, Renée, and Henri were placed in one another's company, although Naomi had to be forced into the venture by her mother. Madame Bourjot realized that Henri wanted to marry her daughter, but she had no idea that he was in love with the girl. It was only Henri's portrayal of Naomi's lover on the stage that revealed the true state of his affections. Rather than lose him altogether, Madame Bourjot, as Henri had anticipated, resolved to help him win her daughter and the family fortune, although tearful and bitter scenes preceded that decision. Through the efforts of his wife, Naomi's father reluctantly consented to the marriage if Henri Mauperin could gain the government's permission to add "de Villacourt" to his name.

In the meantime Naomi had discovered that Henri and her mother had been lovers. Although she loved Henri, she was dismayed by what she had learned. Even so, because of her parents, she had to go through with the marriage. Naomi's only consolation was to tell what she knew to Renée, who was horrified to learn of her brother's actions. When she confronted him with the story, he made no attempt to deny the facts; all he did was tell her curtly and angrily that the affair was none of her business.

A short time later, when, superficially, the antagonism between Renée and her brother had been smoothed over, she accompanied him to the government offices where he received permission to make the addition to his name. While she was waiting for him, she overheard two clerks saying that the real de Villacourt family had not really died out and that one member, a man, was still alive; the clerks even mentioned the address. Her knowledge gave Renée an opportunity for revenge, although she had no idea what might happen if she put her plan into action. What she did was to take a copy of the newspaper announcing that the title "de Villacourt" was to be given to Henri Mauperin and send it to the real de Villacourt, a villainous lout who immediately planned to kill the upstart who dared to appropriate his title.

The real de Villacourt journeyed to Paris and learned that, penniless as he was, he had no legal means to regain his title. Then he went to the apartment of Henri Mauperin and attempted to beat the young man. Henri, no coward, immediately challenged the man to a duel. The arrangements were made by Monsieur Denoisel, a friend of the Mauperin family for many years. He also served as Henri's second in the affair. Henri shot de Villacourt and thought the duel was over, but the man was not fatally wounded. Calling Henri back, he shot and killed him. To Denoisel was given the unhappy duty of reporting to all concerned Henri's untimely death. The one who seemed to take the news hardest was Renée. No one expected her to make so much of her brother's death, since they had never been close.

One day, in a conversation, Denoisel remarked that someone had sent the newspaper clipping to de Villacourt. Renée, fearful that she had been discovered as the author of her brother's death, had a heart attack. For many months she lay ill, apparently with no desire to live. Even the realization, after many weeks, that she had not revealed her guilt made no difference in her recovery. Her father called in the best specialists he could find, but they only remarked that some terrible shock had caused her condition. When told that she had recently lost a brother, they said that his death was probably not the real cause of her illness.

In spite of all efforts on her behalf, Renée Mauperin wasted away and finally died. Nor was the tragedy of the Mauperins yet finished. They lost their third child, Madame Davarande, a few months afterward, when she died in childbirth. Childless and alone, the elder Mauperins traveled abroad, hoping thereby to ease their grief and loneliness.

Further Critical Evaluation of the Work:

Above all, the Goncourt brothers valued truth in literature; in all of their novels, they attempted to find the truth of the subject they chose. In *Renée Mauperin,* they analyzed with shrewdness and precision a particular segment of Parisian society. Viewing this world through the eyes of an intelligent and sensitive girl, they presented the shallowness and pettiness of many of the self-satisfied people who dominated it and who tried to dominate her. In particular, the book illustrates the various conditions of women in mid-nineteenth-century France. First, there is the impetuous young Renée, who as a child cuts Denoisel's hair and smokes her father's cigarette, and who later struggles against the conventions imposed upon young women in the Paris of 1864. Then, there is Mme. Mauperin, with her passion for "symmetry" and her typical overvaluing of her son and undervaluing of her daughter. Mme. Davarande, the society matron, devoted to her position and religious only because she believes that God is *chic,* and Mme. Bourjot, an intelligent woman married to a shallow and petty fool, clearly are intended to represent two typical women of the period. In the society of the day, only a shallow person seems able to find contentment, the authors seem to suggest, particularly if the person is a woman.

Many of the other characters, notably Renée's doting and scholarly father, and the sophisticated and subtle Abbé Blampoix, are well-drawn. The Goncourt brothers were not known for character analysis, but they achieved in this novel a success with their characters above that in many of their other books. Renée's sudden admission of inadvertently causing her brother's death is skillfully and devastatingly handled; the moment reveals the complexities of Renée's character which up to that point had been only suggested. The novel is filled with witty conversations that bring the era to life. The authors knew the value and interest of precise details and skillfully integrated them into the book through conversations and descriptions, often using them to delineate character. Frequently, the conversations are used to suggest a comment on society, as when a room full of people talking is described as "voices . . . all mingled together in the Babel: it was like the chirping of so many birds in a cage." It is this cage which Renée wants to escape, but ultimately does escape only through her death.

The novelistic strength of the Goncourts lay in pure observation. Perhaps they were less broad in their accomplishments than the greatest nineteenth century novelists, but in their best books, such as *Renée Mauperin,* they combined a precise and vivid picture of the society they knew so well with both a sympathetic and touching story and shrewd observations on human nature.

REPRESENTATIVE MEN

Type of work: Biographical essays
Author: Ralph Waldo Emerson (1803-1882)
First published: 1850

Emerson's *Representative Men* was first presented as a course of lectures in Boston in the winter of 1845-1846 and later during his visit to England in 1847. The volume opens with a discussion of the uses of great men and follows with six chapters on men who represent Man in six aspects: Plato as philosopher, Swedenborg as mystic, Montaigne as skeptic, Shakespeare as poet, Napoleon as man of the world, and Goethe as writer.

The book has often been mentioned in connection with Carlyle's *Heroes and Hero-Worship,* published in 1841, but where Carlyle saw the hero as a divinely gifted individual above and apart from the common man, Emerson conceived of the great man as a lens through which men may see themselves. For Emerson the great man is one who through superior endowments "inhabits a higher sphere of thought, into which other men rise with labor and difficulty. . . ." Such men may give direct material or metaphysical aid, but more frequently they serve indirectly by the inspiration of their accomplishment of things and by their introduction to us of ideas. The great man does stirring deeds; he reveals knowledge and wisdom; he shows depths of emotion—and others resolve to emulate him. He accomplishes intellectual feats of memory, of abstract thought, of imaginative flights, and dull minds are brightened by his light. But the true genius does not tyrannize; he liberates those who know him. For Emerson, all men are infinitely receptive in capacity; they need only the wise man to rouse them, to clear their eyes and make them see, to feed and refresh them. Yet even the great man has limits of availability. We get from one what we can and pass on to another who can nourish mind or spirit or titillate a dulled palate. As we are infinitely receptive, so are we eternally hungry; and

as we find sustenance, through us the spirit of the world's great men diffuses itself. Thus, through the ages the cumulative effect of great men is that they prepare the way for greater men.

Emerson views the representative philosopher Plato as an exhausting generalizer, a symbol of philosophy itself, a thinker whom men of all nations in all times recognize as kin to themselves. He absorbed the learning of his times, but Emerson sees in him a modern style and spirit identifying him with later ages as well. Plato honors the ideal, or laws of the mind, and fate, or the order of nature. Plato defines. He sees Unity, or Identity, on the one hand and Variety on the other. In him is found the idea (not original, it is true) of one deity in whom all things are absorbed. A balanced soul, Plato sees both the real and the ideal. He propounds the principle of absolute good, but he illustrates from the world around him. In this ability lies his power and charm. He is a great average man in whom other men see their own dreams and thoughts. He acknowledges the Ineffable and yet asserts that things are knowable; a lover of limits, he yet loves the illimitable. For Plato, virtue cannot be taught; it is divinely inspired. It is through Socrates that we learn much of Plato's philosophy, and to Emerson the older philosopher is a man of Franklin-like wisdom, a plain old uncle with great ears, an immense talker, a hard-headed humorist, an Aesop of the mob to whom the robed scholar Plato owed a great debt.

For Emerson the two principal defects of Plato as a philosopher are, first, that he is intellectual and therefore always literary, and second, that he has no system. He sees so much that he argues first on one side and then on another. Finally, says Emerson, the way to know Plato is to compare him, not with nature (an enigma now, as it was to Plato), but with other men and to see that through the ages none have approached him.

Emerson would have preferred to discuss Jesus as the representative mystic, but to do so would have meant sailing into dangerous waters: the orthodox believers of the time would probably have objected to the inclusion of Jesus as a representative *man*. Emerson chose Swedenborg instead, but in reading this chapter of the book one gets the notion that Emerson was forcing himself to praise this eighteenth century mystic. Emerson remarks that this colossal soul, as he calls him, requires a long focal distance to be seen. Looking more closely, he finds in Swedenborg a style "lustrous with points and shooting spiculae of thought, and resembling one of those winter mornings when the air sparkles with crystals." He summarizes some of Swedenborg's leading ideas: "the universality of each law in nature; the Platonic doctrine of the scale or degrees; the version or conversion of each into other, and so the correspondence of all the parts; the fine secret that little explains large, and large, little; the centrality of man in nature, and the connection that subsists throughout all things." He quotes a passage of Swedenborgian theology which must have appealed to the Unitarian Emerson: "Man is a kind of very minute heaven, corresponding to the world of spirits and to heaven. Every particular idea of man, and every affection, yea, every smallest part of his affection, is an image and effigy of him. A spirit may be known from only a single thought. God is the grand old man." Yet when Emerson comes to the Swedenborgian mystical view that each natural object has a definite symbolic value—as, a horse signifies carnal understanding; a tree, perception; the moon, faith—he rebels at its narrowness. As for Swedenborg's theological writings in general, Emerson complains of their immense and sandy diffuseness and their delirious incongruities. Emer-

son warns that such a book as Swedenborg's *Conjugal Love* should be used with caution, and he suggests that a contemplative young man might read these mysteries of love and conscience once, and then throw them aside for ever. As Emerson continues his examination he finds Swedenborg's heavens and hells dull, he objects to the theologic determination of Swedenborg's mind and to the failure of Swedenborg in attaching himself "to the Christian symbol, instead of to the moral sentiment, which carries innumerable christianities, humanities, divinities, in its bosom." When Emerson imagines the impatient reader complaining, "What have I to do with jasper and sardonyx, beryl and chalcedony," and so on, Emerson's own writing awakes as from a semi-slumber, and one is reminded of his warning in "Self-Reliance" that when a man "claims to know and speak of God and carries you backward to the phraseology of some old moldered nation in another country, in another world, believe him not."

As Emerson perhaps felt relieved after having completed his lecture on Swedenborg, he surely must have anticipated with great pleasure his next on the skeptic Montaigne. He confesses to having had a love for the *Essays* since he was a young man. "It seemed to me," he says, "as if I had written the book, in some former life, so sincerely it spoke to my thought and experience." He is not repelled by Montaigne's grossness, his frank intimacy about himself, because the Frenchman is scrupulously honest in his confessions. As Emerson had found Swedenborg disagreeably wise and therefore repellent, he is in contrast drawn to Montaigne whose motto *Que sçais je?* was a constant reminder to the essayist to stick to the things he did know: such as his farm, his family, himself, and his likes and dislikes in food and friends. Emerson is charmed by Montaigne's conversational style, his calm balance, and his stout solidity. The skeptic is not the impassioned patriot, the dogmatic adherent of creed or party. He is wary of an excess of belief, but he turns also from an excess of unbelief. He is content to say there are doubts. Yet for Emerson, when he turns from Montaigne the man to the skeptic in general whom he represents, the doubter is at base a man of belief. He believes in the moral design of the universe and that "it exists hospitably for the weal of souls." Thus, concludes Emerson, skepticism is finally dissolved in the moral sentiment which remains forever supreme. The skepticism is on the surface only; it questions specifics, but the skeptic can serenely view man's high ambitions defeated and the unequal distribution of power in the world because he believes that deity and moral law control the universe. Emerson himself was at bottom such a believer, though he had passed through his skeptical stage in life to arrive at his belief.

The discussion of Shakespeare as the representative poet begins with the comment that "Great men are more distinguished by range and extent than by originality." Shakespeare, like his fellow dramatists, used a mass of old plays to experiment with. Building upon popular traditions, he was free to use his wide-ranging fancy and his imagination. Borrowing in all directions, he used what he borrowed with such art that it became his.

Emerson touches upon the mystery of Shakespeare's biography, mentioning the paucity of clear facts (only a few more are known today than when Emerson wrote), and then concluding, as have many of Shakespeare's readers, that his plays and his poetry give all the information which is really needed. In the sonnets we find the lore of friendship and of love. Through the characters of his plays we know the man because there is something of him in all of them.

The dramatic skill of Shakespeare is to Emerson less important than his poetry and philosophy and the broad expanse of his book of life, which pictured the men and women of his day and prefigured those of later ages. Shakespeare was inconceivably wise and made his characters as real as if they had lived in his home. His power to convert truth into music and verse makes him the exemplary poet. His music charms the ear while his sentence takes the mind. In his lines experience has been transformed into verse without a trace of egotism. One more royal trait of the poet Emerson finds in Shakespeare: his very name suggests joy and emancipation to men's hearts. To Emerson, Shakespeare was master of the revels to mankind. It is this fact that Emerson regrets: the world's greatest poet used his genius for public amusement. As the poet was half-man in his role as entertainer, so the priests of old and of later days were half-men who took the joy and beauty out of life while they moralized and warned of the doom to come. Only in some future time, says Emerson, will there arise a poet-priest who may see, speak, and act with equal inspiration.

A frequently quoted remark of Emerson's is that he liked people who could *do* things. His expansive praise of Napoleon in the opening pages of his portrayal of the Corsican as the representative man of the world is based upon his belief that Napoleon could and did do what masses of other men merely wanted to. Napoleon was idolized by common men because he was an uncommonly gifted common man. He succeeded through the virtues of punctuality, personal attention, courage, and thoroughness, qualities which other men possess in lesser degrees. Emerson writes of Napoleon's reliance on his own sense and of his scorn of others' sense. To him Napoleon is the agent or attorney of the middle class, with both the virtues and the vices of the people he represented. He was dishonest, stagy, unscrupulous, selfish, perfidious, and coarse. He was a cheat, a gossip, and when divested of his power and splendor he is seen to be an impostor and a rogue.

Emerson finds Napoleon the supreme democrat who illustrates in his career the three stages of the party: the democrat in youth, the conservative in later life, and the aristocrat at the end: a democrat ripe and gone to seed. Napoleon conducted an experiment in the use of the intellect without conscience. But the experiment failed because the French saw that they could not enjoy what Napoleon had gained for them. His colossal egotism drove him to more attempts at conquest, and so his followers deserted him. Yet Emerson asserts that it was not Napoleon's fault. He was defeated by the eternal law of man and of the world. Here, as before, Emerson sees the moral order in the universe. "Every experiment," he says, "by multitudes or by individuals, that has a selfish aim, will fail. . . . Only that good profits which we can taste with all doors open, and which serves all men."

Having considered Napoleon as a man of action who failed after having achieved enormous successes, Emerson turns to Goethe as the representative scholar or writer, a man whose intellect moved in many directions and whose writings brought him fame as the greatest of German authors. Emerson calls him the soul of his century, one who clothed modern existence with poetry. Emerson,

a lover of nature himself, remarks that Goethe said the best things about nature that ever were said.

Realizing the impossibility of analyzing the full range of Goethe's writings, Emerson chooses *Wilhelm Meister's Apprenticeship* for rather brief comment. He describes it as provoking but also unsatisfactory, but though he has considerable praise for this novel in which a democrat becomes an aristocrat, we do not really learn much about it. In fact, one feels that Emerson was struggling with a difficult subject in dealing with Goethe. One comment is worthy of noting, however, since it seems a reference to Emerson himself when he says that Goethe is "fragmentary; a writer of occasional poems and of an encyclopedia of sentences."

Among Emerson's works, *Representative Men* has received modest praise, and such chapters as those on Montaigne and Shakespeare have occasionally been reprinted. One of the aptest statments ever made about Emerson's book is that of Dr. Oliver Wendell Holmes in his *Memoir*: "[Emerson] shows his own affinities and repulsions, and . . . writes his own biography, no matter about whom or what he is talking."

THE REPUBLIC

Type of work: Philosophic dialogue
Author: Plato (427-347 B.C.)
Time: Fifth century B.C.
Locale: The Piraeus, Greece
First transcribed: Fourth century B.C.

Principal personages:
SOCRATES, the Athenian philosopher
CEPHALUS, an old man
POLEMARCHUS, his son
THRASYMACHUS, a Sophist
GLAUCON, and
ADEIMANTUS, Plato's brothers

The *Republic* is Plato's masterpiece, not only because it presents a fascinating defense of the author's conception of the ideal state, but also because it gives us the most sustained and convincing portrait of Socrates as a critical and creative philosopher. Other dialogues, such as the *Phaedo* and the *Apology,* may be superior as studies of the personality and character of Socrates, but the *Republic* is unexcelled as an exhibition of the famed Socratic method being brought to bear on such questions as "What is justice?" and "What kind of state would be most just?"

Although the constructive arguments of this dialogue come from the mouth of Socrates, it is safe to assume that much of the philosophy is Platonic in origin. As a rough reading rule, we may say that the method is Socratic, but the content is provided by Plato himself. Among the ideas which are presented and defended in the *Republic* are the Platonic theory of Ideas—the formal prototypes of all things, objective or intellectual—the Platonic conception of the nature and obligations of the philosopher, and the Platonic theory and criticism of poetry. But the central concern of the author is with the idea of justice in man and the state. The pursuit of this idea makes the *Republic* the longest of the dialogues with the exception of the *Laws.*

The dialogue is a discussion between Socrates and various friends while they are in the Piraeus for a festival. The dis-cussion of justice is provoked by a remark made by an old man, Cephalus, to the effect that the principal advantage of being wealthy is that a man near death is able to repay what he owes to the gods and men, and is thereby able to be just in the hope of achieving a happy afterlife. Socrates objects to this conception of justice, maintaining that whether a person should return what he has received depends on the circumstances. For example, a man who has received dangerous weapons from his friends while sane should not, if he is just, return those weapons if his friend, while mad, demands them.

Polemarchus amends the idea and declares that it is just to help our friends and return to them what they are due, provided they are good and worthy of receiving the good. Enemies, on the other hand, should have harm done to them for, as bad, that is what they are due.

Socrates compels Polemarchus to admit that injuring anyone, even a wicked man, makes him worse; and since no just man would ever sanction making men worse, justice must be something other than giving good to the good and bad to the bad.

Thrasymachus then proposes the theory that justice is whatever is to the interest of the stronger party. His idea is that justice is relative to the law, and the law is made by the stronger party according to his interests. In rebuttal, Socrates maneuvers Thrasymachus into saying that sometimes rulers make mistakes.

If this is so, then sometimes the law is against their interests; when the law is against the interests of the stronger party, it is right to do what is not to the interest of the stronger party.

The secret of the Socratic method is evident from analysis of this argument. The term "interest" or "to the interest of" is ambiguous, sometimes meaning what a man is interested in, what he wants, and at other times what he could want if he were not in error, as when we say, "But although you want it, it is not really to your interest to have it." Socrates adroitly shifts from one sense of the expression to the other so that Thrasymachus apparently contradicts himself. In this indirect way Socrates makes it clear both to the "victim" and to the onlookers that the proponent of the claim—in this case, Thrasymachus—has not cleared it of all possibility of misinterpretation.

Socrates then goes on to say that justice must be relative to the needs of those who are served, not to the desires of those who serve them. The physician, for example, as physician, must make the health of the patient his primary concern if he is to be just.

Socrates suggests that their understanding of justice would be clarified if they were to consider a concrete case, say the state: if by discussion they could come to understand what a state must be in order to be just, it might be possible to generalize and to arrive at an idea of justice itself.

Beginning with an account of what a state would have to be in order to fulfill its functions as a state, Socrates then proceeds to develop the notion of an ideal state by asking what the relations of the various groups of citizens to each other should be.

Every state needs three classes of citizens: the Guardians, who rule and advise the rest; the Auxiliaries, who provide military protection for the state; and the Workers, the husbandmen and other providers of food, clothing, and such useful materials.

In a just state these three classes of citizens function together, each doing its own proper business without interfering with the tasks of the other classes.

Applying this idea to the individual person, Socrates decides that a just man is one who gives to each of his functions its proper task, relating them to each other in a harmonious way. Just as the state has three distinct elements, the governing, the defending, and the producing bodies, so the individual person has three corresponding elements, the rational, the spirited, and the appetitive. By the spirited element Plato means the passionate aspect of man's nature, his propensity to anger or other irrational emotions. He so uses the term anger that he allows for what we call righteous indignation, the passionate defense of reason against desire. The rational element is the discerning and calculating side of man's nature, and it is what enables man to be wise and judicious. The appetitive side of man is his inclination to desire some things in preference to others.

A just man, then, is one who keeps each of the three elements of his nature doing its proper work with the rational element in command. A person is brave, says Socrates in the dialogue, if his spirited element remains always in the service of reason. He is wise if he is governed by reason, for reason takes into account the welfare of the entire person; and he is temperate if his spirit and appetite work harmoniously under the guidance of reason.

In order to discover those citizens best suited to be Guardians, Socrates proposed that the ideal state educate all its citizens in music and gymnastics, continually observing them to decide upon the sort of occupation for which they would best be fitted. He also argued that the Guardians and Auxiliaries should have no private property, and that they each should share a community of wives and children.

These obvious communal features of the ideal state have led many critics to dismiss Plato's construction as unacceptable. But it is well to remember that in the dialogue Socrates tells his listeners that he is not concerned about the practicality of his state; the conception of the state is constructed merely to bring out the nature of justice.

In considering the education of the Guardians, Socrates builds the conception of the philosopher as the true aristocrat or rational man, the ideal ruler for the ideal state. The philosopher is a lover of wisdom, and he alone manages to keep appetite and spirit in harmony with reason. Consequently, the Guardians of the state should be educated as philosophers, supplementing their training in arithmetic, geometry, astronomy, and music with training in the philosophic skills of dialectic. But the prospective Guardians should not be allowed to undertake philosophic education until they are old enough to take it seriously, not as mere amusement. After his philosophic training the prospective Guardian should take part in the active life of his times, so that at fifty he can assume political power with some knowledge of the actual matters with which he shall be concerned.

In connection with his discussion of the philosopher, Socrates introduced his famous myth of the cave. Men are like prisoners in a cave that faces away from the light. Unable to see themselves or anyone else because they are shackled, the men observe only the shadows of things on the wall in front of them, not realizing that the reality is something quite different from the shadows. The philosopher is like a man who leaves the cave, comes to know things as they really are, and returns reluctantly to help the shackled men who think that shadows make up the true world.

The philosopher comes to know reality through a study of the Ideas or Forms of particular things. The world of our experience is like the world of shadows, but the world of Ideas is the true reality.

For every class of objects, such as beds (Socrates' example), there is an Idea-bed, a form shared by all particular beds. The man who studies only the individual beds made by carpenters, or only the pictures of beds made by artists, knows only copies of reality (and, in the case of the imitative artist, only copies of copies); but the philosopher, making the effort to learn the Idea itself, comes closer to reality.

Socrates objects to poetry and to art whenever they are imitative, which they usually are. Although he admits that some poetry can be inspiring in the patriotic training of the Guardians, he stresses the point that imitative art is corrupting because it is misleading Physical things, after all, are merely copies of the Forms, the Ideas; hence they are one step removed from reality. But works of art are copies of physical things; hence they are at least two steps removed from reality. Furthermore, the artist paints only a single aspect of a thing; hence, strictly speaking, art is three steps removed from reality. It is on this account, as well as because of the immoral effect of the poetic style of all but the most noble poets, that Socrates recommends that imitative poets be banned from the state.

The *Republic* closes with Socrates' reaffirmation of his conviction that only the just man is truly happy, for only he harmonizes reason, appetite, and spirit by loving wisdom and the Form of the Good. The soul is immortal, he argues, because the soul's illness is injustice; yet injustice itself does not destroy a soul. Since the soul cannot be destroyed by any illness other than its own, it must be immortal. Socrates concludes by using a myth about life after death to show that the just and wise man will prosper both in this life and "during the journey of a thousand years."